W9-CJP-716

MASTERPLOTS II

POETRY SERIES

B+T
5/93
425.00
set

MASTERPLOTS II

POETRY
SERIES

3

Goa-Lov

Edited by
FRANK N. MAGILL

SALEM PRESS

Pasadena, California   Englewood Cliffs, New Jersey

Copyright © 1992, by SALEM PRESS, INC.
All rights in this book are reserved. No part of this work
may be used or reproduced in any manner whatsoever or
transmitted in any form or by any means, electronic or
mechanical, including photocopy, recording, or any information storage and retrieval system, without written
permission from the copyright owner except in the case
of brief quotations embodied in critical articles and reviews. For information address the publisher, Salem
Press, Inc., P.O. Box 50062, Pasadena, California 91105.

∞ The paper used in these volumes conforms to the
American National Standard for Permanence of Paper
for Printed Library Materials. Z39.48-1984.

Library of Congress Cataloging-in-Publication Data
Masterplots II: Poetry series/edited by Frank N. Magill
    p. cm.
    Includes bibliographical references and index.
        1. Poetry—Themes, motives. I. Magill, Frank
    Northen, 1907-
PN1110.5.M37   1992 v. 3   91-44341
809.1—dc20   CIP
ISBN 0-89356-584-9 (set)
ISBN 0-89356-587-3 (volume 3)

SECOND PRINTING

PRINTED IN THE UNITED STATES OF AMERICA

Themes and Meanings

The poem is one of contrasts: between gross physical lust and true love; between the poet's profligate past and the lovers' present spiritual awakening; between earthly worlds sought by sea-discoverers and the spiritual world discovered by the lovers. These contrasts are brought out in the main themes of sight, awakening from sleep, and earthly versus spiritual worlds.

Renaissance theories saw the sense of sight as central to the birth and continuance of love. In this poem, the sense of sight is seen in two opposing guises: the roving eye of the libertine, and the constant, steady gaze of mature "true" love.

This theme is introduced in the sixth line of the first stanza, where he refers to the attractive women whom he saw, desired, and "got"—a deliberately unsubtle expression. The triumphant opening to the second stanza brings forth the comment that the poet and his lady do not watch each other out of fear, since their true love controls "all love of other sights"—meaning, all interest in the outside world (turning "one little room into an everywhere"). In the third stanza, the lovers gaze into each other's eyes so single-mindedly that they see each other's reflections. Moreover, the steadiness of their gaze is reinforced by the true, plain hearts that "rest" in their faces—an image of openness and trust in each other.

The lovers' lives before they met are discussed in terms of sleep and the unreality of dreams. They were as if asleep in the den of the Seven Sleepers of Ephesus. The pleasures he sought were "fancies," every other woman "but a dream of thee." These images throw into lively relief the radiant greeting that celebrates the lovers' literal and metaphorical awakening into their mature love: "And now good-morrow to our waking souls."

The theme of sea-discoverers and map readers pursuing new worlds was topical in Donne's time, as the boundaries of the old world were broken to include freshly discovered continents. Since the dominant contrast in the poem is between true love and false, it is possible that these explorers carry the additional connotation of sexual adventurers. However this may be, the world that the lovers are shutting out is one of high excitement and romance; how infinitely more attractive, then, must be the self-sufficient universe of their love, which is capable of rendering their small room "an everywhere." Theirs is a perfect world, as opposed to the earthly spheres of the explorers. As such, it is not marred by the seasons' inconstancy, and is of such a fine equal spiritual substance, that it can neither weaken nor die.

Claire Robinson

THE GOOSE FISH

Author: Howard Nemerov (1920-   )
Type of poem: Lyric
First published: 1955, in *The Salt Garden*

The Poem

"The Goose Fish" is a study in irony, and the irony begins with the title. On one level, the title is straightforward and appropriate, because the goose fish occupies center stage in the poem's "story": It is assigned many roles, including onlooker, comedian, optimist, emblem, and patriarch. The irony is that the fish is dead, so one might well wonder how significant any of those roles might be. The poem is in iambic tetrameter and trimeter, in five stanzas of nine lines each (eight lines of tetrameter and the last of trimeter).

The first stanza sets the scene—a moonlit night on the beach—and contains the poem's central action: Two people, believing themselves alone, passionately embrace. For a short time, they believe themselves "emparadised" on the "long shore" where "their shadows [are] as one." In stanza 2, the lovers feel embarrassed afterward, but nevertheless stand united, "conspiring hand in hand." Believing themselves alone, they are shocked to discover that they have been "watched" by a goose fish "turning up, though dead/ His hugely grinning head." This ghoulish discovery not only shocks them but also induces guilt. The presence of the goose fish, in a sense, "gooses" the lovers out of self-centeredness into the realization that their lovemaking did not take place in isolation.

Stanza 3 shows the lovers staring at the dead fish, wondering at its significance. Before discovering it, the lovers had thought that lovemaking would carve for them "a world their own." Having realized that they are not apart from the rest of the world, they try to place a private meaning onto "the observer." Stanza 4 reveals that the lovers, not knowing what the fish symbolizes, decide that its "wide and moony grin" makes it first a comedian, then an "emblem of/ Their sudden, new and guilty love." There is a suggestion in this last line that the fish's observation makes their love "guilty" either because they have been "caught" or because of their modesty at having been watched.

The last stanza ironically stresses the continuing naïveté of the lovers. Not knowing what to make of their grisly audience, the lovers decide that the fish is their friend and their "patriarch," perhaps in an effort to extort a sort of blessing from the fish. The grin, which is so grotesque in death, fails to explain anything. The presence of death, like a bad joke, has accompanied the lovers both before and after their "private" union, just as the moon continues to follow its accustomed path along the sky.

Forms and Devices

The action in "The Goose Fish" is achieved through the lovers' experience of different stages of feeling and knowing, rather than through their experiencing sev-

LIST OF TITLES IN VOLUME 3

MASTERPLOTS II

POETRY SERIES

GOATS AND MONKEYS

Author: Derek Walcott (1930-   )
Type of poem: Narrative
First published: 1965, in *The Castaway and Other Poems*

The Poem

"Goats and Monkeys" provides an excellent example of intertextuality — that is, it relies on an earlier text but in itself becomes an altogether new work, sometimes called the "echo-text." The epigraph from William Shakespeare's *Othello* (1604) announces Derek Walcott's source, one he expects the reader to know. The lines come from act 1, scene 1, of the play and are spoken by Othello's jealous ensign, Iago, as he reveals to Brabantio that his daughter, Desdemona, has run away with the "blackamoor" Othello. In these charged lines, the "black ram" (a male sheep) depicts Othello and the white ewe (a female sheep) Desdemona. "Tupping" means they are "even now" engaging in sexual intercourse; "tupping" is synonymous with "ramming," the kind of pun that would appeal to Walcott, whose poetry abounds in elaborate wordplay.

The poem's title is not altogether clear. Lecherous men are sometimes called goats, and when made to act like fools they are dubbed monkeys; in the play, Iago sees Othello as a lecher, then sets out to make a fool of him. Yet that seems a rather literal and oversimplified reading. Men whose wives are unfaithful to them — as Othello thinks Desdemona is — are derisively called goats. The goat is also part of the zodiac, to which the poem alludes. While Walcott never describes Othello specifically as a goat, he does at one point refer to him as an "ape" and refers to him throughout in bestial terms, most often as a bull. So the title remains elusive, yet extraordinarily suggestive.

In the poem's five stanzas, uneven in length, free in structure, and rich in imagery, Walcott recounts the story of Othello and Desdemona. The first stanza records their sexual union. The next reveals the passion of Desdemona, who has been "Dazzled by that bull's bulk"; still, the poet asks, should not the "poor girl" realize that tragedy awaits her? The third stanza recapitulates the first two, elaborating on their sexual passion and foreshadowing the cruelty that the black Othello will inflict on his white lover. The fourth stanza tells how Othello "arraigns" Desdemona's "barren innocence" by accusing her of infidelity, as though her whiteness "limns lechery" — "limn" meaning to illuminate. In the final stanza, "this mythical, horned beast" — possibly the goat from the zodiac, or maybe the mythological bull — murders Desdemona in a "bestial, comic agony."

While this summary covers the main points of a story already well known, it does little justice to the way Walcott has echoed Shakespeare's text. In fact, he also echoes a number of other texts in a less obvious manner. The sustaining metaphor of Othello as the earth and Desdemona as the moon brings to mind the structure of seventeenth century metaphysical poetry by writers such as John Donne and George

Herbert. Walcott also assumes that the reader knows the Greek myths of Pasiphaë and Eurydice.

This poem, though, comprises no mere retelling of the story Shakespeare had already retold, no mimicry of metaphysical poems, no slavish dependence on mythology. Walcott's impressive exercise in intertextuality holds larger intentions.

Forms and Devices

To underscore Othello's blackness and Desdomona's whiteness, the poet transforms Othello into the earth, Desdemona into the moon. The first stanza, when Othello seduces Desdemona, describes an eclipse: The earth (Othello) covers the moon (Desdemona), and "God's light is put out." The poet compares Othello to Africa, as "a vast sidling [furtive or fawning] shadow" that obscures the moon — or the white world represented by Desdemona. Throughout, this black/white imagery, stemming from the introductory metaphor of earth and moon, accentuates the poem's apparent racial overtones. As Walcott extends the elaborate comparison, he refers to "the sun of Cyprus," an apt allusion in that Othello and Desdemona flee to Cyprus once she has left her father's Venetian home.

Then, to make Desdemona's plight more resonant, the poet compares her to doomed women from Greek mythology, Pasiphaë and Eurydice. Pasiphaë, the daughter of the sun god and wife of Minos, fell in love with a bull that Poseidon had given to Minos. Like Othello, Minos brought about his wife's downfall, for he refused to sacrifice the bull; as punishment, Poseidon cursed the faithless Minos' wife Pasiphaë, decreeing that she would unite with the bull and "breed horned monsters." From this union came the Minotaur, a creature with the body of a man and the head of a bull. Walcott turns Othello into another Minotaur, the beast who wreaked havoc on innocents in his labyrinth — an elaborate maze of passageways — until he was slain by Theseus. In the second stanza, the poet speaks of Othello's mind as a "hellish labyrinth" in which Desdemona's soul will be swallowed.

The other allusion recalls the story of Eurydice, wife of Orpheus, who died from a snake bite and descended into the underworld, from which Orpheus almost rescued her. Like Minos — and Othello — he brings about his beloved's destruction, in his case by looking back at her, which he had been forbidden to do until they reached the earth. Eurydice must return to the underworld, and Orpheus loses her the second time. Thus the "hellish labyrinth" of Othello's mind assumes another meaning, compared now to the Hades that swallows Eurydice and, by implication, Desdemona.

Walcott, perhaps taking his cue from the strong sexuality of the passage in *Othello*, fills the poem with charged sexual imagery, which serves to delineate in another way Desdemona's innocence and Othello's corruption. Othello's "earthen bulk" presses against the white Desdemona's "bosom," his "smoky hand" charring her "marble throat." "Virgin and ape," "maid and malevolent Moor" they are called, as the "panther-black" man violates the "white flesh." Othello's sexuality conjures up "raw musk" (the odorous sexual secretions of various male animals) and "sweat," his penis a "moon-shaped sword" girded by fury, while a "white fruit/ pulped ripe by fondling but doubly sweet" describes Desdemona's sexuality.

Themes and Meanings

Walcott deceives the reader of "Goats and Monkeys," for until the last two lines it appears that the poem follows the traditional view that black is evil, white is good; black is corruption, white is innocence; black is the destroyer, white the creator. In the final lines, the poet contradicts what he has seemingly argued. Othello, the "mythical horned beast" so carefully and effectively drawn to this point, the poet states, is "no more/ monstrous for being black." The words "comic," "mockery," and "farcically" appear in the final stanza, perhaps to hint that the reader is not to take literally what has been presented in the first four stanzas. In effect, Walcott subverts his own poem.

Walcott's ancestors were Africans brought to the Caribbean as slaves to work on sugar plantations; he has some Anglo-Saxon blood as well. Several generations later, Walcott grew up in an educated home, aware of his African heritage but thoroughly schooled in the English language and the British tradition dominating his tiny West Indian island. Walcott was in his early twenties when the Caribbean colonial outposts gained independence from Great Britain. As a child of the faded British Empire, he has often addressed the experience of colonialism in his poetry, an experience he describes as divisive. Yet, unlike many other postcolonial writers of non-Anglo-Saxon origin, he has never promoted a back-to-Africa movement as the panacea for this divisiveness or as a form of revenge for the injustice of British imperialism.

Ironically, long after "Goats and Monkeys" was written—it is one of Walcott's early poems—postcolonial literary-political theorists discovered new meaning in *Othello*, and set out to read it as a racial document. Othello represents the innocent black man, seduced and corrupted by the temptress Desdemona, the white world. Seeking revenge on this white villain, whom he believes to be unfaithful, black Othello rejects her whiteness and destroys it.

Long working to overcome the divisions between black and white through art rather than through political revenge and rejection of his white heritage, Walcott in 1965 appears almost to have foreseen the revisionist reading of *Othello* and, in "Goats and Monkeys," pre-answered and pre-disputed its claims from the 1980's. Walcott concludes that black is no worse than white, that human nature possesses the capacity for cruelty no matter the color of skin. At first this may seem a simplistic way to approach the poem, but not when the first four stanzas are reconsidered in light of the final statement—"no more/ monstrous for being black." These words redefine all that has preceded them and turn the old conception of black and white into a "comic agony" and a "mockery," one that can only be taken "farcically."

Robert L. Ross

GOBLIN MARKET

Author: Christina Rossetti (1830-1894)
Type of poem: Narrative
First published: 1862, in *Goblin Market and Other Poems*

The Poem

"Goblin Market" is Christina Rossetti's most famous poem. In its first stanza, goblins offer fruit for sale. Goblins are traditionally evil creatures who entice human beings into evil. In stanza 2, the sisters Laura and Lizzie hear goblin cries. Lizzie warns Laura that they are not to look, but Laura does not pay heed. Lizzie, however, puts a finger in each ear, perhaps as much to drown out her sister's overtures as to stifle the goblin voices. To be noted here is Lizzie's refusal to allow herself to be overcome carnally. Laura, on the other hand, allows herself to be filled with sight and sound. Lizzie flees; Laura "lingers."

In successive stanzas, the goblins offer their fruit directly to Laura, who responds that she is without money. To this the goblins reply that a golden lock of her hair will be payment enough. Laura yields, and she sucks the fruit insatiably. Lizzie cautions Laura on her sister's return, reminding her of Jeanie, who had pined away after eating the goblin fruit. Laura tells of her own eating, which has not diminished her.

There follows an eloquent stanza depictive of the sisters' oneness, but on the morrow, it is clear that their fates are diverging. Lizzie is happy; Laura longs for more of the goblin fruit, but to no avail. Now, only Lizzie can hear the goblin cries. Day after day, Laura languishes, her health declining, her work neglected.

Lizzie, filled with sorrow for Laura, would like to buy the fruit for Laura, but she remembers Jeanie's fate. Laura's decline, however, forces her to make the reluctant choice. When she meets the goblins, they urge her to eat with them and not simply buy, but she refrains, arousing their ire. They abuse her verbally and physically, pressing the fruit against her mouth. At last, worn out by Lizzie's resistance, the goblins disband.

On her return, Lizzie beseeches Laura to suck the goblin juices from her mouth. The taste of these vestige juices, however, is like wormwood to the responding Laura. Laura falls into a deep sleep, watched over by Lizzie. On waking, she is no longer bound with desire for the goblin fruit.

The poem closes with a description of how, when Laura and Lizzie one day had children of their own, they resorted to this story of the goblins and of a sister's love to show that "there is no friend like a sister" to help one along life's way. Ironically, the same volume in which "Goblin Market" appears also features two poems, "Sister Maude" and "Noble Sisters," depicting (and denouncing) a sister's betrayal.

Forms and Devices

It is the extraordinary capacity of Christina Rossetti to exact profundity from what seems a children's fantasy. It is a trademark of all her poetry, the combining of the simple and the mystical, the ability to see beyond the ordinary.

At its outset, Rossetti entices readers with the hypnotic rhythms of the goblin imperatives, seducing readers into participating in Laura's fall through their reiterated appeal to the senses. This is a poem meant to be read aloud. Though it does not have regularity of rhyme scheme, it has a sensory dimension — not only in the images it presents, but also in the multiple use of *s* sounds in the opening two stanzas, along with the symmetry within lines through the pervasive use of paired dactyls:

> Pine-apples, blackberries
> Apricots, strawberries (lines 13-14).

Rhythms then shift into rhyming iambs midway,

> In summer weather, —
> All ripe together (lines 15-16),

lending a mesmerizing tone that reinforces the temptation motif represented in the goblins' wares.

Frequently Rossetti will employ rhetorical parallelism, with syntax extended for several lines to suggest comparison and contrast between the two sisters through repetition of prepositional phrasing:

> Like two blossoms on one stem,
> Like two flakes of new-fall'n snow,
> Like two wands of ivory (lines 188-190).

She also employs repetition of absolutes, as in "One content, one sick in part" (line 212). In other stages of the poem, Rossetti further spellbinds readers with extensive couplet rhyming. In mood, the reader is in a "once upon a time" world, belying the seriousness of its theme. In short, through technique, Rossetti captures the outer allure of the temptation experience.

There also exists an ingenuous symmetry of plot, conforming to the symmetry found within lines as means to establishing comparison and contrast. In the story, both sisters confront the goblins, though with different results. One indulges and loses part of herself in the yielding of the lock of hair; the other pays nothing and returns with her money. The one is overcome; the other overcomes.

In its imagery, the poem exhibits resemblances to the aims of the Pre-Raphaelite Brotherhood, a movement with which both Rossetti and her brother Dante Gabriel Rossetti were associated, along with William Morris, Edward Burne-Jones, and John Millais. For the Pre-Raphaelites, every detail mattered in the securing of ultimate moral ends. In art, they practiced a narrative painting — sincere, unsentimental, and unadorned. For Pre-Raphelites, color was significant in suggesting spiritual truths. In "Goblin Market," Rossetti employs white, gold and blue in association with Lizzie (lines 408-421), suggesting virginity and saintliness. Orange, which she also employs, had a traditional emblem of purity and fecundity.

Despite the Pre-Raphaelite themes and coloring, Rossetti's poetry never manifests the ornateness of her brother's later style. As befits the religious poet generally, hers is a style reflective of humility and of interest in the afterworld as a reality worth seeking. Ironically, it was her "Goblin Market," with its combination of fantasy and religious moralism, that first won an audience for the brotherhood.

There can be no question but that this deeply pious poet was influenced in her fondness for parataxis (the repetitive use of phrases and clauses without connectors), rhetorical parallelism, and plain diction by the King James Bible. In the dictional element, Rossetti seems to be drawing directly on New Testament themes in association with the sacrificial Jesus, as in the use of the term "wormwood."

Themes and Meanings

"Goblin Market" established Christina Rossetti's reputation early in her career and has remained her most famous poem. One of its principal themes deals with two kinds of love—the profane, which kills, and the spiritual, which nourishes. Pervasive in the poem is the Communion, or atonement, theme, as in "Eat me, drink me" (line 471), another hint of the atoning power of sacrificial love.

At the historical level, the poem should be understood as a tribute to Maria, her older sister, who protected her from making some kind of wrong choice at a very vulnerable time in her life, perhaps over wrongly placed affections. The manuscript itself is dedicated "To M. F. R.," the initials of her sister. According to one version of the poem's origins, Christina nearly eloped with a William Bell Scott, who turned out to be already married. It is known that she loved James Collinson, a painter and original member of the brotherhood, but broke her engagement when he became Catholic. The facts cannot finally be known, since the supposed elopement plan developed nine years after her turning down of Collinson.

At the literary level, it is probable that this poem is meant as Christian allegory. By this norm, Lizzie becomes a rendition of Jesus, who resisted the Temptation and gave of himself for others; at another theological level, she is an aspect of divine grace with power to effect restoration. Laura, on the other hand, emerges an Adam and Eve entity given to moral infirmity. As Christian allegory, it speaks of atoning love, replete with biblical nuance. "Fruit" suggests the Garden of Eden, with its forbidden fruit. "Maids" hints at virginity, or of an innocence before the fall, perhaps a sexual innocence. The prohibition of lines 41-42 replays the biblical Garden of Eden, and the goblins reenact the serpent's role as catalyst to sinning. In line 260, there is mention of "a tree of life." To be noted are the consequences of the kind of fruit to which Laura succumbs. Certainly it is not that of the "tree of life" but points instead to the seven deadly sins in terms of gluttony (lines 134-166), envy (lines 253-255), and sloth (lines 293-296). The poem may be a warning as to how one falls victim to temptation—an allegory on sin and its consequences. Laura flirts with evil. Lizzie "cover[s] up her eyes."

At the psychological level, it may be said that the sisters represent psychic aspects of a single personality. Laura seeks escape from the mundane world through the fruit of self-indulgence. She lives for the wish, or nonreality principle. It is the way of infantile retrogression, yet an impulse in everyone. On the other hand, Lizzie performs a therapeutic role, confronting the dangers of such an approach to life. As such, she represents an objectifying side of the psyche, or the cognitive dimension promoting insight and reintegration.

It may also be said that the poem manifests repressed sexuality with its talk of maids (virgins). Moreover, its depiction of the fruit seems very Freudian in its vehicle of oral imagery. This is not to say that Rossetti was conscious of an inner dissonance regarding sexual issues. Certainly, she was very pious all of her life. The fact remains, however, that she lived in an age that forbade any open sexual expression; Rossetti may have been one of the Victorian era's several figures unknowingly tormented in their sensibility. (Another poem to examine in connection with "Goblin Market" is Rossetti's "Life and Death.") In essence, the Laura-Lizzie polarity may represent a psychical fragmentation between desire and conscience—desire toward this world and conscience toward the next.

Ralph Robert Joly

GOD'S GRANDEUR

Author: Gerard Manley Hopkins (1844-1889)
Type of poem: Sonnet
First published: 1918, in *Poems of Gerard Manley Hopkins, Now First Published, with Notes by Robert Bridges*

The Poem

"God's Grandeur" is a Petrarchan sonnet describing a world infused by God with a beauty and power that withstands human corruption. The poem begins with the assertion that God has "charged" the world with grandeur. It then describes the implications of this "charge." The grandeur is like a physical force, an electric current, a brightness that can be seen.

The poet questions the human response to this grandeur. Why do humans not "reck his rod?" That is, why do they not recognize and accept divine rule? Instead, humans have dirtied this world by using it for mundane purposes. The images work on both the literal and metaphorical level. The poem may be read both as a literal lament for the destruction of the environment by industry, and as a metaphorical lament that humans are more concerned with the prosaic and utilitarian than with spiritual values. In any event, the world seems tarnished, and humans seem insulated, unable to perceive the underlying beauty and grandeur.

The poem's sestet dispels the gloom evoked in the first part. Even though humans are often insensitive to the glory of the world, "There lives the dearest freshness deep down things." The beauty and power of the world remains inviolable, intact. Though the night seems dark, there is a continuing restoration of the light and morning, because the presence of God, like the dove of peace, protects and restores the world.

Although Gerard Manley Hopkins wrote this poem in 1877, he did not seek to publish his poems; he entrusted them to his friend Robert Bridges. Bridges placed some of these poems in anthologies, but it was not until after the poet's death, in 1918, that Bridges published a volume of his friend's poetry.

Forms and Devices

Sonnets are fourteen-line poems built according to strict conventions in a tightly structured form. Hopkins was intrigued with the sonnet form and used it often, sometimes adding his own variations. His poem "That Nature is a Heraclitean Fire and of the comfort of the Resurrection" is a modified sonnet with twenty-three lines.

"God's Grandeur," however, is written according to the conventions of the Petrarchan sonnet, named for the Italian writer Petrarch. This sonnet form has two parts, the initial eight lines, or the octave (rhymed *abba, abba*), and the concluding six lines, or sestet (which here uses the rhyme scheme *cd, cd, cd*). Typically, the Petrarchan sonnet poses a problem in the octave and presents a resolution in the sestet. Hopkins poses the problem of the human response to the beauty of nature, as created by God. The resolution comes through God's grace, for divine concern preserves the beauty of the world intact despite human despoliation.

Hopkins studied Anglo-Saxon and Welsh poetry and drew from them an interest in alliteration, which he believed was essential to poetry. In "God's Grandeur" the letter *g* is associated with God: "grandeur," "greatness," "gathers," and "Ghost." Each line of the poem is knit together through intricate sound patterns that include alliteration (repetition of consonants at the start of words), assonance (repetition of vowel sounds) and consonance (the recurrence of consonants within words). For example, the second and third lines read:

> It will flame out, like shining from shook foil;
> It gathers to a greatness, like the ooze of oil.

Notice how vowels (the long *i* of shining and like: the *a* of flame and greatness) and consonants (the repeated *l*, *sh*, *f*, *m*, *n*, *s*, and *g*) are echoed and re-echoed in the lines. Here and throughout the poem, words are repeated as well. In these lines, the simple words "it" and "like" recur. Elsewhere in the poem, words are repeated for emphasis: "have trod, have trod, have trod" suggests the repetitive, almost marchlike tread of generations of trudging people. The assonance of the vowels in "seared," "bleared," and "smeared" again drives home the ugliness of human destruction. The last line of the poem draws together in a complex pattern the consonants *w*, *r*, *b*, *d*, and *s*, which have echoed throughout the sestet and have come to carry the associations of the gentle, protecting warmth of God as a nesting dove. Further, the word "world" itself brings the reader back to the first line.

Alliteration may have had a philosophical meaning for Hopkins. He believed that the universe is built on the unity of God, which finds expression in the diversity of the natural world. Alliteration is a principle of showing the similarity of sounds in words of different meanings. Thus, alliteration becomes a poetic analogy of the unity underlying the diversity of the world.

Drawing again from the Anglo-Saxon and Welsh traditions, Hopkins made significant innovations in poetic rhythm. He was chiefly concerned with intensity, with capturing the essence of an image, idea, or action. To that end, he would often omit inessential words. Rather than using an even rhythm of stressed and unstressed syllables, as in iambic pentameter, he was interested in the number of stressed syllables. He might omit unstressed syllables for effect or use extra unstressed syllables where they seemed useful. One may scan this poem by counting the number of stressed syllables in each line. These vary from five stresses in the first line to six in the last.

Themes and Meanings

The problem that Hopkins poses in the octave is that of the human response to God: Why do people ignore the beauty and grandeur of God's presence in the natural world? The problem of the world's beauty and its divine origin was a central one for Hopkins, who was a talented artist and musician as well as a poet. His sketch-books are full of detailed drawings of forms he found in nature: shells, twigs, waves, and trees. When he converted to Catholicism in 1866, he gave up his original plan of becoming a painter and decided to become a Jesuit priest. At that time, he worried that his attraction to the natural world and his love of music, art, and poetry was in contradiction to his religious vocation. He feared that his aesthetic impulses would draw him away from the strict asceticism he believed he must practice. He destroyed most of his early poems when he took religious orders.

Hopkins' resolution of his conflict came about when he was deeply moved by a newspaper account of a shipwreck that killed five German nuns. He told his rector about his feelings. The rector remarked that he wished someone would write a poem about the subject, and Hopkins took this casual comment as a personal mandate. He broke his seven-year poetic silence by writing "The Wreck of the *Deutschland*." After that, he continued to write poetry. In his poems, Hopkins explored his compli-cated feelings of faith and doubt. By celebrating the beauty of the natural world as an expression of God's power and "grandeur," Hopkins could reconcile his religious faith with his love of nature.

Repeatedly in his poetry Hopkins used his deep love of nature's beauty to reaffirm his belief in the God who created and maintained the world. In "God's Grandeur," this theme is developed with a great technical virtuosity to create a passionate poem that is somehow both a warning and a reassurance. Although Bridges delayed pub-lication of Hopkins' work, fearing that readers would find it strange and difficult, contemporary readers find Hopkins an exciting and powerful poet. It is difficult to imagine modern poetry without the groundbreaking work of Gerard Manley Hopkins.

Karen F. Stein

GOLDEN VERSES

Author: Gérard de Nerval (Gérard Labrunie, 1808-1855)
Type of poem: Sonnet
First published: 1845, as "Vers dorés"; in *Les Chimères*, 1854; collected in *An Anthology of French Poetry from Nerval to Valéry in English Translation with French Originals*, 1958

The Poem

Gérard de Nerval's sonnet "Golden Verses" relates humankind to the natural world. In its dual suggestions of the dominance of man and the dominance of nature, the poem draws on a conflict that is still very real in modern times, as humanity tries to decide when to control nature and when to leave it alone.

This traditional Petrarchan sonnet in Alexandrine verse concludes Nerval's sonnet sequence *Les Chimères*. The title (chimeras) may refer to the mythological beast or to any imaginary vision. In the light of this definition, one wonders which of the views expressed in his sonnet Nerval held to be true. The first quatrain, with its reference to man as a "free thinker," recalls the scientific positivism of the Enlightenment, when the concept of progress by means of the scientific analysis of nature promised to free man from the superstitions that free thinkers associated with traditional religious beliefs. Both modern science and the Christian views that had preceded it, however, granted to humankind a special status that made it superior to all other things in nature. Both of these schools of thought pushed aside a much older belief in which ancient peoples had seen divinity in nonhuman forms.

In the first quatrain, Nerval seeks to recall the old belief, asking how humans can believe that they alone are capable of thought when "life bursts forth in all things" around them. When he says that the "universe is absent" from human "councils," Nerval's suggestion of a governmental body invokes an area of thought that gives great attention to the rights of humankind and little consideration to those of nature.

The second quatrain asks man to respect the various elements of nature, but a change occurs in the final line when Nerval asserts that "all has power over you." Up to this point, the power in the poem was human power, the "forces that you hold" of the first quatrain. Now, suddenly, humankind must face a strength that is potentially superior to its own. When the sestet begins with the imperative "Fear," the once secure position of humankind is clearly threatened.

Nerval seeks to restore the respect that was once given to nonhuman things. If a "hidden God" resides within each element of the natural world, humankind has a sacred duty to respect the life and growth of these things. When the final line says that "a pure spirit grows," however, it introduces two new concepts into the poem. First, the pure spirit seems to be of a more transcendent nature than that of the animal or vegetable life to which the earlier lines seem to be referring. If this is the case, the growth of this spirit constitutes a form of theological progress that far outweighs the self-centered concerns of humanity.

Forms and Devices

Nerval's choice of imagery in "Golden Verses" reflects the context of the nine-teenth century, but in a way that is distinctly his own. The Romantic poets' concept of nature was strongly pantheistic. Victor Hugo repeatedly invoked such a world, as he does in his poem "To Albert Dürer" (from *Les Voix intérieures*, 1837) in which the forest, to Dürer's "visionary eye" becomes "a hideous monster." This pantheistic life in nature, apparent only to the artist's penetrating vision, also retained a link with its classical origins. (According to Hugo, Albrecht Dürer "saw . . . the faun . . . the sylvan . . . Pan.") Thus it seems strange that, except for his sonnet's epigraph, which is attributed to Pythagoras, Nerval does not cite explicitly classical sources, but presents his pantheism in an entirely modern context.

Paradoxically, the only special degree of insight to which Nerval's sonnet alludes is not that of the poet as seer, but that of the free thinker who believes that humans alone are capable of thought. The only voice that recalls the insights of a pantheistic world is that of Nerval himself.

In the second quatrain, Nerval's generic imagery leads the reader ever further from the initial focus on humankind, first to the beast, then to the flower, and finally to metal. In his choice of categorical references that do not specify which beast or which flower, Nerval parallels a generic form of expression that Charles Baudelaire would develop later in *Les Fleurs du mal* (1857; *Flowers of Evil*, 1909) in which flowers, almost never a specific variety, become emblems of beauty and poetry.

With the final element named in the second quatrain, metal, Nerval draws espe-cially close to Baudelaire. In his poem "To the Reader," Baudelaire describes moral strength as "the rich metal of our will," and references to metal and gems occur frequently in his work. Despite the similar vocabulary, however, this usage serves to pinpoint the difference between Baudelaire and Nerval in their use of generic nature images. For Baudelaire, the importance of either the metal or the flower comes from its role in representing an attribute or a creation of man: will or poetry. For Nerval, the life that exists in natural elements does not depend on man. It has an independent status, resisting human attempts to dominate it, but can nevertheless influence the world.

Given this subordination of humankind's role, the choice of imagery in the sestet contains an apparent contradiction. When Nerval tells the free thinker to "fear in the blind wall a gaze spying on you," not only does blindness conflict with seeing, but also the wall itself seems an unlikely object for this role. Although they may contain natural stones, walls are human construction, but this exploitation of the material is doubtless what Nerval has in mind in his injunction not to make "any impious im-age" of it.

In any case, the progression of objects Nerval invokes in this sonnet takes one far from those in which one is accustomed to imagining life. Plant and animal life are not unusual, but to find sentience in metal or stone, even after the latter has been worked by man, demands a leap of faith. Thus the "eye" born in the final tercet seems that of a chimeric being.

Themes and Meanings

While with his generic imagery Nerval seems to make a simple statement that is devoid of detail and as spare as the sonnet form is brief, when the poem is considered in its context, a further complexity emerges that is perhaps analogous to the sonnet in its detailed structure. Between its autobiographical opening sonnet, "El Desdichado," and this concluding one, *Les Chimères* devotes five sonnets to figures from pagan antiquity and five to the sonnet sequence "Christ on the Mount of Olives." In the context of "Golden Verses," this pagan/Christian dualism may seem to combine views centered on nature and on man. The time sequence of the poems, however, suggests a more coherent view.

Time as it is invoked in "El Desdichado" works backward from the early references to "my only Star," said to be the woman Nerval loved, and the relatively modern Dürer engraving of *Melencolia I* (1514) to classical references to the Acheron and Orpheus. Nerval frequently connected his family to early periods of French history, but here he combines French references with those from a much earlier time. Thus, by the time the first sonnet ends, one is ready to accept Nerval's assertion in the first pagan poem, "Myrtho," that "the Muse made me one of the sons of Greece."

One may wonder how much of Nerval's pagan experience was real and how much was imagined, for while he asserts that he "had drunk the intoxication" of it, the role of the Muse still implies the intervention of imagination. The experience of the sonnet sequence takes Nerval to a number of early cultures, and the nature gods of Egypt in "Horus" parallel the pantheism of the Greeks. In all these settings, however, he finds evidence of a dying world. The "clay gods" of "Myrtho" are broken, and Isis in "Horus" says "the new spirit is calling me." In "Delfica," Nerval seeks consolation: "They will come back, those Gods you weep for!" Inevitably, however, Christ follows the pagan gods.

Nerval shows the reader Christ at his most desperate moment, facing death alone, but his Christ speaks already of a vast experience. Unlike the pagan sonnets, which are rich in flower images that may be linked to the nature invoked in "Golden Verses," "Christ on the Mount of Olives" abandons such imagery for a vaster vision of "worlds," and Christ affirms that "no spirit exists in these immensities." A profusion of life existed in the elements of nature, but it has become invisible to the Christian view that is oriented toward the cosmos but not toward the things of this world.

Thus "Golden Verses" may serve as the moral that concludes the sonnet sequence. Having experienced and compared the cultures of the past, Nerval finds himself in the visionary role of the poet who should advise humanity. The context of the poem may be Greek without specifically Greek references within the text because its message results from the entirety of Nerval's poetic vision. The multiple imperatives of the poem define the poet's role in that it is he who must return humanity to the consciousness of nature.

Dorothy M. Betz

GOLFERS

Author: Irving Layton (Irving Peter Lazarovitch, 1912-   )
Type of poem: Satire
First published: 1955, in *The Blue Propeller*

The Poem

"Golfers" is a short poem in free verse. It comprises three stanzas of three lines each, a parenthetical single-line stanza, and a closing couplet. It belongs to one of the most intensely creative and productive periods in Irving Layton's long publishing career as a poet—the middle to late 1950's and the early 1960's—when he wrote some of the best and most memorable of his poems. Many of his poems of this period celebrate the creative urge so central to Layton's life and writing. The central observation of "Golfers" is one that is voiced over and over in Layton's poetry: contempt for those whom he believes deny the life force by leading lives and taking moral stances that seem to Layton sterile and static.

Of the many volumes in which "Golfers" has appeared since its first publication in Layton's seventh solely-authored collection, *The Blue Propeller* (1955), the one that seems best suited to its tone and intent is F. R. Scott and A. J. M. Smith's *The Blasted Pine: An Anthology of Satire, Invective, and Disrespectful Verse*, first published in 1957 and reissued in a second edition in 1967, Canada's centennial year. In both editions, "Golfers" is included in a section entitled "Solid Citizens," in which Canadians, particularly of Anglo-Scottish descent, and their institutions and mores are the chief target of the satirical verse. Though it is nowhere stated in Jewish poet Layton's poem that the golfers depicted are Gentile, they do seem the epitome of the "country-club set": smug and exclusive Gentile materialists and nation-builders that the professedly atheist but strongly Hebraist and socialist Layton abhorred and whom he has pilloried all of his writing life.

In "Golfers," Layton depicts golf, a slow, mannered game of strategy and precision, as the choice of those people who relate not at all to earthy, Dionysian joy—the sensual, creative principle—but who cultivate a cerebral sterility of morality, mind, and spirit. Wynne Frances, in a critical work on Irving Layton, says:

> Philistinism is the name Layton gives to that compound of smugness, rigidity, gentility, complacency, materialism, and moral apathy that he regards as the most insidious threat to the creative spirit. He attacks it wherever he finds it . . . anywhere in the world.

Forms and Devices

The poem's opening three lines are a simile formed on an allusion to Michel de Montaigne (1533-1592), the renowned French essayist unsurpassed for his thorough, enlightened, and lively observation of human nature with all of its idiosyncracies and folly. Montaigne's "distinction/ between virtue and innocence" differentiates between virtue, a chosen moral position, and innocence, a lack of experience. Layton believes that the creative urge can be best expressed and satisfied through experience, so that innocence is not necessarily a desirable state: virtue seems to him a moral stance that often precludes experience and invites intellectual, moral, and spiritual stasis. The golfers appear to have opted for virtue: irritated, the poet observes, "what gets you is their unbewilderment." The coined word, where "certainty" or "confidence" might have served, implies an attitude of deliberate disengagement from the turmoil and vitality of a headlong encounter with experience, with *life*.

Stanza 2 comprises another simile: The intrusion of the golfers into a pastoral scene is likened to the despoliation of landscape by raw, unfinished houses. The golfers "come into the picture suddenly"; whether this phrase is simply a colloquial expression of the golfers' sudden appearance or is an expression of their assault on the poet's artistic sensibilities and his communion with the natural setting is unclear. In stanza 3, the tone is jeering; the contempt of the poet for these Philistines is intensified. The poem's tenth line, a parenthetical aside, picks up the thread of the moral and spiritual stance that the poet attributes to the golfers in the poem's first stanza, and the reader realizes the extended metaphor on which the satirical structure of the poem is based. "(What finally gets you is their chastity)," complains the poet; the golfers are compared to reluctant virgins, trapped in restraints that prohibit their access to sensual pleasure and fulfillment.

While virtue and innocence can be admired and understood as conditions involving free will or inexperience, chastity is generally viewed as having been imposed and is regarded as an undesirable state. To a poet who embraces Dionysian philosophy with the overt enthusiasm that Layton always has, chastity is practically obscene. Thus in the closing couplet the poet makes a final sardonic observation about the golfers: "And that no theory of pessimism is complete/ which altogether ignores them."

Themes and Meanings

From the beginning of his career as a poet, Layton has defined himself as anti-intellectual, although the profusion of literary, historical, philosophical, and mythological allusion in his poetry speaks to the enormous range of his reading and thinking and belies the anti-intellectual stance he takes. According to critic Eli Mandel, Layton's is "a poetry of profound social and personal concern. . . . Layton belongs with the sort of writer (and artist) [George Bernard] Shaw was prepared to speak of as poet-prophet." In the eloquent "Foreword" to his 1959 collection *A Red Carpet for the Sun*, in which "Golfers" also appears, Layton voices his central concerns, laying out the issues he takes up so aggressively in his poetry. Those concerns are ego- and life-centered; poetry is the artistic medium through which he addresses them:

The free individual — independent and gay — is farther from realization than he ever was. Still, in a world where corruption is the norm and enslavement universal, all art celebrates him, prepares the way for his coming. . . . Poetry, by giving dignity and utterance to our distress, enables us to hope, makes compassion reasonable.

"Golfers," though ultimately too slight a poem to sustain the weight of Layton's vociferous disapproval, does embody what Mandel cites as Layton's central themes: "[T]he nature of the creative process, . . . and the social implications of both human perversity and creativity. . . . But beyond, . . . is the question of articulation itself, the pattern and meaning of poetic form." If Layton's vision is thus understood, the rationale of "Golfers" 's central simile becomes clear. More than being symbolic of a social and cultural group that Layton abhors, the golfers are anathema to his beliefs as a person and a poet. The comparison of the golfers to the "gaps [in subsequent collections amended to the harsher "gapes"] and planed wood" of unfinished houses depicts them as raw, ungainly, without athletic ability or (more significantly) aesthetic wholeness or satisfaction. The poet invites the reader to share his opinion that "among sportsmen they are the metaphysicians." He dismisses golf as an effete game that is contemplative and bloodless, one in which the golfers may strike poses and take attitudes—just as metaphysicians are often regarded as practitioners of a most abstruse branch of philosophy. The golfers are laughable, in the poet's view, because they are "intent, untalkative, pursuing Unity," an aesthetic structure as artificial, empty, and unsatisfying as an unfinished house. (In his *Gulliver's Travels* (1726), eighteenth century satirist Jonathan Swift similarly mocked the fictitious Laputians, scholars so cerebrally preoccupied that they needed "Flappers" to draw their attention to earthly realities.)

The bitter irony of the poem's closing couplet, then, arises from Layton's view that golfers represent almost everything he abhors as a person and a poet. "Why are people so destructive and joy-hating? Is it a perception of the unimportance of their lives finally penetrating the bark of their complacency and egotism?" he asks plaintively in the "Foreword" of *A Red Carpet for the Sun*. It is above all the misplaced arrogance of the golfers on which Layton focuses his satire and defines his own "theory of pessimism" in "Golfers."

Jill Rollins

THE GOOD-MORROW

Author: John Donne (1572-1631)
Type of poem: Lyric
First published: 1633, in *Poems by J. D.: With Elegies on the Authors Death*

The Poem

"The Good-Morrow" is a poem of twenty-one lines divided into three stanzas. The poet addresses the woman he loves as they awaken after having spent the night together.

The poem begins with a direct question from the poet to the woman. Deliberately exaggerating, the poet expresses his conviction that their lives only began when they fell in love. Before, they were mere babies at their mothers' breasts or were indulging in childish "country pleasures." This phrase had a double edge in John Donne's time: it would have been understood as a reference to gross sexual gratification. Perhaps, the poet continues, they were asleep in the Seven Sleepers' den, (referring to an ancient Syrian legend in which persecuted Christians slept for several hundred years in a cave near Ephesus). He asserts that compared with their true love ("this"), all past pleasures have been merely "fancies," and the women he "desir'd, and got" were only a "dream" of this one woman.

The second stanza opens with a triumphant greeting to their souls as they awaken into a constant, trusting love. They have no need to keep a jealous eye on each other because their love subdues the desire to look for other partners; it is so complete, so self-sufficient, that it "makes one little room, an everywhere."

The emphasis moves to the external world that the lovers have abandoned for each other. The poet contrasts the physical worlds sought by explorers and map-readers with the spiritual world of the lovers. When he asserts that each of them is a world in itself, he is referring to the Elizabethan concept of microcosm and macrocosm: the view that every man and woman is a miniature universe, with the same qualities and components as the greater universe.

In the third stanza, the poet's attention focuses even more intimately on himself and the beloved. As they gaze into each other's eyes, each sees a tiny image of the other reflected in the lover's eye, and "true plain hearts" that "in the faces rest." Where, the poet asks, could they find "two better hemispheres" — referring to their faces and to the two lovers themselves as two halves of one world. Their love is spiritual, not earthly, and so is not subject to coldness ("sharp North") or decrease ("declining West").

The concept behind the fifth line is that the earthly sphere is composed of heterogeneous substances which are unstable, ever-changing, and therefore mortal. The heavenly sphere is formed of homogeneous spiritual substance, which is pure and eternal. Sensual love is earthly and subject to change and decay, whereas the love enjoyed by the poet and his beloved is "equal," a state of oneness, a pure and changeless union.

Forms and Devices

Donne is considered an innovator in the area of love poetry. The Renaissance style relied heavily upon convention: the predictable nature of the love affair, the idealized qualities and appearance of the woman, the subservient role of the poet, and the courtly language in which he addressed the woman. Donne broke all these conventions. He shocked readers of his century and the next with his direct, dramatic style, his colloquial language, his open approach to physical aspects of love, and his use of the broken rhythms of real speech. He was also criticized for perplexing the women in his poems (traditionally addressed in terms of uncomplicated emotion) with complex metaphysical matters.

Donne begins "The Good-Morrow" with a typically dramatic opening—no less than three insistent questions to the woman, in the style of everyday speech. The entire poem has the air of being part of an intimate conversation which keeps one always conscious of the immediate presence of the woman. The language and imagery of the poem, however, are deliberately exaggerated, with a strong element of paradox.

For example, love is said to make one small room an everywhere—an image which can be grasped intuitively but which outrages logic. Notice also that the speech rhythms in this phrase work against the basic iambic pattern of a weak stress followed by a strong one: two consecutive strong stresses (a metrical unit called a spondee) fall on the first two syllables of "one little." The effect of this heavy pair of stresses is to undercut the diminution implied by both these words—an effect that is driven home by the most powerful stress of the line, on the first syllable of "everywhere." Another spondee throws into strong relief the first two words of the phrase "true plain hearts"—again, an idea the poet wants to emphasize.

Donne uses strong and weak stresses, and strong and weak verb constructions, to emphasize his thematic contrasts. The "sea-discoverers" and map readers are dismissed in the weak constructions of "Let [them] . . . have gone,/ Let [them] . . . have shown," where the verbs, weakly stressed and in the indirect subjunctive form, allow the ends of the lines to tail off. The threefold repetition of "worlds" also makes the whole adventuring enterprise seem wearisome. In contrast, the lovers "possess" their world—a strong, heavily stressed verb followed by a weighty pause after "world."

The language, line structures, and meter describing the perfection of the lovers' relationship is also worthy of note. The unmusical rhythm and language of "Which I desir'd, and got," contrasts strongly with the lilting rhythm and smooth assonance of " 'twas but a dream of thee." The first and fourth lines of the last stanza are divided into two halves, one in perfect symmetrical balance with the other, reflecting the constant, even nature of the relationship described. The structure of these lines reflects the important ideas of the third line, where the lovers are described as two perfect hemispheres making one sphere, and the fifth line, which asserts that "Whatever dies, was not mix'd equally."

eral external actions. In fact, the movement in the poem is based on their responses after they make love, not on the lovemaking itself. The poem is unified by its images, two explicit—the moon and fish—and one implicit, that of the drama.

This drama image frames the poem. It has been noted that "The Goose Fish" is structured like a drama, with its five verses taking the place of five acts in a play. The lovers are actors upon the "stage" of the long beach. The moon serves as spotlight for an audience of one, the fish. When the lovers are finished with their lovemaking, they are embarrassed, "as if shaken by stage-fright." They stand together "on the sand," "hand in hand" like actors taking a bow on the stage. In this context, the goose fish is considered "a comedian" whose act "might mean failure or success." The moon's decline in the last stanza is like the fall of a curtain on the last act.

Two explicit images dominate and organize "The Goose Fish"—the moon and the fish. "Moon" in some form and the fish appear in each stanza. In the first stanza, the moon is mentioned but not emphasized. The moon serves as a spotlight to convince the lovers that they are alone, as they see no one else in its light. Then the moon becomes "hard" and "bony" in the lovers' perception as they experience embarrassment after their passion; the moon also casts its light upon the macabre fish. Stanza 3 finds the moon also described as hard, although this time it is the hardness of fragile china. Like the moon, the fish is ancient; like the fish, the moon is "bony." This is the beginning of the merging of the images; they blend in stanza 4: The fish has a "wide and moony grin." This merging of the two central images, the earthly and dead with the heavenly and eternal, implies the larger unity of the cosmos, which the lovers finally recognize.

The regular meters of "The Goose Fish" (its iambic tetrameter with each stanza's closing iambic trimeter line) plus its detached, objective narrator give the poem a detached, philosophical tone. Howard Nemerov's successive use of long vowels in the first stanza ("On the long shore, lit by the moon") drags the lines' sounds out in imitation of a stretch of beach. Similarly matching form to content, the energy of the lines increases with the action in his use of shorter, abrupt words, such as "For them by the swift tide of blood" and "But took it for an emblem of." Thus, the metrics of "The Goose Fish" subtly reinforce the content.

Themes and Meanings

"The Goose Fish," a study in irony, deals with the delusions of humankind. On one level, the lovers express the ultimate delusion—that they can make a world apart from the rest of the cosmos. This is what they believe they accomplish by making love unobserved on the sand. Ironically, they are not alone, but are watched by the fish, that simultaneously represents the cosmos and the equally inescapable presence of death. The intruding goose fish, with its oddly comical expression, punctures the romantic mood created by the first stanza, with its description of the moonlit shore. The lovers' queries as to the fish's meaning present further comment on man's egocentricity.

From the lovers' discovery that they are not unobserved follows an implicit comment on the deceptiveness of appearances. The lovers think themselves alone, because of the moon's light and because of their passion, but they are controlled by the very forces they believe they can escape. The fish's sudden "appearance" is not actually sudden at all. It has been there all the time, just as death is always present even in the most seminal situations. In fact, "The Goose Fish" concerns an ironic "love triangle," the lovers and the fish, or the lovers and the rest of life and death.

Another contrast between the worlds of appearances and reality is in the soft sweeping beauty of the beach with its underlying hardness. The moon softly lights lapping waves and warm sand. Beneath this scene of supposed privacy and comfort, however, is a dead fish with brittle bones; the moon's light becomes hard, optimism is rigid, and death grins with "picket teeth," as a bony moon goes down its "track."

Although the central delusion is the lovers' belief that they are unobserved and that through mating they can create a separate sphere, they are also deluded in other ways. Never does the poem indicate that they realize that they are as much of a part of the universe as the moon that goes along its "tilted track" and that they are only "doing what comes naturally" by copulating on the sand as would any other species.

The lovers also think that the fish has special meaning for them, and they try to decipher it. They "hesitated at his smile," but once recognizing that they have been wrong in their presuppositions, they again make a mistake in assuming that the fish's presence is a "sign" which will explain "everything." Here, the lovers fall into another egocentric trap. They assume that the outside world revolves around them and is sending messages. They anthropomorphize the goose fish into "their patriarch," after assuming that it must be "an emblem" of their love.

Although the goose fish "never did explain the joke/ That so amused him, lying there," the lovers enshrine him to legitimize themselves. The joke, actually, is on them; the lovers may grasp that they are part of the whole, but they do not see that they are an insignificant part. The universe does not revolve around them; in fact, their behavior is as programmed and as impersonal as the moon's mechanistic route. The lovers show no recognition of their mortality, even when death "grins" at them. Instead, they transform the obvious into a personal emblem.

"The Goose Fish," one of Howard Nemerov's most anthologized poems, illustrates the poet's philosophical side as well as his realistic awareness of nature as entity in itself, not subject to man's "pathetic fallacy." The poem also contains, implicitly, a wry comment on man's foolishness and life's mystery.

Mary Barnes Bruce

A GRAMMARIAN'S FUNERAL

Author: Robert Browning (1812-1889)
Type of poem: Elegy
First published: 1855, in *Men and Women*

The Poem

Robert Browning's "A Grammarian's Funeral," subtitled "Shortly After the Revival of Learning in Europe," is a funeral elegy in four stanzas. It is written in the first-person plural, suggesting either a group or a single person speaking for a group. It is important to bear in mind the distance between the speaking persona of the poem and the poet himself; throughout "A Grammarian's Funeral," Browning is careful to include elements that make the reader question the objectivity and accuracy of the speaker's (or speakers') observations.

The poem describes a funeral procession for a noted grammarian; the procession leaves a sleeping countryside at daybreak and makes its way to a burial site high on a mountain. The funeral party is composed of students of the grammarian, including the speaker(s), who praise their dead master enthusiastically for his devotion to scholarship and his choice of a life of learning over a more conventional existence.

As the students proceed up the mountain, they describe the grammarian, his early years, his decision to embark on a life of study, and finally, his physical decline and death. They speak with admiration of his contempt for life's more ordinary pursuits and praise his focus on lofty scholarship.

Forms and Devices

Browning uses form and language to heighten the poem's thematic tension between appearance and reality, between the high praise the students lavish on their master and the more shadowy, contradictory portrait of the grammarian that emerges through their posthumous encomium.

The phrasing of the poem is frequently awkward and discordant, and the unusual metrical pattern is distinctly unmelodious: "He ventured neck or nothing—heaven's success/ Found, or earth's failure:/ 'Wilt thou trust death or not?' He answered 'Yes:/ Hence with life's pale lure!' " Such verse seems particularly incongruous in a poem about the great achievements of a man whose life was devoted to the study of the graceful and flowing language of Homer and Sophocles.

The verse seems to undercut the ostensibly serious tone of the poem. The feminine rhymes in the even-numbered lines create a somewhat comic effect, at times resembling strained doggerel more than serious verse. Lines such as *"Calculus* racked him:/ . . . *Tussis* attacked him," and "Fancy the fabric/ . . . Ere mortar dab brick!" are but a few examples of the pat, singsong rhyming found throughout the poem.

Despite the praise of the grammarian's lofty idealism, there is much in the poem that seems to decry his austere way of life. The most apparent is the recurrent imagery of death. In the setting of the funeral, the grammarian is first referred to as "the corpse." He is described rather strangely as "famous, calm, and dead." The students themselves make an unwitting acknowledgment of a connection between death and a life of selfless devotion to scholarship when they say, "Seek we sepulture," implying that the pursuit of knowledge leads to death. It is interesting to note that the only specific reference to the grammarian's field of study (as opposed to more general references to "learning" throughout the poem) occurs at the grammarian's death-bed, as he stammers out Greek grammar through his death rattle.

This physical death, however, is not the only death associated with the gram-marian. The life he leads with such singleness of purpose can be seen as a kind of death-in-life in which he rejects the fullness of an ordinary life for the intense but one-dimensional life of a scholar. At the beginning of his career he determined that "before living he'd learn how to live" — but if he follows this plan he will never begin to live, since, as he himself knows, there is "No end to learning." He seems glad to make this sacrifice, saying, "Hence with life's pale lure!"

Other images add to the ambiguity of the grammarian's portrayal. Despite the students' admiration of him as a heroic figure, the grammarian is described as bald, "cramped and diminished," with "eyes like lead." He was racked with physical disease, and by the end of his life he was "dead from the waist down," hardly the "Lyric Apollo" his students describe. Browning uses imagery such as this deliber-ately to set up tension between the positive and negative aspects of the grammarian and his life's work.

Themes and Meanings

"A Grammarian's Funeral" is marked by ambiguity and division. By contrasting the ideal and the actual and by subtly emphasizing the difference between appear-ance and reality, Browning creates a shadowy, ambiguous character and leaves the reader to decide whether the grammarian is the hero, as his students see him, or a foolishly overzealous scholar who has rejected life for the pursuit of trivial knowledge.

The grammarian's students praise him as a paragon of scholarship and intellectual vigor, and often he is described as an admirable figure striving for lofty ideals. His complete and wholehearted absorption in his studies seems particularly inspiring when he says, "What's time? Leave Now for dogs and apes!/ Man has forever." The grammarian's life of scholarship in this light seems a noble example of the Renais-sance spirit of dedication to the pursuit of knowledge, and Browning's pinpointing of the time in which the poem is set as the beginning of the Renaissance is signifi-cant; the grammarian's close study of Greek grammar may well have paved the way for more accessible and practical products of the renewal of classical scholarship.

The grammarian's chosen field of study, however, is treated with some ambiva-lence. After the students' enthusiastic praise of the grammarian's devotion to an idealized but rather vague "learning," one is surprised to discover that his great achievements are in the realm of particles of grammar. The subject seems comically trivial in comparison with the comprehensive study of "bard and sage" described earlier. Yet, while grammar is perhaps relatively unexciting compared to other aspects of ancient Greek, such as drama or poetry, it is no less valid a field for scholarship, especially in view of the fact that prior to the Renaissance very little was known about the language of the ancient Greeks. Part of the reader's judgment as to whether the grammarian is an admirable or a ridiculous figure rests on this intentionally ambiguous issue of whether the study of Greek particles is a significant or a trivial exercise.

The grammarian's final words on his deathbed further exemplify this ambivalence toward his preoccupation with the minutiae of grammar. In his final moments, the grammarian delivers doctrines on *Hoti*, *Oun*, and *De*. In one sense it is admirable that even at the end of his life he does not waver from his devotion to his subject, instead continuing to the last to contribute to his life's work. At the same time, however, the reader may wonder that at the moment of death the grammarian cannot raise his thoughts to anything higher than prepositions and conjunctions.

The grammarian's choosing "not to Live but Know" is a similarly cloudy matter. He seems to have taken up learning as a prelude to living an enlightened life, only to spurn life after becoming engrossed in his grammar. While his single-mindedness in his scholarship seems laudable, his rejection of a conventional way of life seems foolish and wasteful; the determination is left to the reader.

Browning's equivocal conclusion strikes one last note of ambiguity; the final three lines are capable of multiple interpretations. The grammarian is described as "loftily lying," ostensibly a reference to his burial site, but possibly implying dishonesty — perhaps referring to the grammarian's life of self-denial as he deceived himself about his own human wants and needs. "Leave him," say the students as they depart the summit, possibly a hint that they are rejecting the austere life-style of the devoted scholar who renounced life's pleasures. The grammarian was "loftier than the world suspects," "lofty" here implying "noble" or "idealistic," but also perhaps connoting "haughty" or "arrogant," an appropriate term to describe the grammarian's rejection of everything but his studies.

The final image of the grammarian is of him "Living and dying." The two seem inextricably intertwined for the grammarian. During his life he was dead to the world, living a kind of death-in-life, but he lives on after death in his achievements and in the hearts of his students. This paradox is a particularly appropriate finish for a poem that creates, through the use of contrasts and intentional ambiguities, such a complex and enigmatic figure as the grammarian.

Catherine Swanson

THE GREAT HUNGER

Author: Patrick Kavanagh (1905-1967)
Type of poem: Narrative
First published: 1942

The Poem

The Great Hunger is a fine example of the long poem in the twentieth century. Its 756 lines, primarily in free verse, are divided into fourteen sections, varying in length from twenty-two to 125 lines. The poem, with its oblique title reference to the Great Famine of the 1840's in Ireland, examines the life of Patrick Maguire, an unmarried peasant farmer tied to his small acreage. Maguire starves intellectually, psychologically, and spiritually as he struggles against the tyranny of the soil.

In section 1, Patrick Kavanagh sets a dramatic frame for the whole poem as the narrator invites the reader to watch Maguire and his fellow potato gatherers on the hillside for an hour. That hour figuratively spans Maguire's life through the course of the other thirteen sections. In this section, Maguire is fully introduced, and the bleak Donaghmoyne setting is vividly fixed. The time is October, and Maguire and his men are gathering the potato crop— "like mechanised scarecrows." While detailing the men at work, the narrative voice unfolds the complexities of Maguire's present plight. "Too long virgin," Maguire regrets his unfulfilled promise to himself to marry, sighing, "O God if I had been wiser!" As the section closes, the narrator is ready for the curtain to go up: "Come with me, Imagination, into this iron house/ And we will watch . . . the years run back."

In the next twelve sections, the sixty-five years of Maguire's existence is "run back," somewhat like twelve scenes in a play. Kavanagh projects the "drama" of Maguire's personal, familial, and communal activities, as well as his hopes, illusions, and fears, against a backdrop of a seasonal cycle compounded of the growing season of the Irish potato from early-spring seeding to October harvest and the varied seasonal toils of Maguire and his potato gatherers.

The narrative segments in the separate sections freely range back and forth over the years of Maguire's life and over his fourteen-hour day. Some of these vignettes depict the daily course of Maguire's activities; others re-create earlier moments of his life. Kavanagh augments these vignettes with broader sketches of key moments (usually of psychological importance) from Maguire's life. As the seasons pass and one potato crop follows the next, Kavanagh reveals Maguire's increasing awareness of time's passage— *his* time. Throughout, Maguire's aspirations for a fulfilling life clash with the reality of his thwarted existence.

The climax of Maguire's drama, such as it is, comes at the end of section 13. At this point it is clear that this is a tragedy without a resolution: "No crash,/ No drama./ That was how his life happened." In the poem's final section, now that the "years run back" have completed their course, the narrator steps out of the iron house (the one into which he had invited the reader in section 1): "We may come out into the October, Imagination." The drama has ended: "Applause, applause,/ The Curtain falls." All that remains is a brief epilogue. The poem has come full circle from the opening "Clay is the word and clay is the flesh" — with all the promise in this variant expression of Christian Revelation — to the utter despair of the conclusion, "the apocalypse of clay/ In every corner of this land."

Forms and Devices

The intense, realistic depiction of peasant life in *The Great Hunger* arises directly from Kavanagh's first-hand knowledge of daily existence on his native Monaghan clay hills. To craft his striking and convincing portrait of Maguire's personal hunger, a blend of memory and imagination, Kavanagh employs the techniques now common to modern cinematography. The poem is a carefully crafted editing of close-ups, long shots, and flashbacks; it employs direct and indirect characterization, dialogue, interior monologue; naturalistic narrative vignettes, dramatic sketches, and reflective passages. The fourteen sections are a cinematographic tour de force in poetry.

Kavanagh's re-creation of the natural speech pattern of the Irish peasants is remarkable — and typical of Kavanagh's sharp detailing of particulars throughout the poem. The total effect of the speech passages is more than that of realistic re-creation and more than the ancillary unity they provide. Almost all the talk is of the land — its grip is figuratively at the very throats of these potato gatherers. Their talk reinforces that theme.

A series of key images, or motifs — dream, gap (in the sense of a "way to freedom"), circle, a stone and a handful of gravel — serve structural and thematic functions. Kavanagh's variations on the dream motif illustrate those functions. The poet uses the dream image twice in the first section and returns to it in later sections, with incremental effect. In section 1, Maguire, on the hillside gathering potatoes, reflects associatively upon the moment. Then a shift occurs in Maguire's mental meanderings:

> His dream changes again like the cloud-swung wind
> And he is not so sure now if his mother was right
> When she praised the man who made a field his bride.

The shift is from Maguire's present casual preoccupations to a more reflective contemplation of his past and the factors that have brought him to his present plight. The passage, with the striking simile "like the cloud-swung wind," also implies that Maguire may be more the recipient than the agent in his relations with his fields. The second dream image in section 1 depicts Maguire's youthful suspicious response to the flirtatious laughter of young girls: "He dreamt/ The innocence of young brambles to hooked treachery."

In section 4, the dream motif exposes Maguire's limited and limiting concept of morality and his inclination to be cautious with girls. In the short sixth section, the dream motif reveals broken idealism and, in particular, Maguire's tendency to dream of life (health, wealth, and love) rather than to live it: "Three frozen idols of a speechless muse." Kavanagh concludes this interrelated string of dream images in the final section of the poem, where he ironically speculates on the possibility of Maguire realizing the dream in death: "And the serious look of the fields will have changed to the leer of a hobo/ Swaggering celestially home to his three wishes granted./ Will that be? will that be?"

Themes and Meanings

The Great Hunger is a striking (and necessary) counterbalance to the too-frequently voiced sentimental, romantic exaltation of the Irish peasant. It is a firm refutation of the 'noble peasant' myth.

The poem is not only the depiction of the "sad, grey, twisted, blind, awful" life of one Irish peasant-farmer; it is also a terrible and moving composite image of human frustration. Held by the "grip of irregular fields," Maguire is emblematic of all human beings in their material and spiritual struggle against squalor, emptiness, and sexual deprivation.

The tyranny of the soil dehumanizes Maguire and his fellow potato gatherers. Time for them is measured by the land and its demands; holidays are remembered by the color of the fields. Maguire, only once removed from the beast he drives in that he, unlike them, is aware of his plight, is, in the end, "a sick horse nosing around the meadow for a clean place to die."

Those tied to the land like Maguire become eunuchs, as youthful dreams of love eventually turn to lust, self-abuse, and finally impotence. Promises to marry "before apples were hung from the ceilings for Halloween" are delayed, and in the delay Maguire dismisses "children as tedious" and becomes lost to "passion that never needs a wife." Such deprivation leads to self-deception as a mechanism of survival. Sitting on the wooden gate one July day and "riding in day-dream's car," Maguire is moved to "high ecstasies" by the glory he beholds while, ironically, "Life slipped between the bars."

Religious strictures and rigid communal standards also stifle one's humanity and sense of divine truth. Symbolically, when Maguire leaves Mass, he coughs "the prayer phlegm up from his throat"; ritual without meaning chokes spiritual truth. A puritanical, overactive sense of sin—a part of the general spiritual condition of Maguire's community—operates in his mind. One day as he eyed a passing young woman, he "rushed beyond the thing/ To the unreal. And he saw Sin/ Written in letters larger than John Bunyan dreamt of."

Excessive idealism and the quest for eternal truths also stirred Kavanagh's satiric ire. Too often, like Maguire, people turn "from five simple doors of sense" to the door "whose combination lock has puzzled/ Philosopher and priest and common dunce." Kavanagh would have his reader probe the everyday and the commonplace with common sense.

Glenn Grever

GREEN ENRAVISHMENT OF HUMAN LIFE

Author: Sor Juana Inés de la Cruz (Juana de Asbaje y Ramírez de Santillana, 1648-1695)
Type of poem: Sonnet
First published: 1690, as "Verde embeleso de la vida humana," in *Poemas;* collected in *Anthology of Mexican Poetry*, 1958

The Poem

"Green enravishment of human life" is a sonnet of the Italian or Petrarchan type. It consists of an octave (eight lines rhyming *abbaabba*) and a sextet (six lines rhyming *cdecde*). The sonnet lacks a title; it is identified by its first line. The octave is mainly descriptive of the theme of the poem: hope. The speaker of the poem emerges in the sextet. After describing the attitude of those who, hoping for change, ignore or distort reality, Sor Juana Inés de la Cruz expresses her own positivist attitude about the world.

Sor Juana spent several years of her life at the court of colonial Mexico. There she wrote many poems of circumstance, conventional pieces in which she praised persons of high rank and love poems that might have been written by request. Another part of her lyric poetry, however, conveys her own feelings and worldview. "Green enravishment of human life" is one of those philosophical or moral poems in which Sor Juana expresses her personal ideas. The poem is a good illustration of Sor Juana's rationalism, an attitude that is obvious at other points in her work. For the poet, to hope is to fool oneself, and she distances herself from those who live in the expectation of future improvements or riches. An even more unfavorable description of hope can be found in another of her sonnets, "Diuturnal infirmity of hope," in which she describes hope as cruel, deceptive, and homicidal, since it "inflicts a more protracted death."

In the first stanza of this sonnet, Sor Juana calls hope the "green enravishment." This metaphor suggests the ability of hope to conquer human will. The second line takes up the notion of the irresistibility of hope and relates it to madness ("smiling frenzy of demented hope"). This association sets the tone for Sor Juana's condemnation of such a feeling. The last lines of the first stanza further underscore the unreality of hope by connecting it with dreams, which, according to Sor Juana, usually turn out to be empty.

The second stanza adds more images that underscore the deceitfulness of hope. Hope provides only a false feeling of strength, an illusion of renewed vigor. The last two lines of this stanza mirror each other. Hope makes one who is happy expect more happiness; it makes one who lives in misery expect happiness in the future.

The poet's skeptical attitude is already betrayed by the associations that are implicit in the octave, but her skepticism becomes explicit in the last six lines of the poem. There is a shift of tone in the third stanza. In the first two stanzas, the poem was static, with the author describing hope by means of a list of paraphrases. The third stanza begins with a direct address to hope in the second person: Let those who view reality as they wish, by looking at it through green glasses, chase your shadow, Sor Juana writes. In the last stanza, the poet places herself in opposition to those who filter reality to suit their fantasies. She considers herself to be more reasonable. Rather than chasing the shadow of hope, she considers only that which is tangible.

Forms and Devices

This sonnet is exemplary in its use of conceits which were characteristic of Spanish Baroque poetry. A conceit always implies ingenuity, striking inventiveness, whether in a single original image or in a series of elaborate and witty analogies. This sonnet utilizes several unexpected pairings of terms to describe hope. Paradox and wordplay are also frequently used in Baroque poetry, and Sor Juana uses here the parallelisms, inversions, and repetitions that were favorite ways of syntactic organization in Baroque poetry.

The recurring image that runs through the poem is the traditional association of hope with the color green; this image appears in the first three stanzas. The roots of this association may lie in the rebirth of the world with the reemergence of vegetation in the spring. Sor Juana, however, undermines the positive connotations of the color green by presenting it in contexts that become increasingly negative. It accompanies "enravishment" in the first stanza, which suggests a deceitful, passing state. The falseness of hope is further stressed in the second stanza, in the seemingly paradoxical juxtaposition of images of weakness and strength: "robust old age," "decrepit vigor" (in Spanish, *verdor*, greenness). In the third stanza, hope is described as making the hopeful wear "green glasses" through which they adapt the real world to suit their personal desires.

Furthermore, Sor Juana accentuates the insubstantiality of hope by associating it with nouns such as "dream," "madness," "imagination," "frenzy," and "shadow." The "I" of the poem emerges strongest in the last three lines, and again takes up this notion of the immateriality of hope to underline the poet's own skeptical attitude toward it. Those who hope live in a world of incorporeal desires, but she is firmly rooted in the world of corporeality. The last stanza ends with a striking image: The poet holds her eyes in her hands and only sees that which can be touched.

The poem also reflects the Baroque "spirit of geometry," the delight in calibrated syntactical organization. The first two stanzas are structured almost identically; a list of paraphrases for hope is followed by two concluding sentences that mirror each other: "inextricable dream of them that wake/ and, as a dream, of riches destitute"; "longing for the happy ones' today/ and for the unhappy ones' tomorrow." The last two stanzas also play on each other by juxtaposing the disapproved behavior (of those who live in hope) with the right attitude (Sor Juana's realistic outlook).

The sonnet's careful syntactic arrangement and interconnected metaphors for hope transcend pure lyric ornamentation and give the poet's argument for reason additional weight.

Themes and Meanings

Sor Juana's condemnation of hope might seem excessive, but the poem can be better understood in the context in which it was produced. "Green enravishment" is representative of the pessimism of the Spanish Baroque. The grim vision of life and obsession with death of the Baroque came as a reaction to the optimism and affirmation of humanistic values of the Renaissance. In the poetry of the Spanish Baroque masters Francisco Goméz de Quevedo y Villegas and Luis de Góngora y Argote, one finds as recurring themes a disenchantment with the human being and a preoccupation with the ephemerality of human existence. In her philosophical-moral poems, Sor Juana elaborates on these typically Baroque ideas; she very often describes a deceptive world, the humiliations of old age, and the evanescence of earthly experience.

Such a grim vision of the world and human life precludes relying on hope or expecting future improvements. Sor Juana clearly reproves such attitudes. In the poem, hope is a state that resembles stupidity or madness, implying a voluntary or involuntary distancing from reality. Reality is the only thing one should consider, as Sor Juana states in the last stanza. One should neither project oneself into the future by expecting a change or improvement of circumstances nor impose one's subjectivity on the world.

The poem reminds one of the Greek myth of Prometheus and Pandora. When the Greek gods created Pandora as the punishment for Prometheus' theft of fire, they gave her a box that contained all the evils that would afflict humanity from that moment on. Included in Pandora's box was hope. The myth leaves many questions open. Why is hope an evil? Why did it stop at the box's rim when Pandora opened it and let the evils loose to roam the world? Hope can be seen as that which fuels human ambitions and keeps people going, but it can also be seen as a delusive, blind force that can prolong human misery, inflicting "a more protracted death," as Sor Juana puts it. Sor Juana seems to believe that hope sets one up for greater disappointments and that a rational, positivist attitude is preferable to the ersatz energy provided by a hopeful attitude.

Carlota Larrea

GRODEK

Author: Georg Trakl (1887-1914)
Type of poem: Lyric
First published: 1915, as "Grodek"; in *Die Dichtungen*, 1919; collected in
  Selected Poems, 1968

The Poem

"Grodek" is a free-verse poem of seventeen lines. The title is highly significant;
Georg Trakl served in the Austrian medical services during the World War I battle at
Grodek in Galicia in 1914. He was charged with the care of some ninety wounded
soldiers at an inadequately supplied field hospital; unable to ease their suffering, he
himself broke down and was hospitalized for psychiatric observation. "Grodek"
was the last poem Trakl wrote before his death from a cocaine overdose—perhaps a
suicide—shortly after his breakdown. It quickly became one of the best-known war·
poems of World War I.

Though not separated into stanzas, four complete sentences (in the original) di-
vide the poem thematically as well as syntactically. The first six-line sentence describes the close of a day of battle; as evening comes the sounds of combat—tones
of "deadly weapons" and the "wild lament" of "dying warriors"—are embraced
and surrounded by the approaching night.

Trakl's opening image of the human and mechanical sounds of battle echoing
through the woods into the evening twilight is cut off by the "But" which begins
the second, four-line sentence: "But," says the poet, even though the battle continues, the spilled blood of the day also "gathers" "quietly there in the pastureland"
under the coolness of the moon. This silent return of shed blood to the earth points
to the endless circle of life and death, which is at work even on the battlefield. The
first ten lines of the poem remind the reader of a pastoral scene because of their
familiar nature images such as "autumn woods," "golden plains," "blue lakes," and
"pastureland," yet the pastoral allusions are constantly challenged by contrary images. Just as all the warriors' blood runs together in the low-lying meadows, so too
do all roads lead to "blackest carrion," and the whole second image is also overshadowed by red clouds, "in which an angry god resides," a presence which further
unsettles the poem.

The third, four-line sentence again highlights nature—"golden twigs," "night
and stars," "the silent copse"—as the scene through which now "the sister's shade"
moves "to greet the ghosts of the heroes." This introduction of the shadow or spirit
of an unknown "sister" could imply the soothing touch of an ethereal nurse, or the
peaceful greeting of Woman within the violent male world of the battlefield. Yet in
the context of Trakl's life and poetic oeuvre, in which his own sister plays a very
important role, this "sister" can also represent an intensely personal love, here
shared among the bleeding, fallen heroes. The accompanying sounds of "dark
flutes" could refer to the whistling of nature's cleansing autumn winds, but it is also

a second allusion to the now-distant "deadly weapons" of line 2, that is, the battle's guns. *Tönen* ("to sound," "resound," or "cry out") in line 1 is the same verb Trakl uses in line 14; this repetition, along with the recurrence of "autumn," though as a noun rather than an adjective, signals the closure of the first series of descriptive images.

The vocative "O prouder grief!" serves to set the final sentence apart from the preceding body of the poem. The broken syntax of the last sentence allows for varying interpretations, yet the apostrophized "brazen altars"—for both grieving and sacrifice—seem to be animated by the "great pain" of the tragedy of war. "The unborn grandsons" of the last line serve as a coda to the last sentence and to the poem as a whole; the battlefield images are complete. Yet, the poem implies, what will follow war? Present as well as succeeding generations will be touched by it. The poem's ambiguous attitude asserts itself in the last line, which can mean either "the grandsons yet unborn" or "the grandsons never to be born"; either meaning, however, concludes the poem on a note of mourning and loss.

Forms and Devices

The most obvious formal aspect of Trakl's late poems is their difficult syntax. Like many of his expressionist contemporaries, he bends grammar past the breaking point, a technique which forces the reader to concentrate on the associations between clusters of images. In "Grodek" there is neither a "story" nor pure impressionistic description; instead, Trakl presents a series of images which are at first familiar, then strange to the reader. His images of nature recall a pastoral landscape tradition, yet the traditionally positive connotations of "golden plains" or a "silent grove" are estranged by their unsettling juxtaposition with a "more darkly" rolling sun or warriors' "bleeding heads."

The tradition of the German elegy, a poem of lament for the dead often written in distichs, is recalled by the use of the word "lament" in line 5, as well as by the mention of "grief" and the associations made with sacrifice and mourning through the "brazen altars" in line 15. Yet the poem's free-verse form contradicts the expected metrics of the traditional elegy, and its lack of a dominant personal and subjective voice—an important facet of the modern elegy—defeats further comparison.

The sounds in "Grodek" recall for German ears an important aspect of medieval Germanic heroic poetry, the heroic alliterative line, best known from a ninth century Old High German poem, the *Hildebrandslied* (*The Song of Hildebrand*, 1957). Alliteration—in lines 3 (*Seen/Sonne*), 5 (*Krieger/Klage*), and elsewhere—is the oldest form of Germanic rhyme. Through its use Trakl makes reference to the earliest Germanic war poetry, in which were sung the glories of the solitary warrior in his ultimately tragic search for honor through battle. Trakl's allusions to the past serve not only to recall the heroic tradition in poetry but also to ironize it through the all-too-obvious differences between warriors a millennium apart.

"Grodek" introduces and confounds several well-known poetic modes in its attempt to capture the results and implications of this battle. The complex of images the poem presents, then, is left to stand on its own, outside poetic tradition, and the reader sees but this silent progression of pictures, as in a film; only in the final sentence does the voice of a commentator cry out in grief at the momentous loss.

Themes and Meanings

In the highly politicized German literary world between the two world wars, Trakl's "Grodek" was read and claimed by readers both on the right and on the left of the political spectrum. Although expressionism as a school or style of literature was disdained by the National Socialist regime as decadent in its public associations and indulgent in its subjectivity, "Grodek" maintains enough of the tradition of the elegy to have been read by Nazi readers as a memorial to the dead, to the "ghosts of the heroes." At the same time, those who read closely or were privy to Trakl's difficult private language were able to understand the poem as full of resignation and hopelessness, especially because many of them concentrated on the poem's last line: "the grandsons (yet) unborn." Are the grandsons to come being sacrificed on the brazen altars of war? Is some craving "spirit" of humankind being fed these unborn generations through the act of war? Will these "grandsons" ever be born, or have the deaths of their elders, the "dying warriors," foreclosed their existence once and for all? Trakl leaves the interpretation to the reader.

Trakl's poetry has traditionally been read autobiographically, and this poem— occasioned as it was by his own experience at Grodek— is no different. In general, though, most of his other poetry is far more private and intimate and has consequently been subjected to psychological, religious, sexual, and philosophical interpretations. "Grodek" presents readers with something of an exception among Trakl's works since, unlike many of his poems which are grounded in some intensely private ordeal (experiences of religion, drugs, and incest), it has its roots in the common historical experience of World War I.

Because "Grodek" has been anthologized in collections of war poetry so often over the years, readers have been forced to interpret it in this context. So although academic readers and Trakl specialists like to trace the poem's key words and images throughout Trakl's oeuvre— to determine, for example, the various associations of "blue lakes" or of the "sister" in all his other poems— and interpret "Grodek" as the culmination of a consistent poetic journey, the poem actually stands well on its own as perhaps the most important German war poem of all. Within the context of twentieth century German history, Trakl's mourning call, "the unborn grandsons," might force readers to consider all the dead of the next war and to mourn them as well.

Scott D. Denham

THE GROUNDHOG

Author: Richard Eberhart (1904-   )
Type of poem: Meditation
First published: 1934; collected in *Reading the Spirit*, 1936

The Poem

"The Groundhog" is a poem in free verse; its forty-eight lines are marked by no formal divisions. It traces a process of development in four main stages, however; the first stage occupies the first twenty-four lines, while the last three are allotted eight lines each.

The speaker, the "I" of the poem, is never clearly identified but is probably a man of thoughtful, even scholarly, habits. He recounts a series of four encounters with a dead groundhog, ending in the present, three years after his first sight of the lifeless animal.

Strong emotions dominate stage 1, the speaker's first reaction to the groundhog, which has died recently. It is June, the height of the season of fullest life, but the three heavy stresses of line 3, "Dead lay he," arrest and shock the speaker. Senses shaking and mind racing, the speaker nevertheless focuses carefully on the busy, "ferocious" process of the groundhog's decay. He even takes action, angrily poking the body, which is seething with maggots. His anger may stem from his disgust at seeing the maggots or it may be the anger of denial, a cold rage against death. The emotion is pointless, however, for the heat of the localized natural scene becomes generalized and cosmic, as the "immense energy" of nature—from maggots to the sun—dwarfs and disarms the speaker. Standing silently, the speaker tries to make sense of his experience, hoping to balance his initial passion with understanding. He hopes for a spiritual benefit as well, for the first stage ends with the speaker "Praying for joy in the sight of decay."

Stage 2 occurs during the autumn of that same year, when the speaker returns intentionally to see the groundhog's remains. He revisits the scene "strict of eye," but finds only a disappointing, shapeless hulk. Consciousness predominates and seems to have inhibited or destroyed the man's emotional powers. He concedes that he has gained wisdom, but at an excessive cost. The next summer, in stage 3, the speaker chances upon the site of the groundhog's corpse, of which only hair and bones remain. In line 39, the speaker sees the groundhog objectively, "like a geometer." He cuts a walking stick, a steadying contrast to his angry stick of the previous summer.

The speaker reports on his fourth and final stage of development in the present, three summers after his first sight of the carcass. By now, the groundhog has decayed completely, leaving the speaker to recapitulate the whole process. The poem's last six lines summarize the process and compare it to historical figures, from its physical stage of vigorous summer and the conqueror Alexander, through the intellectual stage of withered emotion and the detachment of the ironic thinker Michel Eyquem de Montaigne, to the spiritual stage of Saint Theresa.

Forms and Devices

As a whole, "The Groundhog" is a complex and unresolved metaphor, pairing two processes: the universal mortality of nature and the growth of human awareness. As the carcass of the groundhog decays and disappears, so do the speaker's reactions develop. He moves from initial shock to intellectual paralysis to dispassionate objectivity, then ends with a recognition that combines, but does not wholly reconcile, feeling and thought.

Richard Eberhart reinforces the poem's controlling metaphor with an equally complex treatment of the ancient poetic convention that associates the seasons of the year with the stages of individual human life. Traditionally, this convention matches spring with youth, summer with early maturity, fall with late maturity, and winter with death. "The Groundhog" modifies the convention, since its four main stages enact scenes that take place in summer, fall, summer, and summer, respectively. The sequence is fitting, for the action of the poem encompasses only three years of the speaker's life — most likely, years of early manhood.

Outwardly, the speaker has changed very little. Inwardly, however, the process of growing awareness has been much fuller. Near the end of the poem, the speaker brings both processes together, standing "in the whirling summer" of external nature, his hand capping the "withered heart" of his internal realization that death's power is terrible and complete.

Thus the poem's main metaphor involves both parallels and juxtapositions of man and nature. At first, the speaker registers the parallel of shared mortality. Viewing the dead groundhog, he is shocked to note "our naked frailty" in line 4. This early insight, however, is only momentary, as the speaker shifts to intense visualization and desperate action. After he pokes the carcass, the speaker sees the power of nature expand from the tiny maggots to a universal fever, a cosmic power that leaves him feeling powerless. His only refuge is silent contemplation, as he tries to control his emotions, hoping that he will come to understand the relationship of universal death and human awareness.

His return in fall is subdued, since he has allowed his intervening intellectual pursuits to wall out his earlier emotional response. The speaker himself is aware of the seasonal metaphor, for during this stage — the only one not to occur in summer — he recognizes that "the year had lost its meaning" (line 29).

The next summer's visit owes little to conscious effort; the speaker chances upon the site. In this brief scene, the speaker replays his first visit, but with important differences. He views the disintegrating carcass, but his vision is calm and objective. Again, he uses a stick, not as an angry goad, but as a walking stick, an aid to steadiness and direction.

The poem's fourth and last stage recapitulates and combines both metaphorical parallels and juxtapositions. The season is again summer, with the speaker at a new height of awareness, a state that includes both emotional loss and increased but chastened thought. His conclusion, expanded by allusions to human civilizations and exemplary individuals, testifies to the omnipotence of death.

Themes and Meanings

"The Groundhog" is a poem about death. More specifically, its theme may be put best as a question: What does the knowledge of death do to a human being, the only creature blessed and cursed with consciousness? This theme is as ancient as poetry and as persistent as human thought.

As noted above, Richard Eberhart explores and traces the intricate relationship of mortality and awareness, but he does not resolve it. The completed processes of the poem form a neat synopsis — summers whirl, hearts wither, men think — but such a synopsis is only an invitation to further speculation. Such speculation is a recurrent theme in Eberhart's work. In his first book, the long autobiographical poem *A Bravery of Earth* (1930), the poet explicitly describes three levels of "awareness," linking them with "mortality," "mentality," and "coming to understand." Much of his later work, especially "The Groundhog," represents a deepening and enriching of this powerful theme.

Two great principles animate "The Groundhog": the grand mortal energy of nature, and the smaller but equally recurrent energy of human thought. The first three sections of the poem present the reader with two sets of facts: the natural process of decay, and the human task of trying to make sense of mortality from within the larger cycle of death and disintegration.

The reader who notices the repetition of "in" during the poem's last six lines, one long sentence, might come as close as possible to resolving the relationship of death and consciousness. Line 43 presents the last sight of the speaker, "there in the whirling summer," contained within the larger natural process. Line 46 shows "Alexander in his tent," the world conqueror at rest before confronting once again the physical action and death that brought him a short-lived empire. This allusion also echoes the physical action of the speaker's first stage.

Line 47 focuses on the quiet intelligence of "Montaigne in his tower," contemplating life and death. The French thinker also suggests the speaker's "intellectual chains" of stage 2, as well as the "geometer" of stage 3. The poem's last line seems to add a new dimension, spirituality, with "Saint Theresa in her wild lament." In its way, however, this line recalls and extends the prayer that ends the first section, lines 23 and 24. Whether by means of the speaker's quiet prayer or the saint's loud protest, the human being strives to understand the mixed gifts of life and awareness.

Thus the speaker and the reader of "The Groundhog" both achieve a kind of recognition. The dead creature has provided the occasion for recognition. Contemplating dead civilizations and heroic individuals could have done no more. An understanding of death comes only at the end of a complex process of realizing and fusing flesh and spirit, reason and passion, outward and inward nature.

Terry Lass

GUNSLINGER

Author: Edward Dorn (1929-   )
Type of poem: Poetic sequence
First published: Gunslinger I, 1968; *Gunslinger II*, 1969; *The Cycle*, 1971;
  Gunslinger Book III, 1972; collected in *Slinger*, 1975

The Poem

Gunslinger (or *Slinger*, as it is called in the 1975 Wingbow Press complete edition), owes some of its strategies to the modern long poems that preceded it. In particular, its form and perspective derive from an extraordinary new kind of epic poem, *The Maximus Poems* (1953-1975), by Charles Olson. Olson was Edward Dorn's teacher at Black Mountain College, an experimental arts school in North Carolina famous for its stellar faculty and gifted students. The college, under Olson's rectorship, gave its name to a movement in experimental verse that used ancient myth and principles from theoretical science in poetry. Olson's intense relationship with Dorn profoundly influenced Dorn's writing.

Other works that have influenced Dorn's poem include Ezra Pound's formidable epic on twentieth century culture, *The Cantos* (1919-1970), William Carlos Williams' *Paterson* (1946-1958), which celebrates the common man of New Jersey's small towns, and even Hart Crane's lyrical paean to John Augustus Roebling's engineering wonder, the Brooklyn Bridge, in *The Bridge* (1930). All these and other poems turned away from the English literary tradition to forge a new American epic literature based on the materials of modern American life and the symbols and archetypes of ancient Western literature.

Unlike its predecessors, however, Dorn's long poem is explicitly a satire on contemporary Western thinking; its humor and hyperbole distinguish it from the sonority and somber vision of Olson's *The Maximus Poems*, which ends on a note of frustrated hopes and beleaguered visions of the ideal. The American tradition of extended lyric works calls for the probing philosophical analysis of American life, the exploration of religious ideals, and the construction of a utopian republic drawn from elements of contemporary social reality. Dorn departs from these conventions by satirizing the bedrock of American social gospel — the notions of sensible reality and of individual autonomy and privilege that Americans distilled from British and continental thought. Instead of proposing his own ideological program, Dorn punctures the philosophical illusions of empirical causality, simple time and space, realism, and dichotomy, the underpinnings of awareness that Americans have inherited from the European Enlightenment.

Dorn's satirical assault on the social gospel aligns him with a much older tradition of philosophical debunking. *Slinger's* parentage includes Geoffrey Chaucer's *Canterbury Tales* (1387-1400) and Miguel de Cervantes' *Don Quixote* (1605, 1615), works in which a cast of characters set out on a journey and share long humorous tales exposing the foibles of their age. The journey itself is only a pretext for the complex dialogues that ensue among the leading characters.

Dorn's *Slinger* is thus a patchwork of influences that have been combined to form a modern version of the ancient quest narrative. The plot involves a cast of colorful twentieth century stereotypes — among them a talking horse, a talking barrel, a Western saloon-keeper named Lil, a poet, an LSD-toting hippie called Kool Everything, and a character referred to simply as "I" — marginal beings who might well populate a George Lucas film, who set out by stagecoach for Las Vegas and after several days' travel stop at Cortez, Colorado, near Four Corners, the common boundary of New Mexico, Colorado, Utah, and Arizona that has long been held sacred by the Hopi Indians as marking the center of the world. Here they say farewell and go their separate ways.

Their journey begins in Mesilla, New Mexico, a small town south of Las Cruces that houses a museum devoted to the cowboy outlaw Billy the Kid. The protagonist of the poem, the Gunslinger, is a campy updated version of Billy, less an outlaw than a philosopher-maverick whose targets are all the dregs of materialism and linear thinking that have been antiquated by the intellectual revolutions of the post-World War II era. His weapon is his quick, aphoristic speech, which he directs at anything that cannot exist on its own terms. His most deadly "shot" is to *describe* a thing, to obliterate its autonomy by drawing it into a sentence, thus imprisoning it in another mind's perspective.

Gunslinger's horse, modeled after Quixote's Rocinante, enjoys its own privileged autonomy as a member of the group; the animal talks a combination of rant and wisdom and calls itself Claude, after the great French anthropologist of primitive culture, Claude Lévi-Strauss. The character "I," who comes into the discourse as the authorial or narrative voice, is "deconstructed" into a hapless minor figure who stumbles about in an LSD-induced daze for much of the poem. At one point, the poet declares, "I is dead," a double entendre referring to the character "I" and to the fate of the imperial ego in literature. These are a few of the upendings or anticonventions that Dorn establishes at the outset of the quest.

The poem opens as Gunslinger, his horse Claude, "I," and Lil set out for Las Vegas by stagecoach. They are soon joined by the poet and Kool Everything as they make their way slowly across New Mexico into southwestern Colorado, the Hopi *axis mundi* (axis of the world), where several of the characters soar off into the Hopi visionary cosmos and return just as the group is breaking up. Their pilgrimage to Las Vegas is diverted to Cortez, the county seat of Montezuma County, Colorado. These names suggest the Spanish Conquest of Mexico by Hernán Cortes, the first imperial soldier of Western expansion into the Indian New World. Montezuma was the last Aztec emperor, who mistakenly trusted the Spanish on their arrival. The Cafe Sahagun is Dorn's allusion to Fra Bernardino de Sahagún, the Spanish monk who feverishly copied down several of the Mayan codicils or parchment scrolls before the whole of Mayan literature was thrown on the fire by the conquistadors.

Thus the journey from New Mexico to Cortez, Colorado, follows a path from white settlement and an outlaw's museum to an Indian shrine shrouded in the symbols of conquest and devastation. Everyone grows in spirit as a result of the journey, though Dorn's use of hyperbole, bombast, ridicule, and comic detachment conceals the serious motives of the poem.

Forms and Devices

Long twentieth century poems are formally eclectic and attach almost any kind of structure to their segmental design. *Gunslinger* is no exception. Among its many forms are those of song, set speech, narrative episode, dialogue, anecdote, and fable. Comedy abounds in all of its tonalities: hyperbole, sarcasm, witty punning, visual wordplay, philosophical in-jokes. Verbal exuberance underscores the work throughout; the poem's comic progenitors include François Rabelais, the sixteenth century French master of broad farce and caustic exaggeration, and even Lewis Carroll and Edward Lear, the great English satirists of social philosophy at the turn of the nineteenth century. The poem is a catchall of erroneous thinking in the century, which it ruthlessly parodies throughout the poem. One is never permitted to literalize the discourse of the poem; it operates on several levels at once to both propose and then explode egocentric intellectualizing and lyric gush.

Slinger is divided into four numbered books, each taking up a segment of the group's journey as its narrative frame. Book 1 sets up the quest and introduces the main characters, announcing the sudden turns in the plot by imitating an old soundtrack device of cowboy films, in which an ominous guitar chord is struck. "Strum" is posted in bold, silhouetted type at various junctures of book 1. In book 4, the strum turns into a manic "thwang!" Dorn tries out other "dramatic" clichés, such as the use of italics to introduce different voices into the dialogue.

The songs that punctuate parts of the dialogue are broad parodies of Western film songs. Gunslinger's song about the girl from La Cruz proffers such pseudolyrics as "she stood and she stared like a moose/ and her hair was tangled and loose."

One must think of cowboy crooners such as Gene Autry and Roy Rogers to get the full flavor of these burlesques. When nonsense and absurdity reach a peak, Dorn slips in a quasi-serious digression on a point of vision, a sobering comment on contemporary morality, or a surprisingly beautiful snippet of lyric that pulls the reader up short.

Suspense, as in much of Olson's poetry, is rich here, and it is used playfully to distract the reader from "believing" anything in the text. Dorn knows that the reader is well-versed in the clichés and formulaic plots of cowboy stories; he works against them by mockingly following their conventions, turning them inside out when the Gunslinger or his horse Claude or Kool Everything expounds casually and knowledgeably on an obscure point of epistemology or uses an absurdly decorous eloquence in speaking of a trivial matter.

Dorn uses every pretext to spoof, deride, or simply toy with literary monism in this poem. When the Drifter is introduced in Lil's bar, the narrator slips into archaic speech and stiffly describes the guitar-strumming bard, using all the hyperbolic figures of epic poetry. Dorn's humor moves from farce and slapstick to subtle jibing at classic poetry; the reader is always conscious of the poem as a parodic tour de force as well as a brilliantly crafted yarn about the modern West.

"The Cycle," which fills the latter half of book 2, is a stylized sequence of songs delivered by the poet in numbered, unrhymed quatrains that mimic Elizabethan song "cycles." These "heroic" songs, paced out in ragged iambic pentameter, narrate the bumbling adventures of the Cheez, the song's antihero, who is the very opposite of a knight or his cowboy counterpart; instead, he is among the myriad anonymous, faceless citizens in industrial urban life. His name signifies his lowly function as part of a cheeseburger made by the local fast-food franchise.

Book 4 starts with a prolegomenon, an invocation to the muses, and moves on to the narrative proper, a journey into space rendered in computerese and regional slang. The characters stop at the Cafe Sahagun in Cortez, Colorado, the terminus of their journey, and another comic dialogue on contemporary life takes the reader to the end of the poem. The second half of book 4 contains a series of quick comic sketches featuring several new minor characters, including Portland Bill and the "talking barrel." Reality has been transformed by drugs and mind travel into a looking-glass world in which any object can suddenly spring to life and deliver a comic monologue on the absurdities of conventional life. Even these spoofs on reality have their serious purpose, however — showing the "ensouled" world of Indian mysticism against a backdrop of Western skepticism and literal reality.

Themes and Meanings

Slinger takes the cowboy film or story as its subject because it is the essence of modern Western ideology: The subject of the cowboy film is a white male hero who overcomes the forces of evil in other white men, the adversities of the environment (wolves, raging fire, storms) or the perversities of so-called primitive peoples such as American Indians and the "half-breeds" south of the border. What is said to triumph in such heroic tales is reason itself — cold, empirical logic set against wild nature. Dorn's perspective runs directly counter to each of these assumptions. His sympathies are squarely with Indian America, with wilderness, the unspoiled frontiers of the New World that European man contaminated and largely destroyed.

Dorn's purpose in this mock epic is to puncture his readers' illusory certainties and attack their cultural assumptions. The Gunslinger is modeled on the figure of Charles Olson, a kind of philosophical and ideological outlaw who is opposed to the conventional roots of modern reality. Behind Dorn's beliefs lies the century's heritage of new thinking, which is redefining nature as harmonious balance and creativity, and rediscovering in the primal societies colonialized by Western imperialism secrets to living in harmony with the earth. The new villain of modernism and postmodern writing is not the wild Indian or the savage beast of the forest, but the predatory ingenuity of Western man himself.

The cowboy story is the place to set up Dorn's mocking denials; here is the lode of images and themes by means of which Western society propagandizes audiences, preaches its gospel of progress and rationality. All of Dorn's figures derive from the typical cowboy tale but reverse their stereotypical roles. "I" ceases to be a hero and becomes a mere vessel to hold lysergic acid; he is "retired" from literature in this tale. Even the drifters get a new image; they are not menacing, but rather helpful marginal figures. The horse, Claude, is intelligent, witty, wry, and more rational than a man. Nature itself is intelligent, more balanced in its dynamic than is human thought.

The journey that begins at Mesilla, New Mexico, is intended to reach Las Vegas, the mecca of Western greed and artificiality in the desert, but it gradually turns into a pilgrimage to the Hopi shrine at Four Corners. This shift in goals is the serious point buried beneath the poem's satirical surface: It marks in the characters a turning away from the neon-lit excesses of contemporary urbanism toward the ineffable mysteries of nature encoded in Hopi religion. The characters themselves are a microcosm of fringe culture in America—the hippies, gurus, poets, and artists who have been composing alternative visions since the end of World War II. Indeed, *Slinger* belongs to the "drug culture" of the 1960's, which is now thought to have mocked and satirized rationality itself by means of "trips," descents in the mind, visions, psychedelic hazes, and similar methods.

Slinger's place in contemporary literature is with other bohemian classics of the era: with the work of the Beat writers Allen Ginsberg and Jack Kerouac; with the plays of Sam Shepard, which treat the modern West from a similarly jaundiced viewpoint; and with Thomas Pynchon's satiric novels, all of which explode the underlying psychology of destruction in Western thought and propose antidotes in the form of primitive mysticism and myth.

For a time in the early 1970's, *Slinger* enjoyed the reputation of a cult text and was passed around reverently by younger readers who shared the passionate conviction that the West was hurtling toward technological suicide. *Slinger*'s outrageous satire has faded over the years, and its views seem a bit quaint and light-hearted in an age that is reeling from environmental catastrophes and ravaging plagues. Like many good works of literature, *Slinger* was prophetic in sounding the alarm.

Paul Christensen

HAP

Author: Thomas Hardy (1840-1928)
Type of poem: Sonnet
First published: 1898, in *Wessex Poems*

The Poem

Thomas Hardy has structured "Hap" to meet all the requirements of the form of an English sonnet: Its fourteen lines are written in iambic pentameter, the rhyme scheme *abab, cdcd, efef, gg* is complied with, and the three quatrains are followed by a rhymed couplet to conclude the poem.

The title suggests all the readily identifiable characteristics connoted by the word "hap" (used as a noun until early in the twentieth century). The word itself has nearly disappeared in modern English except as a clipped form of the verb "happen" (as in "It then came to us to hap upon the drunken sailor"). At the time the poem was written, however, the word still functioned commonly as a noun meaning chance, luck, fortune, or coincidence.

Hardy's use of the first person leaves no doubt about the poem's existence as a personal expression of the author's own attitudes about and experiences with life, here a certain resigned bitterness attributed to chance or bad luck. The poet is posing hard questions about life (particularly humankind's relationship to a possibly existing god).

The poem has an "if-then-but" structure which exactingly adheres to its division into quatrains. Hardy asks an indirect question in the first stanza, gives a "then" answer in the second one; and follows it with a dismissal in the third. The couplet at the end serves to answer the question embedded in the beginning of the poem.

The opening line of the poem is an expressed desire for "some vengeful god" to communicate to him and laugh, at least, at the poet's condition and suffering. The stanza reveals that Hardy would take satisfaction—though assuredly not joy or delight—in knowing that some omnipotent cosmic force was pleasuring itself in his own pain. This expression actually questions whether such a god exists.

In the middle stanza, Hardy indicates that he would accept such cosmic causes of his suffering by embracing death. He wishes to take some intellectual comfort, at least, in knowing that his pain has been willed by entities in the universe stronger than himself and over which he has absolutely no control.

The final quatrain begins with a loud "But not so." Hardy concludes that the gods are not willfully subjecting him to pain and suffering in order to pleasure themselves. His anguish is not manifested in plan or design or thought. Rather, it can be explained only in terms of "Crass Casualty"—a phrase he uses to mean "chance," or, more nearly correctly, "bad luck." The couplet at the end serves to reemphasize this point: "purblind Doomsters" have indifferently, probably unknowingly, given his life "pain" rather than "blisses."

Forms and Devices

The sonnet is basically constructed around a simplistic metaphor: Life is a pilgrimage through which Hardy journeys, experiencing pain and suffering only. While making this journey, the poet is aware of the existence of God, but he is seemingly unable to determine whether he is a "vengeful" one. Hardy refers directly to God four times, citing him first as "Powerfuller than I," a means of recognizing his own hopelessness and helplessness in the face of whatever God has in store for him. He later refers to God as "Crass Casualty," by which, again, he means "chance" or "bad luck." The reference to "Time" is to mention yet another universal force against which he is sheerly helpless. Finally, Hardy shifts to the plural when he writes of "purblind Doomsters" who will manipulate and control his own life yet who are totally devoid of any care or concern for him. Not only are they more powerful than he, but they also outnumber him.

This metaphor is couched in the form of the English sonnet. The content of the sonnet, both structurally and thematically, adheres to the pattern of the form; specifically, the theme and exposition follow requirements of form. The first stanza introduces the subject and the question, essentially, "Life is a pilgrimage of pain—why so?" The answer is that such suffering is not intentionally willed by a "vengeful god." The second stanza elaborates this idea by repetition and denial. One "Powerfuller than I" has not with thought and deliberation "meted" out his tears. In the third stanza, this perception of and explanation for human suffering is finally made explicit: The poet's "joy lies slain," and his hope is gone, the reader is told, after learning "But not so." That is, the denial that the gods are willing this suffering by plan or with reason is made irrevocably clear. Finally, the couplet spells out emphatically that the poet's suffering can only rightly be explained as indifference and blindness on the parts of the gods themselves, now called "Doomsters."

Other than this basic metaphor, which finds a parallel in the sonnet form, the poem is rather straightforward. "Crass Casualty" obstructing both sun and rain suggests that the gods would block out all, good and evil alike, in human nature and environs; "dicing Time" casting a moan functions similarly. A few examples of alliteration appear ("love's loss" and "meted me"), but with no overall discernible purpose.

Themes and Meanings

Hardy's impetus in writing the poem, surely, was to explore and explain the reasons for his own suffering. The poet asks this question explicitly at the beginning of the third stanza: "How arrives it joy lies slain . . . ?" The problem is not merely that joy is slain but also that pain is plentiful on his pilgrimage of life. Hardy takes up the question of God's existence, or, more to the point, the nature of the relationship between God and man.

He variously describes himself, either directly or indirectly, as a "suffering thing"; as one whose "sorrow" gives the gods "ecstasy"; as bearing "it" (life, and suffering in life), clenching, and dying; as shedding tears; as possessing "slain" joy and "unbloomed" hope. At the same time, he sees himself encapsulated by omnipotent cosmic forces described as "some vengeful god," "Powerfuller than I," "Crass Casualty," "dicing Time," and "purblind Doomsters."

Hardy denies that humans are as flies to wanton boys. He sees his condition as worse: The gods are deriving no pleasure from the pain of humans. If the gods were inflicting, or even permitting, human suffering with some purpose or purposes of their own (even self-indulgence or sadism), then the poet says that he could "bear it, clench [himself], and die." He can find, however, no evidence that this is the case; the universe is malign through chance and indifference — through "hap" — not through any purpose, even an evil one.

One quality of Hardy's poems, also immediately recognizable in his novels, is that they often evidence fatalism. In the classical sense of the word, "fate" would be either good or evil; the gods gave some people one of these, while others received the opposite allotment. Individuals did not always, or even usually, understand how or why, but purpose and design eventually became evident. Hardy's universe, however, is one in which the gods are merely half-blind "Doomsters," inflicting pain and suffering through indifference and total neglect. Human pilgrimages are entirely haphazard.

Fate, then, reigns supreme in Hardy's perception of the universe and in humanity's recognition and acceptance of the lots not assigned but received anyway. The gods seek neither vengeance nor ecstasy. They slay joy indiscriminately and undoubtedly provide pleasure, fulfillment, and meaning to others in the same way. Chance is "Crass," and Time, arguably the most indifferent of all cosmic dimensions, is seen simply as determined by a toss of the die.

The amounts and degrees of human suffering are determined by matters over which individuals have no control or even perspective. Beyond this, humans not only cannot control their own destinies — their cast of the die — but they also cannot even comprehend their destinies. Hardy is left with a total inability to change or to effect changes in his condition, his pain and suffering. He is only partially able to understand it. Finally, he is left with only a fatalistic bitterness. He is evidently not envious of those whose lot is different from his own. He can neither control nor understand his suffering; he can only accept it in order to live with the terms that the "purblind Doomsters" have unwittingly provided him.

Carl Singleton

HARLEM

Author: Langston Hughes (1902-1967)
Type of poem: Lyric
First published: 1951, in *Montage of a Dream Deferred*

The Poem

"Harlem" is a short, reflective poem, somber in tone, with an ominous, pointedly italicized ending. It appeared originally as the first poem in the last sequence of poems ("Lenox Avenue Mural") in the book *Montage of a Dream Deferred*. Sometimes *Montage of a Dream Deferred* has been reprinted in its entirety, (as in Hughes's *Selected Poems*); sometimes "Lenox Avenue Mural" has been reprinted separately; often "Harlem" has been reprinted alone.

The poem can stand alone. Although it is part of a suite of six poems ("Lenox Avenue Mural") and of a book of ninety-one poems (reduced to eighty-seven in *Selected Poems*), it is self-contained and autonomous. It consists of seven short sentences, the last six of which respond to the opening question, "What happens to a dream deferred?" Of the six responses, all but one are themselves framed as rhetorical questions. The whole of *Montage of a Dream Deferred* is set in Harlem, yet only two of its ninety-one poems mention Harlem in their titles ("Harlem" and "Night Funeral in Harlem"). Simply being titled "Harlem" gives this particular lyric a special recognition in the sequence.

The "dream deferred" is the long-postponed and, therefore, frustrated dream of African Americans: a dream of freedom, equality, dignity, opportunity, and success. This particular poem does not define or give examples of the dream (many other poems in *Montage of a Dream Deferred* do this); it concentrates, instead, on possible reactions to the deferral of a dream, ranging from the fairly mild-mannered ("Does it dry up/ like a raisin in the sun?") to the threatening (*"Or does it explode?"*). The first five potential responses to frustration are essentially passive, the last one active.

Langston Hughes first made his home in Manhattan's Harlem in 1922. He was a leading figure in the Harlem Renaissance, the 1920's flowering of African-American literature and art. Although he traveled widely and often, he kept circling back to Harlem. He lived there, on a more-or-less permanent basis, from the early 1940's on, maintaining a home on West 127th Street for the last twenty years of his life. *Montage of a Dream Deferred* is a product of the late 1940's, when Hughes had at last settled in Harlem.

The variety of responses that "Harlem" suggests as reactions to the deferring of a dream may be taken as a sort of cross-section of behavior patterns Hughes saw around him among the citizens of Harlem. The poem reflects the post-World War II mood of many African Americans. The Great Depression was over, the war was over, but for African Americans the dream, whatever particular form it took, was still being deferred. As Arthur P. Davis wrote in a 1952 article in *Phylon*, "with Langston Hughes Harlem is both place and symbol. When he depicts the hopes, the aspirations, the frustrations, and the deep-seated discontent of the New York ghetto, he is expressing the feelings of Negroes in black ghettos throughout America."

Forms and Devices

The most striking features of "Harlem" are the vivid, even startling, metaphors that Hughes introduces as possible answers to the poem's opening question, "What happens to a dream deferred?" Each metaphor could be taken as suggesting a pattern of behavior. Drying "up/ like a raisin in the sun" could refer to the gradual shriveling of a dream or a person, still sweet but wrinkled, desiccated. (Lorraine Hansberry's 1959 play, *A Raisin in the Sun*, ruminates on this sort of response to a dream deferred—taking its title from Hughes's poem.)

To "fester like a sore—/ And then run" suggests something considerably more unappealing—and dangerous—than drying up, obviously implying infection: a wound not healing. Eventually a limb or a life may be lost. Worse still among its implications is that it will "stink like rotten meat," for now life is gone from the organism entirely and putrefaction has set in. "Stink" is used as an intentionally offensive, vulgar word, suitable for the occasion.

So far there has been a kind of logical progression, from dehydration to localized decay ("fester") to wholesale decomposition, but here the poem takes a surprising turn. To "crust and sugar over—/ like a syrupy sweet" seems anti-climactic at first, after rot; "sugar" and "sweet" recall the concentrated sweetness of a raisin.

Hughes may have been thinking of a false, "syrupy sweet" form of behavior—what Paul Laurence Dunbar, in his poem, "We Wear the Mask," called "the mask that grins and lies"—an outer "crust" that hides. The poem does not say what it hides, but one may be reminded of the narrator's grandfather in Ralph Ellison's novel *Invisible Man* (1952), a grinning, subservient old man who, on his deathbed, "had spoken of his meekness as a dangerous activity"—who had told his grandson "to overcome 'em with yeses, undermine 'em with grins, agree 'em to death and destruction, let 'em swoller you [like too much sugar, perhaps] till they vomit or bust wide open."

Each of the last two answers to the question, "What happens to a dream deferred?" is set off from the others. Penultimately, there is the statement, "Maybe it just sags/ like a heavy load"—perhaps the saddest of the responses, suggesting depression and despair. Finally, there is the overtly warning question: *"Or does it explode?"* When violence broke out in America's inner cities in the 1960's, Hughes's poem proved to have been prophetic.

By no means are the metaphors in "Harlem" meant to exhaust the number of possible responses to the deferring of a dream. Indeed, another poem in *Montage of a Dream Deferred*, "Same in Blues," uses a repeated refrain to state that in a dream deferred there is "A certain/ amount of traveling," "A certain/ amount of nothing," and "A certain/ amount of impotence." The poem notes that "There's liable/ to be confusion/ in a dream deferred." Even with "traveling," "nothing," "impotence," and "confusion," the list of responses is nowhere near exhausted. There may be as many dreams deferred as there are residents of Harlem or as there are African Americans.

Themes and Meanings

Although "Harlem" can stand alone, it is best understood in its original context as a key part of *Montage of a Dream Deferred*. Hughes conceived *Montage of a Dream Deferred* as a single, long poem made up of many parts, some as short as three lines (or fewer than ten words), some as long as two pages.

The word "montage" suggests analogies with a visual design consisting of many juxtaposed smaller designs or, better (since a series of poems exists in time more than in space), with a rapid sequence of related short scenes in a film. The most useful analogue of the work is, however, neither pictorial nor cinematic but musical. In a prefatory note to *Montage of a Dream Deferred*, Hughes wrote that "this poem on contemporary Harlem, like be-bop, is marked by conflicting changes, sudden nuances, sharp and impudent interjections, broken rhythms, and passages sometimes in the manner of the jam session, sometimes the popular song, punctuated by the riffs, runs, breaks, and disc-tortions of the music of a community in transition."

Hughes had long been interested in and knowledgeable about African-American music. Beginning in the 1920's, he wrote poems about—and sometimes in forms influenced by—the music. His first book, *The Weary Blues* (1926), took its title from such a poem. Bebop, the innovative jazz of the late 1940's, with its emphasis on the successive improvisations of individual instrumental voices, most strongly influenced the form and the flavor of *Montage of a Dream Deferred*.

If the book were conceived as one long bebop tune based on chord changes on the theme of "a dream deferred," then "Harlem," strategically placed at the beginning of the end of the book, marks the point at which the theme is restated in preparation for the end. Dreams are mentioned in more than a dozen individual poems in the book; the phrase "dream deferred" appears in a half dozen poems prior to "Harlem" (and in three poems that follow). "Harlem" is the first poem to ask, "What happens to a dream deferred?" (The succeeding poem, "Good Morning," repeats the question.)

The dream that "Harlem" (and *Montage of a Dream Deferred*, in general) asks about is the African-American version of the American Dream: A "Dream within a dream," as "Island" (the last poem in *Montage of a Dream Deferred*) calls it. In the course of the book, individuals imagine the dream in many different ways. Some merely dream of things (a stove, a bottle of gin, a television set, a diamond ring); other dreams also require money, but they are less specifically material (to have a nice place to live, to get an education, to be able to afford a proper funeral). Some intangible dreams require the cooperation of another person or other people (to be fed, to be appreciated, to be respected, to be loved); other intangible dreams can be solitary (to be safe, to be independent, to be happy). Whether one's dream is as mundane as hitting the numbers or as noble as hoping to see one's children reared properly, Langston Hughes takes them all seriously; he takes the deferral of each dream to heart.

Richard Bizot

HASIDIC SCRIPTURES

Author: Nelly Sachs (1891-1970)
Type of poem: Lyric
First published: 1949, as "Chassidische Schriften," in *Sternverdunkelung;*
 collected in *The Seeker and Other Poems*, 1970

The Poem

"Hasidic Scriptures" consists of twenty-nine lines divided into tercets, couplets and one quatrain, all written in free verse. The title refers to the teachings of Rabbi Israel Ba'al Shem Tov (1700-1760), the founder of Hasidism, and draws the reader immediately into the context of Jewish mysticism. An epigraph preceding the poem comments on the mystical relationship between the Law of the Commandments and man's physical experience. The first line, "All is salvation in the mystery," which repeats throughout the poem, indicates Nelly Sachs's belief that it is inappropriate, if not impossible, to attain spiritual truth through logic. The poem unfolds as a meditation on this relationship between the Creator and the created world, in which Sachs transforms theological and metaphysical concepts into a deeply personal artistic vision.

The poem's first eleven lines place the reader at the beginning of Creation as light is born of darkness in the protective, nurturing matrix of the universe. The entire process is distilled into images of night, stars, water, and sand. For Sachs, who was inspired by mysticism, the agent which initiates and sustains the Creation is language: "and the word went forth/. . . Names formed/ like pools in the sand." These "names" refer to the formative power of language and recall man's role in naming the animals (Genesis 2:20), which implies a personal participation in language. In the syntax of the poem, the names' arrival follows an undefined longing felt by all creatures. The reader is led to make the connection between this longing and the attempt by man to share through language in the creative process, thereby becoming one with the Creator.

The next eight lines both close the Genesis material and introduce the next phase of the poem, which depicts the experience of exile and the promise of the covenant (as in the biblical Exodus and Deuteronomy). This section presents images of death connoting the expulsion from Eden: bones, bleeding veins, sunset, and pain. Yet upon these images are superimposed the concepts of the Commandments and laws which transcend individual mortality. Memory, the foundation of tradition, offers another way to transcend death, the death caused by forgetting. In Sachs's poetry, forgetting and remembering are always functions of the Holocaust's historical burden.

The final ten lines interweave images from God's promise to Abraham, Jacob's vision, and the exodus from Egypt into a composite vision of the Jewish experience. The biblical incidents are arranged in a backward chronological order that represents the reversal of the journey away from God. Sachs first records the crossing of the Jordan and the transport of the Hebrew laws and Scripture, which together imply the end of national exile. Following is a description of a barren wilderness of stones, quicksand, and darkness. Even here, God's presence, the flash of revelation, is immanent: "the dwelling place of buried lightening." The poem closes with the image of the sleeping Jacob, known as "Israel, the fighter of horizons" after his battle with God, dreaming the promise of a nation born "with the seed of stars," which signifies the promise to Abraham. The writing of this poem coincided with the development of Israel's nationhood, and the final lines bespeak a political and historical hope as well as a spiritual one.

Forms and Devices

Hans Magnus Enzensberger wrote in his introduction to *O the Chimneys* (1967) that Sachs's poems are "hard, but transparent. They do not dissolve in the weak solution of interpretations." The most powerful aspect of her poetry is her use of symbols and metaphors in which are concentrated layer upon layer of meaning drawn from her life's experiences and Jewish mysticism. The complexity of her system of signs is further enriched by the associations brought to it by her readers. Her translators face the difficult task of selecting words that evoke at least some of the many nuances found in the original texts. They are further challenged by the complicated and ambiguous syntax of her verses: New clauses begin without markers, subjects and objects are blurred, and inserted modifiers distend the sentence's structure. These strategies alter the pace of reading. The reader is sometimes slowed and sometimes propelled by the use of anaphora (here, the repetition of "and" at the beginning of eleven lines) in a chain of associations.

The broken rhythm of Sachs's syntax is replicated in the arrangement of her lines of verse. The repetition of the poem's first line, "All is salvation in the mystery," weaves through an irregular pattern of couplets, tercets, and a single quatrain creating an unpredictable emphasis. Another unifying element is the recurrence of simile after each repetition of the opening line.

The simile is only one of the many forms of metaphor encountered in this poem. Metaphor, especially metaphor developed from biblical or mystical imagery, is the cornerstone of Sachs's system of poetic expression. She has observed of her own poetic craft: "Images and metaphors are my wounds. Death has been my teacher. I wrote to be able to survive." (She escaped the fate of her fellow Jews in the concentration camps by fleeing to Sweden in May, 1940.)

In this poem, darkness and light have universal significance, but Sachs expresses her hopeful belief in transformation when she imagines the night giving birth to the stars. Dark and light, good and evil, are not in perpetual conflict; rather, one can engender the other. Similarly, she transforms the image of the stone — hard, lifeless matter and symbolic of exile in the barren desert — into a petrified darkness that still contains the promise of divine movement and light. Even threatening quicksand becomes a metaphor of the potential for change on the most elemental level. In conjunction with the final images of fertile seeds and stars, sand assumes yet another dimension inspired by the Bible: God promises Abraham, "I will shower blessings on you, I will make your descendants as many as the stars in heaven and the grains of sand on the seashore" (Genesis 22:17). Sachs allows the conventional, sometimes negative connotations of certain images to stand while exploring the promise hidden within.

Themes and Meanings

Nelly Sachs, described as the "poet of the Holocaust" when she was awarded the Nobel Prize in Literature in 1966, challenges the view that poetry is impossible after Auschwitz. To untangle the disorder left in the wake of World War II, she turned to the works of Jewish mysticism. The Book of the Zohar (The Book of Light), a thirteenth century commentary on the Pentateuch, provided a new way to envision the metaphysical order of the world, a way to make sense of a system fallen apart. She posed the essential question: How could the Holocaust have occurred in a world supposedly under the care of a supreme Divinity? Mysticism provided the keys to putting the shattered world back together again. Within the darkest experience had to be found a new light. The alternative would be nihilism or deep pessimism, and both are untenable positions in a theology based on the Covenant.

Sachs was acutely aware of the dilemma that writing in German posed for her. The German language was discredited because it had been the language of the oppressors. She developed a strategy for salvaging her means of expression and communication—her system of metaphors, which is, in effect, a reinvention of language. Her system affirmed the existence of bonds between words and their meanings, while opening up a new range of meanings, and it challenged words to describe what had been termed indescribable.

In view of Sachs's quest to transform her native language into an appropriate vehicle for poetry, her vision of the Creation is striking. In it the world is essentially created through language. In "Hasidic Scriptures," the indescribable is not directly the horror of the concentration camp but the world's (especially man's and specifically Israel's) relationship to God. She envisioned this relationship in terms of Hasidic mysticism infused with elements of Christian mysticism which seemed to provide answers to the existential questions raised by the events of World War II.

The central aspect of this relationship is the experience of exile, of separation from the Divine. Juxtaposed with this spiritual exile are the historical exiles of the Hebrews and Sachs's own exile in Sweden. Sachs combined the metaphysical, the Biblical and the biographical concepts of exile into a totality of associations. However, just as sand is a metaphor not only for barrenness but also for the constant transformation and movement in the created world, exile contains within it the ever constant hope of return or reunification.

Elisabeth Strenger

HE WHO DOES NOT HOPE

Author: Gunnar Ekelöf (1907-1968)
Type of poem: Meditation
First published: 1945, as "Den som inte hoppas," in *Non serviam;* collected in
 Songs of Something Else, 1982

The Poem

In "He Who Does Not Hope," the simplicity of Gunnar Ekelöf's diction belies a highly dense thought process. It is a brief poem—thirty-two lines of free verse, divided into four eight-line stanzas—which begins calmly and rationally with two statements, the first of which echoes the title. The first four lines state that the absence of hope also means freedom from the despair that comes from disappointed hope; correspondingly, believing in nothing frees one from the torment of doubt. In the second half of the stanza, however, this passive but untroubled view is contrasted with its opposite. As soon as one breaks out of unthinking passivity and tries to find a goal or a meaning in life, one is flung into conflict. One begins an unending struggle with the "dragons" of doubt and despair which breathe their poison into one's consciousness.

Stanza 2 also shifts between opposites. It evokes the picture of a winter day, when snow is falling outdoors and a fire is burning in the hearth indoors. These seemingly contradictory elements, snow and fire, both suggest the brevity of life. The fifth line draws together the contradictory elements of snow and fire, heat and cold. The "play" of life—the double suggestion occurs of the *theatrum mundi* ("world theater") and of aimless movement—is like the play of both the snow and the fire. A renewed paradox ends the second stanza, with the statement that the "meaning" of life derives from its meaninglessness.

The third stanza begins on a profoundly negative note. Life has no inherent plan or order. While the disasters of Greek tragedy can at least be ascribed to the preordained workings of fate, twentieth century life lacks even this order. People are the victims of haphazard "combinations" of circumstances and the undifferentiated actions of natural disasters ("whirlwinds") and the forces of history (worldwinds). Struggle alone is insignificant; the only important aspect is a change from one form of struggle to another.

With the fifth line of the third stanza, the poem takes on an anguished urgency. The images of fire and snow recur; now, however, they suggest the cycle of destructive forces in human life: "Let the fire thaw the drift./ Let the drift put out the fire"—since disintegration and death are inevitable, let them proceed. The two concluding lines of the stanza raise the poem to a crescendo of agonized questioning. The poetic speaker uses second-person address: "Life, where is your meaning now?/ Life, where is your point now?"

The fourth stanza obliquely answers the intense questioning of the previous one. The focus moves inward, and the tone becomes lyrical. The heart and soul are orphans, born without parentage, nurturing, or guidance. In their bond, however, they find the relationship that their orphan birth has denied them, for they are "brother" and "sister." The soul is superior to the heart or emotions, for it fills the yet more important role of "mother."

In the final four lines of the last stanza, the poem rises to its most lyrical and most personal note. The objective tone is now fully shed with the use of the first person— "me" and "my." The poetic voice invokes the sister-mother to rock him back and forth and sing for him. This "song without end," it is implied, counterbalances the meaninglessness and brevity of life with meaning and eternity.

Forms and Devices

In spite of the free verse and the simplicity of the diction, "He Who Does Not Hope" presents a complex use of paradox, tightly bound by metaphorical development and verbal devices. The structure of the stanzas in both the Swedish original and the excellent translation by Leonard Nathan and James Larson reflects this underlying tightness. In each stanza, a major modification in the thought development occurs halfway. In stanza 1, this shift is introduced by "but" and sets apart two contradictory life views. In the second stanza, the last four lines synthesize paradoxical elements only to posit yet another paradox. The role of the mid-stanza shift in stanzas 3 and 4 is that of lyrical reinforcement: The second half of stanza 3 offers an emotional response to the destructiveness and brevity of life, while the concluding lines of stanza 4 address lovingly the sister-mother.

The syntax reflects the above pattern, for in each stanza, a full stop concludes the fourth verse. In addition, the first two stanzas, with their objective tone, form a subunit, as do the more subjective third and fourth stanzas. The first four lines of stanzas 1 and 2 are subdivided into two statements of two lines each, terminated by periods. The final four lines, however, are uninterrupted by stops and propel the thought forward with the smoothness of their flow. Similarly, the third and fourth stanzas are interlinked by a pattern of statement in the first four lines and rhetorical address in the concluding four. The third stanza, in which the content rises to a peak of questioning, is the most fragmented, both in sentence structure and by breaks or caesuras. The first four lines consist of sentence fragments, marked by the repetition of "not" and "but," separated by stops at the end of each line.

In structure as well as in content, the fourth stanza is the point of final synthesis. Thematically, an abrupt shift occurs from images of the outer to images of the inner world, from images of brevity and destruction to images of endurance. The effect of this revelation is epiphanic. To underline the exultation of the conclusion, a marked caesura separates the fourth and fifth verses, as the poem breaks forth into a lyrical address to the soul/sister/mother and, for the first time, first-person pronouns and adjectives are used.

Not only the structure but also the verbal devices reflect the tightness of this free-verse meditation. In lines 5 and 6, the repetition of "he who seeks" causes the diction to linger emphatically before the theme of conflict is broached. The third stanza is a feat of translating skill. Transposed, as noted above, is the repeated "not . . . but"; in a verbal echo of the sweeping forces of disaster, the second line lingers on "whirlwinds and the drift of world winds." Here, as with the transposition of "fire . . . drift" and "drift . . . fire" in the fifth and sixth lines of stanza 3, the all-embracing cycle of struggle is suggested.

Themes and Meanings

"He Who Does Not Hope" is a poetic search for a goal and meaning in life. In this way, the poet is like a knight who, as did the chevaliers of the Round Table, rides forth on his quest. Like them, he has setbacks and fights mightily with poison-breathing dragons before he arrives at his goal. Unlike them, however, his dragons are not supernatural creatures but are inherent in life itself.

The poem shifts between paradox and antithesis. Beginning in stanza 1 with the absence of both search and struggle, it moves rapidly to the opposite state: the search which transforms man into a knight in combat. Another rapid shift in metaphor introduces two natural images, fire and snow. Within the sphere of nature as of man, one finds brevity and the omnipresence of disintegration and death. At the end of stanza 2, the search seems to have ended in failure, for the only "meaning" to be derived from life is that of "meaninglessness"; paradoxically, however, the words also suggest that "meaning" is implicit in its absence.

Heat and cold, fire and water have to this point been the antithetical elements which suggest transience in the natural world as well as in human existence. In the third stanza, however, the elements of air and earth ("whirlwinds" and "world winds"), along with the interaction of fire and snow, epitomize the destruction wasted upon humanity.

The "goal" and "meaning" of the quest are found, the final stanza implies, not in the external world, but in a mystic inner region. Although the heart and soul are "orphans" within the world of physical existence, their cohesion yet provides the meaning and eternity which the outside world denies. With the image of the cosmic mother whose infusion of the outer world can only be accomplished by means of the vision within—a recurrent motif in Ekelöf's poetry—the poem ends in paradox. Even more significantly (and here the poet reaffirms the exalted nature of his calling) the eternal meaning expresses itself in the song of the sister/mother/soul.

Anna M. Wittmann

THE HEART

Author: Georg Trakl (1887-1914)
Type of poem: Lyric
First published: 1914, as "Das Herz"; in *Die Dichtungen*, 1919; collected in
   Poems, 1973

The Poem

"The Heart" is written in thirty-one lines of free verse. Its three stanzas represent three stages of an emotional experience that moves from fear to a vision and a sense of reconciliation. The title emphasizes the image that occurs in the first and the last two lines of the poem and is a metonym for feeling. In the first and third stanzas, the heart is nevertheless personified. Wild with passion, unruly, and unnerved by fear and anguish, it represents the persona in the first line. In the last two lines, however, it belongs to a female figure, who brings about reconciliation and hope.

In the first stanza, the persona describes feelings that accompany a walk near the woods on a November evening. The poem begins with the anticipation and fear of approaching darkness and death. As the persona enters the outskirts of town, he observes a group of poor women, who buy cheap food at the slaughterhouse. They receive innards and decaying meat, nourishment that can clearly bring on illness. On the symbolic level, the nature of this food evokes the inner decay and disintegration of society, because nourishment that sustains life is traditionally blessed, rather than cursed, as this food is in the persona's thoughts.

Fear, defeat, and mourning for a destroyed past are the predominant feelings of the second stanza. Instead of experiencing the hoped-for peace of the evening, the persona observes a storm, which he uses as an extended metaphor for war and destruction. Thunder appears as the dark call of a trumpet that runs through the wet, golden leaves of elm trees, which suddenly appear as a torn flag, yellow as the flag of the Austrian Empire, the poet's native land. This flag seems to be both bloody and smoking, as if ruined in battle. A man is mourning as he listens to the sounds of the storm in wild sorrow. The stanza concludes in an exclamation calling for past ages that have been destroyed and buried following a conflagration, represented by the red evening sky.

The third stanza is devoted to a vision of a young woman, who appears from the darkness of a door and transforms the devastated environment by means of purity and love. Sublimation—that is, a vision of her moral elevation and a sense of her supernatural strength—is indicated by the gold that characterizes her figure. The pale moons that surround her are reminiscent of traditional Catholic light symbolism pertaining to the Virgin Mary, particularly in her associations with light that shines through the darkness of the night and suffering. Additional images of nature—of pines felled by the storm on the side of the mountain, which appears as a fortification—are closely related to the Austrian landscape and suggest a royal court, through which the young woman attains high social, or even royal, stature. The radiant heart, which illuminates the cool atmosphere of a snowy peak, sharing its clarity, purity, and calm, belongs to her, not to the persona, who nevertheless finds consolation and awe in this vision.

Forms and Devices

"The Heart" consists of a series of brief descriptions of scenes that the persona selects as if to convey a state of mind informed by social and historical awareness of the world. This approach lends expressionistic style to the first two stanzas of the poem, which nevertheless remains primarily symbolistic.

Symbolic dimensions are introduced by means of a fusion of several literary devices—personifications, metaphors, a rich web of adjectives, and color imagery—which resonate with both traditional associations and new connotations acquired through context. Beginning with the "wild heart" of the first line, almost every image is personified. Most images also involve movement and change. Through the multiple associations of the imagery, the poet stresses that traditional associations or expectations no longer hold. Whereas "wild" suggests daring and independence, for example, here it is transformed by fear. Even the evening, presented in the metaphor of a blue dove, arrives without bringing peace or reconciliation.

The interchangeability of inside and outside, observation and feeling, natural phenomenon and historical event, expressed by means of an intricate fusion of imagery, lends the poem emotively rich texture. In the second stanza, for example, a storm is described in metaphors that suggest war, but it is the battle that appears overwhelmingly real, even though it may be only anticipated or feared by the persona. Again, metaphoric structure prevails as historical time, the past that has disappeared, seems to be buried by the evening sky, and the real conflagration of war is suggested.

Color, both named and implied, as in snow, as well as suggested by its absence, as in dark and bare in the first stanza, contributes to the resonance of the poem. The same color tends to recur and absorb new connotative values from the context. Therefore, in addition to their visual effect and symbolic overtones, colors support the poem's movement on the emotive level. For example, in connotations of prosperity and royalty, gold dies into gray in the first stanza and suggests spiritual impoverishment, which is continued in the images of a bare countryside in November and of the group of poor women. In its reference to the monarchy, introduced through the connotations of the golden autumn trees that appear as a torn and besmirched yellow flag, it is destroyed, emphasizing the expected consequences of war. Gold recurs a third time, as a symbol of transcendence brought about by the strength of the human spirit, and contributes to the affirmation of the value of feeling at the end of the poem.

A similar function is performed by the exclamations, which separate descriptive units of the poem, emphasize emotions that accompany the persona's observations, and delineate the poem's structure. Through them, the poem moves from anguish to horror in the first stanza, through intense regret and mourning in the second, to clarification and reconciliation at the end of the poem. The exclamations also add lyric intensity to the poem.

Themes and Meanings

"The Heart" is about social disintegration and the destruction of not only an empire but also a way of life and a historical period, as well as about the strength of the human spirit, which can transcend adversity by means of goodness of the heart. This is the basic theme of the entire oeuvre of the Austrian Georg Trakl, who, prior to his death during the first year of the war, gave an apocalyptic interpretation of the impending collapse of the Austrian Empire. In Trakl's poetry, the doom of his native country is foreshadowed by a sense of decay and the social disintegration that affected both the family and the individual.

Trakl's vocabulary denoting decay and his extensive use of color were strongly influenced by the French Symbolist poet Arthur Rimbaud. In the context of Trakl's poems, this imagery acquired new significance, as it came to cluster around his premonitions of the social and political disintegration of his country and his search for personal resolution in poetry and feeling, which he considered redemptive.

Trakl's sense of social disintegration is often conveyed in his presentation of a polarized sister-brother relationship, the friendship, love, guilt, and suffering of two figures who are envisioned as both the same and irrevocably divided. The female figure, which may be associated with the *anima* or spiritual part of a person, is usually sublimated or envisioned as a consoling superior being in Trakl's poems.

This theme is based on the poet's passionate and tragic relationship with his sister, but it is strongly influenced by the Russian novelist Fyodor Dostoevski's figure of Sonia, the heroine of *Prestupleniye i nakazaniye* (1866; *Crime and Punishment*, 1886): Sonia's innate goodness contributed to the preservation of the purity of her heart in spite of adverse and debasing circumstances in her life and to her recognition of the redemptive capabilities of love and the human spirit.

In "The Heart," polarization in the context of the brother-sister theme takes the form of a movement from a wild, fearful, enervated heart that is aware only of decay to the image of a radiant heart that spreads its light over white snow. The associations of redemption touch upon an awareness of the Austrian landscape, the sense of stability and firmness of the past, conveyed by the image of the fortification, and Catholic associations of the pale moons that surround the youthful female figure to whom the radiant heart belongs. Thus Trakl gathers his tradition and heritage in a few lines and extends the hope for personal redemption in spite of a tragic historical event.

Marie Gerenday Tamas

HEART OF AUTUMN

Author: Robert Penn Warren (1905-1989)
Type of poem: Lyric
First published: 1978, in *Now and Then: Poems, 1976-1978*

The Poem

"Heart of Autumn" is a poem of twenty-four lines about an old man who, aware of the limitations of human knowledge, searches for intimations of a divine purpose in the universe. He does this by observing the migrations of wild geese instinctively accomplishing their destiny in the heavens as they fly southward every year in the autumn.

Appearing last in the volume, *Now and Then: Poems, 1976-1978*, "Heart of Autumn" was chosen to round out a group of poems in part 2 of the book containing "Speculative" verses, in contrast to "Nostalgic" works in part 1 of the collection. The poem is a compelling exercise in philosophical speculation about the ultimate meaning of human life, in keeping with Robert Penn Warren's remarks about the purpose of literature in his Jefferson Lecture in the Humanities, entitled "Democracy and Literature," delivered in 1975: "What poetry most significantly celebrates is the capacity of man to face the deep, dark inwardness of his nature and fate." The title of the poem bears the double meaning of the ultimate significance of the dying season of autumn for man and nature, and the oneness that the aged speaker comes to affirm between the migratory geese and himself in his pursuit of transcendence at the close of his life.

Stanzas 1 and 2 describe the southward migration of wild geese from the northwest, somewhere in the United States, when suddenly a hunter's shotgun blast violently breaks the V-shaped formation of the birds but cannot for long prevent their recovery of flight and the resumption of the order of nature ("the season's logic").

Stanzas 3 and 4 begin to decipher the lesson of this description of nature for humankind and its mysterious destiny. The aged speaker perceives a difference between unerring brute instinct guiding the geese's heaven-directed flight and his own limited human intelligence in deducing the purpose of his existence.

Stanzas 5 and 6 at first mock human intelligence as a catalyst for error and deception ("Path of logic, path of folly, all/ The same"), contrasting sharply with the laws of nature that govern the instinct of geese on the right "path of pathlessness" in the mysterious beyond. The mocking quickly subsides under the ecstatic experience of the speaker's identification with nature and his transformation into a wild bird winging his way toward the ineffable finality of a heavenly hereafter, in a sunset glow that makes the fall of his life a climactic rising of the human spirit. The mortal words of the poet wind down into a simplicity that is a prelude to the sound of silence ("the imperial utterance" of the geese) in the awesomeness of eternity.

Forms and Devices

"Heart of Autumn" is a lyric poem of six four-line stanzas without end rhymes and without a regular metrical system. Instead, Warren employed relaxed free verse in run-on lines, capturing the speculative, ruminating quality of his exploration of self, nature, and destiny.

Warren's earlier poetry had been strongly influenced by the formal control and the elegant, well-mannered rationality of John Crowe Ransom's verse. Beginning with the volume *Promises* (1957) and revealed fully in the major book-length poem, *Audubon: A Vision* (1969), however, Warren's poetic line became more free-flowing and energetic in the modernist mode. A distinguishing mark of his poetry is a passion directed toward the physical world and toward a knowledge of truth. He was a writer full of yearning for more than what life normally discloses and yet full of appreciation of the world that instigated that yearning. In fact, "Heart of Autumn" is the beautiful culminating swan song of a singer who loved life but lusted after intimations of immortality.

Assonance and consonance permeate the poem and help to make up for the absence of metrical rhythms ("Wind-flicker of forest, in perfect formation, wild geese"). An example of metonymy — the use of one word for another, suggesting the effect for the cause — appears in "the *boom*, the lead pellet" (line 4), representing the hunter's shotgun firing at the geese.

Paradox, an apparent contradiction that is somehow true, appears twice: first, in the "path of pathlessness" (line 14), representing the geese's instinctive flight to a mysterious, heaven-directed destiny in accordance with the order of nature; and second, in the "Path of logic, path of folly" (line 17), signifying the error-prone intelligence and foolish wisdom of human beings out of touch with the natural order of things.

The language of the poem alternates between a colloquial informality ("the *boom*") of extreme simplicity ("fall comes") and a philosophical formality ("Process of transformation") that embraces technical vocabulary ("the sounding vacuum of passage"). There are neologisms; Warren turns a noun into a verb ("arrows") and creates other new words by compounding ("Sky-strider," "Star-strider," and "wing-beat"). Warren is also elliptical, reducing the poetic communication of concepts to the briefest spurts of words and phrases, as in lines 4, 14, 17, and 24.

Symbols lie at the heart of the poem's stunning effectiveness. The autumn indicates the speaker's age, the sunset represents death and eternity, and the migratory geese embody the heaven-directed destiny with which the aged speaker identifies through a process of birdlike transformation at the end of the poem.

Themes and Meanings

"Heart of Autumn" is a poem about the discrepancy between the heaven-directed destiny in the natural order of things and a human being's initial ignorance of this eternal fate, which the speaker comes to realize in the end. The poem is a wonderful way for Warren, late in his career, to have presented a statement about the purpose of his long life dedicated to art.

It is, after all, a modern American Romantic poem, following a well-established tradition of searching for meaning about life now and in the hereafter through literary meditations about birds. The motif has been especially popular during the past two centuries in works such as John Keats's "Ode to a Nightingale," Percy Bysshe Shelley's "To a Skylark," Thomas Hardy's "The Darkling Thrush," and Robert Frost's "A Minor Bird."

Particularly close to the subject matter of "Heart of Autumn" is the content of William Cullen Bryant's "To a Waterfowl" and William Butler Yeats's "The Wild Swans at Coole." Unlike Yeats, however, Warren affirmed an identification with the birds being observed to the point of undergoing a birdlike transformation that Keats would have envied. If anything, Warren is more of an escapist Romantic poet than either Yeats or Bryant had been. Bryant may have similarly worried about the hunter's damage to waterfowl but never assimilated himself with the birds. His moralizing observations about God's providence over humans and nature anticipated but did not duplicate Warren's total identification of humans and nature with providence at the conclusion of "Heart of Autumn."

Even before the later poetry appeared, M. L. Rosenthal, in *The Modern Poets: A Critical Introduction* (1960), had noted in Warren's work "a refusal, against the tangible evidence, to accept the tragic irrevocability of the disappointed hope." A hopefulness about human destiny marks "Heart of Autumn," despite the dark notes suggesting a cleavage between humans and nature in the hunter's shooting of geese (lines 4-7) and in the speaker's initial detachment from the geese and his initially limited understanding of them and himself (lines 9-17). Happily, his detachment and ignorance dissolve under a Romantic "Process of transformation," ending the broken bond between humans and nature and speeding the birdlike poet to his rendezvous with destiny in the heavenly beyond.

Thomas M. Curley

HEART'S NEEDLE

Author: W. D. Snodgrass (1926-　　)
Type of poem: Poetic sequence
First published: 1959, in *Heart's Needle*

The Poem

"Heart's Needle" explores a father's struggle to remain a father to his daughter who, though separated from him by her parents' divorce, maintains regular visits over a two-and-a-half year period. The child is almost three years old at the beginning.

The title comes from an old Irish tale, "The Frenzy of Suibne," about the death of an only daughter, who is "the needle of the heart." In the poem, W. D. Snodgrass suggests that the daughter's presence as well as her absence is a needle in the heart, since both intensify his sense of loss. In a sequence of ten poems, the father speaks to his daughter as she develops into a petulant, asthmatic child whom he must scold; at the same time, her curiosity and independence bring him as much pleasure as pain. In the end, he cannot imagine his world without her.

The poem begins in the winter of 1952, during the Korean War and after the speaker's first marriage has collapsed. Snodgrass is often grouped with the "confessional" poets of the 1960's who wrote autobiographical poems, and parallels with his own marital break-up and separation from his daughter Cynthia are apparent. Throughout the poem, however, Snodgrass clearly establishes that his concerns are as much universal as personal and particular.

In the first four sections, both father and daughter suffer the consequences of the divorce. The daughter (in section 1), once like "a landscape of new snow," gradually forms (in section 2) similarities in behavior with destructive forces (strange dogs, moles). Between a mother who must be appeased and an unhappy father, the child swings like a heavy weight. Her father realizes that she is "love's wishbone" (section 3) and that he, as the seasons pass, remains a nerveless man and an unproductive poet (section 4).

In sections 5 and 6, as a chilling winter turns into spring, the relationship becomes more complex. The child begins to "chatter about new playmates, sing/ Strange songs." He tells her that he has "another wife, another child." As she forgets their old songs, he remembers in more detail — when she was first born, a storm on July 4, a pigeon they caught and let go. The more he remembers, the more he cannot free her, and the more he feels that he should.

The potential destructiveness of this relationship becomes quite evident in section 6. The father says, "You bring things I'd as soon forget"; one of those things is her severe asthma attack one fall. He recalls the scene and believes that she is giving up, passively drowning. He urges her to understand that one is only free when one chooses the time and place for one's death. Yet a major gap exists between what he says and what he does: "Yet I,/ who say this, could not raise/ myself from bed how many days/ to the thieving world." The danger is that they will try to live their lives on ideas unfounded on experience.

Sections 7 through 9 are dominated by increasing emotional contortions for them both. Delightful times remain, but they diminish in number and intensity. The child whines more; she becomes more willful and demanding. He, rising "back from helplessness," becomes "local law" and punishes her (section 8). In the ninth poem, after a three-month absence from his daughter, the poet/father finds himself writing bitter poems and wandering "among enduring and resigned/ Stuffed animals" of a natural history museum. Among the fixed postures of bobcat, bison, elk, and malignancies encased in jars, the father projects his self-loathing onto the world and its history, wishing that nothing had ever been born. He and the world's "diseased heart" become one.

In the tenth and final poem, the father's experience confirms that only change is permanent: "The vicious winter finally yields/ the green winter wheat." Among the stirrings of spring, father and daughter are together again, briefly but happily. They will not leave each other to separate lives, but like the coons "on bread and water" reach after each other.

Forms and Devices

In an essay on his revisions of "Heart's Needle," particularly of the sixth section, Snodgrass says that he sought a poem that would be both personal and universal, and styles and forms that would adequately express its depth of feeling. The relationship between father and daughter and the considerable grief in the poem, he knew, could lead to sentimentality. He met the challenge, in part, by establishing a formal structure and developing rhymes, accentual syllabics, and varied verse forms that would balance the emotional content. Thus, the poem gives a sense of deep but controlled feeling.

He also made the poem a metaphor. For example, from the outset, section 1, the poet begins to establish the process of seeing one thing as another. The child is born in winter during a war, and her mind is like new snow; here, she is contrasted with the "fouled" snow in which the soldiers freeze. The father's mind is cramped in "that cold war" of marital stand-off, thus connecting him with inert soldiers. Innocence versus experience is suggested. The personal parallels the global. Other images expand this motif: The father is analogous to a tenant farmer viewing his unplowed field or a poet his uncreated drafts. In a world in which survival of the fittest is the norm, the speaker relishes a brief moment of tranquillity before the new variation begins. Throughout the ten sections, the father/child relationship is persistently connected to broad human and natural processes. A matrix of images is established that expands the limits of possible interpretation.

One of Snodgrass's favorite devices is the leitmotif—an image that reappears and becomes more complicated in its associations and meanings. The soldier image, for example, which is identified in section 1 with adults at war and reaffirmed in section 3 through the figure of soldiers grinding their teeth in trenches, reappears in section 8.

This time it is associated with the daughter who, for not eating her evening meal, is sent to her room where, as prisoner, she grates her teeth. The father says that "Assuredly your father's crimes/ Are visited on you." The human and natural processes continue, and she inevitably enters a cold war.

When grinding teeth is linked to cavities, the meaning is modified. The father's reaction to his daughter's pain is as it was for the soldiers—rotting teeth are an expression of sympathy. In section 8, however, when her departure from him as well as her growing independence provide him both pleasure and pain, he says, "Indeed our sweet/ foods leave us cavities." In the civilian world, and especially in that of father/daughter relationships, cause and effect are more ambiguous than on the frozen turf of war.

Other motifs that Snodgrass develops in this way are the bird, fox, bed, and snow which define event and emotion and provide the sense that meaning evolves from image rather than generalization.

Snodgrass' voice—his tone and attitude toward his subject—is aptly described by critic William Heyen as "urgent but controlled, muted but passionate, unassuming but instructive." To this should be added "reflective but wry." Snodgrass is a witty poet whose language resonates with tropes that deepen one's sense of his sincerity rather than deflect it. His exaggerations—"We huff like windy giants," or "Bad penny, pendulum,/ you keep my constant time," or sitting "like some squat Nero at a feast"—not only are playful but also define mood and relationships at particular moments. Since such figures appear throughout the ten sections and interact with harsher images, the overall tone is not only ironical—balancing between humor and horror—but also consistent with the narrator's search for the basis on which father and daughter can honestly relate to each other.

Themes and Meanings

"Heart's Needle" is about possibilities and limits. On the narrative level, Snodgrass asks if it is possible for a father and daughter to be physically separated, with the attendant distortions of the psyche for both, and still remain a father and daughter. At various points it appears impossible, particularly when the child has asthma attacks, quarrels with her new stepsister, or goes off to another state. Similarly when the father remarries, has a new child, or sinks into paralyzing bitterness, the odds for maintaining a family relationship diminish.

Snodgrass finds that the continuing union, on this level, remains either mysterious, unexplainable, or the result of willful action alone. In section 10, father and daughter go on a picnic and feed the animals, where he reaffirms that "you are still my daughter." The narrative throughout, however, has been sustained by a pattern of interlocking images which from the beginning raises this question: Is it possible in this world for the world to stay together? In Snodgrass' realm, father and daughter are microcosms, parts of a broader network of actions and meanings.

The answer to both questions is finally yes; however, the affirmation is painfully won and quietly expressed. One misses the point of the struggle if one does not understand the connections between different forces at work in the universe. Everything "wails on its oval track." Seasons, war, the food chain, festival holidays, birth and death—all, within the experience of the poet and his daughter, come "back once more/ like merry-go-round horses." That means that shattering storms, frozen soldiers, trapped foxes, cramped minds, and inert emotions—as well as all the viciousness manifested in the fixed, stuffed animals in the museum—are inescapable. "The malignancy man loathes/ is held suspended and persists," the poet says.

The change of seasons brings spring, however; Canada geese return, Easter arrives, peace replaces war, and a child, new seeds, and piglets "come fresh." This, too, remains ineluctable. Monotonous and mechanical the cyclic process may be, but it is experienced reality.

In an early essay, Snodgrass says about ideas in poetry that the discovery of them comes in a variety of ways. The most common and significant ones are inherent in the patterns and language of the poem. To discover that idea, says Snodgrass, "is one of the most exciting events in our world; it has a value quite distinct from any value inhering to the idea *as* idea." He means that paradigms and systems of ideas (political, economic, or theological) are not important, because they are imposed on reality; they frame attitudes and conduct, requiring that a person subordinate individual experience to them. Those ideas that are real and useful actually happen to a person.

The relevance of this observation to "Heart's Needle" is that the experience of father and daughter teaches the father an idea which he applies. He did not come to the relationship with established ideas of The American Family or prescribed codes of conduct. Their particular situation forces them to come to terms with each other. When he tells her that "We try to choose our life" (quite different from saying we are free only when we choose our death), he affirms a range of possibilities that he has discovered: One can choose separation and bitterness, because that is natural and one is free to do so; however, one can also choose union, because that choice is real and as deeply embedded. Thus, the final line, "And you are still my daughter," understood in this context, is both the father's expression of his choice and the undeluded reality that his experience confirms.

Philip Raisor

THE HEAVY BEAR WHO GOES WITH ME

Author: Delmore Schwartz (1913-1966)
Type of poem: Lyric
First published: 1938, in *In Dreams Begin Responsibilities*

The Poem

Delmore Schwartz has been described by the editors of *The Norton Anthology of Modern Poetry* (1973) as a poet concerned about "divisions within his own consciousness," and "The Heavy Bear Who Goes with Me" dramatizes that division. In the poem, Schwartz personifies his own body and gives it a life apart from his consciousness. The speaker of the poem is actually the disembodied mental consciousness of the poet, who offers observations on the physical part of his humanity as if it were a separate being. To dramatize the differences between mind and body, Schwartz describes the body as if it were a bear.

The three irregular stanzas of the poem offer an analysis of the "heavy bear" that seems to accompany the speaker wherever he goes. This "Clumsy and lumbering" creature (line 3) that loves "candy, anger, and sleep" (line 6) carries on an active existence at the speaker's side. The speaker describes the bear as a "factotum," one that acts on behalf of another—in this case, the bear is acting for the speaker, as if the speaker were giving directions but not directly taking part in the experiences which the bear undergoes.

This constant companion that eats and sleeps with the speaker does not seem to be able to communicate coherently; instead, the bear howls to express its feelings. This animalistic cry signals its hunger—for sugar and other sweets—and also its fear. Breaking the spell he has created by suggesting that the bear is simply an unconscious animal who has attached himself to the speaker, Schwartz notes how such fear is engendered by terrifying dreams in which the bear is confronted with notions of death and the nothingness that waits after death. The awareness that "his quivering meat" will one day "wince to nothing at all" (lines 18-19) causes the bear to "tremble"—a word Schwartz uses twice in the same stanza, perhaps to suggest the existential nature of the bear's (and man's) existence.

At the beginning of the final stanza, the narrator stresses that this "inescapable animal" (line 20) which "Moves where I move" (line 22) appears to be a caricature of the self. The flesh-ridden creature is almost an embarrassment to the rather sophisticated narrator, who sees his companion getting in the way when the narrator wishes to be most human. For example, when the narrator's beloved is near, the bear touches her "grossly" (line 30) just at the moment when the narrator wishes to convey some expression of tenderness; the narrator cannot "bare [his] heart" and make his feelings clear to his loved one (line 31). No matter what he does, the narrator is unable to rid himself of his earthy companion, that "drag[s] me with him in his mouthing care" (line 33)—that is, off to satisfy his visceral needs—amid "the hundred million of his kind" (line 34) that have the same bodily desires and demands. The recognition that the bear is but one of so many exactly like him is a subtle reminder that humans, too, no matter how unique they believe they are, share many of their human characteristics with millions of others.

Forms and Devices

"The Heavy Bear Who Goes with Me" is in some ways reminiscent of the short tales that compose the popular medieval *Bestiary*; as the authors of *A Literary History of England, Vol. I: The Middle Ages* (1967) note, in that work descriptions of various animals are "followed . . . by a Christian application or moral." Schwartz uses a similar technique in associating the physical qualities of the bear with those of the human body in order to make a point about the inseparability of the two parts of human nature: the physical self and the spiritual or mental self.

Schwartz follows traditional rules of poetic composition only loosely in this lyric. The irregular stanzas are more like verse paragraphs, each providing separate descriptions of the bear's physical characteristics and his relation to the speaker. Some use is made of rhyme, but no strict patterns emerge; for example, the rhyme scheme of the first stanza is *abcbdeffa*. More common is Schwartz's reliance on some form of stop at the end of each line. All but six of the poem's thirty-five lines are punctuated at the end, and the syntax of the poem demands that the reader pause at the end of three of the unpunctuated lines. This technique mirrors the sense of clumsiness, the halting, lumbering attitude of the bear; readers will find themselves stumbling from line to line, dragged along in the same way the speaker says the bear is "dragging" him along as a constant companion through life.

Schwartz makes extensive use of active verbs to describe the bear's behavior. The animal "climbs," "kicks," "howls," "trembles," "stumbles," and "flounders." He couples these words with nouns and adjectives that further emphasize the bear's physical, brutish nature: The bear is "clumsy," "lumbering," a "central ton" that, wearing a fine suit, ends up "bulging his pants." He is a "caricature," a "stupid clown" that touches someone "grossly." Readers may be reminded of the famous line in Alfred, Lord Tennyson's "Ulysses" in which the hero, back from his twenty years' wandering about the Mediterranean, expresses his disgust with his subjects in Ithaca by calling them "a savage race/ That hoard, and sleep, and feed, and know not me" — the ten monosyllables striking the note of disdain for the same kind of animalistic qualities and lack of consciousness and intellectual sophistication that characterize Schwartz's bear.

The stress on the physical qualities of the bear and the subtle use of end-stopped lines combine to convince readers of the essentially materialistic nature of the body. Schwartz wants readers to understand that the body is different from the spiritual side of man but that there is no way for the spirit or consciousness to escape from its constant companion.

Themes and Meanings

Schwartz provides a clear indication of the theme of "The Heavy Bear Who Goes with Me" in the phrase he affixes to the poem as a kind of subtitle: "the withness of the body." Usually attributed to the philosopher Alfred North Whitehead, this short descriptive epigraph suggests the complex nature of the human condition. Man is a dual creature; he is possessed of a consciousness that gives him a sense of time and of "otherness," but at the same time he is an animal like other animals. Human consciousness exists within a body that demands the same kind of life-sustaining materials and is subject to the same kinds of appetites — for food, for physical comforts — as other, lower creatures. Further, no matter how unique any man thinks he is, he cannot deny that he has bodily needs remarkably similar to the "hundred millions of his kind" (line 34); this sobering thought is meant to counterbalance the vanity men feel in promoting their own individuality.

The poet is dramatizing the long-debated issue of man's dual nature. The only creature on earth possessing a sophisticated consciousness that gives him a moral sense and an understanding of the consequences of his actions, man is nevertheless compelled to exist in a material body that is really as much a part of him as is his higher intelligence. No matter how hard he tries, man is never able to separate his spiritual nature from his physical side.

Schwartz's extended descriptions of the bear are intended to suggest the physical conditions under which the human body exists. All animals — including the human animal — crave the physical comforts that this bear seeks. Further, many of the actions that humans take are indeed reminiscent of the clumsy behavior of this dumb bear; humans, Schwartz is saying, are often embarrassed by their bodies. At those moments when consciousness wants people to be most human — when a situation calls for erudition or sensitivity, for a clear statement to others that would help one express exactly what one thinks or feels — the material side of human nature seems to get in the way, to be like the lumbering bear, a creature that fumbles and gropes in a most unhuman way to make the expressions of consciousness apparent to the outside world.

Laurence W. Mazzeno

HEBREW MELODIES

Author: Heinrich Heine (1797-1856)
Type of poem: Poetic sequence
First published: 1851, as "Hebräische Melodien," in *Romanzero*; collected in *The Complete Poems of Heinrich Heine*, 1982

The Poems

"Hebrew Melodies," Heinrich Heine's series of three poems, written in 1851, constitutes the third and final section of *Romanzero*, a collection published that year and also containing groups of "Historien" (Tales) and "Lamentationen." The title *Romanzero* suggests old-fashioned romantic ballads, but the volume is actually a compendium of sophisticated mid-nineteenth century poetry. The title of the sequence was suggested to Heine by the "Hebrew Melodies" of George Gordon, Lord Byron (1815), though the two sets of poems have little or nothing in common. Heine's poems reflect both continuity and change as far as his attitude toward Judaism and his Jewishness was concerned.

The first poem, "Prinzessin Sabbath" ("Princess Sabbath"), consists of thirty-eight unrhymed stanzas that present a warmly appreciative picture of the Sabbath observance in a synagogue. On the eve of the Jewish day of rest, Israel—that is, a Jew—is freed temporarily from the witch's curse that has transformed him into a dog, and he enters the synagogue as a prince ready to meet his princess, the personification of the Sabbath, who is as humble and quiet as she is beautiful. The poet describes the richly symbolic festive bustle in the house of worship as the cantor intones the traditional chant *L'khah dodi likrat kallah* ("Come, beloved [or my friend] the bride awaits you"), which Heine erroneously credits to Don Jehuda ben Halevy. (The real author is Salomo ben Moshe Alkabez). Instead of a smoke, which is prohibited on the Sabbath, the princess promises her beloved the culinary delight of *schalet* (or cholent, a slowly simmered bean stew). Such treats evoke visions of biblical scenes, but the waning of the Sabbath threatens to force the observant Jew to resume his dog's life. Heine ends his poem with a description of the traditional havdalah ceremony: Smelling a spice box keeps the worshipers (whom the need to bid the Sabbath farewell has saddened and weakened) from fainting, and a few drops from a goblet of wine serve to extinguish the candle and, with it, the Sabbath.

In a letter dated August 21, 1851, Heine called "Jehuda ben Halevy" his most beautiful poem. It is the longest in this sequence—four sections containing twenty-four stanzas and almost nine hundred lines—yet it is a fragment. The poem has an elegiac beginning and undertone as the poet, in his mourning for the devastated Jerusalem, invokes the exemplary figure of Jehuda ben Halevy (more properly, Judah Halevi, a scholar, physician, and poet who was born in Toledo around 1075 and is believed to have died in Cairo around 1141). In flowery fashion, Heine describes the making of a poet and his study of the Torah and the Talmud—the latter divided into the polemical, legalistic Halaka, which is likened to a fencing school for dialectical athletes, and the Agada, the didactic part, which Heine compares to a phantasmagoric garden. Yet Halevy is not viewed as a parochial poet; Heine integrates him into the mainstream of Christian medieval Europe by calling him fully equal to the great Provençal poets—though his muse was not some lady love but Jerusalem, whose destruction he deplores. Following an old legend, Heine has the poet killed by a Saracen horseman while in the holy land as a penitent, but his conjecture that Halevy's killer may have been an angel in disguise sent by God to take the poet to his eternal home is original with him.

In a lengthy digression, Heine concerns himself with jewels found by Alexander the Great after his victory over the Persian king Darius in 331 B.C., specifically the wondrous wanderings of a pearl necklace. The poet says that if he owned Alexander's golden casket, he would use it to store the teardrop pearls of lamentations. Another digression involves Heine's French wife, whose limited education did not include the poetic golden age of Spanish Jewry. Heine uses this excursus to pay tribute to the other great poets of that age, Salomon ben Judah ibn Gabirol of Malaga and Moses ibn Ezra of Granada. After musing about the origin of "schlemiel," the word and the concept, Heine ends with the story of Gabirol's death in Cordova at the hands of an envious Moorish neighbor.

"Disputation" consists of 110 rhymed stanzas, the rhyme scheme being *abcb*. The witty narrator gives a grimly hilarious account of a fourteenth century public debate between the Franciscan friar José and Rabbi Juda of Navarre at the Toledo court of King Pedro I of Castile and his queen, the fragile Frenchwoman Blanche of Bourbon (Donna Blanca). The question to be settled is which is the true God, the threefold Christian God of love or the Hebrews' stern one God, Jehovah. Since the loser will have to adopt the religion of the winner, each debater has eleven assistants standing by with baptismal basins or circumcision knives. After exorcising some Jewish devils, the friar gives an absurd account of Christian beliefs, crudely likening Jews to various beasts. His vulgar rhetoric and violent threats conflict with his promises of gentleness and love. Making little more sense, the more rationalistic rabbi emphasizes that Jehovah is a strong, living presence and holds out the prospect of the faithful feasting on the succulent flesh of the legendary Leviathan, God's favorite fish. The arguments and counterarguments of the two zealots having become increasingly heated and vituperative in this twelve-hour marathon, the king asks the queen for her judgment, and her somewhat unsettling decision is that both of them "stink."

Forms and Devices

Writing about "Hebrew Melodies," Louis Untermeyer, one of numerous poets and scholars who have undertaken to render Heine's poetry into English, states that Heine's background, diction, and emotions are characteristically Jewish in his celebration of the senses and that the poet's Jewish flavor is not bittersweet, as has often been observed, but sweet and sour, the heritage of generations of cultural pungency. Such a statement may not evoke universal agreement, but it is suggestive, for these particular poems reflect Heine's complex sense of Jewishness and contain a variety of devices that serve to reveal as well as mask his ambivalence about his Jewish background. The poet does so through exceptionally colorful and luxuriant language and with abundant biblical and broadly cultural allusions. When Heine was working on the "Hebrew Melodies," he had been living in exile for two decades and wasting away in what he called his *Matratzengruft* ("mattress grave," or "crypt") for more than three years, slowly dying of a venereal disease. This circumstance gave his late writings heightened immediacy and urgency. "Jehuda ben Halevy," and to some extent "Princess Sabbath," the only melodious poems of the sequence, were inspired by a book published in 1845, *Die religiöse Poesie der Juden in Spanien*, a magisterial study of the religious poetry of medieval Spanish Jewry by Michael Sachs, a Berlin rabbi and pupil of Leopold Zunz, a scholar to whom Heine had been close prior to his conversion in 1825.

In the "Hebrew Melodies," the mercurial, often impish poet, a practiced dispeller of moods and destroyer of illusions, delights in juxtaposing different worlds in ingenious and amusing, sometimes confusing fashion. Heine's ingenious wordplay, linguistic drolleries, stylistic shifts, discursiveness, abrasive diction, and mixture of the exalted and ironically deflated are deliberate and sometimes brilliant poetic devices. His penchant for digressions and discord is in evidence throughout as Heine superimposes an irreverent nineteenth century perspective on older traditions. Facts and legends, as well as symbols and reality, intermingle wondrously as pathos and trivia alternate, heartfelt sentiments give way to critical comment, and discussions of momentous events and important figures deteriorate into private gossip and satiric sniping. For example, in "Jehuda ben Halevy," Heine, who tended to ridicule his Jewish contemporaries, satirizes Julius Eduard Itzig, a converted Jew (and noted Berlin jurist) who changed his name to Hitzig, and the poet wonders whether the additional letter indicates a pretension to holiness.

Heine's exploration of the luckless schlemiel, an exercise in mock scholarship, leads him to ask whether the poet, particularly the Jewish poet, is not the quintessential schlemiel, the innocent, the scapegoat. In "Princess Sabbath," the poet's praise of cholent, that kosher ambrosia, culminates in a parody of Friedrich Schiller's "Ode to Joy" (known from Ludwig van Beethoven's Ninth Symphony). The reference to *Tausves-Jontof* (more correctly, *Tosafot Yomtov*), a sixteenth century critical commentary, in the context of a fourteenth century disputation, may have been a deliberate anachronism, but other slips, such as his reference to a mezuzah (which is not found at the entrance of a synagogue), are indicative of Heine's limited knowledge of Hebrew and Jewish lore. "Disputation," a grotesque variant of a medieval tournament or athletic contest, has a deliberately discordant, sardonic, and sinister tone, because an unsparing exposure of the clerical mind, as bombastic as it is intolerant, clearly calls for black humor. It is hardly accidental that the last word of that poem, and the entire collection, is *stinken*.

Themes and Meanings

In an afterword to *Romanzero*, dated September 30, 1851, Heine says that, like a prodigal son, he has returned to the idea of a personal God and, having dwindled down to a spiritual (as well as physical) skeleton, he is ready to make his peace with God and the world. It is tempting to believe that after yielding to the blandishments of atheism, Hellenism, and polytheism, Heine is returning to his Jewish roots. There is evidence that the ailing Heine did return to monotheism and identify with the suffering Jewish people, but this identification was paralleled by continued inward detachment from significant aspects of the Jewish religion. In "Princess Sabbath" and "Jehuda ben Halevy," Heine gives a sympathetic account of Jewish religious practices and cultural contributions, and he sensitively delineates the tragically dualistic existence of the Jewish people. The second poem contains a paradigmatic picture of an idealized poet with whom Heine seems to feel a spiritual affinity; Jehuda ben Halevy's writings appear to be divinely inspired, and he acts as a pillar of fire in the desert of the Diaspora. "Disputation," however, contains a clear-cut rejection of Jewish (or any other) dogmatism, proselytic fanaticism, and hidebound self-righteousness. As S. S. Prawer has pointed out, "Princess Sabbath" presents a skillful fusion of caricature, allegory, realism, and symbolism, of light and darkness, the poetic and the prosaic—a poignant insight into what centuries of oppression, persecution, and martyrdom have done to the Jewish psyche. "Hebrew Melodies," then, begins with a touching tribute to the spiritual and aesthetic qualities and rewards of Judaism and ends with a condemnation of what may be called an extreme representative of the Jewish faith. The poet was a free spirit and an ambivalent person to the end, and Heine would not have been Heine if he had been otherwise.

Harry Zohn

THE HEIGHTS OF MACCHU PICCHU

Author: Pablo Neruda (Neftalí Ricardo Reyes Basoalto, 1904-1973)
Type of poem: Narrative
First published: 1946, as *Alturas de Macchu Picchu*; in *Canto general*, 1950;
  collected in *Pablo Neruda: Five Decades, a Selection (Poems, 1925-1970)*,
  1974

The Poem

The Heights of Macchu Picchu is a long narrative poem forming book 2 of Pablo Neruda's monumental choral epic, *Canto general* (general song), a text comprising 250 poems and organized into twelve major divisions, or cantos. The theme of *Canto general* is humankind's struggle for justice in the New World. "The Heights of Macchu Picchu" is itself divided into twelve sections; it is written in free verse.

The poet, adopting the persona of the native South American man, walks among the ruins of the great Inca city Machu Picchu, built high in the mountains near Cuzco, in Peru, as a last, and vain, retreat from the invading Spanish conquerors. It is a poem of symbolic death and resurrection in which the speaker begins as a lonely voyager and ends with a full commitment to the American indigenous people, their Indian roots, their past, and their future.

The first poem of the sequence opens with the image of an empty net, sifting experience but gathering nothing. This opening reveals that the speaker is drained by the surface of existence; he searches inward and downward for a hidden "vein of gold." He then sinks lower, through the waves of a symbolic sea, in a blind search to rediscover "the jasmine of our exhausted human spring," an erotic symbol associated with a lost paradise.

The second poem contrasts the enduring world of nature with the transitory goals of human beings, who drill natural objects down until they find that their own souls are left dead in the process. The speaker recalls that in his urban existence he often stopped and searched for the eternal truths he once found in nature or in love. In city life, humans are reduced to robotlike machines with no trace of the "quality of life" in which Neruda still believes. The question of where this quality of life can be found remains unanswered for three further poems; the search for truth, in the poet's opinion, is a gradual and humbling process.

This search for truth is the subject of the third poem, which confronts modern humankind's existence directly. This existence is likened to husking corn off the cob; urban dwellers die "each day a little death" in their "nine to five, to six" routine life. The speaker compares a day in the life of the urban people to a black cup whose contents they drain while holding it in their trembling hands. In this poem, Neruda prepares the way for the contrasting image of Machu Picchu, which is later described in its "permanence of stone."

The fourth poem shows the speaker enticed by not only "irresistible death" but also the life and love of his fellowman. This love remains unrealizable, however, as long as all he sees in his fellowman is his daily death. His own experience in the urban context progressively alienates him from others, dragging him street by street to the last degrading hovel, where he ultimately finds himself face-to-face with his own death.

The short fifth poem defines this kind of death even more closely in a series of seemingly surrealistic images, leaving a final vision of modern life with nothing in its wounds except wind that chills one's "cold interstices of soul." In this poem, the speaker is at his lowest spiritual point in the entire sequence.

Then, quite abruptly, the mood of the poem begins to rise in the sixth section as the speaker climbs upward in space toward the heights of Machu Picchu and backward in time toward the moment when that ancient city was created. At that moment in time, all lines converge, past and present. Here, "two lineages that had run parallel" meet and fuse, that is, the line of inconsequential human beings and their petty deaths and the line of permanence in the recurring cycles of nature.

Machu Picchu is the place where "maize grew high" and where men gathered fleece to weave both funereal and festive garments. What endures in this place is the collective permanence those men created. All that was transitory has disappeared, leaving only "the lonely precinct of stone."

Section 7 picks up this contrast between what endures and what has vanished. The speaker sees "the true, the most consuming death" as having slain those ancient men—their death being nobler because it was a collective experience. What they left behind was their citadel "raised like a chalice in all those hands," their blood to make "a life of stone." The speaker believes that he can "identify" with the absolute "Death" he finds on the heights, but his search for this death also has been a search for a more positive kind of identity and for identification through nature with his fellowmen. The speaker's journey teaches him—more by means of feeling than by means of thought—to see new facets of the truth, both about himself and about the nature of existence. The journey does not end, however, with the discovery of the city.

The speaker's hopeful mood lasts through the next two poems: the eighth poem, with its vivid evocation of nature, pre-Columbian man, and his gods all fused together in an all-embracing love that the poet summons up from the past to transform the present and to anticipate the future; and the ninth, a solemn chant, building up to a final pair of lines that bring the reader starkly back to both the ancient men who built the citadel and their destination—time.

The poem's last major turning point comes with the question opening its tenth section: "Stone within stone, and man, where was he?" The speaker begins to speculate about whether the people who built ancient America may not have been similar to modern urban people and whether the citadel might not have been erected on a base of human suffering. The speaker wonders in what conditions these people, possibly slaves, lived.

In the eleventh section, the speaker attempts to go beyond the weave of matter until he can hold "the old unremembered human heart" in his hand, seeing behind the "transcendental span" of Machu Picchu to the invisible "hypotenuse of hairshirt and salt blood" implied by the geometry of those ruins. The speaker concludes that humankind is what matters because "man is wider than all the sea"; the poet wishes to acknowledge all the people who died building this city so that they may be reborn with him and through them as his "brothers."

What really matters to the speaker at the end of the poem is that which his own experience has in common with the experience of other human beings. He also needs to reveal people to themselves in such a way that they can feel the identity behind their separate lives and share his insight.

Forms and Devices

The major symbol of the poem is that of Machu Picchu itself. In Neruda's poem, Machu Picchu becomes the center of a tangled web of associations with disparate and intertwining strands. It is by no means a clear-cut symbol, for its meaning shifts as the poem's strong current of emotions alternates between past and present, but the speaker's journey gradually takes on the nature of a highly personal "venture into the interior" in which he explores both his own inner world and the past of the Latin American people. There is no explicit mention of the city until the sixth of the twelve poems that form the sequence, the earlier sections covering not the poet's physical journey but a kind of pilgrimage through human life in search of meaningful truth. When the poet does reach Machu Picchu, its heights turn out to be the place from which all else makes sense, including his own continent.

Machu Picchu as a natural and human symbol is the pivotal force around which both the natural and religious imagery of the poem is focused. During the speaker's descent into the heart of meaning, the presence of matter, both inorganic and organic, is significant as a symbol of inescapable reality. The speaker touches stone, earth, roots, trees, rain, clouds, and space in the course of his journey. Each line of the poem, each metaphor, brings this matter closer to human experience, specifically to human sexuality, until the speaker says, "I sank my tempestuous sweet hand/ into the most genital recesses of the earth."

Christian symbolism and imagery also inform the poem. Yet Neruda does not embrace theology in his epic and philosophical vision. Although the speaker has questions about the nature of humankind during his search for truth, there is no God or gods beside him or above him. He will reach the high stone pinnacles of the sacred city Machu Picchu, a city built by humans to the greater glory of their gods, but the gods have departed. No mention is made of the divine forces that moved the Incas to haul huge stones to build the sacred city as a last refuge from the advance of the Spaniards and the religion they wanted to impose. Only the stones remain, an echo of the ancient fervor of the old faith.

Neruda often uses Christian imagery in the poem to heighten a vital point, bringing in varied associations without implying the literal truth of the concepts. In line with the Christian imagery, the language of the ninth poem of the sequence is that of a solemn chant, or litany, to Machu Picchu, describing the site with eighty-four epithets. Not a single verb appears in this fragment, which is composed in the style of a liturgical litany, with an abundance of repetitive phrases. Also, when in the final poem, the speaker asks the builders of the ancient city to show him the places of their agony, he uses language that links their sufferings to the stations of the cross.

Themes and Meanings

The major themes of Neruda's poem are death and regeneration. These themes are primarily realized through the speaker's cyclic journey (similar to those in the Bible or in Dante's *The Divine Comedy*, c. 1320). The speaker explores the cosmos, penetrates the earth to its secret chambers, ascends toward light from the roots through the stems of plants, and identifies with the stones of the huge sacred city. The speaker serves as primitive human, as prophet, and, ultimately, as semidivinity, searing through space and through history, bringing the reader with him on an incredible voyage, an adventure to the end of the earth. A strange poetic time machine allows the speaker to swim upstream in the flow of time, exploring nature, humankind, history, and visions of the future.

The speaker's magic powers have taken him first down into the earth, through seas of darkness. Then, he ascends up the ladder. Climbing, he goes through the thickets toward the tall city rocked in a "wind of thorns," the city that is like a spade buried in primordial sand, the city made out of stone. The speaker beckons to the reader to "climb up" with him.

On this journey, the overwhelming presences are those of nature in all of its power and those of ghostly ancient men who came to terms with nature many centuries ago. Both presences fuse in a moment of love and recognition, and the past becomes the present.

What the speaker finds in his vertical pilgrimage is not God or the gods, however, but the traces of a destroyed civilization: the ashes of a ruined kingdom and the signs of its priests, its women, its children, and its slaves. Everywhere, the footprints of humankind are present: everywhere, matter has been penetrated. Beneath each stone, the speaker senses a presence from the past, and the initial sense of loneliness gives way to joy. The gods may have vanished, but the presence of humankind endures. Identity and brotherhood infuse the key words of the poem's climactic end: "I am here to speak for your dead lips." Only thus are the ancient ghosts placated. In the speaker's identification with his ancestors, he becomes one of them. The speaker has come into contact with death and resurrection. It is the awakening of an identification and a commitment of solidarity with the Americas past, present, and future.

Thus, *The Heights of Macchu Picchu* is a poem of symbolic death and resurrection in which the speaker himself participates as an actor, beginning as a lonely voyager and ending with the manifestation of his full commitment to the collectivity of the American indigenous people: their cultural roots, their past, and their future.

Genevieve Slomski

HELIAN

Author: Georg Trakl (1887-1914)
Type of poem: Lyric
First published: 1913, as "Helian"; in *Die Dichtungen*, 1919; collected in *Modern German Poetry 1910-1960*, 1962

The Poem

Georg Trakl wrote "Helian" in December of 1912 and January of 1913, in the darkest time of the year. Shortly afterward, he referred to it in a letter as the most precious and most painful thing he had written. As is all of his work, it is highly autobiographical.

"Helian," at ninety-three lines, is Trakl's longest poem. The stanzas are short and of irregular length, ranging from two to seven lines, and are grouped into five main sections. Some of the material from the "Helian" manuscripts subsequently found its way into shorter poems, so critics now speak of the " 'Helian' complex," which consists of "Helian," "Evening Song," "Rosary Songs," and "Decline."

There has been considerable speculation about the origin and meaning of the title, with critics comparing it to names and titles having variant spellings. Only Gunther Kleefeld has been able to relate the name Helian as it stands to a discernible pattern in Trakl's work; namely, the linguistic juxtapositioning of brother and sister pairs. Elis is the brother of Elisabeth, Georg of Georgine, Narziss of Narzisse, and Helian of Helianthus. Helianthus is the botanical name for a sunflower, which Trakl identifies in one poem as Helian's sister. He himself often appears in his poems as the sun god or the sun boy. He expressed the need for the sort of living conditions in which sunflowers thrive: plenty of light, plenty of warmth, and a quiet beach. In reading "Helian," one should keep in mind that it was written at the time of the year when the sun boy would feel most alienated.

The opening lines of the poem establish the positive effects that the sun, its color, yellow, and the summer have on Helian. He is at peace with himself, his friends, and the world. Likewise, the almost parallel account of autumn that follows contains mainly realistic descriptions of the beauty of the season. The sun is still present, shining into storerooms, and one is almost inclined to disregard the few lines that seem ominously out of place.

The second section of the poem, lines 22 through 38, is framed by depictions of a ravaged garden and black November destruction. Nature is no longer beautiful, but threateningly ugly. Only when walking past friendly rooms does Helian experience harmony that is reminiscent of his mood in summer. Once fully inside, however, in the house of his fathers, Helian is horrified by the decline of his family. His sisters are degraded. His soft eyes are beaten with nettles, and he falls ill. Winter follows.

Section 4, lines 60 through 80, is tripartite. Visions of idyllic existences are contrasted with the agonies of the tortured, the leprous, and the decomposed. The poem ends with Helian's madness in black rooms. He ponders the darker end, and God silently sinks his blue eyelids over him.

Forms and Devices

"Helian" is an extraordinarily complex poem. The overall process it describes is one of tragic personal decline. One may assume that the poetic persona is Trakl. In the progression of the poem, there is a complete inversion in outlook. The first section contains only two negative lines, the last only two positive ones. Serenity and clarity give way to horror and blackness. The most beautiful landscapes yield to nightmarish visions. The best of the outer world is replaced by the worst of the inner world. Trakl has carried to extremes the literary convention of using the changing seasons to represent the human life cycle. In "Helian," the warmth and light of summer turns into the cold and dark of winter, forcing the main character from the healthy outdoor environment back into his parents' house, from extroversion to introversion, from sanity to madness.

Walls play a major role in "Helian." The transformation they undergo in the first half of the poem parallels Helian's mental deterioration. Walls are rigid constructions that in Trakl's work represent self-control and the successful repression of certain urges. The fact that Helian is not surrounded by walls but is walking along them indicates that he is continuing to function with a sense of direction.

In the opening lines, the walls are yellow, a reflection of Helian's sunny mood in the summer season. In autumn, he walks along red walls, perhaps a warning signal, since red is the color of fire and of blood. It is not entirely clear that things have gone wrong, however, until in November he walks along walls full of leprosy. Trakl views ugliness as a product of hatred. He is beginning to resent the self-imposed restrictions and describes the veneer of civilization as loathsome. Significantly, there follows a sympathetic reference to the poet Hölderlin, the "holy brother," who became mad. Finally, in the third and central section of the poem, the walls come down. Black walls collapse on the spot. Helian has let down all restraints; he enters the empty house of his fathers, and malign elemental forces are unleashed.

Just as warm, sunny days may occur in late autumn, "Helian" derives much of its poignancy from the fluctuations between sanity and madness within the overall process of decline. Repeatedly, the poet presents the reader with positive images that give rise to the hope that Helian will be able to pull himself back up out of the depths. Each time, however, he sinks back lower than he was before. These are the steps of madness to which he refers in the fifth section. The suspense one feels in view of these sustained vacillations is heightened by Trakl's repeated references to evening and to night, which keep the poem hovering symbolically on the edge of light.

Themes and Meanings

The meaning of Trakl's poetry eluded critics for more than seventy years. His surprising and apparently unconnected images were dismissed by frustrated readers as the word salad of a schizophrenic whose problems were exacerbated by his dependency on cocaine. Yet the poems continued to be read for the compelling beauty of their language, which in the original German is unequalled.

A breakthrough in understanding Trakl came in 1985, with the publication of Gunther Kleefeld's monumental psychoanalytical study *Das Gedicht als Sühne* (the poem as penance). Based on the known facts of Trakl's biography and remarks in his letters, it presents Freudian interpretations of his poetic images as products of conflicting primal forces in Trakl's mind. The recurrent themes that emerge are Trakl's hatred of his mother for withdrawing from her children, his resultant incestuous relationship with his sister, and his criticism of his father for not providing enough guidance and control. Dark thoughts and demoniac actions stem from the id (the unconscious, instinctual area of the psyche), which may be restrained or punished by the superego (the moral, social area of the psyche and seat of the conscience); hence, the extreme contrasts in the imagery.

Applying this schema to "Helian," one encounters the id first of all in line 5, personified as the son of Pan asleep in gray marble. It is impossible for this side of Trakl's personality to be banished completely. The best the superego can do is to encase the demon in stone and hope that he continues to sleep. In this opening description of summer, Helian gets through the evening and even the night safely. In the evening, he drinks brown wine in the company of friends.

Once the season turns to autumn, however, increasing the distance between Helian and the sun, on which he is so heavily reliant, the dark thoughts surface. Line 5 of this part at first seems quite out of place and nonsensical in itself: "In the evening, the white water sinks into burial urns." This, however, is clearly the first resentful reference in "Helian" to Trakl's mother. Reviewing the context of the preceding lines, one sees that Helian actually has three reasons to feel abandoned. Not only is the sun slowly drawing away from him, but Helian has also just witnessed the flight of the birds, who are going south for the winter. Furthermore, although it is evening again, the drinking parties on the terrace seem to have stopped for the year, leaving a void. There is nothing to drink, just as there was nothing to drink when he was denied his mother's milk, when the white water, intended as the food of life, was misdirected to the ashes of the dead, when things went wrong right at the start. Now, everyone is leaving him again, the sun and the birds and his friends. The present emotional state is symbolically associated with a similar emotional state from early childhood. The line makes perfect sense.

As "Helian" progresses, the poem consists increasingly of such images from the subconscious, so that a very close reading is required—one, in fact, that presupposes familiarity with Trakl's oeuvre.

Jean M. Snook

HENCEFORTH, FROM THE MIND

Author: Louise Bogan (1897-1970)
Type of poem: Lyric
First published: 1931; collected in *The Sleeping Fury*, 1937

The Poem

The four brief six-line stanzas of "Henceforth, from the Mind" express a sense of the sublimation of passion and emotion integrated into the life of the mind and imagination. Throughout, an unidentified speaker addresses an unnamed "you": The meditative and contemplative language and tenor of the poem suggest that "you" is really the speaker, addressing his or her interior life.

The first stanza is a single sentence. The first line is the same as the title, and the speaker tells the listener that from this point in time all happiness to be enjoyed will come from the mind. Although the source of such joy may be traceable to material things—which would include the pleasures of the flesh—the future enjoyment of these pleasures will be an imaginative and mental one. The last two lines add an independent clause, making the assertion that it will be the speaker's thought that will endow time and place with significance and honor. The implication is that such time and place may be present in fact, or in memory and imagination; in either case, it is the mind that creates their meaning.

The second stanza makes a parallel statement with regard to language, asserting that language alone will, in the future, produce the kind of happiness that the listener had formerly thought, in youth, would be the concomitant of passionate desire. The speaker elaborates on the youthful illusion of the power of passion in a set of parallel clauses suggesting the violence of emotions that seem to wrench the person physically, to stab one to the heart even to a sense of dying.

The last of the poem's three sentences comprises the twelve lines of the last two stanzas. Here, the speaker varies the "henceforth" that has opened the first two stanzas by introducing the third stanza with "henceforward." The speaker elaborates a description of a seashell, which, held to the ear, seems to reproduce the rhythmic sound of the ocean surging back and forth over the sand. The sound is characterized in an interpolated clause as a subdued, almost suppressed sound that speaks to the listener from profound depths, but that nevertheless marks the changes of time, notes growth and ripening, and brings forth beauty from a state of agitated calm. In the last two lines, the speaker returns from the interpolated clause with two more repetitions of the word "henceforth"; the shell that began the sentence is now seen to be the source of the speaker's mental, emotional, and cognitive life. From this shell, the entire universe will "echo": that is, the listener's world will, henceforth, be one composed entirely of the inner experience of mind and imagination.

Forms and Devices

"Henceforth, from the Mind" has a particularly tight metrical scheme. The basic rhythm is iambic trimeter, with few, but subtle, variations. The first lines of the first and second stanzas, each opening with the word "henceforth," are headless, beginning with a stressed syllable and containing only five, instead of six, syllables. The third line of the last stanza, "Will sound you flowers," and the penultimate line of the poem, "henceforth, henceforth," are iambic dimeter. There is one foot that deviates from the iambic pattern: The antepenultimate line begins with the trochee "Born under," a stressed syllable followed by an unstressed one, reversing the iambic pattern throughout the rest of the poem. The second and fourth lines of the fourth stanza, however, end in feminine rhymes: "wondered" and "sundered." The meter is highly regular and supported by a close rhyme scheme. The first four lines of each stanza rhyme in a quatrain pattern of *abab*, with the last two lines forming a couplet. The only variation is the slight off-rhyme of the last couplet pairing "henceforth" and "earth."

Such a strongly marked rhythmic and rhyme scheme in a poem with very short lines often produces a mechanical, sing-song effect. That rule does not hold true in this poem because of the interplay between long-vowel syllables in unstressed positions. In the second line, "whole joy," and in the third line, "may find," are feet in which the unstressed syllable (whole, may) contains a long vowel: This attenuates the distinction between the stressed and unstressed syllables and makes the rhythm less heavily marked, less "bouncy" than is often the case with a heavily accented trimeter line. The same is true in the second stanza with the foot "you to" in the fourth and fifth lines, and in the third stanza with "wherein" and "you heard." This device— together with the variations in rhythm obtained from lines that employ enjambment, variation in placement of caesura, and slight differences in line length from headless lines and feminine rhymes—creates a graceful, nuanced rhythm with a subtle music.

"Henceforth, from the Mind" is an example of the plain style identified in Renaissance poets such as Ben Jonson and continuing through the tradition of English poetry down to twentieth century exemplars such as Louise Bogan. The style is characterized by controlled emotion—which may nevertheless be extremely intense—by precision of diction and by little or no figurative language or rhetorical ornamentation. Bogan uses only one extended metaphor: the shell of the last two stanzas, which is said to contain the "smothered sound" that acts as a clock, "chiming" the passing of time to the listener and that will "sound" the listener "flowers." What these flowers stand for specifically is never really clear, simply as a single tenor for the metaphorical shell is not explicitly indicated: Whether it is meant to be the listener's ear as the organ of hearing (corresponding to speech implied in the "tongue" of the second stanza), or whether it stands for the whole of the listener's imaginative and intuitive faculties, the poem does not explain.

Themes and Meanings

The theme of renunciation rings strongly in this poem, balanced with equal strength by the sense of peace and dignity that comes with acceptance and knowledge of what is being renounced, and pleasure in the alternative gains that renunciation of physical pleasures may bring. In the first stanza, for example, the speaker may belittle the possibility of finding much joy in "earthly things"; the listener's mind, however, in endowing time and place with the "grace" (of attention, esteem, or memory), which mind and imagination can give, will actually create a much richer experience than the meager joys that any mere "thing" can afford. The contrast being drawn between "thing" and "thought" focuses the speaker's argument. The promise of future serenity emerges through the sentence structure in the description of the speaker's mind as the peaceful ground of an experience that will happen of itself: "Joy" will spontaneously "spring" from the mind, as "time and place will take" the listener's thought in an equally spontaneous experience of "grace."

The second stanza continues the sense of peaceful detachment from struggle, even though the struggle would have brought joy that—in the past, in the listener's imagination—would have had almost physically painful effects. There is the merest hint of the figure of cupid in the figure of joy that could "pierce you to the heart," but the clichéd picture remains entirely subordinated to the more inclusive sense of "joy." Indeed, here the speaker seems to promise that a purer delight may emerge from "shallow speech alone," for such happiness, the speaker says, "will come," and without the wrenching pain of erotic passion.

The last two stanzas are the poem's most complex statement, both rhetorically and grammatically. The powers of the imagination are invoked in the figure of the shell, which can create in the listener's mind a whole universe physically distant from the material world—the "oceans . . . so far from ocean sundered" that seem to roar within the seashell far removed from the actual ocean.

The interpolated clause in the last two lines of stanza 3 and the first four lines of stanza 4 suggests the creation of alternative worlds by the imagination. The sound is "smothered," and "long lost," and the growth and blossoming of the listener's imaginative gifts takes place in a "troubled peace." The metaphor here, and its grammatical placement embedded deep within the speaker's authoritative lecture on the future, suggest something of a poet's life of the imagination. Louise Bogan was troubled at various times in her life with depression and emotional turmoil, and she underwent psychotherapy to confront her emotional and creative demons. The undersea metaphor of the sound that is both "smothered" and deep, that yet brings forth creations of beauty, suggests the concept of the psyche's unconscious, buried, as it were, below the ego's functioning everyday life, but the source of creative and imaginative gifts. The "flowers" in this reading could stand for, among other things, the speaker/listener's own poems, the spontaneous products of imagination.

The poem's last two lines complete the sentence by arriving, finally, at the verb and its subject, and sum up the entire poem. The joy that the speaker will no longer find in external things or in fleshly pleasures comes not from the world and what it gives or shows the listener, but from the echo produced by the listener's own imagination. To renounce the material world, the speaker implies, is to gain the world of the imagination: an echo, perhaps, more than the real thing.

Helen Jaskoski

HERO AND LEANDER

Author: Christopher Marlowe (1564-1593)
Type of poem: Epic
First published: 1598

The Poem

Hero and Leander is a short, amorous epic written in rhymed couplets of iambic pentameter. It is divided into cantos called "sestiads," after a verse form which gains its name from the isle of Sestos, where the action takes place. Apparently, Christopher Marlowe wrote the entire first two sestiads of 484 and 334 lines. Some believe these two chapters were meant in themselves to be a complete poem; others believe that Marlowe did not live to finish his work. In any case, George Chapman, the famous translator of Homer, took up the work and completed it by adding four more sestiads. Although appreciated, the Chapman augmentation is not cherished, venerated, or studied with the same interest as the Marlowe chapters, which are considered the best poetic work in that genre during the Elizabethan period.

Hero and Leander could be called an "amorous epic" to distinguish it from the longer Homeric epics which are on heroic subjects. It lacks the sober dignity and solemn tragedy of classical Greek tragedy and epic. Some critics have suggested calling it an epyllion, which carries the sense of a shorter and less serious narrative work. The classical models for these works, so popular in the sixteenth century, were the long, sensuous, and humorous poems of Ovid, particularly the *Amores* (c. 20 B.C.), the *Heroides* (before A.D. 8), and the *Metamorphoses* (c. A.D. 8). Ovid was popular in the Middle Ages, providing the literary material for a cult of love which expressed itself in verse romances and the poetry of the troubadours, though the explicit sections of his works were treated as allegory.

The English Renaissance — gay, vigorous, delighting in the senses and a newly discovered sense of personal freedom — disrobed classical love literature of its embarrassed indirection, and sensual, worldly, playful poetry abounded. Marlowe's *Hero and Leander* was one of the most popular and influential works following this tendency. It describes the brief and illicit courtship of Hero, a young priestess of the temple of Venus on Sestos, and Leander, a handsome young man of the city of Abydos. The two are separated by the rough seas of the Hellespont, and Leander braves the waters in order to spend evenings with Hero.

The complete legend involves the tragic death of the lovers. Neptune, the god of the sea, becomes enamored of Leander as he swims across the Hellespont. Leander rejects Neptune's love, and the god drowns Hero in anger. This tragic tale was told by the Greek fifth century poet Musaeus, and it is the Greek or a Latin translation of this poem which is the textual basis for Marlowe's work. Marlowe, however, barely foreshadows the lovers' unhappy fate in his two sestiads; this grave duty has been left by history to Chapman. It is possible to read Marlowe alone, therefore, and see nothing but a bright, humorous, sexy poem about two young lovers enjoying their first carnal knowledge, as well as Leander dealing embarrassedly with the homosexual love interest of Neptune, who, showering Leander with jewels and lasciviously fondling him as he swims, seems the picture of an aroused, wealthy, older bon vivant.

The poem begins with a straightforward exposition and then veers instantly into a florid description, full of classical allusions, of Hero's beauty. Marlowe fills the text with such allusions, an ostentatious display of knowledge of antiquity that is part of the genre. Hero's beauty is so great that the god Apollo once offered her his throne. Her sleeves are decorated with a representation of naked Venus chasing her beloved Adonis; the figured border of Hero's dress is stained with the blood of desperate lovers who killed themselves because she rejected them. In a spirit of humorous exaggeration, Marlowe describes her breath as so sweet-smelling that bystanders praise it and honeybees swarm about her mouth. Marlowe calls her "Venus' nun," which means literally that she is a virgin serving the cult of Venus in the temple at Sestos. Yet, "Venus' nun" is also an Elizabethan expression for a prostitute.

The description of Leander is equally exaggerated and even more replete with classical allusions. The allusions recall stories from Homer, Vergil, Ovid, and Greek tragedy. Leander's tresses are like the Golden Fleece—the Argonauts would have traveled to Colchis for them. Cynthia, the moon, is pale in grief that she cannot have Leander. His body is as straight as the magic wand of Circe, the enchantress from the *Odyssey* (c. 800 B.C.). Jove would have accepted drink from Leander's hand and replaced the lovely servant Ganymede with him. Hippolytus, who preferred hunting to love and died rather than accept improper amorous advances, would nevertheless have fallen in love with Leander.

The narration is taken up again with a description of the annual festival at Sestos of Adonis, the boy loved by Venus. Since the festival is in honor of the goddess of love, guests journey there to find new lovers. Hero stands out as the most beautiful woman there. She is compared with the stars and all sorts of heavenly bodies. People rush to see her; many fall in love with her and die of her indifference (to "die" is, in Elizabethan parlance, colloquial for sexual climax).

There is a moment of tragic foresight when Hero and Leander first see each other, but instead of continuing with a description of the meeting of the lovers, Marlowe provides an elaborate digression by describing the fabulous temple of Venus. It is adorned with representations of mythology; these frescoes and bas reliefs, a convention in heroic literature, are usually an evocation of battle and heroic deeds. Yet in this light, amorous epic, they are a list of amorous indiscretions by the gods— appropriate adornment for a temple to Venus. The courting scene begins tenderly with commonplaces about love at first sight. Then, however, follows a long speech by Leander against virginity. One sophism after another, it is designed to seduce Hero at all costs.

Hero's answer expresses her maidenly ambivalence, for although she is attracted to the young man, she nevertheless makes a show of defending her virtue. She supplicates Venus to save her from this threat to her chastity, but Cupid, the god of love, hovers above her and beats back her prayers from heaven. He then flies to the "palace of the Destinies," where the Fates, three old women, weave each person's fortune and future. Cupid asks the Fates to arrange a happy outcome for Hero and Leander, but they will not, because of an injury received from the god at an earlier time. The story of this ancient insult to the Fates, another lengthy digression, ends the sestiad.

The second sestiad is devoted to the actual seduction of Hero. She flees to her tower on Sestos. Leander follows. They kiss and embrace, but no more than that, because Leander does not yet know the facts of life. As instinct instructs him further, however, he again presses Hero to have intercourse with him. The narrator describes in delicious detail their amorous contention and Hero's attempt to maintain her virginity. This level of description proceeds throughout the entire poem as an alternative to the mythological allusions and classical tone. Leander leaves without having completed "the rites of love." Soon, however, he swims again to Sestos, this time attracting Neptune as his naked body cleaves the waters. Leander's rejection of the sea god is the basis for his downfall, which will occur in the Chapman section of the epic.

The rest of the sestiad is the actual final seduction of Hero and an evening of lovemaking. In the morning, the sun rises to find Hero standing by the bed, watching Leander. Marlowe achieves a grand climax by paralleling her early rise with the rise of the sun, which chases away embarrassed night. The 1598 edition contains at this point a cryptic Latin expression, *Desunt nonnulla*, which means "something is lacking." That probably indicates the publisher's understanding that Marlowe broke off in his composition before it was completed.

Forms and Devices

Hero and Leander has been considered by many to be the finest of the English Renaissance's "mythological poems." One of the chief devices of a mythological poem is classical allusion, references to texts and legends of Greek and Roman antiquity. The allusions in *Hero and Leander*, however, are uneven in tone and often have an unmeasured quality. For example, in praising Leander's beauty, Marlowe writes, "Even as delicious meat is to the taste,/ So was his neck in touching, and surpass'd/ The white of Pelops' shoulder." Pelops' shoulder is indeed white, because it is made of ivory, a god having in fact eaten the fleshly shoulder when it was served up by Tantalus, Pelops' father, in a stew. Yet there is also the poet's description of the carvings on the walls of Venus' temple: "There might you see the gods in sundry shapes,/ Committing heady riots, incest, rapes." The poet then tells of Zeus's seduction, as a golden shower, of Danae; his marriage to his sister, Hera; his love play with the boy Ganymede; and his appearance as a bull to rape Europa. Marlowe then describes Mars and Venus, who were trapped in an iron net by Vulcan after they committed adultery together; and the destruction of Troy because of the rape of Helen.

Nineteenth century critics such as A. C. Bradley saw in the sensuality of Marlowe's imagery and the flamboyance of his classical allusions a certain Renaissance enthusiasm and "frank acceptance of sensuous beauty and joy." M. C. Bradbrook introduced in the mid-1930's, however, a new reading of Marlowe's poem which sees these allusions as ironic, parodic, and generally humorous. The reference to Pelops, for example, is not infelicitous or inapt but sharp-edged and complex; it means that Marlowe is not taking Leander's gratuitous beauty utterly seriously. He creates an ironic distance and does not uncritically portray Leander's amoral sensuality. The poet's list of rapes, incests, and acts of sexual violence by the gods could be seen as sarcasm or at least not the acceptance without regard to taste and decorum usually attributed to Elizabethan "enthusiasm."

In general, the devices of Marlowe's poem parallel those of true heroic narrative, but because the subject is love, not war, there is a deliberate contrast as well. When aggression is replaced by passion, romantic wooing replaces mighty heroic deeds.

Themes and Meanings

During the Renaissance, respect for classical antiquity, for Greek and Roman culture, expressed the idea that mortal man with his abilities and limitations should be at the center of human perspective, that is, should be the measure of human values. This view contrasted with medieval thought, in which the Christian god and theological absolutes were the measure of all things. *Hero and Leander* is an expression of the Renaissance "humanistic" perspective, for the work takes human physical love as its subject and gives the reader a psychological portrait of the development of passion and romance in callow youth. The classical references and constant evocation of antique mythology underscore the humanistic point by posing a nonmetaphysical, nontheological cosmology instead of the allegorical Catholic Christian worldview.

Recent criticism has improved scholars' understanding of the humanity of this approach by pointing out the complexity and ambivalence of Marlowe's acceptance of classical models. He does not receive the violent and irascible sexual life of the Greek gods as a model of authenticity or self-liberation; he regards it with a critical eye. Expressing Renaissance enthusiasm, he rejoices in the richness of the story materials, the colorful tales of the loves of the gods. Yet there is also irony and parody, subtle shifts of perspective and changes of voice, which indicate that his moral perspective is complex.

Hero, for example, is beautiful but disingenuous. Her defense of her virginity is half-hearted. She spurns Leander but drops her sixteenth century fan so that he will follow. Leander's behavior reflects no moral position but rather pure concupiscence. Hence Marlowe's harsh aphorism: "Love is not full of pity (as men say)/ But deaf and cruel where he means to prey." Moreover, Leander may be beautiful and winsome, but he is also embarassingly naïve. He does not know even the basic facts about human intercourse. He fails to recognize Neptune's homosexual love for what it is and ignorantly says, "You are deceiv'd, I am no woman, I."

Robin Kornman

THE HEROES OF CHILDHOOD

Author: Thomas McGrath (1916-1990)
Type of poem: Elegy
First published: 1947, in *To Walk a Crooked Mile*

The Poem

An "elegy" at one time indicated a poem of mourning for an admired member of the nobility or for a deceased loved one. Though this meaning sometimes still holds, the term is now applied to virtually any verse meditation on loss. "The Heroes of Childhood" is a modern folk elegy which romantically laments, not a particular human death, but the death of childhood and the illusions of youth. Written in five five-line stanzas, the poem's end rhyme and regular metrics contribute to its innocent, songlike quality. That quality reinforces the poem's very subject—with mounting irony.

The "childhood heroes" of the poem's first stanza are immediately described in terms of the American West: "their pearl-handled six-guns never missed fire," and "In a town full of badmen they never lost face." The point of view is first-person plural, which serves to generalize or universalize the subject. Faith in human goodness and infallibility is a typical experience of childhood, and the objects of admiration are like frontier heroes with their perfect aim and absolute goodness.

Stanza 2 continues the fictitious Wild West analogy but introduces two names from nonfictitious history: "Big Bill Haywood" and "Two Gun Marx." Marx is Karl Marx, the father of socialism and Communism, and Haywood was William Dudley Haywood, the American labor leader. These are the outlaw heroes who "stood against the bankers" to give to the poor. (From about the time of his college years, Thomas McGrath himself was a Marxist, and he was even blacklisted during the McCarthy era.) At this point in the poem, the speaker seems to be describing the heroes, not of childhood and myth, but of young adulthood and history, the perspective of youth coming to an awareness of real-world events and politics.

Even this faith in historical heroes, however, is eventually disturbed: "But we in our time are not so sure." When "we"—as opposed to childhood's god-heroes—are called to account, "our hearts" are "strung up" by hard thought about the realities of attempting political revolution. The childhood analogy of Wild West heroes is continued here, but the speaker now acknowledges the difficulties of living up to childhood ideals. The efforts this speaker has made to eliminate social injustice (through the labor movement and socialist reform) are condemned by the very society those efforts were meant to assist.

The natural next step in disillusionment is to examine anew one's childhood heroes and to consider whether, indeed, they too awaken at night, feverish with doubts. The tone of this fourth stanza is distinctly elegiac: "Perhaps we were mistaken, it has been so long. . . ." Each sentence here ends with a question, and the stanza is itself about raising ultimate questions. The speaker ends with an admonition that

"The heart must build its own direction —/ Which only in the future has a permanent shape." The fall from faith has left only a romantic hope for future revolution, one constructed out of the "heart" rather than faith in human gods. Childhood and this poem itself thus come to their grim, though stubbornly idealistic, conclusion.

Forms and Devices

McGrath's poems are characterized by incredible formal variety. Though much of his later work is free verse, he sets an adroit pen to seemingly any formal exercise, including "The Heroes of Childhood." The poem is written in fairly regular iambic tetrameter, with an end-rhyme scheme of *aabba*. Though these formal choices contribute to the folk-songlike quality of the piece, the meter is never so regular and the end rhyme never so direct as to reduce the poem to pure playfulness or silliness. The first stanza, in fact, demonstrates his skill at slant rhyme: "austere," "fire" and "there," as well as "dice" and "face." The second stanza includes "pure," "car," and "poor," as well as "Marx" and "works." These off rhymes blunt the potential singsong effect of true end rhyme. In a poem about both childhood innocence and hard adult realities, McGrath's rhyme scheme seems here to be just right.

Typical also of McGrath's work is an impersonal point of view. Though some of his poems are indeed intimate, he more often employs distancing devices to address universal political issues. In the case of "The Heroes of Childhood," McGrath accomplishes this distance through a first person plural angle of vision. One could easily substitute "I" for each "we" in this poem; the particularly American childhood, the conversion to Marxism, the subsequent doubts and even blacklisting — these are biographical elements of McGrath's own life. His choice of the plural pronoun, however, generalizes the poem, and underscores the universality of social concerns he felt took precedence over personal biography.

Point of view and sound patterns are important devices in "The Heroes of Childhood." More than anything, however, the poem relies on a central, extended figure: the American West as an emblem of American innocence. The Hollywood-style Wild West described in this piece, with its "Dead Eye Dans" and pure-hearted outlaws, is like the philosophic childhood of the speaker, and perhaps America generally. The key feature of such a philosophy, as of Hollywood popular film, is illusion. According to this vision, morality is unambiguous, the good guys always win and the good guys are always on our side. By the end of the poem, however, the figurative West has become "this dead world's Indian Nation." The immature vision of the speaker thus gives over to a single, real, and terrible image: the mass grave of America's native people.

Themes and Meanings

At the center of McGrath's poem is the idea of direction and its loss, or illusion and disillusion. This is a well-worn theme. In the work of writers from every part of the globe, there appears in imaginative writing some notion of the Fall, a loss of original innocence and faith, and the subsequent troubles of mortality and incapacity.

The first illusion for McGrath is the American Dream—Hollywood-style heroes with their white hats and horses—but this is soon replaced by a young man's Communist ideals. In the Marxist view, direction is all-important because it is predetermined. The world is on an inevitable course toward a workers' utopia, free of class struggle. Yet in stanza 4, the speaker's faith in absolute direction, absolute ideals of any kind, is eroding: "Did they too wake at night . . ./ And wonder when direction would be clear if ever?" At the far end of both the American and the Marxist dream is loss of moral certainty and purpose.

Interestingly, "The Heroes of Childhood" ends with a reaffirmed faith in a new type of direction through what McGrath calls "the heart." This is not the heart of any particular person, group, or view, but is *the* heart, and so is perhaps intended as some essential self, a romantic source or spring. It might be the imagination as well, casting forward its shapes and building its own spontaneous paths, independent of worldly change and ideologies. "The heart must build its own direction—/ Which only in the future has a permanent shape."

Such indefinite, rather wistful sentiments are not necessarily typical of McGrath. Throughout much of his work, he seems to insist on tangible, earthly remedies for tangible human problems. He is critical of Platonic idealism and notions of afterlife salvation. He wants change right here and now, in the world we know. Nevertheless, in such poems as "The Heroes of Childhood," efforts to change the world are found to be untenable, fraught with ambiguities. He thus comes to rely on the less practical redemption of "the heart."

Certainly no other American poet has demonstrated such an unlikely interlocking of elements as we find in McGrath. Few poets write from both artistic expertise as well as overt political convictions—and Communist ones, at that—but despite those life-long convictions, in this poem McGrath seems to affirm, instead, creative imagination as the source of change and goodness. The imagination is of course an imperfect assurance, and some readers may find the poem's conclusion unconvincing, or at least difficult: The heart "left hanging" must somehow now start building.

Cynthia Nichols

HIGH WINDOWS

Author: Philip Larkin (1922-1985)
Type of poem: Lyric
First published: 1974, in *High Windows*

The Poem

"High Windows" consists of five quatrains; it has a variable metrical pattern and an irregular but discernible rhyme scheme (basically *abab*). Like many of Philip Larkin's poems, "High Windows" is written in the first person with no attempt to separate himself from the speaker. "I write poems," Larkin has said, "to preserve things I have seen/thought/felt (if I may so indicate a composite and complex experience) both for myself and others."

In "High Windows," an older man describes his thoughts and feelings on seeing a young couple during the late 1960's at the height of the sexual revolution. With cynical envy, and in blunt language, the speaker assumes that they have sex and that "she's/ Taking pills or wearing a diaphragm."

It is a situation that to him (and his generation's way of thinking) seems like the "paradise/ Everyone old has dreamed of all their lives" — without consequences and free of shame. All social restraints of "Bonds and gestures" have been thrown aside like "an outdated combine harvester" in favor of this new freedom, and now everyone can go down the "long slide/ To happiness."

At this point, the speaker wonders whether anyone looked at him when he was young, "forty years back," and thought the same things: *"That'll be the life;/ No God any more, or sweating in the dark/ About hell and that."* The church and its priests, too, *"will all go down the long slide/ Like free bloody birds."* Here it is unclear whether the slide leads to happiness, hell, or (in the absence of God) simply into nothingness.

The speaker concludes enigmatically by refusing to state his conclusion in words. "Rather than words comes the thought of high windows." Larkin is conveying (in words) the idea that some mental processes are beyond words. In this case, there is only the image, like a revelation, of the "sun-comprehending glass,/ And beyond it, the deep blue air, that shows/ Nothing, and is nowhere, and is endless."

Forms and Devices

It is one of the privileges of the contemporary poet working in traditional forms to play with those forms for ironic effect. Larkin once said that "Deprivation is for me what daffodils were to Wordsworth"; his tone is typically that of a cynic for whom life has not made good on its promises. Larkin's technique in "High Windows," as elsewhere, is based on the frustration of form, just as his theme is often frustration itself.

At first glance, "High Windows" appears to be written in traditional quatrains, but the first stanza immediately frustrates such an assumption. Whatever one may have assumed about the decorum of lyric poetry is contradicted by the opening lines, as much by the tone set by the vulgar and technical diction as by the lack of perfect rhyme.

Like Wilfred Owen, Larkin is a master of slant or off rhyme, setting up sonorous expectations that turn out to be as off-key as life itself is. The "she's/paradise" slant rhyme makes sense in that it displays the speaker's envy; the "kids/diaphragm" pairing does not rhyme at all. Its dissonance is as much a thing of sense as of sound, implying the irony of kids using birth control to keep from having kids. After this unconventional opening, the poem becomes increasingly traditional, in diction and meter as well as rhyme, as the speaker begins to make sense of a situation that at first merely baffles him. His conclusion, though, is startling.

The three verbs of the opening stanza set the agenda for the stages of the poem: the speaker can "see" the couple, can "guess" what they are doing, and can "know" that they are in paradise. His initial observation reveals more about his own desires and fears than theirs. Through an imaginative shift in perspective, he is able to look at himself more objectively. This double perspective inexplicably leads to the vision of high windows.

Tonally, the speaker moves from a cynical stance of envy (stated in vulgarly degrading diction) to a more reasonable viewpoint (mildly blasphemous in comparing priests with "bloody birds"), until he comes to rest in the meditative reconciliation with the world and himself in the high-toned final stanza.

This tonal modulation is matched by the poem's thematic development. It moves from a literal interpretation of the couple's freedom (the freedom from restraint to couple as they please), to an act of imaginative speculation (if there is no God, then the priests have no power), to a symbolic interpretation of freedom that acknowledges that beyond the physical and social realm lies another sort of freedom— beyond desire, envy, and everything transient and human.

Themes and Meanings

"High Windows" is a poem about the nature of freedom. The technology of birth control has granted sexual license to the young couple by freeing them from the inevitable sequence of love-marriage-children, but old "Bonds and gestures" die hard. A generation reared on the restraints of religion envies the young's relative "paradise." Deeper than envy, however, is the fear of freedom. Without restraints, society dissolves into anarchy, and the universe becomes meaningless. Such fears are what William Blake called "the mind-forg'd manacles" of self-enslavement. In the course of the poem, the speaker casts off envy and fear to accept the absolute freedom promised by the endless emptiness of "the deep blue air."

The poem (dated February 12, 1967) takes as its point of departure the free love of the sexual revolution. Old and new views of sex are contrasted in a pair of images: the combine versus the slide. The old view of sex has been "pushed to one side/ Like an outdated combine harvester." It suggests something mechanical, useful, and economically profitable, and it carries the symbolic baggage of a moralistic grim reaper: Ye shall reap what wild oats ye sow. The new view re-forms the old metal into a smooth playground slide, down which the young are going "To happiness, endlessly." The mechanical social duties of sex have been replaced by the free play of the pleasure principle.

With the obsolescence of social bonds, the power of the church, the chief agent of restraint, is lessened. The priests, too, will go down the long slide, like "*free bloody birds*," but not to happiness. In the existential philosopher Jean-Paul Sartre's phrase, they will be "condemned to be free." They will disappear into the empty heavens.

In situation and point of view, Larkin's poem resembles "Sailing to Byzantium" by William Butler Yeats. An old man observing "the sensual music" of "The young/ In one another's arms" decides that "That is no country for old men." Leaving the sensual world to the young, the speaker finds his solace in "monuments of unaging intellect" and is left contemplating "God's holy fire/ As in the gold mosaic of a wall" in the ideal city of Byzantium. Yet Larkin's tone is wryer, drier, and more down to earth. Larkin's speaker finds neither monuments of culture nor God in his "high windows." For all their majesty, they are not the stained glass of an old church, but clear "sun-comprehending glass."

The absence of God in Larkin's sky, as well as the absence of culture, has led some critics to see Larkin as a pessimist. Far from conveying any sense of hopelessness, however, the transparency of the glass, the purity of the blue sky, and the clarity of the vacant heavens are supremely peaceful. Above and beyond any thoughts of youth or age, unsullied by human desire or deprivation, social or even divine expectations, are the sun and sky—nature, pure and brutally simple, without judgment or explanation.

The image is a vitalistic, life-affirming view of nature. The "sun-comprehending glass" may be uncomprehending, leaving the big metaphysical questions unanswered, but it does understand the sun's life-giving warmth. The pagan sun god of sensual joy has replaced the Christian God of restraint and punishment. The last word of the poem is "endless," but the poem's motion does not end there. Instead, it circles back to the young couple "going down the long slide/ To happiness, endlessly." The linkage affirms the connection between their literal freedom and the absolute freedom of the speaker's vision beyond the "high windows."

The revelation suddenly reconciles the speaker not only with the couple (he now seems free of envy for their slide to happiness) but also with the priests (who may be pitied for their illusory slide into a vacant heaven). For him there may be "Nothing" in the way of transcendental or metaphysical solace above and beyond man and nature, but with the disappearance of God there is also the disappearance of shame and therefore a rediscovery of "paradise." Instead of "sweating in the dark/ About hell and that," the speaker stands in the light of a new kind of peace and freedom, where he must find, or make, his own meaning of a seemingly meaningless universe.

Richard Collins

THE HOLLOW MEN

Author: T. S. Eliot (1888-1965)
Type of poem: Dramatic monologue
First published: 1925, in *Poems, 1909-1925*

The Poem

"The Hollow Men" is both a single hundred-line poem and a sequence of five poems (or parts). Although almost entirely lacking in simple narrative cohesiveness and linear development, and defying simple classification ("The Hollow Men" is at once dramatic monologue, soliloquy, choric ode, lyric, elegy, and meditation), T. S. Eliot's highly and at times allegorically abstract text nevertheless achieves a remarkable unity of effect in terms of voice, mood, and imagery. The simplicity and seeming transparency of the title—a conflation of William Shakespeare's *Julius Caesar* (c. 1599-1600) and poems by Rudyard Kipling and William Morris—serve as an ironic indicator of Eliot's rich and complex texture. The two epigraphs—one from Joseph Conrad's novel, *Heart of Darkness* (1899), and the other a child's line from the yearly observance of Guy Fawkes Day (November 5) in England—serve a similar purpose; they contextualize the poem literarily and historically while underscoring the poem's thematization of spiritual hollowness and failure of will.

The poem is chiefly narrated in the first-person plural; a "we" that serves to broaden the speaker's predicament beyond the individual to encompass a more nearly universal figure who is emblematic of his age and who may well be speaking for, as well as to, the reader. Against the dying Kurtz's last words, "The horror! The horror!" in *Heart of Darkness*, Eliot's narrator can only rouse himself to utter a "quiet and meaningless" "Alas!" of resignation and despair.

The very fact that this "we" does speak (although monotonously) holds out at least the possibility that this "we" is not yet completely resigned to human inconsequentiality and to a spiritual void—that, whether from guilt or from need, "we" yearns for something more. The wasteland depicted here looks back to Eliot's 1922 poem *The Waste Land* but more especially to Dante's *Inferno* (c. 1320). "We" are modern-day versions of Dante's tormented souls suffering in "our" low-grade way the pain of loss, whispering rather than howling. The Dantean allusion helps to explain the otherwise inexplicable shift from plural "we" to singular "I" in part 2 and helps explain the intensification of wasteland and inferno imagery here and in part 3. Part 4 holds out the distinct, slight possibility of redemption for those otherwise condemned to groping blindly "in this valley of dying stars," of dying hope.

On the very verge of entering the saving (baptismal) waters of "the tumid river," of crossing over Eliot's version of the River Styx from the land of death in life to that of life in death, the choric narrator fails to make the necessary Kierkegaardian leap of faith. He remains where he is, poised between the horror of spiritual as well as sexual sterility and the promise of a redemption, which, he also perceives, holds the threat of judgment and damnation.

The fifth and concluding section is structurally the most complex and thematically the most disturbing. The unresolved mix of pronouncements, prayer, and nursery rhyme (with its substitution of "prickly pear" for "mulberry bush") offers no entry into purgatory, no glimpse of paradise. Instead, it leaves speaker and reader alike still poised between two states of being and therefore still very much in the grip of paralyzing despair.

Forms and Devices

In his review of James Joyce's prototypical high modernist novel, *Ulysses* (1922), written at the very time he began work on the poems that would later make up "The Hollow Men," Eliot explained that "in manipulating a continuous parallel between contemporaneity and antiquity, Mr. Joyce is pursuing a method which others must pursue after him. . . . It is simply a way of controlling, of ordering, of giving a shape and a significance to the immense panorama of futility and anarchy which is contemporary history." Eliot had himself already employed the mythic method to devastating effect in *The Waste Land*. That method, along with the richly allusive style to which it is closely tied, plays a less insistent but arguably more integral role in giving shape and direction to the considerably less diversified but still disconcerting flux of materials (or "stuffing") from which Eliot assembled "The Hollow Men."

Rudyard Kipling, William Morris, Joseph Conrad, William Shakespeare, Ernest Dowson, and Paul Valéry play their parts, but none so importantly, pervasively, and unobtrusively as Dante. His *Divine Comedy* (c. 1320) serves as both the foundation upon which Eliot's otherwise fragmented text rests and as the yardstick by which the choric speaker's spiritual plight may be measured. The point of the mythic method is not to show how far modern man has fallen from some nostalgically regarded golden age, but to show how similar, even static, the human condition actually is. Such a procedure transforms Eliot's paralyzed narrator into a figure capable of Dantean grandeur—and anguish.

In addition to perfecting the mythic method, Eliot began structuring his poetry in dramatic terms. The two procedures are in fact clearly connected, for Eliot's interest in drama focused on its origin in primitive rituals. The choric voice and "drumbeat" rhythms of "The Hollow Men" manifest a dramatic quality that Eliot adds to and plays against the Dantean parallel. The prevalence of short lines, of elliptical and fragmentary phrasings, and the repetition of a handful of key words and images (eyes, shadow, and kingdom, for example), as well as the inclusion of two framing quasi-rituals (the children begging on Guy Fawkes Day and the "here we go round the mulberry bush" children's rhyme), highlight the poem's dramatic quality, even if they do not direct attention to it overtly, and add not only to the work's incantatory effect but also make it at once mythic and modern, strangely primitive yet remarkably up-to-date.

Themes and Meanings

Although sufficient evidence exists to warrant reading "The Hollow Men" as autobiographical revelation, Eliot's commitment (particularly at this point in his career) to an "impersonalist" aesthetic and to finding "objective correlatives" that would transform private experience into subjective terms requires a less narrow approach. "The Hollow Men" reflects the lingering post-World War I malaise that affected not only Eliot but his age as well.

The poem succeeds admirably in registering a mood not merely of disillusionment but of personal weakness. The choric speaker, either speaking in unison with others about their common condition or speaking alone for them, perhaps because they do not yet perceive or understand their plight, wearily yet, in his own way, steadfastly resists the self-knowledge to which his whispering leads him. This resistance is, however, tempered by the fact that he mocks himself for his failure. He fears the judgment that will expose his failure of nerve to others and to himself at least as much as he fears the death that will just as surely expose the meaninglessness of his life as a spiritual coward or zombie.

Although he fears the "eyes" that will know and pass sentence on his evident inadequacy, he also longs for the "eyes" that see what he does not. These are the eyes (of Dante's Beatrice and Christ's mother Mary) evoked in the poem's most intensely lyrical moment: "The eyes [that] reappear/ As the perpetual star/ Multifoliate rose/ Of death's twilight kingdom/ The hope only/ Of empty men." The moment—"Alas!"—does not last; it is followed by the highly fragmented fifth and final section, which ends, as does *The Waste Land*, with a shoring of fragments against the ruin. Unlike *The Waste Land*, however, here poetic word and world end not with madness and not "with a bang but a whimper." The shadow of spiritual death—doubt and despair—falls; the mood of spiritual paralysis prevails.

Robert A. Morace

HOMAGE TO SEXTUS PROPERTIUS

Author: Ezra Pound (1885-1972)
Type of poem: Poetic sequence
First published: 1919, in *Quia Pauper Amavi*

The Poem

Homage to Sextus Propertius is essentially Ezra Pound's translation of books 2 and 3 of the *Elegies* by the Roman poet Sextus Propertius, who lived during the latter part of the first century A.D. Calling this poem a "translation," however, is misleading. Although many of Pound's lines are accurate translations of the Latin verses, other stretches of the English-language poem depart widely in sense from the Latin original. Nevertheless, the subject matter of *Homage to Sextus Propertius* is that of the original books of the elegies, though the ordering of the various sections is often Pound's own.

Section I encompasses the standard elegiac introduction of classical poetry: Propertius establishes his credentials as a young poet, with a new way of saying things. He acknowledges that his fame might be some time in coming, but when it does come, he will have a better memorial than the finest, most elaborate tomb. Part of Propertius' novel poetic manner is his subject matter: Instead of glorifying the exploits of Imperial Rome, he intends to be part of the lyric tradition of classical poetry, which emphasizes love and intense personal emotion.

In the first stanza, Propertius calls up the ghosts of past lyric poets, thereby establishing his poetic heritage. He then contrasts the lyric tradition, in the second stanza, with popular contemporary poets whose subject is war. In the third stanza, he heightens the contrast through irony, speaking with contempt of poets whose chief role seems to be publicists of the Roman state and its "celebrities." Propertius concludes this section with the traditional prediction that those who are mentioned in his poems will enjoy eternal fame along with the poet.

In section II, Propertius extends his opening theme, explaining how he came to turn from the currently popular subjects of war and conquest to poems having to do with pining lovers, sorcery, and midnight trysts. The impetus behind his change of heart, Propertius claims, comes from two visions: one of Apollo ("Phoebus") and one from Calliope (the Greek muse of epic poetry). These two supernatural beings, both of whom were traditionally associated with poetic inspiration, remind Propertius that his gifts do not lie in the area of public poetry.

In section III, Propertius turns, then, to what he does best—writing about love. In this section, he receives a late-night invitation from Cynthia, his lover, to visit her. Out of timidity, however, he refuses.

At midnight, Cynthia demands that Propertius come to her—the implication is that their meeting will be for lovemaking. Propertius experiences a conflict, however; on the one hand, he is eager to visit his mistress (and he knows how angry she can be if he fails her). On the other hand, he worries about muggers. The unlit streets of ancient Rome were probably no safer at midnight than those of modern New York City, and Propertius imagines his robbery and death.

He tries to bolster his courage in the third stanza by recalling that lovers are sacred. Even if he does meet violence, he tells himself, such a death is worth dying for Cynthia's sake. Still, in the end, he decides he would rather not die on a public street.

In section IV, Propertius talks with his slave, Lygdamus, who is his go-between with Cynthia. During this conversation, he imagines how Cynthia has received his rejection of her earlier offer. Throughout this section, Propertius implies that Cynthia is little more than a prostitute and that she has been unfaithful to him with Lygdamus. Evidently, Lygdamus has described the desolation that has fallen over Cynthia's household as news of Propertius' rejection has reached her. Lygdamus tells him that his mistress remains in bed, copiously weeping, dressed simply, without her usual ornaments. Moreover, Cynthia accuses Propertius of unfaithfulness.

In stanzas 3 and 4, Lygdamus quotes Cynthia's description of Propertius' quite literal enchantment by another woman: The other woman has used potions and spells to snare her lover. This is followed by Cynthia's curse on her rival, and the prediction of her own death following Propertius' rejection. Propertius, however, responds sardonically to these histrionics. He believes neither in Cynthia's protestations nor in Lygdamus' fidelity.

Meanwhile, in section V, Propertius proves to have other problems besides those with his mistress. His patron, Maecenas, is pressuring him to write martial epics in the manner of Vergil. In classical Rome, poets commonly were supported by rich men eager to add to their own fame by being associated with well-known writers. Such patrons often lent their financial backing to several writers. Maecenas was perhaps the most important of such men because he included in his literary circle such great writers as Vergil and Horace. Propertius, however, struggles to maintain his poetic integrity. He stubbornly restates his initial intention to write lyric poetry instead of the public verse of Maecenas' other poets.

In the first part of section V, Propertius gives Maecenas a literal example of why it would be a bad idea for him to attempt Vergilian epics. Propertius makes a pretended attempt to write on "great" subjects — the extensions of the Roman Empire, the triumphs of Augustus Caesar, the battles of the Roman legions. The result is bombast, badly written, and ridiculously described.

In the second part of this section, however, Propertius turns to his true gift: love poetry. He explains to Maecenas that his muse is his lover, that everything she does provides him with material for volumes of poetry. Her lyre playing, the way her hair falls on her forehead, the clothes she wears, and especially, her lovemaking — all these are so fascinating to him that he has no time for writing poetry about war and history. In fact, Propertius tells Maecenas in the final part of this section, his lover disdains epic poetry, especially Homer. Her distaste for the greatest of ancient writers, Propertius ironically reveals, is that she disapproves of Helen of Troy's "conduct."

Section VI introduces a somber note to the course of the poem. Propertius imagines his death and funeral and Cynthia's response to his death. Much of the content in this section is conventional to classical poetry. In death, the high and the low, the conqueror and the conquered, are equal, sharing Charon's ferry over the river Acheron in the underworld. As far as Propertius himself is concerned, his death will be humble. His funeral cortege will comprise few followers, and those will be not very distinguished. Cynthia will lament her dead lover, to be sure, but perhaps only because "it is a custom." In any case, Cynthia's cries of grief will be in vain, since, obviously, the dead are past hearing.

Section VII is also conventional in theme: Love is contrasted to death. Propertius is keen to assert that lovemaking—the sensory joy of the physical—is the only antidote to mortality. The poet describes Cynthia's insistence on a lighted chamber so that the lovers can see each other, thus increasing their joy. Their nightlong embraces have great variety, and these are interspersed with intimate conversation and with each gazing into the other's eyes.

In contrast to section VI, in which Propertius reflects on his own death, in section VIII, he imagines Cynthia's death. The content here is gently ironic. The poet imagines the jealousy of the goddesses over Cynthia's arrival in the afterworld. He briefly retells the stories of other mortal women who suffered the goddesses' wrath: Io, who was turned into a cow by Hera because Zeus admired her; Andromeda, whose beauty incurred the wrath of Poseidon; Callisto, whose affair with Zeus spurred Hera to change the mortal girl into a bear. Nevertheless, Propertius claims, Cynthia's beauty is so great that, once she arrives on Olympus, the goddesses may permanently lose favor.

Propertius continues this theme in section IX, where he implores the gods to extend Cynthia's life. He argues that there are already enough beautiful women in the underworld and that, besides, he himself will die if Cynthia perishes. He then goes on to admonish Cynthia to keep up her devotions to the gods in thanks for her continued life, and he also insists that she show her "thanks" to the poet by spending ten nights with him.

In section X, Propertius describes his kidnapping by a group of small boys who have been commissioned by Cynthia to bring him to her. The poet has been up most of the night carousing, and so he is fairly drunk when the boys accost him. They drag him to Cynthia's house at daybreak, and he enters. He finds Cynthia asleep, and he stands gazing at her, stunned by her beauty. As his senses return, so do his doubts of Cynthia's fidelity. He carefully inspects her bed for signs of a rival. At this point, Cynthia awakes and knows what her lover is thinking. She haughtily denies having other lovers; in fact, she implies, she's tired of love—so tired, in fact, that she is on her way to make her devotions at the temple of the vestal virgins and will have nothing more to do with Propertius.

The aftermath of Cynthia's rejection is described in section XI. Tormented by love, Propertius glumly reflects on the fact that there is no escaping desire. Even if he could mount Pegasus or wear Perseus' flying sandals, he could not escape his love for Cynthia. Meanwhile, Cynthia herself seems to have forgotten him. He hears tales of her other affairs, but he tries to dismiss these as the inevitable rumors surrounding beautiful women. In an attempt to forget his worries, he reconsiders old stories of the loves of gods and mortals, but even in retelling these he finds no escape. In the poem's conclusion, section XII, Propertius discovers that his worst imaginings are true: His best friend, Lynceus, another poet, is conducting an affair with Cynthia. Nevertheless, Propertius reaffirms both his love for Cynthia and his intention to continue to write love poetry against the contemporary fashion for epics.

Forms and Devices

Like nearly all Pound's poetry, *Homage to Sextus Propertius* uses free verse — poetic lines that have no set rhythm or consistent number of feet and that do not rhyme. This does not mean, however, that the poem lacks strong verse structure. Moreover, certain distinct rhythms recur, which often suggest certain classical patterns. For example, anapestic feet (two unstressed beats followed by a stress) occur frequently, as in the poem's first stanza: "Who hath taught you so subtle a measure." Such rhythms were used in classical poetry for a variety of purposes, especially for Latin comic drama.

Generally, however, the rhythms here are those of speech: Pound believed that Propertius' lines were meant to mimic the rise and fall of conversation, in the same rhythmic fashion as Pound's own verse. The result is often a rhythmic line, or sequence of lines, followed by an ironic, nonrhythmic conclusion. The generally anapestic rhythm of "And expound the distentions of Empire," for example, is interrupted by the lack of distinct rhythm in the line immediately following: "But for something to read in normal circumstances?" In the preceding example, Pound uses structural irony — the pompous beat of the first line contrasted with the idiomatic rhythm of the second — to reinforce the thematic irony, which contrasts the windy subject matter of Imperial Rome with Propertius' own more personal verse.

The other striking structural feature of the poem is its use of allusion. Such use would obviously be natural to any classical poet. Although Pound, through Propertius, makes reference to a number of contemporary historical events (mainly the conquests of the Roman emperors), generally the poem's allusions are to the loves of the gods, discussed above.

Finally, the poem includes many lyrical, imagist passages, especially in lines describing Propertius' love for Cynthia. Imagism was a poetic movement, largely "invented" by Pound himself, that sought to impart to the reader highly vivid sensory impressions of natural images. These impressions were to be appreciated for their own sake and not for any symbolic weight they might hold. The images were usually coupled, so that two distinct impressions might together create a third. In section III's first stanza, for example, "Bright tips reach up from twin towers,/ Anienan spring water falls into flat-spread pools" combines two distinct sensory images — the glowing tops of the Roman cityscape with the trickle of water into shallow pools. This juxtaposition of images is done for its own sake, to instill in the reader a feeling of the reality of the sensory world.

Themes and Meanings

The thematic basis of *Homage to Sextus Propertius* is reflected in the poem's most obvious feature: that it is a creative translation by one poet of another poet's work. The key, then, to what Pound was attempting with this poetic form lies in the word "homage" of the title. The poem is an attempt by Pound to recapture the living spirit of Sextus Propertius, to enable a modern English audience to understand how an ancient Latin audience would have read, and appreciated, this classical poet. Thus, "homage" means "a loving tribute" by the modern writer "in the manner of" the ancient one.

Moreover, Pound has chosen to translate Propertius' *Elegies* because the Latin poet's themes coincide closely with Pound's own cultural concerns. A clue to this coincidence lies in Pound's many modern, idiomatic renderings of Latin passages having to do with Roman Imperial politics. Pound's "celebrities from the Trans-Caucasus," for example, uses the twentieth century "celebrities" to focus on the parallels between ancient imperialism and the modern British variety.

Like Propertius, Pound believed that many popular contemporary writers were little more than public relations experts for the powerful. *Homage to Sextus Propertius* was written during the close of World War I, when the war's futility and horror had become widely known. In the aftermath, the prewar colonial empires began to collapse, making poetry that glorified imperial power seem highly ironic. So Pound discovered in the works of the first-century Roman poet a precursor to his own concerns.

Among these concerns was the conflict between public and private in literature. *Homage to Sextus Propertius* exalts the permanence of highly personal lyric poetry and emphasizes the transience of "public" verse. Pound's lively re-creation of Propertius' life and milieu is itself proof that individual experience is poetry's most enduring subject. Gifted people, the poem implies, will always be underestimated by the ruling elite; yet those writers who fully record their own emotions will enjoy fame long after the conquests of empire are forgotten.

As Propertius/Pound turns to examine the private life, the poem introduces themes having to do with love and with the subtleties of personality. As the reader learns of Propertius' joys, sorrows, and ironic doubts in love, he or she also begins to learn much about the poet's personality. In fact, as the poem develops, the psychology of the poet himself will turn out to be a main theme. Propertius is a complex, "modern" figure — at once passionate and timid, self-reflective and naïve, sincere and ironic. Through this Latin poem, Pound gives voice to a twentieth century sensibility.

John Steven Childs

HOMECOMING

Author: Paul Celan (Paul Ancel or Antschel, 1920-1970)
Type of poem: Lyric
First published: 1959, as "Heimkehr," in *Sprachgitter*; collected in *Paul Celan: Poems*, 1980

The Poem

"Homecoming" is a free-verse poem of nineteen lines. Its title is somewhat ironic, suggesting a joyous return, a celebration of reunion. The actual "homecoming" that Paul Celan describes in the poem is a bleak return to a landscape of the dead.

The poem comes from a collection that marks the point at which Celan became renowned throughout Europe. The title of this collection, *Sprachgitter* (speech-mesh), illustrates the increasing darkness and obscurity of his work. The title suggests the difficulty of speaking through a mesh or grid, and perhaps implies that speech itself is a mesh or grid, filtering and distorting the feelings it attempts to represent, perhaps causing pain and injury to the one who attempts to speak. The word is Celan's invented compound, and such inventions abound in his later work.

In the case of many poems, it is important to distinguish the speaker of the poem from the poet. In Celan's case, however, no such division is necessary. Celan's life speaks through his poems. They tell of the loss of his parents in the Holocaust and of his attempts to factor this loss into his life and come up with a product other than zero. They also tell of his failure to do this, describing again and again the void left by the Holocaust and the silence of God in response to his anguish.

The poem refers to an unidentified "you," but the "I" is suppressed. The word "I" is used once, but it is not the usual use of the first-person singular—it refers to "an I," a consciousness. The English version has only about seventy-five words (the total depending on how compounds are counted), and although "Homecoming" is not as sparse and compact as his later poems, no word is wasted.

The opening three-line section provides the basic scene and coloration of the poem: snowfall, gray-white or "dove-coloured." The second segment lifts the vision upward, but there is no change in mood. Above the landscape stretches the white sky, "the sleigh track of the lost." There is no respite from this overall blankness in a downward glance either, for there, "hidden," are "what so hurts the eyes," presumably the graves of the dead, which are what the speaker most sees although they are hidden by the snow.

Each of these "hills" represents "an I slipped away into dumbness." In the snow and ice, "a feeling" blown across the cold and empty scene ceases its drifting and plants its gray-white flag: Perhaps the flag is the poem, a grave-marker for the unnamed dead.

Forms and Devices

"Homecoming" is spare and stark, having little use for ornament. The truth it describes trivializes conventional attempts at ornamentation. Its nineteen lines contain a number of words that have a falling rhythm—words such as "hidden," "dumbness," and "feeling," each of which contains a stressed syllable followed by an unstressed one. These words, often placed at the ends of lines, contribute to the mood of snowfall and of sadness. (The words in the original German have the same effect.) The other patterns of stressed and unstressed syllables in the poem produce the effect of chords in a minor key, and contribute to the overall impression of grief. The musical quality of "Homecoming" is also found in many of Celan's other poems, some of which make specific reference to musical forms and themes.

Metaphor in this poem is very basic. Snow and winter traditionally suggest death, and here the snow is becoming "denser and denser"—obscuring more and more the possibility of any vision of light. The snow is described as "the sleigh track of the lost." One of the recurrent images in Celan's earlier poems is the picture of the ashes of the dead rising over the Holocaust ovens, and this suggestion is recalled by the image of the dead rising in this poem into the air in a sleigh. The gray of the remembered ashes pollutes the purity of the snow, so that although the snow should be white, it is seen as gray, "dove-coloured."

The gray and white colors of this poem, combined with the insistent snow and ice, produce a feeling of isolation and desolation, the lowest level of the psyche. It is a mental state not far removed from the coldness at the center of Dante's inferno, where the deepest damned are immobilized in a pit of ice. At the level of complete loss, all freezes to "dumbness." This paralysis comes not from sin but from total grief, deprivation of all that centers one in the world and makes it livable.

At the conclusion, the only sign of life is a "feeling"—an emotion divorced from the speaker who experiences it. The poem combines the concrete with the abstract to explain how this feeling attaches "its dove-its snow-/ coloured cloth as a flag." The feeling has thus been brought into the world of real things.

By the end of "Homecoming," the reader has been led through a series of winter images to a closure that is ambivalent. The last image is the "flag," which suggests labeling, identifying, or claiming. The speaker may be using the poem to reclaim his lost loved ones by memorializing them. On the other hand, this attempt may be vain. The flag is barely discernible from the snow, its color almost indistinguishable from the surroundings of the same neutral hue.

Themes and Meanings

All Celan's poems are about loss, even those rare ones that carry some glimmer of hope, a possible substitution, such as love, for past losses. The deaths of his parents in the concentration camp, as well as those of all other victims of the Holocaust, haunt the poems. His best-known works ("Death Fugue," for example) are direct treatments of the Holocaust. The colors of all of his poems are gray and somber; his works reflect the experience of one who has survived the ordeal and at the same time not survived it, because so much has been lost that not enough is left to sustain him. Celan committed suicide in 1970, despite having married and having become internationally famous as poet and translator.

The death-in-life theme is present from the onset of "Homecoming." The title suggests meetings and greetings, but neither is forthcoming. The dense snow, suggesting death, is thickening. The third line is mysterious, but it too suggests death in life: The snow falls "as if even now you were sleeping." The "you" is addressed nowhere else in the poem and, as usual in Celan's poems, is indeterminate; but the lines state that the addressee is "as if" sleeping. He (or she, or they) is not sleeping; the suggestion is that he is absent, dead.

The white and gray of the scene extend from the top to the bottom of the field of vision, and everything the speaker sees in the sky or on the earth connotes death. The sky is the "sleigh track of the lost"; the ashes of the incinerated Holocaust victims rose skyward. The snowy hills on the ground are the graves, and each one contains "an I slipped away into dumbness." The use of "I" gives two suggestions to the line: Each individual consciousness has been silenced, and the speaker is identifying with each one of the lost. "I" in this poem may mean both "ego" and "self." (The German "Ich" also has this dual meaning.)

The final four lines raise the issue of the possibility of the speaker's survival. He has come "home" to homelessness; everything is frozen and dead. The earth and sky are full of graves. Still, something moves in this bleak landscape—a feeling, which finds its substance in cloth, white or gray-white. A question might arise from this enigmatic conclusion: Is the flag thus formed visible enough to identify the landscape? So much of the speaker has been lost, drained away, identified with the dead, diffused into the earth and the sky. Can there be enough self left to sustain him?

The question of how poetry could be written at all after the Holocaust has been raised, and some critics have accused Celan of aestheticizing the death camps— making them into art and thus glossing over their horror—but critic and translator Michael Hamburger's comment on another Celan poem could also be applied to "Homecoming": "[T]he personal anguish was transposed into distancing imagery and a musical structure so incompatible with reportage that a kind of 'terrible beauty' is wrested from an ugly theme."

Janet McCann

HOMECOMING: ANSE LA RAYE

Author: Derek Walcott (1930-   )
Type of poem: Lyric
First published: 1969, in *The Gulf and Other Poems*

The Poem

"Homecoming: Anse La Raye" is a poem of moderate length, with sixty lines of free verse divided unevenly into four stanzas. The title of the poem indicates the work's subject: the speaker's return to the village of Anse la Raye on the Caribbean Island of St. Lucia. This island is the birthplace of Derek Walcott, who can be identified as the speaker in the poem.

The poem begins in the first-person plural, but by the second stanza the voice shifts to the second person as the speaker begins to address his poetic self. The speaker states that his poetic self experiences many difficulties when he attempts to fulfill his desire to return and be an intrinsic part of his birthplace. The speaker's tone is imbued with estrangement and meditative reflection as the problems of his return to Anse la Raye are examined.

The first stanza begins by linking the peoples of the Caribbean region with other cultures. The speaker indicates that in the island's school the works of antiquity were taught but that these works and their mythological associations, although significant in some ways, were products of other cultures and soon forgotten. For the moment, the speaker's poetic self concentrates only on the sea and a "well-known passage." The speaker views the setting without romantic illusions. The "well-known passage" mentioned in the first stanza becomes a "fish-gut-reeking beach." The ominous tone suggests something more threatening and less comforting is taking place, not what one would expect for a homecoming. As the speaker's poetic self looks over the scene, children appear. The children think that he is a tourist and hope to receive money from him. A feeling of disenchantment is apparent as the speaker tries to interpret and react to what he sees.

The third stanza begins with another reference to the children who "swarm like flies" around the speaker's poetic self. At first, he does not reject the children but pities them, because they are unaware of the larger world and that the "silvery freighter" might "pass them by." Their ignorance is met with an equal amount of ambivalence as the speaker muses on what it would be like to share their lives. For a brief moment, he imagines a return to a physical state where the sea and island life are enough. A tone of resignation, however, enters as the stanza concludes with the thought that the experience of homecoming can be bereft of feelings of warmth and security.

The final stanza brings the reader back to the children. The speaker's poetic self has given them nothing, and they curse him for his lack of generosity. The natural environment remains threatening. He is tired and walks back to the village past an esplanade where "dead/ fishermen move their draughts in shade," probably a reference to the game of checkers rather than the fishermen's hauls. One of the fishermen smiles and nods in recognition, but the speaker views this gesture with the same detached mood, sarcastically commenting that the fisherman who nods gestures "as if all fate/ swayed in his lifted hand."

Forms and Devices

Walcott employs a tone of detachment in "Homecoming: Anse La Raye." At the beginning of the poem, the speaker uses the pronoun "we," implying that the speaker is addressing others who happen to share similar experiences. By the end of the second stanza, the speaker begins using the pronoun "you," referring to his separate poetic self. Because the poem plays on the idea of detachment and even alienation, the use of "you" is more effective but not totally exclusive: The speaker maintains a connection between the "we" of the first stanza and the "you" of the remainder of the poem. As a partially detached observer who uses the second person to observe his own actions, the speaker creates another less-subjective level of interaction with the surrounding environment and its people. This objectivity allows him to remove or dismiss most of the illusions one might possess when considering the experience of homecoming, especially on a Caribbean island.

The speaker gives the island and its people a voice. In a way, the speaker becomes the island. He employs alliteration, as in the use of the "s" sound to mimic the hissing sound of the surrounding sea as well as the ever-present trade winds. The repetitive nature of this device creates a lulling effect for the reader that imitates the constant and somewhat prosaic rhythms of island life.

The imagery in the poem is also symptomatic of the speaker's unbridled and sometimes harsh view of his home. Early in the poem, he refers to "Afro-Greeks" and "Helen." As the poem progresses, the speaker maintains contact with the world of antiquity and the world at large through the use of metaphor, simile, and personification. The fronds of the coconut palms are "salt-rusted/ swords," while the shells of sea crabs become "brittle helmets." The "barbecue of branches" on the beach are like "the ribs/ of sacrificial oxen on scorched sand." The use of these rather violent images strikes an unpleasant chord, as the reader is forced to wonder why the speaker thinks of his home this way. Yet the connection of the Caribbean culture with the cultures of the outside world is positive. The Caribbean region is associated with the "Middle Passage"—not a separate entity but part of the larger European, African, and American whole. The island and other islands like it, however, are encircled by an "infinite, boring, paradisal sea," an ocean that "sucks its teeth," where "frigates tack like buzzards." The black cliffs are not majestic, but they do "scowl" at the speaker's poetic self. This imagery gives the reader a glimpse at the actual place with its gloom, decay, and connection to the historical past.

Themes and Meanings

"Homecoming: Anse La Raye" is about estrangement from one's own culture as well as from the larger world. The title of the book in which this poem originally appeared supports this idea of separation or division. At one point in the poem, the speaker's poetic self becomes poignantly aware of the fact that "there are homecomings without home." His quandary is not easily explained. The island is viewed with an unbiased eye but also with a restrained rage. He attempts to see its natural beauty, but his attempt is stifled by the decay around him. The ocean becomes boring; its movement creates "the doom-/ surge-haunted nights." The comfort that one might associate with the constant caress of the sea gives way to rumbling turmoil. Standing on the beach with the children, he contemplates their fate and suggests that they may never get a chance to ride the "silvery freighter," which appears on the horizon as a symbol of human potential and freedom.

When the speaker's poetic self leaves the beach, he sees the "dead/ fishermen." One of the men appears to greet him, but the speaker's poetic self remains aloof. In one last reference to the fishermen, the speaker states that one of the men has "a politician's ignorant, sweet smile." This smile is benign, at least on the surface. The speaker possesses a negative yet sympathetic attitude toward these men. He has already pronounced them "dead." They are racked by a pervasive and destructive apathy. Their lack of concern creates a dilemma that borders on cannibalism—they are described as "eating their islands." Yet the speaker's pronouncement is paradoxical; fishermen are part of his personal history, but their apathy only reinforces his bittersweet feelings of estrangement. The gulfs that exist between the speaker and his past, the speaker and his island home, the speaker and the environment, the speaker and his people, and the speaker and himself all add to this alienation.

Another theme that is preponderant in the poem is the theme of rage, especially the rage that manifests itself as a reaction to the political, social, and economic domination of the Caribbean region by the old colonial powers. In the first stanza, the speaker refers to the lessons once learned and now forgotten involving "borrowed ancestors." He refers to himself (and others such as him) as "Afro-Greek." The speaker seems to relish the idea of cultural pluralism yet also finds it slightly distasteful. He is a victim, a castaway, the product of a colonial past. The resignation that he sees around him—the children who respond to the lure of the tourist's money and the dead fishermen who do not seem to find their lives bankrupt—is disturbing. He moves among his people as if he is a stranger, always guarded, never indicating that he feels totally comfortable or at ease. When the "silvery freighter" appears but then becomes a "silvery ghost," hope vanishes as well. The islanders' dreams and ambitions are dependent on a world still dominated by outside forces. The larger world seems content to ignore this island even though a few of its people, including the speaker, would welcome the opportunity to embrace it with a renewed spirit. Ultimately, their dilemma is emblematic of a far greater issue: The world abounds with all types of recognizable gulfs, and these gulfs, whether personal, cultural, or political, are not easily bridged.

Robert Bateman

HOMESICKNESS

Author: Marina Tsvetayeva (1892-1941)
Type of poem: Lyric
First published: 1936, as "Toska po rodine . . ."; in *Izbrannoe*, 1961; collected in
   Selected Poems, 1981

The Poem

"Homesickness" is a short lyric poem in ten stanzas, each composed of four irregular lines. The meter of the poem is fundamentally iambic, but, as is character- istic of Marina Tsvetayeva's lyrics, there are breaks formed by the ellipsis of verbs and nouns as well as by emotional exclamations. The rhythmical intonation creates a counterpoint to the formal metrical pattern.

"Homesickness" was written immediately before Tsvetayeva's return to the Soviet Union. Tsvetayeva had emigrated to Europe (first to Berlin, then Prague, and finally to Paris) in 1922. Although the title of the lyric suggests that the poet is longing to return to her homeland, it becomes clear that the poem actually expresses the poet's ambivalence about returning to a place that may no longer be home. The title, in- stead, concerns the poet's desire to find a place where she and her poetry will be understood and welcomed.

Although Tsvetayeva often projected herself in the image of mythic or literary figures, this poem is written in the first person with no distinction implied between the poet and the speaker. Tsvetayeva's work is often noted for its intimate tone and emotional candor. Considering that most of Tsvetayeva's work is autobiographical in nature, and often confessional, it is helpful for readers of her poetry to be aware of certain biographical details.

Tsvetayeva left the Soviet Union, like many of her contemporaries, disillusioned with the outcome of the October Revolution. The time she spent outside her country, particularly the last decade in Paris, was also difficult. She found little acceptance for her writing in either the Soviet Union or among the Russian writers in the Pari- sian émigré community, which made her living situation difficult for most of her life. Ultimately, Tsvetayeva chose to return to the Soviet Union, where she later committed suicide.

The first four stanzas of the poem describe the alienation she feels from society: She has no place to call her own. The next three stanzas elaborate on the isolation she feels from other human beings. She exclaims that she will be misunderstood in any language, implying that she'll be misunderstood in Russia as well as in Europe. People with someplace to call their native land and with a nationality to serve as an identity will not understand her since she lacks this sort of "native stain." Further- more, she will be misunderstood because she seeks to escape everyday reality, while the nameless, faceless "they" of the poem are immersed in it.

In the seventh stanza, she explains that her soul is outside the measure of time, so she will never be understood by readers of the twentieth century. In the last two stanzas, she emphasizes her detachment from her homeland in particular. In the last two lines of the poem, however, she suggests that, if she had to call someplace home, she would choose Russia, which is symbolized by the rowanberry bush.

Forms and Devices

The meaning and language of Tsvetayeva's later lyric poetry is concentrated. It is designed to frustrate the reader looking for standard poetic forms and formulae. Since experimentation in sound and rhythm is vital in Tsvetayeva's poetry, much of the poem's charm is lost in translation. Tsvetayeva's experimentation with language, in combination with her unofficial status in the world of Soviet literature until the 1960's, explains why much of her work is not yet translated into English.

Tsvetayeva's elliptical style is striking. Because of the inflected nature of the Russian language, the omission of verbs and nouns (as well as flexibility in word order) is possible and common in everyday speech. Tsvetayeva exploits this aspect of the Russian language to experiment with new rhythms. Her language is bound closely with the expression of feeling. The feelings expressed in her poetry always seem intense because of its highly personal content.

Many of her lyrics are syntactic and thematic variations on one theme. Repetition of certain words and sounds is an important element of Tsvetayeva's poetry. The phrase that is repeated throughout this lyric is "it's all the same." This repetition functions in several ways. It emphasizes the indifference of the world toward the poet, but more significantly, indicates the poet's detachment from society. While every other person is part of a group, she remains an outsider. Other people have an identity defined by nation, yet the poet has no nationality. The repetition of "all" and "every" also emphasizes the lack of distinction between all people and places. Places and people seem to merge into one amorphous whole. The poet remains an outsider to this group.

The isolation of the poet is further emphasized by the use of plurals and the images of the crowd. While the rest of society is compared to a group of trees, she is the log that is left behind. Other people are "readers of newspapers," signifying not only their uniformity but also their attachment to the reality of present time. In contrast to this group, she is a poet who lives in all centuries.

Tsvetayeva's employment of plurals to describe people with whom she shares nothing in common and places to which she does not belong seems to present a dehumanized world. Houses are no longer homes. Instead, they are described as hospitals or barracks. People are not human. They have become "readers of newspapers" or part of a forest. Tsvetayeva's portrayal of herself is also dehumanized but in the sense that she is not part of the human world. She describes herself as a "captive lion." She adds that while her body may be trapped in this century, her soul is beyond time. The poet seems to be the only one with a soul and with an individual identity.

Notably, only one another image that does not directly refer to the poet is mentioned. The one thing that emerges out of the uniformity is the rowanberry, a bush indigenous to Russia and significant in the Russian literary tradition. Even though she does not truly feel a part of any society, Russia is the closest thing to a home that is possible for her in this world.

Themes and Meanings

"Homesickness" is a lyric about the poet's alienation from society, and about Tsvetayeva's alienation from society in particular. Tsvetayeva often takes a broad theme that has been traditional to lyric poetry and personalizes it. She was very familiar with the Western European literary tradition as well as the Russian tradition. The theme of the poet as an émigré from all nations is common in Romantic poetry, in which the poet is considered to be a visionary. The poet essentially is different from other human beings. In that respect, the poet is isolated from society.

Tsvetayeva herself reiterates this idea in the essay "Poet i vremia" (1932), or "The Poet and Time." She writes that "every poet is essentially an émigré, even in Russia." Tsvetayeva, however, personalizes this theme by expressing her own alienation as well. Not only is she isolated from others by her status as a poet, but she is essentially exiled from her homeland. She felt—although her poetry actually did have many admirers—that her poetry was not accepted or understood among the Russians living in emigration and, in later years, that there was no place for her poetry in the Soviet Union either. Tsvetayeva sought escape in her poetry, which, in effect, isolated her to an even greater extent.

Her conception of the poet in exile differs from that of other Romantic poets in an important respect. Even though she often seems proud of the way in which she stands out from the crowd, Tsvetayeva also admits that her role is a burden to herself and to others. The Symbolists, who were also writing while Tsvetayeva was active, saw poets as prophets in an almost religious sense. Tsvetayeva may have considered the poet's role to be like that of a prophet, but she emphasized the loneliness and misery rather than the glory of the poet.

Pamela Pavliscak

THE HORSES

Author: Ted Hughes (1930-   )
Type of poem: Lyric
First published: 1957, in *The Hawk in the Rain*

The Poem

"The Horses" is a thirty-eight-line poem in free verse, written mostly in two-line stanzas. Like many of Ted Hughes's poems, it reflects his fascination with nature, especially animals—their appearance and behavior, their own peculiar places in the world. The poem begins with the narrator in a bleak state of mind. Taking a walk in the dark before dawn could be invigorating, but he perceives "Evil air, a frost-making stillness," and his breath leaves "tortuous statues in the iron light." In these first few lines, Hughes paints a stark, dreamlike picture in black and gray.

Horses, a familiar enough sight during the day, become strange when the narrator sees ten of them in the gathering dawn. They do not react when he passes by. They seem to be objects, not living beings, chiseled out of a frigid landscape: "Grey silent fragments/ Of a grey silent world." The narrator, who listens "in emptiness on the moor-ridge," appears emotionally depleted.

His spiritual emptiness leaves him vulnerable to the morning breaking dramatically around him. He hears a bird (a curlew) cry out in the stillness. He sees the sun light up the landscape in orange and red. The single sound and the vibrant colors expose a new world—complete with water and distant planets in the sky—lurking immediately below the winter night's seemingly impenetrable surface.

In this poem, the sun does not rise; it erupts: "Silently, and splitting to its core tore and flung cloud,/ Shook the gulf open, showed blue,/ And the big planets hanging." As is often the case in Hughes's poems, a familiar occurrence in nature takes on a muscular force, a startling violence. The narrator, having watched the landscape erupt into color, turns again to the horses. Like the landscape, they are waking up. Their stony stillness gives way to small signs of life: "Their draped stone manes, their tilted hind-hooves/ Stirring under a thaw." The horses, however, remain stoically silent, at one with their surroundings.

The horses shape the observer's memory of the scene. He is overwhelmed by their appearance in a landscape transformed so swiftly from icy desolation to apocalyptic beauty. Described early in the poem as "huge" and "megalith-still," the horses are powerful creatures with the will to remain controlled and quiet even as the "frost showed its fires." While the narrator has described himself as empty and stumbling about as if he were "in the fever of a dream," the horses appear calm, sure of their place in the world, able to endure all things. The poem ends with the narrator hoping, in a sentence construction reminiscent of prayer, that he will always remember the horses. Significantly, he now identifies them as "my memory." They have become something both personal and abstract, and they seem to embody a spiritual resilience of which the narrator did not seem capable in the first lines of the poem.

Forms and Devices

"The Horses" is somber in style as well as content. Its many monosyllabic words help create its weighty, serious sound. It is necessary to pause repeatedly in a monosyllabic line such as "The frost showed its fires. But still they made no sound." The rhythm is further slowed in this instance by the long vowel sounds and the full stop in the middle of the line. Frequent alliteration adds to the poem's intensity. The repetition of initial sounds ("draining the darkness," "making no move," "hung heads patient as the horizons") creates a solemn, lingering echo.

The repetition of key words is also significant to the poem's overall effect. In stanza 6, for example, Hughes describes the horses with their "draped manes and tilted hind-hooves," and in stanza 15, he again mentions their "draped stone manes, their tilted hind-hooves." The repetition of words and images heightens the horses' unchanging quality. They have a permanence about them that is both unnerving and awe-inspiring.

Hughes also repeats the word "still" to great effect. It first appears as a noun in the second line, "a frost-making stillness," paradoxically suggesting a kind of active stasis. Then the horses are portrayed as "megalith-still." Though alive, the animals seem as fixed and static as enormous stones. After the sun rises, the description of the horses ("still they stood") suggests resilience as well as lack of movement. The next time they are described as still ("But still they made no sound"), the word evokes restraint, the power to resist the upheaval of the overwhelming sunrise. In its last use, "still" describes the poet's desire to remember the horses' quiet power ("May I still meet my memory").

Such a shift in usage is a subtle analogue to the shift in the poet's perceptions of the horses and the landscape. One can see a similar effect in Hughes's use of color imagery. In the poem's opening lines, everything is black and gray, dark and empty. Then the sunrise brings violent orange and red into the picture and exposes the blue gulf.

The colors are so powerful that the poet attempts to retreat to the dark woods where he had been earlier. Outside the woods, however, he sees the horses calmly tolerating the exposure that comes with daylight. In this new context, "the red levelling rays" and, in the last stanza, "the red clouds" are transformed into images as beautiful and memorable as the horses.

For a poem so loaded with visual images, "The Horses" places an intriguing emphasis on listening. This emphasis is underscored by the poem's own echoes and solemn rhythms. Yet the landscape described is profoundly silent, except for the curlew's cry in stanza 9. At the end, the speaker (in the "din of the crowded streets") wants to remember not only "hearing curlews" but also "Hearing the horizons endure."

The silent horizon, paradoxically, becomes an enduring sound in the poet's mind. Sight and sound, sound and silence, shape his memory of a scene. Hence his memory — to continue the process of silence naturally evolving into sound — becomes the poem that is read silently yet heard in one's own mind.

Themes and Meanings

While Hughes's longstanding interest in animals, birds, and fish does not always provide him with positive imagery — one thinks of his macabre "Crow" poems, for example — this early poem portrays horses in an admirable light. Horses, in fact, stand up better to Hughes's scrutiny than most other creatures. They seem to represent a strength of will and a natural grace that humans would do well to emulate.

Cold and darkness are initially supplanted by the feverish brilliance of red and orange light. Then the horses, lit by these fiery hues, give the revelation some substance. They are stoic figures capable of surviving brilliant light as well as gray silence, and the narrator seems to identify with them. He wants to remember their resilience, their ability to endure.

This poem is, in retrospect, rather poignant, because not much of Hughes's later work provides for redemption. Many of his poems, in fact, contain grotesque analogies highlighting human shortcomings and self-degradation. In "Crow's First Lesson" (1970), for example, God attempts to teach the bird to say "love." The experiment is an abject failure, as these two strange lines suggest: "Crow retched again, before God could stop him./ And woman's vulva dropped over man's neck and tightened." Unlike the majestic horses, the crow evokes all that is sordid and unresolved in man's relationship with God, as well as in men's and women's relations with each other.

Another perspective on Hughes's animal poems is presented by the poem "Roe Deer" (1979). Similar to "The Horses" in its first-person consideration of animals at dawn, the poem describes two deer making their way past the narrator. Impressed with "their two or three years of secret deerhood," he wants to enter their world but cannot do so. "Roe Deer" ends with the animals vanishing in the snow.

In the later poem, Hughes seems preoccupied with the fleeting quality of inspiration. Although the deer are depicted in a positive light, they vanish before the narrator can grasp their full meaning. "The Horses," by contrast, depicts an emblem of endurance. Like the fleeting image of the deer, however, the horses now exist only in memory. The poet must evoke the huge, silent animals in words in order to savor that memory fully.

It is hard — particularly in the light of Hughes's later work — to ignore the poem's equally memorable images of despair and emptiness. The narrator's vulnerability in the face of the sunrise and the horses is extreme. There is not much separating the sustaining image of the horses and the poem's other images of violence and despair.

It seems possible, given the attention he pays to the frigid darkness, that he will recollect the "evil air" as often as he recollects the horses. The poem's prayerful conclusion may also be interpreted as unfulfilled longing, since even the powerful memory of the horses may not stem the tide of noise and years.

Hilary Holladay

THE HORSESHOE FINDER

Author: Osip Mandelstam (1891-1938)
Type of poem: Ode
First published: 1923, as "Nashedshii podkovu"; in *Stikhotvoreniya*, 1928;
   collected in *Modern Russian Poetry*, 1967

The Poem

"The Horseshoe Finder" is an ode patterned, to a degree, after Pindar, as attested by its subtitle, "A Pindaric Fragment." Its ninety-seven lines compose nine stanzas of various length. It is the longest poem written by Osip Mandelstam; it is also one of the very few poems he wrote in unrhymed free verse.

The poem opens with a choruslike description of a pine forest with numerous tall trees. The observers look at the forest primarily from a utilitarian point of view, wondering how many ships could be built from these pine trees and how the trees would fare in storms. The seafarer, "in his thirst for space" and eagerness to go to sea, is also trying to figure out how a ship can be built, comparing the raggedness of the sea to the firmness of the earth.

In stanza 2, the point of view is again that of the "we" of the chorus. They empathize with the planks and boards of the ship built long ago, not by the peaceful carpenter of Bethlehem but by another one, the father of wanderings and friend of seafarers. They envisage, now in retrospect, that the boards were once tall trees standing on a mountain ridge. Having completed the introduction, the poet is ready to "tell his story," but he is uncertain at which point to begin. The perspective shifts to a more modern time, in which everything "cracks and rocks" and the ships are replaced by two-wheeled carts breaking themselves to pieces at a racetrack.

In the next stanza, the poet hails the maker of a song, not the anonymous one but the one who put his name to it, thus assuring its long life and gaining for himself a headband reserved for heroes of antiquity. The fifth stanza presents the poet's musing about the transformation of the air into water, of water into crystal, and finally of crystal into earth, tracing the normal process throughout history. Suddenly, after he has been concerned with the course of history and the passage of time, in the sixth stanza the poet makes a statement that divides the poem in half: "The fragile chronology of time comes to an end." Expressing his gratitude for all that has transpired in the past, the poet, switching to the first person, complains that he is confused, that he has lost count, and that an erstwhile glorious era now rings hollow. Even though the sound is still ringing, the stallion lies in the dust, unable to run anymore.

In the last two stanzas, the poet seems to be resigned to his fate. He has nothing more to say, even though his lips still keep the shape of the last word; yet not everything is hopeless. Someone finds a horseshoe of the stallion long gone, polishes it, and puts it over his threshold. Thus, even though time and the era have cut the poet like a coin, so that "there's not even enough of me left for me," the final prognosis is that there will still be horseshoes and coins to be found by later generations.

Forms and Devices

"The Horseshoe Finder" is an ode to the nameless horseshoe finder—and to Mandelstam's poetry. It was written at a time when Mandelstam thought that his poetry had become a fossil itself.

Connections with Pindar are obvious. Among the Pindaric features is, for example, a tendency to leap from one subject to another without transition. The myths are presented only in their essentials, while the rest is left for the reader to supply. The subject of a horse is also very Pindaric, as is the elegiac mood. Mandelstam's own poetic power, though, makes the poem distinctly his own.

As in most of his poems, Mandelstam relies here on images and metaphors as his strongest poetic devices. The image of stately pine trees, "free to the very top from their shaggy burden," adds beauty to their usefulness as material for ships. The poet returns to this image to point out once again that they are living beings as they moan under the saltless downpour, clamoring for a pinch of salt—that is, flavor. When describing the transformation of the elements, the poet says that "the air is kneaded until thick as earth." Perhaps the most beautiful image is that of a dying horse; the sharp arch of the neck still preserves the memory of a race, but the legs are now gone.

The most important metaphor is that of a ship, which has been used often in literature, both classical and modern, to represent poetry, among other things. When coupled with another metaphor, the racing two-wheeled carriage, which stands for modernization, the antithesis is complete. Furthermore, the change from boundless seas to a limited racetrack signals a loss of great proportions. Two other metaphors, the horseshoe and the coins, also play important roles in the poem. The horseshoe stands for two things: the glory that has been lost, and the value that has been recovered. While all glory must eventually pass, the value resulting from it can be preserved forever, provided it has been passed on to new generations. The horseshoe represents the preservation of great achievements in general, and of Mandelstam's poetry in particular. The fact that the horseshoe has been found and restored to its original beauty speaks for the validity of the poet's expectations.

The coin metaphor is somewhat less important and more negative; the poet seems to reverse himself and begins to doubt the permanence of things. Just as the coins can lose their value or be cut and disfigured, so the poet feels that "the era, trying to gnaw them in two, left the marks of its teeth on them." Through this metaphor, Mandelstam voices his pessimism about the future, in contrast to the optimism expressed by the horseshoe.

Themes and Meanings

By placing his emphasis on history and art in "The Horseshoe Finder," Mandelstam defines the poem's two basic themes: the passing of an era, and the capacity of art to survive throughout the ages.

Mandelstam often warned against the demise of civilization, most notably in his prose work "Gumanizm i sovremennost" ("Humanism and the Present," 1923). In many of his poems ("A Wandering Light at a Fearful Height," "The Age," and others), he raises the same issue, bemoaning the fact that the values of "the Golden Age" on which Western civilization is based are in danger of being replaced by a new, barbaric age. "The Horseshoe Finder" is the best example expressing those thoughts and sentiments.

The first two stanzas reveal Mandelstam's basic concept of history. The pristine world of antiquity, with its uncomplicated ways and closeness to nature, is personified by stately pine trees and ships, as well as by daring seafarers who were at home on boundless seas. Ships were built not by the peaceful carpenter of Bethlehem—a clear reference to Christ—but by an unnamed carpenter who loved travel and was a friend of sailors. The latter figure has been variously identified by critics as Joseph, Poseidon, and Peter the Great. Whichever interpretation is correct, the shipbuilder is a man of action, daring, and adventure—a mover of history.

The poet shifts to a different view of history when he states that the reckoning of the years of our age is coming to an end, presumably referring to the drastic changes in modern times in general and to the revolution in his own country in particular. The era now rings hollow, supported by no one, revealing indecision and hypocrisy. The deterioration of values is further underlined by a change from seafaring ships to race carts.

This pessimistic view of history is alleviated by the possibility that true values will survive, after all, as depicted by the metaphor of a horseshoe, which gives Mandelstam a chance to express his view of art. By finding a horseshoe, a future finder will be able not only to gain a correct picture of the past but also to realize the indestructibility of true art.

Toward the end of the poem, Mandelstam modifies the metaphor from a horseshoe to coins, undoubtedly to give vent to his despair about his personal situation in the 1920's and about his doubts of the survival of his own poetry. This momentary faintness of heart notwithstanding, Mandelstam's faith in the ultimate survival of art has been justified (by this poem, among others) and confirmed by the esteem he now enjoys more than ever.

Vasa D. Mihailovich

THE HOUSE IN THE HEART

Author: Naomi Shihab Nye (1952-   )
Type of poem: Lyric
First published: 1982; collected in *Yellow Glove*, 1986

The Poem

"The House in the Heart" is a free-verse poem with lines and stanzas of irregular length. The poem is written in the first person, with no particular distinction being made between the author and the one speaking; thus it takes on a confessional or private tone. The opening statement presents the problem of the poem—how to get through the day (and life) when one feels spiritually and emotionally empty. One does not know the specific occasion for this feeling of emptiness. It seems to exist almost like a form of weather, a depression that moves in like the "dark rain" outside. The speaker makes chamomile tea and watches the "little flowers" as they float in hot water. The chamomile flowers are desiccated and dead, inanimate, something the water uses. She says, "the water/ paint[s] itself yellow," while the flowers merely "float and bob"—a projection of her own feelings.

The speaker seems detached from life as the cars outside go "somewhere," but she does not venture to guess where. She feels no connection with them. Looking for some way to escape her depression, she makes the odd statement, "This is my favorite story," then talks about a "man with a secret jungle growing/ in his brain" who "says chocolate/ can make him happy." At this point, it is not clear whether her "favorite story" refers back to the cars swishing past or ahead to the man with the jungle in his brain. One is curious as to why either should be a "favorite story," especially since there is no real feeling of enjoyment here; perhaps she is simply trying to cheer herself up as one would distract and cheer a child by telling a story. Whatever the "favorite story" is, the reader does not get to hear it because when she imagines how much chocolate it would take to overcome her gloomy feelings, she says it would have to be "a bar/ heavy as a brick." The heaviness of the image conveys the heaviness of her mood. In an afterthought that is oddly amusing, given the melancholy tone of the poem, she adds that this chocolate bar would also have to have almonds. Then, she says, she would begin to whisper about "the house in the heart."

This "house in the heart" is a literal image of the chambers of a human heart, the "moth-wing ceilings" suggesting the heart's flutter and beat and the "cat-lip doors" its opening and closing valves. At the same time, the heart is a symbol of emotion. When one imagines the "penny-size rooms" of the heart, it becomes an image of diminution of feeling, small in size and in value.

At this point, at the center of the poem, there is a short, four-line stanza in which she tries to confront and accept the situation. Up to this point, she has been imagining some solution in making tea or eating chocolate—actions to satisfy the body. Now she rejects the importance of the body and says, "it's a porch, that's all." Her frustration is summed up in the words, "but I don't know/ what to do about it."

The wording at the beginning of the next stanza parallels that in the beginning of the poem as she returns to the problem of how to deal with the emptiness she feels. Common objects, such as the tea strainer she uses daily, seem unfamiliar. Some unhappy event has taken away the comfort and meaning of ordinary daily life so that her body is nothing but an envelope carrying messages she cannot remember.

She looks out the window at the darkness and bad weather, reflecting that the streetlights "will stay on late" in the unusual darkness. The poem ends with an image of the "house in the heart" in which there is "no one home." Love, emotion, maybe someone who once lived there—all are gone. One still does not know exactly what happened to bring things to this state, but the heart is an empty house, and the speaker is painfully aware of that emptiness. The word "cries" in the next-to-the-last line and the repetition of the words "no one home" end the poem on a note of mourning.

Forms and Devices

The form of the poem is open and improvisational: Line and stanza breaks are used to emphasize and to control the pace of the poem. The third stanza is a pivotal one, and the rest of the poem is organized around the resignation in that stanza.

Naomi Shihab Nye uses a fragmentary statement punctuated with a dash in the first stanza to give a questioning, inconclusive feeling to the poem. In general, punctuation and line breaks give a somewhat rambling feeling to the language, as if thoughts come slowly and with difficulty. When the speaker says, "With almonds," the two words come as an afterthought, simulating the speaker's meandering thoughts. Punctuation in the fourth stanza, which also ends with a dash, similarly contributes to this feeling.

Dramatic metaphors and startling images are extremely important in this poem, particularly the extended metaphor of the house as a heart and the body as its porch. Images of the "moth-wing ceilings" and "cat-lip doors" of the heart are beautiful and fantastic, yet slightly morbid.

Other objects and actions in the poem work metaphorically as outward signs of inner feelings. The act of brewing tea, the rain at the window, and the cars going by outside are used to externalize the speaker's state of mind. As her house feels strange to her and isolated by rain, darkness, and cold weather, so, too, her feelings are cut off by some sort of emotional bad weather. The frozen palm fronds outside suggest a death or loss. The dried flowers of the chamomile, the imagined bar of chocolate, and the idea of herself as an envelope containing no message she can remember all externalize her feelings dramatically. This is particularly important in a poem where the writer gives little specific information about any events that led to the poem and where the poem focuses on some pivotal moment extracted from some larger picture. Nye is particularly adept at such vivid capsule dramas, full of concrete detail and action, economical in development. One can only infer a world outside the focus of the poem—for the moment, the poem is the world. The repetition of "no one home, no one home" at the end simulates the ghostlike echo in an empty house and dramatizes the emptiness expressed by the speaker.

Themes and Meanings

Nye's poem is about dealing with grief or depression and the process of sustaining life when it seems that there is neither joy nor the will. One knows that the speaker is someone who in the past has brewed tea and has gone about her life full of "messages." She lives in a house in a neighborhood somewhere and has believed the body to be "important." What has gone wrong? One does not know, nor does one know how permanent this state is.

Presumably, people recover from grief and depression, but in the depths, it is hard to see past the moment and to imagine that things will ever be any better. If there is any hope in the poem, it is in a subdued feeling of amazement in the speaker's voice. The opening lines are not a question but a statement— "it is possible," the speaker says. No matter how empty one feels, it is possible to go through the motions of living, moving "through your own kitchen," trying to make sense of life.

The poem may be dealing with a spiritual crisis, or it may be an existential statement about the loss of meaning in life. Images of absence and the image of the palm tree injured or killed by cold weather suggest that this is about a particular loss— the loss of love or the death of a loved one— in which case, "no one home" means that someone is actually missing from the speaker's life, someone who occupied that place she calls the house in the heart.

Finally, however, one cannot know what circumstance gave rise to the poem, nor does one need to know. Like a piece of music that conveys a mood or state of mind, the poem uses concrete images to depict a state of profound depression. Though the speaker maintains an effort to go through the motions of life— making tea and looking out the window— the poem ends without any real comfort.

Barbara Drake

HOWL

Author: Allen Ginsberg (1926-   )
Type of poem: Elegy
First published: 1956, in *Howl and Other Poems*

The Poem

Allen Ginsberg's own description of "Howl"—"A huge sad comedy of wild phrasing"—is an accurate summary of its largest structural outlines and predominant moods. Written in a version of open verse that employs as its fundamental unit a series of individual image clusters, it is divided into three parts, each marked by a specific rhythmic pattern. The first part, with its fervent declaration that "the best minds" of a generation have been driven to madness, immediately establishes the poet as an engaged witness, while the compelling claim that opens the poem, "I have seen . . . ," is a conscious parallel to Walt Whitman's active participation ("I was the man; I suffered; I was there") in the critical moments of his time.

Taking as his subject the "angelheaded hipsters" who represent an undiscovered underground community of artists, junkies, street people, mutants, and other outcasts, Ginsberg uses the first part of "Howl" to tell, in compressed form, the life highlights of people who have been damaged or destroyed by their inability to fit into American society during the Eisenhower years. Using the word "who" to begin each miniature biographical fragment, Ginsberg gradually develops a picture of an entire counterculture, the separate images building toward a mosaic of madness and desperation, but a mosaic which is informed by the manic energy of inspiration and excitement that made these people so distinct.

The motive behind the actions he describes is the achievement of a transcendent vision of existence, and the range of experience he covers is transnational, including urban jungles and open plains, academic settings and back alleys. His "angelheaded hipsters" use every available transformative agent, as well as their untapped mental capacity, to reclaim a world that has gone awry. Part 2 of the poem is an attempt to identify the reasons that society has become so hostile for these "remarkable lamblike youths," and after asking what "bashed open their skulls and ate up their brains and imagination," Ginsberg locates the core of corruption as a "monster of mental consciousness" that he designates "Moloch" after the Canaanite Fire God (in Leviticus) whose worship required human sacrifice.

The entire section is written as a composite of images that coalesce into the supersymbol of monstrosity which stands for every negative element in American life. Each long-breath line is set off by the word "Moloch," and the repetition of the word within the line as well generates a cascade of doom overwhelming the political realm ("Congress of sorrows"), the social ("Whose blood is running money"), the sexual ("Lacklove and manless in Moloch!"), and the personal ("who frightened me out of my natural ecstasy!"). The inventory of ugliness culminates in a series of staccato statements, a chant of wrath—"demonic industries! spectral nations! invincible madhouses!"—that suggests a swirl of chaos in which people are engulfed, their lives governed by forces beyond their ken.

The third part of the poem is an attempt to set the spiritual strength of an artistic intelligence against the materialistic forces responsible for this spiritual desolation. This section is addressed to Carl Solomon, a man Ginsberg met when they were both patients in Columbia Presbyterian Medical Center, and places the poet in a kind of solidarity with Solomon, who is being treated in Rockland Hospital. Solomon stands for all the "lambs" of part 1, and each line in this section begins with the affirmation "I'm with you in Rockland," which is modified by aspects of Solomon's ingenious, creative, and anarchic method for spiritual survival. The poem concludes with a presentation of what Ginsberg called "the answer," followed by the last image, an extension of the community of love and brotherhood into a dreamlike future of promise and hope.

Forms and Devices

Before writing "Howl," Ginsberg had worked primarily on what he called "short-line free verse" in the measures of American speech and in more traditional forms based on centuries-old British prototypes. Describing himself as "sick and tired" of what he was doing, and fearing that his work was not "expressionistic enough" because he could not "develop a powerful enough rhythm," he decided to follow his "romantic inspiration" and write without concern for precedents or conventions of any kind.

He thought that his subject ("queer content my parents shouldn't see") would probably prohibit publication, so he felt free to compose without preconception or limitation. Guided by what he called his "Hebraic-Melvillian bardic breath"—a version of Old Testament prophetic proclamation, modified by Herman Melville's conversions of those rhythms into the syntax of American prose narrative—Ginsberg worked out an effective, original formal structure which was completely missed by most critics at the time of publication. Noting in a letter that none of the reviewers had "enough technical interests to notice" what he considered the "obvious construction of the poem," Ginsberg explained (or taught) the poem himself in his "Notes for *Howl and Other Poems*."

According to his account, after his initial declaration of his subject, the fate of the "best minds" (his narcotics-using bohemian community), Ginsberg depended on repetition of the word "who" to keep the beat, an approach influenced by Jack Kerouac's ideas about improvisation akin to modern jazz. He then built "longer and shorter variations on a fixed base," elaborate images lifting off each basic measure that were written for their meaning as well as "the beauty of abstract poetry" and the latent energy found in "awkward combinations . . . disparate things put together." The repeated "who" operates as a ground beneath each "streak of invention," but even with this technique, Ginsberg worried that it would be difficult to sustain a long line in a long poem. To put "iron poetry back into the line," Ginsberg believed that his "concentration and compression of imagistic notations" such as "hydrogen jukebox" or "bop kaballa" would function like a haiku, in which juxtapositions encourage the brain to make a connection in a leap of energy, which he called "lightning in the mind." Ginsberg also likened this method to the "cubist phrasing" of Cezanne's painting. In a further attempt to keep the line moving, he employed "primitive naïve grammar," which condensed phrases by removing words not totally necessary, and eliminated what he thought were "prosey articles" that dulled the rhythm. The goal of his efforts was to "*build up* large organic structures," and he believed that all of his previous work as a poet was involved in balancing the lines to avoid any loose or dead areas that would leach energy out of the poem.

Parts 2 and 3 follow a similar strategy. The framing question of the second part calls forth the series of images of Moloch, Ginsberg's ultimate symbol of the evil and destructive forces of the modern world. Each line operates as a separate stanza, with the line itself broken into "exclamatory units" or "component short phrases"; the repeated use of the word "Moloch" acts as a "rhythmical punctuation." The whole section builds toward a climax in which the poet intones individual concepts as exclamations of mental fixity ("Dreams! Adorations! Illuminations!"), concluding part 2 in an explosion of psychic energy leading to a mood of ecstatic abandon developed by a chant designed to approximate or induce frenzy.

Part 3 is conceived as a "litany of affirmation" that restores the tranquillity which the Moloch passages have disrupted; Ginsberg based it to some extent on the model of Christopher Smart's "Jubilate Agno" ("rejoice in the lamb"), just as the Moloch structure is partially based on Percy Bysshe Shelley's *Epipsychidion* (1821). Smart's use of statement-counterstatement lies behind Ginsberg's repetition of a phrase base ("I'm with you in Rockland") as an anchor, with the response or extension that begins "Where . . ." "elongating itself slowly" to form a pyramidal structure. The individual units are often surrealistic, as Ginsberg attempts to convey the imaginative, often oblique sense of existence for which Solomon stands. The final unit in the pyramid is purposefully too long for one line, or one breath unit, and its textual density is developed to carry the full weight of Ginsberg's last revelation ("where I open out and give the answer"). This final unit is open-ended, containing no rigid punctuation device, as if to suggest the beginning of a journey "in the Western night" that replaces the initial journey into nightmare that was introduced as the poem began with an image of "streets at dawn."

Themes and Meanings

During the 1950's, American literature seemed to reflect the mood of life in the postwar world. The general ethos of caution, conformity, and complacency that marked the political and cultural climate was reinforced by mainstream writing cited by reviewers and celebrated by academicians. Yet an alternative tradition, as authentically American as the more prominent conservative one, was gaining energy and substance, and the landmark reading at the Six Gallery in 1955 signaled its emergence into public consciousness. The central feature of this event was Allen Ginsberg's first public performance of "Howl," a moment recognized by most of those present as a turning point in American literary history.

What Ginsberg accomplished was the creation of a territory for writing that was radically different from the narrow, nearly exhausted modes of expression approved by the literary establishment. By example, he validated a literary possibility that ran counter to, or way beyond, the prevalent positions on form, style, and subject. The ardor of his voice—the overwhelming, unreserved expression of his commitment to a vision of enlightenment—stood in almost shocking contrast to the generally accepted modes of ironic distance, elevated diction, and formal argument. To the critics who reacted with dismay or derision, "Howl" seemed like a regression to a subliterary realm of vulgarity and excess. Ginsberg's poem, which demanded an oral presentation to achieve its full effect, however, reclaimed the power of the poet's singing voice from those who emphasized the appearance of the poem in print as its most important placement. He used chants to accumulate rhythmic power and modulated moods through schemes of sound, contributing to an audience involvement that compelled a participation beyond a measured critical evaluation. By devising a structure that was uniquely suited to this purpose, Ginsberg was also forcing a reconsideration of the whole idea of form, an agenda which he shared with Charles Olson, Robert Creeley, and others who agreed with Whitman's idea that "Old forms, old poems . . . here in this land are exiles."

"Howl" not only captured the spirit of an underground culture but also conveyed it in a specifically American voice, employing not only a version of American vernacular speech but also elements of street slang, the argot of the junkie and the hipster, conversational modes, an amalgam of jazz cadences, and the tempo of several species of sermon. By demonstrating that poetry could include styles of language hitherto regarded as inappropriate for literary expression, Ginsberg drew informal, even "improper" speech into the poetic field. Concomitantly, his subject, "the remarkable lamblike youth" he describes in part 1, is part of a world ignored by "serious" writers circa 1950, and Ginsberg's attention to radical activists, outrageous artists, sexual "deviants," and experimenters with forbidden substances prefigured the explosion of variance and defiance of the 1960's. "Howl" presents this nascent counterculture and attempts to explain its meaning and importance, extoll its values, celebrate its moments of beauty, and defend its seemingly aberrant and rebellious behavior. The thrust of the poem is an insistence on the importance of plurality and tolerance as components of an ideal America—an America in which examples of individuality and eccentricity would be accepted so that a society built on greed and materialism might be transformed and redeemed.

Like Walt Whitman, Ginsberg has always written toward the restoration of a "lost America of love," and the style of "spiritual revelation and prophetic certainty" he devised for "Howl" was crucial to this goal. A poem begun as a celebration of creativity and subversion ends as an anthem of vision and enlightenment.

Leon Lewis

HUGH SELWYN MAUBERLEY

Author: Ezra Pound (1885-1972)
Type of poem: Poetic sequence
First published: 1920

The Poem

Hugh Selwyn Mauberley is a sequence in two parts. The first part consists of thirteen poems dated 1919; the second part contains five additional poems dated 1920. The quatrain is the dominant stanza in both parts.

The title concerns the career of Hugh Selwyn Mauberley, an aesthetic poet of the old school. The name, like "J. Alfred Prufrock" in T. S. Eliot's poem, suggests a somewhat stuffy, old-fashioned, Milquetoast character (*mauviette* means "Milquetoast" in French). The subtitle, "Life and Contacts," suggests affinities with the tradition of the novel, and also a certain modern superficiality to Mauberley's career.

Mauberley is only one of the poem's poet personae. As K. K. Ruthven explains in *A Guide to Ezra Pound's Personae* (1969), "Self-analysis produced the two personae in the poem, Mauberley and E. P., each of whom is an oversimplification of radically different elements in Ezra Pound himself." E. P., the poet concerned with renewing rather than reiterating the poetic tradition, is the dominant persona in part 1.

Sections I-V introduce E. P. and state the present situation of poetry after World War I. Having studied poetry in the "obstinate" British isles, the American E. P. is "out of key with his time" in striving to "resuscitate the dead art/ Of poetry" and to wring "lilies from the acorn," an impossibility in an age of "tawdry cheapness" which demands an image of "its accelerated grimace." The modern age believes only in "the market place," not in the beautiful, in either pagan or Christian form. The apostrophe to Apollo asks, ironically, who deserves the "tin wreath" in this "botched civilization," which sacrificed a generation "For a few thousand battered books."

The next four sections (titled but unnumbered) assess the recent history of English poetry, from the Pre-Raphaelite aestheticism of Dante Gabriel Rossetti and Algernon Charles Swinburne in "Yeux Glauques" to the raptures of the Decadents Ernest Dowson and L. P. Johnson in "Siena Mi Fe'; Disfecemi Maremma." "Brennbaum" caricatures the "stiffness from spats to collar/ Never relaxing into grace" of the dandy Max Beerbohm as a ridiculous posture for the poet, whose business is grace, not polish. It is better than the view of "Mr. Nixon," however, for whom avarice is greater than aesthetics: "The 'Nineties' tried your game/ And died, there's nothing in it." In other words, poetry does not pay.

The final group of poems before the envoi (sections X through XII) is a series of portraits. The "stylist," true to Mr. Nixon's analysis, remains "Unpaid, uncelebrated" for his artistic accomplishments and leaves the "sophistications and contentions" to raise pigs in the country with an "uneducated mistress." The middle-class woman of section XI, with her superficial education, is bereft of any aesthetic passion (much less eroticism), her only "instinct" being limited to what "her grandmother/ Told her would fit her station." The only instinct in dully respectable Ealing is the instinct for social survival. For Lady Valentine of section XII, poetry is fashion, "her border of ideas," such as they are in her literary salon. The poet concludes that poetry has been ousted in favor of journalism and commerce.

The "Envoi" is the poet's swan song, a tour de force that incorporates the poetic tradition in the free-verse adaptation of a seventeenth century song. Unconverted to the tawdry cheapness of the Mr. Nixons, the poet reasserts his belief in the erotic and the aesthetic, figuring himself and his beloved as "two dusts": "Siftings on siftings in oblivion,/ Till change hath broken down/ All things save Beauty alone." In the end, for him at least, beauty remains the goal of art.

In part 2, beginning with "Mauberley: 1920," the poet Hugh Selwyn Mauberley appears for the first time. Unlike E. P., with his wry critique of aesthetes and philistines, Mauberley is not ready to break out of the ivory tower of his aesthetic reveries. He is a minor artist, "lacking the skill/ To forge Achaia." Section II shows that he is also unable to seize on passion, except in "retrospect," so his art is like the "epilogues" of "the still stone dogs" whose mouths are left "biting empty air." "The Age Demanded" shows Mauberley unable to apply his art "to the relation of the state," because to him beauty is a way of making the month "more temperate." This inability results in his neglect of his craft in favor of "maudlin confession/ Irresponse to human aggression," and finally to his "Exclusion from the world of letters." In section IV, Mauberley finds himself washed up (in more ways than one) on the shore of one of his own tropical reveries, with this epitaph: "I was/ And I no more exist;/ Here drifted/ An hedonist." "Medallion," which ends *Hugh Selwyn Mauberley*, has often been thought to be Mauberley's only poem, but it is more likely that it is Pound at last throwing off the masks of E. P. and Mauberley (if not uniting them) and speaking in his own voice, an example of his vision of the future of poetry.

Forms and Devices

Pound is a master of poetic technique. T. S. Eliot called him "the superior craftsman." As a student, Pound vowed to know "everything" about verse and meter, and in *Hugh Selwyn Mauberley* he gives a virtuoso performance. The "Envoi," for example, is a creative adaptation of Edmund Waller's seventeenth century "Go, Lovely Rose," to his modern purposes. Pound offered *Hugh Selwyn Mauberley*'s quatrains, modeled on Théophile Gautier's *Émaux et camées* (1852), as a "countercurrent" to the excesses of free verse. Pound's quatrains are masterful in their fluidity and in their variation of meter and rhyme.

Off-rhyme is used to satiric effect, often bilingually or in conjunction with an ironic use of myth. In part 2, the modern age's "accelerated grimace" is contrasted with the ancient Greek's "Attic grace." A similar effect is achieved in "The sale of half-hose has/ Long since superseded the cultivation/ Of Pierian roses." Ancient names are rhymed with present vulgarities: "Samothrace" with "market place"; "Pisistratus" with "rule over us"; "Milesien" with "Englishmen." Bilingual rhymes are also used: *"Tpoin*/leeway" and *"Oeou*/upon" (Greek); "later/*patria*" and "slaughter/*decor*" (Latin); *"trentuniesme*/diadem" (French).

At first glance, *Hugh Selwyn Mauberley* may seem to be an intimidating web of foreign phrases, quotations, literary allusions, and impenetrable puzzles. The poem is dense with Pound's erudition, but the reader should not be deterred. This erudite scaffolding, while adding to a full understanding of the poem's architecture, need not detract from one's appreciation. The foreign phrases, for example, may seem formidable, but they are rarely essential. Their very presence is, in a sense, more important than their meaning. Like glass fragments in a kaleidoscope, they reflect upon one another for their color.

The allusions to the poetic tradition, however, are essential, since *Hugh Selwyn Mauberley* is a poem about poetry, especially modern poetry's relationship to the tradition. Pound believed that poetry should incorporate all that culture had to offer in the way of language, philosophy, history, religion, myth, and literature. His one proviso was that the poet should "Make it new."

The poem is not written from a single point of view. Instead readers overhear Mauberley and E. P. thinking or composing, snatches of conversation, or omniscient pronouncements, not unlike the variable point of view in a novel. (Pound even called the poem "an attempt to condense the [Henry] James novel.") Still, the poem manages to present a unified consciousness against the background of its time, even though E. P. and Mauberley are distinct halves of that consciousness.

One way of making the tradition reflect upon the present is the ironic use of myth. Like James Joyce and T. S. Eliot, Pound invokes myth to contrast the lusterless present with the heroic past. Daphne in the drawing room in section XII has a precedent in Alexander Pope's mock-epic *The Rape of the Lock* (1712), but what is original in Pound is the collage effect achieved by juxtaposing quotations of dead and living languages, real and fictional poets, myth and history. From such a kaleidoscopic range of allusion one really does get a sense of the vital presence of the supposedly dead past, a quality that Pound insisted was at the heart of a living culture.

Themes and Meanings

Hugh Selwyn Mauberley is a poem about poetry. Unlike many such poems, however, it is not so much a justification of its own existence as a speculation into what poetry might become. In Pound's poetry leading up to *Hugh Selwyn Mauberley*, Hugh Kenner has said in *The Poetry of Ezra Pound* (1951), one can see "the history of the purification of our post-Victorian speech." In this poem, Pound self-consciously charts that purification by evaluating the state of the art (part 1, I-V), discussing the recent history of English poetry (part 1, VI-IX), examining the cultural climate of poetry's audience (part 1, X-XII), recapping the tradition ("Envoi"), exorcizing one aspect of his own poetic weaknesses in the form of Mauberley himself (part 2, I-IV), and then, dropping the masks of E. P. and Mauberley, finally offering an example in his own voice of what the future of poetry might be in "Medallion."

As Pound's own footnote to the poem explained, *Hugh Selwyn Mauberley* is a "farewell to London," but it is also a farewell to all that the "obstinate isles" of Britain offered him in the way of literary influence and society. Like John Ruskin's "Kings' Treasuries," this is Pound's indictment of a society inimical to the arts. E. P. had come to London from a "half savage country," it is true, with only the rudiments of a poetic sensibility: He had the passions without the craft, and so was "wrong from the start." As his craft grew, the age demanded something more than the "obscure reveries" of the Romantic's "inward gaze," but something less than "the 'sculpture' of rhyme."

World War I, with its grotesque wastage, only underscored the bankruptcy of the civilization with its prizing of statues and books over human life. Yet one laudable result of the war was the shock that breeds honest expression, "frankness as never before," although this expression for some comes as "laughter out of dead bellies." The problem is that those who fought in the trenches are not those who control the literary salons of the postwar period, the hollow laughter of which competes with the grotesque laughter of the dead.

Pound's interest in the Pre-Raphaelites and Decadents was based on their devotion to art for art's sake, a faulted view but one in which passions could be sincerely explored, unlike the views of their critics, the moralistic Buchanans and the materialistic Mr. Nixons. In the "yeux glauques" of Elizabeth Siddal — the ill-fated wife and model of Pre-Raphaelite poet and painter Dante Gabriel Rossetti, and model for Edward Burne-Jones's *Cophetua and the Beggar Maid*, which "preserved those eyes" — one sees reflected the beginning of the late-Victorian conflict between the aestheticism of Rossetti and Swinburne and the prim respectability of Robert Buchanan, who in his "Fleshly School of Poetry" attacked them for their pagan sympathies. In such a society, Edward FitzGerald's 1859 translation of the *Rubáiyát of Omar Khayyám* could only be "still-born."

Yet it is the hedonism of the *Rubáiyát* and the English Decadence that Mauberley's (and in part Pound's) own expression is based on. Like Brennbaum, whose art is a posture, stiffness never relaxing into grace, Mauberley's art consists of "Firmness," but "Not the full smile." It is "an art/ In profile." When he tires of the extra effort it requires to go beyond technique into new beauties of grace, he relaxes not into grace but into "maudlin confession." He regresses into the kind of *egoism a deux* that Rossetti had with Elizabeth Siddal, except that Mauberley has only his own reverie to keep him company.

Only in "Medallion" does Pound show the purity of poetry "in porcelain." Reminiscent of Rossetti's prefatory sonnet to his sequence *The House of Life* (1869), "Medallion" has the effect of turning the language into what Rossetti calls "a moment's monument." It is in this way that Pound shows one direction, within the strictures of the tradition and before his experiments with the *Cantos* (1917-1970), that the purified language of post-Victorian speech can go in poetry.

Richard Collins

THE HUMAN ABSTRACT

Author: William Blake (1757-1827)
Type of poem: Lyric
First published: 1794, in *Songs of Innocence and of Experience*

The Poem

"The Human Abstract" is a short poem of twenty-four lines divided into six quatrains. The title refers to the human capacity to create false structures of belief through excessive use of the rational part of the mind.

In the first quatrain, the speaker offers his opinions on moral and social issues in a way that justifies the existing order. He says that without poverty, there would be no way for people to exercise pity or compassion, and that if everyone were happy, there would be no opportunity to relieve the suffering of others.

The same speaker, who obviously includes himself among the compassionate and merciful, continues in the first two lines of the second quatrain. He gives his explanation of how order is preserved in a society. When there is "mutual fear" among people, the result is peace; fear keeps everyone from breaking the rules of society. Although self-love (what the speaker here calls "selfish loves") always predominates, it is in everyone's interest to accept the social order and the restrictions it imposes. If every individual were allowed to gratify every personal desire, everyone would feel threatened and insecure.

In line 7, another speaker takes over, and the poem is given over to his attack on the views of the first speaker. This is clearly William Blake's own voice. He states that when people accept the views of the first speaker, the result is a cruel society. A false philosophy spreads its tentacles everywhere and traps the innocent. In the name of religion and compassion, the seeds of Christian "humility" are planted. The word has a bitter edge to it, because humility to Blake meant only subservience to a pernicious and illusory view of God and human nature. The seed grows into a tree, an imposing edifice that overspreads everything and cuts out the light of the sun to produce a "dismal shade/ Of Mystery." Mystery was another pejorative term for Blake. Taking his cue from the Book of Revelation (17:5), in which the Whore of Babylon is said to be named Mystery, Blake often used the term to refer to false religion. Here the speaker adds that caterpillars and flies (the representatives of organized religion) feed on this Tree of Mystery.

In the fifth quatrain, the speaker explains what this tree of false religion and false morality produces: deceit, but it is a deceit that seems sweet and healthful to those who are under its spell and appears to provide them with all the sustenance they need. The speaker, however, points to what he sees as the truth of the matter: In the tree, where its branches are thickest, lives the raven, a symbol of death.

The final quatrain brings the speaker's point home with considerable force. The tree that contains such poison is not to be found in nature or in anything that exists outside the mind of man; it grows in the human brain itself.

Forms and Devices

Blake's poems often grow in meaning when the illustrations that accompany them are taken into account. The design for "The Human Abstract" shows a bearded old man sitting under a tree, tangled up in its fallen branches. The branches resemble ropes or chains and seem to sprout directly from his brain. They also seem to be arranged to resemble part of a human skeleton, which brings out the idea implied in the text of the poem that conventional religion sucks the life out of people. The old man is an early depiction by Blake of his mythological figure Urizen, who represents the rational faculty of man when it no longer works in harmony with man's other faculties. Setting himself up as the sole God, Urizen becomes a tyrant, but, as the design shows, the enslaver is himself trapped by his own creation. This illustrates the images of snares and baits in the poem. Even the lines of Urizen's beard seem to suggest the branches of the Tree of Mystery.

"The Human Abstract" is the first poem in which Blake used the symbol of the Tree of Mystery. He was to use it many times afterwards, notably in *The Book of Ahania* (1795), in which Urizen, having broken away from the other faculties, finds the Tree springing up from under his own heel. The symbol is derived from the tree of the knowledge of good and evil, of which Adam and Eve ate the fruit, as recorded in Genesis 2:9. Blake interpreted this tale as indicative of a fall into the strictures of conventional morality, under which human desires and actions were classified into good and evil. To Blake this was a piece of judgmental nonsense that perverted the innocence and purity of human desire and led to corruption and self-deceit. The Tree of Mystery, for example, also appears in another of the *Songs of Experience*, "The Poison Tree," in which the devastating effects of the self-restraint known as "Christian forbearance" (the original title of the poem) are laid bare.

The other symbols in this heavily didactic poem are related to the tree symbol and form a straightforward part of the poem's allegory. The seed of the tree is Cruelty, and the seed forms a root, Humility, which develops into branches. The identification of the caterpillar as a symbol of the priesthood is clear when the following passage in Blake's *The Marriage of Heaven and Hell* (1790-1793) is noted: "As the caterpillar chooses the fairest leaves to lay her eggs on, so the priest lays his curse on the fairest of joys." Continuing the allegory, the fruits of the Tree are Deceit, and the true nature of the tree is revealed by the presence in its branches of the raven, ready to prey on those who have fallen victim to the great illusion.

Themes and Meanings

When Blake published *Songs of Innocence* (1789) and *Songs of Experience* together, in 1794, he subtitled the collection, "Shewing the Two Contrary States of the Human Soul." The state of experience is shown as a cramped, fearful, and introspective attitude to life, completely opposed to the free-flowing, open, joyful impulses enjoyed by the speakers in the *Songs of Innocence*.

Many of the poems in the two books are deliberately paired. In a draft version of "The Human Abstract," Blake called it "A Human Image," which shows that it was intended as a contrast to "The Divine Image" in *Songs of Innocence*. Blake altered the title to convey, more directly, the true nature of the human image portrayed in the poem.

"The Divine Image" celebrates the virtues of mercy, pity, peace, and love as divine qualities dwelling within man. "The Human Abstract" satirizes each of these virtues, showing what happens to them when calculation replaces spontaneity and self-righteous morality usurps innocent joy and self-understanding. In "The Divine Image," mercy and pity are innocent expressions of the essence of humanity — the natural tenderness that flows from one human being to another and makes the human divine. The qualities do not depend for their existence on the presence of unhappiness or suffering. In "The Human Abstract," all this is changed. Mercy and pity somehow must be manipulated into existence and can be manifested only in an imperfect society created by human beings; they are not intrinsic to the soul.

The other two virtues become even more sinister. Peace results only from fear, quite unlike the sense conveyed in "The Divine Image," in which peace is "the human dress," its natural state of being. The same applies to love, which, in the innocent poem is "the human form divine," but in "The Human Abstract" is a state of mind that seeks its own advantage in everything and all love is self-love. The tragedy that Blake conveys with such force is that to those who are enmeshed in this web of limitation, self-deceit, and man-made cruelty it seems normal, inevitable, divinely ordained, and good, while the speaker who attacks these premises with such withering scorn is fully aware of the battery of interlocking rationalizations and phony arguments that are used to seduce the minds of the unwary.

Although Blake would later develop a complex mythological system to convey his ideas, this short poem contains the essence of his vision in stark simplicity: his opposition to any philosophy or creed that diminishes man's capacity to enjoy the unbounded bliss that is his birthright.

Bryan Aubrey

HUSWIFERY

Author: Edward Taylor (c. 1645-1729)
Type of poem: Meditation
First published: 1960, in *The Poems of Edward Taylor*

The Poem

"Huswifery," written in the late seventeenth century, is perhaps the best known work of Edward Taylor's poetic canon. It is meditational in form, one of several periodic exercises designed to place Taylor in a correct spiritual posture for communion with Christ, literally through the Lord's Supper and metaphysically through a spiritual union brought about by faith. Almost always religious, Taylor's poetry is influenced by the great English Metaphysical poets John Donne, George Herbert, and Richard Crashaw. Like them, he joined disparate fields of experience and often offered bizarre juxtapositions of images.

"Huswifery" takes its unusual rural imagery not only from the primitive location of Taylor's pastorate but also from his memories of his boyhood home in England, where he earned a living from the soil and perhaps sheared and spun wool as part of his daily labor. In his early youth, Taylor may also have been employed in the weavers' shops of the nearby town of Hinckley.

Stanza 1 implores God to use Taylor as His spinning wheel and to provide a holder for the flax of faith in the words of Holy Scripture. Taylor breaks down the weaving image further by associating functions of the parts of the spinning wheel with various human characteristics. His affections become the "flyers" (revolving arms which twist the wool into yarn); the soul is the spool which collects the thread; and conversation is seen as the reel which winds the spun wool.

Stanza 2 continues the clothes-making metaphor as Taylor becomes the loom whereon the refined thread is transformed into cloth. As in stanza 1, a part of the Trinity, the Holy Spirit, is necessary for this new function to occur. The Spirit will wind bobbins or spindles, and God Himself will create a web, an organized pattern in the material. The speaker will weave the pattern of faith into the fabric and will complete the materials needed to construct the garment of salvation. Ordinances (God's law) will then shrink and thicken the cloth (the fulling process) by means of moistening, heating, and pressing. Finally, the finished product will be dyed in radiant and heavenly colors and ornamentally patterned with a lustrous finish of Edenic beauty.

The third stanza portrays the transformation of the cloth into a garment that will cover humanity's rebellious nature: his "understanding, will, affections, judgment, conscience, memory." Wearing the garment will also illuminate and affect Taylor's words and actions so that they will glorify God and lead Taylor himself to the ultimate glory of heaven. There, clothed with the holiness provided by the Father, Son, and Holy Spirit, he will be ready for the final judgment and eventual translation into eternal glory.

Forms and Devices

"Huswifery" may be placed in a category of emblematic poetry—collections in which engravings or woodcuts of moral symbols or types were printed with a motto or a series of short verses. Although the poem is grammatically simplistic, it revolves around a complex metaphysical conceit, the art of clothes making. Taylor's three stanzas (a Trinitarian reference) break down the conceit, extending the meaning by an analytic comparison of its parts. Thus Taylor first portrays the spinning of the yarn, then the weaving of a fabric on a loom, and finally the construction and completion of a finished garment or robe. Other rhetorical devices used by Taylor are polyptoton, the repetition of a word functioning as different parts of speech (for example, "reel" in lines 5 and 6 as both a noun and a verb), and ploce, a core or base word modified by various affixes (for example, "glory" becomes "glorify" in line 16 and returns to its original form in line 18).

Rhyme in the six-line stanzas follows an *ababcc* pattern, with some near rhyme illustrated in the use of "memory" and "glorify" (lines 14 and 16) and "choice" and "paradise" (lines 11 and 12). Taylor also utilizes syntactical inversions ("my conversation make," line 5) and stylistically parallels Old English alliterative verse by maintaining a caesura or pause at the middle of each line.

Since Taylor has been known to use anagrams and acrostics in his verse, some mention should also be made of the first and last letters in each line. The letters *m*, *t*, *a*, and *e* occur consistently and may be rearranged to form the words "team" and "mate," suggesting the symbolic joining of God and man that is mirrored in the text.

Although there is an occasional roughness in Taylor's word choice and awkward rhyming, the colloquial diction often attains the cosmic meaning desired by the author. It symbolizes the joining of the sinner with the Savior, the eventual union of the elect with Christ, and the predestination of all saints, no matter how lowly, to transcendent glory.

Themes and Meanings

A close reading of "Huswifery" suggests a variety of meanings for the central conceit of clothes making. In fact, the extended metaphors reveal an obsession with typology, finding theological meanings in ordinary events. Thus the coat or dress taken from Job 29:14 in the Bible can be seen as a symbol of righteousness. Other biblical referents include Psalm 30, where clothes equal joy, and Psalm 31:25, where clothes equal strength and dignity. Isaiah 61:10, however, offers the most specific parallel: Here the chosen is clothed in "garments of salvation and arrayed in a robe of righteousness as a bridegroom adorns his head like a priest and as a bride adorns herself with jewels." This passage also invokes the New Testament reference to being clothed with Christ (Galatians 3:27).

The robe, like Joseph's coat of many colors in Genesis, is a symbol for being the chosen one of God and for having put on Christ's flesh and His robe of blood through faith and baptism. The biblical associations with robes thus recall Jesus' roles as prophet, priest, and king, all of which require a ceremonial garment. The associations also suggest a sacramental preparation for receiving the Lord's Supper. Like several of Taylor's preparatory meditations, "Huswifery" also implies the necessity to be clothed in Christ before approaching the eucharistic table.

A meditation, the form "Huswifery" takes, is a secret prayer composed of praise and petition. By using this form, Taylor acknowledges the complete sovereignty of God and the inefficacy of good works to attain salvation. He implores God to use him as a pastor and as a poet to spread the Gospel. The poet becomes a weaver of lovely cloth, Christ's truth made more attractive in verse. As an artist, Taylor decorates theological images, utilizing speech as a cloth for constructing thought and English as a literary yarn to create a linguistic web of beauty. This writing image is also reinforced in the double meaning of the word "quills" (line 8), which indicates the inspiration of written verse by the Holy Spirit.

The transformation of wool into yarn and then into cloth and a garment also suggests a type of spiritual marriage. Here, putting on the robe suggests an assumption on Christ's honor and accomplishments. At the marriage feast, Christ becomes one with Taylor, imputing redemption through the sacrament. This creates a mystic union, a close and personal relationship that Taylor desires to share with others. Taylor appeals to God to continue to robe him with the sanctification necessary to minister, the grace needed to attend the nuptial feast of Christ and His Church, and the forgiveness required to participate in communion. The analytic breakdown of the clothes-making process mirrors the achievement of a state of grace. It too is gradual and Christ-centered in its reliance on God to bring about conversion, motivate repentance, and offer divine grace.

Ultimately, the title not only reflects Taylor's desire to parallel what he saw as a woman's tasks of spinning, weaving, and sewing but also displays his goal of becoming the bride of Christ, integrated and perfected as both pastor and poet by the sacrifice of the Lamb. Taylor's puns on "dye" and "die" as well as "pinked" (cut, or punctured as in the wounds of Christ) emphasize that the robed priest's sacrifice satisfies God's requirement for justice, at the same time pleading for His grace and for humanity's salvation.

Michael J. Meyer

HYMN TO INTELLECTUAL BEAUTY

Author: Percy Bysshe Shelley (1792-1822)
Type of poem: Lyric
First published: 1817; revised and collected in *Rosalind and Helen*, 1819

The Poem

"Hymn to Intellectual Beauty" is written in seven twelve-line stanzas with an *abbaaccbddee* rhyme scheme. The word "intellectual" means nonmaterial, and "intellectual beauty" refers to an "unseen Power" that shines on "human thought or form." As a mental phenomenon, intellectual beauty is an ideal that transcends "This various world," which it visits like an "awful shadow." The poem's religious attitude toward this power is reflected in the use of the word "hymn" in the title.

In the first stanza, the speaker of the poem uses a series of similes to describe intellectual beauty to the reader. Its main characteristics seem to be universality and evanescence: Intellectual beauty visits "This various world" and "Each human heart and countenance," but it is "inconstant" and fleeting, "Like memory of music fled." The number of contrasting similes in the stanza suggests that this power is essentially ineffable, "yet dearer for its mystery."

The second stanza mourns intellectual beauty's inconstancy. The poem asks why this "Spirit of BEAUTY" is not always present to illuminate "our state,/ This dim vast vale of tears, vacant and desolate," but decides that this question is unanswerable. In the third stanza, the poet considers the sages and poets who use the names of "Gods and ghosts and Heaven" in a "vain endeavour" to explain away "Doubt, chance, and mutability." He insists, however, that "life's unquiet dream" will be given "grace and truth" by intellectual beauty, not by the myths of religion.

Stanza four continues the praise of intellectual beauty which, according to the poet, has the power to make man "immortal, and omnipotent" if it remains in man's heart. Although intellectual beauty does not provide people with ideas, it does nourish "human thought . . ./ Like darkness [does] a dying flame." The stanza ends with a prayer to the spirit to stay with man, "lest the grave should be,/ Like life and fear, a dark reality." The poet turns to autobiography in the fifth stanza, describing himself as a boy searching for ghosts and hoping for "high talk with the departed dead." He "called on poisonous names," which in the context of the poem are words such as "God and ghosts and Heaven," and was not answered, but then the shadow of intellectual beauty fell over him and he "shrieked, and clasped [his] hands in extacy!" Stanza six goes on to describe how he dedicated himself to intellectual beauty in the hope that this "awful LOVELINESS" would liberate "This world from its dark slavery."

The seventh and final stanza shifts to a "solemn and serene" autumn afternoon. Having given the reader a sense of intellectual beauty and his own relationship to that mysterious power, the poet asks it to give an autumnlike "calm" to his "onward life." The poem ends with a prayer reaffirming the poet's allegiance to intellectual beauty and his commitment "To fear himself, and love all human kind."

Forms and Devices

"Hymn to Intellectual Beauty" takes the form of a religious address to an object of worship, beginning with an invocation, in which intellectual beauty is described and praised, and ending with a prayer. Moreover, the language used throughout the poem is religious. With its "own hues," the invisible power "consecrate[s]" everything human, giving "grace and truth to life's unquiet dream"; it has the power to make man "immortal, and omnipotent" and may even be able to redeem "This world from its dark slavery." The poet presents himself as having been intellectual beauty's ardent follower from the time the spirit's shadow fell over him when he was a boy. In fact, the poet's conversion is nearly hysterical in intensity: He shrieks as he clasps his hands in an attitude of prayer. Even in the present, the older poet dedicates himself to the "awful LOVELINESS" with "beating heart and streaming eyes," and his final prayer is for intellectual beauty to grant him "calm."

Although the poem uses religious terminology, it does not advocate an established religion. The beliefs of Christianity, for example, are described scornfully as "Frail spells," and the poet describes the religious phrases he learned as a child as the "poisonous names with which our youth is fed." According to the poet, intellectual beauty teaches him "To fear himself, and love all human kind"; God is not included in this formula. Thus the religious language of "Hymn to Intellectual Beauty" serves to express both the poet's reverence for the spirit of ideal beauty and his repudiation of traditional beliefs.

While the religious sentiments of "Hymn to Intellectual Beauty" are clear, intellectual beauty itself remains a vague concept, and Percy Bysshe Shelley uses similes throughout the poem to suggest, but never to limit, intellectual beauty's qualities. Some of these similes describe the invisible power as being "Like moonbeams . . . behind some piny mountain shower," "Like clouds in starlight widely spread," "like mists o'er mountains driven," and "like the truth/ Of nature on my passive youth." Since intellectual beauty is invisible, it cannot be given an exact physical description, so Shelley uses imagery that is partially obscured, cloudy, or misty. At times he even turns to another abstraction, such as "the truth of nature." When it manifests itself to the poet, intellectual beauty is described as an "awful shadow." The image of the "shadow" must be taken in a figurative rather than literal sense — it gives the reader a sense of the spirit's mysteriousness and indicates that intellectual beauty can never fully manifest itself in the physical world. At most, the poet can apprehend its reflection or shadow.

Shelley's decision to write a hymn to a nonmaterial power is typical of the poet, who believed that the physical world was less important than "human thought or form." Moreover, it is significant that "Hymn to Intellectual Beauty" is a prayer to an invisible spirit rather than to the kind of anthropomorphic deity that Shelley deplored.

Themes and Meanings

The central problem of "Hymn to Intellectual Beauty" has to do with the meaning and significance of intellectual beauty, in terms of both humanity as a whole and the poet's life in particular. Although many readers of the poem have tried to define intellectual beauty, it cannot be identified with any one ideal. In fact, the poem links this spirit with several abstractions, including beauty, grace, thought, form, harmony, and calmness.

Perhaps the key to understanding intellectual beauty is to focus on what it is not, and it is clear that it is not part of the physical world. Many of Shelley's philosophical notions derive from Plato's, and in his poetry Shelley often uses (and transfigures) Plato's belief that there are two kinds of reality: the visible or physical realm, made of constantly changing matter, and the intelligible realm of forms, or such purely mental phenomena as truth and beauty. Intellectual beauty resides solely in the intelligible realm and can only be apprehended in the visible world as an obscure, shadowy presence. It is nevertheless important to humankind, because it contains the ideals toward which each person must strive in order to achieve perfection. That is why Shelley associates intellectual beauty with human thought and insists that it is a crucial element in the attainment of human immortality and omnipotence, and the abolition of "dark slavery." The fact that intellectual beauty is identified with man suggests that this power, despite its divine attributes, does not derive from God or the supernatural. It teaches humanity to love, esteem, and fear itself rather than a separate divinity—in essence, "Hymn to Intellectual Beauty" is an attempt to replace traditional worship with a religion that celebrates humankind and its potential to perceive and attain perfection. The role of intellectual beauty in this religion is to dispel the fears and sufferings associated with the physical world by revealing to its disciples the deeper truth of the realm of ideals.

Beyond intellectual beauty's significance to humanity as a whole, the poem describes the importance of the spirit in the poet's life. As a boy, the poet sought to communicate with beings existing beyond the physical world, ghosts and heavenly spirits, but was not answered. When the boy turned to philosophy, however, "musing deeply on the lot/ Of life," the shadow of intellectual beauty fell over him in a sudden visitation. This suggests that intellectual beauty is to be found through philosophy rather than simple religious faith in "God and ghosts and Heaven." The autobiographical section of the poem is important because it allows the poet to speak with the authority of a prophet who has had direct communion with the object of his worship. Inasmuch as he represents humanity, the poet's experience supports the idea that humankind as a whole could be inspired and transfigured by intellectual beauty, escaping through this spirit the "dark reality" of death.

William D. Brewer

HYMN TO PROSERPINE

Author: Algernon Charles Swinburne (1837-1909)
Type of poem: Dramatic monologue
First published: 1866, in *Poems and Ballads*

The Poem

"Hymn to Proserpine" is a dramatic monologue of 110 lines, not divided into stanzas. The mythological Proserpine, the daughter of Zeus and Demeter, became queen of the underworld; Algernon Charles Swinburne invokes her in the title and throughout the poem as the goddess of death.

The poem is supposed to be spoken by the Roman Emperor Julian the Apostate (A.D. 331-363), who opposed Christianity and supported the traditional Roman pantheon. The poem has as an epigraph the Latin phrase *Vicisti, Galilaee* (thou hast conquered, Galilean), supposed to be Julian's dying words. The Galilean is Jesus Christ, and Julian meant that Christianity had triumphed. Although the hymn is ascribed to Julian, it presents Swinburne's own views rather than a historical reconstruction of Julian's doctrines.

Most people fear death, but the Julian of the poem does not. He states that death is greater than "the seasons that laugh or weep" (line 3). Life has its joys and sorrows but is ended by death. Yet this view of the world, Julian claims, has come under challenge. A new religion denying that life is cruel appears to have triumphed; Julian means Christianity, which under his ancestor Constantine had become the state religion of the Roman Empire. Julian looks with dismay at the strife caused by religious conflict, and he calls for an end to it: "I say to you all, be at peace" (line 21).

As for himself, the new religion has no appeal. It cannot destroy the pleasures of life or offer anything as good as they are. Although life has pleasures, however, everything is changeable, and death brings a welcome relief. Death ends all, and Julian rejects reincarnation and resurrection: "For no man under the sky lives twice, outliving his day" (line 31).

The poem shifts around line 40 to a sharp assault on Christianity. Julian mocks the worship of Jesus, who was beaten and crucified. To the Romans, the gods were beings of superhuman strength. Worshiping a being whom humans could injure and kill made no sense to the devotees of ancient paganism.

Julian declares that Christianity will eventually be overthrown; nothing can withstand the power of fate, which changes everything. A long comparison between fate, "impelled of invisible tides (line 54), and the sea concludes with the prophecy that the new religion will perish: "Ye shall sleep as a slain man sleeps, and the world shall forget you for kings" (line 70). Julian turns to a comparison between Mary, the mother of Jesus, and Proserpine, very much to the advantage of the latter. He concludes with the declaration that Proserpine is greater than all other gods, because she brings death.

Forms and Devices

The reader of "Hymn to Proserpine" will immediately be struck by Swinburne's unusually strong rhythms. This is characteristic of his poetry: "Hymn to Proserpine," like most of his verse, was written to be declaimed dramatically, not read silently.

In the line "Thou has conquered, O pale Galilean; the world has grown gray, from thy breath" (line 35), the stresses on the first syllable of "conquered," the third syllable of "Galilean," "gray," and "breath" have the effect of a continued drumbeat. Again, in "For these give labour and slumber; but thou, Proserpina, death" (line 104), the accents on "thou" and "death" jump at the reader. By his use of this device, Swinburne turns the poem into rhetoric: Although no audience is indicated, one can imagine Julian delivering it as a speech. Twentieth century poets such as T. S. Eliot turned away from this declamatory style, instead seeking to reproduce the sound of natural conversation. In spite of its artificial character, Swinburne's tone achieves great force.

The poem uses another technique characteristic of Swinburne — alliteration. When one encounters the line, "O ghastly glories of saints, dead limbs of gibbeted gods!" (line 44), the repeated *g* sounds capture one's attention. Swinburne grabs the reader by the lapels to put forward his view of Christianity. This line also uses contrast effectively: "glories" are usually the opposite of "ghastly," and "gibbeted" is hardly the first adjective that comes to mind for "gods." The unexpected adjectives add to the alliteration in highlighting the line.

Swinburne uses alliteration several times. In speaking of the sea, he says: "Waste water washes, and tall ships founder, and deep death waits" (line 50). Several lines later, one finds "And bitter as blood is the spray" (line 60). These phrases accent the importance of the sea, a key theme. In some of his poems, Swinburne overuses alliteration (the device is basic to the frequent parodies of his verse). In "Hymn to Proserpine," he keeps it under control.

Reference to the sea brings out another basic technique of the poem — symbolism. Much of the work presents the sea as a symbol of change; Swinburne makes it clear that he does not mean the literal sea. He speaks of it as "impelled of invisible tides" (line 52). He draws out the symbol in detail: The spray is "bitter as blood" (line 60); its crests are "fangs that devour" (line 60); it is "shark-toothed and serpentine curled" (line 53).

Swinburne's depiction of the sea displays another characteristic touch. The symbol has metaphors and similes included within it. It is not the crests of the real sea that he calls "fangs"; it is the "crests" of his symbol that are characterized by a further literary figure. The "foam of the present that sweeps to the surf of the past" (line 48) and the "whitening wind of the future" (line 54) are other metaphors lodged within the symbol.

Themes and Meanings

The poem presents an unusual view of life. Proserpine, the goddess of death, is celebrated. She has destroyed previous gods and will, Julian alleges, destroy Christ as well. Destruction and cruelty receive praise and are welcomed. The repeated "but thou, Proserpina, [give] death" praises the goddess rather than laments her effects. The poet turns to her—"Goddess and maiden and queen, be near me now and befriend" (line 92)—because she brings death.

One might think that if Swinburne welcomed death, then he hated life, but this mistakes the precise nature of his pessimism. He does not say that because life is bad, one should welcome death as a release. Rather, it is the destructive power of death that is welcomed. Swinburne admires the "poisonous-finned, shark-toothed" sea creatures (line 53). Although "grief is a grievous thing" (line 33), and death brings this to an end, life in itself is not exclusively evil. It includes many sensual pleasures; these, even—or perhaps especially—when destructive, are the chief glories of life. Not even these pleasures can withstand death.

Given his praise for destruction, it is hardly surprising that Swinburne scorned Christianity. It teaches that the world is governed by love and that death is a prelude to resurrection. Nothing could be more alien to Swinburne than these tenets. He notes, "They are merciful, clothed with pity, the young compassionate gods./ But for me their new device is barren" (lines 16-17). To replace wrath with pity and compassion is no step forward.

To Swinburne, those sentiments express weakness. Christianity's "ghastly glories" consist of the fact that its saints are martyrs. Jesus was executed as a criminal. The spread of the new religion thus represents the triumph of weakness. In speaking of "compassionate gods" and "gibbeted gods," Swinburne uses the plural to denigrate Christianity further. Although it taught belief in one God, the poet holds this of no account and simply refers to the new gods.

The view of death presented in the poem provides an even more essential reason to reject the new religion. Life may not be entirely, or even preponderantly, bad, but eventually people tire of it. Death is a permanent sleep and releases men from care. Christianity defies this key to the world's nature by teaching that death is not final. Fortunately, in Swinburne's view, this doctrine will fall before life's "mutable wings" (line 30).

To understand the poem, one must take account of the period when Swinburne wrote. Many of the Victorians questioned Christianity. Historical criticism of the Bible and the publication of Charles Darwin's *On the Origin of Species* (1859), which challenged the account of creation in Genesis, led to furious battles about religion.

Another issue arose from this one: Without belief in Christianity, what was the basis of morality? Swinburne's poem gives a decisive response to this question. The rules of morality inhibit pleasure; Christianity, by teaching compassion and self-sacrifice, has made the world grow gray. Had the times been less given to religious doubt, Swinburne's praise of destruction might have been easily dismissed as an aberration. Given the actual situation, high-minded humanists such as John Morley anxiously distanced themselves from the poem's message and condemned Swinburne.

Bill Delaney

HYMNS TO THE NIGHT

Author: Novalis (Friedrich von Hardenberg, 1772-1801)
Type of poem: Lyric
First published: 1800, as *Hymnen an die Nacht;* collected in *Hymns to the Night and Other Writings*, 1960

The Poem

Hymns to the Night is a group of six organically related poems or hymns of praise and religious devotion. The hymns record the poet's struggle to overcome his grief at the death of his young fiancée, Sophie von Kühn, in 1797, shortly after her fifteenth birthday and shortly before they were to be married. The death of Sophie, the inconsolable loss of an unspoiled and idealized love, becomes for Novalis the occasion of a spiritual awakening, the opening of a new religious vision. The spiritual world opened to Novalis is represented as the world of the night.

Though the first hymn opens with praise of light, the inexpressible, secretive night soon exceeds the lavish wonders of day. As the world darkens and the busy activity of daytime fades away, distant memories, the wishes of youth, childhood dreams, and brief joys, reemerge. The soul stirs its heavy wings and comes to life, returning to spiritual matters of its deepest concern. The night opens our spiritual eyes, which look at last toward the depths of the soul. Night becomes the realm of the life of the spirit.

Late in this hymn, the poet addresses night's messenger as his beloved. This messenger is Sophie, who "called the night to life" for him and opened his eyes, and to whom he owes his spiritual birth. Her love and her death broke the hold of the practical daylight world. He calls upon her to consume him with spirit fire, so that he may join her in the pure spiritual world of night, where the union denied them in the daylight world can be everlasting.

The second hymn laments the interruption of night by the return of day and entreats the night not to abandon her intimates utterly to the affairs of daylight. Novalis, however, comes to see that the daylight world secretly depends on the hidden processes of the night, which make a grape fill with juice or bring a young girl to her flowering. Similarly, the hidden processes that created the oldest stories and even the concept of heaven have their origins in the night world. Night and darkness bring the keys to our most infinite mysteries.

In the third and most personal hymn, Novalis recalls standing at the foot of Sophie's grave with nowhere to turn, consumed in grief. At the depths of despair, "Night inspiration" comes to him. The mound becomes transparent (in the next hymn it is called a "crystal wave"). As he gazes into it, he sees his beloved. In her eyes he first glimpses eternity.

This timeless moment, also recorded in Novalis' journals, is the point of origin of the hymns, which explore and develop the new vision this experience opened to him. Sophie's grave thus becomes symbolic, the crossover point from the world of daily preoccupations to the mysterious and infinite world of the spirit.

In the fourth hymn, Novalis attempts to reconcile his new vision with the practical demands of life. He resolves to work untiringly in his daytime pursuits yet adds that his secret heart will stay true to the night and to "creative love, her daughter." In this hymn, the author finds a mission that gives meaning and direction to his life and art. His mother, the night, sends him, and his brothers and sisters in this religious awakening, to transform the world with creative love and infuse it with spiritual meaning. The fourth hymn ends: "I live by day/ Full of faith and courage/ And die by night/ In holy fire."

In the fifth hymn, Novalis constructs a brief history of religion. He begins with the emergence of Greek gods, whose reign is pictured as a classical feast. Such early mythologies failed to address adequately the issue of death. The immortal gods were not concerned with it. For mortals, once life in the daylight world ended, there was only a dull dream in a world of shades. Death of a loved one brought sadness without consolation. The problem remained unresolved until the birth of Christ. A poet from Greece, present at the Nativity, sings of Christ as the savior whose death will open the world of the eternal spirit to humanity. Death, which once plunged humanity into despair, will now draw humankind forward in longing for eternal life.

Like Sophie, Christ opens the realm of eternal night, and like Sophie, Mary becomes the blessed virgin, the merciful messenger of the night world. The classical feast parallels the daylight world before Sophie's death. The larger context of cultural history thus parallels and illuminates the poet's new religious vision, and his revelation attains a broader cultural significance as a guide to a new spiritual awakening.

The sixth and final hymn, entitled "Longing for Death," envisions death as a desirable passage to the realm of the night. Remote from the time when Christ was in the daylight world, humankind's spiritual thirst can be quenched only in the world of the night. The poet praises night because in it individuals may join their lost loved ones, and, guided by Mary and Christ, be settled forever in the lap of God.

Forms and Devices

The hymns are extremely innovative, formally mixing prose poetry and several forms of metrical, rhymed verse in a single work. In manuscript, the hymns were even more innovative, for the entire first hymn and several other lengthy passages were originally written in free verse. In the *Athenäum* version, on which almost all translations are based, the long passages of free verse were reorganized as paragraphs of poetic prose, or prose poems.

In the *Athenäum* version, the first three hymns are prose poems, the fourth begins in prose and shifts to rhymed verse, the fifth alternates forms, and the sixth is entirely rhymed, metrical verse. Thus, as Novalis' vision becomes more developed and unified in the hymns, his poetry becomes more formalized.

Novalis first introduces rhymed verse in the fourth hymn. In the second section, the speaker addresses the light, insisting that he will remain true to the night without which day is nothing. Then, in one of the highest moments of inspiration of the hymns, the speaker's point of view becomes identified with eternal spirit. Still addressing the light, he says, "Truly I was, before you existed. . . ." The speaker has become identified with pure spirit, which, unlike the body, can be said to be older than light itself, because it is eternal. In a way, he speaks with the voice of the night. This important shift in point of view reflects a leap of faith and is closely related to the shift in poetic forms.

From this inspired perspective, this union of the higher self and night, Novalis sees clearly his mission in life as an apostle of night. Shortly hereafter, Novalis breaks into rhymed verse, in a poem of devotion and celebration of the mission he has discovered. Written with inspired confidence in his vision, this poem is a part of Novalis' private litany, written as an expression of a confirmed faith.

Much of the fifth hymn, the historical one, is printed as paragraphs of prose poetry. Death's arrival at the table of the classical feast becomes the subject of an allegorical ballad, reminiscent of medieval morality tales. It is composed in rhymed iambic pentameter, in eight-line stanzas that end in a rhymed couplet. The form is reminiscent of folk song. The same stanza form is used for the song of the poet who attends Christ's nativity later in the hymn.

When the history is completed, the fifth hymn, again from a position of commitment to the vision and mission, breaks into metrical verse very much like that which closes the fourth hymn in line-length, measure, and rhyme scheme. As at the end of the fourth hymn, the shift in verse form corresponds to the construction of a liturgy of devotion to the night, the beloved, Christ and Mary. The sixth hymn, similarly, is an extended song of devotion written entirely in rhymed, metrical verse.

Thus, as Novalis gains certainty of his vision and the mission of the hymns, he leaves the exploratory forms of free verse and prose poetry in which he has developed his vision and the history that confirms it. He turns to forms in which a liturgy to sustain devotion and commitment may be created. The formal trend also marks a transition toward his metrically regular, rhymed *Geistliche Lieder* (1801-1802; *Devotional Songs*, 1910), which Novalis completed after the hymns. Some of the *Devotional Songs* later became hymns in German hymnals.

The symbolic connotations of night and day, of light and dark in religion, and the usual ascent associated with spiritual enlightenment are inverted in the hymns. Novalis attains his vision looking down into the grave and descending into the night. Christ and Mary are enthroned in the darkness, and daylight and light are, for the most part, reserved for the banal affairs of daily living. At the end, the movement toward God is downward. Readers soon become naturalized in this imagery, however, and even come to accept the premise that darkness, since very much larger than the realm of daylight, is perhaps a better metaphor for the realm of the eternal spirit.

An important romantic symbol is also introduced in the fourth hymn as Novalis finds his mission. He and his spiritual brothers and sisters are to plant the world of light with flowers that will never fade. Of course, the flowers of the daylight world always fade, and fade quickly. Only through creative love, perhaps through creative arts, or imagination, can there be flowers that never fade. This is the germ of the idea for the famous "blue flower" of Novalis' novel *Heinrich von Ofterdingen*, (1802; *Henry of Ofterdingen*, 1842), an unfading flower that became a central symbol of the German romantic movement.

Themes and Meanings

The inversion of light and dark imagery raises important questions about the relation between Novalis' vision and the Christian tradition that he invokes, as does the predominantly artistic mission the hymns outline. The mission of creative love, of transforming the world and giving it meaning rather than discovering an already existing meaning, emphasizes the importance of the individual imagination in religion. Like other Romantics, Novalis identified the soul with imagination, and the religion he would propound must be internalized and transformed, as it is in the hymns. It must awaken the soul. Also like other romantics, Novalis believed that poets must create the religious texts of the new awakening.

The emphasis on darkness and night tempts one to place Novalis in a lineage of Christian mystics that would include Saint John of the Cross. The role of Sophie as the virgin messenger who opens the realm of the spirit to the poet suggests a comparison with Dante, who is led through the world of the afterlife by the grace of Beatrice, who died in her youth. Yet the romantic emphasis on creative individual imagination and the absence of the concept of sin from Novalis' vision distinguish him from these more Catholic religious poets.

The last stanza of the fifth hymn contains one of the most problematic passages in the hymns. Novalis writes of the pure realm of the night, of the paradise of spiritual life, which he says is "Just a Single Night of Ecstasy—/ An eternal poem—/ And our sun of all suns/ Is the countenance of God." Many commentators find this passage problematic or offensive, since it blends sensual and aesthetic pleasure with religious devotion in language that lovers might apply to an earthly paradise. Novalis' highest paradise seems, to many commentators, not too high, and more an expression of perverse fantasy than of truly religious devotion and insight.

These questions point out the uniqueness and originality of the *Hymns to the Night*. In them, Novalis creates a magnificent romantic religious vision with a courage and height of inspiration few romantic writers were able to equal. His hymns resonate with passionate grief, love, and religious longing, and ultimately attain an aspiring faith in a compelling personal vision of the spiritual message and the life of Christianity. Novalis died young, at the age of twenty-nine, and the hymns stand as perhaps the purest expression of his youthful creative power and as a monument for his beloved, Sophie von Kühn.

Von E. Underwood

HYPERION

Author: John Keats (1795-1821)
Type of poem: Epic
First published: 1820, in *Lamia, Isabella, The Eve of St. Agnes, and Other Poems*

The Poem

Hyperion is a fragment of an epic poem in blank verse, divided into two complete books and a third incomplete book: Book I contains 357 lines, Book II has 391 lines, and Book III leaves off in mid-sentence at line 136. John Keats turned from this poem to compose his great odes in the summer of 1819 before returning to the subject of *Hyperion*. Instead, however, of completing this epic, he began an entirely different poem (also incomplete) called *The Fall of Hyperion* (1856).

The title of *Hyperion* indicates the name of its hero, the ancient Greek god of the sun. Hyperion was one of the Titans, offspring of Coelus (the sky) and Tellus (the earth). Saturn was ruler of the Titans, overthrown by his three Olympian sons, Jupiter, Neptune, and Pluto. Keats's epic is based upon this episode of mythology, when the Olympians overthrew the Titans and Olympian Apollo took the place of Titanic Hyperion. The story of the poem begins at the point when all the Titans except Hyperion have been defeated.

Book I opens in a dark valley of great stillness, where Thea (wife of Hyperion) is searching for Saturn. She finds him alone, massive in size but deeply dejected and utterly stunned. Thea urges him to look up; then she ceases, realizing that theirs is a hopeless cause. The two of them do not move for four months. Then Saturn opens his eyes and asks Thea to help him understand what has happened; he is supposed to be king of the gods, but he is so impotent he must have lost his identity. He makes himself believe that he can still command a force to recover his throne. Thea feels hope and urges Saturn to follow her to where other fallen Titans have gathered.

The poem then shifts to observe the behavior of the only Titan not yet fallen. Hyperion is in his sky-palace, stalking its hallways nervously, feeling great dread. He asks if he is also about to fall, like all of his brethren. He cries out in defiance that he will attack the rebel Olympians. Hyperion threatens to drive the sun through the sky to start the day at an unnatural time, but not even a god can disturb "the sacred seasons." His father Coelus sympathizes, urging Hyperion to use his remaining powers to help the Titans, to act and not wait to be acted against: "Be therefore in the van of Circumstance." The first book ends with Hyperion plunging into the darkness below, "like to a diver in the pearly seas."

Book II describes the arrival of Saturn and Thea at the dark den where the Titans have congregated. It is a woeful scene, where giant forms lie listlessly about in angry astonishment. They are roused when Saturn appears. He cannot explain their defeat, but he asks them how to respond to the Olympians.

The first to give advice is Oceanus, who counsels resignation. The triumph of the

Olympians is a phase in the process of natural law, which governs history and creates progress, as the old must give way to the new in all things. The Titans should be wise and recognize the truth of natural process. Oceanus says that the Olympian gods are young and beautiful, a new generation of advancing truth; "first in beauty should be first in might." The only consolation available to the Titans, he says, is to "receive the truth, and let it be your balm."

While the other Titans remain quiet, little-regarded Clymene timidly ventures to express her feelings. She describes how she had tried to console herself by blowing into a seashell to make music. She threw away the shell when she heard a strange, enchanting "golden melody" that seemed to drift across the ocean. She tried to stop her ears, but she heard the cry of a sweet voice, calling "Apollo! young Apollo!" Clymene tells her tale without interpreting it, simply illustrating the fact of a new regime.

Her brother Titan, huge Enceladus, is indignant at both the timidity of Clymene and the resignation of Oceanus. Enceladus offers to lead an assault on their conquerors, and he reminds them that Hyperion remains unfallen. At that moment, Hyperion appears, brightening the dark den with his burning presence. The Titans see that Hyperion is himself dejected, so they are tempted to become despondent again despite the fighting words of Enceladus. Some shout out the name of Saturn, and Hyperion answers the same. On this note, the second book ends.

Book III shifts to the young Apollo, about to assume his divine mission. He is wandering alone, perplexed about the strange emotions he feels. He sees a goddess approach, and he believes that he knows her from his dreams. She announces that she has been watching over his growth for some time, that she has forsaken her own people to be with him. Suddenly, Apollo recognizes that she is Mnemosyne (memory, mother of the Muses), and he struggles to control his feelings of sadness even as he speaks. Apollo explodes with a barrage of questions, asking Mnemosyne to account for the universe itself. Abruptly he halts his questioning and exclaims, as he looks into the eyes of the goddess, "Knowledge enormous makes a God of me." Then he writhes in pain, his face grows pale, and even his hair begins to move. He shrieks in agony, and the poem stops without completing its last sentence.

Forms and Devices

Hyperion was designed to follow the epic form of John Milton's *Paradise Lost* (1667). The opening is an imitation of the scene that opens Milton's epic, describing the army of angels who have followed Satan in their rebellion against God and who have been cast down into Hell. The summoning of the Titans to a conference by Saturn is a repetition of the call by Satan. Keats's poem strikes a new direction, however, by leaving its titular hero unfallen, awaiting the challenge from young Apollo. Yet perhaps there is an imitation here also, with some similarities between Hyperion/Apollo and Satan/Christ. Where the poem would have gone if finished cannot be known, and perhaps Keats abandoned it because he could not take it beyond Milton's epic in a way satisfactory to Keats himself. When he returned to the subject in *The Fall of Hyperion*, Keats chose a new form and adopted a new style altogether, as he made himself the heroic medium for the transfiguration of Apollo into a god.

There is more to *Hyperion*, however, than an imitation of the narrative introduction and heroic characters found in *Paradise Lost*. The blank verse is "Miltonic" in its construction, using similar metric design and sentence structure. The normal subject-verb order is inverted, and the subject comes at the end of a long sentence, following a series of parallel modifying phrases. This device is a typical way to imitate the classic English epic style; thus, the poem opens in Book I with "Deep in . . ./ Far sunken from . . ./ Far from . . ./ Sat gray-hair'd Saturn." This sentence is still not finished with the identification of its subject, for it continues with more balanced clauses for another two-and-a-half lines. The catalog of identifying features used here, and elsewhere, is representative of epic style as well.

There are distinctive figures of speech, usually similes, which mark *Hyperion* as a poem of epic ambition. The most common kind of epic simile is the extended comparison, as when Thea is compared (or contrasted) with an Amazon in Book I and when the forest where Saturn lies is compared with a meeting of a senate, also in Book I.

Long set speeches, particularly in the first two books, contribute to the epic form of the poem. These occur in Book III as well, but they are interrupted by exclamations and hurried expressions of surprise and recognition. The style of Book III seems deliberately varied, then, to reflect the changes which are occurring in the character of Apollo as well as in the order of divine government. The poem further imitates classic epic form by setting its action throughout the cosmos, transcending human affairs, and exploring all possible realms of being. When Keats wants to suggest how far the Titans have fallen, in fact, he compares them with human beings, as in Book II, when he says, "As with us mortal men," Saturn moves with a heavy heart.

The poet's apostrophe to the Muse to ask for inspiration is another typical device of the epic, and it is employed, with some individuality, in *Hyperion* to open Book III: "O leave them, Muse! . . ./ Leave them, O Muse!" The poet who calls out to the muse actually is commanding rather than pleading or requesting. This aggressive and demanding attitude by the speaker as epic and prophetic poet is maintained through most of the poem, as Keats uses the privileged voice of a bard to pass judgments on his characters and to surround them with an understanding which surpasses their own—even if they are gods and he is merely human. This attitude will be more completely realized as a shaping form of the poem when it is presented as dream and vision in the later *The Fall of Hyperion*.

Themes and Meanings

The three main themes of *Hyperion* are: process, power, and poetry. The epic narrative examines how change in status and perception is a characteristic of all process. The conflict between generations of gods is a dramatization of the resistance of the past to claims of the present; while the poem focuses on the utterances of the Titans as signs of recovering energy, its thrust is toward the futility of efforts by the Titans to prevent their defeat. History is a succession of discrete generations, governed by a universal law of change. Whether Oceanus' interpretation of this process as progressive is correct, the poem does not confirm, because it does not conclude.

Certainly, however, the poem confirms the pain of dislocation and disorientation which occurs in the process of transferring power, as the Titans are impressively miserable in their monumental, static condition. They barely relieve their misery by talking about it, yet that is the only means available to them for mitigation of their humiliation. There is irony at work in the poem's use of changing point of view, because the huge Titans ineffectively bluster about revenge while the young, troubled Apollo wanders aimlessly toward his divine destiny. In all instances, furthermore, the heroic gods are guided by heroic goddesses, to suggest that the physical power of males is administered by the greater powers of females (manifested in their pity, their sensitivity, and their respect for the past).

The feelings of Thea, Clymene, and Mnemosyne are focused by their responses to the new powers of beauty manifested in the Olympian gods; that beauty is especially promised by the young Apollo, who will inspire a new era of civilized loveliness. Since Apollo is particularly the god of poetry, his birth into divinity is a fitting climax to a poem which ends without concluding. A new kind of poetry is born with the birth of a new god.

The meaning of *Hyperion* is caught by the crossing of these three themes. History and nature command change as a universal law of process, affecting the gods themselves. Natural process passes through discontinuous stages of self-awareness (the generations of gods and creatures), but it is also continuous, because it is a passage of power. The assumption of power by a new generation, a new body, and a new consciousness is the responsibility of all successive life, including the poets who, like Keats, suffer for their talent as they follow their inspiration by Apollo and reject the past of Hyperion.

Richard D. McGhee

I AM

Author: John Clare (1793-1864)
Type of poem: Lyric
First published: 1848; collected in *Poems of John Clare's Madness*, 1949

The Poem

"I Am" is a short poem of three six-line stanzas. Each stanza is regular iambic pentameter, rhyming *ababab*. The verse form is slightly unusual, not surprisingly for John Clare who experimented freely with different meters and forms. The poem begins with the simplest assertion of identity — "I am." The reader knows only the bare fact of the speaker's existence — no particulars are given. One does not learn who this speaker is and what his specific conditions are, though one is told in the first stanza that the speaker is friendless and forsaken. This speaker, paradoxically asserting his identity but providing no identification, repeats "I am" three times more in the opening stanza; however, he does so with qualifications that increasingly diminish his strange self-assertiveness. He tells the reader that no one cares who he is, that he has no one with whom to share his sorrows, and that he merely "lives," tossed about as aimlessly as "vapours." The aimlessness suggested by "vapour" in this final line of stanza 1 is powerfully reinforced by the enjambment, or running over, of the grammatical focus of its verb "tost" into the first line of stanza 2.

In the second stanza, the speaker is thrown helplessly "into the nothingness of scorn and noise." This paradox of a "nothingness" that is noisy and scornful is immediately followed by the pure oxymoron of "waking dreams." In this uncanny and contradictory world, the speaker likens himself to a shipwrecked sailor awash in a nightmare "sea" without a "sense of life or joys." The speaker, drifting insensibly in this "nothingness," now propounds his most fearsome paradox: Those whom he loves dearly are the most estranged from him. Although this stanza draws upon the conventional metaphor of shipwreck, with its suggestions of isolation and loneliness, there is evidence in this stanza that the speaker is not alone in his strange suffering. In fact, it appears that he suffers, in part, because he is not alone. Hostile ("scorn") or indifferent ("strange") witnesses may be present, but the speaker is separated from them as if lost at sea.

The concluding stanza confirms this, for the speaker now expresses a desire to escape to a world without men or women, without either joy or sorrow — a refuge of passive peace and detachment. This paradise is the past, the early years of childhood when the speaker imagines he was in unity with God and nature: "untroubling and untroubled." In "I Am," one encounters a nameless and faceless sufferer entertaining the impossible wish to return to the innocence of childhood. Exactly what and why he suffers is not known, but the terror and hopelessness of his sufferings are plain.

Forms and Devices

John Clare was the son of poor English farmers. At various times, Clare was a farmhand, a militiaman, a kiln stoker, and a mendicant. His formal schooling was slight, and until late in life, his access to books was limited. One book Clare knew early and well was the Bible, and its influence is especially evident in "I Am." The Psalms are perhaps the best analogue for Clare's testament of sorrow, for like the Psalms, "I Am" is at once personal and impersonal, impassioned yet restrained. Like the Hebrew Psalmist, who expressed his *de profundis* within a highly formal system of poetic parallelism, Clare closes his lyrical passion and despair in almost perfectly regular iambic pentameter. The speaker of the Psalms is often uniden- tified, as is the speaker in "I Am," and both tell much about the speakers' sorrows but little about the speakers themselves. The characteristic plea of the Psalmist to be delivered from his "gathered enemies" is also echoed by the speaker of "I Am": He is surrounded by "scorn" and "noise" and, finally, in the closing lines, looks toward God for his deliverance.

The opening phrase of the first stanza, "I am — yet what I am," may allude to the divine tautology of Exodus, "I am that I am" (Exodus 3:14). If this is so, however, the allusion is ironic, for the speaker of this poem asserts his identity despairingly, emphasizing his impotence and helplessness. The speaker's description of being "tost into the nothing of scorn and noise" recalls biblical language describing the damned thrown into hell: "cast into the lake of fire" (Revelation 20:10). Finally, the idyllic image of the sleeping child "abiding" with God echoes the confidence of the Psalmist who hopes to "abide before God for ever" (Psalms 61:7). Certainly, in a more general sense, the simplicity and grandeur that have so often been noted in this poem owe a debt to the lofty cadences of the King James Bible.

From another perspective, "I Am" is a poem intimately connected with the sensi- bilities of its own era, for it expresses with great intensity the Romantic conflict between innocence and experience, a theme central to the poetry of Clare's contem- poraries. Clare is often compared to William Blake, since both were mystics who suffered eventual madness, but there is a more significant link between them. Clare shares Blake's Romantic exhaltation of childhood. In "I Am," childhood is figured as paradise before the Fall, a region in which there is no man (Adam) and no woman (Eve), only the isolated consciousness alone with God. The poem's speaker seeks to recover the infantile condition of moral neutrality and irresponsibility free of the knowledge of sexual distinctions and the emotional extremes of either joy or sorrow. Recognizing Clare's Romantic division of innocence and experience, one can appre- ciate the terrible irony of his reiterated "I am," for the poem is really a passionate longing after "I was." For William Wordsworth, Clare's other Romantic analogue, adult experience involves a falling away from the glories of childhood, a diminish- ment with compensations of greater knowledge; but for Clare, adult experience is a virtual hell from which the only escape is a fantasy of return to childhood, even to a prenatal unconsciousness.

Themes and Meanings

It has been said of Clare's lyrics, of which "I Am" is perhaps the greatest, that they possess "a penetrating simplicity which neither requires nor permits of analysis." In a sense, this is true. "I Am" is a cry from the depths, an utterance of terrible sorrow passing into an imagined calm that is as deep and absolute. Part of its power is its perfect directness; it is not a confession so much as a prayer, and its language is unmarred by sentimentality or ornament. It is perhaps too profound for literary criticism and strains the limits of secular literature. What does cast light on the poem—as is not the case with many poems—is the author's biography.

Clare was a man who crossed many boundaries. Son of a semiliterate father and a wholly illiterate mother, he began life in terrible poverty. His schooling was meager and brief, and his first poems were written on chance scraps of paper while he worked as a farmer or laborer. When a collection of these poems was published in 1820, he came to the attention of a sympathetic nobleman who helped raise an annuity for his support. For a time, Clare was a celebrity, a kind of "natural wonder," appealing in his uncouthness to the current taste among intellectuals for primitive genius. The farmer's son toured London and met the literati, but the "peasant poet" soon found himself on the outs again trying to sell his books door-to-door.

At this time, an unhappy love affair of Clare's youth began to haunt him. He began to have delusions, added to a serious drinking problem, so his family placed him in an asylum. Clare remained in various asylums for the last twenty-seven years of his life, writing poetry in the brief lucid intervals of his madness. The "living sea of waking dream" in "I Am" is a vivid image of a madhouse common room where patients act out delusions and fantasies that the sane experience only in dreams. Thus, the reader can now recognize that the oxymoron of "waking dream" is really no more than a matter-of-fact description of a terrible reality. The obsessive return to assertions of identity in "I Am" is the desperate affirmation of a self threatened by disintegration into madness, into "the nothingness of scorn and noise" from which the poet briefly emerges through the clarity and nobility of his poem.

Clare was not the only poet of humble origins in this time who found fame only to die miserably. Robert Burns, Robert Bloomfield, and William Thom suffered much the same fate. This group is sometimes known as the "unlettered poets," and the name is indicative of the kind of condescension and half-comprehension they often encountered. Clare's repeated "I am" may share something—but far more mournful—of Burns's angry "a man's a man for a' that," which Burns wrote in defiance of all the monied privilege and pretension he grew to hate. Having escaped the confines of their class, these poets had a need to assert their identities, because this assertion was all the identity they had: "I am—yet what I am, none cares or knows."

Whitney Hoth

I CANNOT LIVE WITH YOU—

Author: Emily Dickinson (1830-1886)
Type of poem: Lyric
First published: 1890, as "In Vain," in *Poems by Emily Dickinson;* collected in
The Poems of Emily Dickinson, 1955

The Poem

"I cannot live with You— "(the title is not Emily Dickinson's, since she did not title her poems) is a poem of fifty lines divided into eleven four-line stanzas and a concluding twelfth stanza of six lines. The poem—more than twice the length of many of Dickinson's poems—is an unusually long poem for Dickinson. It is written in the first person from the point of view of a speaker addressing a lover.

Structurally, the poem is a list of things the speaker and her lover cannot do together and the reasons why they cannot. In the first three stanzas, the speaker announces to her beloved that she cannot "live" with the person because of the nature of "Life" itself. Life as it is ordinarily conceived of by those who deal with it daily on its most basic levels—the "Housewife" and the "Sexton" who locks up and unlocks ("keeps the Key to") both earthly possessions and the graveyard—is something subject to decay: It can "crack" and be "Discarded."

The speaker goes on to assert in the fourth and fifth stanzas that neither could she "die" with her beloved, because one of them would have to remain alive in order to close the other's eyes ("For One must wait/ To shut the Other's Gaze down"). The speaker asserts further that logically it would be impossible for her both to "see" the beloved die ("freeze") and to be dead at the same time (to have her "Right of Frost").

In the sixth and seventh stanzas, the speaker explains why she could not "rise," or be resurrected, with her beloved. Her reason is that resurrection to the "New Grace" of Jesus requires placing Jesus at the center of one's life, acknowledging him to be, metaphorically, the brightest sun. The speaker's "homesick Eye," however, is focused on her beloved: "Because Your Face/ Would put out Jesus'." The beloved not only is more central than Jesus to the speaker's life but also entirely blots out the face of Jesus. The eighth and ninth stanzas then predict the inevitable judgment that would be brought about by the speaker's blasphemy. The speaker's only defense, however, is a reiteration of her blasphemy: Her beloved "saturated" her "Sight" so completely that she could no longer see ("had no more Eyes/ For") more shadowy, "sordid" types of "excellence" such as God's "Paradise."

In the tenth and eleventh stanzas, the speaker cites further difficulties that could arise should the two lovers be resurrected and judged together: One of them could be damned and the other saved. Regardless, the speaker insists, her own "self" would be a "Hell" to her if she were separated from her lover. It is these reasons that lead to the conclusion of the final and longest stanza: "So We must meet apart." Since the two lovers cannot be together, they can only be with each other by being apart and sustaining themselves with the only things they share: distance and "Despair."

Forms and Devices

One of the most important devices used in the poem is metaphor, a figure of speech in which one thing is seen in terms of something else. The speaker of the poem uses the language of love — specifically, that of the renunciation of love — as a way of both denouncing and renouncing the traditional paradigm for human life set forth by Christianity.

The poem is structured according to the stages of human life as defined by this traditional Christian paradigm: life, death, resurrection, judgment, damnation/salvation, eternity. Rather than overtly criticize the adequacy of this model for human life, however, the speaker considers the value and "Sustenance" afforded by this paradigm through an examination of its implications for a love relationship.

Within this larger metaphorical structure, the poem incorporates a parallel metaphor of sensory experiences that underscores the speaker's rejection of both traditional definitions of "Life" and conventional modes of experiencing and perceiving "Life"; the speaker invokes images of eating, seeing, hearing, physical proximity, and again, at the end, eating. The first three stanzas employ images associated with eating in order to develop a metaphor for human life as it is traditionally viewed: "Life" is a piece of "Porcelain" or a "Cup" that contains the human spirit for a while until it cracks, breaks, or becomes outmoded ("Quaint") and needs to be "Discarded." The speaker implies that she and her lover require "A newer Sevres," a finer piece of porcelain — in other words a newer, more elaborate metaphor for "Life."

The fourth through the ninth stanzas focus on the process of seeing in order to critique traditional notions about death, resurrection, and judgment. In the traditional Christian paradigm, death is not subject to human intervention, resurrection is contingent on the "New Grace" of God, and judgment is solely the province of God. Through metaphors of sight, however, the speaker undermines God's authority and power in all of these realms. In stanzas 4 and 5, death is redefined as the freezing of sight, and only the lovers have the power "To shut the Other's Gaze down." Similarly, in stanzas 6 and 7, it is the vision of the beloved's face — not Christ's — in the "Eye" of the lover that shines brighter and "closer" and that, therefore, makes possible resurrection.

Finally, in stanzas 8 and 9, the implications of this metaphor of the sun (with a pun on "son of God") are fully developed. The speaker — in a dazzling metaphor of blindness — discounts conventional judgment and defends herself: She has been so ecstatically blinded ("You saturated Sight") by the beloved that she no longer has "Eyes" and can no longer see such "sordid" things as traditional "Paradise." In the final stanza, the speaker returns to the metaphor of eating to assert the lack of nourishment provided by the traditional model for human life; she and her lover have created a new form of "Sustenance" — "Despair."

Themes and Meanings

This poem is a critique of the traditional paradigm for human life set forth by Christianity. By means of the metaphor of a love relationship, the speaker delineates the inadequacy of this paradigm as a model for human existence and affirms a superior, individual definition of "Life." What first appears in the poem to be a renunciation of love becomes, in fact, a renunciation of those ways of viewing life that interfere with the higher vision of the lovers.

The speaker renounces those definitions of life which do not provide "Sustenance." "Life" that is susceptible to decay, mutability, and—more important—the authority of others (the "Sexton," the "Housewife," "They," or God Himself) is life that can be and needs to be "Discarded." The speaker, from the beginning, implies that the two lovers can create a different kind of life that is not perishable—an eternal life: "A newer Sevres pleases." Similarly, power over death is appropriated by the lovers. If, as the speaker metaphorically asserts, to die is to have one's sight "freeze," then the lovers will be looking at each other so steadfastly that only they can stop the gaze of each other, only they can bring about death.

The speaker goes on to eradicate the possibility of traditional resurrection when she says, in effect, that her beloved is brighter, more enlightening, and more of a "sun" to her "Eye" than Jesus: Her lover, in other words, is the source of true vision. Furthermore, the speaker argues, trying to fit into this traditional paradigm only makes the lovers vulnerable to the judgments of others. Once her beloved becomes vision itself—"You saturated Sight"—she is blinded and unable to perceive lesser, "sordid" things such as "Paradise." Both lovers thus are freed to develop their own criteria for damnation and salvation: To be together is to be "saved," to be apart is "Hell."

In the final stanza, the speaker arrives at the conclusion that the poem has been building up to: Because the traditional paradigm available to the lovers for expressing life, love, salvation, vision, and eternity does not work, they "must meet apart." Because the lovers now create the terms of their own life, death, and salvation, they are free enough and powerful enough to redefine, too, both the traditional love relationship and the conventional meanings of language.

In this way, the poem can be viewed as a critique of God's divine plan for human life, in which Christ will be "that bread of life," "the light of the world," and "the resurrection, and the life" (John 6:48, 9:5, 11:25). In accordance with God's plan, Christ asserts in John 14:6: "I am the way, the truth, and the life: no man cometh unto the Father, but by me." By means of the poem, however—which is disguised as a renunciation of love—the speaker creates a "Life" to rival God's traditional plan for life; by developing their rival definitions of life, death, and salvation, the lovers arrive at their self-determined "judgment" and "Paradise." They become their own saviors. Christ as the sustaining "bread" of life has been supplanted by the lovers' self-derived source of nourishment: "that White Sustenance—/ Despair." Finally, the last stanza of the poem—with its additional two lines—literally and metaphorically adds one more stage to the traditional Christian paradigm for human life—an augmentation that is both a further act of blasphemy and a final assertion of the speaker's ultimate power and triumph.

Angela M. Estes

I FELT A FUNERAL IN MY BRAIN

Author: Emily Dickinson (1830-1886)
Type of poem: Lyric
First published: 1896, in *Poems: Third Series;* collected in *The Poems of Emily Dickinson*, 1955

The Poem

Like all Emily Dickinson's poems, this one bears no title. The usual way of referring to a Dickinson poem is therefore through either its first line or its assigned number in Thomas Johnson's definitive edition. "I felt a Funeral in my Brain" is vintage Dickinson in both form and theme, given to homely illustration from life — here a funeral — simplicity of construction, irregular rhyme, and a preoccupation with death in a context of somber meditation. Outwardly a simple poem, it is one of several that Dickinson wrote not only to note the pervasiveness of death as ending, but also to explore the very nature of death itself.

The initial stanza commences with what is fundamentally a conceit through which the persona, or speaker in the poem, attempts to articulate what death is like through an unusual analogy — that of a "Funeral in [the] Brain." Intriguingly, and not an uncommon stance in Dickinson, the viewpoint is that of one who has already died. In recall, the funeral is sufficiently vivid nearly to transport the persona back to the realm of sense — or, as the speaker says, "it seemed/ That Sense was breaking through."

Stanza 2 continues the poem's emphasis on the ritual of death with a movement from sense to numbing, as if underscoring death's inexorable onslaught on life. The analogy is to the funeral service. As in the opening stanza, the third line reinforces death's macabre finality in its repetitive insistence, here by using the participle "berating."

Stanza 3 moves toward burial with the lifting of the coffin "across [the] soul," a way of suggesting not merely the disembodiment of the soul, or psyche, the coffin passing through its immaterial substance, but also an obliteration of human and immortal significance. This fact lies behind the stanza's mournful clarion, "Then space began to toll," depicting both the resonance of the church bells and the thunderous fact of the grave as the ultimate separator from the senses.

Unusual here is Dickinson's use of a run-on stanza, leading into the penultimate fourth stanza, in which the persona is metonymized as an "Ear" forced to take in this overwhelming proclamation of the bells — "As [though] all the Heavens were a bell." Death empties one of personhood, and one is joined to an eternal silence, countermanding that of the world of sense above. Thus, the persona suggests the analogy of shipwreck in "Wrecked solitary" to depict the disintegration and isolation of the dead.

In the final stanza, the persona recalls her interment in the ground, and here the true crisis of the poem is waged with the breaking of "a plank in reason." Death represents a fall from rationality into nothingness—hence, into nonbeing. Cryptically, the persona speaks of the consequence of this fall as one of "hit[ting] a world at every plunge," perhaps suggesting the hellish worlds of mythological and biblical import and their traditional association with the earth's interior. Death is thus the legacy of man's first Fall and its own hell, in which humankind has "finished knowing."

Forms and Devices

Noteworthy in the poem is the employment of near rhyme in lines 2 and 4 of the initial stanza to suggest disintegration. In the ceremonial observances of the next three stanzas, regularity asserts itself in the rhyming of the second and fourth lines, as if the poet were suggesting that it is in human rite that humans attempt to assign meaning to death. The final stanza, however, is ominous in its breaking of the "plank of reason," as if implying the folly of such attempts to bridge, or transcend, death's chasm through the imposition of a rationale upon the cosmic scheme of things. Accordingly, there is not even near rhyme, for death is the ultimate cessation of any kind of knowing, the consummate disintegration of sense.

Repetition is pervasive in the first three stanzas to underscore both the solemnity of the occasion and the ominous truth that death represents. There are "mourners to and fro" who keep "treading, treading"; there is a service that is like a drum that is "Kept beating, beating," while in stanza 3, the persona hears "those same boots of lead again." Behind this repetition lies the implication of death as an inexorable process undoing everyone. Thus, while the time aspect of the poem is ostensibly one of past tense, the persona reminiscing, one finds the irony of a repetition affirming time's slow but inevitable movement toward human dissolution in which time itself will die. It is a theme similar to that of Dickinson's more familiar poem "Because I could not stop for Death."

As always in a Dickinson poem, the imagery of the poem is arresting, both for its sources in the commonality of everyday life and for its assigned function in the poem as the weave of a conceit, or extended analogy. Here the real event is inner, not outer. The poem deals not with what death means to mourners, but with what death means for its victim: the loss of that which makes life possible, the senses. That loss is referred to in the poem as a "funeral in [the] brain" or a "mind . . . going numb," or "a plank in reason" that breaks.

This last image is the most striking of all. In the context, the plank suggests a means of passage over a chasm. It breaks, hurling the persona into the depths below. Dickinson may be suggesting the insufficiency of rationality to prepare one for the "fall" into death. Quite certainly, death marks the ending of all rationality and, hence, of all knowing. Strikingly, it is with the breaking of the plank of reason that the reader returns full circle to the poem's startling opening, "I felt a Funeral in my Brain."

Themes and Meanings

Dickinson often objectifies death through a narrator who recalls her own death. This occurs, for example, in poems 449, 465, and 712. Along with God, nature, and love, death is a favorite theme. At times Dickinson's position toward death seems contradictory. On one hand, she seems nearly to celebrate it as an anodyne to life, as in "Because I could not stop for Death," where death appears in the guise of a suitor and the grave is a "House" in the ground. On the other hand, death is that stain upon the cosmos, an act of a "burglar" deity. In one of her letters, she exclaimed, "I can't stay any longer in a world of death."

The poem is notable for its lack of a consolatory element, a departure from the custom of the time. Indeed, it offers no message of any kind, either about how to live or how to prepare for Eternity. The emphasis is upon death, its stark reality as a divorcer from the senses and as life's ultimate ritual. A person has no source of promptings for its content. Clearly the poem is not Christian in its depiction of death as ultimate extinction rather than as passage into glory.

It is possible that the poem deals with a psychical death—that is, with the desperate attempt of the mind to ward off pain through repression, or the forgoing of consciousness. In this vein, the analogy of burial is an appropriate one. Elsewhere (poem 777), Dickinson writes of "The Horror not to be surveyed—/ But skirted in the Dark—/ With Consciousness suspended—/ And Being under Lock." In poem 341, Dickinson writes that "After great pain, a formal feeling comes—/ The Nerves sit ceremonious, like Tombs." In the same poem, she writes, "This is the hour of Lead," which may be compared with the "boots of lead" in the present poem.

It is also conceivable that the poem depicts the mind's downward journey into madness or psychological dislocation. In this connection, poem 435 speaks of "Madness" as the "divinest Sense" and of "Much Sense—the starkest Madness." Indeed, some critics have argued for a psychotic disturbance in Emily Dickinson or for some kind of severe loss in her life that created a devastating emotional aftermath.

Ralph Robert Joly

I HAVE A TERRIBLE FEAR OF BEING AN ANIMAL

Author: César Vallejo (1892-1938)
Type of poem: Narrative
First published: 1939, as "Tengo un miedo de ser un animal," in *Poemas humanos*; collected in *Human Poems*, 1968

The Poem

"I have a terrible fear of being an animal" is a poem of twenty-seven lines that is divided into four stanzas. It is in free verse and makes ample use of internal rhyme and assonance in the original Spanish. One of the dated poems in *Poemas humanos*, this poem bears the date of October 22, 1937.

The poem is actually untitled; using its first line as its title is a convenience for scholars, critics, translators, and students, not the wish of the poet. The first line, however, does reveal more about the poem and the poet in what it does not say than in what it does. It is not "becoming" an animal that the persona/poet fears, but "being" one. With that acknowledgment, he gives credibility to his grosser animal self, the more profoundly sensual self that he carries within. Although the animal exists, it is one of "white snow."

The first stanza also expresses the idea that each positive natural element has its negative aspect; each object of strength has its implied weakness. The animal has power, but that power is ameliorated by its snowy substance. The same is true of the other elements of nature. The splendid and supremely sunny day, because of its brilliance, has implicit within it the equally supreme and pervasive night.

The second stanza explores the absurdity of man—his fragmentation, his emptiness, and his implicit and unfulfilled dual nature. In the third stanza, César Vallejo seems to appeal more to the senses than to the mind. In nostalgic reminiscence of the early Symbolist poets' perfume concerts, he seeks "aromatic logic." The unusual juxtaposition of aroma and logic serves to infuse each with the qualities of the other, thus negating the pure quality of both.

The fourth stanza centers on the essential struggle in which each person is engaged: the basic struggle to bring together the elements of the transcendent and the prosaic, the physical and the ephemeral, the mind and the senses. The poet exhorts one to act, to remain within and without at the same time. For Vallejo, the intangibility of existence can be seen in the consistent verbal destablization of concept and sensation. Therefore, "to thrash, to exist, to cough, to secure oneself" is to be in constant flux, but the function of existence is to try to capture the essential reality that exists somewhere between all oppositions.

Forms and Devices

When reading Vallejo, and particularly the poems in *Poemas humanos*, it is useful to be aware of the figure of speech called synecdoche. Synecdoche is the use of a part of something to represent the whole—an individual for a class, a material for a thing—or vice versa. In "I have a terrible fear of being an animal," Vallejo makes extensive use of synecdoche. The purpose of using this device is to expand the evocative power of language by calling up all of the associations and consequent allusions that each fragment contains, and in so doing to build the levels of meaning of the poem. Another reason, especially noteworthy in Vallejo, is to confuse the reader.

In the first stanza, for example, there are several synecdochic fragments accenting light and darkness; day and night are obvious. "Archepiscopal" is less obvious but no less germane. This metonymic device relating to the church hierarchy may imply both light and darkness depending on the needs of poet and poem.

There are repeated allusions to power or powerlessness in the references to the "animal," to "snow," to earthly and unearthly forces, as in the ecclesiastical reference, to the animal's "veiny circulation," to his ability to "breathe" and transform himself, and finally in the terrestrial but significant emblem of "money," which leads both power and powerlessness to the man/animal.

The story that the poet tells by linking all these elements is neither direct nor easy to follow. It is almost like a series of verbal mirrors, each of which reflects and absorbs the light of the others in order to create a more rich and varied impression. In the second stanza, Vallejo refers to man as an "absurd" creature, a "premise" rather than a person. By using synecdoche, placing a hinge at his waist, separating his neck from the rest of his body, and giving him a snout rather than a nose, Vallejo shows just how fragmented and perhaps even puppetlike the animal/man is.

By including a reference to the "tabla of [John] Locke," Vallejo at once calls up the philosophical notion of the human entity born as a blank table, an empty slate, without heavenly gifts, and its author, who claimed that logic could be obtained through the association of ideas. The reference to "Bacon" is to Francis Bacon, the English philosopher, who established the technique of scientific inquiry based on what is observable and, therefore, deducible. By means of those various synecdochic juxtapositions, Vallejo underscores how absurd any creature—even a "premise" who is a man—actually is.

When Vallejo calls upon aromatic logic in the third stanza, the reader knows that he is drawing on the earlier mentioned technique of sensory stimulation of literary efforts by perfume, but he is also alluding to what foolishness the animal, man, has made of the idea as well as the operation of logic. There is further use of the sense of smell, but in a reality in which day is night— "lunar day" — and life is equal to death: "the alive absurdity and the dead absurdity." The pervasive scent there is putrid.

The last stanza compounds synecdochic and metonymic confusion, and the poet now can be seen thrashing about within the existence of the poem, using numbers as a further abstraction of the illusory power of words.

Themes and Meanings

"I have a terrible fear of being an animal" encapsulates the multiple spiritual, social, and aesthetic struggles of Vallejo the man and Vallejo the poet. From his earliest days, Vallejo struggled with the traditional and acceptable forms of spirituality. He rebelled against the imposition of the moral and ethical values of his family and society by listening to the promptings of his interior life. He tried to make sense of the disparate nature of theory and practice whether at work in theology, life, or literature.

Vallejo uses this poem to explore the conflicts between art and life, the earth and beyond, man and god. The poem itself becomes an analogue, a reflection of these various systems and bodies.

Vallejo says in "Los dados eternos" ("The Eternal Dice"), for example, that God is dead, at least in his supremacy over man, but he acknowledges the existence of God in a diminished form. In that work, he elevates man, but in this poem, he reduces man by exposing his frailty and his invincibility simultaneously. In his theoretical writing on the avante-garde, Vallejo deplores the capitalist intelligentsia's control of the ostensibly new in poetry. In this poem, however, he laments the animal's inability "to change itself and have money." Vallejo also repeatedly uses many of the techniques of the movements he reviles.

Vallejo says in his essay on "New Poetry" that new poetry that is based on new words or new metaphors is new only in the sense of novelty or complication, but new poetry that is based on "new sensibility is . . . simple and human and . . . might be taken for old." Nevertheless, his own poetry retains all the conventions of the modern.

The poem, then, can be seen as a duel between Vallejo and himself. Essentially, he fulfills Arthur Rimbaud's idea that his self is an "other." The poem is his battleground, and rather than drawing the reader into the fray, the poet further distances and alienates his audience. He uses numbers at the end, when words have lost their meaning. They become cheap, valueless in their ability to communicate. Ultimately, the poem is left open to as many possibilities as man is. As Vallejo has said, one must be careful of the human substance in poetry.

Heather Rosario-Sievert

I HAVE FORGOTTEN THE WORD I WANTED TO SAY

Author: Osip Mandelstam (1891-1938)
Type of poem: Lyric
First published: 1922, as "Ia slovo pozabyl, chto ia khotel skazat'," in *Tristia*;
  collected in *The Eyesight of Wasps*, 1989

The Poem

"I Have Forgotten the Word I Wanted to Say" is a poem of six stanzas, each composed of four lines. Its rhythm is created by the placement of a regular number of accented syllables before and after the caesura, the pause in the middle of the line. This style of tonic verse is called *dolniki* in Russian and was the verse form preferred by some innovative Russian poets of the early twentieth century.

The poem, as is frequently the case in Russian lyric poetry, depends very much on its form to convey the poetic content. By writing in *dolniki* instead of a stricter accentual-syllabic meter, Osip Mandelstam enjoyed greater flexibility in the number of unaccented syllables he could use in a line. As a result, the lines vary in length from nine to thirteen syllables while echoing consistently in four beats. This irregularity in the line length allows the poem to assume a more individual nature where shorter lines add tension and longer lines develop the thought. The caesura, while helping to organize the sound pattern by dividing the lines into two sound groups with two accents each, also inserts a pause into the often rather long line. Since the poem is philosophical and laden with profuse symbolism, the caesura gives the reader/listener some extra time to visualize or reflect on the poem's meaning.

The persona begins relating his experience using a phrase very much like one used by everyone at some time: "I have forgotten the word I wanted to say." In this first line (which serves as the title), in Russian, the "word" is emphasized. This emphasis at the very beginning hints that it is not only that the persona has forgotten what to say, but also that there is a special importance to the word, that the word is invested with a special value. Resounding throughout the remainder of the poem is the frustration and anguish this experience causes the persona.

For the poet, the loss of a word is catastrophic, since the dominant force in his life is communicated in words. Thus, in the second stanza, as "the word swoons," life itself seems to cease: "No birds are heard. No blossom on the immortelle." Similar images of the void and bleakness echo this one — for example, "An empty boat floats on an arid estuary."

Nor can the persona find that word for all his searching. It takes on varying attitudes, becoming a "tent or shrine," acting like the mourning Antigone, or falling "like a dead swallow." He bemoans his predicament and wishes for a return to a former state of being, in which he was able to command his words and never let down the creative expectations of the muses. Having forgotten what he wanted to say, he has become lifeless. He associates only with death, and can only articulate a sense of muteness and loss.

Forms and Devices

Mandelstam wrote during a period very heavily influenced by Russian Symbolism, a type of writing in which profuse images that take on the aspect of symbols are greatly instrumental in conveying the artistic designs of the poet. Some of Mandelstam's images may appear strange, and their sheer density with respect to the content of the poem makes for difficult reading. To the reader uninitiated in classical poetry, the repeated evocation of swallows and shadows may seem quite foreign, but other images may be more akin to the reader's experience, such as singing absentmindedly, which conveys the mental destitution the poet feels at his powerlessness.

The entire poem revolves around an extended metaphor laden with symbolic imagery. "The word" represents expression, which, particularly to a poet but also to every mortal, is life itself. When the persona says he has "forgotten the word," he is saying figuratively that he has lost his ability to create or express and, thus, the power to live in a human sense.

The word in this metaphorical sense is symbolized by the swallow. Thus, either the word (in stanza 5) or the swallow (in stanza 1) must "fly back" to the "palace of shadows"; the symbol for "the word" becomes interchangeable with what it symbolizes.

Flying would seem to be a mixed metaphor used with "the word," but since "the word" has been clearly identified with the swallow, the figure transfers successfully without any confusion. Moreover, many romantic notions of creativity involve the metaphor of flying to achieve inspiration. Among these, Plato's chariot of winged steeds (in *Phaedrus*, fourth century B.C.) is very important to Mandelstam. On this chariot, the artist can be drawn above the mundane, everyday world into the heavens, where the ideal from which to model one's artistic vision can be found. The swallow naturally embodies an experience outside everyday human life, the ability to fly, and thus symbolically represents the poet's power of inspiration, which must also draw on experience outside daily human existence. The blind swallow, however, has no power; indeed, her wings are clipped. Similarly, Mandelstam's persona is powerless, and his position is much like death.

The "shadows" and the "transparent ones" represent the insubstantial remains of the dead in Hades, the place where Mandelstam's word is detained. The "palace of shadows" is thus the edifice of the realm of the dead. "Stygian affection" (stanza 3) and "Stygian clamour" (stanza 6)—from the river Styx, in Hades—repeat the motif of the realm of the dead.

The profusion of symbols throughout the poem does not obscure its pure, lyric beauty. "Oh to bring back the shyness of clairvoyant fingers,/ Recognition's rounded happiness!" Somehow, the numbness that has overtaken the persona cannot obliterate the former state of grace in which even his fingers could see and memory connected properly with its original sensation.

Themes and Meanings

"I Have Forgotten the Word I Wanted to Say" is a poem about creation, about the act and paramount importance of creating. "The Word made flesh" is the biblical metonymy for God's most unique creation, His son, Jesus. Also in the Bible, "the Word" was the first, and thus arguably the greatest, thing created by God. In the Russian Symbolist world view, to which Mandelstam ascribed in many respects, the poet is like a god. Although, like any human, the poet is forced to exist in the domain of everyday life, during the act of poetic creation, he or she is lifted above the crowd (as though by the chariot of Plato's *Phaedrus*) to the lofty heights usually accessible only to deities. Losing the ability to create, then, condemns the poet to an earthbound existence with the gray masses, symbolized by the shadows of Hades. There is something godlike in creating with words. There were special reasons, however, that creation was important to Mandelstam—not only because he aspired to attain some exalted status as a god-man.

Expression in the Soviet Union after the Bolshevik Revolution of 1917 was becoming less and less free. Schools of writing were initiated to teach the proper social class, the so-called proletariat, which was often constituted more of agrarian types, the proper production of a new type of literature that was really mythologized propaganda. People were writing panegyrics to Lenin, to socialism, to factories, hydroelectric stations, tractors, combines, collectivization, and the most pedestrian of topics imaginable, which the authorities claimed fulfilled the real mission of literature: to inculcate "correct" culture into the masses. Some poets joined the bandwagon and began writing propagandistic verse, most notably Vladimir Mayakovsky ("Eat your pineapple and chew your veal/ Your end is coming soon, you bourgeois!"). Poets such as Mandelstam were under pressure to conform to this unaesthetic, institutionalized norm. Thus, the symbols of the world of the dead—the shadows or shades of Hades, the river Styx—really symbolize the fate of all expression, the death of the ability to create. Mandelstam's earliest fears were, unfortunately, well-founded. Twelve years after the writing of this poem, he would be arrested for the first time, and four years after that he would die in a transit camp in Siberia.

Creativity is the very essence of life, but it is a latent human talent; creation is its active principle and supplies the necessary vessel for the embodiment of that creativity. The word left unembodied is not a part of a creation; if forgotten, perhaps the word does not exist at all. If kept from writing, perhaps the poet is not alive at all. Mandelstam conveys this damnation poetically: "I have forgotten what I wanted to say/ And a thought without flesh flies back to its palace of shadows."

Christine D. Tomei

I HEARD A FLY BUZZ—WHEN I DIED—

Author: Emily Dickinson (1830-1886)
Type of poem: Dramatic monologue
First published: 1896, as "Dying," in *Poems: Third Series*; collected in *The Poems of Emily Dickinson*, 1955

The Poem

Emily Dickinson did not give titles to most of her poems. They are usually labeled by their first lines, and her modern editor, Thomas H. Johnson, has numbered them according to his conclusions about their order of composition (this poem is numbered 465). Publications of the poem before Johnson's *The Poems of Emily Dickinson* (1955) are usually of the text as it was altered by Mabel Loomis Todd when she published *Poems: Third Series* (1896).

"I heard a Fly buzz—when I died—" consists of four stanzas, with Dickinson's characteristic slant- or near-rhymes in the second and fourth lines of each quatrain. The first-person speaker of the poem is at some remove from Dickinson's lyric voice; these words come from beyond the grave. Dickinson wrote a number of poems from this point of view; perhaps the most famous is "Because I could not stop for Death—" (poem 712). This subject held a particular fascination for Dickinson, in part because she was interested in resolving religious doubts about life continuing after death. In this poem, the dead speaker looks back at the moment of death.

After announcing that she heard a fly buzz when she died, the speaker describes the moments that led up to this event. The first stanza describes the silence of the room before she died as like the quiet between two phases of a storm. The second stanza describes the people present at the deathbed. They are also quiet, exhausted from their watch and preparing now for the final loss. In the third stanza, she says she had just made her last wishes known when the fly "interposed." The last two lines of this stanza begin the long sentence that continues through the final stanza. This sentence describes how the fly seemed to blot out the light, and then all light ceased, leaving her conscious but utterly blinded.

The poem announces at the outset that sound will be important. The middle of the poem emphasizes the silence as temporary, as a fragile period between storms of suffering and weeping. The end of the poem returns to the sound of the fly's buzz, seemingly quiet and inconsequential, not a storm at all and yet marking indelibly the momentous instant of transition.

Forms and Devices

Dickinson's stanza form is not remarkable in itself; indeed, students of her poetry take delight in finding comically inappropriate melodies for singing her poems, the majority of which follow the rhythms of familiar hymn tunes. (This poem, for example, works equally well with "Oh God Our Help in Ages Past" and "The Yellow

Rose of Texas.") What makes her stanzas remarkable is the contrast between their conventional rhythms and the striking metaphors, symbols, and points of view they contain. Two complexes of comparison are especially interesting in this work: those conveying the silence before the fly appears and those characterizing the fly.

When Dickinson compares the stillness in the room to the "Stillness in the Air—/ Between the Heaves of Storm," she conveys at least three interesting things about this quiet moment. First, it is a temporary lull that follows violence and is expected to precede more violence. That violence, being associated with a storm, seems to exceed the capacity of a mere room to hold it. By giving the storm "heaves," she begins a second comparison between the storm and weeping. This comparison is taken up in the second stanza by means of synecdoche, in which a part of something is used to signify the whole. She says "The Eyes around—had wrung them dry." Eyes signify the mourners as do the breaths in the following line. Just as the mourners have been heaving in their weeping, their eyes have been wringing themselves dry, like wet cloths, or like clouds in a storm. By this means, Dickinson asks readers to imagine both the room and each individual mourner as filled with a storm of grief that is beyond encompassing. Finally, she reveals that the mourners are awaiting "the last Onset," the image of the storm is extended to the speaker herself, for there is a storm taking place in her as well, a storm of suffering that might also be compared to a battle, in which this lull signals the final, fatal onset.

What is expected next, then, is momentous sound, the climax of mourning, grief, and suffering. When the expectation of painful climax is clear, the poem turns to the idea of compensation or comfort. The second stanza says that when the last onset comes, the "King" will manifest himself. In the conventional view of death in nineteenth century America, that "King" (capitalized for emphasis and to indicate divinity) would be Christ, come to reap the soul of the dying Christian. By not naming this "King" however, Dickinson creates an ambiguity that reverberates through the whole experience of the poem. The figure might just as well be Death as Christ. Furthermore, what actually appears to the dying woman is not any recognizable king at all but a fly.

When the fly appears, a double reversal takes place. The storm metaphor and the expectation of a king lead the reader to anticipate something momentous at the end of the poem. This expectation is answered by the fly. These reversals invite the reader to explore the connections between the fly and the king. Such explorations lead into further shocking violations of expectation regarding meaning in the poem.

By exploring the metaphor of fly as king, one comes to the realization of the fly as a symbol. The best-known "fly king" is Beelzebub, lord of the flies and prince of devils. There is nothing in the poem to suggest that the woman should expect eternal damnation, yet Dickinson seems to have made this connection with its surprising connotations. Furthermore, flies are conventionally associated with death; they swarm on carrion, and their larvae thrive there. The most terrifying possible meaning for a religious person in the substitution of a fly for a king is that death is final, that the soul dies with the body and there is no afterlife.

Dickinson's technique emphasizes the violation of expectations. In addition to the primary substitution (of fly for king), she enacts a similar violation when she rhymes "me" and "fly" in the third stanza, reintroducing the fly with a near-rhyme. Finally, she repeats this pattern by shifting from sound to sight at the end of the poem, when the buzz of the fly seems to blot out the speaker's light so that the windows fail to let light into her room, and her consciousness, still apparently operational, loses its connections by means of sight and sound to the familiar physical world.

Themes and Meanings

Dickinson, like many of her contemporaries in the middle of the nineteenth century, was deeply concerned about the truth of the conventional Christianity taught and generally believed in her culture. Like that of Ralph Waldo Emerson, Nathaniel Hawthorne, and Herman Melville, her religious questioning resulted in part from the general decline of the authority of Christianity in Western civilization. This decline had begun most visibly perhaps with the rise of rivals to the Roman Catholic Church's secular power in nation-states and had continued through the splintering of that church in the Reformation, the intellectual and scientific critique of Christianity's traditional interpretations of history and nature during the Enlightenment, the challenges to Christianity's moral and political power in the American and French revolutions, and the spread of knowledge about powerful rival religious systems partly as a result of advancing world trade and communication.

Many of Dickinson's poems are about the various problems of faith and doubt that would occur to a brilliant and imaginative mind in her culture. This poem is an attempt to pierce through the absolute barrier that stands between the poet and the life beyond death. It attempts to answer the question: What comes in the moment that follows death?

Dickinson places herself in the mind of a woman who has died. She relives the moment of death, trying to imagine it and the hoped-for illumination that should follow. She finds at the instant of death a clarity of perception that she tries to extend through that instant. Yet what her imagination provides at that crucial instant is the fly, which ends illumination and leaves the consciousness in utter darkness.

Nevertheless, consciousness remains. The voice speaks from beyond the grave, but all it can reveal is what its senses could apprehend before death, that instant when the senses ceased to operate. Beyond that is a blank, toward which the fly as a symbol points but about which it reveals nothing but questions: Who is the King? Is it death? Is it Christ? Is it something unimaginably terrifying, like Beelzebub? The fly ushers the poet across the threshold suggested by its "Blue—uncertain stumbling buzz." The fly points the way, but the living cannot interpret its buzz, and her voice stops.

Terry Heller

I KNOW A MAN

Author: Robert Creeley (1926-   )
Type of poem: Lyric
First published: 1957, in *The Whip*

The Poem

There is a deceptive simplicity to many of Robert Creeley's poems which tends to camouflage the power the poet brings to his subject and temporarily delay a full apprehension of the work's psychological penetration. A typical example is "I Know a Man," one of Creeley's most anthologized early lyrics, which is written in the discursive and reflective voice Creeley often uses. Its four stanzas are essentially a continuous expression in which nearly every word is a unit of meaning, its position and location amid punctuation, space, and other words crucial to its purpose.

This poem is an example of "open verse" or "composition by field," which Creeley developed through his friendship and correspondence with Charles Olson; it is employed throughout the poems collected in *For Love* (1962) to permit Creeley an "obsessive confrontation with solipsism" (as Charles Altieri identified it) and an occasion for close scrutiny of the psychological mood of the speaker.

The opening lines, beginning "As I sd to my/ friend," plunge into what appears to be an ongoing dialogue. Although there is a suggestion that the poem is part of a conversation, it is also a version of an inner dialogue in which dual components of the poet's psyche are involved. The ambiguity is introduced in the second stanza when the speaker observes, after what seems like a direct address to his friend—the person called "John"—that it "was not his/ name." When the second stanza asserts that "the darkness sur-/ rounds us," it is evident that this is as much a statement of psychic perception as a literal account of a specific occurrence.

When the poet asks, "what/ can we do against/ it," the second stanza joined to the third by the query, a mood of resignation begins to develop, but it is immediately challenged by a reversal that pivots around the phrase "or else" and abruptly moves toward direct action in the proposal to "buy a goddamn big car." This assertion links the philosophical with the physical, and the bold proposition to do something is both a specific possibility and a figure for choosing to take action. After the word "car," the third stanza concludes with a comma, a more significant pause than the previous connections between stanzas, which lack any punctuation; this sets off the last stanza, making it almost a response to the previous ones.

Once again, the opening line, "drive, he sd," maintains a dual focus, referring both to the "I" who speaks first and the "he" who is the other part of the dialogue. There is a momentary agreement that action is necessary, but this is fractured almost immediately when it become evident that the word "drive" more properly belongs to the "I" who suggests buying the car, while "he" is warning "look/ out where yr going." This admonition to retain an awareness of direction while acting reinforces the initial division in consciousness, but from an altered position.

Forms and Devices

The spare and urgent lyricism, as Charles Molesworth described it, which is the essence of Creeley's style in "I Know a Man," is developed through the employment of a vernacular mode of speech, by the arrangement of this language into tightly controlled rhythmic patterns, and by the organization of these rhythms into a structural frame that permits abrupt changes in psychic mood.

One of Creeley's governing poetic principles is the precept that a poem cannot be arranged in any previously anticipated form, but that its shape develops from the circumstances of its composition. In "I Know a Man," the concise, monosyllabic terseness of the first line establishes a clipped form of utterance in which the weight of each unit of meaning is important. Creeley is particularly attentive to nuances of stress, so that the opening statement moves toward completion in the second line, underscoring the importance of the "friend" who is addressed. The line then continues toward the phrase "I am," intensifying the personal nature of the declaration, a point pushed further by the third use of the word "I" to conclude the stanza. At the same time, the thought is carried directly to the next stanza by the power of the third "I" reaching across the space to the second use of "sd."

This firm control of perspective culminates in the brilliant ambiguity of the last stanza, where, as Creeley has described it, "the poem protects itself" through syntax which compels a reflective consideration of the conclusion:

> why not, buy a goddamn big car,
> drive, he sd, for
> christ's sake, look
> out where yr going.

While it is a legitimate interpretation to regard the directive "drive" as a part of the proposal that "he" has made, as some critics have done, Creeley's explanation that "[i]t's the 'I' of the poem who is saying 'why don't we get out of here'. . . it's the friend who comes into it, who says 'take it easy, look out where you're going,'" shows how concerned he is about carefully controlling meaning. Creeley further observes that he could have placed a period after "drive," but he believed that the "actual impulse" of the poem would eventually make the same point. His constant alertness to the complexity of language is also expressed in his choice of such abbreviations as "sd," "yr," and "&," which help to carry the tension of the speaker's voice throughout the poem, and which are in consonance with the compact nature of the speech as it moves from an arresting hesitancy to impulsive action. The division of the word "sur-/ rounds," with its use of a hyphen, conveys not only the tentativeness of the speaker but also the sense of enclosure from which he is trying to escape.

The third stanza moves toward this escape as the poet considers possibilities. The rapid change of mood is captured by the positioning of the threatening "it, or else," (suggesting unknown danger), followed by the sudden proposal, "shall we," which includes both members of the dialogue. This moves toward the almost manic assurance of "&/ why not," which is followed by the plunge into the specific, "buy a goddamn big car." The success of the poem depends on the relationship of words and on Creeley's sensitivity to the subtlest nuances of pitch, timbre, and sound duration. The absence of metaphor, metrical form, rhyme, figurative language, and other familiar technical devices places the total burden of meaning on word placement.

Themes and Meanings

Robert Hass has described "I Know a Man" as "the poem of the decade about a world gone out of control," while Creeley has spoken of the "senses of confusion and muddiness and opaqueness that people obviously feel in their lives" and which he tried to express in the poem. These insights together represent the dual focus of the poem—it is a reaction to chaos surrounding the poet and a response to the uncertainty that he regards as a prime component of his own psychic makeup. As Charles Altieri has observed, one of Creeley's goals is to construct "an aesthetic space for the multiple facets of the self," and in "I Know a Man," the conversational exchange is both a dialogue with another person and a reflective interior monologue in which alternative courses of action are debated. The friend called "John" is a representative of what Creeley sees as a fixture of friendship, a quality he values, and the phrase "I know a man" is used as a form of compliment that implies the friend's usefulness for both support and caution. In other words, the poet is describing an intimate encounter in which he feels close enough to the "other"— whether an aspect of his mind or an actual person—to share some of his deepest concerns.

The poem approaches the problem of stasis, a condition of dread that requires a bold stroke summoning energy from any available source. The "goddamn big car" is both a literal means of escape and a figure for seizing and using whatever power is accessible. The admonition to "look/ out where yr going" is part of a recognition by the "friend" (or inner voice of conscience) that the impulse to act is very human and must be respected, but that this type of spasmodic action does not really accomplish much.

The uncertainty (as well as the necessity) of the proposed solution is also an aspect of one of Creeley's most crucial aesthetic considerations: the relationship of the poet to his primary instrument, his language. It is through words that the poet attempts to reconcile the conflicting impulses of the self, but the words he uses carry their own inherent ambiguities, their implications of uncertainty. Therefore, just as it is sometimes necessary to "drive" without direction, it is also necessary to begin a poem without any assurance about its conclusion. The driver (or poet) may discover his destination (the poem) in the course of the act of driving (writing). The poet knows that merely getting into a "big car" is not sufficient; it is also crucial to watch "where yr going," and the admonition from the useful "friend" is as much a part of the poet's practice as the commitment to begin the poem to overcome the surrounding darkness. The parallel between writing and driving—an instant by instant awareness of where one is, a process requiring constant attention—is part of

Creeley's desire to exercise his craft as "an immediate relationship with the experience at hand," as Robert Kern has put it.

The poet is aware that he is "always talking" to combat the darkness, whether his voice is inner or externally directed, but he also knows that he is committed to an ultimately inexact solution. Language itself, the words of the poem, may be a barrier as well as an entrance, and the compulsive speech, replete with self-reflection, may be a kind of overcompensation for this limitation. When the poet says that John "was not his/ name," the poem shifts into a realm composed of words beyond direct connection to the outer world—a form of reality, but one with the potential for further abstraction. In this sense, the closing "look/ out where yr going" has implications for psychic stability that are almost as ominous as encouraging. This is why the friend prefaces it with "for/ christ's sake" and why the entire vehicle seems dangerously close to the edge of disaster.

Leon Lewis

I LIKE TO SEE IT LAP THE MILES—

Author: Emily Dickinson (1830-1886)
Type of poem: Lyric
First published: 1891, as "The Railway Train," in *Poems: Second Series*; collected in *The Poems of Emily Dickinson*, 1955

The Poem

As the title given to it by the first editors of Emily Dickinson's poem suggests, "I like to see it lap the Miles—" is about a train. It was not unusual for Emily Dickinson to write short descriptive poems of this kind, although she more often wrote about natural objects than mechanical ones. In this poem, she uses natural images to describe a thing which is only nearly named in a pun.

Dickinson first describes the thing as if it were like a cat, lapping and licking so many miles like so much milk. When it stops "to feed itself at tanks," however, one must adjust one's image from a household pet to something much larger. The next line reinforces this impression, as this thing is something "prodigious." It is big enough to go around not only one but many mountains in a single "step." When in the second stanza the reader is told that it looks into the windows of houses, one might even imagine a giant leaning down with his eye to a window. In line 8, however, the poem shifts focus from size to power: This thing can "pare" or carve a "quarry" out of rock.

In the first line of the third stanza, one's impression of the largeness of the thing shifts from height to length: It is something that "crawl[s]" and is noisy. In lines 10 and 11, the reader is told that its "complaint[s]" are "horrid" and "hooting," but because its noise is referred to as a "stanza," it is known somehow also to have a poetic or musical quality.

In the last line of the third stanza, the thing once again takes on a kittenish, playful quality—it "chase[s] itself down hill" like a kitten chasing its tail—but then, in the fourth stanza, it take shape as a horse that "neigh[s]" and returns to its "stable." Here, Dickinson makes a pun: In the nineteenth century, because the railroad had only recently replaced transport by cart horse, the railroad was referred to as the "Iron Horse" and its storage buildings as "car barns." Rather than being a reference to horses, "Boanerges" in the fourth stanza is a name applied to the disciples James and John, who were called "sons of thunder" when they cursed the Samaritans for not believing in the mission of Jesus. Presumably this reference in the poem is to the fearfulness of the thunderous "neigh" of the "Iron Horse."

The movement of the train is like clockwork. A natural image serves to communicate a sense of the mechanical: The train's movements are as regular as those of stars. The image of the shining star also suggests the metallic shininess of the train. At the end of the poem, the train abruptly ends its headlong journey with a "Stop—." When it is still, it seems "docile" and without aggression, but its force is only dormant, because it is still "omnipotent."

Forms and Devices

The poem's four stanzas are quatrains (they are four lines each). The pattern of beats, syllables, and rhymes in each stanza is called ballad meter, because this form is found in most traditional musical ballads: four iambic feet in the first and third line, three iambic feet in the second and fourth line, and a rhyme scheme of *abcb*.

It is difficult to analyze exactly what causes Dickinson's poems to have what one of her editors called a "strange cadence of inner rhythmical music," but one way to approach the matter is to trace the pattern of sounds in her poetry. For example, the consonance that begins with the repetition of certain letters in the first line carries through the entire poem. The repeating *l* of "like," "lap," and "miles" continues through the stanza with "valleys" and "itself"; one also finds it in "pile" and "supercilious" in the second stanza, in "crawl," "all," "while," and "downhill" in the third, and in "punctual," "docile," and "stable" in the fourth.

In each stanza, the words that have approximately the same sound at the end of the second and fourth lines—up/step, peer/pare, while/hill, star/door—are called near-rhymes; they are characteristic of Dickinson's poetry. Moreover, the pair of near-rhymes in the second stanza forms a near-rhyme with the pair in the fourth stanza: Both pairs end with *r* but have different vowel sounds.

Both of these consonants, *l* and *r*, are also part of internal near-rhymes in the second and third stanzas. In line 6, one finds a near-rhyme formed by the second syllable of "supercilious" (*per*) in the middle of the line and "peer" at the end of the line, and in line 5, by the first syllable of "quarry" (*quar*) with "pare." In line 10, there is an internal near-rhyme of "all" with "while," and in line 12, of "-self" with "Hill." The internal rhyme of "lap" in line 1 with the end rhyme of the stanza, "up"/"step," is repeated again with "stop" in line 15. The end consonant of those words also appears at the beginning of the end-rhymes of stanza 2.

One finds this same kind of extended repetition with certain vowel sounds, (that is, assonance), particularly with the long *i* that appears with the first word in line 1, "I." This sound reappears throughout the poem, with "like" and "miles" in line 1, "pile" in line 5, "sides" in line 9, "while" in line 10, "like" again in line 13, and depending upon how one pronounces it, possibly "docile" in line 15.

The question of how a word is to be pronounced is behind the elusive musiclike quality of the poem. Following a certain sound pattern may call for words to be pronounced one way, while another calls for the same words to be pronounced differently. These various sound patterns pull at individual words—for example, the word "docile": The *i* sound begun in line 1 calls for the second syllable to be pronounced with a long *i*, but the nearer sound of "Hill" calls for the *i* to be short. At the same time, the end sound of "punctual" in the preceding line presses for a *schwa* sound for the vowel.

Themes and Meanings

This economical single-sentence poem manages to propose various images for the locomotive. Some of them are natural, playful, and benign, while others are threatening or overwhelming. Between these two very different representations arises an ambiguity that is one of the themes of the poem.

In one sense, this ambiguity is a question of perspective. Seen from afar, perhaps, the train is a small, toylike thing, but at close range, it is gigantic. To step around piles of mountains is to pass beyond boundaries, which is in a sense to dislocate the horizon. To peer in windows is to intrude past other kinds of boundaries, to cause private life to become public, which is to violate the border between interior and exterior realms. A star is a thing which looks tiny but which science states is in fact huge almost beyond comprehension, so that comparing the locomotive to a star is to make a thing that appeared small and yet became huge seem infinitely small again. The poem, by playing with perspective, reveals the ambiguity that is intrinsic to the seen world.

In another sense, the ambiguity is one of attitude. The beast described does much consuming—it laps, licks, feeds, and pares rocks like vegetables. "Prodigious" is only one step away from prodigality, or excessive consumption. In addition, at the end of its breathless ride, like a horse, it arrives at the stable door, inside which it will presumably be fed. Meanwhile, it is "supercilious," or haughty, and "complain[s]" throughout its journey. The impression created by this series of images is that of a demanding, arrogant taskmaster.

Yet, ironically, the locomotive was invented to serve man, not to be served by him. So the poem, without explicitly saying so, questions the relationship between man and machine. This representation of the railroad as something of potential runaway power is strengthened by the references to the Boagernes, the star, and omnipotence. These images cast the locomotive in the role of a god. It resembles the disciples of Christ; its coincidence with a star associates it with the arrival of a messiah; its all-powerfulness is like God's. Nevertheless, the train is a thing made by man, not by God, as the many natural objects which represent it are. The problems of perspective which the poem raises call into question humankind's ability to see accurately at all and thus to know enough to undertake such creations.

The poem exaggerates this uncertainty by expressing itself in metaphors—images which are understood to portray a subject not explicitly but by suggestion. At the same time that the poem questions the wisdom of such creations as locomotives, however, it is itself a creation. Therefore, the subtle monstrosity of the poem—its shifting, protean metaphors—comes to mirror the possible monstrosity of its subject, and the presumption of divinity on the part of the inventors of the railroad is the same presumption claimed by the poet.

Laurie Glover

I MARRIED

Author: Lorine Niedecker (1903-1970)
Type of poem: Lyric
First published: 1976, in *Blue Chicory*

The Poem

"I married" is short and untitled; by convention, it is referred to by its first line. The simple declaration of the opening line is followed by a stanza break, and then by twenty short lines arranged in four stanzas. Though this is a free-verse lyric, the third and fourth lines of each stanza are linked by a rhyme or near-rhyme. Sometimes the focus of the poet's attention shifts dramatically within a given stanza, as well as from one stanza to the next.

In the first stanza, Lorine Niedecker speaks of her motivation for marrying—she sought a refuge of human kindness in a world whose deplorable condition she characterizes as a state of "black night." She next says that she expected "warmth" from her marriage but could not realistically hope for "repose." In this context, "warmth" is also something one desperately seeks in the face of a society that is "cold" like nighttime, and "repose" is something that is difficult to come by in a world that seems organized for the benefit of evildoers, just as nightfall is the time when criminals gain advantage and malevolent supernatural spirits are thought to stir. Niedecker concludes the stanza by noting that "at the close" she has found a companion. She was indeed sixty years old in 1963, when the marriage she speaks of took place.

In the second stanza, one gains a clearer sense of "the world's black night." Here Niedecker speaks of herself and her husband seeking shelter from "the long range guns." This phrase is packed with menacing significance. It suggests the deadly trajectory of a long-range nuclear missile launched at a target from somewhere far across the planet. It also evokes the wounding of concerned and knowledgeable persons by their awareness of armed conflicts occurring in other parts of the globe. Finally, the poet may be thinking of the electronic mass media: the television and radio stations that send their signals across long distances in every direction, seeking to addict as many people as possible to their inane offerings. The conclusion of the stanza turns from this evocation of violence and manipulation to another matter—it comments, amusingly, on the cramped condition of the apartment shared by the poet and her husband.

The opening of the third stanza speaks of "A slit of light/ at no bird dawn—." The first line evokes the stripe of brightness visible on the horizon at daybreak, but this dawn, presumably in winter, is unaccompanied by the delight offered by a chorus of birds. This suggests a moment when one feels a sense of spiritual renewal that is not as sweet as one had anticipated such a moment might be. Niedecker is telling readers that such vivifying, if not totally radiant, moments are typical of her marriage. The stanza then veers toward another consideration—the poet discusses the history of her attitude toward her husband's drinking habits.

In the final stanza, Niedecker builds on the poem's opening declaration to state that "I married/ and lived unburied." That is to say, the marriage has helped her to avoid sinking into a demoralized state of half-deadness. The poem ends not with this conclusive-sounding sentence, but rather with the enigma of the broken-off statement, "I thought— ."

Forms and Devices

"I married" is a challenging poem—it forces one constantly to maintain one's interpretive alertness, and one may be puzzled or even exasperated by its sometimes quirky movement from subject to subject. If one listens well to Niedecker's tone, one finds that it is also an engagingly friendly poem, for it radiates a feeling of candid and calm personal revelation, in which there is self-assurance without a trace of pompous self-importance, and meditation without brooding or abstraction.

Avoiding any theatrical outcries or effusions, the poet speaks quietly of the renewal she gained from her marriage and displays unembittered acceptance of the inherent limitations of human relationships and lives. Even wrenching societal horror is addressed in a calm manner. The poem's tone of amiable stillness and strength can be seen in the following lines:

> for warmth
>   if not repose.
>   At the close —
> someone.

The phrase "at the close" speaks of a potentially devastating fact: not having many more years to live. Yet these lines are arranged for the word "close" to be lightened by fitting into a cheerful rhyme. If one pronounces the lines aloud, one rushes eagerly to this rhyme once one has spoken the word "repose," for "at" and "the" are not syllables the tongue lingers over. One feels that Niedecker is facing her advanced age without terror.

There are odd shifts of attention in "I married" and sections that seem only loosely connected to the themes of the whole. Listening to the rhythms and other sonic aspects of the poem is relevant to this concern also; one perceives that, as in an excellent piece of music in which each passage grows logically from the notes that precede it, each moment of the poem sounds as if it fits exactly where it is. This tends to wear down any resistance one might have to the way the poem is constructed.

If one shifts one's attention from sound to meaning, resistance is also challenged by the vibrant nature of each portion of the poem. The passage about living in unroomy lodgings charms with its comical exaggeration, and when Niedecker writes

>   Untaught
>   I thought
> he drank
>
> too much,

the phrase "too much," isolated after the pause of a skipped line, links with the previous words of the sentence in two different ways. The sentence can mean, "Inexperienced, I thought he drank excessively," and, less obviously, "Inexperienced, I thought too much about his drinking." Both meanings are intended. The double duty performed by the simple words "too much" is an example of the condensed nature of Niedecker's poetry. She saw the compression of much meaning into few words as central to her poetic activity.

From beginning to end, "I married" is terse in its expression. One may note especially, however, the way in which the phrase "long range guns" encapsulates various frightening realities, and the curious manner in which the compact phrase "no bird dawn" is crafted by wrenching the noun "bird" into adjectival usage.

Themes and Meanings

"I married" sets its love story against the backdrop of a tragically unenlightened human race whose actions allow the "long range guns" to gather strength. Reference has already been made to the phrase "long range guns" as pointing both to warfare and to the broadcasts of the mass media. This interpretation may seem far-fetched; however, turning to other works of Niedecker, one finds that she often takes note of radio and television, sometimes quite negatively. In "Alone," for example, she celebrates being without a television set with the statement, "At last no (TV) gun." The gun metaphor in "Alone" refers to the way in which the public uses electronic entertainment as a weapon against meditation, anxieties, and other things it wishes to avoid.

Niedecker states in "I married" that her relationship to her husband has brought her much of the comfort she had sought. She speaks of the somewhat disappointing but still invigorating "dawn" moments and states near the end of the poem about eluding, through her marriage, a "buried" feeling of death in life.

In the latter passage, there is also another possible meaning: When Niedecker states, "I married/ and lived unburied," she can be seen as expressing thanks that the marriage itself has not crushed her spirit. The tangles and perils that must accompany the attempt to mingle two human lives are an important concern of this poem. The passage about drinking can be viewed as relevantly exhibiting one of the tangles of Niedecker's married life.

This leads, finally, to a possible added significance of the passage about "a slit of light." In addition to the meaning already discussed, Niedecker indicates in these lines that her dawnlike moments of spiritual renewal, and her experiences of literal sunrises, cannot be characterized as "bird dawn[s]," because she cannot feel the simple elation one imagines a bird to experience when it senses sunlight or otherwise feels invigorated. Her happiness, like her other emotions, can only be human and complex, intertwined with intellectual conceptions and the details of a complicated life.

Stephen M. Baraban

I SING OF OLAF GLAD AND BIG

Author: E. E. Cummings (1894-1962)
Type of poem: Elegy
First published: 1931, in *W* (ViVa)

The Poem

According to Richard S. Kennedy's biography of E. E. Cummings, *Dreams in the Mirror* (1982), "i sing of Olaf glad and big" grew out of Cummings' experience at Camp Devens, Massachussetts, shortly after he was drafted into the Army in July of 1918. Cummings' memories of the camp remained vivid until 1930, when he composed *W*, a grifitto for a collection of poetry also entitled *W*, standing for "ViVa," meaning "long live," which was published in October, 1931. The book began darkly, dealing satirically with the sordidness of the world, and ended more happily, with an emphasis on the earth and lyrical love poems.

This poem, one of the satires, is number 30 in the series; it has a strongly negative emphasis. Usually considered the most hard-hitting antimilitary piece written by Cummings, it is based on his brief acquaintance with one soldier at Camp Devens who shared his disgust for violence and his unwillingness to participate in war or to use a gun. After a confrontation with the commanding officer, Olaf (not his real name) was seen no more, but rumor persisted that he had been transferred to the Army prison at Fort Leavenworth and would be brutalized for his pacifistic stance.

The poem consists of seven stanzas of inconsistent length, and it praises those individuals whose conscience compelled them to resist war and its destruction. The poem's beginning parallels the *Aeneid* (c. 29-19 B.C.), in which Vergil sings of arms and the man. Olaf is a new kind of personal and private hero who refuses to merge his will with the gods and persists in maintaining a gentle and patient rather than warlike attitude. Nevertheless, Olaf cannot be classified as passive, since he combats his ignoble humility with brutal obscenities, invectives that his tormentors will understand. The poem offers an alternative to violence: the heroic value of moral strength. This strength allows Olaf to achieve epic stature even when his torturers try to strip him of the last vestige of human dignity. These attempts to destroy him are countered by Olaf's love and courage, traits which are misinterpreted by the masses as weakness or cowardice.

The poem closes by forcing the reader into more intense involvement with Olaf and a recognition that Olaf's plight is a universal dilemma. If the qualities that society prizes are epitomized in the poem's officers and noncoms, readers will no doubt see more value in Olaf's renunciation of renown, reputation, and life in the face of their repressive actions. His courage allows him to die not for a cause, but because of a cause, not for his country but because of his country. The value of individualism and integrity is stressed, and Cummings' humorous contempt for the military establishment reiterates his approval of nonconformity, both in life and on the printed page.

Forms and Devices

E. E. Cummings' work is characterized by unorthodoxy, invention, and especially by experimentation with language. Some of the unusual writing techniques normally present in Cummings include pun, paradox, inversion of cliché, grammatical turning, and typographical experiments. The purpose of these techniques is their immediacy of effect: Cummings wishes to surprise the reader into a new and unique vision about the topic under discussion.

Several evidences of Cummings' unorthodoxy are evident in "i sing of Olaf glad and big." Cummings avoids traditional capitalization. The narrative "i" is in lower case to indicate his own humility, while the importance of Olaf is indicated by the fact that each "I" referring to him is capitalized.

Word choice is yet another indicator of Cummings' refusal to follow the norm. For example, there is formal speech ("being of which/ assertions duly notified," lines 34-35) which is appropriate for legal documents, while there are also colloquialisms such as "yellowsonofabitch." Obscenities seem to be included for shock value, yet there are also archaisms which seem out of place in a modern poem.

Syntactical changes exemplify Cummings' unique approach to poetry. The most obvious is the reversal of the common "noun, verb, direct object" pattern to noun, direct object, verb, or direct object, noun, verb. Examples of such inversions include "officers// their passive prey did kick and curse" (lines 22-24) and "Christ . . ./ i pray to see" (lines 38-39). Cummings also uses redundancies, "bayonets roasted hot with heat" (line 30); shift in parts of speech by adding adverbial suffixes, "preponderatingly" (line 40); and words broken into component parts, "object-or" (line 3) to draw attention to his message. Typographically, he removes spacing to increase speed and indicate mood. The technique appears in line 5, "westpointer"; line 27, "firstclassprivates"; and line 36, "yellowsonofabitch."

Several puns appear in this poem as well, including "grave" (line 20) and "firstclassprivates" (line 27). In addition to their regular definitions of "serious" and "military rank," the words also suggest death and sexual organs, respectively, expanding their potential meanings.

Finally, Cummings' unusual use of punctuation—semicolons, commas, and colons—allows him to control where his readers pause and how long they meditate on a certain idea. Yet despite these nonconformist features, the poem utilizes a traditional rhythm (iambic tetrameter) and a traditional rhyme scheme.

Cummings thus combines experimentation with traditionalism, exploring new uses of typography, syntax, ellipses, and visual arrangements while retaining relatively normal rhythm and rhyme. The resulting tension in form and style parallels the situation depicted in the text, pitting the individual against society, peace against violence, and nonconformity against conformity. This merger of methodology and meaning is at the heart of Cummings' accomplishments.

Themes and Meanings

This poem presents a strong antiwar statement as Cummings lauds a conscientious objector for his resistance and eventual refusal to participate in battle. Although Olaf's actions eventually result in his death by torture, the narrator believes that he will see Olaf in heaven: Olaf has chosen a Christ-centered path and will be forgiven for his lack of "patriotism," since in this case patriotism is evil.

The poem begins with a positive picture of Olaf—his massive physical frame, his joyful attitude, and his warm heart—but in line 3, Cummings hyphenates the word objector ("object-or"). This hyphenation establishes a new mood in the poem by suggesting that Olaf is merely an object, manipulated by society to meet its own ends. Cummings sarcastically describes Olaf's colonel as "well beloved" and "succinctly bred"; these two back-handed compliments play against the word "erring," used to describe Olaf. The real intent is to evoke pity for the nonconformist and to portray the military figures as inhumane and cruel. This purpose continues with the sarcastic description of the noncoms employed to convince Olaf of the war's correctness as "overjoyed" (line 7) and "kindred intellects" (line 13): These men are happy being brutal. Olaf, in contrast, is calm and controlled. He recognizes that he is "a corpse"; these men will eventually kill him, but he coolly (without annoyance) replies to their abuse with defiant words.

Eventually, Olaf's case is referred to the commander-in-chief of the Army, the president, who sadly agrees about the "yellowsonofabitch" and decides on imprisonment—no doubt solitary confinement—in a dungeonlike prison, reiterating both the medieval/war images and the tactics of torture used in the Dark Ages. Line 42 associates Christ, also punished and killed for his nonconformity, with Olaf. Despite the fact that Christ faced opposition to His actions, Cummings implies that he attained heaven and conquered both torture and death; similarly, Olaf will gain this reward for his fortitude and perseverance. The poem maintains that the American ideal of patriotism has been perverted to depraved cruelty as the war machine grinds any opposition to pulp. On the other hand, Olaf is portrayed as a heroic example of true perfection, a perfection which defies warlike society and advocates peace and pacifism.

Michael J. Meyer

I SING THE BODY ELECTRIC

Author: Walt Whitman (1819-1892)
Type of poem: Lyric
First published: 1860, in *Leaves of Grass*

The Poem

"I Sing the Body Electric" appeared in the 1860 third edition of Walt Whitman's revolutionary volume of poetry, *Leaves of Grass*, as poem 3 of the "Enfans d'Adam" (later Anglicized to "Children of Adam") sequence. It is a celebration of the beauty of the human body, both male and female, that dwells on its physicality, its many forms, its sexuality, and its divinity. The poem—in the final, 1892 edition of *Leaves of Grass* discussed here—is composed of nine numbered sections of free verse.

The title, joyously proclaiming the poet's intent, is also the first line of section 1, which introduces the poem. The first four lines speak of the connectedness of everyone the poet loves; the next four are a series of rhetorical questions that stress the evils of corrupting the body and proclaim a direct link between the body and the soul: "And if the body were not the soul, what is the soul?"

Section 2 states that the body of the male and of the female is "perfect" and that the expression of the human face "balks account"—its beauty simply cannot be explained. Whitman proceeds from the face to other parts of the body, describing movement and grace as seen in people of all ages and walks of life: grown men, babies, women, girls, swimmers, wrestlers, laborers, the "farmer's daughter," "two apprentice-boys." He concludes by again proclaiming his unity with them all: "I loosen myself . . . am at the mother's breast with the little child,/ Swim with the swimmers, wrestle with wrestlers."

In section 3, Whitman reminisces about an old farmer he knew who was the father of five sons. He describes him as vigorous, calm, beautiful, and handsome; he was a man that anyone would want to be with—and would want to touch. Section 4, one of the shortest in the poem, speaks of the delight of being among those that one likes, of being "surrounded by beautiful, curious, breathing, laughing flesh." Again, the soul is mentioned; physical things, Whitman states—the touch and the odor of the body—"please the soul well."

Section 5 describes the female form, and it contains explicitly sexual imagery. The female has a "fierce" attraction, Whitman declares, then goes on to describe the activities resulting from that attraction—the "love-flesh swelling and deliciously aching," ejaculation, and the "night of love working surely and softly into the prostrate dawn." The sexual imagery is also tied to birth, to the creation of the new generations of the future. Section 6, depicting the male, ascribes action, power, passions, and pride to the male. Both male and female have their places in the procession of the universe. At the end of the section, Whitman asks another series of rhetorical questions, arguing forcefully for the equality of all humans.

Sections 7 and 8 begin by picturing a man's body and a woman's body, respectively, "at auction." The mention of a slave auction in this hymn of praise to the human form is jarring (and, to modern sensibilities, repugnant), but Whitman uses the setting as another avenue for observing the body's perfection, musing on the basic equality of all people, and imagining future generations: "How do you know who shall come from the offspring of his offspring through the centuries?"

The final section, one of the poem's two longest, consists mostly of a long catalog of parts of the body, with descriptions of the activities and movements they can perform. It both begins and ends by linking, once again, the body and the soul. More than that, however, the body and soul are united as one, and they are united with the poem itself: Bodies "are the soul," and "they are my poems," which are also everyone's poems. The soul, Whitman concludes, can be nothing but the body and the parts of the body.

Forms and Devices

Whitman's poetic style in the poems of *Leaves of Grass* (the first edition appeared in 1855) stood nineteenth century poetic convention on its ear. In order to approximate the rhythms of oratorical speech, he wrote in long lines that do not fit on one line on the page. He generally avoided the use of regular stanzas and rhyme. He wove together vocabularies from many walks of life, speaking in a voice larger than life, a bardic voice he meant to represent both himself and all of America.

In a series of vignettes, "I Sing the Body Electric" presents image after image of the body and its movements, portraying swimmers, rowers, laborers, wrestlers, and firemen. They seem almost Olympian figures, and the figures are nearly always in motion; the swimmer, naked, "rolls silently with the heave of the water," apprentices wrestle after work, and firemen march. The female figure, too, is idealized, as woman soothes a child or "moves with perfect balance." Whitman is observing acutely throughout the poem—he worked for a time as a newspaper reporter and editor—and he reports his observations one after another with emotion and immediacy. He views scenes of the body from a distance, then moves to small parts of the body, both seen and unseen, such as "eye-fringes," "tongue, lips, teeth," "scapula," "arm-pit," and "heart-valves." The small and the large are united, none seemingly more important than the other, as no one person is more "equal" than any other.

Whitman uses the technique of the catalog to great effect in this and other poems. The technique goes back to the lengthy catalog of ships in Homer's *Iliad* (c. 800 B.C.) and was used effectively by John Milton in the seventeenth century, yet Whitman makes it his own. In the poem's ninth and final section, he creates an apparently endless list of parts of the body, and the cumulative effect is to emphasize the wonder of the body—in its totality and in all of its parts.

Leaves of Grass was intended by Whitman to be a poetic text that he would expand and revise throughout his life; he published numerous editions of the work between 1855 and 1892, with most of the revision occurring prior to the 1881 edition. There are therefore differing versions of many of the poems, and critics have disagreed as to which edition represents Whitman's finest achievement. "I Sing the

Body Electric" first appeared in the book's third edition and was subsequently revised. The 1860 version, in fact, was untitled, and it did not begin with that incantatory phrase. Instead, it directly addressed readers immediately—"O my children! O my mates!"—and, instead of the 1867 version's reference to "armies of those I love" (line 2), addressed the "bodies of you, and of all men and women."

Themes and Meanings

Walt Whitman was not reticent about proclaiming his beliefs (or, in fact, his own talents). "I celebrate myself, and sing myself," he wrote in "Song of Myself," yet that self was always seen as a part of all humanity and particularly of the people of the United States. Sexuality, he believed, was not something to be left unspoken or concealed; it was one of the most vital aspects of life. Again in "Song of Myself," he described himself as "hankering, gross, mystical, nude" and said that, like a hawk, he would sound his "barbaric yawp."

The celebration of the physical and the sexual in "I Sing the Body Electric" was indeed too barbaric for the sensibilities of many people in the nineteenth century. Even Whitman supporter Ralph Waldo Emerson supposedly advised him not to include the poem (or the sexual and homoerotic "Calamus" poems) in the 1860 edition, but Whitman held to his artistic vision. Many readers were outraged. A few years later, Whitman was fired from a government post after a superior read the sexual poems.

Whitman presents his glimpses of the body almost as quick snapshots, and he is both observer and participant in the scenes and experiences. The poem is not concerned with the intellectual question "What is beauty?" but observes beauty at the physical and sensual level—one recalls John Keats's description of a life of sensation rather than thought.

Whitman's responses are immediate, bold, and unapologetic. They almost swoon with the joy of the human form—both the joys of living in his own body and of being surrounded by others: "I do not ask any more delight," he says, "I swim in it as in a sea."

The body transcends the mundane; it leads to artistic experiences and even mystical understanding. Whitman's sort of transcendence differs from that of Transcendentalists such as Emerson, however, in that Whitman is not concerned with a dualism of matter and spirit: "the parts and poems of the body," he concludes, "these are the soul." They are one. Like nineteenth century English poet Gerard Manley Hopkins, Whitman sees the body as a wonder, as sacred; unlike Hopkins, he does not see that divinity as explicitly Christian.

Whitman frequently meditated on future generations and on the future of the United States, and the sexuality of "I Sing the Body Electric" and the other "Children of Adam" poems is seen as part of the cycle of procreation; the poems reflect his projections into the future. When he looks at the man or the woman standing before him, he sees "countless immortal lives" and "the start of populous states and rich republics"; he sees "the teeming mother of mothers." Whitman celebrated the joy of the moment and the ecstasies of the physical, but the present was united with the future and the physical was one with the spiritual.

Clarence McClanahan

I TASTE A LIQUOR NEVER BREWED—

Author: Emily Dickinson (1830-1886)
Type of poem: Lyric
First published: 1861, as "The May Wine"; collected in *The Poems of Emily Dickinson*, 1955

The Poem

Emily Dickinson did not give titles to most of her poems, so they are generally referred to by their first lines. The editor of the 1955 edition of her poems, Thomas H. Johnson, attempted to number them according to the order of their composition; "I taste a liquor never brewed— " is listed as number 214. Dickinson sometimes left alternate versions of her poems, and the version discussed here is what Johnson believed to be her final one.

"I taste a liquor never brewed— " consists of four stanzas, the second and fourth lines rhyming in each quatrain. This is a poem of visionary experience in which the richness of a natural setting in summer is the cause. Speaking in her own lyric voice, Dickinson describes the exhilaration of going outdoors in summer in terms of getting drunk in a tavern.

In the first stanza, she asserts that she is drinking an unusual kind of liquor, one that has not been brewed but that is superior to the finest Rhine wine. In the second stanza, she says that she has become drunk by consuming the air and the dew of summer days. This consumption has taken place in "inns of Molten Blue," or under the hot summer sky. In the third stanza, she claims that her capacity for this liquor exceeds that of the most dedicated of summer's drinkers, the bees and the butterflies: When they have ceased drinking, she will continue. In the final quatrain, she affirms that she will drink until seraphs—the six-winged angels that stand in the presence of God—and saints as well run to Heaven's windows to see her, "the little Tippler/ Leaning against the—Sun—."

The last image of the poem, which grows out of the central comparison between drunkenness and her experiences of the summer day, humorously conveys a spiritual expansion of the self. Through this expansion, she comes to the notice of divine spirits, calling them away from their usual adoration of God in order to see this smaller god who, though perhaps a little unruly, has grown momentarily toward her true stature and importance.

Forms and Devices

Dickinson employs careful placement of pauses and an implied phrase repetition to break up what would otherwise be a steady marching rhythm. By this means, she conveys a dual sense of staggering, of the drunk losing physical control and the mystic stumbling into the presence of divinity. She makes her conventional stanza serve the unconventional, even the daring juxtaposition of drinking alcohol with nature as an inspiration of sublime perceptions.

Dickinson's central device is the metaphor that brings together drunkenness with visionary perception. She establishes that, for her, the air and dew of summer constitute a liquor and that she is a drunkard, reeling through days that are like streets, after drinking in the inn of the sky. Therefore, she has prepared the reader for the whimsical and surprising development of this comparison in the final two stanzas.

In the third quatrain, the foxglove flower becomes the tavern of the bee. Dickinson produces fanciful humor in this comparison by inventing "landlords" — placing the word in quotation marks — who will turn the bees out of the foxgloves when they have become too drunk. She continues in this vein by speaking of butterflies that, after drinking deep, "renounce their 'drams.' " The language of these comparisons evokes one of the many popular crusades of Dickinson's lifetime, the temperance movement. Often, the temperance movement called for total abstinence from alcohol, and it temporarily succeeded in legally enforced abstinence with the passage of national prohibition within forty years after Dickinson's death. By playing at opposing both abstinence and temperance, Dickinson pokes fun at the seriousness of the predominantly Protestant and conservative culture in her native Amherst, Massachusetts, where the rhetoric of temperance was familiar. This seeming irreverence extends to serious religious ideas as well.

A playful irreverence appears in the final stanza. Here, her drunken antics call to their windows not the upright citizens of the town, who might observe disdainfully the loud drunkard leaning against a lamppost in a sorry state. Instead, the observers are the angels and saints, and the tippler who they see is not leaning against something stabilizing in the street. Rather, she leans against the sun itself (capitalized for emphasis and to suggest divinity), the blazing source of summer and of the wine of the air and dew, the visible symbol of the God from whom these divine beings presumably have turned their attention in order to watch her. There is implied irreverence in making a spectacle of oneself and disturbing the heavens, but the final comparison between a mere lamppost and the sun seems to resolve this irreverence by asserting that the one who becomes drunk on summer comes ultimately to lean upon God.

The final stanza exhibits fairly clearly a technique that Dickinson used often in her poems: the implied repetition of a line or phrase. The last line of the second stanza may be implicitly the first line of the third stanza, but it is much clearer that the last line of the third stanza is implicitly repeated at the beginning of the fourth. Repeating "I shall but drink the more!" grammatically completes the lines that follow. In this way, one reads the line once to complete the third stanza and then must think it again in order to understand the beginning of the following stanza. One of the more striking uses of this technique in Dickinson's work is at the beginning of the fourth stanza of "A Bird came down the Walk — " (poem 328), where the first line both completes the previous sentence and begins the next one.

The repeatable lines and the placement of dashes in this poem give it a spasmodic gait which parallels the drunkard's staggering and thereby underlines the poem's central comparison.

Themes and Meanings

One of the main themes of Dickinson's poetry is the religious quest. She wanted to know with some certainty true answers to the questions that human beings repeatedly ask about the meaning of life: How did we come to be? Why are we here? What is our ultimate destiny? In her poems, she uses the poet's tools, a powerful imagination and a command of language, to seek in her own experience the answers to these questions. In this way, she associates herself with the Romantic poets, giving primary authority to personal experience, especially in nature, rather than to that of previously written words in scriptures and commentaries. Her work as a whole suggests that she was not comfortable with having to depend on nature and personal experience as sources of knowledge about God and religious truth, but that she was less comfortable with simply accepting what others believed because they had lived before her or occupied positions of authority. Among the more revealing poems about this quest are "I had not minded—Walls—" (398), "Me prove it now—Whoever doubt" (poem 537), and "Those—dying then" (1551).

Her humorous irreverence in this poem regarding her culture's attitudes toward alcohol and the seriousness of religious subjects reflects her rebellion against authority. Her presentation of the experience of nature as uniting her with divinity illustrates her hope that, through personal experience, she might gain true religious knowledge.

Although Dickinson wrote often about the power that she found in nature to heal and reveal, her discoveries were not unambiguously positive. Indeed, poems such as this one about the possibility of joyous vision in the contemplation of nature are roughly balanced by those about its more dangerous and unsettling mysteries, not the least of which are those questions evoked by the presence of death.

A poem closely related to "I taste a liquor never brewed—" is "The Soul has Bandaged moments—" (poem 512), in which Dickinson illustrates the contrast between moments of paradise, "When bursting all the doors—/ She dances like a Bomb," and "retaken moments—/ When, Felon led along,/ With shackles on the plumed feet,/ And staples, in the Song." "I taste a liquor never brewed—" captures a moment of paradise, when Dickinson believes that she is at home in the world and is certain that this world is a sure route to heaven. In many other poems, Dickinson tells of the "retaken moments," when she seems to be a prisoner in the world, with impenetrable, dragon-guarded walls between herself and what she wants most to know.

In this poem, Dickinson's blend of joy and humor in her controlling metaphor of drinking to excess conveys vividly her perception of a benevolent deity in the natural beauty of a summer day.

Terry Heller

I WANDERED LONELY AS A CLOUD

Author: William Wordsworth (1770-1850)
Type of poem: Lyric
First published: 1807, in *Poems in Two Volumes*; expanded in *Poems* (1815)

The Poem

"I Wandered Lonely As a Cloud" resulted from an experience of William Wordsworth and his sister Dorothy while on a walking tour of the Ullswater region in April, 1802. Dorothy wrote of it at length in her journal; when the poet began to compose the present poem two years later, his wife Mary Hutchinson Wordsworth contributed what are now lines 21-22, which William correctly identified as the best two in the poem. While rearranging his works for an 1815 publication, Wordsworth added the second stanza. As it presently stands, this poem is reputed to be the most anthologized poem in the world.

The "I" of the poem is explicitly a poet (line 15); the implied "you" is therefore explicitly a reader of a poem. Such clear roles doubtless add to the poem's illusion of simplicity.

The final stanza confers poetic meaning upon the experience of the previous three descriptive and narrative stanzas. In his famous preface to the second edition of *Lyrical Ballads* (1800), Wordsworth said that poetry results from "emotion recollected in tranquillity," and in the fourth stanza the poet, in tranquillity, recollects an earlier experience and sees more deeply into it. Suddenly the poem's simplicity is complicated by the addition of an explicit program: Wordsworth is exemplifying his contention that the events and emotions of the first three stanzas must recur in an altered mode of existence, neither in nature nor in history but in memory, if they are to occasion a poem.

Returning to the beginning of the poem, one finds the poet hiking on a windy day. He has no set destination. Happening upon innumerable wild daffodils, he compares them to a crowd of people and to an army ("host" implies that the flowers are the heavenly army of the divinity). He compares the densely packed flowers to the stars in the Milky Way and to a multitude of dancers engaged in a spirited dance. This stanza, added in 1815, balances the original event more evenly between isolated subject ("I") and communal object (daffodils) by concentrating on the external scene. The other three stanzas rely heavily on the first-person singular.

The poet had enjoyed the event even while he experienced it, but in later years, when he is more mature, he comments that at the earlier time he had not recognized its full value. In the final six lines, the poet moves into the present tense, using the key Wordsworthian word "oft" to generalize about the reiterated and enduring effects of recollection. The word "vacant" usually connotes for Wordsworth positive things such as vacations. "Pensive," by contrast, implies melancholy, the serious, gloomy, earthbound humor among the four humors; but it mainly serves as a dark foil to set off the bright and joyful conclusion.

Forms and Devices

The poem contains four six-line stanzas of iambic tetrameter, rhyming *ababcc*. The usual metrical substitutions (trochee or anapest for iamb) are very sparingly used. Wind characterized the original experience. Dorothy Wordsworth made it a strong unifying motif of her journal entry. It endured while her brother deleted and altered other particulars, and it continues to unify the reader's experience of the poem.

The wind enhances almost every visual aspect of this highly visual poem. The visual words that imply movement— "fluttering," "dancing," "shine," and "sparkling"—all imply the motion imparted by the wind. The Milky Way stars even "twinkle" because of the instability of the upper air. The one visual image that suggests no motion, "golden," perhaps devalues literal material wealth in favor of the aesthetic wealth of the last eight lines.

The wind also occasions the poem's powerful kinesthetic images—images of the tactile sensation of one's own motion or empathy with another's. The first three forms of a key word— "dancing," "dance," and "danced"—literally name the wind's past effects, and the fourth, "dances," names the continuing effect of remembering the past wind; "flash" does the same. Even more important, the wind unites the many individual flowers, waves, or stars by making them perform together some single action; they are not a multitude of separate and isolated beings, for although they are originally perceived merely as "a crowd,/ A host," they soon form a community.

As such they can be company for the lonely poet: Since he was a cloud at the beginning of the poem, he was also subject to the wind's motion. The wind has brought him to the destined meeting. His condition at the end of the poem involves no literal wind but, instead, the psychological results of the original experience: Emotion-charged memory is the psychic wind that often blows the poet and the daffodils together again. Moreover, the poet relives the experience so much more deeply in later years that this psychic wind sets his heart dancing with his old friends the daffodils, even though he had not danced with them during the original encounter.

The three main groups—daffodils, waves, and stars—both as they were and as they are remembered, create some correlatives that make the poem applicable to vast ranges of space and time: as below (daffodils), so above (stars); as on sea (waves), so on land (daffodils); as in day (waves and daffodils), so at night (stars); as in the past (daffodils, waves, and stars), so in the present (they and their associated emotions when recollected in tranquillity).

Themes and Meanings

One can conjecture that the earthbound melancholy of the poet's pensive mood (line 20) is transformed into its opposite, the sensual, cheerful sanguine humor which is associated with the element air. As fire and choler are the opposites of water and the phlegmatic humor, so air and the sanguine humor are the opposites of earth and melancholy. Since air (wind) and water (waves) are so prominent in the poem, one finds oneself with another Garden of Eden built of the same two elements that John Milton used to build his doomed Eden in *Paradise Lost* (1667, 1674). It is no accident that five lines near the start of the 1805 version of Wordsworth's *The Prelude* (1850), written within a few months of "I Wandered Lonely As a Cloud," subtly echo the final five lines of Milton's *Paradise Lost*. At the end of *Paradise Lost*, Adam and Eve leave the Garden of Eden with the world "all before them"; providence is their guide as they take their "solitary way." In *The Prelude*, Wordsworth writes that the "earth is all before me"; even if his guide is only "a wandering cloud," he says, "I cannot miss my way."

Wordsworth plainly anoints himself as the new Adam; two Eves, Dorothy and Mary, saunter with him into the new post-lapsarian world of Romanticism. Not the Judaeo-Christian providence but Nature — or more precisely, the wind, as the holiest spirit remaining — will bring the poet who abandons himself to it to his daffodils, his destiny, for their sprightly (spirited, inspired) dance. During hours of apparently aimless sauntering, the wind will lead him away from melancholy into the sensual and sanguine Eden of a post-Christian, nearly pantheistic cosmos.

The reader might suspect "I Wandered Lonely As a Cloud" to be guilty of the "pathetic fallacy" — of attributing human emotions to subhuman things. Wordsworth's pantheistic Nature, however, is poles apart from the totally demythologized nature of late nineteenth century naturalism, which has no traits of consciousness. Instead, it is an all-inclusive cosmic entity of which the attributes of any of its parts may be affirmed.

David Hartley, an influential British psychologist and philosopher in the eighteenth century, had a major impact on Wordsworth. In Hartley's psychology (empirical associationalism), sensory data begin to associate and synthesize themselves within a passive and unreflective mind; the poet's initial aimlessness in this poem probably reflects that childish condition. Wordsworth, who was no systematic thinker, supplemented Hartley with some transcendental intuitive idealism. The resulting self-contradictory jumble makes some sense in practice if one sees passivity as a program, aimless wandering as a conscious discipline, and memory as being extremely important to Wordsworth. Once Nature has impressed itself on the poet's senses, especially by eliciting pleasure or pain, his memory and intuition continue to associate, unify, and refine the impressions long after the sensory objects that caused them have disappeared. In the sensitive mind, these products eventually flower into ideal forms, poetic ideas, and aesthetic emotions.

In "I Wandered Lonely As a Cloud," then, a holy wind brings the poet to the place of meeting that Nature has appointed, Nature reveals itself to him through the daffodil host (as if the flowers are a multitude of angelic messengers of the divine), and the wind of Nature finally empowers the poet to utter his enduring inner experience.

Thomas J. Steele

ICE

Author: Ai (1947-   )
Type of poem: Narrative/dramatic monologue
First published: 1978; collected in *The Killing Floor*, 1979

The Poem

The free-verse poem "Ice" is a monologue that dramatically narrates the speaker's experiences as a cast-off teenager, her killing of her child and her man, and the warm memory she has for this man as she comes to reconcile her adolescent confusion. The poem consists of four stanzas, the first three having thirteen lines each and the last, twelve. The title word proceeds into the first line, with the thought that will compare the conditions on a river as a harsh winter ends with the chilly and irresolute emotions she felt toward her new family.

The speaker is a young woman. Throughout the poem she addresses her lover, beside whose grave she stands. She had strangled their first child, which the reader discovers only after being confronted with the oddly juxtaposed images of the sun-rise surrounding her man and the baby's skull in the box. Despite having violently attacked and killed him, she finds that her affection for him strengthens. In this monologue, Ai creates an effect similar to that achieved by Robert Browning in "My Last Duchess," except that Ai dramatically relates the specific details of the speaker's actions.

The opening stanza establishes the fact that, as an adolescent Choctaw Indian girl, she is far from home, living in Minnesota. The Choctaws were called one of the "Five Civilized Tribes" of the southeastern United States; however, taking up the white man's ways did not exempt them from being forcibly removed from their original homelands in northern Alabama and Mississippi and relocated to the Indian Territory, which later became the state of Oklahoma, in the 1830's. The speaker resents her father for considering her already "a burden" at twelve, and her feelings of resentment at his giving her away during her menses are powerful.

At fourteen, the speaker, literally a child-woman, is ill-disposed to the roles of mate and mother (nowhere in the poem is marriage explicitly stated or implied). She describes her man's warmth and disposition as he enters their abode, hugged by the sun, in stanza 2. The rocking horse he made for her is subtly placed in that stanza; it introduces details such as "the ebony box/ with the baby's skull inside," the husband combing his hair with a casual gesture, and the dramatic action in stanza 3 that may shock the reader. She dismounts from the rocking horse, which is essentially a toy, to attack, maim, and slay him.

Reopening her eyes in the last stanza, she recalls how "I wanted you then and now/ and I never let you know." Together—he in death, and she vibrant and filled with mixed emotions about their past—they will "slide forward" into an eventual and eternal realm of the spirit.

Forms and Devices

When using first-person points of view, poets often adopt a persona or mask in order to create a character that seems mentally and physically active and real. Creating this persona does not mean that the poet intends to veil autobiographical details. The figurative devices in "Ice" may be drawn from oral history, readings, historical documents, and the like. Ai may feel close to the images she creates, and her Native American, Asian American, and mixed black and white ancestry makes her imagery, details, and emotions more profound.

Images of remembrance, retribution, distrust of males, and killing abound in "Ice." The ice on the river breaks into "obelisks," which as tapered monolithic structures bear a phallic significance. Ice metaphorically reflects the speaker's attitude toward her man, her distrust of him, just as its breakage results from the onset of warm conditions.

Juxtaposed to the poem's bittersweet memory and dramatic violence are images of soft materials such as "that shawl of cotton wool," the "white smock," the piece of velvet, and "the pony-skin rug," all of which convey nonthreatening surroundings. Ai balances this set of images, however, by introducing early in the poem the material central to the speaker's rage— "the roll of green gingham" she had to use to absorb the blood of her menstrual flow, a flow that confirms that she is ready for childbearing. This bloody roll of gingham embodies her child-woman's humiliation over being disposed of for being a burden to her father. In the second stanza, the horse she rides has a "black mane cut from my own hair," a mane she strokes, but which, because it is her hair, fills her with mixed emotions. The clashing of these images corresponds to the speaker's inner turmoil over what are also natural and utilitarian events and practices. Ai's perceptions of serenity balanced by physical acts of rage characterize other poems in her books *Cruelty* (1974) and *The Killing Floor* (1979).

Ai gives "Ice" a cyclical narrative structure. A poet achieves a cyclical structure by connecting historical events with present emotions in a fashion that is neither chronological nor linear. Reminiscence, flashback, and an organic sense of the relationship of events across or despite temporal realities distinguishes such a poetic structure. T. S. Eliot's lengthy sequence, *The Waste Land* (1922), is one example of this kind of circular construction. The cyclical character of "Ice" may derive from Ai's heritage, in that this nonlinear form is common in storytelling narratives among indigenous peoples, and is particularly important to Native American and certain Indonesian groups. The expressionist does not attempt a deliberate shaping of the form to meet a cultural demand. The form results from the people's nonlinear and nonchronological perception and understanding of time.

Early in "Ice," the speaker by the graveside holds back her head and remembers, then closes her eyes, taking the reader to the second stanza's memory of being a mate and the mother of a dead child. Closing this stanza, the speaker blocks out the cries of the new infant, cries that provoke finally her rage against her man. The "row of bear teeth" image seems less clear regarding her intentions than the closing of her eyes and the covering of her ears, both of which are avoidance gestures. Thus one may infer that these bear teeth are part of a rug or a pelt similar to the pony skin. As the speaker manipulates these teeth, she parallels the masticating imagery of the previous lines, and completes the image of attempting to crush the gingham roll, her man nailing shut the black box, and the strangulation imagery in the third stanza as a whole. When she opens her eyes in stanza 4, she completes a cycle of memory and physical position. In the two closing lines, she affirms her feelings of growing warmth toward him "without bitterness," emotions she grasps more keenly and can better articulate. "Everlasting," the poem's final word, reaffirms the seasonal breaking up of river ice, and her perpetual reminiscence.

The number of stanzas and lines is probably not arbitrary. The four stanzas reflect the seasons and the cardinal directions. That stanzas one through three have thirteen lines each seems to suggest not ill luck but the thirteen moons in a year as understood by the Choctaw girl. Each menstrual period is called a "moon." The twelve lines of the last stanza suggest that she has jettisoned the hurt and humiliation she recalled earlier in the poem.

Themes and Meanings

This poem might be misinterpreted if the reader finds its violent imagery gratuitous. Ai's juxtaposition of the soft materials and the man, who is low-key and caring, with verbs of force and destruction actually reveals the speaker's adolescent confusion and hurt.

The onset of adolescence brings forth a variety of conflicting emotions that teenagers cannot articulate or understand. Male readers of "Ice" can become sensitive to the fact that preteen and adolescent girls find the onset of menstruation a dynamic physical change and an emotionally terrifying experience. The speaker resents her father for having no need for her, and for casually giving her away to a man who seems to be gentle to her, but toward whom she enacts a displaced violence.

She resents the blood-producing menses, and her anger compels acts of crushing and squeezing. Curiously, the first infant was a girl; the second, a boy, she does not harm. Like the bear's teeth, this is an intangible detail in the poem. A child herself at twelve or thirteen, the speaker can be interpreted as saving her daughter from "the curse" and the boy for a later vindication.

The sexuality suggested by the obelisks evolves to a less threatening aspect as the speaker's attitude toward the man softens. The core of distress and anger from stanza 1 through stanza 3 is nevertheless framed by the serenity of stanza 4 and the opening of the poem. Even her mate's ".45 you call *Grace of God* that keeps you alive," which enables him to survive and provide for his family is, after all, empty, making him defenseless and vulnerable.

Ron Welburn

THE IDEA OF ORDER AT KEY WEST

Author: Wallace Stevens (1879-1955)
Type of poem: Meditation
First published: 1934; collected in *Ideas of Order*, 1935

The Poem

"The Idea of Order at Key West" is a meditative poem in a relaxed iambic pentameter. Its fifty-six lines are broken into groups of uneven length that define the major points of its argument. The poem examines the interaction between imagination and reality through the figure of a woman who sings beside the sea and whose voice neither violates the reality of the sea nor simply reproduces it. She is the creator or "maker," not merely a mirror. She puts the sea's "dark voice" into human words, drawing it into the realm of human experience: "When she sang, the sea/ Whatever self it had, became the self/ That was her song, for she was the maker." Her song is not an exact reproduction of nature's own utterances. If it were it would not be meaningful to the human listener, but "would have been the heaving speech of air." Nor could it be simply her own voice; "it was more than that." The woman's voice is a translation of the natural into the human, which allows her listeners to perceive their world anew. It is her song of nature that heightens the listeners' sense both of the world itself and of their uncertain position in it: "It was her voice that made/ The sky acutest at its vanishing."

The listeners find that at the conclusion of her song, the world has been re-ordered for them: The lights in the fishing boats at the harbor have created a new arrangement of the natural. These lights have "mastered the night and portioned out the sea,/ . . . Arranging, deepening, enchanting night." The speaker of the poem, after hearing the woman's song, asks "Ramon Fernandez" to explain, if he can, why this reordering has taken place. Ramon Fernandez was an actual French critic, but when Wallace Stevens was asked about the allusion he claimed that he chose the name at random. (Since Stevens was acquainted with Fernandez's work, the disclaimer may be suspect.) One can think of the Fernandez in the poem as "the critic" or simply as an intelligent listener. In the last five-line section, the speaker, still addressing Fernandez, answers his own question by referring to the "blessed rage for order" which is responsible for the transformation. This "maker's rage to order words of the sea" causes humans to search for more precise definitions of their points of arrival and departure. In studying the obscure hints of the nature of humanity, humans seek more exact and intense poetry: "In ghostlier demarcations, keener sounds."

The poem's title is reflected in the title of the collection, *Ideas of Order* (1935). At this point in his work, Stevens had turned from the Florida images of fecund nature that dominated his earlier poems to more active poems exploring and defining the act of creative perception.

Forms and Devices

The iambic pentameter of this poem is not, strictly speaking, blank verse, but irregular rhyme. The use and abandonment of rhyme seems appropriate to the poem's portrayal of the creative act as an attempt to impose order—the system of language—on chaos, the reality of the sea. The rhymes themselves, often identical rhymes, suggest the motion of the waves.

The poem begins with two seven-line segments containing rhyme; the second is the most tightly structured, its lines concluding with the words "she," "sound," "heard," "word," "stirred," "wind," and "heard." As the reader believes that a pattern has been established, however, the sections become more irregular and the vocabulary more varied. The flow of the poem becomes less artificial, more subtle, as it changes from rhyming iambic pentameter in the direction of more flexible blank verse. The last five lines, which make up the exalted address to the critic, conclude with the words "Ramon," "sea," "starred," "origins," and "sounds."

The overall form of the first part suggests the subject: the sea put into words. The images and metaphors in this description of sea and singer emphasize their difference through imaginative combinations of them: "The water never formed to mind or voice,/ Like a body wholly body, fluttering/ Its empty sleeves." The comparison is both physical and intellectual, and it illustrates Stevens' agility in embodying aesthetic concepts in poetry. The sea's inhumanness is ironically demonstrated by comparing it with the human, giving it attributes of "body" and clothing—"empty sleeves." Lines such as "The grinding water and the gasping wind" bring the sea graphically into the poem as the backdrop and source of the woman's song.

When the poem describes the song's ending and the listeners turning "toward the town," the tone and imagery "turn" too, in the direction of the final affirmation of poetry and humanity both. As the rhymes diminish, the images change from the sea's repetitions to the ordering power of the lights on the boats—lights (and flames) tending to represent consciousness. From the disordered sea of reality one moves to geometric structures of light, "emblazoned zones and fiery poles," which art has created by changing the way the real is envisioned.

Themes and Meanings

In 1954, the year before his death, Wallace Stevens was asked to define his major theme for a contributor's column. His clear, direct statement might have been taken from almost any of his earlier critics' analyses. His work, he said,

> suggests the possibility of a supreme fiction, recognized as a fiction, in which men could propose to themselves a fulfillment. In the creation of any such fiction, poetry would have a vital significance. There are many poems relating to the interactions between reality and the imagination, which are to be regarded as marginal to this central theme.

This summary statement encapsulates the general thrust of Stevens' poetry and the motivation behind "The Idea of Order at Key West," a relatively early poem.

One of the characteristics that establishes Stevens' modernism is the self-reflexiveness of his work. His poems are all about writing poetry; they reflect themselves. This poem explores three questions, all relating to the creative act. It asks, What is the relationship between the imagination and reality in art? What does art do for, or to, its perceiver? Where does art originate?

The relationship between sea and song, as described in the first part of the poem, illustrates that ideally art puts reality into a human structure without violating the nature of that reality—that is, without falsification. The speaker emphasizes the role of the imagination as "maker" but suggests that the "she" who is the singer of the poem is being as true as she can to what she observes, considering the limitation that she must express her vision in the human vehicle of words. (That the imagined world must be bound by the real is suggested in other of Stevens' poems, such as "The Ordinary Women.")

The question of what art does for its perceiver is given a double answer. Art provides an understanding of what would otherwise be the alien language of nature. Moreover, art increases one's sense of one's place in this world, although this position may be one of isolation and filled with uncertainties. In other words, art gives a heightened sense of both one's world and oneself.

Finally, the source of art is represented as desire, as a human need that transcends logic. The source of art is a desire for truth and poetry at once. The poetic impulse is a furious need (a "rage") to "order words of the sea," or create order from the chaos of the world. Yet it is also a need to explore human origins and points of departure, "fragrant portals" barely perceived and shrouded in mystery. The pursuit of such understanding leads to both greater knowledge and more acute poetry ("In ghostlier demarcations, keener sounds"). The poet alters how he or she and others perceive reality, and the source of this change is the "blessed rage" that is the poet's curse and gift.

Janet McCann

IF YOU ASK ME

Author: Gunnar Ekelöf (1907-1968)
Type of poem: Dramatic monologue
First published: 1955, as "Frågar du mig var jag finns," in *Strountes*; collected in
Selected Poems of Gunnar Ekelöf, 1967

The Poem

"If You Ask Me" is a short dramatic monologue in free verse. The speaker seems
to be identical with Gunnar Ekelöf himself. In the opening lines he anticipates—
and answers—a question posed by his unidentified interlocutor about where he
exists—*finns*, the Swedish verb Ekelöf uses, means something between "abide" and
"reside." As the monologue continues, the reader becomes closely identified with
the silent friend to whom the poet is speaking. Using the familiar *du* form of address
(which in 1955 still implied a certain degree of intimacy), the poet explains that he
lives beyond the mountains in a world that is at once far away and nearby. He admits
that he inhabits another world but insists that the friend—perhaps without knowing
it—lives there too. Like the earth's atmosphere, this other world is everywhere; but,
like helium, it only exists in minute quantities in relation to some of the other permanent constituents of the atmosphere like nitrogen, carbon dioxide, and hydrogen.

The poet's friend has apparently believed this other world to be some sort of
mystical, transcendent realm; therefore he has asked for an airship (a helium-filled
dirigible) to take him there. The poet tells him that what he really needs for the
journey is a filter—that is, some sort of gas mask that will eliminate noxious gases.
He tells him to ask for a filter that will take out everything that separates people from
each other, a filter that will even separate them from "life," in other words, from the
mundane concerns that prevent them from entering the other world. The meaning of
this metaphoric filter becomes one of the cruxes of the poem.

Having apparently received and donned the requisite filtering mask, the friend
next blames it for the fact that he finds it difficult to breathe. The poet reproves him
by pointing out that everyone who uses the filter to attain the purer air of the other
world has difficulty breathing, though most of the time they tolerate this condition
without complaint. As a final reproof to his friend, the poet implicitly—and
ironically—compares him to a certain "wise" man who blamed the darkness for the
difficulty he had in seeing the stars. Whether or not the friend feels the sting of the
poet's irony and understands that darkness is the necessary precondition for seeing
stars the reader never learns.

Forms and Devices

Strountes, the curious title of the collection in which "If You Ask Me" appeared,
points to one of the most striking stylistic aspects of this poem: its plain, unpoetic
diction. The word *Strountes* appears to be a French transliteration of the Swedish
word *strunt*, which means "rubbish" or "nonsense." One of the epigraphs Ekelöf

chose for this collection was a statement by the great Swedish Romantic poet and novelist, C. J. L. Almqvist, that it is unbelievably—almost insuperably—difficult to write *strunt*. Göran Printz-Påhlson has observed that in this volume of poems, Ekelöf is "attempting to make poetry by counterposing completely uncorrelated styles and in that way to find out his own 'style' " (*Solen i spegeln*, 1958). Leif Sjöberg's rendering of *Strountes* as "Tryflings" captures something of the Joycean wit Ekelöf doubtless intended the title to convey to his Swedish readers (introduction to *Selected Poems of Gunnar Ekelöf*). The casual, free-wheeling style of the *Strountes* poems allows Ekelöf to steer a course that moves between the cosmic and the comic. "If You Ask Me," which was also translated by Robert Bly in his anthology *Friends, You Drank Some Darkness: Three Swedish Poets* (1975), lies closer to the comic pole. Like most of the forty-eight poems in this collection, it has no title, no punctuation, and no identifiable form.

What, then, makes it a poem? Poetry, according to Ekelöf, arises not from the contents of the poem, but from the counterpoint of its words. In one of his most important essays, "En outsiders väg" ("An Outsider's Way," 1941), he explains this principle: "Seen in one light a group of words means something that was clear as day, seen in another the meaning of the same words is uncertain—as night. And poetry is this very tension-filled relationship *between* the words, *between* the lines, *between* the meanings." An example of Ekelöf's ability to create such tensions is evident in the way in which we glide by association from "helium" to "airship" (which is usually filled with helium). His skill at creating the kind of counterpoint he requires in a true poem is much more evident in the original Swedish text, however, in which the first syllable of "helium" may suggest *hel* ("whole")—and consequently the kind of *helhet* (wholeness) that can only be found in the "other" world. Similarly, the banal Swedish phrase he attributes to the "wise" man, *nätt och jämnt* ("barely"), interacts with *natt* ("night") and *jämnmod* ("equanimity") in a way that highlights the significance of these two key words in the poem.

Themes and Meanings

A first reading of this poem about the other world inhabited by the isolated poet might tempt the reader to see it as a restatement of the Nature-Art dichotomy, a traditional theme that is perhaps best known to readers of modern poetry in "Sailing to Byzantium" (1928) by William Butler Yeats. But Ekelöf is not seeking to replace mutability with the permanence of art. Indeed, he appears to reject the idea that one can sail away by airship to a world that might be filled with "monuments of unageing intellect." He is isolated, not because he is old or because he is a poet, but because isolation is the human condition. What he is saying in this poem is that though he is daily in close, but superficial, contact with other people, he is really totally isolated, deeply confined within his own self. Quite satisfied with his shallow relations with other people, the addressee fails to realize that he has no real self. What Ekelöf says to his reader in "Tag och skriv" ("Open it, Write") applies equally to the friend in "If You Ask Me":

In reality you are no one.
Your suit; a place, a name —
all else is merely your wish,
your 'I' a wish, your lostness one, your savedness another:
you have taken it all out in advance!

In "If You Ask Me," breathing (or difficulty in breathing), a common theme in Ekelöf, vividly concretizes the desperate inadequacy of the atmosphere ("sphere of breath")—that is, of reality. Merely living in this atmosphere fragments one; not only does it separate people from one another, it also keeps them from themselves. This is why he recommends the filter with which to isolate the helium that is diffused among the other components of the air. This "helium," this "other world," is Ekelöf's metaphor for the self. What one can hope to find after filtering out everything that keeps people from entering this pure self is best stated in "An Outsider's Way":

A writer's first task is to resemble himself, to become a person. His duty, or rather, his best way of attaining this, is to acknowledge his incurable loneliness and the futility of his wandering on Earth. It is only then that he can strip away all the stage scenery, decorations, and disguises from reality. And it is only in that capacity that he can be useful to others — by placing himself in the predicaments of others — of everyone! It is futility that gives life its meaning.

This short dramatic monologue is a concise poetic restatement of that credo. It involves a paradox that, as Printz-Påhlson has pointed out, recurs in many of Ekelöf's poems: only in the depths of the self does one find what is common to all. Because the poet has found this kind of wholeness in his self, he urges a "filter" upon his friend. Even though the quest for wholeness involves considerable discomfort, the potential reward should encourage the reader to undertake the filtering process with equanimity. The final fillip in the poem comes when he discredits the "wise" man who blames the darkness for the fact that he can barely see the stars, traditional symbols of aspiration and of direction. Implicit in the last word in the poem, "night," is the idea, frequently expressed in Ekelöf's poetry, that all of the familiar polarities — day and night, good and evil, life and death, meaning and meaninglessness — are complementary concepts that only acquire meaning when considered in relation to each other.

Barry Jacobs

THE IMPALPABILITIES

Author: Charles Tomlinson (1927-   )
Type of poem: Lyric
First published: 1963, in *A Peopled Landscape*

The Poem

"The Impalpabilities" is a short lyric in one stanza of twenty-two lines, written in free verse. It does not have a traditional lyric subject, such as a person, place, or object. Instead, it is concerned with the subtleties involved in the way what is outside oneself is perceived.

The poem is written in an impersonal mode. It uses the first-person plural "we" in order to include the reader in the statements it makes about the nature of experience. By describing shades and tones of his perceptions in as detailed a manner as possible, the poet hopes to remind readers of moments in their own experience that are similar to his.

The poem starts by directing readers to the "things we must include/ because we do not understand them." It is the impalpable things that cannot immediately be grasped and molded into shape by humanity that will concern the poet. Not being able to understand impalpable things with the ease and readiness with which one knows the palpable, does not mean that the impalpable can merely be passed by. That which is beyond one's knowledge is still encountered, and its mystery is tempting rather than daunting.

The impalpabilities, as one would expect, never take final form in the poem, but the poet finds suggestions of them in various half-realized events or objects. In the fifth line of the poem, the impalpabilities linger in the "marine dark" like an uncanny sea creature. In the nine lines that follow, there is a sustained evocation of musical chords. These chords do not end in a harmonious closure. Instead, they remain suspended in a kind of frozen, perpetual dissolution. This dissolution does not mean, however, that the chords vanish into nothingness. They may be impalpable, but they are still there, exacting and requiring one's attention.

The next image in the poem is unfolded in the succeeding four lines: It is a wood which "advances before the evening takes it" — a forest glimpsed at twilight. After the sun has set, the wood is no longer illuminated as an independent and palpable phenomenon. Yet, as long as the dark has not fully advanced, it retains a distinct atmosphere of identity. This identity is not merely a vestige of its daylight one, but possesses shadowy, fascinating meanings of its own.

In the final lines, the branches of the trees in the forest are compared to "extended fingers" dipped in water that seem to become detached from the rest of the body, supporting "the cool immensity" of the external shadows and not the human form of which they were originally a part. They have passed into a distant and foreign sphere of perception, yet they are never completely separated from the human.

Forms and Devices

Much of the poem's formal effects are embodied in its appearance on the page. This is a poem whose visual aspect is not only in the images within the poem but in the poem's external shape. It is composed of short lines that are organized in groups of three apiece. In each group of three, the first line is fixed in the standard left-hand margin, while the next two lines each begin with a sharp indentation to the right. This form mirrors the subject matter of the poem, where the possibility of different perceptual shapes for different varieties of experience is acknowledged. The poet uses another device as a counterpoint to the formal organization of the lines. By varying the length of each line (from as short as only two syllables to as long as nine), he supports the poem's assertion of the whirling patterns of experience.

The poem is recognizable as a product of modern free verse, yet its agenda is not as much to depict chaos or disorder as to show ideas of order existing where one ordinarily would not suspect them to be. The poem filters its impalpable content through a tightly organized network of form. The two parentheses that appear in the eleventh and nineteenth lines remind one of the author's presence and display a layer of conscious awareness against the inchoate areas that the poem chronicles. The potential for chaos is also held in by the eloquence and reserve of the poet's language. His language is exact while being austere and reflective. Words are displayed in a way that maximizes their force. When, for example, the poem speaks of the chords that "hang/ in an orchestral undertow," the position of the word "hang" at the end of a two-word line is subtly suggestive of the action of hanging performed by the chords themselves.

Charles Tomlinson, a musician and an artist as well as a poet, skillfully combines different sense and sensory processes. Although the dominant motif in the poem is a visual one, much space is also given to hearing and to touch. The idea of the impalpable refers to something not amenable to touch, yet the powerful concluding image of the fingerlike branches implies that there is as much of a tangible sensation in failing to grasp something as in fully seizing it. The tableau of the wood standing in near darkness is a visual one, as is the previous image of the marine dark. The central orchestral metaphor brings in the element of sound. Yet these senses often seem to merge into each other, as in the previously quoted image of the "orchestral undertow." Here sound and touch are gathered together, yoked with one another in meaning, yet never merged or dissolved into a shapeless mass. By holding different senses in poised juxtaposition, the poet creates the impression of complexity and ambiguity without collapsing into confusion. Ironically, the language of sensory perception is used to convey a quantity—the impalpable—that is inherently beyond the senses. The sensory language can never hope to convey fully what is beyond us, yet it can depict this very effort at understanding.

Themes and Meanings

In his early poetry, Tomlinson concentrated on a meticulous observation of the external world. The subjects of nature and of art were especially prominent. In poems such as "On the Hall at Stowey" and "Farewell to Van Gogh," Tomlinson combined a gorgeously exact scenic vividness with a declared poetic goal. This goal was to take the lead from the masters of the Modernist movement, Ezra Pound and T. S. Eliot, who were prominent influences on Tomlinson, in rejecting a purely subjective view of experience. Tomlinson was far more sensitive to nature and to visual detail than the earlier poets, yet their influence combined with his own distinct personality to create an unusual and fascinating way of approaching the world. Instead of placing the self at the center of the universe, Tomlinson wished to direct his attention to objects whose appeal lay in the fact that they were external to the self. Tomlinson rejected what he saw as the Romantic self-indulgence of painters such as Vincent van Gogh. Instead of advertising himself, Tomlinson sought to enter into a proper relation with the world, one that would not simply subjugate all phenomena to an egoistic self-infatuation. This does not mean the self is renounced. For the poet to humble himself before the outside world is still a gesture of the poetic self. It is Tomlinson's dedicated poetic mission to move readers closer to the world as it is.

In this poem, though, Tomlinson is not depicting tangible objects, such as houses, trees, or paintings. Instead, he concentrates on their very opposites: the impalpabilities. He regards the impalpabilities in a cool, discriminating light, not with an excess of emotional energy. They do not reside in a distinct landscape, the way objects would ordinarily, yet they are placed in a sharply contoured landscape, not in a free-floating void. The poet's aim here is to break down the barrier between the opposites of the knowable and the unknowable. Tomlinson does not celebrate the impalpable because it cannot be fully known, nor does he resign himself to looking merely at what is apparent because it is all that can be fully understood. Tomlinson makes a distinction between what can be approached and what can be explained, and insists that the latter should not be mistaken for the former. To retrench from the orchestral ˈndertow or from the looming wood at twilight would be shallow; to fantasize about it as something dark and inexplicable would be overly heated and melodramatic. Tomlinson takes the middle course, but he does not achieve a simple reconciliation between extremes. The tension and liveliness in the poem convey the strange paradox that what may be most gripping are those very phenomena on which the readers find it hardest to maintain a stable grip. In a sense, things are most palpable when they are impalpable.

Nicholas Birns

IMPERIAL ADAM

Author: A. D. Hope (1907-   )
Type of poem: Narrative
First published: 1955, in *The Wandering Islands*

The Poem

"Imperial Adam" consists of eleven quatrains. The quatrain is a traditional English verse form of four lines with various rhyme schemes; A. D. Hope has chosen to rhyme the first and third lines, then the second and fourth. The lilting rhythm is altogether appropriate for the erotic subject matter, and the poem derives a pervasive sensuality from its voluptuous diction and imagery.

"Imperial Adam" starts out by retelling the story from the second chapter of Genesis in which Eve emerges from Adam's rib so that Adam will no longer be alone. The poem dwells, however, on what the Old Testament writer fails to record in the blunt statement, "Adam knew Eve," and it offers a vivid account of the initial sexual encounter enjoyed by the father and mother of humankind. Once extracted from Adam's rib, Eve sighs and smiles at her male counterpart as she lies on the grass of paradise with "the honey of her flesh" shining in the sunlight and her "place of love" beckoning to him. Understanding what he should do through watching the animals copulate, he takes Eve into his arms and "Like the clean beasts, embracing from behind," begins the joyful work of founding "the breed of men." He plants his seed in the woman that "Jahweh" (Jehovah) had given him, then watches her breasts ripen and her "belly" swell and grow.

The final stanza records the birth of their child, and it contrasts sharply with what has gone before. Vanished are the eroticism, the paradisaical aura, the bliss. In their place emerges the ugly reality that accompanies loss of innocence: The child who crawls from between Eve's legs is a pygmy and is named "the first murderer."

"Imperial Adam" stands as the best of Hope's series of erotic poems written in the 1950's. On one level, the poet is celebrating — much in the way earlier English writers such as Andrew Marvell (1621-1678) and John Donne (1572-1631) did — female beauty and sexuality. Hope's attraction to such poetry and his imitation of it in his own fashion are typical of his art because he is thoroughly schooled in the English tradition and often relies on it as a source.

Had "Imperial Adam" not contained that final, jarring revelation, it could be considered an imaginative re-creation of Adam and Eve's first sexual encounter and might be placed in the earlier English tradition of erotic poetry. The horror of the final quatrain, however, destroys the sense of pleasure generated by the sensual imagery in the preceding stanzas, and the poem becomes a distinctively modern one.

Forms and Devices

The main device lending "Imperial Adam" its erotic quality in the first ten stanzas is diction. Loaded phrases such as "naked in the dew," "brown flanks," "virile root," and "spurt of seed" distill Adam's masculinity. The major part of the poem, however, focuses on Eve, who has skin like honey—even richer in texture than the "golden breasts" of the papaw, a fruit noted for its fleshiness. She lies on the grass like a "plump gourd," loosens "her sinuous thighs," and reveals breasts rising "softly." Even her "place of love," its dark hairs covered with dew, "winked crisp and fresh."

Another method Hope employs to imbue the poem with an air of sexual abandon is the use of animal imagery. As Adam and Eve "Began in joy" their sexual union, the animals in the Garden of Eden watch. The elephant is "gravid"—that is, pregnant—or distended and enlarged by pregnancy, which this rare word connotes. The "hind"—a red deer—is calving, the "bitch" breeding, the "she-ape big with young." As Eve lies on the grass after the "lightning stroke" of sexual pleasure, she enjoys the licking of "The teeming lioness"—teeming used in the archaic manner to mean breeding and producing young. Then the exotic vicuña, an animal famous for its fine, silky fleece, "nuzzled" Eve as she slept.

The poet has conjured up a fecund and fruitful place in his narrative, using the only devices he has at his command: words formed into images. They are exactly the right formations to extend and give life to the scant details Genesis provides. It does appear that the writer of "Imperial Adam" took his cue not from Genesis but from another book of the Old Testament, the Song of Solomon, which exults in the female body and sensuality. Biblical imagery and allusions abound in Hope's poetry.

The abrupt juxtaposition in the final stanza of "Imperial Adam" devastates the mood the poet worked so hard to create, and the question arises in the mind of the reader: Why does Hope seemingly defile the pleasure-filled garden? In the last quatrain, even the soft sounds disappear, and Adam sees Eve's "water break," then watches her "quaking muscles" as she gives birth to a monster destined to become a murderer. This sudden switch in mood effectively places side by side beauty and ugliness, light and dark, good and evil, pleasure and pain—in essence, all those contrasting elements that make up the mosaic of human experience.

Themes and Meanings

The poem's title is problematic. Why should Adam be called "imperial"? The word most often denotes an emperor or the empire itself—for example, an imperial nation, led by the emperor, wields power over scattered colonies. To interpret the poem as a protest against imperialism seems farfetched, however, considering the time in which it was written and Hope's own attitude toward colonialism. On the other hand, an obsolete meaning of imperial is "sovereign," and it could describe someone, emperor or not, who exercises supreme authority. A feminist reading, with this definition in mind, might see Adam as guilty of subjecting and corrupting Eve and Adam as the agent of authority. While such an approach is possible, it too, appears unlikely to be Hope's intent. Finally, imperial means "outstanding in size or quality." Perhaps this last definition is the right one to apply in order to approach the poem best.

Adam and Eve are considered in Christian mythology to be the father and mother of the human race, so this rather literal definition of imperial seems appropriate. Once they, in their supposed superiority, give themselves over to animal pleasure, they awaken to the terrible knowledge of evil, thus being reduced from their imperial status to that of ordinary humans. The animals gained no similar awareness as the result of their coupling; to possess such knowledge is the curse of humankind.

The final stanza raises significant questions: Why should their child have "a pygmy face"? What is notable about an undersized face? In addition to delineating physical smallness, when capitalized, pygmy describes African and Asian people four to five feet tall; in Greek mythology, the Pygmies were a tiny race noted for their warlike and barbaric ways. Right or not, the word does carry the connotation of ferocity, barbarism, abnormality, or physical aberration. This meaning comes not only from the mythological source, but also from the early explorers who encountered the real Pygmies during their forays into Africa and Asia. The explorers found these small people distasteful, seeing them as ugly, fierce, and uncivilized. Pygmy also contrasts with the "imperial stature" of Adam—and of Eve by implication.

Because the word pygmy immediately creates revulsion in the reader, it works splendidly as a metaphor that unfolds without effort. The effect is then compounded by the final line: "And the first murderer lay upon the earth." According to the fourth chapter of Genesis, the eldest son—not a pygmy—of Adam and Eve was called Cain, and he killed his brother Abel out of jealousy. Hope obviously expects his reader to know the rest of the story and to extend its meaning. Cain has evolved into the personification of evil, containing in his person the seed of destruction, of war and enmity, of hostility and rancor among humans. The poem's conclusion brings to mind the final lines of William Butler Yeats's (1865-1939) "The Second Coming": "And what rough beast, its hour come round at last,/ Slouches towards Bethlehem to be born?" Hope is obviously an admirer of Yeats, whose "noble, candid speech" he praises in his poem "William Butler Yeats." Because Hope draws constantly from earlier sources for his inspiration, he may well have had the famous lines from "The Second Coming" in mind when he concluded his own poem. Not consciously imitating, Hope more likely wanted his reader to be aware of the connection. Certainly, when the haunting Yeats lines echo in the background, the conclusion of "Imperial Adam" gains resonance.

What begins, then, as a joyful amplification of Adam and Eve's first encounter evolves into the history of the human race. In one respect, "Imperial Adam" recounts in an economic and suggestive way the whole story told in Genesis—moving from innocence to awareness, from ignorance to knowledge, from good to evil.

Robert Ross

IN A DARK TIME

Author: Theodore Roethke (1908-1963)
Type of poem: Lyric
First published: 1960; collected in *The Far Field*, 1964

The Poem

In this confessional poem, Theodore Roethke describes a passage through a "dark time" in his life and his emergence from this episode, not into peace and quietude, but at least into wholeness. The journey to and out of the psychic pit described in the poem may be a metaphor for personal tragedy, spiritual emptiness, or, more likely, because it is known that Roethke suffered from periods of psychosis, a poetic attempt to deal with a mental breakdown.

The poet insists that a plunge to the bottom of the abyss of psychological disorientation and dislocation of identity is necessary to achieve clarity: "In a dark time, the eye begins to see." There must be painful struggle, though, before this end is reached. In the first stanza, the poet has glimpses of his personality, but he finds only fragments and pieces, meeting not himself but his shadow, hearing not his voice but his echo. As he says later in the poem, "The edge is what I have." He also finds that he is not sure of his place in the larger scheme of life because he "live[s] between the heron" (a stately, beautiful creature) "and the wren" (an ordinary bird), between "beasts of the hill" (highly placed, but brutal animals) "and serpents of the den" (associated with evil and danger, but also with knowledge).

In the second stanza, the poet specifically identifies his problem as mental illness but implies that it is not he but the world which is out of joint: "What's madness but nobility of soul/ At odds with circumstance?" In fact, madness may not necessarily be "a cave" in which one is lost, but may be "a winding path" to a new awareness. Despair experienced completely may lead to "purity."

Meanwhile, there is the chaos described in the third stanza, in which daytime is suddenly replaced by midnight, ordinary objects blaze as if lit from within, and images are thrown one upon another at such a dizzying pace that the experience is described as "a steady storm of correspondences." Nevertheless, the confusion is necessary because the old personality must be destroyed before a new one can be born: "Death of the self in a long, tearless night."

Although the paradoxes ("dark, dark my light") and the unanswered questions ("Which I is *I*?") continue in the final stanza, there is an apparently unexpected resolution of the conflict, as the poet touches the bottom and then begins to rise: "A fallen man, I climb out of my fear." At last, there comes a mystic union with God and the poet feels a part of everything ("one is One"), but there is no safe haven. The poet has been born again into a violent world, but this time he is able to face it "free in the tearing wind."

Forms and Devices

Although, at first glance, "In a Dark Time" seems to be a collection of outbursts and slapped-together images which is less a description of madness than an example of it, the poem is really a carefully crafted work in which its conclusion is implicit in all of its elements, beginning with the rhyme pattern of the poem. Roethke uses a six-line stanza, the rhyme scheme of which is *abcadd*. This pattern, which appears at first glance to be no rhyme scheme at all until the stanza's last three lines, reinforces the point of the poem, which is that disintegration may be necessary to achieve unity. There appears to be no rhyme after the first three lines, but with the end of the fourth comes a resonance of the first—the suggestion that there is order where there had appeared to be none. The last two lines of the stanza, a strongly rhymed couplet, imply that the poet is drawing his world together again into a type of order.

The *a* rhyme of the first stanza ("see" and "tree") is strong and definite, but the same element of the second stanza ("soul" and "wall") is only a near rhyme, as is that of the third ("correspondences" and "what he is—") and fourth ("desire" and "fear"). These near rhymes reinforce the idea that the poet is only barely in control of himself and the poem, but the strongly rhyming last couplet of each stanza pulls the poem and the reader away from formlessness. As a final seal on the idea that to endure this kind of psychic torment is to break through into a new kind of reality, the last two lines of the poem, the ones which in each stanza had borne a strong rhyme, themselves yield to near rhyme ("mind" and "wind"). It is as if the poet is telling his readers that they thought they had his poem figured out, but that they do not. To experience fully the reality that the poet is describing, it is necessary to see things in a totally new way.

The imagery of the poem, at first confusing, also reinforces the idea that from apparent paradox and nonsense come new knowledge. Some of the images embody contradiction, such as the serpent with its double meaning in Western culture. Others lose their paradoxical quality when seen in the terms of the poem's entire statement. It seems impossible that a "light" could be "dark," but Roethke means that one must embrace all elements of one's personality in order to integrate them, even those parts which one does not regard as admirable ("beasts of the hill") and even if the process is confusing ("Which I is *I*?"). Confusion and disorientation are necessary, Roethke says, for only by asking the question and admitting ignorance can one begin to find new ways of learning.

Themes and Meanings

In "In a Dark Time," Theodore Roethke uses one of his own major themes—the renewal of the human spirit through contact with the natural world (a theme which unites him with the Romantic poets of the early nineteenth century)—in company with a major theme of modern literature—the theory that it is necessary not merely to test limits but also to break past limits in order to become fully oneself.

In many of his other poems, Roethke comes to the creatures and the milieu of the physical world to renew himself and give his life meaning during a time of crisis. Roethke is primarily a poet of small nature, reveling in the existence of little creatures such as sparrows, snails (as in "Elegy for Jane"), tiny fish, and even amoeba ("The Minimal"), and feeling a sense of kinship and brotherhood with them. In "In a Dark Time," however, the representatives of the natural world are threatening beasts and serpents, and the poet is unsure of his place in the scheme of things, as he lives "between" the various living things that he mentions. Furthermore, the natural world is no longer an ordered, understandable place: The moon is "ragged," and midnight descends during day. The creature with which the poet finally chooses to identify "my soul" is the not only despised but wretched "heat-maddened summer fly" which, "buzzing at the sill," can see the world that it wants to enter but is unable to do so.

One of the points made by the poem is that the world is not understandable, not only by logical means, but also by any kind of ordinary human perception or judgment. Perhaps the path of insanity or psychic disintegration, feared and shunned by most people with good reason can, instead of leading to destruction, provide a gateway to a new kind of reality. At the end of the poem, Roethke says that he "climb[s] out of [his] fear" and becomes "free in the tearing wind" but does not offer the reason that this change has occurred because the process is incomprehensible by the usual methods of evaluation. The poet has not arrived at a quiet place, such as the eye of a storm, but is still in the midst of the tearing wind which unsettles and jumbles everything. At least he himself is whole— "one" —and can endure what he had previously feared. It is also unclear just who or what is the "God" which the poet encounters at the end of the poem. Roethke was neither conventionally religious nor consistently mystical; in his other poems in which he speaks of union with all life, he does not maintain that he is thereby always contacting a divine spirit, as did one of his poetic heroes and ancestors, William Blake.

"In a Dark Time" is, after all, not a philosophical treatise but a highly charged description of an emotional storm. As Roethke states in another poem: "We think by feeling. What is there to know?" ("The Waking"). Roethke would also say that poetry is not read for answers but for experiences. Even as the only way to find the world that lies beyond ordinary human consciousness is to push sanity past its limits, so the only way to understand a lyric poem such as "In a Dark Time" is to push reason past its limits and *feel* the poem.

Jim Baird

IN CALIFORNIA

Author: Louis Simpson (1923-   )
Type of poem: Lyric
First published: 1963, in *At the End of the Open Road*

The Poem

"In California" consists of six unrhymed stanzas of four lines each, with irregular line lengths, in which the speaker reflects on his geographical and historical situation. Louis Simpson, though born in Jamaica, settled in New York City in 1940 — hence, the reference to his protagonist's "New York face" in line 2 of the poem. He begins the poem on the California coast ("the dream coast"), having come from New York and finding himself among business and outdoor types ("realtors/ And tennis-players"). He feels out of place on this western edge of the nation. What he has seen, and how he feels, has left him with a "dark preoccupation."

The second stanza recalls the westward movement, the "epical clatter" (line 5) of the pioneers making their way through Tennessee and Ohio, toward where the speaker stands, reflecting on the music and spirit ("Voices and banjos") of their quest to settle the new land. Then, heaven regarded this westward advance favorably. Now, the "angel in the gate" (line 8) above the Western coast witnesses the "dream" unfolding, not becoming involved in human affairs.

Stanza 3 opens with an address to Walt Whitman, who celebrated the American pioneering spirit in the nineteenth century and wrote exuberantly of the westward expansion. The "King and the Duke" (line 10) are characters in Mark Twain's novel *The Adventures of Huckleberry Finn* (1884); these clownish charlatans call themselves the Duke of Bilgewater and King Looy the Seventeen of France. The poet tells Whitman to step down from his poetic promontory overlooking the march west and join the fictional King and Duke on their journey down the Mississippi with Huck Finn and the escaped black, Jim. Placing the great poet of the American dream with two charlatans suggests that the speaker sees the epic voice mocked by the reality of what the dream has become: a collection of realtors and tennis players and rows of sailboats in a marina facing Alcatraz Island with its notorious (but defunct) federal penitentiary. Here, he says, the pioneers should turn back.

Still addressing Whitman, the speaker in the fourth stanza continues to explain why he believes the pioneer spirit of early America has vanished: "We" have lost the capacity — courage, intellectual scope, vision — to "bear/ The stars . . . those infinite spaces" (line 14). Capitulate, he tells Whitman; give up the mountain from which the American dream was envisioned. It will be parceled up and sold for tract homes as the valley has been. This thought reminds the poet of past civilizations that have died: Babylon and Tenochtitlan. Those cities were but precursors to what the poet sees around him, a dying empire.

In the final stanza, the poet realizes that the human spirit can neither "turn" nor "stay"; it must be ever in motion. The American pioneer has been stopped at the western gate, has fallen into a materialistic sleep, and has lost the spirit to surge onward. The poet's final lines separate the somnolent populace from the pioneering spirit itself, which the poet sees in a final vision as a train of "great cloud-wagons" advancing beyond the Rock, the Marina, and the subdivided valley. Its spiritual pioneers continue "dreaming of a Pacific."

Forms and Devices

The poem's structure combines convention with free form. A quick glance reveals evenly spaced and numbered stanzas, each line begun with a capital letter, each stanza consisting of exactly four lines. On closer examination, however, the form opens: The lines do not rhyme, have no regular length, and lack conventional metric form. The poet clearly wants phrasing to determine line length and keeps the rhythms near natural speech. The regular stanzaic structures provide secure parameters in which the reflective spirit can move back and forth geographically and historically. Visually, the poem advances evenly and surely, while the emotions stir in phrasal eddies.

Attention is thereby divided between conventional structure and the poet's voice and mood, between ideas and conventional techniques. By fencing the open linear form with regular stanzas, the poet exactly suits his mood and theme, which dwell on the abandonment of an ideal, of a defunct dream that could not—or did not —hold up under the advance of the pioneer spirit.

The poem's allusions give symbolic weight to the poet's argument. California, its realtors, yacht clubs, and subdivisions, all symbolize the failure of the dream, a vulgar distortion of the epic vision of which Walt Whitman sang and which he symbolizes here. The poet's vision sweeps over thousands of years of history, with specific allusions to Babylon and the ancient Aztec city. In this way, the poet's ideas do not fade in a welter of abstract concepts. Despite the generalized diction—phrases such as "the fabulous raft" and "those infinite spaces" are characteristic of the poem as a whole—the pictures that emerge from the language and the allusions are sufficiently clear. The poet's ideas are sustained by suggestion rather than by graphic detail, by allusion rather than by vivid imagery. Though "epical clatter" (line 5) is alluded to, one does not hear it in the "Voices and banjos," nor does one smell the "incense" or see very distinctly the "angel in the gate." If Babylon "astonished Herodotus," one does not see his astonishment, but one feels the weight of the ideas nevertheless, because the voice of the poet brings the reader into his vision with his allusions, moods, and rhythms.

One feels from the start that one is hearing the reflections of a somewhat demoralized witness to a sad reality—that one is overhearing him. He assumes that someone is listening, absorbing his mood as his phrases carry the poem along: "Here I am, troubling the dream coast." His mysterious voice awakens a desire to know, to follow along, listening to the echoes of his despair reverberate through history as he sweeps the reader along toward his final apotheosis. His commanding tone reinforces this march forward: "Turn round the wagons here," he says, then, "We cannot turn or stay," and if the poem tells more than it shows, the final vision nevertheless leaves the reader with a majestic image of "great cloud-wagons" floating beyond the dying land where the poet is left with his "dark preoccupation."

Themes and Meanings

The poet speaks through visions as he reflects on the remnants of a dream that inspired a nation before it dwindled into subdivisions, tennis games, and sailboats. The failure represented by the realtors and tennis players may be attributable in part to a hard reality: Whenever the human spirit is brought to material considerations, its death is assured. Looking back, he sees the pioneers, hears their voices and banjos, and sees their spirit rising to heaven; now he sees it stopped by a great barrier, the Pacific. It appears to be time to surrender the dream and settle into comfort, to acquiesce to the inevitable: decay and death. The great singer of this dream, Walt Whitman, should "Lie back," for the pioneer voice is quieted. In the silence, one hears the speaker's "dark preoccupation," dark because he is reminded of other civilizations, once astonishing, now only names.

The "I" in the first stanza represents the poet's sense of alienation from his surroundings. He has a specific identity, a "New York face," but by the end of his grand sweep through history, foreign and domestic, the solitary figure has become the "we" that is possessed of a spirit that "cannot turn or stay." The poet sees a separation of physical manifestations from the human spirit itself. People, things, places — these objectify the spirit, but they eventually die and are sloughed away, like dead skin. The elevated spirit moves onward, drawn by another dream, another Pacific. Irony tempers the poet's voice in this final vision without deflating the grand vision entirely, for the Pacific has become a symbol of a physical barrier that stops people, nations, and dreams. Humankind, the poet seems to be saying, will always surge outward, following the lofty dream that spirit forever discovers in its quest for perfection, but as long as it finds physical expression, it will be halted by the great imponderables of reality, such as the Pacific Ocean. Material forms die; the spirit survives.

The final vision seems to revive the poet's spirit; he rejects the death of spirit while accepting the death of the dream that Whitman celebrated. The poet's final mood is plaintive. Uplifted by the vision of the "great cloud-wagons" moving outward, he is also aware that "we" are not in them. A twinge of regret and a bit of irony remain: As the pioneers sleep and surrender to the great reality before them (represented by the Rock, Alcatraz Island, the human spirit moves on, a dream itself, a dreamer still. Though elevated by the final vision, the poet is also doubtful. He seems to be asking what good all that pioneer effort is if it comes to this — a dead place that is abandoned finally by a spirit that surges toward another dream coast, which will eventually meet the same fate.

Bernard E. Morris

IN COLD HELL, IN THICKET

Author: Charles Olson (1910-1970)
Type of poem: Meditation
First published: 1951; collected in *In Cold Hell, in Thicket*, 1953

The Poem

"In Cold Hell, in Thicket" is a sequential poem in two parts: Each part is subdivided into numbered sections that work like the movements in a musical score, each developing an aspect of the theme of the whole poem. The title of the poem is taken from images used in the *Inferno*, the first book of Dante's epic poem *The Divine Comedy* (c. 1320), in which Dante describes his descent into the Christian underworld by entering a dense thicket covering the gate of hell. The "cold" hell refers to the winter day of the poem and to the snow that is falling on the fields.

The situation of the poem is of a speaker walking across the frozen ground of a fort, most likely the battlefield at Manassas, Virginia, now the Manassas National Battlefield Park, where the battles of Bull Run in the Civil War (1861-1865) had been fought. Manassas is near Washington, D.C., where Charles Olson was living at the time he wrote this poem in August, 1950. A letter to his friend, Edward Dahlberg, reports his car trips out to various Civil War sites.

The most striking characteristic of the poem is its visual appearance on the page, what the French call the *mise en page*, or layout of a poem. It is marked by strophes, long stanzas in open form, some beginning at the left margin of the page, others beginning at indented margins. Every section has a different spatial order in which the thinking process is given a typographical signature or formal design. Indenting in Olson's poetry means the thought has drifted inward toward memory or dreamy reverie. The sum of his techniques is explained in his essay "Projective Verse," written in 1950, in which he discusses his metrical strategies and his use of a "breath" unit for the line, a nonmetrical unit of speech based on the length of breath needed to utter a phrase or completed thought.

The tone of the poem is one of heightened oratory, a formal discourse marked by stately rhetorical assertions and questions, complex syntactical structures in which long dependent clauses intersect direct questions. This form of oratory, notable in other poems Olson wrote in the early 1950's, was partly influenced by his brief career in politics (1940-1946), when he served in various offices under Franklin D. Roosevelt's administration. One may detect some of Roosevelt's eloquent style of delivery in this language; Olson was himself a talented orator in youth, and he won several state and national awards for public speech.

Part I of the poem opens on the subject of war, a frequent theme of Olson's poetry. His keèn sensitivity to history makes him reexperience the bloodshed of the Civil War battles fought on the snowy ground over which he trudges. The poet is middle-aged, forty years old, and he compares his situation with that of Dante, who wrote his epic poem "in the middle way" of life. The "cold hell" of the title is the confusion and directionlessness the poet feels as he meditates on the subject of bloodshed and death. At the back of his mind is the imminent death of his mother, who died several months later, on Christmas, 1950.

The first numbered section sketches in a new theme: the speaker as Osiris, the Egyptian god who was murdered and dismembered, his limbs scattered over the Nile river. Osiris' mother, Nut, is the night sky, whose breasts are the stars. His sister, Isis, gathers up the limbs and brings her brother-husband back to life. The poet, however, looks up into the night sky and cannot organize his perceptions to see the form of a god overhead. He is fractured within and cannot sort out the meaning of his own surroundings or his experience. Like Osiris, he is dismembered body from soul in his grief.

In section 2, Olson's major theme emerges: the role of imagination as builder of forms out of the fragments of nature and lived experience. The snowy grounds of the fort are a vast array of unassorted particles that he must shape and invest with understanding. After the first stanza, the language is indented to suggest a deepening thought process, as the poet asks himself directly how he will regain control of his emotions and overcome his grief. He feels that he must do so without the aid of his figurative sister, Isis.

Section 3 goes to the heart of the problem by asking, "Who am I?" He notes that the "scene" before him is organized by its own inherent principle; all but himself seems to participate in natural form. Only he is isolated, set apart from the form nature assumes in any landscape. The word "abstract" comes to him in this passage and suggests not only the root meaning of things dragged from their context, but the human tendency to remove the self from its surroundings, to contemplate its own subjectivity in isolation of other events and influences. One must take a "fix," or reading of the self within the natural landscape, he argues, to enter the order of natural events and to take one's place among them.

The second half of the poem, part II, is divided into two movements. The first, unnumbered, part opens with a phrase from the *Inferno*: "*selva oscura*," or dark wood. Olson, however, puns on the *selva* to suggest "self," or dark self. He asserts that the darkness of the self is psychological; all grief comes from within the self and not from the world. Nature is a perfectly ordered system, a paradise in which individual human beings suffer privately from their gross illusions and selfish concerns.

Section 2 formulates the rest of the argument by noting that hell and paradise are functions of human subjectivity, attitudes formed from cultural and psychological factors having little or no bearing on the actual state of the world. Hell is a projection of personal despair that distorts the appearance of the world. Accordingly, he can begin to resolve his despair and confusion by accepting that his remorse is purely subjective, a form of self-grieving. This leads to the final section of the poem in which he remarks that men "are now their own wood," an image taken from Ezra Pound's poem "A Pact," in which Pound pays homage to the poet Walt Whitman by acknowledging him as having cleared a path through the American wilderness, and that the fallen trees may now be carved, shaped by the poets who follow. The "wood" in Olson's poem is also figurative, a material of mind and imagination to be "wrought, to be shaped, to be carved, for use, for/ others."

The speaker overcomes his remorse after having reasoned that his depair is a product of selfish emotions and that the "world" remains the same despite an individual's personal mood or attitude. The way forward is to recognize that emotion is a vague generality and that reality is always a tissue of detailed and precise elements woven together in a pattern enclosing the world. Thus death has its place, even his mother's coming death and the son's anticipatory grief; they are not isolated events but part of the unity of nature. The speaker can now move again and begin his further pilgrimage through the "wilderness" toward greater understanding of the unity of life. The reader is again reminded of Dante's *The Divine Comedy* as the speaker moves out of the field to the next stage of his journey: The way forward out of hell is toward purgatory, and finally, into paradise.

Forms and Devices

Olson is skillful in balancing his use of images in the poem. On the one hand, the fort mentioned in the second stanza of the poem is literal, identified by a number of facts about its location and structure on the landscape; but almost immediately after, the description of the setting widens into allegory, characterizing the scene as "unclear," a "hell." The landscape on which the figure meditates is both exterior and interior at once, an actual place and a metaphorical setting in which the speaker explores his own inner psychological terrain. The language moves back and forth between the two poles of reference and sustains the dual nature of the setting throughout the poem.

The thicket mentioned in section 3 of the first half of the poem is simultaneously the trees on the battlefield and the state of the poet's own consciousness as he looks out over the setting. The black branches in the winter sky are like nerves "laid open"; they strike the poet and generate the words that form his language in the poem, line by line. Thus, each image of the poem is the result of an impinging datum from the surrounding fields; the poet stands mutely in the center of a landscape that acts upon him detail by detail, which he then composes as language in the poem. The poem, therefore, is the reenactment of the scene. Somewhere in the abstract ordering of the words is the ghost of the actual trees and their wiry branches, "these black and silvered knivings."

It is this device of turning each objective item into its subjective equilavent that makes the poem a meditation. The word itself describes that act of internalizing an object until it fills the mind with its influences. The restless self-exploring that goes on in the poem worries each datum until it is elevated to a complex psychological issue, as in the final resolution of the poem in part II, stanza 2, where even the field becomes a "choice," a "prayer."

Themes and Meanings

"In Cold Hell, in Thicket" is about the process of understanding. The poem begins in a state of utter desolation brought on by the adverse circumstances in which the poet finds himself. These feelings have nothing to do with the actual setting he confronts, but his perception or misperception of what he sees is an indication of how far removed he is from the world. As the poem unfolds, one watches the procedure by which the landscape comes to represent the speaker's inner turmoil. The second half of the poem, however, reverses the flow of Romantic meditation by refusing to accept this view of the world as real. Instead, the speaker renounces his despair and searches to discover how the world is not only different from himself, but of a form that remains perfect and inalterable in its integrity.

By accepting the primacy of the natural order of things as the true picture of the world, Olson's persona decides he must rediscover the order within himself, beneath the emotional chaos of his feelings. As he remarks to himself near the close of part I, only by exact and precise attention can the real underlying form of self be discovered. The poem is a lesson in self-analysis, a way of confronting the pains of experience without ending in pity and remorse. The meditation demands of the speaker a clear, open attention to the details of feeling, and when properly traced, will reveal that the single self, the isolated human in the landscape, is a fiction. The truth of human nature is that it belongs within the matrix of other life, and that its responsibilities are to others, not only to the isolated individual. The poem renounces that aspect of individuality in which selfish desires are primary. Instead, the concept of the individual is redefined in the poem to mean an originality of attention focused on a world of connected life and its system of relations. The poem ends with the speaker reentering the world as an imaginative participant, no longer the grieving outsider.

Paul Christensen

IN MEMORY OF SIGMUND FREUD

Author: W. H. Auden (1907-1973)
Type of poem: Elegy
First published: 1940, in *Another Time*

The Poem

"In Memory of Sigmund Freud" is an elegy to the famous psychologist written in twenty-eight alcaic stanzas. W. H. Auden read works by Sigmund Freud when he was very young, and Freudian theories played an important part in Auden's poetry throughout his life. Although the poem is a fitting tribute to the creator of psychoanalysis, it is better studied as a description of Freud's importance to Auden and his influence on Auden's own psychological, political, and aesthetic theories than as a precise description of Freud's character or theories.

The first two stanzas remind the reader that Freud died during World War II, when many others were dying, and strike the moral note that will dominate the poem. Stanza 6 records Freud's death in England, where he had fled when the Nazis occupied his native Austria in 1938. The remaining stanzas shift back and forth among metaphoric descriptions of Freud's theories, Auden's evaluation of those theories, and his discussion of his contemporary world. The "problems" of stanza 4 anticipate the complexity of Freud's theories and Auden's description of them.

Freud's psychoanalysis rests upon the belief that psychological problems are provoked by emotions repressed in the unconscious. Stanza 3 concerns the lack of control of the unconscious and its determining effects upon individual lives. In stanzas 5 and 25, the unconscious is compared to "shades" and the "night." Patients are cured through uncovering repressed emotions by probing their pasts through free association. Stanzas 8 through 11 describe this process of "looking back . . . to recite the Past" in order to heal the "unhappy Present" and the well-known "Freudian slip," by which the unconscious inadvertently betrays itself in describing the past "falter[ing] . . . at the line where/ long ago the accusations had begun." This illumination frees one to be less inhibited and to accept many facets of oneself, which Auden illustrates in stanzas 20 through 22.

Freud also identified certain instincts that govern conscious and unconscious behavior. Central to his theories—and to the tremendous controversy that they incited—is Eros, or the sex/love instinct, which (like the Greek god for which it is named) is both creative and destructive. Eros is implicit in many details of the poem, such as the jealousy portrayed in stanza 4 and the appeal of the unconscious' "creatures" in stanza 26. It appears explicitly in the last two lines of the poem, which also invoke Aphrodite, the goddess of love and mother of Eros. Auden believed that Eros, together with the release of unconscious emotions, allows one to reconcile internal conflicts, including the tension between the reason and the emotions. He describes this in stanzas 23 through 27.

Auden celebrates these theories because he believes that they enable people to live more virtuous lives; he makes this claim in stanza 2 and elaborates upon it throughout the poem. They allow one to escape involuntary behavior and make self-conscious, moral decisions. Because Freudian theory reconciles warring contraries and makes a person whole, the synthesis that Auden describes in the last six stanzas of the poem is, to him, inherently moral.

Forms and Devices

"In Memory of Sigmund Freud" is an elegy in alcaic stanzas. Auden uses Freud's death not only to commemorate him, but also to meditate upon good and evil and to comment upon the malignity that infested the Fascist powers in World War II. This is typical of elegies, which traditionally reach beyond their immediate subjects to broader, often social, concerns. Usually this comment is in the form of protest. John Milton, for example, took the occasion of the death of Edward King to attack the corrupted clergy (as well as materialism and the aspiration for fame) in "Lycidas."

The poem also resembles other elegies in that it offers consolation for Freud's death: His theories, like art and literature in earlier elegies, survive him. It elaborates upon this consolation in much less detail than most elegies do, however, and it observes very few other elegiac conventions. Most elegies, for example, are really meditations upon death and upon human effort to deal with life's transience. Auden spends very little time reflecting upon death itself. Nor does he use pastoral elegiac conventions, such as the pathetic fallacy or the procession of mourners. This nonconformity marks the difference between earlier, traditional, coherent cultures and the troubled modern world.

Auden was one of the most brilliant and innovative prosodists among modern poets. No other twentieth century poet uses as many old and new verse forms. An alcaic stanza has four lines: The first two have eleven syllables; the third, nine; and the fourth, ten. Auden and Marianne Moore are two of the very few poets in English successfully to employ syllabic meter rather than accentual-syllabic meter. Determined by the number of syllables per line rather than the number of syllables and number of accents, syllabic meter is common in languages such as Italian and Japanese but is rare in English.

The verse of "In Memory of Sigmund Freud" is also technically unusual because of its heavy use of enjambment or run-over lines, in which the sense of a line and its punctuation do not pause at the end. The enjambment is so extreme that many stanzas are not even end-stopped. This creates a ruminating, meditative effect, which is reinforced by the fact that—contrary to normal practice—the first words of most lines are not capitalized. This enjambment means that, in spite of its contrived form, the poem lacks strict demarcations, and its ideas are fluidly connected.

The importance of connection can also be seen in many of the poem's metaphors, the most distinctive of which are topographical. These geographic metaphors are typical of Freud, who often explained the psyche by dividing it into different territories. The most sustained use of these metaphors describes Freud's pervasive influence by comparing him to a "climate of opinion" or a "weather" which "extends" everywhere and penetrates "even the remotest miserable duchy" (stanzas 17 through 21). This metaphor and its enjambment create an impression of expansion, dispersal, and flow.

Themes and Meanings

The expansion and connection characteristic of the poem's images and its verse are central to the meaning of "In Memory of Sigmund Freud." The poem is in large part about modern alienation and fragmentation and how to overcome them. The isolation and disjunction of modern lives are highlighted by Freud's having been a Jew in exile, the unconscious' "delectable creatures" being "exiles," freedom's loneliness (stanza 23), and the description of "unequal moieties fractured" (stanzas 23 and following). These themes preoccupy many modernist writers, including T. S. Eliot, Virginia Woolf, and James Joyce, whose works imitate their subjects through subjective, unconnected voices and disjointed syntax and structure. Auden resembles these and many other modernists in blaming rationality—and the elevation of reason—for these modern malaises. Auden, however, has chosen to imitate the connection he recommends instead of the fractured world around him.

Alienation and fragmentation can be cured through recognizing repressed problems. This acknowledgment results in free choice, a virtue which threatens evil because it empowers the individual to determine his or her own fate. His contemporary world gave relevance, even urgency, to Auden's message. Implicit in the capitalization of the "monolith[ic] State" (stanzas 13 and 20), for example, is a criticism of World War II's autocratic, Fascist countries, such as Germany and Italy. The reminder in stanza 6 that Freud was Jewish and the comparison in stanza 7 of Hate's repression of emotions to killing and burning call up the Nazis' slaughter and burning of the Jews.

Generosity contrasts with evil's tyranny and grounds the recognition that frees humankind. If one is generous to oneself by accepting one's acts and stopping the "accusations," one will be made whole: "long-forgotten" parts of oneself will be restored. If one is generous to others, then modern ills will be cured. One also needs to be open and generous to the surrounding world in order to have the sense of wonder acclaimed in stanza 25. Such unselfishness results in the love personified in Eros and recommended in stanza 26. By reaching out to others, we can rescue "the future that lies in our power"—in other words, save civilization.

Freud is an example of the magnanimity that Auden describes. He is one of those who "hoped to improve" and help humankind in spite of his own persecution. By underlining Freud's persecution, Auden stresses modern humanity's alienation and protects Freud against the charge that his methods were too authoritative. This also reminds the reader that it is often very difficult to be forgiving and altruistic, but that people must love and forgive one another even when fact and reason seem to justify hate and resentment. Auden's praise of and appreciation for Freud is itself an example of the love and generosity he promotes.

Laura Cowan

IN MEMORY OF W. B. YEATS

Author: W. H. Auden (1907-1973)
Type of poem: Ode
First published: 1939; collected in *Another Time*, 1940; revised in *Collected Shorter Poems 1927-1957*, 1966

The Poem

The Irishman William Butler Yeats was the most famous and important poet writing in English at the time of his death in January, 1939, and W. H. Auden sought to make a living memorial to Yeats through this ode. The ode form is traditionally reserved for important and serious subjects and is written in an elevated style, so Auden gave Yeats great value and dignity by using this genre. The poem was written within one month of Yeats's death and published shortly thereafter. It has three distinct parts; Auden radically revised the third part by eliminating three entire stanzas which were part of the original when he included it twenty-seven years later in his *Collected Shorter Poems 1927-1957* in 1966.

In part 1, Auden paints a dark, frozen, wintry landscape as the backdrop for Yeats's death; it is almost as if the earth mourns his loss. The animals in the forest and rivers, however, run their usual courses unaware of the magnitude of the loss. Yeats's poems are treated as being human, like part of his family; the news of his death is withheld from his poems, which live on. On his last afternoon, his whole being, like a city under siege, is invaded by death. His body revolts, his mind is emptied, silence overcomes him, and he is stilled. After he is physically dead, Yeats's poems still live and are scattered across the world; the dead poet loses control over their meanings and over the kinds of affection they will excite. The poems are "The words of a dead man," which, after his death, are reinterpreted "in the guts of the living." Auden repeats that one might try to measure the loss of Yeats with scientific "instruments," but they only can tell one that "The day of his death was a dark cold day." He implies that Yeats had a value much greater than any "instrument" can measure.

In part 2 of the ode, Auden switches to Yeats's life and contrasts the man to his work: The man dies, but his poetry lives forever. Yeats's poetry survives Yeats's silliness and mysticism, his own physical decay, his insane country of Ireland, and even the damp and sometimes miserable Irish weather. Auden claims that poetry "makes nothing happen" in a practical sense but that it survives in the human imagination, far from the control of business executives. The poetry flows through imagination and unites humankind, which may be isolated, grief-stricken, and living in crude towns. Even though Yeats dies physically, he lives on in the imagination through his poetry.

Part 3 is beautifully formal and rhetorical. Auden begins by directly addressing the earth, into which Yeats will be placed. He instructs the earth to accept an "honored guest," not a dead man; the section is decidedly celebratory rather than grim.

In the later (1966) version of the poem, Auden eliminated three entire stanzas, which in the original followed the first stanza. In these stanzas, Auden explains that time, meaning history and chronological time, pardons poets and does not fully claim them, since it "worships language" and those who write it. Yeats was therefore to be pardoned any personal idiosyncrasy, and such a pardon by time presumably would make him one of the immortal poets. Auden's speaker then compares the nightmarish days of 1939 immediately before World War II broke out with the ability of Yeats to create art and poetry out of disastrous times.

Yeats is looked up to as a role model for other poets, because he had an unconstrained voice which would tell the truth even during times of "intellectual disgrace" when nations were barking at each other like threatening curs. Even in dark times such as those of 1939, when human pity seems "frozen," Auden asks the spirit of Yeats to "Still persuade us to rejoice." He wants the "poet," either Yeats or himself, to make something fruitful (a "vineyard") from the distressing period by "farming" it in his poetry. In the last stanza, he wants poets to help start the "healing fountain" which will teach free men to endure even in hateful and evil days and will teach them again "how to praise." Poetry needs to give life and hope even in the darkest days.

Forms and Devices

Auden begins this ode with an archetypal image cluster that links winter and death. The setting is desolate and filled with winter, death, and negative words, which often are linked by alliteration of *d* sounds. Alliterating negative words and phrases include: "disappeared" and "dead" (line 1), "deserted" (line 2), "disfigured" (line 3), "dying day" (line 4), and "day," "death," and "dark," (line 6). This repetitive cluster of alliterating negative words in conjunction with the frozen, wintry words creates a powerful scene of desolation in which the world's dead time seems to mirror the poet Yeats's death. In an extended form of personification, the wintering earth itself seems to mourn the loss of the poet.

In addition, Auden makes good use of other extended metaphors by establishing a different central metaphor for almost each stanza in part 1. He compares death to an invading army that takes over Yeats's whole being in stanza 4. The "invasion" is preceded by "rumours," then "revolt" in the provinces of his body; then the "squares of his mind" are emptied, silence pervades the "suburbs" of his existence, and lights go out when the "current of his feeling failed." Auden uses a cluster of geographic terms (provinces, squares, and suburbs) to illustrate the personal world of Yeats being shut down. These linked geographical comparisons metaphorically make Yeats a whole country unto himself, which magnifies the gravity of the loss.

Auden also uses individual metaphors with great cleverness. One example is his use of "mouth" at the end of part 2 to talk about poetry and the poet simultaneously. Poetry is a "mouth" in that it metaphorically speaks to the reader. Since the "mouth" is also the organ of speech, the word is used as a form of metonomy to refer to the poet himself. Like a mouth, poetry is an open potential from which words can issue. Mouths, like poems, are eternal features of mankind—one, the mouth, is a permanent physical feature, while the other, the poem, is an imaginative creation that endures beyond the poet's death.

Themes and Meanings

Auden seeks to immortalize W. B. Yeats by writing a poem about his memory and its value. He celebrates the immortality of Yeats's great poetry instead of mourning the man's demise. One of Auden's main points is that once an artist creates his art, the art develops its own autonomy and life and is not limited by the artist or his intentions. To Auden, as he makes clear in part 3 of the poem, poetry needs to teach humankind to rejoice and to endure the hideous times of life. Poets, following Yeats's example, must create great eternal art from the disasters of their times as they "farm" and perfect their verse. Writing poetry about painful experiences can be healing both for the poet who writes and for the reader who reads. Yeats presumably did write painful and healing verse in his own "unconstraining voice." He transmuted disasters in Ireland, such as the violently repressed Irish rebellion against the British during Easter, 1916, into poems of great beauty and dignity. Auden seeks to follow that example in this ode. The disaster that Auden comes to "celebrate" is the death of the greatest living English poet, W. B. Yeats. In his memorial ode, Auden tries to transform the "curse" of Yeats's physical death into an occasion for rejoicing. Yeats's personal death ends his production of new poems and permanently closes his "mouth," but, paradoxically, the poet does not die. Yeats lives through his monumental poems and takes his place with the other immortals. By reminding readers of the paradox of death not being final for a poet, Auden implies that one should not be sad at Yeats's passing. The poet lives forever in and through his poetry. Art is eternal, and that is an encouraging thought even in the darkest of day.

David J. Amante

IN PARENTHESIS

Author: David Jones (1895-1974)
Type of poem: Epic
First published: 1937

The Poem

The 187-page poem *In Parenthesis* is in seven sections, and it tells the story of a group of British soldiers of all ranks as they proceed from England to the trench warfare at the battle of the Somme. The action, therefore, is set during World War I but extends only from December, 1915, to July, 1916.

The preface and the thirty-five pages of footnotes, both written by David Jones, should be considered a part of the poem. In the preface, David Jones explains that the title refers, first, to the war itself as a "space between," a turning aside from the regularity of one's ordinary business. Second, he implies that life itself, "our curious type of existence here," is a space between nonexistence and the future.

T. S. Eliot's "A Note of Introduction" was added in 1961 and suggests that readers will have to "get used to" this unusual poem. Eliot puts his literary mantle over Jones by including him in a quartet of modern writers (Eliot himself, James Joyce, and Ezra Pound being the other three) whose lives were altered by the war, but he singles Jones out as the only one of the four who had actually been a soldier.

The first section introduces the reader to the principal characters: Major Lilly-white, Captain Gwynn, Lieutenant Piers Jenkins, Sergeant Snell, Corporal Quilter, Lance-Corporal Aneirin Lewis, and Private John Ball. They, and others, are members of the Royal Welsh Regiment, 55th Battalion, "B" Company, No. 7 Platoon. They are somewhat clumsy and apprehensive of the new role that has been thrust upon them, as they move across the Channel and disembark from "cattle trucks" on French soil.

In section 2, the platoon sees its first, impersonal, action, coming with an explosion of "some stinking physicist's destroying toy." This literal explosion interrupts a personal "explosion" by Sergeant Snell, who is caught in mid-sentence in a diatribe against Private Ball. The explosion rips up the dirt and plants, covering in disorder the invading "order" of the soldiers' camp.

Section 3 is a nightwatch. Little happens, and very little can be seen. The men cannot see one another clearly enough to recognize their companions. Private Ball, who has by now become the principal figure in the poem, particularly feels a sense of isolation. In section 4, the soldiers are in the midst of the waiting for something to happen. Even as the rain falls miserably down, Lance-Corporal Lewis stands up and offers a paean to all the war heroes in Western history. His speech is somewhat surrealistic in its grandeur and scope, as if he were temporarily possessed by the valor of so many who died in catastrophes similar to World War I.

In section 5, several soldiers get promotions (Quilter, Watcyn, and Jenkins, though Watcyn soon loses his for drunkenness). The troops see more action, and the platoon has its first death. Meanwhile, the focus of each individual becomes increasingly narrow: Each day becomes more important; each minor celebration, like a food parcel from home, seems more significant. Tension increases beneath the "ordinariness" of it all.

Section 6 is the final preparation of the battalion for its turn on the front line. Private Ball sees his friends from back in England, from back before this parenthetical war, one final time. The battalion moves forward and sees, along the road, dead mules "sunk in their servility." The soldiers cannot help but think of themselves in similar terms.

In the concluding section, characters from the opening of the poem are killed. The killing seems arbitrary, not for any didactic or balancing purpose. Lance-Corporal Lewis dies anonymously, unobserved. Jenkins leads the platoon into battle and is quickly mowed down. Next to die is Sergeant Quilter, who had assumed temporary command. Lillywhite also dies. Private John Ball survives, however, having been wounded in the leg. In the end he discards his rifle and lies down by a fallen oak, hoping the stretcher-bearers will find him and noticing in a cloudy way the many other soldiers who surge past him.

Forms and Devices

From the time of its publication there has been controversy over the genre of this "writing," as Jones himself called it. Large portions read very much like narrative prose, and at least as many read like lyric poetry. In his preface, Jones describes his work in terms that seem to refer to sculpture rather than song, and he suggests he has carved out a new "shape in words" from an otherwise amorphous welter of experience. The emphasis on physical description is not surprising, since Jones was a painter before he wrote any poetry.

The materials he uses for this new shape derive from "the complex of sights, sounds, fears, hopes, apprehensions, smells, things exterior and interior, the landscape and paraphernalia of that singular time and of those particular men." This is clearly, therefore, a poem of mixed styles, some imitative of colloquial speech, as though the poet were standing in the field of battle with a tape recorder, surrounded by the welter of British accents and vocabularies. At other points in the poem, however, Jones's style becomes highly crafted and careful, far more dense and lyrical than common speech. This poem, he writes, "has to do with some things I saw, felt, and was part of." Therefore, it might be described as autobiography, though it is impersonal and not confessional writing; it shares much, as well, with the genres of historical writing, philosophy, and even theology.

It is significant, however, that Eliot in 1961 added his introduction to the poem, since, in doing so, he put his imprimatur on the "Eliotic" stitching together of allusions, myth, history, snatches of conversation, songs, and the other elements that had come to be associated with his own poetry, and especially with *The Waste Land* (1922). It is unlikely that Jones's poem would have been recognized at all before the experimentation of Eliot and James Joyce: Since it is even less obviously generic than their creations, it would have been too apparently shapeless even for discerning readers. Following the lead of these modernists, Jones seems consciously to be expanding the generic poetic tradition he has inherited, allowing a topic as brutal as World War I to explode old categories and to reflect in the lines of *In Parenthesis* the slippery, arbitrary, and confusing experience of modern warfare, as well as its eclectic mix of conflicting emotions.

The topic itself and the time in which the poem was written both contribute to its form, but there are other significant factors in Jones's biography that shape the poem's allusions and voice. These, in a more traditional way, break out of the limited setting of one man's experience of a specific war and let the poem address all such "parenthetical" human experiences. Jones was a Londoner of Welsh and English descent, and a convert to Roman Catholicism. He draws on historical and ritualistic elements from all these sources and lets them influence the form of the telling.

Jones never mastered the Welsh language but hoped he might use this poem and his later *The Anathemata* (1952) as vessels to preserve a portion of the vast Welsh literary heritage. The most intimidating aspects of this poem often can be clarified with reference to the notes Jones provides. These indicate the Welsh allusions, the early epic *Y Gododdin*, *The Mabinogion*, *Kulhwch ac Olwen* (the Welsh version of the Waste Land myth), and others.

There are Latin references as well, to the Roman invasion of Britain, the battles and heroism of that early period, and the language used to express that heroism. There are Elizabethan allusions and quotations from Shakespeare's iambic pentameter, Victorian ditties such as Lewis Carroll's *The Hunting of the Snark: Or, An Agony in Eight Fits* (1876), and contemporary slang. The result is an amalgam of the historic languages of Great Britain — a human voice, timebound and amorphous, but expressive of the grandeur and pain common to all, regardless of the age.

Jones's Roman Catholicism also influenced the form of the poem. (He converted in 1921, three years after leaving the army and seven years before beginning writing *In Parenthesis*.) This is particularly true in section 3, with its liturgical references to the service for Good Friday and frequent allusions to a battle between light and dark. Section 7, with its early reference to the canonical hours of prime, terce, sext, and none, sets a ritualistic context for the slaughter soon to follow, suggesting participation in a larger mystery beyond the confusion of human violence.

Themes and Meanings

The title page of section 7 quotes from a sixth century Welsh poem: "Gododdin I demand thy support. It is our duty to sing: a meeting place has been found." This suggests the complex theme running through the "shape" of this poem and the war it records: As horrible as war is, there is something here to celebrate. This is not a classic antiwar poem in the same vein as that of a Rupert Brooke or a Wilfred Owen. *In Parenthesis* is graphic in its depiction of the horrors of war, of the mindlessness of much of the violence resulting from nationalistic pride, but it also speaks with an aesthetic voice and wonders if some beauty can be found even in the very instruments of human destruction. Jones is skeptical that this will be possible but sees the attempt as part of his responsibility as a poet in the twentieth century, an age that now must live with "increasingly exacting mechanical devices; some fascinating and compelling, others sinister in the extreme."

Jones's poem speaks with a profoundly humanistic voice, transcending the grotesque suddenness of individual deaths in battle and finding in history a common thread connecting all soldiers to the nobility of being a man or a woman. *In Parenthesis* deals with powers that tap into the life-force itself, the incomprehensible energies that bring humans into existence and dispatch them just as quickly. The poem, might be said to be basically religious, using the war as a metaphor for life itself—to Jones, each is a parenthesis. His poem suggests that war helps people become more aware of that larger parenthetical condition called life, a condition ultimately as sudden and individually crafted as the war would have been for each soldier.

"It is our duty to sing," as the Welsh poem states, because "a meeting place has been found." It is a sad and grim meeting place, but there, at the bloody battle of the Somme, humanity meets its past, and in some sense its future. In the search for this meeting place and in the preparations for this bloody battle, Jones's characters take their place in an oddly liturgical procession, each rank knowing its proper place. This arbitrary, human-imposed order finally becomes ineffectual in the face of the war's blind aggression.

The new level of alienation forced upon soldiers by modern weaponry is, on one level, imitated by Jones's insistence, like Eliot's, on stitching together a tapestry from the colored threads of many unfamiliar cultures. The need for footnotes in major works by both poets emphasizes this growing ignorance. Most readers, after all, will know few of the details of the Arthurian legend, let alone the lesser known Welsh myths and the ramifications of other literary and liturgical allusions.

Use of theological language reminds the reader of a sacrament, and reading the poem becomes something of a ritual of remembrance. Common humanity is certainly a thematic strain running throughout this poem; the increasing difficulty modern men and women have in maintaining this sense in the face of cultural disintegration necessitates the poem's melancholy tension.

The poem produces a sense that history, as well as the individual, is slipping through the cracks even as Western civilization concentrates its attention on "toys" of destruction. In such a porous world, simple goodness becomes heroic, and salvific. This seems to be what Private John Ball learns as he observes the various sorts of British fighter. Wounded and waiting for rescue, watching an endless stream of fresh-faced soldiers streaming by, he remembers past Welsh heroes and the *Song of Roland* (c. 1100).

Jones seems finally to offer up to God the entire poem and all it represents: the history of the British Isles and much of Western civilization. The formal poem is followed by footnotes (and the cultural history they embody), and then Jones offers a concluding frame: a final page of scriptural quotations, equating the soldiers throughout history with sacrificial victims and with the Sacrificial Lamb of Christianity, Jesus. *In Parenthesis* is, finally, a poem about the "mystical body of Christ."

John C. Hawley

IN SANTA MARIA DEL POPOLO

Author: Thom Gunn (1929-   )
Type of poem: Lyric
First published: 1958; collected in *My Sad Captains and Other Poems*, 1961

The Poem

"In Santa Maria del Popolo" is composed of four stanzas, each containing eight lines of iambic pentameter, with the rhyme scheme *ababcdcd*. The title refers to a famous church in Rome, Italy, which houses the painting *The Conversion of Saint Paul* by Caravaggio (1573-1610). The painting depicts the moment in the biblical story (Acts 9) in which Saul of Tarsus is blinded by a heavenly light and falls to the ground. Later, Saul is cured of his blindness by Ananías and converted, eventually to become Saint Paul. The poem's title, however, focuses on the painting's location and, therefore, on the poet's experience of viewing the painting.

"In Santa Maria del Popolo" opens with the narrator waiting in the dim church for the light to strike the painting in just the right way. His knowledge of the artist makes it clear that he has sought out the painting in a kind of pilgrimage. The dim light is fortuitous because it shows something essential about the painting: "how shadow in the painting brims/ With a real shadow, drowning all shapes out." Only the horse's backside and the "various limbs" of the fallen rider are highlighted. These dominant physical details seem to put in doubt "the very subject" of the painting, supposedly the conversion of Saint Paul.

The second stanza completes the description of the painting. Then the narrator begins to interpret the painting by asking the "wily" painter what he means by "limiting the scene" to the "one convulsion" of Saul lifting his arms "in that wide gesture" toward the horse.

The third stanza's mention of Ananías reminds the reader that Saul's sight has not yet been restored, nor has he been converted. The painter sees not what is to be, but only "what was," including "an alternate/ Candor and secrecy inside the skin." This enigma is somewhat clarified when the second half of the stanza mentions Caravaggio's models, "pudgy cheats" and "sharpers," who may have led to the artist's death in a brawl.

The poem concludes with the narrator turning away from the painting, "hardly enlightened." In the "dim interior" of the church, he sees old women praying, their arms "too tired" to make the "large gesture of the solitary man." Unlike Saul, or perhaps the narrator, they cannot make the heroic act of "Resisting . . . nothingness" by "embracing" it.

Forms and Devices

The practice of writing poems about paintings is common, especially in the twentieth century. Examples of the practice are W. H. Auden's "Musée des Beaux Arts," William Carlos Williams' "The Dance," and John Ashbery's "Self-Portrait in a

Convex Mirror." Poets often use such poems to state their affinity with the artist's sensibility or aesthetic. A poet will approach a painting in a way different from that of a scholar, yet if his poem is to be more than impressionistic description, he must know some of what the scholar knows.

Thom Gunn, who has done his homework, translates the artist's pictorial effects into poetic devices. The poem, for example, sets the painting within a narrative frame: The poet enters the church, waits for the good "oblique" light, views the painting, and then, upon leaving, considers how he has been "enlightened."

This play of light and dark is echoed in other dualities, such as the identity of "Saul becoming Paul" and the stanzas' two-part structure. Caravaggio is known for his manipulation of light and dark, a device called tenebrism, or the "dark manner." He creates highly dramatic, realistic effects by highlighting physical forms that seem to lurch out of the darkness toward the viewer, often at unusual angles. Gunn re-creates this angular effect first by describing the light in the church with an unusual syntax: "the sun an hour or less/ Conveniently oblique makes visible/ the painting." He then highlights the physical forms of the "dim horse's haunch and various limbs" of Paul.

Paul's figure is "Foreshortened from the head, with hidden face." Caravaggio uses this over-the-shoulder point of view to encourage the viewer to identify with Paul, just as Gunn allows the reader to see the painting through his eyes, never putting himself in the foreground of the poem.

Caravaggio was also known for his disregard of convention. His figures, composition, and color were pictorial heresy to his contemporaries. His depiction of Paul beneath his horse lacks the decorum of most treatments of scripture. His composition can be defended by pointing out that in the moment depicted, Saul has not yet become Paul. Unconverted, Saul is still in the realm of the profane. His future conversion is unavailable to the artist, whose subject is the visible world: "The painter saw what was."

Gunn notices that Caravaggio's emphasis on the horse's backside detracts from the supposed focus on Paul, whose "various limbs" hardly identify him as the saint of the painting's title. It is this compositional decision to shift the focus away from Paul that intrigues Gunn, however, and becomes the center for his own interpretive re-creation of the painting.

Themes and Meanings

"In Santa Maria del Popolo" is a poem about blindness and revelation and the relative abilities of religion and art to enlighten human experience. Gunn wrote in "My Life Up to Now" (1977) that he was "forever grateful" that he was "brought up in no religion at all." Attracted to existentialism for its philosophy that each person makes his or her own meaning in an absurd universe, and to poetry as his chosen vehicle for creating that meaning, Gunn confronts the relative power of religion, art, and poetry.

Gunn undoubtedly identified with Caravaggio, a violent, sensual, risk-taking individualist known for his homoerotic renderings of traditional motifs. Gunn addresses the painter as one artist to another ("O wily painter"), complimenting him on his daring artistry: "limiting the scene/ From a cacophony of dusty forms/ To the one convulsion." The word "cacophony" is the poet's word of sound, not the painter's of sight, and it seals their artistic fraternity. What Gunn wants to know, though, is "what is it you mean/ In that wide gesture of the lifting arms?"

The focus of the painting for Gunn is the "Candor and secrecy inside the skin" that leads to Saul's conversion. But what secret? The second half of the stanza seems to suggest that Saul's secret may have something to do with Caravaggio's homoerotic paintings, specifically "that firm insolent/ Young whore in Venus' clothes" and the "pudgy cheats" and "sharpers" of such paintings as *Concert*, *Lute Player*, and *Bacchus*. Accounts of Caravaggio's death disagree, but Gunn accepts the account of violent death at the hands of one of these male prostitutes "picked off the streets." The suggestion is that Saul (a famous misogynist) harbored a sensual secret, perhaps not unlike the homoerotic tendencies of Caravaggio and Gunn himself.

It is not Paul's specific erotic preference that is important, however, but the "alternate/ Candor and secrecy" that caused him to be an outsider. Paul is representative of the "solitary man" of existential philosophy who resists "nothingness" by "embracing" it. Unlike the women in the church who keep their secrets "closeted" in their heads, as in the confessional, the artist confesses the "Candor and secrecy inside his skin." The saint, too, admits his fallen state. Finally, the poem's narrator, who leaves the church "hardly enlightened," also admits his failure to achieve revelation through religion. This may only mean, however, that he leaves with the dark burden of what Caravaggio's painting has shown him and that what enlightenment it has inspired in the creation of his own poem has not been easy.

Richard Collins

IN TENEBRIS

Author: Thomas Hardy (1840-1928)
Type of poem: Lyric
First published: 1901, in *Poems of the Past and the Present*

The Poem

"In Tenebris" is a sequence of three meditative poems, divided into six quatrains in poem I, four in poem II, and five in poem III. Each poem is headed by a Latin epigraph or motto from the Psalms that expresses alienation and despair. The title is Latin for "in the darkness," anticipating the light and dark imagery in all three poems. The original title in *Poems of the Past and the Present*, "De Profundis," or "Out of the Depths," also reflects the speaker's gloomy vision and his preoccupation with physical and spiritual death.

"In Tenebris" is an intensely personal expression of grief and isolation written in the first person. It was written in 1895-1896, when Thomas Hardy was despondent about the decline of love in his marriage and the public's rejection of *Jude the Obscure* (1895), his last novel before he gave up fiction and devoted himself to poetry. Biographers and critics disagree about the extent to which this poem expresses Hardy's bitterness about his own experience and conveys an attitude of unrelieved pessimism, "pessimistic" being a label Hardy himself rejected. Although the speaker claims to be emotionally dead in poem I, the energy with which he mocks the optimistic majority in poem II and questions his own fate in poem III suggests that he is exploring alternative responses to the harsh realities of life that he faces unflinchingly.

The motto of the first poem, which translates as "my heart is smitten and withered like grass," introduces a series of terse poetic statements comparing the cruel catastrophes of nature as winter approaches with the speaker's stoic assertions that he cannot be hurt by these signs of approaching death; he is already dead, having lost friendship, love, and hope.

The mottoes of poems II and III place the speaker and his woe in the context of a society in which he has no place. Poem II is headed by lines which translate as "I looked on my right hand and beheld, but there was no man that would know me. . . . no man cared for my soul." The tone of derision throughout this poem is obvious from its opening lines, as the clouds echo the shouts of the "stout upstanders" who assume all is for the best. Each stanza begins by mocking the masses, with their "lusty joys" and smug Victorian belief in progress, and ends with the speaker's denigration of himself as one born at the wrong time. This contrast climaxes as the entire last stanza mimics the crowd's rejection of the speaker's insistence on facing "the Worst" to find a "way to the Better." He imagines them casting him out as one who is deformed, who "disturbs the order here."

Poem III's opening Latin reference to warlike ancient tribes in distant places reinforces the speaker's sense of alienation: "Woe is me that I sojourn in Mesech, that I

dwell in the tents of Kedar. My soul hath long dwelt with him that hateth peace."
The first and last stanzas repeat his notion that his life might as well have ended
before his disillusioning realization that "the world was a welter of futile doing." The
middle stanzas recall three different moments in his youth that might have been
more fitting times for him to die, while he was welcoming spring, feeling secure
with his mother on Egdon Heath, or suffering a childhood illness. Thus "In Tenebris" concludes with the speaker daring to question even the divine law that deter-
mines when life begins and ends.

Forms and Devices

The three poems of "In Tenebris" combine a number of the poetic techniques that
distinguish the large and diverse body of poetry written throughout Hardy's life. His
adaptions of traditional meters can be seen in the contrast between the short lines of
poem I, with its heavy use of spondees and trochees in the first and last lines accenting the funereal theme, and the much longer lines of poems II and III that imitate
heroic and alliterative verse as the speaker mocks society and questions fate. The
poem's diction, in addition to blending colloquial, formal, and archaic words, includes original coinages such as "unhope" and "upstanders." The biblical quotations and the images from the events and landscape of Hardy's childhood show the
influences of his past in relation to the modern social and philosophical themes of
the poem.

The structure of each poem of "In Tenebris" is regular and repetitive, reflecting,
perhaps, the speaker's entrapment in his own vision of despair and alienation, but
also his persistent assertion of that vision in defiance of all opposing forces. The
common patterns of language and imagery that unite the three poems follow the
movement of the speaker's thoughts as he views himself in the context of nature,
society, and the universal laws of time and fate.

Every stanza of poem I begins with an image from nature showing the harm done
to flowers, birds, and leaves by the cold and tempests of winter, except that the last
stanza uses the black of night to introduce another symbol of death that reappears
later. Every second line (all except one beginning with "But") stresses the speaker's
immunity to these rhythms of nature, since he is permanently enervated, heartless,
and hopeless—past the stages of grieving or doubting for a season. The occurrence
of one or two phrases of negation in every stanza further emphasizes the speaker's
insistence that he is beyond the reach of the horror and dread that winter, night, and
death usually evoke.

Poem II also contains a number of negative statements and images from nature in
every stanza, but they have become part of a more expansive and energetic outcry
against society. Statements such as "the clouds' swoln bosoms echo," "breezily go
they, breezily come," and "their dawns bring lusty joys, it seems" add a mock-heroic
flavor to this exposure of the easy optimism of the masses. The speaker's more
sensitive view that "delight is a delicate growth cramped by crookedness, custom,
and fear" relates to the other images of deformity he attributes to himself. The fact

that this poem not only uses the same rhyme in the second half of every quatrain, but repeats the same word— "here" — at the end of every stanza, however, suggests that the speaker is determined to stand his ground with his unpopular but honest compulsion to face "the Worst."

In poem III, the images of nature are associated with specific memories of home near Egdon Heath. The heavy use of alliteration, along with some archaic language, gives this poem a more dignified and ponderous tone, as the speaker turns from his satire of contemporary society in poem II to question universal laws of time and death. The images of light and dark culminate in the realization that, since true vision and knowledge bring pain and frustration, it would be better to have been overtaken by the darkness of death earlier in life. This idea is repeated throughout the first and last stanzas, with three occurrences of the same phrase indicating the persistent desire to consider a better time when "the ending [might] have come," creating an especially emphatic ending for a series of poems that explores various dimensions of spiritual and physical death.

Themes and Meanings

In a poem with so many images from nature and biblical references, it may seem ironic to find no suggestion that nature or religion offers comfort to one as lonely and dejected as the speaker of "In Tenebris." Although the indifference of God or nature is not discussed as explicitly as it is in many other poems by Hardy, this speaker's view that he is isolated from the cycles of nature, from society, and from the entire world of darkness and chaos shows that he rejects all conventional sources of support. Nevertheless, this poem demonstrates that Hardy never stopped seeing in the Bible and in nature powerful sources of inspiration and reflections of the human condition.

Hardy's vision of human life in this poem seems to be one of unrelieved gloom and hopelessness. He asserts that life is not worth living once childhood innocence is replaced by the disillusionment that comes from experiencing pain and futility. It is important to recognize, however, that this despair is just one of many moods expressed in Hardy's poetry. He stated in his preface to *Poems of the Past and the Present* (1901) that this collection "comprises a series of feelings and fancies written down in widely differing moods and circumstances, and at various dates. . . . the road to a true philosophy of life seems to lie in humbly recording diverse readings of its phenomena as they are forced upon us by chance and change."

Twenty-five years later, in the "Apology" that prefaced his new volume, *Late Lyrics and Earlier* (1922), Hardy again stressed the mixed character of his collections of poems. He responded to criticisms that he was too pessimistic by quoting a line from "In Tenebris," reminding his readers that facing "the Worst" was a necessary preliminary to seeking a "way to the Better." In spite of the predominance of negative statements in this poem and its preoccupation with death, it contains implicit revelations of much that Hardy did value in life. His isolation from the cycles of nature in poem I is overshadowed by the strength of his own independence and assertion of individual will. His alienation from society is balanced by his skill at satirizing its smug optimism with wit and irony in poem II. His questioning of his own fate in poem III is accompanied by reminders of the value of memory and individual life. Although he is unable to see any fulfilling order in society or the world, the poem itself demonstrates that he is able to create a meaningful artistic order out of his frustration and despair.

Tina Hanlon

IN THE BLUE DISTANCE

Author: Nelly Sachs (1891-1970)
Type of poem: Lyric
First published: 1957, as "In der blauen Ferne," in *Und niemand weiss weiter;*
   collected in *O the Chimneys,* 1967

The Poem

"In the Blue Distance" is a haunting meditative lyric. Its intense images are presented in free verse. Like most of Nelly Sachs's painfully beautiful poems, it is a
variation on her basic theme, the Holocaust. This poem searches for a way to go on
afterward, reflecting the theme of the book's title, translated as "and no one knows
how to go on." The poem's travelers look toward "the blue distance" where "longing
is distilled" or where one can recognize and find deliverance from longing. Exactly
what one longs for (peace, forgiveness, love, death?) is not determined by the poem,
but its mood is one of acceptance. This mood of quiet reconciliation, in the last
stanza, offers the possibility of transcendence from hate and bitterness. That offer is
perhaps made with reference to the suffering of the Holocaust, if only implicitly.

The first stanza presents a vista—a metaphorical view from a valley. Those who
live below can see far away a row of apple trees with "rooted feet climbing the sky."
In this image, the juxtaposition of "rooted" and "climbing" suggests a tension between two longings, perhaps. One is to remain earthbound, and the other looks
toward the blue distance, skyward. In Nelly Sachs's vocabulary, flying—one way to
interpret "climbing the sky"—often signifies transcendence or re-creation. "Those
who live in the valley" might feel some comfort knowing that another higher realm
exists.

The apple trees in one sense signify the hope and abundance of such a spiritual
place. Perhaps it can be as simple as those on earth wishing to see heaven, or simply
to know one exists. Thus the poem in stanza 1 seems to consider another way
(among all the ways in Sachs's poetry) for those hurt by the insanity of the war to
expiate their terrors, and to relieve longings intensified by the losses they suffered.

One could also say that "rooted" and "climbing" allude to the magic of organic
growth—the magic that all plants possess. Such organic growth, or regeneration,
would mean, in human terms, spiritual healing. Apple trees also are heavily laden
with mythology: They are the forbidden fruit of the tree of knowledge, but they also
bring blossoms in spring, and thus hope. Thus, stanza 1 suggests the necessity for
those who are suffering from their pasts to find some way to regenerate their spiritual balance and inner peace, the way plants are able to come back after being cut
back. There seems to be a yearning for some way to grow toward the sky, out of the
low valley.

"The sun, lying by the roadside" is, on the one hand, a descriptive image of the
sun lying low on the horizon, at sunset: it appears to lie by the road. Yet on the other
hand, the image is frightening. For if the sun really lay by the roadside, like some

suffering or ambushed traveler, such eerie displacement would suggest the worst kind of chaos. The "magic wands" could suggest that this sun is an impostor, a prankster, or a sorcerer. If so, perhaps the travelers are being deceived. Perhaps even nature is not to be trusted in a world so prone to chaos and pain.

In a lighter and more positive interpretation, these magic wands could simply suggest the regenerative magic of the natural world, of which the sun is a part. It provides light, so basic to life, and in a figurative sense, knowledge. Perhaps the stanza reflects the wrenching uncertainty of life during the Holocaust — the command "to halt" could come at any time, from any quarter. Life during the Holocaust had become so unpredictable, so unnatural, one might not be surprised to see the sun collapse, and become earthbound.

In stanza 3, the travelers have halted, although they seem alone "in the glassy nightmare." One cannot be sure why or for whom they have stopped. This lack of certainty compounds the eeriness that arose in the second stanza. "Glassy" lends an apt sense of distortion and again, uncertainty, to the poem's increasingly nightmarish atmosphere.

An image from the natural world characteristically rescues people from the nightmare and barely breaks the silence of this poem. A cricket "scratches softly at the invisible" — a beautiful and redeeming, although practically inexplicable, image. The mystical quality of Sachs's work is exemplified here in that the relief this profound image bestows upon the reader must be felt, rather than understood. No easy explanations exist for "the invisible" (eternity? the unknown? the deity?). These attempts at explanation dilute the power of the image itself, which is effective primarily in its emotional impact.

The poem ends with a second such image, which again, characteristic of Sachs's poetry, relies on emotion to complete what it communicates. "Stone" and "dust" reverberate in their earthboundness back to the tension in stanza 1 between being rooted and "climbing the sky." In Sachs's poetry, images of earth, dust and sand often signify the past, specifically here, the human suffering of years past. In the transcendent spirit-filled final lines of this poem, the stone does fly — it dances and "changes its dust to music." The transformation signifies that out of suffering, upheaval, or even death can come a spiritual insistence on life and beauty, only two ideas that "music" might suggest here. The stone thus dances a dance of renewal and life, not of death.

Forms and Devices

"In the Blue Distance" is highly imagistic. Its impact comes from the visual intensity of its metaphors, as well as their eerie, mystical reverberations. In this sense it compares to most of Sachs's work.

Known for its enigmatic quality, Sachs's poetry is not "easy" to read. Whatever difficulty the reader confronts, however, is not attributable to the technical devices of her poems. They are not written in encoded language, nor are they riddles to be solved. Readers may experience difficulty laying aside their demands to have the poem's "meaning" made easily comprehensible. Her concentrated and emotional language, its allusions and metaphors, unfold only slowly, and the reader must be prepared not to rely on a need for explicit meaning, but to experience the mystery of the poem. That is, as with the cricket image, one feels her poetry better than one can hope to understand it in the analytical sense.

Yet Sachs uses masterful craftsmanship in her poems. The earthy images in this poem manage to root the poem itself in good warm soil. Its movement from section to section seems almost, again inexplicably, like natural growth. Each stanza has an image central to its movement and the "narrative" movement of the poem. The climbing apple trees, the "lying" sun, the cricket scratching and the dancing stone are simple pictures yet profoundly intriguing and suggestive. These images, one to a stanza, move the poem forward with sure quiet steps, as if the delicate thread of emotion spun stronger by each new line is being handed carefully along.

Personification is also used; it lends an eerie yet somehow friendly quality to otherwise mysterious images—the cricket scratching "at the invisible" and the stone dancing. Since the stanzas are not regular in number of lines or line length, the images that reside within the poem provide its form. The interplay between them unifies the poem.

Sachs speaks in simple language, and the rhythm of "In the Blue Distance" is relaxed and unassuming. In fact, the low-key conversational tone the poem has is amazing, given the otherworldly intensity of the images. That it breaks down into three relatively simple sentences shows Sachs's ability to comb away the wool surrounding an emotion she wishes to convey and to find a beautifully simple correlation in the imagery. Her concrete images are the key to this fertile simplicity.

Themes and Meanings

"Death gave me my language," Sachs said. "My metaphors are my wounds." Such a statement implies an intensely private poetry, and there is perhaps a sort of arrogant folly in searching for "meanings" in images whose very strength comes from their wildly errant suggestiveness. Her images suggest many directions, many meanings. Yet Sachs's statement also simplifies a discussion of meaning. Her basic theme, the Holocaust, leads her to explore all avenues of thought and emotion in terms of the great mystery, death.

One could read this poem as a meditation on arriving at the edge of death. The stillness, approaching silence, at the heart of this poem certainly suggests that the travelers teeter between worlds—where language becomes unnecessary. The momentary yet strong break in movement after stanza 2 ("The sun . . . commands the travelers to halt") suggests an interface between the worlds of life and death. In the "glassy nightmare," the travelers are fairly on the edge of a world. The "invisible" at which the cricket scratches suggests an entrance point, if one follows this theme, into the next world.

Yet death in this poem is neither fearsome nor terrible. In a sense, it has already happened, for there is no escape from the sun. The poem is really a reckoning, an acceptance of the inevitable event of death, which seems to approach almost tenderly in this poem—as softly as the cricket scratches at the door. Sachs has written harshly accusatory poems about the Holocaust, but this is not one of them. Her work has been called forgiving, and the calm lyricism of this poem certainly demonstrates that quality. In it, even death seems forgiving. The stone is cold and hard, but "dancing," transforming dust, and the past with all its anguish, to music.

JoAnn Balingit

IN THE EVENING

Author: Anna Akhmatova (Anna Andreyevna Gorenko, 1889-1966)
Type of poem: Lyric
First published: 1914, as "Vecherom," in *Chetki*; collected in *The Complete Poems of Anna Akhmatova*, 1990

The Poem

Opening with a reference to music, a garden, and grief, the first of the poem's sixteen lines places a man and a woman in a romantic setting, as seen from the woman's point of view. She is recollecting a meeting with a friend, and the mood is sorrowful, perhaps because of the music, which provides an emotional context as well. By mentioning the music, the poet hints at unspoken suffering. It is suggested by the music, or the music prompts sad memories, here unexpressed, in her own past. Abruptly, another detail is remembered. The second pair of lines uses the image of "oysters in ice," whose smell reminded the poet of the sea. The couple is at dinner at a seaside restaurant—the title suggests a romantic time of day—and the memory is rich in sensory detail: the sound of sad music, the smell of the sea brought in by the oysters. The mood is bittersweet.

The second stanza continues the romantic moment, the poet recalling what her friend said and his simple gesture of touching her dress. The next two lines dwell on the peculiar quality of his touch, which the poet remembers as "unlike a caress." The negative comparison interrupts the romantic mood that has so far been sustained. Its significance captures her attention for the moment as she begins stanza three. She compares the man's touch to stroking a small, delicate creature—a cat, for example, or even a bird. Leaping further in an imaginative comparison, the next line compares the gesture to watching young ladies ride horses. A distance between the two people is suggested. His avowal—"I am your true friend"—is not that of an ardent lover. Love is not mentioned or hinted at, and his gesture, "unlike a caress," is like the kind one uses on other creatures—a cat, a bird—not a lover. It reminds her of watching slender women ride, not of the passionate gaze of a lover. She remembers the smallest details, the slightest movement, subtle shades of expression and color, as the next two lines demonstrate, describing "the light gold lashes" and "the laughter in his tranquil eyes." A true friend he may be, but his eyes are tranquil, not lovesick or fiery with passion.

The final stanza returns to the music, which is still dolorous, but now the violins "sing," and their "voices" are remembered through a visual image—that of drifting smoke. Perhaps they are expressing the poet's own sorrow. The vision prompts her to express sudden emotion, gratitude for the time when "You're alone with the man you love." The poem ends on an ambiguous note: The poet may be addressing heaven on the reader's behalf or she may be inviting the reader to join her in thanking heaven. The poem addresses the reader throughout in standard lyrical fashion, but the final address, "You're alone with the man you love," suggests that the poet, knowing what it is like not to enjoy such moments, is telling the reader to praise heaven for such time as the reader will have.

Forms and Devices

The primary devices of the poem are somewhat unconventional to the lyric. As the poem opens, it appears to be a love poem focusing on a fond recollection of a meeting between two lovers, but after the speaker mentions "Oysters in ice," music ringing out with "inexpressible grief," she focuses on the man's seemingly casual gesture for five of the poem's sixteen lines. The man's comment that he is the poet's "true friend" suggests that something other than love is in question or on his mind, perhaps only loyalty, not the passion of a lover. The poem's drama, then, unfolds in a series of details that hint at something other than what is directly expressed in the poem. Juxtaposing images, the poem invites inference while seeming to deliver a simple recollection of a meeting between two friends, if not lovers. The poet remembers signs of emotions—sorrowful music, tranquil eyes—without appearing to feel any herself. Her attention seems to be deflected from any direct recognition of her own emotions toward more distant elements, letting the reader surmise rather than see.

The poem develops in a way that is reminiscent of the haiku, using juxtaposed images that create, by means of their interaction, a significant perception. The poem surprises the reader with its placement of detail and imaginative leaps. The third stanza illustrates these effects most clearly as the poet associates the man's touch with stroking a cat, or a bird, or—making a dramatic leap to a sensory image of a very different kind—the act of watching slender horseback riders. The poet seems to be searching for an objective correlative to that momentous gesture, a trifle that merits unusual attention because it seems to have extraordinary meaning. To find the right evocative correlative is to discover and reveal the significance of a poem. The image also suggests the nature of the poem itself—a performance watched by the poet as she recollects; as she performs, the reader watches her, a slender equestrienne.

The weight given to minute matters in this poem is evident in the little that happens between the beginning and ending references to sad music: The man says he is a true friend and touches her dress. The moment is fixed in a nest of details, the way one remembers a first kiss, a birth, a death. The poem challenges the reader to find that significant event—is it the man's remark, the peculiar gesture, the music, or all together? The whole may be greater than the aggregate of parts, or else the parts do not make a significant whole. The colon setting off the poet's final words in line 14 suggests a summary comment, perhaps an ironic moral: Thank heaven for a time like this one—or unlike it. The instability at which the ambiguities hint corresponds to a changing rhyming pattern in the final stanza. In the original, the first three stanzas rhyme *abba, cddc, effe*, but the final stanza rhymes *ghgh*. It may be that the final alteration in rhyme scheme parallels the poet's own changing attitude toward the preceding situation.

Themes and Meanings

Undeniably, the poem is about a meeting between two people. Loyalty appears to be an issue, and the mood is not cheerful. It is difficult to know the source of the sorrowful emotions the poet mentions at the start and returns to in the final stanza. The lines say that the music is sad—the violins are "mournful"—and without commentary, the poet lets the reader associate the sadness with the speaker's mood, as though she recalls those details that reflected her own feelings. The poem is intriguing because it appears to develop a romantic meeting without providing enough confirmation for the reader to be certain. The speaker's attention to subtleties and her sensory awareness contrasts with the poem's understated quality. Rich with detail, the poem lacks emotional commitment to any single statement or point of view other than that of the poet, whose attitude is noncommittal. For all the reader knows, the poem may be about a profound disappointment. The man's avowal speaks of friendship, not love. His gesture is not that of a lover. Rather, it reminds the speaker of a spectator watching others. The man's apparent emotional distance from her—he is a "true friend," not a lover—may be a response to her own detachment. The poem seems to contradict itself, appearing to describe a romantic moment while creating ambivalence, doubt.

The poem's meaning, then, may be inferred not from what the poet says but from what she does with a handful of details. The poem's true subject is not the remembered meeting between two friends but how the poet remembers the meeting, how she felt then and how she feels as she remembers. Since she gives more attention to the setting and to the associations a gesture causes than to her male companion, the reader loses sight of him, sees the hands gesturing and the slender equestriennes riding, hears the mournful music, sees the drifting smoke, and hears the poet's voice praising heaven, or telling the reader to praise heaven. The man's one remark—"I am your true friend!"—stands out because it lacks motivation and has no definite relationship to the rest of the poem. The reader is not told what prompted it or what the speaker thinks of it. It is a non sequitur, like watching young women riding on horseback—like the final two lines, in fact. The poet has managed to express her own ambivalence toward the male friend by collecting disparate images in a poem that refuses to focus on any one meaning. The poem is about what was or what could have been. Anna Akhmatova might also be advising the reader, based on her own disappointments, about the value of time alone "with the man you love."

Bernard E. Morris

IN THE NAKED BED, IN PLATO'S CAVE

Author: Delmore Schwartz (1913-1966)
Type of poem: Lyric
First published: 1938, in *In Dreams Begin Responsibilities*

The Poem

Like many other poems by Delmore Schwartz, this—the author's most frequently anthologized piece—takes its title from its first line, which provides the work with an intriguing and memorable opening. This is matched by an equally powerful, if dispiriting, concluding statement. The poem is thus securely framed.

Structurally, the poem is made up of two compact blocks of text, each about fourteen lines long. Hence, one might regard it as a rhymeless double sonnet. It would be perhaps more accurate to say that each half of the poem behaves like a double octave and like a double sestet, as considerable tension and interaction is going on between the two parts.

Indeed, the first half can be seen to break further into two verse paragraphs in the middle of line eight. In this way, the author points out a slight departure from the main thrust of the preceding seven and a half lines. Similarly, in the poem's very last line, a break occurs that marks off the concluding statement or capstone of the work. A more decisive turning point is indicated by the continuous break separating the two halves of the piece.

Although the poem is written in the first person, the speaker keeps himself in the background as much as possible. The poem's chief concern is not so much to give an account of a unique personal experience as to focus on what binds humanity together. Thus the "I" in the first half of the poem is referred to as "son of man" in the latter. In spite of this generalizing impulse, however, the author is at pains to fill in with a wealth of particulars the state he is trying to define, evoke, and describe: that is, insomnia or sleeplessness by night, followed by the drowsiness attending pulling himself together in the waking hours of morning.

The title of the poem provides a good entry into the poem. Its first half, "In the Naked Bed," conveys the feeling of an insomniac's futile tossing. This is suggested by the rather unexpected and seemingly superfluous attribute "naked." The other phrase, "in Plato's Cave," reminds the reader of the famous myth of human consciousness depicted by Plato in the *Republic* (388-368 B.C.). In its early stages of becoming, humanity but dimly realizes its condition. Perceptions are like shadows projected onto the wall of a cave. Only later, according to the ancient Greek philosopher, is humanity capable of escaping its delusions and getting out of the cave to confront reality as it really is, in broad daylight, by dint of the tools of abstract reasoning. Schwartz seems to require one to regard his poem as dealing alternately with the delusional and obsessional aspects of both insomnia and waking. The twin phrases making up the title are thus complementary and, up to a point, synonymous. The two stages—sleeplessness and drowsiness—are consecutive and therefore separable, each being dealt with analytically and at length. One cannot, however, draw the dividing line so neatly, for as early as the middle of the first part, the figure of the milkman might be taken to herald the break of day, providing a transitional moment in the poem.

Forms and Devices

The poem is characterized by a sustained unidirectional movement with a break between its two parts that stands for a brief interlude of sleep. The continuous string of verbs—all in the past tense—ensures the even pace of the unfolding narrative. Many realistic details are touched upon in passing, each contributing to the density of the text. The accumulation of tangible facts provides the poem's momentum and its self-transcending transformation toward the end: the conversion of past into present, and the abandonment of the sequential development. Instead, the speaker points now to a pattern of recurrences and cyclicity that define human history.

Both parts are replete with visual and auditory images. Alone in his room, the insomniac is aware of the amplified noises of the street below, as well as of the flitting shadows chasing themselves along the ceiling and down the wall until the milkman's sound makes him aware of the impending dawn. Drawn to the window, the speaker is struck by the eerie emptiness of the cityscape whose atmosphere seems to descend from the early metaphysical paintings of Giorgio di Chirico.

This effect is further matched and enhanced in the second part by such compelling metaphors as the waterfalls of hooves and the coughing of a car's engine. Further, the image of the half-awakened bird tentatively testing the reality of the dawn by means of its song recalls poetic moments in Alfred, Lord Tennyson ("Tears, Idle Tears") and Wallace Stevens ("Sunday Morning"). Finally, the sensation of one's self as being "still wet with sleep" creates a singular graphic moment in which the reader is, so to speak, invited to recognize the poetic as the chief constitutive feature of the work in hand. By contrast, the concluding sentence restricts the figurative tendency of the language to a minimum. "So, so"—the very first words of this section—show the reluctance of the speaker to indulge in the figurative game again. The time has come to conclude. Such epithets as "ignorant" qualifying "night" and "the travail of early morning" aptly sum up and contrast the oppositions developed in the poem. Then, in a totalizing gesture, they are blended into a formula of recurrence, "the mystery of beginning/ Again and again," which is an attempt to define historical time as a sequence of half-realized moments.

Themes and Meanings

"In the Naked Bed, in Plato's Cave" is a poem about the workings of the half-conscious mind in its strivings to extinguish itself in sleep and in its trials to refocus while awakening. Out of this twofold struggle man emerges "perplexed," sleepy, "affectionate, hungry, and cold." It is in this sense that history, in the end, remains "unforgiven" or unredeemed—an ever-renewable mystery. While in the making, history can be neither comprehensible nor controllable, the poet seems to intimate. It is sheer activity, somehow escaping man's moral aspirations toward truth, order, and justice.

"Plato's cave" is reenacted (ontology repeats philogeny) in the insomniac's "naked-bed" struggle to obliterate the stubborn or obssessional contours of the hard material facts of outer reality. Likewise, it still provides a valid analogy to the exhausted mind's attempts to regather itself and its sense of identity (in terms of reconstituting familiar surroundings) while trying hard to wake up.

This dramatization of the mental ebb and flow provides the forcefulness of the work. The reader is bound to leave it with a heightened awareness of her or his own subjectivity—the first essential step toward the light of reason and out of the chimeras of one's cave. This daily struggle to regain and reconquer one's mind's sovereign control is aptly introduced by the figure of the milkman, who, like an unobtrusive minister, enables one to connect again to the source of innocence and well-being. The milk of human kindness is there, in Delmore Schwartz's poem, ready to bestow its miraculously redeeming vitality—but for how long? Its promise seems to loom there only for History to "dismember and disremember" it in its eagerness to tarnish and undo.

Stefan Stoenescu

IN THE RUINS OF AN ANCIENT TEMPLE

Author: Yánnis Rítsos (1909-1990)
Type of poem: Lyric
First published: 1979, as "Sta ereipia archaiou naou," in *Ritsos in Parentheses*
  (includes English translation)

The Poem

"In the Ruins of an Ancient Temple" is a free-verse poem in two stanzas of nine and six lines. The title shows a concern shared by much modern Greek poetry with its ancient inheritance, although here that concern is ironic and unromanticized.

The first stanza presents a series of short, declarative sentences, almost one per line, describing the life of common people in a modern Greek rural setting. These straightforward statements set the tone of the down-to-earth life depicted. Each subject has its own verb, just as each worker has his or her own distinctive action to perform. The museum guard observes, the women wash, the blacksmith hammers, the shepherd whistles.

When the animal and mineral worlds are introduced, the lines are longer, enjambed, and colored with metaphor. Responding to the shepherd's whistle, "The sheep ran to him/ as though the marble ruins were running." The water of the river is personified, its "thick nape/ shone with coolness."

The final sentence of the first stanza is more than two lines long and focuses on a woman hanging clothes to dry. She spreads them on "shrubs and statues," her husband's underpants hung from the shoulders of a statue of the goddess Hera. Her action might appear satirical (imagine someone hanging their underwear from a crucifix), except that it is an action, not a gesture.

The second stanza consists of only two sentences. The first is a fragment: "Foreign, peaceful, silent intimacy—years on years." Like the ruins, the fragment has no verb to animate it. Time is stopped, spanned, to suggest the long years that have gone into the easy relationship between these people and their ancient landscape. The Greeks go about their business, as they have for thousands of years, without undue respect for the archaeological and artistic ruins around them.

The final sentence's complex structure fits the complexity of the poem's conclusion. Fishermen carry on their heads "broad baskets full of fish," but it is "as though" they are "long and narrow flashes of light:/ gold, rose, and violet." These are the same colors as the "richly embroidered veil of the goddess" carried in a procession, which the communal "we" have cut up "to arrange as curtains, and tablecloths in our emptied houses."

As in many of Yánnis Rítsos' poems, the simplicity of the description is deceptive. Each of the actions carries symbolic cargo made more substantial by the reality of the activity being described. In the end, a texture of meaning has accrued, so that one understands, however vaguely, that something of importance has taken place before one's eyes, even in the simplest of scenes.

Forms and Devices

The poem's thematic tension between ancient and modern is developed through a series of contrasts. From the very beginning, the tension between dead stone and living flesh is established. Yet their identity is suggested in the off rhyme of the lines' endings: *marmara* (marbles) and *mantra* (sheepfold). This contrast is fused, if not erased, when the sheep's movement makes the marbles appear to be moving also. The image is a simple metaphor on the surface, but the optical illusion has the surrealistic effect of making the ordinary landscape magical.

The dualities the poem addresses are embodied in the two-part structure. In the first stanza, ancient and modern collide and merge, like overlapping transparencies: the museum guard "in front of" the sheepfold; the sheep "among" the marbles; the water's sculptural nape and marmoreal coolness "behind" the oleanders. In the second stanza, the duality is less visual than temporal (years "on" years). Spatial positioning gives way to symbolic layering: fishermen "on" the shore with baskets "on" their heads; the procession "bearing" the veil; the curtains and tablecloths "in" our houses.

In the first stanza, Rítsos uses sound and movement to contrast the ancient-contemporary scene. The present is animate with the sound and motion of work: the plash of washing in the river, the beat of the hammer, the whistle of the shepherd. Even the museum guard, whose job is to protect by observing, moves, though minimally. Silence and stillness dominate the second stanza.

In both stanzas, however, color is used to contrast the vibrancy of the present with the colorlessness of the temple ruins. The oleanders give color to the statuesque water, while the underpants give color back to the statue of Hera. The fish in the baskets illuminate the landscape with "flashes of light," and the veil of the goddess, like the fish of "gold, rose, and violet," illuminate the interiors of the houses.

Rítsos never uses imagery or metaphor for mere decoration. Each stanza's symbolic significance turns on a metaphor: "as though" the marble and the sheep were the same; "as though" the fish and the goddess' veil were identical. These are finely observed details, but they are also optical illusions, symbolic sleight of hand, which turn one thing into another, alluding to traditional religious symbolism, both pagan and Christian.

Rítsos avoids using these symbols for didactic purposes. His technique is to suggest an ambiguity inherent in the thing itself. By working up a visual and symbolic texture, he allows readers to draw their own conclusions about the poem's meanings.

Themes and Meanings

"In the Ruins of an Ancient Temple" is a poem about the role of the gods in the modern world, and the role of humans in their creation or perpetuation. It can be read as an ironic expression of how the gods — both pagan and Christian — have lost all color, life, and vibrancy in the modern world. Such a reading, however, turns the poem into a satire instead of an exploration of the role (even the responsibility) the imagination has in giving life to gods, statues, and poems.

Statues appear in many of Rítsos' poems, almost always as a life-affirming reminder. "The Statues in the Cemeteries," for example, "don't copy us; they are alone too; they suffer; they contradict nonexistence." One should keep in mind that the marbles in the landscape are not the gods themselves, but only works of art, sharing in the imaginative project that the poet himself is working on. If they have no life of their own, they remind readers that they are the ones who are alive.

The careless way the woman spreads her husband's underpants on Hera's shoulder is designedly comic. Far from showing a lack of respect, however, this easy famil- iarity is more in line with the ancients' view of the gods than the modern-day museum mentality of reverence for anything classical. (The gods had no amnesty from the barbs of Aristophanes' comedy, and Greek statuary was painted to make it appear more lifelike.) As the sheep animate the marbles, the cloth gives back to the statues some of their original coloring.

In the ancient fertility ritual of *sparagmos*, the god was "cut up" and distributed among the fields to ensure a bountiful harvest. Rítsos evokes the ritual of sparagmos in a political sense when the communal "we" cuts up the "richly embroidered" veil of the goddess and redistributes this aesthetic wealth to the people for "our emptied houses."

The word "emptied" instead of "empty" is a political, or economic, choice. "Empty" would signify a simple lack, perhaps an ascetic renunciation of the material world, consonant with Christian orthodoxy, while "emptied" signifies a fullness that has been taken away. It is an indictment of those who have "emptied" our houses in the name of the gods to fill the coffers of the church or state.

In examining the museum guard, an employee of the state, standing as sentry at the beginning of the poem, one may ask What is he guarding? His casual attitude shows that there is nothing really to protect. It is not as though the sheep or the washer women are going to run off with the statues, which are, if not meaningless, valueless to them, except as mannequin drying racks.

The real riches are highlighted by the colorful patches in the poem. "The water's thick nape" concealed "behind the oleanders" is more valuable to the people, both for its utility in their work and for its intrinsic aesthetic qualities. The fishermen bearing "flashes of light" have more power of religion, like Christ's fishers of men, than the dead formalities and useless processions of the church.

These riches need no museum guard. These are the flashes of perception that Rítsos considered the job of the poet—living among the things of the world in a "Foreign, peaceful, silent intimacy . . . years on years"—to cut from the cloth of the "long, richly embroidered veil" of culture and to redistribute to the people to brighten their emptied houses.

Richard Collins

IN THE THIRTIETH YEAR

Author: J. V. Cunningham (1911-1985)
Type of poem: Satire
First published: 1960, in *The Exclusions of a Rhyme: Poems and Epigrams*

The Poem

The title of "In the Thirtieth Year" is clearly significant; it points to the time and moment of choice when the speaker elects to take his "heart to be his wife." It also indicates that the normal search for someone to give his heart to has been ended. It is a choice, instead, of solitariness and self-sufficiency. The reason this choice comes at the "thirtieth year" is not explained, but it suggests a deliberate choice after earlier failures in love, failures to find someone to whom his heart may be given.

The speaker of the poem is not the poet, J. V. Cunningham. He is an ironic speaker who seems not only to explain but also to justify his choice of separateness. Cunningham is usually a straightforward poet who despises the fashionable use of irony. Here, however, he uses a mask to represent a way of thinking and living that is quite different from his own. He is satirizing the type of man who would make such a choice to protect himself from the pain and risk of human relationships.

Only eight lines long, "In the Thirtieth Year" is a very precise poem. It begins by describing an unusual wedding of the speaker to his heart; this substitute for a "wife" is announced as a reasonable and viable option. Yet a person who keeps his "heart" to himself, who actually weds it, is an egoist who feeds upon himself rather than risk the effort involved in developing a relationship with another person.

The second couplet clarifies this solipsistic union: "And as I turn in bed by night/ I have my heart for my delight." The "heart" has not been given away to another, a situation about which many poets have written. Instead, his "heart" is there at his call and command and gives him the only delight he will receive. Indeed, there is a parody of a sexual relationship as the speaker turns to meet not his beloved but his own heart.

The "heart" in the third stanza remains a part of the speaker. There is, at least, the assurance of fidelity. "No other heart may mine estrange" since it is a part of him. It alters as he alters, forming a perfect union. The "heart" is an echo of its solitary possessor, changing and mirroring its owner and sole proprietor.

The last section of the poem produces an interesting disjunction: "And it is bound, and I am free." The "heart" cannot wander to another; it cannot leave the speaker. The speaker, however, has attained his freedom by excluding all other possibilities, a very illusory freedom based on the imprisonment of his heart.

The last line brings the poem and the relationship to an appropriate close: "And with my death it dies with me." They are joined together in life in an exclusive relationship, so it is only appropriate that they perish together at death.

Forms and Devices

"In the Thirtieth Year" is written in rhyming couplets that are appropriate for the balance and antithesis that Cunningham uses to trace the relationship between self and heart. The union is complete and will allow no one else to intrude. The heart has been joined to the self in alternating lines of verse in nearly every couplet. For example, in the second couplet the first line has the speaker touch on his turning in bed and the closing line of the couplet has the heart turn to the speaker.

The meter is iambic tetrameter, but there are a few significant variations. The first line of the poem, for example, has slack syllables at the beginning of the line, and the sixth line ("For my heart changes as I change") violates the iambic pattern in the first and second feet. The regular meter is quickly reestablished, however, in the next line ("And it is bound, and I am free"). The poem is also divided into stanzas of two lines in which the first runs on and the second is end-stopped, making each couplet a separate and complete unit.

The rhymes of the poem are also interesting. For the most part, they provide effective contrasts. For example, "estrange" is rhymed with the very different "change." Change suggests freedom and estrange a fracturing. Best of all, perhaps, in the last couplet "free" is rhymed with "me." The supposed freedom is only the result of a relentless concentration on the self by excluding all others.

The language of the poem is the language of love; "wife," "delight," and "estrange" all suggest a close love relationship, although the relationship that is established in the poem is very different from usual. It is protective self-love that will not risk itself by reaching out to another.

Of the few poetic devices used, the metaphor of taking "my heart to be my wife" frames the whole self-contained parody of a relationship. The images of turning in bed to meet not a loved one but one's own heart for "delight" is appropriately derisive. The image of the heart being "bound" is also interesting, especially since that binding is the means to the speaker's freedom, which would be impossible in a true relationship.

The most important device, however, is the personification of the speaker's heart. It assumes the characteristics of a person as it substitutes for a wife in its fidelity and companionship; it also provides the only delight that is possible for the speaker.

Themes and Meanings

The primary theme of "In the Thirtieth Year" is that of the egoism and isolation of a man who would close in on himself because of the pain a struggle for love would involve. He escapes the struggle into a smug self-satisfaction.

Cunningham powerfully portrays the seemingly reasonable choice of the speaker. The tone of the poem is also noteworthy, as Cunningham does not reveal the satiric nature of the poem directly; he describes the choice of heart for wife as if it were commonplace. It is only when the reader begins to look beyond the choice into its consequences that the poem can be seen in a very different light.

The poem as a whole portrays a complete relationship, bizarre as it is. It begins at the moment of the choice of the beloved. It develops into the closeness of an intimate relationship, swears fidelity, and finally completes itself with a mutual death.

The poem is a satirical exposure of a certain way of life. Cunningham does not satirize a specific individual but a more general type. The type that is represented here is one that seems to interest him frequently as a satirical subject. For example, in an earlier poem, "The Solipsist," he writes of the type of person who recognizes no "others." Everyone is subsumed into the demanding self. It is a position of absolute certainty that is achieved by the exclusion of the very existence of others.

It is interesting that in the same group of poems, Cunningham has written a poem on a very different relationship. "To my Wife" speaks of the difficulties and joys of love. In this poem, love is not a static relationship as it is in "In the Thirtieth Year"; it changes as "affections alter" the two partners. Even though there is constant change, the creation of a real relationship is impressive.

> So love by love we come at last,
> As through the exclusions of a rhyme,
> Or the exactions of a past,
> To the simplicity of time,

This achieved love is both "quiet as regret" and "like anger in the night." It is a complex love that can include opposites and still sustain itself.

Cunningham is best known for his epigrams, and all of his poems are terse and compressed. In this poem, the reader will not find any of the witty turns and surprises found in the epigrams. To understand it, the reader must see it as the encapsulation of a life in very few lines. Such economy is appropriate because it is a life that rigidly excludes the possibility of anything other than the self. So the unity of the poem is the unity of a deliberately reduced and restricted life. Cunningham does not intrude his own voice into the poem. The "I" of the poem tells his own story and condemns himself with his own words.

James Sullivan

IN THE WAITING ROOM

Author: Elizabeth Bishop (1911-1979)
Type of poem: Lyric
First published: 1976, in *Geography III*

The Poem

"In the Waiting Room" describes a child's sudden awareness—frightening and even terrifying—that she is both a separate person and one who belongs to the strange world of grown-ups. The poet locates the experience in a specific time and place, yet every human being must awaken to multiple identities in the process of growing up and becoming a self-aware individual.

Elizabeth Bishop wrote about this experience as it had happened to her many years before she wrote the poem. Published in her final collection, it is considered one of her most important poems. The speaker in the poem is Elizabeth, a young girl "almost seven," who is waiting in a dentist's waiting room for her Aunt Consuelo who is inside having her teeth fixed. In the manner of a dramatic monologue or a soliloquy in a play, the reader overhears or listens to the child talking to herself about her astonishment and surprise. She tries to reason with herself about the up-welling feelings she can hardly understand. The result is a convincing account of a universal experience of access to greater consciousness.

In the long first stanza, of fifty-three lines, the girl begins her story in a matter-of-fact tone. The place is Worcester, Massachusetts. On a cold and dark February afternoon in the year 1918, she finds herself in a dentist's waiting room. In plain words, she says that the room is full of grown-ups in their winter boots and coats. She picks up an issue of the *National Geographic* because the wait is so long. She is proud that she can read as the other people in the room are doing.

She looks at the photographs: a volcano spilling fire, the famous explorers Osa and Martin Johnson in their African safari clothes. Then scenes from African villages amaze and horrify her. A dead man (called "Long Pig") hangs from a pole; babies have intentionally deformed heads; women stretch their necks with rounds of wire. Their bare breasts shock the little girl, too shy to put the magazine away under the eyes of the grown-ups in the room.

To recover from her fright, she checks the date on the cover of the magazine and notes the familiar yellow color. Suddenly, a voice cries out in pain— it must be Aunt Consuelo: "even then I knew she was/ a foolish, timid woman." The voice, however, is Elizabeth's own, and she and her aunt are falling together, looking fixedly at the cover of the *National Geographic*. One infers that Elizabeth might have slipped off her chair—or feared that she might—and tried to keep her balance.

In the second long stanza of the poem (thirty-six lines), Elizabeth attempts to stop the sensation of falling into a void, a panic that threatens oblivion in "cold, blue-black space." She reminds herself that she is nearly seven years old, that she is an "I," with a name, "*Elizabeth*," and is the same as those other people sitting around her.

She does not dare to look any higher than the "shadowy" knees and hands of the grown-ups. She understands that a singularly strange event has happened. Questions arise in her mind. Why is she who she is? Why should she be like those people, or like her Aunt Consuelo, or those women with hanging breasts in the National Geographic? She heard the cry of pain, but it did not get louder—the world sets some limit to the panic.

Two short stanzas close the monologue. The first, in only four lines, reverts to a feeling of vertigo. The hot and brightly lit waiting room is drowned in a monstrous, black wave; more waves follow. Then, in the six-line coda, her everyday consciousness returns. It is wartime (World War I lasted from 1914 to 1918) on a cold winter afternoon in Worcester, Massachusetts, February 5, 1918. The experience that disoriented her is over. Here, at the end of the poem, the reader understands that Elizabeth Bishop, a mature and experienced poet, has fashioned the essence of an unforgotten childhood experience into a memorable poem.

Forms and Devices

For the voice of Elizabeth, the speaker of "In the Waiting Room," the poet needed a sentence style and vocabulary appropriate to a seven-year-old girl. Bishop relied on the many possibilities of diction and syntax to create a plausible narrator's tone.

The words spoken by Elizabeth in the poem reveal a very bright young girl (she is proud of the fact that she reads). Almost all the words come from Anglo-Saxon roots, with few of the longer, Latin-root forms. The plain verbs—I went, I sat, I read, I knew, I felt—are surrounded by the most common verb, to be: "I was." The last two stanzas, for example, use "was" and "were" six times in ten lines. A beginner in language relies on the "to be" verb as a means of naming and identifying her situation among objects, people, and places. "What is that?" comes early to a one-year-old with a vocabulary of very few words. In her reliance on the verb "to be," Bishop shows an exact ear for children's speech.

The nouns and adjectives indicate a child who is eager to learn. She names the articles of clothing: "boots" appear in the waiting room and in the picture of Osa and Martin Johnson in the *National Geographic*. Perhaps the most "poetic" word she speaks is "rivulet," in describing the volcano. She could be quoting from the article she is reading—the caption under the picture. Similarly, "pith helmets" may come from the writer of the article. In the next line, Elizabeth does specify that the words "Long Pig" for the dead man on a pole comes directly from the page.

Along with a restricted vocabulary, sentence style helps Bishop convey the tone of a child's speech. Most of the sentences begin with the subject and verb ("I said to myself . . .") in a style called "right-branching"—subordinate descriptive phrases come after the subject and verb. Short sentences of three to six words are frequent: "It was winter"; "I was too shy to stop."

Bishop's skill in creating an authentic child's voice may be compared with the work of other modern authors. Henry James created a novel in a child's voice, *What Maisie Knew* (1897). The child Maisie learns that even if adults often tell her "I love you," the real truth may be just the opposite. Another modern author, Joyce Carol Oates, has written a novel in a child's voice, *Expensive People* (1968). Ideas of violence and antagonism to adults are examined in a child's experience.

Themes and Meanings

"In the Waiting Room" asks eternal questions: Who am I in the world? Where do I fit in? Like a kaleidoscope, life presents fractured levels of existence in a single moment. The individual feels divided and yet united to each level. The experience can be frightening. Poets and philosophers from Socrates to William Butler Yeats, in all religious traditions, have expressed the paradox of the person being at one time individuals and members of a whole society.

The religious overtones of the poem begin in the title; the visible world is often seen as a vestibule or waiting room in which one gradually comes to understand the larger dimensions of one's dwelling place. While one is in "the waiting room," one is, in a sense, an exile, away from home, a child among grown-ups.

As children, people begin their understanding with homely, familiar objects—the boots and coats of the people in the dentist's office on a wintry afternoon. Like Elizabeth in the poem, people feel that they know securely when they exist. "Now" is Worcester, Massachusetts, February, 1918.

Soon the larger world comes in, as one learns about other places and times. Strange and alien events disturb one's serenity: those "others" are not like me. The child's world is invaded by violent scenes—to Elizabeth, a dead man being carried on a pole, women's breasts exposed. The world begins to swing as her experience of the "far" finds an echo in the "near." Her Aunt Consuelo's voice is *her* voice. Between these poles of the far and near, where does an individual belong? Vertigo sets in, the angst of modern life, Søren Kierkegaard's "fear and trembling," and, further back, the Fall of Adam. Only an effort of the conscious will can stop the descent.

The poet as child conquers the experience and arrests the fall by asserting her uniqueness. The three levels of "otherness" suggested by Aunt Consuelo (the intimate family), those sharing the waiting room (those in boots seated around Elizabeth) and the far-off people (those in boots in the *National Geographic* picture) must be pushed away. The access to adult ego-consciousness comes with the lines, "you are an *I*,/ you are an *Elizabeth*,/ you are one of *them*." The idea is similar to the Hindu phrase, *om tot sat om*, "I am that I am"—both an individual and one with the other.

Yet people continually want to trace that boundary of the self and society. In the poem, vertigo again assails the poet. Like a hell, the waiting room of this world is too hot, too bright. Uncomfortable waves of emotion roll over it. The poem ends on another religious analogy about the question of existence in the world, life as a battle: "The War was on." Everyone, like a soldier, faces unknown and alien forces from the many levels of the real and imaginary world. Everyone continues to orient themselves with all the power they can muster in the "night and slush and cold."

Doris Earnshaw

IN THE WINTER OF MY THIRTY-EIGHTH YEAR

Author: W. S. Merwin (1927-   )
Type of poem: Lyric
First published: 1967, in *The Lice*

The Poem

"In the Winter of My Thirty-Eighth Year" is a free-verse, unpunctuated, twenty-two line meditative lyric, divided into five unequal sections. The speaking "I" is clearly the author. The title of the poem calls to mind the famous opening line of Dante's *The Divine Comedy* (c. 1320), "At midpoint of the journey of our life." The Florentine poet meant by that midpoint the age of thirty-five, regarded—in biblical terms—as the apex of manhood and creativity. Viewed in this light, the poem might be said to hold that central place in W. S. Merwin's *Selected Poems* (1988).

The first section of the poem makes the reader feel at ease by adopting from the very beginning a familiar tone. The feeling is further strengthened by the ordinariness of the situation. It is indeed true that the border between young adulthood and middle age is a blurred one, and consequently one does not experience it as something actually dividing or cutting one off from younger days.

The poet has made the first section, which belongs to the past, "*when I was young*," spill over into the second—dealing with his present condition, in which the speaker can still afford to toy with the idea of appointing his own age in spite of what the calendar says. He is still not showing his age; his understanding seems to have been both affected and untouched by the passage of time.

There is a more clearly marked break after the second section. Each of the remaining three sections deals with an isolated aspect of biography: age (youth), speech, and stars (fate). These sections, though discrete, are constructed in keeping with the same rhetorical pattern. Each is meant to be reassuring by dismissing a negative assessment. Eventually they add up to an odd, undefinable feeling that leaves the poem open-ended and ambivalent.

Forms and Devices

The poet muses in a relaxed tone of voice. The object of his meditation is the nature of experienced inner or subjective time and its relation to chronological or mechanical time. To emphasize this imaginative effort of grasping the twofold nature of time, the poet makes sparse use of imagery. The first section is conspicuously devoid of concreteness. The aim of the speaker is to establish temporal relationships with which to capture his sense of his own selfhood. Yet he feels remote and disoriented, "As far from [himself] as ever."

The same dearth of figurative material (there can be no metaphorical activity in the absence of tangible imagery) can be encountered in the third and fourth sections. Both rely on an impeccable logic by means of which the speaker hopes to achieve a clearer and more stable view of his whereabouts.

This is even more true of the second section, which contains a more elaborate design of hypothetical and guarded statements in which time is shown to be both relative and elusive. Its functions or effects are no less difficult to evaluate. This rather artificial and contrived textual space—a kind of hall lined with reflecting mirrors—is introduced by two lines that carry the whole weight of poetic figuration available in the first half of the poem: "Waking in fog and rain and seeing nothing" describes the speaker's condition now that middle age has overtaken him. The only certainty available is that there is practically nothing to grasp or to lean on. Hence, the speaker goes on, "I imagine all the clocks have died in the night." This is perhaps the most compelling statement in the whole poem, creating a sense that time has come to a stop and has ceased to matter.

The concluding, fifth section rounds off the picture by contributing its powerful description of stars as drifting "farther away in the invisible morning." The concluding image—if it can bear that name—"the invisible morning," is arguably more pregnant than that of the waking self "seeing nothing" and that of the imagined death of all clocks "in the night." "Invisible morning" is but another way of naming the ungraspable. Yet "morning" is morning, and it sounds a kind of a hopeful note at the end of the tunnel.

The poem is therefore quite telling by the very way in which is eschews direct perception by one's senses. On the other hand, the figures of thinking—or the way temporality is hurried or arrested, hypothetically juggled and surveyed—make up for the rarefied concreteness of the text. This in itself is a remarkable achievement: To be simultaneously in and out of time, forgetful of its flow and yet mindful of its consequences, is not an easy task for neutral, transparent syntax to accomplish.

Themes and Meanings

"In the Winter of My Thirty-Eighth Year" is a poem about manhood and its problems. The sense of achievement is definitely there, for "speech"—the most precious tool of the poet—has already "lent itself to [the speaker's] uses." There is also a sense of impending crisis in spite of the disclaimer: "There is nothing wrong with my age now." The speaker feels at odds, as the reader has seen, with his present condition. Moreover, his "emptiness" is freely floating among the receding stars. This levitation and boundlessness is what ultimately prevails.

The difficulty the speaker faces is one of definition. The speaker's age has been imagined, anticipated, and, like his youth, indefinitely deferred. The perplexity and confusion results from the fact that the observer's vantage point does not lie outside the moving system of reference (Albert Einstein's theory of relativity comes to mind here) but is part and parcel of it. One cannot experience directly both the river of time and its relative speed with respect to stationary objects along the banks.

On the other hand, the thirty-eighth year in the life of an American poet, as a critic of Merwin's oeuvre has pointed out, is an important landmark. At that very age, Walt Whitman completed his first edition of *Leaves of Grass* (1855). Consequently, later poets of the self—and Merwin is one of them—may be tempted to measure their own achievement against Whitman's time scale.

Many poems in *The Lice* are concerned with Merwin's own maturity and its problems: "Looking East at Night," "December Night," "After the Solstice," "December Among the Vanished," "Glimpse of the Ice," "The Cold Before the Moonrise," "Early January," "Dusk in Winter," and "For the Anniversary of My Death." (Indeed, Merwin "must have the mind of winter," as Wallace Stevens might say.) Read as a sequence, these poems provide an illuminating context for a deeper grasping of this poem. What seems to be missing from it is a direct reference to death. The tone of "In the Winter of My Thirty-Eighth Year" is, or seems to be, free of metaphysical anxiety: "Of course there is nothing the matter with the stars." Nor is it fraught with longing or hope, as is Dylan Thomas' "Poem in October," its most kindred forerunner. Merwin's sense of his own individual destiny seems to bask suspended in a relativity of his own making: "Now no one is looking I could choose my age/ It would be younger I suppose so I am older." The arbitrariness of the gesture is supported by the fluidity of the syntax, unmonitored as it is by any punctuation markers.

In giving his 1967 volume the title *The Lice*, Merwin believed he should unravel for the benefit of his public the context from which he had lifted this rather unusual reference. He printed an epigraph from the pre-Socratic philosopher Heraclitus on the left-hand side of that volume's title page:

> All men are deceived by appearances of things, even Homer himself, who was the wisest man in Greece; for he was deceived by boys catching lice: they said to him, "What we have caught and what we have killed we have left behind, but what has escaped us we bring with us."

No better illustration of this observation could be provided than Merwin's meditation on his own mid-term balance of gains and losses. Yet in Merwin's poem there can be no easy discrimination between such opposites, for the reason that his losses and his gains are on the move themselves, continually shifting and changing their own significances.

Stefan Stoenescu

THE INDIAN BURYING GROUND

Author: Philip Freneau (1752-1832)
Type of poem: Lyric
First published: 1788, in *The Miscellaneous Works of Mr. Philip Freneau*
  Containing His Essays and Additional Poems

The Poem

"The Indian Burying Ground" is a short lyric poem of forty lines celebrating the spirits of Native Americans haunting their sequestered graves in the North American wilderness. It is an early American example of the Romantic movement in Western literature. Although its elegiac subject matter harks back to the eighteenth century British school of "graveyard" poetry, Philip Freneau adds a Romantic twist to the sepulchral theme of human mortality. This writer displays a Gothic fascination with supernatural phenomena and moonlit scenes of fancy, a primitivistic attention to unspoiled natives and pristine nature, a nostalgia for a legendary past, and an interest in the spellbinding powers of the imagination (or "fancy") as superior to the reason of the European Enlightenment. In lyric form and fanciful poetic theme, Freneau bears close comparison with William Collins in eighteenth century England.

The poem opens with a primitivistic speaker in the guise of a common man challenging civilized burial customs, which betray what a culture thinks of the state of death. When civilized culture demands burying a corpse in a prone position, death is seen as an eternal sleep for the soul.

If readers consider not the European past but the antiquity of the New World, however, they contemplate America's primordial race of Indians, whose sitting posture in their graves suggests that their souls actively continue the simple pursuits of their former mortal lives, as depicted on their pottery and as indicated by their weapons. For example, an Indian arrowhead, or "head of stone," symbolizes the opposite of a European headstone—namely, the enduring vitality of the dead person's spirit, unlike the cold, engraved memorial for a dead white man.

Almost midway through the poem, there is a shift from commentary about burial rites to an exhortation to an unnamed stranger forbidding any violation of a secluded Indian grave site where the dead were buried sitting, not sleeping, and whose corpses therefore left a noticeable swelling in the grass-covered landscape. This Indian graveyard lay in a setting of Romantic sublimity, set off grandly by a boulder of native carvings and sheltered by a venerable elm tree that once witnessed Indian pastimes.

Let the passerby and local farmer ("the shepherd") beware of disturbing the ghosts of these departed Indians, who haunt their burial site and ward off injuries done to the hallowed place. One such spirit is the ghost of an Indian maiden as beautiful as the darker-skinned Queen of Sheba in the Bible.

At the haunting time of midnight in a dewy moonlit setting, the passerby will let reason be overpowered by imagination, or "fancy," so as to be able to see a frightening supernatural vision of deer hunters and an Indian chief wearing war paint and riding perpetually in night's shadows.

Forms and Devices

"The Indian Burying Ground" is a lyric poem consisting of ten quatrains with alternating end rhymes. The prevailing meter is iambic tetrameter with variations. A lyric poem tends to be a simple evocation of a single, simple experience and/or emotion, and such is this poem's aim and achievement. Freneau's lyric poetry, though minor, is often haunting in its beauty. Using contemporary themes of nature, evanescence, interest in an unspoiled humanity and solitude, primitivism, and the supernatural, he evoked a real charm that is at odds with the harsh satire for which he was best known in his own time.

His lyric poems are rooted in the eighteenth century seedbed of British "graveyard" poetry, and especially in William Collins' more formally ornate Romantic poems that pay homage to the new European interest in fancy, fantasy, Gothic supernaturalism, and nostalgia for remote national history. Freneau's accomplishment was to naturalize these English literary trends and European artistic impulses to help give impetus to a national literature for the burgeoning United States of America.

As Freneau lamented in his "Advice to Authors" (published in the same year, 1788, as the poem under discussion), the United States was as yet a very thin, rocky soil for cultivating the fine arts and for nurturing starving poets. It was a miracle that any literature emerged at all in a nation that was too young and too rude to have developed a fully civilized culture sustaining poetic creation:

> In a country, which two hundred years ago was peopled only by savages, and where the government has ever, in effect, since the first establishment of the white men in these parts, been no other than republican, it is really wonderful there should be any polite original authors at all in any line, especially when it is considered, that according to the common course of things, any particular nation or people must have arrived to, or rather passed, their meridian of opulence and refinement, before they consider the professors of the fine arts in any other light than a nuisance to the community.

Even outside the context of an uncultured United States, "The Indian Burying Ground" should be considered a good performance, if not a great poem; it is a lovely piece, of European inspiration and idealistic American sensibility.

Themes and Meanings

"The Indian Burying Ground" is a poem about the admirable ways of Native Americans, here viewed essentially as "noble savages," a fairly common eighteenth century idea, as exemplified in their custom of burying the dead in a sitting position symbolic of their pristine vitality in life and for eternity.

The poem indulges in a nostalgia for the primitive, the past, and the fantastic as envisaged through the poet's and the reader's imagination, which is deemed more powerful than the faculty of reason in the human mind. Freneau begins his poem with a declaration of independence from received notions of European civilization respecting burial rites, and ends, appropriately, with a declaration of allegiance not to fact-based reason but to the new Romantic imagination: fancy-bound and therefore capable of conjuring up Indian spirits that are shown to be forever alive in the sublime realm of mist, moonlight, and shadow. The growing interest of Americans such as Freneau in their own past and in the original natives of the country may be seen as the result of an impulse similar to the one that made the Germanic and Celtic past an important topic of English Romanticism. Veneration of the "noble savage" was also widespread in England and on the Continent in the eighteenth century.

It must be pointed out, however, that Freneau's worship of the noble American savage is unconsciously compromised by large doses of implicit condescension toward Indians. Compared to white men of European background, the Indians are written off as "a ruder race" (line 24) and as the "children of the forest" (line 28) who in death produce "many a barbarous form" (line 31) to haunt their graveyard and punish unwary intruders. Hence, critics and readers alike must be cautious about ascribing an enlightened primitivism to Philip Freneau and his poetry.

Thomas M. Curley

INSOMNIA. HOMER. TAUT SAILS

Author: Osip Mandelstam (1891-1938)
Type of poem: Lyric
First published: 1916, as "Bessonnitsa. Gomer. Tugie parusa," in *Kamen*, second
edition; collected in *Modern Russian Poetry*, 1967

The Poem

"Insomnia. Homer. Taut Sails" is a short poem of only three stanzas, told in the
first person. It is untitled, like many of Osip Mandelstam's poems, although the very
first word, "Insomnia," fits the mood of the entire poem. It is one of his early poems
and one of many poems in which he used classical motifs. The lines are six-foot
iambic, rhymed regularly *abba*.

The poem opens with three noun sentences, setting the stage in a most concise
manner. The persona is suffering from insomnia and is reading the list of the ships
of Homer's *Iliad* (c. 800 B.C.), most likely hoping that it will help him fall asleep. He
has read half of it when, in his imagination, the sails of the ships on the list turn into
white cranes, which are now flying high above Hellas. The connection between the
first words of the poem becomes clear: Insomnia leads to Homer, and Homer leads to
white sails and the ships.

In his imagination, the poet sees the ships as a flock of cranes and follows them as
they fly off in wedge formation to distant lands. They are compared, parenthetically,
to royalties whose heads are covered with the foam of gods. The poet then unexpect-
edly asks where they are flying, even though he gave a hint in stanza 1. He immediately gives another hint, after suddenly shifting the perspective, by asking the
Achaeans another unexpected question: What would Troy be to them without Helen?

In the third stanza, the poet provides further elucidation about the mystery by
shifting his focus again to the sea and Homer. He flatly states that both the sea and
Homer are governed by love, but now he is faced with a dilemma: Should he listen to
the sea or to Homer? The dilemma resolves itself when Homer falls silent and only
the majestic roar of the sea is audible.

By now, sleep is taking over as the sea inundates the persona's pillow: He has sunk
into drowsiness after the dilemma has been resolved. The perspective shifts back to
the persona and the bed, where it all began.

Forms and Devices

In this poem, as in most of Mandelstam's poems, metaphors and images reign
supreme, beginning with the opening metaphor of Homer. Homer serves not only as
the provider of reading material (the catalog of ships), but also, in a much more
important role, as a guide toward the revelation that the persona (poet) is seeking.
This metaphor also opens the door for other metaphors, all of which are closely
connected with Homer.

The sea is the second important metaphor. At first, it is a beautiful, calm sea on which the ships/white cranes sail majestically. Toward the end, it turns into "the dark sea" that roars and crashes heavily, the dominant sound before the persona sleeps. The sea metaphor also contains a clue to the central message of the poem.

The third important metaphor is that of the cranes, which clearly stand for the ships. They are seen as beautiful white creatures sailing gracefully through space. They are not used here merely for description, however—nor is their geographical destination particularly important, or else the poet would have told the reader about it immediately. By sailing to Troy, as the poet hints by mentioning the Achaeans, the cranes direct the reader's attention toward the focal point of the poem.

Helen is used as the fourth metaphor, in which the three previous metaphors converge. Although she is mentioned only once, she provides the all-important clue to the rationale of the poem.

Thus the four main metaphors work in harmony not only to bring sleep to the persona of the poem but also to provide the answer he is seeking. All four are therefore indispensable; remove one and the whole edifice collapses.

There are several striking images in the poem. The description of the long-extended flock of cranes and their wedge formation adds grace to the significant role of the birds. The white vision of their graceful sailing amid the blue sky and the sea lends them a touch of royalty. The crane image is reinforced by the image of the kings, who are sailing on and guiding the ships. The kings' heads are covered with foam produced either by the swift sailing of the ships or by clouds descending upon their heads. Moreover, the foam is modified by "divine"—no doubt a reference to Aphrodite, the goddess of love, who was born out of sea foam. (Mandelstam has used this motif in another poem, "Silentium.")

The poem concludes with the image of a dark, roaring sea that crashes and thunders against the pillow, providing a fitting climax to the search and to the solution. It is interesting that the whiteness of the cranes contrasts with the darkness of the sea, as if to underscore the change of focus of both the persona and the reader from the lightness of the pre-sleep condition to the heaviness immediately preceding the sleep.

Themes and Meanings

"Insomnia. Homer. Taut Sails" is a poem about love. It takes an unconventional approach to the subject, to be sure, as Mandelstam's poems often do.

It is not easy to determine that the poem deals with love, since the reader's attention is captivated by the beauty of the metaphors and the images of Homer and the white ships/cranes. The reader is also puzzled by the seemingly incongruous association of insomnia and Homer (although the association between Homer and ships is quite apparent).

The first hint that love is the main theme occurs in the reference to the "divine foam," which immediately conjures up the vision of Aphrodite, the goddess of love. The next hint is contained in the innocent and apparently pointless question about where the ships are sailing. Certainly, the royal sailors—that is, those who command the ships — know their destination. The poet does not wait to provide the answer, even though it is a cryptic one. By acknowledging the fact that the sailors are Achaeans sailing toward Troy, and by asking rhetorically what Troy would mean to them without Helen, Mandelstam supplies a one-word answer, love, as Nils Ake Nilsson points out in his book *Osip Mandelstam: Five Poems* (1974). After all, did not the Achaeans fight a battle at Troy primarily to liberate Helen? Was not Helen the symbol of love, worth going to war and fighting for?

After providing the simple, if cryptic, answer, the poet further complicates his own answer by stating in the first half of the next line, very forthrightly, that "both sea and Homer" are moved by love, a statement requiring further elucidation. The aphorism used to complete the verse, "all is moved by love," may be seen as a lame truism or as a safety valve. The fact that he shifted his attention in the closing lines away from the issue altogether may indicate that Mandelstam thought that he had made the point clear, but additional explanation is necessary.

Aside from the euphonic similarity, perhaps relatedness, in Russian of the two words, sea and Homer (*more* and *Gomer*), there are other possible explanations. Victor Terras, in his article "Classical Motives in the Poetry of Osip Mandelstam" (1966), finds examples in classical literature that express the belief that the entire universe (including sea) is governed by love. Nilsson quotes additional examples from other literatures, including the work of Dante. Certainly, the primary moving force of poetry is love. Homer, the epitome of a poet, composed some of the best passages of his works, especially those concerning Helen, on love. The logic of the juxtaposition of sea and Homer becomes clear now. By deciding in the final lines of his poem to "listen" to the sea rather than to Homer, Mandelstam opts for the stronger of the two, having used Homer metaphorically to proclaim the divine force of love.

Vasa D. Mihailovich

THE INVITATION TO THE VOYAGE

Author: Charles Baudelaire (1821-1867)
Type of poem: Lyric
First published: 1857, as "L'Invitation au Voyage," in *Les Fleurs du mal*;
  collected in *Flowers of Evil*, 1963

The Poem

"The Invitation to the Voyage" is number 53 in *Les Fleurs du mal* (*Flowers of Evil*, 1909), part of the book's "Spleen and Ideal" section. Written in direct address, the poem uses the familiar forms of pronouns and verbs, which the French language reserves for children, close family, lovers and long-term friends, and prayer.

Charles Baudelaire was a master of traditional French verse form. In this poem, he chose to employ stanzas of twelve lines, alternating with a repeating two-line refrain. Each stanza is divided into distinct halves built on an *aabccb*, *ddeffe* rhyme pattern. An initial pair of rhyming five-syllable lines is followed by a seven-syllable line, another rhyming couplet of five-syllable lines, then a seven-syllable line which rhymes with the preceding seven-syllable line. The pattern of five- and seven-syllable lines is repeated with new rhymes then followed by the refrain couplet of seven-syllable lines. The regular alternation of long and short lines produces a gently syncopated rhythm, difficult to duplicate in translation.

The poem opens gently, addressing the beloved as "My child, my sister." She is invited to dream of the sweetness of another place, to live, to love, and to die in a land which resembles her. The tone is intimate, the outlines gently blurred. The lady and the destination are described with ambiguity: The suns there are damp and veiled in mist; the lady's eyes are treacherous and shine through tears. The refrain promises order, beauty, luxury, calm, and voluptuous pleasure in the indefinite "there."

In the second stanza, the poet describes an interior scene, a luxurious bedroom where time, light and color, and scent and exoticism combine to speak the secret language of the soul. The description is made in the conditional form; this dream interior has not yet been realized. Again, the refrain returns with its promise of order and beauty, now in reference to the room which has just been described.

The last stanza presents a landscape, an ideal scene of ships at anchor in canals, ships which have traveled from the ends of the earth to satisfy the whims of the lady. Although vagabond by nature, they are gathered to sleep on canals which, unlike the untamed sea, are waters controlled and directed by human agency. As in the first stanza, the tone is generalized; the poet speaks of sunsets in the plural. The light of the sunsets, which dresses the fields, canals, and town, is described in terms of precious stones ("hyacinth," as a color, may be the blue-purple of a sapphire or the reddish orange of a dark topaz) and gold, recalling the luxury of the second stanza. The stanza ends in warm light and sleep as the refrain returns with its promise of order, beauty, and calm.

Forms and Devices

"The Invitation to the Voyage" makes full use of the music of language as its carefully measured lines paint one glowing picture after another. A successful translation must approximate as much as possible the verbal harmony produced in the original language, with its gentle rhythm and rich rhymes. Equally important appeals are made to the senses of sight and smell in the images employed by the poet.

The three stanzas of "The Invitation to the Voyage" correspond to three visual images, three landscapes. The first is vague and hazy, a "somewhere" where the poet emphasizes the qualities of misty indistinctness and moisture. There is sunlight, but it is diffuse. The "suns" of the imaginary landscape are doubled by the lady's eyes. The beloved and the imaginary landscape are alike mysterious and indistinct.

In the second stanza, the interior scene is also distinguished by its light, reflected from age-polished furniture and profound mirrors. It is also distinguished by the rare perfume of flowers mixed with amber. As with the light, the amber scent is "vague." The emphasis is on complexity of stimuli: many-layered scents and elaborate decoration enhanced by time and exotic origin. The intimate tone of the first stanza is preserved through this descriptive passage; it is "our" room which is pictured, and the last line of the stanza echoes the "sweetness" of the beginning of the "Invitation" by describing the native language of the soul as "sweet."

In the third stanza, a second exterior landscape is presented, with many elements of a Dutch genre painting: ships, with their implied voyages behind them, slumbering on orderly canals, the hint of a town in the background, the whole warmed by the golden light of the setting sun. The eye is invited to enjoy this picture, a glowing visual image painted with words. The environment is not the enclosed, hothouse atmosphere of the second stanza. The light is wider, more expanded, the poignant hyacinth and gold of sunset. Still, the gem quality of the "hyacinth" light recalls the opulence of the second stanza, as the "sunsets" of the third stanza echo the "suns" of the first.

The three visual images presented by the main stanzas of the poem are connected in many ways. The most obvious is the repeated refrain, with its indefinite "There," which refers simultaneously to each separate scene and to the imaginary whole. With each return of the refrain, the poet tightens the embrace that holds the poem together in an intimate unity.

The complex pattern of rhyme in the original version is also an instrument of the poetic unity, especially since it is doubled by an interior structure of repetition and assonance. The fourth and fifth lines begin with the same word, *aimer* ("to love"). No less than nine lines begin with *d* and fourteen with *l*. Moreover, there is a striking incidence of *l*, *s*, and *r* sounds throughout the poem, forming a whispering undercurrent of sound. Even when this effect is lost in translation, the formal structure of the poem and the strength of its images ensure that the reader will be struck by its unified construction.

Themes and Meanings

In *Flowers of Evil*, and most particularly in the "Spleen and Ideal" section, Baudelaire explored self-destruction and exaltation, beauty in its most sordid and ethereal forms, and the place of the poet in interpreting human sensation and knowledge. "The Invitation to the Voyage" is one of the most beautiful of his "ideal" poems, a tour-de-force of seductive appeal, a love poem which offers the beloved a world of beauty. The more beautiful and desirable the world of the poem, the greater the compliment to the lady, since the poet declares them to be alike. The complexity and richness of the formal structure of rhyme and rhythm are echoed in the thematic structures of the interior and exterior landscapes, where ornament and exotic luxury are highly valued. Adventure and the outer world are at a distance, exotic themes which perfume the dream without troubling it. The wandering boats are still and asleep on canals, not the wild ocean. The "ends of the earth" send their treasures, but they are to be protected in a closed space, not diffused.

The "voyage" to which the beloved is invited is an imaginary and interior one. The qualities of warmth, diffused light, vague perfume, order, and luxurious and exotic ornamentation are cultivated beauties, neither wild nor natural. Everything within this enclosed paradise is united by an intimate harmony and communicates in the intimate and secret language of the soul.

The beloved must be convinced to enter this ideal world, where every desire is fulfilled. The first stanza presents the invitation in gentle terms, addressing the beloved as "my child" and "my sister." Yet, in contrast to the later stanzas, suffused in light and warmth, the first stanza speaks of ambiguities: love coupled with death, sunshine with dampness, misty skies. The beloved herself is the prototype of the imaginary world—charming but mysterious and treacherous. She is also the "sister" of the speaker, intimately known and like him. Readers meet her especially through the image of her eyes, shining through their tears.

Eyes are a frequent image in Baudelaire's poems. In "Autumn Sonnet" (number 64 of *Flowers of Evil*), the eyes of the beloved are "clear like crystal." In "The Cat" (number 51 of *Flowers of Evil*), the poet gazes into a cat's eyes with astonishment and sees fire, clear lights, living opals—which stare back at him. In "Beauty" (number 17 of *Flowers of Evil*), Baudelaire ends the sonnet with the image of the eyes of the goddess Beauty, pure mirrors which fascinate poets. In many of these poems, the eyes are inscrutable sources of light or living mirrors and a means by which the poet's gaze is turned back upon himself. In gazing at the Other, be it cat or goddess, the poet is thrown back on his own yearning soul.

The diffuse light and misty eyes of "The Invitation to the Voyage" conceal the pain implicit in the bond of poet and lady, the betrayal and tears present in the formation of the imaginary world of the poem. The beloved, the speaker, and their world are intimately bound in a unity where luxury, calm, order, and sensual beauty are a means of control over the ambiguous mystery and sorrow of life. The poetic text itself is emblematic of the promised paradise. The beauty, formal order, and musical appeal to the senses fulfill that promise and build that world.

Anne W. Sienkewicz

AN IRISH AIRMAN FORESEES HIS DEATH

Author: William Butler Yeats (1865-1939)
Type of poem: Dramatic monologue
First published: 1919, in *The Wild Swans at Coole*

The Poem

"An Irish Airman Foresees His Death" is a short dramatic monologue, originally one of four poems written by William Butler Yeats to commemorate the death of Major Robert Gregory, son of Lady Augusta Gregory (Yeats's onetime patron and later his colleague). Gregory, never a close personal friend of Yeats, was a multi-talented Renaissance man, titled Irish gentry, athlete, aviator, scholar, and artist who, even though over the age for compulsory military service, enlisted in World War I. He did so because it was a magnificent avenue for adventure.

The poem is equally divided into two eight-line sentences with four iambic te-trameter quatrains. Yeats writes in the first person, donning the persona of the air-man as he prepares to go into battle in the sky. In the first quatrain, Yeats shows the airman's ambiguous feelings about fighting in the war; he has no strong emotions concerning either those he is fighting against or those he is fighting to protect. Even with these mixed sentiments, however, he is sure that he will die in this adventure. Not only is death from enemy contact possible but also, with aviation in its infancy, the chances for mechanical error multiply the dangers he faces.

The second quatrain continues this ambiguity as the airman realizes the fruitless-ness of his participation in the war. He knows that no matter what the outcome of his personal battles, they will not affect the overall war effort—nor will the outcome of the war affect the lives of the Irish peasants with whom he identifies.

The third quatrain indicates the selfish desire for adventure that was the airman's reason for enlisting to fight. His rugged individualism made his choice preordained; only his method of fighting was open. True to a romantic tradition, the airman chose the imagined "chivalry" of single combat in the rarefied heavens over the anonymity of the wholesale slaughter which the ground soldier confronted on the battlefield when faced with the advancements of modern warfare. Gone were the traditional concepts of bravery and honor; the arbitrariness of artillery, machine-gun fire, and poison gas killed randomly.

In the final line of the last quatrain, Yeats leaves the first person when he says, "In balance with this life, this death." Particular attention should be paid to Yeats's shift to "this" life, "this" death as opposed to using "my." He is universalizing the air-man's experiences, transcending the politics of World War I and moving to the real-ization of the futility of all wars, all waste of human life.

Throughout the poem, the airman feels no sense of disappointment, no misgiv-ings about his fate, no disillusionment about his outcome. He has accepted the chal-lenge in the tradition of the romantic hero and will continue on toward his preor-dained end.

Forms and Devices

At first glance, the structure of the poem seems awkward, almost as if Yeats made punctuation errors by omitting periods. There are also two locations where he has used semicolons rather than commas (after "clouds above" in line 2 and after "clouds" in line 12). Yeats uses these semicolons to provide positive links with the thoughts immediately following. He links (and contrasts) the serenity in the line ending "clouds above" with the agitation among the populace, figuratively "below" him both in space and temperament. In line 12, he uses the semicolon to link (and contrast) the "tumult in the clouds" with the clear, rational balancing of his mind.

Yeats, always the quintessential Irish nationalist, uses this poem as a vehicle to allude ironically to the part that the Irish played in World War I. When the airman states, "Those that I fight I do not hate,/ Those that I guard I do not love," he is showing implicitly that the Irish, who were constantly at odds with British domination, were forced into the war on the Allied side with ambivalent feelings. They had no more sympathy for the British than they had for the Germans.

Voluntarily fighting as a British ally, the airman may be grouped with the "Byronic heroes," the literary epitome of Romantic individuality. True to this metaphor, the airman comes to realize his own self-destruction and embraces it with composure and aristocratic nonchalance. He did not have to fight, but when "A lonely impulse of delight/ Drove to this tumult in the clouds," he joins the legions of Byronic heroes (Robert Browning's Childe Roland, Alfred, Lord Tennyson's Ulysses, and Lord Byron's Manfred, to name a few) who are a combination of boundless energy and fatalistic recklessness.

The airman knew that his death was predestined; it can be compared to the death of Icarus from Greek mythology. Icarus, ignoring his father's (Daedalus') warnings as they were escaping from Minos in Crete, flew too near the sun on the wax and feather wings that he and his father had constructed. The heat from the sun melted the wax, and Icarus fell to his death. The airman knows that as he continues to be driven to the "tumult in the clouds" he, too, will eventually meet his death.

This foreknowledge of fate is effectively used, as is the juxtaposition of contrasting thoughts throughout the poem. Two prevalent examples are the airman not hating the enemy and not loving the Allies. The airman is placing himself above such emotions and continuing on his personal "quest" for adventure. In the age of technologically advanced weaponry, it would be impossible for the Byronic hero to pursue his adventures on the ground; it was left to the Yeatsian hero to turn to the skies.

Themes and Meanings

In "An Irish Airman Foresees His Death," Yeats uses the dramatic monologue to accomplish a dual purpose. Yeats is using the death of an Irish hero to further the prestige of Irish nationalism; Gregory was well-suited for the purpose. He was of the nobility; he was a volunteer in the truest sense of the word; he was a worldly, sophisticated Renaissance man; he was a war hero (recipient of the Military Cross); and he was an Irish patriot. No matter what the true reason Gregory chose to fight in World

War I, he was an ideal vehicle for Yeats's propaganda.

Several ironic facts may be noted about Gregory's death and about the possible influence that he may have had (if his life had continued) on both the public and private sphere. Gregory was accidentally shot down by an Allied war plane, a fact that Yeats did not know at the time he composed this poem. Gregory also had been active in Irish politics prior to his enlistment. After the war, England sent in the hated Black and Tans to enforce order in Ireland. Because of Gregory's prestige and power, he may have been able to exert some mollifying control over the chain of events that immediately followed the armistice. His death also led his impoverished wife to sell his ancestral home, Coole, because she was unable to manage the estate.

Yeats's second purpose is to explore the futility of war and the waste of human life that results. The airman balances his past life and his future, and decides that they are equally wasteful. War will have no effect either on him or on the populace for whom the war is supposedly being fought. The banality of the situation is that the airman is able to see this and is able to ignore the emotional pleas that are normally used to entice men to fight. Yeats was confronted with a complex problem. The traditional language of poetry was of no use in conveying the ghastly horrors of modern trench warfare. Many poets, such as Siegfried Sassoon, Wilfred Owen, and Edward Thomas, developed a new language and form to meet these new demands. For Yeats, an escape back to the traditional romantic hero allowed him to voice his own poignant protest in a world gone mad.

Stephen H. Crane

IRREPRESSIBLY BRONZE, BEAUTIFUL & MINE

Author: Ntozake Shange (Paulette Williams, 1948-   )
Type of poem: Lyric
First published: 1987, in *Ridin' the Moon in Texas*

The Poem

Ridin' the Moon in Texas, the collection of poems containing "irrepressibly bronze, beautiful & mine," responds to particular works of art. The artwork to which "irrepressibly bronze" specifically responds is an untitled photograph of a man's back by acclaimed and controversial photographer Robert Mapplethorpe. The poem, occupying four and one-half pages, is not an extended description of the photograph; rather, it is a poem on a topic—black men—inspired by it.

The poem is divided into three sections, all written in free verse. The first section, written in the first person, itself seems to break up into two parts. The first part provides a history of the speaker's sexual awakening. It begins with a childhood crush on a friend of her father who used to arrive in St. Louis each summer with different white women. The speaker thought of this man as hers because he was black, as she is. This memory triggers another, of laughing and playing with young boys who would grow up into black men "if they lived so long." She remembers the sexual excitement and mild sense of danger of dancing with black men as a young woman.

This leads into a part of the poem, written in the present tense—a portion that reads like a seduction. "Look at me pretty niggah," she says, and "bring it on baby." The language in this part of the poem is explicitly sensuous, clearly sexual, and full of images of "holding your heart" and other representations of love. When the speaker says, "you rode off & left/ your heart in the palm/ of my child hand," it seems that person she is addressing is still the friend of her father who used to visit in the summer.

In section 2, the poem begins a transformation. Grammatically, this section expands outward, from the first-person singular to the first-person plural. By the end, the narrator is talking about "our beauty" and "our heroes." Similarly, the personal tone of the first section becomes political when she identifies the man who used to arrive each summer as "of course george jackson," referring to the black militant and writer who died in prison. The line *"soledad, soledad"* is at once a reference to the Soledad Prison, where George Jackson served time; to his book, *Soledad Brother* (1971), written in prison; and to the literal translation of this Spanish word, "solitude." Ntozake Shange pictures Jackson fighting for air in prison and associates him with two other slain black activists, Malcolm X and Martin Luther King, Jr. This triggers a chain of associations of black men whom she considers beautiful for their courage, including Bob Marley, the legendary reggae performer, and Jackie Wilson, the popular soul singer of the 1960's and 1970's who died in the 1980's. The closing line of this section, *"soledad mi amor soledad,"* seems to be a meditation not only about George Jackson and his imprisonment but also about the solitude of assassination, or simply neglect, visited upon many of the strongest black men of her youth.

Section 3 is a brief description of lovers making love under palm trees. Against the mournful, almost elegiac background of the second section, this description of petticoats and panties being pulled down, of the music of muscles, of shoulders and bodies in motion, and of jaguars prowling "when their/ eyes meet" is presented as a life-affirming image. Under these trees, young black women make love with young black men whose lives are threatened and often cut short by the violence of a racist society.

Forms and Devices

Ntozake Shange is perhaps best known as a playwright who infuses her plays with poetry. It should come as no surprise, then, that her poetry has its own theatricality; that is, it is poetry which is best read aloud.

In "irrepressibly bronze, beautiful & mine," she does not use standard punctuation. The only punctuation she allows herself is a slash mark (/), which she uses to indicate a slight pause but not specifically to replace other forms of punctuation. These slash marks can be seen as analogous to the marks of a conductor's sheet that indicate the pace of the music. The effect is that some of Shange's lines of poetry seem to contain several lines within them.

The shift in person the poem undergoes, from first-person singular in section 1 to first-person plural in section 2 to third person in section 3, indicates a similar shift in the perspective of the poem. In the first section, Shange speaks from the point of view of a woman recalling her own sexual awakening and excitement with black men. Thus, the tone is personal. In section 2, she remembers the struggles and deaths that black men have faced in her lifetime. The identification of the man about whom she was specifically speaking in section 1 as George Jackson should not be taken too literally. Rather, she is painting a collective picture of the black man: The black man is Jackson, Malcolm X, Martin Luther King, Jr., Jackie Wilson, and many others. Thus, she speaks in a plural voice. The third section tries to put the erotic excitement of young black men and women in perspective. Following the descriptions of men who have had to struggle for life, this section looks approvingly on young men and women taking pleasure in life. The metaphors she uses in this section— of tongues wrapping around each other, of "dew like honey" slipping from lips, and of jaguars prowling when eyes meet— makes it clear not only that making love is a life-affirming act but also that it is an act that can productively express the ferocity of the lives of black youths.

Themes and Meanings

The reader of "irrepressibly bronze, beautiful & mine" should recall that the late 1980's, when the poem was written, was a period of raging political and literary debate about the depiction of black men in novels by black women—and in the media at large—as brutal rapists and victimizers. This debate frequently centered on Alice Walker's novel (and the film adaptation of) *The Color Purple* (1982). Shange often found herself in the middle of the debate because of her widely popular play, *for colored girls who have considered suicide/ when the rainbow is enuf* (1976), which depicted black men as potential rapists and killers of black women. Against this backdrop, "irrepressibly bronze, beautiful & mine" can be seen for what it is— a political love poem to black men.

The basic message of the poem is that the speaker has for all of her life felt intimately connected to black men. The black man she is addressing toward the end of section 1 is literally the friend of her father, who used to appear every summer, but is also an image of black men she has known throughout her life. All of her life, she says to him, she has been holding his heart in her hand. This is a turn on the cliché of holding "*my* heart in my hand" and implies not that she has always wanted to give herself to him but that she has always felt that she had a part of *him* she wanted to give to him. It also implies that the man in question, who is a stand-in for black men in general, has a lot of heart, so much that he could leave some with her.

The list of black male heroes in section 2 is a tribute to the hearts of these men and an appreciation of the way they have defined the black spirit of which she feels a part. It is to the struggle and pain of defining this spirit that she pays tribute.

The third section of this poem should also be read historically. A widely expressed belief of the time held that the lack of moral values within the black community was responsible for the ongoing economic subjugation of blacks and that sexuality in young people was best repressed. Opposed to this, Shange stresses the sense of vitality, excitement, and completion in sexuality.

The title of this poem provides a good clue to understanding the poem itself. That the person is "irrepressible" implies a vitality of spirit that cannot be contained. The element of sensuality implicit in describing him as "bronze, beautiful & mine" conveys not only the deep intimacy the speaker feels for her subject but also contains in language the sensuousness of spirit celebrated and infused by the poem.

Thomas J. Cassidy

ISRAFEL

Author: Edgar Allan Poe (1809-1849)
Type of poem: Lyric
First published: 1831, in *Poems*; revised in *The Raven and Other Poems*, 1845

The Poem

"Israfel" is a lyrical poem of eight uneven stanzas, each stanza ranging from five to eight lines in length. The title is the name of an angel mentioned in the Koran, the sacred book of the Muslims. Edgar Allan Poe appended a note to this poem to make sure that his readers understood Israfel's significance; the note read: "And the angel Israfel, whose heartstrings are a lute, and who has the sweetest voice of all God's creatures— KORAN." Israfel's importance as a singer or artist is central to the poem, and Poe's consideration here of creativity—singing and music-making—reflects a typical concern of other Romantic poets such as George Gordon, Lord Byron, Percy Bysshe Shelley, and John Keats. The poem is written in the first person from the point of view of someone—perhaps Poe himself—who is also a singer or creator of some sort, but readers do not discover this important information until the last stanza of the poem. The poem begins by stating that an angel lives in heaven and that his name is Israfel. Israfel, who is so creative that his very heart is a musical instrument, is such a wonderful singer that, according to legend, the stars even stop their own "hymns" to listen to him. The moon is, moreover, in love with him, while the lightning and constellations such as the "Pleiads" listen as well.

In the third stanza, Poe begins to explain what makes Israfel's music so lovely that even the heavens take notice: His singing is exquisite and passionate because of the instrument he plays—his own heart ("The trembling living wire"). In this stanza, Poe refers to this instrument as a "lyre" (a stringed instrument like a harp), but in the first stanza he calls it a "lute" (a stringed instrument more like a guitar or mandolin). In the fourth stanza, Poe explains that where Israfel lives ("the skies that angel trod") is extraordinary ("deep thoughts are a duty") and beautiful (the Houri, beautiful women who wait in heaven for the devout Muslim, are as lovely as stars here).

For these reasons (because his surroundings are so lovely and because he plays his music from his heart), Israfel is not wrong to despise inferior art ("An unimpassioned song"); he deserves the reward of being called "Best bard" (the greatest singer), and he deserves to wear the honorary crown of the most skillful—the laurels. Here the poem shifts slightly in that Poe addresses Israfel directly; he writes, "thou art not wrong." In the last two stanzas, the tone of the poem changes dramatically, and we see the speaker emerging more forcefully and somewhat bitterly. Poe tells Israfel that all that is in Heaven is there for Israfel while people on earth live with both pain and pleasure: in "a world of sweets and sours,/ Our flowers are merely—flowers." The poem concludes with the somewhat angry observation that if the speaker of the poem could live in heaven and Israfel on earth, Israfel might not be such a wonderful singer, and he—the speaker or Poe—might be much better.

Forms and Devices

At the center of "Israfel" is the figure of the angel, Israfel. Since Israfel sings and plays music, since he is referred to as a "bard," and since — by the end of the poem — he is compared to the speaker of the poem who is himself a poet, one can safely assume that Israfel serves as a representative for the artist or the creative spirit. As such, one might refer to Israfel as a metaphor for the artist, as a stand-in which allows Poe to develop his ideas about art, writing, and creativity. Involved in this metaphorical framework are other important aspects of the poem. First, Israfel's instrument — or his means to create — is represented variously by a lute, a lyre, and his human heart. The fruits of Israfel's creativity are rendered as singing and as music so that these two creative efforts become emblematic for all creative efforts. Finally, those who listen to Israfel's music are the heavens; his audience includes the highest and most unreachable elements in the physical world — stars, lightning, the moon, constellations.

Although the rhymes in "Israfel" are unpredictable, conforming to no particular formal pattern, each stanza is intricately and skillfully set to rhyme. Most stanzas have only two distinct end rhymes (the first stanza rhymes "dwell," "well," "Israfel," "tell," and "spell" as the first rhyme and "lute" and "mute" as the second), but occasionally a stanza has three different rhymes (the second stanza rhymes "above" and "love," "noon" and "moon," and "levin," "even," "seven," and "heaven"). Sometimes Poe uses near rhymes, words which do not quite repeat the same sounds (in the last stanza, "I" and "melody"); and sometimes he uses visual rhymes, words which look alike but sound different (in the second stanza, "even" and "seven").

Like the rhymes in "Israfel," the meters and the stanza structures are uneven and refuse to conform to a particular pattern. Occasionally, the poem establishes a regular rhythm only to interrupt the pattern it sets up. In the first stanza, for example, the opening four lines have three beats each, while the next two lines carry on and increase the momentum with four beats per line. Suddenly, however, the stanza ends with an abrupt line of only two beats. Sometimes readers feel a little disrupted and surprised by such techniques.

Several sets of polarities or oppositions are set up in "Israfel," and these become central to Poe's focus in the poem. There is, first, the distinction between heaven and Earth: Israfel, an angel, lives in heaven, and the speaker of the poem is an inhabitant of Earth, Israfel's world is so far superior to the speaker's that what is "shadow" for Israfel becomes "sunshine" in the earthly realm. Israfel is, moreover, a "spirit" while the speaker, again, is flesh and blood. There is also the opposition between singing and silence, since those who are most moved by the artistry of Israfel are moved to listen and to remain "mute." Finally, there is the beauty of the heavens, the "deep thoughts," the lovely Houris, and the sense of love as mature and fully developed ("Where Love's a grown-up god"). This excellence is set against the real world of "sweets and sours" where even beautiful things are limited: "Our flowers are merely — flowers."

Themes and Meanings

During the Romantic period in both British and American literature the attention of many writers—especially poets—turned to the issue of creativity itself. By the end of the eighteenth century an emphasis on individualism prevailed, and creativity was seen as an expression of the imaginative spirit of an intensely feeling and expressive soul. In "Israfel," Poe displays many of these attitudes about creativity, creative genius, and art. In his very concern with what makes a superior artist, he finds himself in harmony with other poets and writers of the Romantic age.

Israfel represents the ideal Romantic artist for many reasons, the first of which is that his very heart is his instrument. He plays and sings, in other words, "from the heart," from his passions and his emotions. The Romantic writer trusted emotions; he had turned from the eighteenth century's emphasis on the mind, on logic and reason, to a veneration of feeling, sensitivity, and even sensation. Thus, not only does Israfel play with passion, but he also sings "wildly" with "fire." He is not held back by decorum or inhibition; he sings what he feels.

Like the consummate artist that he represents, Israfel commands respect from the rest of the universe; somehow, what he does when he sings causes all of creation to take notice. Even the inhabitants of the heavens take notice, for Israfel's art is so perfectly an expression of his singing heart that all acknowledge his gift. Finally, Israfel's art is enhanced by his closeness to perfection; he lives, after all, in heaven. He is an angel. The Platonic notion that the world is an inferior representation of some ultimate, perfect ideal informed the thought of many Romantic writers, and Poe reveals himself to be no exception. Heaven and perfection belong to Israfel, so he can sing beautifully.

What of the earthbound artist, however—what of the writer who is not an angel and who does not own heaven and all of heaven's glories? This is the question that the poem seems to raise, for the poem is spoken by just such an artist. The speaker of the poem—probably Poe—reminds Israfel that writing poetry on earth is more difficult than writing poetry in heaven, and he asserts that Israfel would himself not be such a great artist were he "mortal." Even more significantly, the speaker boasts that if he were in Israfel's place, he might sing "a bolder note," a more beautiful song.

Since the speaker, who also is the creator of the poem, is only mortal, his work—this very poem—must be flawed. It will not be the perfect song that Israfel sings. In fact, this might even explain some of the oddities of this poem. Perhaps Poe's use of unmatched stanzas, his irregular patterns of meter and rhyme, and his use of two different words for Israfel's musical instrument ("lute" and "lyre") are simply his evidence of imperfection. Perhaps he indicates, with these reminders of his mortality, that he is still far from the ideal that an artist should seek. His poem is merely—a poem.

Kathleen Margaret Lant

IT WEEPS IN MY HEART

Author: Paul Verlaine (1844-1896)
Type of poem: Lyric
First published: 1874, in *Romances sans paroles*; collected in *Romances Without Words*, 1921

The Poem

"It weeps in my heart" is actually the first line of an untitled work in the group of poems called "Ariettes oubliées" ("Forgotten Melodies"). This sixteen-line poem, composed of hexasyllabic quatrains in the original French, contains a very musical rhyme scheme known as *rimes croisées*, or what might be noted as the following pattern: *abaa, cdcc, eaee, fdff*. The epigraph, "It rains gently on the town," attributed to Arthur Rimbaud, Paul Verlaine's companion and literary confrere, is not found among Rimbaud's known body of work, and the tribute's origin, therefore, remains a mystery. Many critics have made suppositions as to its source, but nothing has been verified positively.

Many of Verlaine's poems have musical titles, as his artistic credo (from his poem "Art poétique") was "De la musique avant toute chose" ("Music first and foremost"), and his emphasis on the musicality of the poem is evident throughout his career. The title of this collection, "Romances," connotes sentimentality, and the echoes of such sounds as "heart" and "rain" (in French, *coeur* and *pluie*) are reminiscent of the simple medieval ballads and troubadour songs.

The poem is written in the first person and is a lyric poem in the classical tradition that expresses the intensely personal feelings of the narrator. The first quatrain sets the mood, explaining that the poet's weeping heart is mirrored by the exterior world as it rains on the town. He asks, "What languorous hurt/ thus pierces my heart?" He cannot locate the source of his suffering.

The second stanza demonstrates how the falling rain provides music: "a sweet sound," "the song of the rain," but his heart remains "dulled with pain." Both sentences that compose the quatrain are exclamatory, demonstrating the relief that the poet hopes the rain will bring to his aching heart. He cries out to the rain that he hears, grateful that its music offers him diversion.

The third quatrain reveals the poet's agony: Although he is longing to find the cause for his suffering, the heart will not betray itself to him. He seeks a rational answer to an emotional problem that is not forthcoming. This causes greater agitation.

The fourth quatrain confirms the poet's anxiety that the worst pain "is not to know why." He suffers neither from "love" nor "disdain." The exterior world may possess music, but his "heart has such pain." The mood at the end of the poem is consistent with the state of being that was expressed at the beginning. There is no relief provided by outside forces nor is the poet's own understanding of his situation ameliorated. The ache is overpowering and lingers. His song is a lonely, single melody, a lament that bemoans unhappy solitude.

Forms and Devices

In its original French, the poem's rhyme scheme ends in mostly soft feminine vowel sounds. The tonality is a light one; the poet tries to emulate the sound of softly falling rain. Such consonants as *pl* and *t* that echo throughout the original French poem are also reminiscent of the "song" of the rain that drops onto the roofs and the ground—*tois* and *terre*.

Verlaine uses metonymy: The heart is given the function of representing the whole human being filled with pain. Although the exterior rain falls gently, the weeping in his heart is certainly not as pleasant; therefore, his use of the simile comparing the tears of the heart with the rain on the town really serves to show a dissimilarity rather than an equation. The alliterative devices of the "sweet sound" contrast with his pervasive unhappiness.

The poem's only resolution is the declarative statement that "It's far the worst pain/ not to know why." The poet expresses no newfound knowledge during the poem. He continually questions: What is the cause of my pain? There is no answer. The questions merely echo the pain and his ponderings provide no relief. This device of using rhetorical questions shows the poet's attempt at blending rationality with emotion. Because there is no transformation, it is clear that the poet is stating that logical answers can not be applied to unnameable feelings. His "grief's without reason."

In his quest to examine the possible reasons behind his state of sadness, the poet tries to distance himself from the emotions and expresses this through his poetic imagery. "It weeps" is as impersonal as "it rains," displaying an analytic posturing on the part of the narrator. The oxymoron "disheartened heart" and the use of "love or disdain" as a paradox to explain the extremes of sensation by the heart further demonstrate a scientific stance by the poet, who is trying to study the source of his pain. As his experiment is failing, so too his metaphors reveal an evaporation through words such as *pénètre* (the translated word "pierce" is deceptive—*pénètre* means to penetrate, not to prick); a heart *qui s'ennuie* (the translated world "dulled" is also inappropriate, because *s'ennuie* means to lapse into boredom, which clearly demonstrates the passivity of this person); and, again, the *coeur qui s'écoeure* (the heart that simply languishes).

The poem's sensorial imagery reveals how sight ("weeps in my heart/ as it rains on the town"), touch ("pierces my heart"), hearing ("song of the rain"), taste, and smell paralyze the poet from actively and methodically tempering these strong perceptions that conquer his mind and taunt him by flaunting their power.

Themes and Meanings

An aria is an elaborate melody for a single voice with accompaniment. Verlaine placed this poem in a group of poems called "little arias" that lie within the framework of the larger group called "ballads." The importance of music in "It weeps in my heart" is unquestionable. The solo is sung by the narrator whose melody—one of sadness—is in disharmony with the sweet sounds of life around him. The epigraph attributed to Rimbaud that appears as the introduction to the poem, "It rains gently on the town," portrays a simple and almost peacefully somnambulant scene that, the reader discovers, is a counterpoint or descant to the woeful tune that measures discord within the man. As there is no satisfactory resolution for the narrator because the heart will not betray the cause of its melancholy, so, too, the two melodies never assonate. Although the ballad and the aria are both traditional vehicles to express unrequited love, the homophonic structure of the ballad and the labeling of the poem a "little aria" are ironic, as the poet seeks to empty generic norms with this theme of pervasive depression attributable to unknown causes: There is no grand passion *d'amour* here, simply a lack of comprehension. This particular "arietta" is a psychological portrait and not at all a sentimental one, despite the fact that structurally the poem is composed like a ballad.

One reason that Verlaine's poetry does not translate well is his emphasis on musicality. It is possible to translate the metaphors, the imagery, and themes, but his technical ability to create music of the French language is out of reach to English-language readers. The French language has masculine and feminine rhymes and other sounds that can not be duplicated. To read Verlaine in French is to understand what made him not only a writer but a symphonic composer as well. Generations of readers can recite "Il pleure dans mon coeur/ Comme il pleut sur la ville" almost as if it were a song and not a poem.

"It weeps in my heart" reveals a state of ennui that Verlaine chose to treat in many of his poems. This portrayal of the passive intellectual is a unifying thread among the French symbolist poets of his day. Here, Verlaine does not attempt to confuse the senses as was typical of the symbolist craft, but rather he presents a perplexed human being who aches for clarity. It is the spirit of the narrator more than anything else that allows this poem to be characterized as symbolist. Verlaine, here, is certainly a less radical alchemist than his friend Rimbaud, whose uncharacteristically simple and charming quote serves as the inspiration for the poem.

The explosive relationship between Verlaine and Rimbaud (at one point, Verlaine shot Rimbaud and was imprisoned in Belgium) and its effect on Verlaine's sanity is not, despite some critics' claims, depicted in content or form in this poem, regardless of the selected epigraph. "It weeps in my heart" reveals impeccable and methodical craftsmanship by a writer who is in command and in control.

Susan Nagel

THE JEWELS

Author: Charles Baudelaire (1821-1867)
Type of poem: Narrative
First published: 1857, as "Les Bijoux," in *Les Fleurs du mal*; collected in
  Baudelaire: Selected Verse, 1961

The Poem

In "The Jewels," a poem composed of eight quatrains in regular Alexandrine lines, Charles Baudelaire records a portrait of his mulatto mistress dressed only in her jewelry. While the description will not seem excessively graphic to the modern reader, this poem was one of the ones responsible for the censure and withdrawal from sale of the first edition of *Les Fleurs du mal* (1857; *Flowers of Evil*, 1909).

The principal development of the poem follows a seduction scene in which the woman seduces, and thus psychologically dominates, the poet. The stage is set during the first two quatrains while the woman remains relatively passive. The poet is attracted to her, but his attention remains focused on her jewels. The only indication that the woman already controls the situation comes in the first line, where she is said to wear the jewels because she knows the poet's heart. Yet rather than conveying a form of manipulation, this phrase may also be read as her desire to please him.

The description of the jewels contains elements that will fascinate the poet through a simultaneous appeal to his various senses. By the third quatrain, this fascination begins to have its effect. The poet appears below the woman, in a position suggesting adoration, while she smiles at him from the "height of the sofa." Still, she remains passive, merely accepting his love that "rises up" to her.

In the fourth quatrain, the woman becomes active. Her eyes are still those of a "subdued tiger," but they contain all the implicit danger of the beast. As she moves in an increasingly sensual manner, the poet notes her "metamorphoses." These movements continue through the ensuing quatrains until the poet must admit that she can "trouble the repose" of his soul.

Although the poet must see the danger the woman presents when he describes her breasts as more seductive than "the Angels of evil," he does not heed the warning implicit in this insight. His admiration continues in the seventh quatrain, where he is still fascinated by the contradictory elements, combining feminine and masculine allusions, that make up her beauty.

Thus the final image of the lamp "resigned to its death" figures both the passage of time and the final disposition of the poet. The ebbing lamplight signals an end to the love scene, but a fire in the hearth, also dying to embers, continues to flare up periodically with a "flaming sigh." The sigh may echo the poet's satisfaction or his resignation. If it contains elements of the latter, he has accepted the troubles to his soul as the price of pleasure. Danger and beauty remain inextricably linked in the last line, where the firelight "inundated with blood [the woman's] amber-colored skin." The blood, a clearly symbolic application of the red color imparted by the dying fire, suggests the threat of violence, but the poet's attention remains fixed on the beauty of the mingling colors.

Forms and Devices

The poet's fascination with the woman's "sonorous jewels" reflects the importance Baudelaire accorded to synesthesia as a source of poetic inspiration. In his sonnet "Correspondences," he defined this fusion of appeals to various senses, specifically the harmony of perfumes, colors, and sounds, as "having the expansion of infinite things." Thus objects capable of producing synesthesia offered a special opportunity to the poet to grasp those transcendent ideas that should be expressed in poetry.

The poet desires the woman in "The Jewels" both for her own beauty and for her potential role in his inspiration. He reminds the reader in language reminiscent of "Correspondences" that he loves "things where sound is mixed with light." The light caught by the "radiant world" of the gems is joined by sound as the woman moves. The jewels striking against one another "throw off while dancing a lively, mocking sound." Characterizing the jewelry as a "world" and its sound as "lively" emphasizes its importance. It seems to be alive, but it depends on the movements of the woman to animate it.

With the adjective "mocking," however, Baudelaire introduces an element of uncertainty. Why would the sound of the jewels mock the poet? If the poet desires inspiration from them, would these living jewels somehow foresee that his creative desire would be frustrated? The mockery Baudelaire perceives in the jewels reflects his failure to find his increasingly elusive poetic vision.

Although Jeanne Duval had come to Paris from the Caribbean, a source of her appeal to Baudelaire could have been that she reminded him of a trip he had taken around Africa to the islands of Mauritius and Reunion in 1841-1842. Baudelaire first met his mistress some three months after his return to France. As he suffered from the cold of cloudy, northern Paris, Baudelaire increasingly saw the sunny, tropical climate he had known only briefly as an emblem of the vision that he sought.

A consistent theme of exoticism in *Flowers of Evil* links Baudelaire's desire to distant lands. Thus the jewels give the woman "the triumphant air that the slaves of the Moors have on their happy days." Not only does this phrase draw on the concept of exotic locales, but it also contains very conflicting suggestions concerning the role of the woman. She is cast as a slave but at the same time is triumphant. The ambiguity can be resolved if one realizes that by submitting to the poet's desires, the woman is actually controlling him.

Exoticism continues in the use of animal imagery to describe the woman. She is, in a sense, the poet's pet. Yet the animals that represent her, a tiger and a swan, are far from domesticated: the one dangerous and the other silent and enigmatic. The animals' strength is echoed in the allusion to Antiope, sister of the queen of the Amazons in Greek legend, who further shares the element of exoticism as part of a temporally remote and foreign culture. The images combine to convey the woman's strength and her potential fascination to the poet.

Themes and Meanings

Baudelaire's hero in *Flowers of Evil* strives for a poetic vision that parallels Christian salvation. Just as the Fall resulted from the temptation of Eve, woman becomes the agent of the poet's separation from his vision of the ideal. Immediately before "The Jewels" in the first edition of *Flowers of Evil*—the only edition where it was to appear in Baudelaire's lifetime—a series of three sonnets, "Beauty," "The Ideal," and "The Giantess," defines an ideal of beauty presented in female form. Following "The Jewels," "Exotic Perfume" continues the association of synesthesia with the woman saying that her perfume causes the poet to "see happy shores spread out" before him.

The vision the woman offers, however, is one of a false paradise. Only ten poems later in the 1857 edition, the poet both literally and figuratively awakens. In "One night when I was with a frightful Jewess . . . ," Baudelaire sees the act of love linked with death and dreams of "the sad beauty of which my desire is depriving itself." The vision of beauty, represented in the earlier sonnets by a statue or a giantess, cannot be translated into a living woman.

Because various elements of female beauty cause Baudelaire to believe, for a time, that he can regain transcendent vision through love, he is drawn into distractions that cause him to waste his life in this false pursuit. The central attraction of woman in this regard is her eyes—eyes that often reflect the light of heaven and thus become confused with it. Consequently, in "The Jewels," it is especially significant that the woman dominates the poet through her hypnotic eyes.

In the same way, the choice of the jewels themselves as the focal point of this poem underlines the deceptive elements that, from the first, have impeded the poet's vision. The poet's only direct access to celestial light occurs at the beginning of *Flowers of Evil*, when "Benediction" offers him a glimpse of his "mystic crown." Poetry, however, which is incapable of portraying this pure light, must fall back on images of the crown and the jewels that compose it, translating the celestial into earthly images.

The light reflected by the gems in "The Jewels" thus recalls to the poet images, though false ones, of his initial vision. Yet the gems in this poem are not confined to the ones worn by the woman. As the poet compares her charms to evil angels, he says they remove his soul from its solitary "crystal rock." The contrast between the purity of this single crystal and the multiplicity of the woman's jewels parallels the concentration of transcendent experience compared with the fragmentation echoed in the numerous and contrasting images used to describe the woman.

Dorothy M. Betz

THE JEWISH CEMETERY AT NEWPORT

Author: Henry Wadsworth Longfellow (1807-1882)
Type of poem: Meditation
First published: 1854; collected in *The Courtship of Miles Standish and Other Poems*, 1858

The Poem

"The Jewish Cemetery at Newport" is a lyric meditation in fifteen rhymed quatrains. The title indicates the location where Henry Wadsworth Longfellow focuses his reverie on time, history, and death. As in the tradition of English meditative poetry of the eighteenth century, the poem at once paints a visual portrait of the cemetery yet also uses the place as a way to explore the poet's own reflections.

The poem is set in Newport, Rhode Island, at the oldest Jewish burial ground in America, one long since abandoned. It is written from the perspective of a solitary observer basically identical with the poet himself. In the first two stanzas, the poet regards the cemetery, muses over its desertion, and thinks not only of the desolate present but also of its hallowed past.

In the fourth stanza, reading the names chiseled on the gravestones, the poet is caught by the incongruity between the biblical first names of the deceased and their Spanish and Portuguese surnames. This leads him to imagine the people behind the names, initiating the central movement in the poem, from the fourth to the eleventh stanzas. In this part of the poem, the poet conjures up a vivid spectacle as he contemplates the story of those now dead. He envisions the people worshiping in the synagogue, chanting Psalms, and mourning for their dead. He asked what prompted the Jews to emigrate, what "burst of Christian hate" led them to undertake the perilous voyage to America. The poet is eloquently aware of the oppression and suffering they had undergone in their lives, "The life of anguish and the death of fire," as well as the pathos of their deaths. With a historical sensitivity rare for his time, he mentions the many persecutions Jews had suffered at the hands of Christians who had accused the Jews of killing Christ.

In the final four stanzas, the poet takes a more detached point of view. Shifting from his imaginative vision of the experiences of those buried in the cemetery, he reflects on the implications of their fate. The poet feels pity for them, but he also admires their ability to persist through such obstacles. The persistence of their faith through the centuries moves him deeply. Because of their persecution, however, the Jews have had to bury themselves in their past. They read the "mystic volume" of the world "backward, like a Hebrew book." Instead of investing their hopes in the American promise offered to others who have made a similar journey, the Jews focus on the study of their religion and their laws. The poet sees this immersion on the past as grim and deathlike, yet he respects the learning and commitment this past inspired and is even astonished at its determination to endure in a new and strange land. Death, though, overtakes even the most determined of human traditions. The poem ends with the realization that, despite the sympathy and regret of the poet, "the dead nations never rise again."

Forms and Devices

Longfellow adapts his stanzaic form from poems in the English tradition, such as Thomas Gray's "Elegy Written in a Country Churchyard." These poems, like "The Jewish Cemetery at Newport," are concerned with the presence of death in the midst of a human landscape. The first and third lines of each four-line stanza rhyme, as do the second and fourth. This variety of stanza gives the impression of ceremony and dignity. The rhyming words are usually of one or two syllables and often contain very sharply defined vowels and consonants. This effect contributes to the sense of enclosure and reflective weight to be found in the poem. Longfellow departs from the tradition by his own highly individual stress and meter, which do not always follow the largely iambic patterns expected in English prosody since the Renaissance, and the poem's forms convey a sense of familiarity and ease. This ease assists in transmitting the very specific subject matter of the poem to an achieved poetic level.

The poem is filled with many strong visual images. These images do not point as much to the physical reality of the cemetery before the poet's eyes, but rather to the scenes in the life that the poet imagines for the dead who are buried there. Much of the imagery is, either implicitly or explicitly, biblical. Longfellow, who was not Jewish himself, drew upon the knowledge of the Old Testament he possessed by virtue of his Christian background to supply the detail for his picture of the Jews buried in Newport. Longfellow assumes that the reader is educated and shares this knowledge. By comparing the lives of the Newport Jews to those of their biblical forebears, Longfellow lends the poem an aura of emotion and reverence. There is a sense that the cycle of life and death related in the poem has occurred not once but many times since biblical days. Longfellow's skillful choice of words (for example, when he rhymes "Synagogue" with "Decalogue," the Latin phrase for the Ten Commandments) combine specifically Jewish and biblical images with more universal poetic ones. An instance of this practice occurs when he speaks of the Jews living in "Ghetto and Judenstrass, in mirk and mire."

When specifically biblical terms are not being employed, Longfellow uses a diction that aspires to rhetorical heights. Longfellow's words express feeling, yet also decorum and gravity. By using words that even at the time seemed old-fashioned, such as "climes" and "spake," the poem exudes a sense of respect for the importance and venerability of its subject, and also of the tragic, somber level of its theme.

Although the poem is basically a monologue by the poet-observer, at times the poet seems to be speaking not only to himself, but also to a more general reader. This is especially true when exclamation points are used in the first and final stanzas. The punctuation in both cases seeks to arouse the reader into responding intellectually and emotionally to the subject.

Themes and Meanings

"The Jewish Cemetery at Newport" is about death and about the past. These are themes to which Longfellow was unusually sensitive among poets of his age. Although Longfellow's reputation has never recovered from the drastic fall it took during the era of modernism, it should be recognized that the concern about history and memory this poem shows is rare during a period in which literature was often more concerned with an examination of the American present. Longfellow looks into the neglected odds and ends of history and finds meanings there that others overlook.

The poem contains well-researched, accurate information. It is true, for example, that the first Jews in America were Sephardim from Southern Europe. Longfellow, though, does not passively rely on this knowledge, but incorporates it into his own imaginative meditation. The story that the poet sees and finds in the cemetery in the end seems far more noteworthy than more contemporary ones that are more immediately attractive. The sensitivity of the poet is all the more impressive in that his positive regard for the Jews is notable at a time when anti-Semitism was unfortunately still not totally unrespectable.

The poem is not sentimental about the Jews of Newport. It does not try to pretend that their lives were ideal, nor does the poet become overly optimistic about what he can learn from them. There is no sense of breakthrough to a greater or inner truth at the end of the poem. His experience of the cemetery does not teach the poet about the nature of life. What he contemplates enriches his imagination, yet also warns it of the reality of suffering and of loss that has occurred in the past. Longfellow is vitally interested in the past, but he does not think this interest can save or redeem the present.

Although the poem is immersed in the details, real and imagined, of the Jewish cemetery, it is not exclusively about the place where it is set. In the final stanza, in which the poet makes the more universal point that "The groaning earth in travail and in pain/ Brings forth its races, but does not restore." Though one may learn from history, one finds that it is not full of endless creativity, but instead, of loss and sorrow. The final reference to the "dead nations" does not mean the poet sees the extinction of the Jewish people. He is referring more broadly to the impossibility of bringing the past into the present. The poet's empathy with the people buried at Newport can only go so far. They and he in the end are separated by the most crucial boundary of all: that between life and death.

Nicholas Birns

JOURNEY OF THE MAGI

Author: T. S. Eliot (1888-1965)
Type of poem: Dramatic monologue
First published: 1927; collected in *Collected Poems, 1909-1935*, 1936

The Poem

From the time that he prepared "The Hollow Men" for publication in 1925 until he wrote "Journey of the Magi" in July, 1927, T. S. Eliot wrote virtually no poetry at all. His personal convictions underwent enormous upheaval during that two-year hiatus, culminating in his baptism into the Church of England on June 29, 1927. Shortly thereafter, the editor at Faber & Gwyer Publishers, for whom Eliot worked as an editor, asked Eliot to write a Christmas poem as one in a series of short, illustrated poems called the Ariel Poems. The result was "Journey of the Magi," published on August 25, 1927. It was, as Eliot said in an interview published in *The New York Times Book Review* (November 29, 1953), the poem that released the stream for all his future work. Thus the poem bears personal as well as artistic significance for Eliot.

"Journey of the Magi" is a first-person recollection of a Magus, one of the Persian Magi who came to visit the Christ child as recorded in the second chapter of Matthew. The poem is narrated, however, from the perspective of many years later, after the Magus has returned to his home country. He is an elderly man, reflecting on events that occurred many years prior.

The recollection is divided into three parts. The first stanza recalls the journey itself, the long and demanding ordeal of the caravan to Judea. The weather was very cold and sharp; the camels had sores and often balked; the camel drivers were unhappy at their deprivations and ran away. There was little shelter, and the people they met were unfriendly: "A hard time we had of it." The second stanza describes their arrival, at dawn, at the Judean valley, where they at last find a hospitable landscape with water and vegetation. In the stanza's last two lines, they arrive at Bethlehem, "not a moment too soon," and find the infant Christ.

The third stanza consists of a reflection on the meaning of the event. Here the Magus struggles with the significance of birth and death. He is aware of the prophecy that the Christ was born to die as an atonement, but he also reflects on his own approaching death.

It is helpful while reading the poem to remember that the Magi were king-priests of the royal tribe of Medes and that their primary tasks were to understand astronomical signs, to interpret dreams, and to understand prophecy. Their entire knowledge of the Christ derived from the Hebrew kingdom during its exile in Babylon beginning in 605 B.C., when Nebuchadnezzer conquered Judah. The most influential figure of that period was the Hebrew Daniel, who lived for sixty-six years in Persia and who prophesied the Messiah (Daniel 7:14).

Forms and Devices

This relatively simple story of the Magi is tightly packed with significance, particularly in Eliot's use of allusion and symbolism.

The poem bears echoes of authors who influenced Eliot's own spiritual journey, most notably Lancelot Andrewes. The poem opens with a quotation taken from Lancelot Andrewes' Nativity sermon, preached in 1622 to the Jacobean court. As he pointed out in his essay "Lancelot Andrewes" (*Selected Essays*, 1934), Eliot admired Andrewes' intellectual achievement, his ability to hold both intellectual idea and emotional sensibility in harmony, and his leadership in the church of seventeenth century England. Andrewes seemed to validate church membership for Eliot at a time when he was contemplating his own baptism into the church.

Furthermore, the staccato-like lines of the last section of the poem—the hesitation, repetition, and acceleration—were all techniques that Eliot admired in Andrewes' prose style. Eliot's lines in stanza 3, "but set down/ This set down/ This" also derive from patterns that Andrewes used in his Nativity sermons of 1616, 1622, and 1623.

"Journey of the Magi" creates more interest, however, by its complex pattern of biblical symbolism, which intensifies in stanza 2 as the Magi approach Bethlehem and the birth of the Christ. The symbolism seems to accelerate, as does the journey itself, toward its fulfillment.

The valley they enter is cut by a flowing stream, suggesting Jesus' claim to be the Living Water in John 4:10-14, and this living stream powers a mill that seems to beat away the darkness, further suggesting Jesus' claim in John 8:12 to be the Light of the World. With the dawning of this light, however, the Magi see first of all a symbol of death—"three trees on the low sky," or on the western horizon.

As they enter the valley, an old white horse gallops away. The reference here cannot be to the white horse of Revelation 19:11, as some have assumed, since that horse bears the Christ at his second coming. Rather, it refers to the white horse of Zechariah 6:5, whose task it was to announce the coming of the Messiah. That task now completed, the horse gallops away.

The Magi arrive at the first outpost of civilization and see, at a tavern, vine leaves over the lintel, suggesting the Old Testament Passover and Christ's fulfillment of it in his claim that he is the True Vine (John 15:1, 5). The next two lines were recorded earlier than the drafting of the poem in a notebook that Eliot kept, but they do fit the biblical pattern. The hands dicing for silver suggest the bartering for Christ (Matthew 26:14-16), and the feet kicking the empty wine-skins suggest Jesus' parable of the new wine in Matthew 9:17.

Led by such signs, the Magi arrive at the Christ child, finding the place and deeming it "satisfactory." The adjective satisfactory has troubled some readers, since it seems to understate the event, or to show some disappointment. That may be so. After all, the Magi were kingly priests seeking a king, and they found instead a rude stable. It may also be that Eliot employs the term "satisfactory" based on his study in philosophy, drawing upon the philosophical definition as a necessary and sufficient fulfillment of the signs given. As such, it is a statement of resolute conviction.

The Magus who tells the poem is, in any event, so powerfully taken by the event that years later it still disturbs him profoundly. The disturbance arises from the paradox of birth and death, the fact that this Messiah was also the one destined to die on one of the "three trees on the low sky." In fact, the crucifixion may already have occurred and come to the Magus' knowledge. Thus he puzzles over the paradox: The Christ was born to die, and believers are dying to an old way of life, to be born again. He does not fully understand the puzzle, but he takes considerable solace from it, claiming that he would now be glad of his own physical death.

Themes and Meanings

Two important themes of Eliot emerge, and they link the poem to both his earlier and his later work. Like so many of Eliot's patterns, they are themselves in tension: light and dark, water and aridity.

Eliot's earlier poems are full of hot sunlight blasting across arid landscapes. It is a destructive light, seeming to drive people inward toward a spiritual isolation and darkness. "Journey of the Magi" begins in such a darkness. In fact, the Magi, after their guides desert them and they meet hostilities along the way, prefer to travel in darkness. The pattern signifies a lack of spiritual direction, a mere wandering, but it is only by the traveling itself that one can hope to apprehend the light. Moreover, their seeking is reciprocated. The power of the stream drives a water mill that drives away the night. Light does come, and with it comes revelation. A way is given; an end to the seeking is arrived at.

Concomitantly with the dawning of light comes the presence of renewing water. Although the travel of the Magi is not through the parched landscape of *The Waste Land* (1922), it is through an equally sterile and arid landscape of the cold winter. With the dawning, however, they meet the stream of running water. The two patterns work synchronously: the light signifies illumination; the water, renewal. Light and water are both notably absent in Eliot's earlier poems; they appear in significant ways, however, in the poetry he wrote following "Journey of the Magi." The poem represented a crossroads in Eliot's poetic career, providing a direction for his work to follow.

John H. Timmerman

JUNK

Author: Richard Wilbur (1921-   )
Type of poem: Lyric
First published: 1961, in *Advice to a Prophet and Other Poems*

The Poem

"Junk" is a thirty-line poem written in Anglo-Saxon strong-stress meter. Each line is alliterated and broken into two halves, the second of which is indented, making each full line two-tiered. In a note to the poem, Richard Wilbur provides a rough translation of the epigraph, which is excerpted from an Anglo-Saxon fragment: "Truly, Wayland's handiwork—the sword Mimming which he made—will never fail any man who knows how to use it bravely." The epigraph gives an example of the alliterative, accentual meter of the original.

The poem begins with the narrator's detailed description of a neighbor's trash, viewed with a frown of disapproval. It is a critic's notice: "hell's handiwork," inferior wood, the grain not followed in its construction, broken tumblers, warped boards. The cool appraisal is interrupted by an exclamation in line 11: "Haul them off! Hide them!" The speaker can hardly stand to look at this deplorable "junk and gimcrack," or to think of those responsible for the shoddiness, "men who make them || for a little money." He likens these craftspeople to dishonest boxers and jockeys, but he thinks more favorably of the things themselves. Somehow they retain their honor, their composure, since they are not to blame for their sorry condition. They are prisoners whose consignment to the dump is a release, a purgatory in which they shed their junkiness and become like new again, unspoiled, ready to be used properly.

The elements will gradually transform these objects back to something close to their original states. The dump is a compost heap, a place where time and depth can pressurize the materials into diamondlike purity. The poem ends by referring to the mythic smiths Hephaestus and Wayland, immortal craftspeople as opposed to the immoral tricksters responsible for the junk. "Junk" describes a return to origins and proclaims a faith in something good and creative in the "making dark" of the human psyche.

Forms and Devices

Each line of Anglo-Saxon strong-stress meter contains four stresses, or accents, three of which are usually alliterated. The number of unstressed syllables is not counted. There is a strong caesura (pause or break) in the middle of each line. This caesura can be indicated by space between the two hemistiches (half-lines), but Wilbur chooses to drop the second half down so that each full line has a two-step arrangement. As Wilbur's first line shows, assonance (vowel repetition) can be used instead of consonant repetition: "axe angles," "ashcan." His second line, as well as the remaining twenty-eight, repeats consonants: "hell's handiwork," "hickory." Any three of a line's four stresses can alliterate. Sometimes all four do, as in the fifth line ("plastic playthings," "paper plates") and the nineteenth ("Talk," "torture," "tossed," "tailgate"). Lines 22 and 30 repeat the *w* sound in all four stresses. No adjacent lines alliterate on the same sound.

On the framework of the poem's thirty lines, Wilbur winds a series of ten sentences. A reader can chart the poem's tone and temper by noting how full and steady or how brief and fragmentary those sentences are. The poem begins with three long sentences, each three or four full lines long. Then two exclamations burst out in a single half-line and are followed by the longest sentence of the poem, which runs five and one-half lines. The next two sentences also include half-lines, but the poem ends with the steadiness of two sentences that are both four full lines in length. On a seismograph, the poem would begin calmly, register tremors in the middle, and end calmly after a gradual return to regularity. That structure supports the dramatic or emotional "plot" of the poem, which begins with detached observation, erupts with disgust, then comes to reassurance, to a recognition of good after all.

Rhetorically, the poem turns on the word "Yet" in line 17, slightly after the halfway point. After that, Wilbur emphasizes the passivity of the objects, which are unable to speak on their own behalf. They are tortured, "tossed," and will "waste in the weather ‖ toward what they were." They need an advocate, just as they need an honest craftsperson to bring out the lasting beauty latent within them, the "good grain" that can be rediscovered.

Wilbur, as advocate of these things, uses similes to describe their construction and quick disposal presenting a little morality play: the villainous makers, "like the bought boxer" or the "paid-off jockey," versus the things themselves, "like captives who would not/ Talk under torture." The poem describes dishonesty countered by honor, but it is not especially comforting that the heroes are inanimate, simply able to withstand or outlast punishment, better off buried than out in the open.

The alliteration tends to cluster words that are palpable, words that have heft and flavor, even when they refer to the deplorable junk: "shivered shaft," "shattered tumblers," a "cast-off cabinet/ Of wavily-warped ‖ unseasoned wood." In describing ugliness, the poem rises to beauty. It is an illustration of how this ordinary junk really does have the potential to be more than "jerrybuilt things." Wilbur himself shows how.

Themes and Meanings

"Junk" is a poem about renewal. On a literal level, it envisions the recycling of shoddy goods into good raw materials. By extension, however, it also foresees the regeneration of the human soul. It is a paean to biodegradability as well as a meditation on culture, both a lament for American planned obsolescence and a hymn to natural process and artistic dedication.

Although the poem begins with an ironic, detached view of a banal, commercialized hell, a scene of wastefulness on an ordinary sidewalk, it ends with a lofty, impassioned vision of a different underworld, the "making dark." Between the dull, discarded objects and the "depth of diamonds" there is an all-important illumination, the sun glorying "in the glitter of glass-chips." This sunlight will act literally and figuratively like a paint stripper, a purging light in which both object and spirit can be cleansed.

The image of an axe at the poem's opening represents a means of breaking into pieces, chopping down, and gathering materials, yet it too is simply junk headed for the dump. The axe also echoes the sword mentioned in the epigraph, a weapon for a hero, an instrument of deliverance. Knowing how to use a sword bravely is analogous to the poet's task of cutting through the appearances of things to the truth they embody—or could embody.

A number of words in the poem suggest Anglo-Saxon culture: "axe," "angles," "shaft," "shellheap," "dolmens," "barrows." As in most of Wilbur's poems, the vocabulary is rich, precise, and evocative. The Anglo-Saxon form reflects a rough culture; the alliterative line clangs noisily. It is physical, hefty, pushy, combative, primitive, almost berserk on words, almost incantatory and hypnotic. It brings Beowulf to suburbia. One of the marvels of the poem is the blending of this tough, hardy, oar-splashing, sword-wielding form with the characteristic elegance of Wilbur's argument, his steady pacing of sentences interrupted in line 11 by two exclamations that are the dramatic heart of the poem: "Haul them off! Hide them!"

One of the twentieth century's poetic dilemmas has been the difficulty of bringing the industrialized world into poems without losing the poetry. Poetry that ignores its actual surroundings is merely escapist, yet poetry that uncritically embraces cultural trash might not be poetry at all. Wilbur presents the junk of mass production directly as evidence of industrial degradation, but he also imagines a way out, a way that is not merely a nostalgic return to a buried vitality but also a vigorous recapturing of it.

The poem is about discarding and recovering—and the transformation that time, earth, and the decay of the compost heap can bring about. One of the things recovered here is the poetic form itself, the Anglo-Saxon meter, revived from obsolescence into something contemporary and American. Other twentieth century English and American poets have used the form, notably W. H. Auden in his long poem, *The Age of Anxiety* (1947). As if to demonstrate that writing in the form was more than a tour de force, Wilbur began his next collection, *Walking to Sleep: New Poems and Translations* (1969), with "The Lilacs," another poem in Anglo-Saxon meter.

"Junk" is a kind of *ars poetica*, suggesting a view of the art of poetry, which similarly begins anew in the "making dark." The Scots call a poet a *makar*, or "maker," and Robert Graves has likened the craft of poetry to smithcraft. The two deities allied in this restorative enterprise are the Germanic Wayland and the Greek Hephaestus, both smiths. The poem begins (in the epigraph, a recovered fragment) and ends with Wayland, who gives a sense of mythic transformation, which is the goal and reward of honest craftsmanship.

John Drury

THE K

Author: Charles Olson (1910-1970)
Type of poem: Lyric
First published: 1948, in *Y & X*

The Poem

"The K" is a lyric poem of twenty-six lines written in free verse. It interprets the letter *K* as a physical symbol of the fully realized human being who, in harmony with the moon's gravitational force, moves beyond conventional limitations conditioned by Western civilization and bridges the gap between the subjective and the objective and between the self and the natural realm of total reality.

The escape from the partitioning of reality characteristic of the modern Western mind to the attainment of a wholeness of being marked the principal aim of Charles Olson's art and thought. As he stated about ultimate human aspirations in *The Special View of History* (1956), "each one of us has the desire for the good (Love), we move to beauty (Aphrodite), we care for the Real (Truth or Idea), and we have to do something about it, whatever we do (we Will)." Poetry is meant to assist humanity in the process of such self-realization by reimagining the world, reorienting readers, and thereby dissolving the separation between the delimited self and the outer, total reality.

The poem begins with an energetic and upbeat interpretation of "The K" as, literally, an alphabetical symbol of the "tumescent I" that is the fully realized self in harmony with the external natural force of the moon acting on the tidal energies and potentialities of a human being. The upward linear stroke of the letter *K* represents the flowing out of the self in response to the moon's gravitational pull. The *K*'s downward linear stroke signifies the ebbing of the self under relaxation of the lunar force. The "tumescent I" is a vital, ever-expanding and contracting flowering of one's identity.

Such self-actualization is a revolutionary new goal for humanity ("The affairs of men remain a chief concern"). Reaching the goal brings harmony ("We have come full circle") and promises a millennial victory for the liberation of the self, provided one transcends boundaries, such as delimiting gender identity ("the fatal male small span"), and integrates opposites, like male and female, into a wholeness of being ("I shall not see the year 2000/ unless I stem straight from my father's mother"). If that integration is humanity's fate ("what the tarot pack proposed"), then the speaker will sing a fitting song integrating opposites: He sings "as she" does and weds silence and sound in "one unheard liturgy."

Self-actualization is not a prophecy for the future: It is happening now, as inner tidal energies inherently reach out to bond with the lunar-driven forces of the outer natural world. Such harmony of being ("Full circle") is attainable. Therefore, discard the delimiting culture of Western civilization, and end all rule-mongering derived from Roman, Greek, and Christian systems of thought. Put a stop to "romans" (meaning "Romans" as well as restrictive conventions signified by "roman types, letters, and print"). Rid the world of "hippocrats" (the conflation of "hypocrites" and of "Hippocratic" followers of stifling Western codes embodied in the medical oath). Finally, go beyond the stifling Western creed of "christians" imitating ("ecco" for "echo") their misery-loving Christ crucified ("Ecce homo!" for "Behold the man!")

Genuine self-realization requires rejecting the lessons of the civilized past and pursuing a "simpler" route to oneness with the natural world's lunar forces ("The salts and minerals of the earth return"). The speaker's final advice is for humanity to embrace the moon, its shadows and its night, as the way of reaching wholeness of being ("a bridge, a horse") and as the way of ending ("the gun, a grave") the old conventional life of the circumscribed self of society's making.

Forms and Devices

"The K" has an exuberantly affirmative mood that bears comparison with the hortatory tone of Walt Whitman's *Song of Myself* (1955) and Friedrich Nietzsche's *Also sprach Zarathustra* (1883-1885; *Thus Spake Zarathustra*, 1896).

Olson's poetry was directly influenced by the poetic techniques of Ezra Pound. Pound had helped spearhead the modernist revolution in early twentieth century poetry of the Western world, and Olson was perhaps the most prominent, if critical, follower of the methods practiced in Ezra Pound's *Cantos* (1917-1970). Both men shared an abhorrence of vague abstractions (Olson considered them the major obstacle preventing the attainment of a totality of being).

Both poets strove for the exact word (*le mot juste*) and the precise image and discarded discursive poetic statement. Both favored intense compression and ellipsis—the deletion of all unnecessary words—to achieve a complex suggestiveness of meaning with an absolute economy of language (for example, "Assume I shall not" or "Our attention is simpler"). Both had a flair for neologism and created new words out of familiar ones. Olson invents "hippocrats" by conflating "hypocrites" and adherents to "Hippocratic" oaths, and he invents "ecco" by conflating the verb "to echo" in English with the Latin adverb "ecce" as in the phrase "ecce homo!" or "behold the crucified Christ!" in the Gospel passage.

Both Pound and Olson indulged heavily in allusions to literary and historical figures and events to lend a mythic richness and universality of meaning to their poems (for example, Olson's "romans, hippocrats and christians" and "the cross/ ecco men and dull copernican sun").

Olson imitated Pound's penchant for the literal and pictorial character of words that reached its zenith with the use of ideograms (word signs capturing a physical actuality, in place of detested abstractions). Hence, Olson's poem focuses on the letter *K* to signify the gravitational ebb and flow of the fulfilled human spirit (the "tumescent I") in harmony with the lunar force of nature. Word signs of moving toward integration ("a bridge, a horse") and of ending old habits ("the gun, a grave") conclude the poem.

The major symbol of the poem is the moon. With its gravitational effect on tides, it is used to express the harmony between the self and the totality of the natural world of being and becoming.

Themes and Meanings

"The K" is about remaking oneself into a "tumescent I" by moving into a wider world of being and becoming, beyond the conventional boundaries of Western civilization and in harmony with nature's lunar force.

Olson's influential essay "Projective Verse" (1950) rejected the partitioning of reality separating the human from the natural world. Poetry is to assist readers in breaking down conventional boundaries and in experiencing the totality of things: "A poem is energy transferred from where the poet got it, . . . by way of the poem itself to, all the way over to, the reader. Okay. Then the poem itself must, at all points, be a high energy-construct and, at all points, an energy discharge." Thus, the poem must go beyond the representation of meaning and seek a presentation of reality to end the estrangement between the socially conditioned self and the totality of the objective world of nature.

In another of Olson's experimental essays, *"Human Universe"* (1965), there is an attack against Socrates for fathering the delimiting Western system of education: "We have lived long in a generalizing time, at least since 450 B.C. And it has had its effects on the best of men, on the best of things. Logos, or discourse, for example, has, in that time, so worked its abstractions into our concept and use of language that language's other function, speech, seems so in need of restoration that several of us go back to hieroglyphs or to ideograms to right the balance. (The distinction here is between language as the act of the instant and language as the act of thought about the instant.)" Olson's poetry, indulging in a regular use of ideograms influenced by Pound, aimed to retrieve language's supposedly lost function of speech for a vivid communication of actuality ("the act of the instant") transcending the cognitive detachment of abstraction and generalization. "Art does not seek to describe but to enact": "The K" attempts to fulfill this artistic imperative.

Thomas M. Curley

KADDISH

Author: Allen Ginsberg (1926-   )
Type of poem: Elegy
First published: 1961, in *Kaddish and Other Poems*

The Poem

"Kaddish" is a long elegy infused with stream of consciousness; it is divided into six parts with long poetic lines and passages of prose. The title comes from the Judaic prayer, recited in daily services, in praise of God and in memory of the dead. The term itself sets the elegiac tone of the poem, announcing principally that the poem is in memory of the poet's mother, Naomi Ginsberg, who had died three years earlier.

The title also anticipates the poem's first-person point of view and suggests a confessional tone. To say that the poem is confessional is to suggest that the poet directly addresses the reader (or, in this case, his mother, as a posthumous reader) without the mediation of a persona. More important than the confessional stance, which could imply simply an autobiographical approach, is that Allen Ginsberg is revealing intensely private experiences that have not only shaped his life but also formed the muse of his poetic sensibilities. Thus, he claims early in the poem that "Death is that remedy all singers dream of." Singer here represents the poet, whose historic duty has been to sing the truth. This concept of the singer brings to mind the beginning of Vergil's *Aeneid* (c. 29-19 B.C.), which begins "Arma virumque cano" (I sing of arms and the man). "Kaddish" becomes a song for the dead, begun, as the first six words indicate, in present tense, but with the distance of recollection: "Strange now to think of you."

The first section of the poem, called "Proem," acts as a prelude for what follows in the other five sections. It has the aura of a musical overture, highlighting the themes and motifs that will come forth in their full complexities later. The first two lines announce the poem's modus operandi, as the following words suggest: strange, think, you, eyes, walk, village, winter, night, Kaddish, blues. The poet is in a singularly peculiar state. He believes that it is strange to think of his mother while walking on a sunny day in New York City's Greenwich Village; he has been up the night before reading the Kaddish aloud and listening to the blues. In these two images, Ginsberg unites the larger backdrops of this elegy: his Jewish heritage and the private suffering, as depicted in blues music, of living painfully and in isolation. Readers familiar with Ginsberg's poetry will recognize that these two ideas create the foundation of his canon.

What follows is a recollection of his mother's immigration and early life in America, ending with the invented prayer, written in prose lines, that he sings to the "Nameless, One Faced, Forever beyond me, beginningless, endless, Father." The second section, called "Narrative," recounts his mother's bouts with insanity, from the time the poet was twelve until her death in 1956, three years before the poem was written. The story of her paranoia ends at the moment of her final sickness and ultimate death. Infused in these final passages about her life is the poet's sudden dramatic address to her, where he writes: "O glorious muse that bore me from the womb, gave suck first mystic life & taught me talk and music, from whose pained head I first took Vision." Here Ginsberg reveals what he only implied in the poem's first few lines—that his mother's life, and death, comprise the source of his poetic energy.

The third section, called "Hymmnn," is a complete and invented prayer, a return to the song motif, recited both to "He who builds Heaven in Darkness" and to the mother-muse Naomi. The fourth section, "Lament," is a list of regrets. The poet wishes he could have understood his mother's painful, paranoiac visions better and not have resisted the uncontrollable way that she brought pain on him and his family. The fifth, called "Litany," reiterates the poem's major episodes of his mother's illnesses and relapses into an incantatory prayer which begins "O mother/ what have I left out" and ends with a list of the various "eyes" of her life, from the "eyes of Russia and the "eyes of Czechoslovakia attacked by robots" to the "eyes of lobotomy" and the "eyes of stroke." The final section, "Fugue," ends in an utter rending of emotion with the poet unable to articulate anything more than "Lord Lord Lord caw caw caw."

Forms and Devices

Ginsberg's two principal formal devices in "Kaddish" bring about the poem's impression of sadness and remorse. The first is what could best be called stream-of-consciousness writing—that is, the unending and unyielding movement of thoughts and emotions. One can see this stream of consciousness most obviously in the poem's punctuation, in particular the dash. The use of the dash is relentless; in each use, it announces an associative and subsequent thought or emotional condition. For example, in the second section, "Narrative," a prose stanza reads: "Once locked herself in with razor or iodine—could hear her cough in tears at sink—Lou broke through glass greenpainted door, we pulled her out to the bedroom."

Lou is the poet's father. What is typical of this passage is that the dash separates images into categories that resemble the pattern in which the poet remembers them. By not relying on traditional syntactic constructions or regular sentence patterns, Ginsberg heightens the tension between memory and experience. He intensifies the severity and the unswerving nature of the narrative itself. Because he leaves out the expected punctuation of periods, for example, thoughts never end but keep moving, the way the poet himself keeps moving by walking on the streets of New York City, as announced at the beginning of the poem.

A second device is the poet's simultaneous juxtaposition and linkage of song and prayer. Both song and prayer are expressions of celebration, be they joyous or sorrowful. If one thinks of song as the more secular and prayer as the more religious, one can see how Ginsberg uses these two forms to mediate the pathos of the poem. Ultimately, as the title of the poem predicts, prayer wins out—as the final sections of the poem give way to an outpouring of emotion and recitation of mourning.

Still, the poet is constantly trying to use the motif of song as a remedy for his grief. Thus, as he says at the beginning of section 2, images "run thru the mind—like the saxophone chorus of houses and years." By returning to the texture and sound of blues, the poet can resist his sorrow. Yet in a moment of self-blame and self-guilt later in the same section, the poet breaks from the narrative to recite a line in Hebrew from the Kaddish itself: "Yisborach, v'yistabach, v'yispoar, v'yisroman, v'yisnaseh, v'yishador, v'yishalleh, v'yishallol, sh'meh d'kudsho, b'rich hu." Here, the recitation of the Kaddish perhaps eases his suffering; or, if not that, since the song of the poem is not the remedy he had sought, the recitation of the actual Kaddish—rather than the poem as a form of Kaddish—reminds him of his sorrow, and in that he finds a kind of solace.

Themes and Meanings

Ultimately, a prayer for the dead is recited to cleanse the pain of the speaker. Yet it appears in "Kaddish" that Ginsberg only makes things worse for himself. One theme of the poem is the double nature of remembrance: how it both heals and hurts. This juxtaposition is typical for the elegy. For the speaker, remembering his mother is a method for praising her life—except that here, her life is revealed as one that incurred such immense pain that remembering and retelling the horror of it becomes another form of pain, a reiteration of past sorrows, a recapitulation of the poet's loss.

In one moment, Ginsberg describes his whole poem as a lament. If one thinks of lament less as regret or mourning and more as wailing—and in that sound it is a song of grief—one comes closer to the poem's overriding theme of calling out, of moaning. This crying is articulated at the end of the "Proem": "Death, stay thy phantoms!" Ginsberg suggests that living is painful enough, full of psychological adversities such as those experienced by Naomi, that death would be helpful if it simply did not unleash its gestures of remorse. In a larger context, her suffering embodies the fear of the unknown, everyone's fear of the unaccountable. Perhaps that fear in and of itself is a reason people say prayers for the dead.

In that, one finds another theme of "Kaddish": the poet's need to write poems. Ginsberg has always filled the role of the prophet-poet, and those familiar with his work will recognize the bardic nature of "Kaddish." In this sense, the poem is an act of primordial utterance, spoken to the dead out of respect for the dead.

David Biespiel

KALEIDOSCOPE

Author: Paul Verlaine (1844-1896)
Type of poem: Lyric
First published: 1883, as "Kaléidoscope"; in *Jadis et naguère*, 1884; collected in
  Selected Poems, 1948

The Poem

The twenty-eight lines of "Kaleidoscope" are divided into seven four-line stanzas
of Alexandrine verse (twelve-syllable lines). The rhyme scheme (*abba*, *cddc*, and so
on), with alternating masculine and feminine end rhymes, is traditional in French
poetry. In these seven quatrains, fragments of diverse sensory impressions of the
past are presented to the reader in juxtaposed images that change like bits of colored
glass in a kaleidoscope.

Paul Verlaine composed the poem during his incarceration in Brussels, after being
arrested for firing at and wounding his lover, the young poet Arthur Rimbaud. The
two poets had returned from London, where they had spent several months. The
poem recollects images from this period spent wandering the streets of London with
Rimbaud, reality obscured by alcohol, time rendered timeless by love and pleasure.

In the first stanza, the locale of the poem is established: a city street. Neither the
street nor the city is real, though: It is a dream city, yet one that evokes a sensation of
past experience, of déjà vu characterized by vagueness and clarity at the same time.
A single image, "sun shining through a fog," appears in the first stanza and confirms
the inspiration for the poem: The sun suggests physical desire, the fog suggests
London.

The second stanza opens with two auditory images. There is a "voice in the
woods" and a "cry on the sea." These sounds are surprising, for they seem contradictory to the city street locale of the first stanza. The contradiction is resolved
when one wakes up from these "metempsychoses" (transmigrations of the soul,
used here in the sense of altered states, or dreams) only to find that things have not
changed. Reality is, then, in a woods, near the sea. The city is the dream.

The third stanza plunges the reader back into the dream city streets where organ
grinders and marching bands are heard, where cats sleep on tavern countertops. Two
of these three images are musical ones and show the importance of music in Verlaine's poetry. "Music above all," he would write later in his "Art poétique."

In the fourth stanza, a polarity of human emotions—joy and sadness, laughter
and tears—are "invocations to death." In the dream city, one experiences emotional
extremes that are viewed as inevitable and fatal. Such was indeed the case of Verlaine's relationship with Rimbaud. Verlaine claimed to have been born under the
malignant influence of a dark star. His escapade with Rimbaud was both agony and
ecstasy. Verlaine considered it his ineluctable fate.

The next two stanzas continue to present colorful sights, sounds, and smells of the
city: Widows, peasant women, and prostitutes mingle with soldiers and dandruff-

laden old men; dance-hall music and firecrackers are heard; the odor of urine is in the air.

The final quatrain is a return to the states of dreaming and waking mentioned in the second stanza. One wakes up and falls asleep again into the same dream, but this time the dream is not the city. It is the summer, the grass, and the buzz of a bee—the bucolic decor of woods and seashore in stanza 2. Reality and dream have changed places.

Forms and Devices

The poem is an example of poetic impressionism: Verlaine suggests with verbal imagery the same way Debussy suggests with music and Monet suggests with pastels. Verlaine veils his meaning, deliberately obscuring contours in order to create an enchanting vagueness in which there are elements of both the unknown and the familiar. "Kaleidoscope" is written in accordance with Verlaine's personal system, which he developed around the time the poem was written (1873, ten years before publication). In this system, Verlaine sought to eliminate entirely the first person, the poet, the "moi," from poetry. In this poem, the "I" is replaced by the more nebulous, nonspecific pronoun "one."

Although the poem is set visually in quatrains, it is knit together verbally. Three stanzas are joined by the continuation of a sentence from the last line of one to the first line of the next without a syntactical pause. Others are joined by repeating first words (lines 4 and 5 begin "Oh this . . . !"), which allows Verlaine to blur the traditional boundaries of the poetic stanza.

Except for the word "metempsychoses," the vocabulary of the poem is simple, almost childlike. The phrase "It will be as if . . ." ("Ce sera comme quand on . . .") is a colloquialism Verlaine often used. In keeping with this puerile simplicity, he uses much repetition, especially at line beginnings (in French, "Où" begins lines 10 and 11 and "Des" opens lines 14, 15, 16, and 17). There are alliterations (a *v* sound in the first stanza and an *f* sound in the fifth); internal rhyme (the "on" and "or" of line 26: "Et que l'on se rendort et que l'on rêve encor"); consonances; and weak end rhymes that function primarily as assonance with a preponderance of "open" vowels. These devices create sonorities that enhance the suggestivity and musicality of the work.

Of all the figurative language in "Kaleidoscope," the most striking are the two oxymorons in the fourth stanza. In line 14, the tears rolling down his cheeks are qualified in French as "douces" ("sweet"), the opposite of "salty." The oxymoron in the next line is easily translated as "laughter sobbed." The apparent contradiction in terms serves to heighten the degree of each emotion and, simultaneously, to cloud the reader's perception of the causes for the extreme joy or sorrow. After all, "It will be as if one had forgotten the causes" (line 6).

Since music was extremely important to Verlaine, the rhythm of his verse is particularly interesting. His favorite rhythmic innovation was the displacement of the caesura. (In French poetry, this mid-line pause is after the sixth syllable.) It is displaced in most of the lines of "Kaleidoscope." In several lines, there is no place at all for the caesura (notably in those lines beginning "It will be as if one . . ."). As the poem progresses, the number of pauses increases. By the final stanza, there is a caesura in the first three lines and two caesuras (reinforced by commas) in the last line. The effect is that of a musical ritardando, a slowing down of the rhythm for the conclusion.

Themes and Meanings

Verlaine was a Parnassian poet (that is, believing in art for art's sake) in the sense that he was horrified at the idea of using poetry as a vehicle for preaching ideas or indulging in self-pity, as was often the case with the Romantics. He wrote to the poet Stéphane Mallarmé that his poetry was an effort to render sensations drawn from a personal world of memory and illusion. It is helpful to keep this purpose in mind when interpreting Verlaine's work.

Many poets through the ages have dealt with the theme of the passage of time. "Kaleidoscope" looks to the future in using the repeated line "It will be . . ." ("Ce sera . . .") and by the predominance of the future tense throughout the poem in French. Yet the dream is about the past "as if one had lived there." The verbs "wakes" and "falls asleep" are in the present tense. By obscuring the division of time into past, present, and future, the poem presents time as an illusion, irrelevant, because it is subject to distortion by the senses.

Like Charles Baudelaire (1821-1867), a poet of the preceding generation, Verlaine chose as his primary subject modern man, who must copy physically with the refinements of an excessive civilization, more specifically, the sentient creature confronted with the lure of the city, the vices of the social underworld. In "Kaleidoscope," the city is London, but it is also Paris, Brussels, any city. The reader enters the poet's personal world of sensation, which immediately becomes the reader's personal world, "one's" own experience. It suffices merely to hint at, to suggest, meaning in muted tones and minor keys.

"Kaleidoscope" is a poem about the dichotomy of the human condition, the contrasts and contradictions inherent in human beings. There are dream states and waking states, both of which seem to be reality at the time. There are experiences of great joy and extreme sadness. There are moments of clarity ("this sun") and moments of dim perception ("a fog"). There is a longing for the purity of nature and a fascination with the corruption of the city. There is the will to live and the will to die. In the poem, lines distinguishing one from its opposite have been obscured; it is impossible to differentiate reality from dreams, pleasure from pain, past from present or present from future, or, by extension, good from bad and right from wrong. One is no more than the reflected image of the other. Viewed in this light, the poem is truly a kaleidoscope in which the mirror of poetry creates symmetrical patterns out of random pieces of sensation.

Judith Barban

THE KING OF HARLEM

Author: Federico García Lorca (1898-1936)
Type of poem: Ode
First published: 1940, as "El rey de Harlem," in *Poeta en Nueva York*; collected
in *Poet in New York and Other Poems*, 1940

The Poem

In his "Lecture on New York," Federico García Lorca said that he wanted to write a poem about black people in North America that would emphasize the pain that they experience for being black in a contrary world. García Lorca accomplishes his goal in his long poem entitled "The King of Harlem," collected in the volume *Poet in New York and Other Poems*. This long poem (119 lines) is an ode (an elaborate lyric directed to a fixed purpose and theme); its twenty-four stanzas are divided into three sections, and it is written in free verse.

The title of the poem is ironic. The black man, who was respected as a king in his ancestral land and who was the master of his own destiny, is now the "king" of an alien land and culture: New York City's Harlem.

Section 1 of the poem contains seven stanzas. The first stanza opens with a violent image: The black man uses the white man's ineffectual tool, a wooden spoon, to overcome crocodiles — symbols of evil. The black man dares to gouge out the "eyes of crocodiles" with a wooden spoon.

In the next two stanzas, the natural world (exemplified by fire and water) that the black man once inhabited either lies dormant ("age-old fire slept in the flints") or putrefies ("vats of putrid water arrived"). In the fourth stanza, the loss of feeling and identity with nature continues. Instead of children being initiated into the hunt of majestic beasts, they perversely "flattened tiny squirrels."

In the fifth stanza of the poem, a bridge appears. The whites are exhorted to "cross the bridge" to the world of the blacks in order to understand what they have lost in the process of civilization. The descent into the underworld (classically symbolized in the works of Dante and Vergil by the crossing of a bridge) progresses in the next stanza; however, the powers to be fought and conquered in the wasteland of New York are not typical forces of evil but a "blood vendor of firewater" or "Jewesses" in their bubble baths. Among the absurd visions that are encountered in the descent is "the infinite beauty/ of feather dusters, graters, copper pans, and kitchen/ casseroles."

In the final stanza of the first section, the black man is hopelessly enslaved in a doorman's uniform by the millionaires of New York. His suppressed energy has become pent-up anguish as a result of his "red" oppression. This stanza relies heavily on red imagery to convey its mood of suppressed violence; for example, the black man's blood shudders with rage, and his violence is "garnet."

Section 2 of the poem contains nine stanzas. The first two stanzas describe American girls and boys in Harlem who "stretched their limbs and fainted on the cross,"

Christlike sacrificial victims of white civilization. The third stanza echoes a stanza in section 1 of the poem. The king of Harlem once again digs out the crocodiles' eyes, not with a wooden spoon this time but with "an unbreakable spoon," a tool even more unnatural than wood.

The blood motif dominates the next six stanzas of the poem's second section. The rage in the blood that rushes through the black man cannot be seen because of the darkness of his skin; it surges beneath the surface. Yet "There must be some way out of here," the ninth stanza begins.

The third and last section of the poem is even more emphatic in its denial of escape from the situation and in its affirmation of an ultimate victory of sorts by the primitivism of the black man over the rational. In the first stanza of the section, blacks seek their king in the streets. In the fourth stanza, however, a wall rises in the black man's path, blocking any creature's escape. The poet exhorts the black man not to look to its cracks for escape but to "the great central sun" for the answer. The black man must wait in his "king's jungle" until the tide turns against the forces that contain them and the highest rooftops are devoured by the primeval forest. Then, they will be able to return to their natural order and dance free of doubt. The white man's Moses will be engulfed by flowers and put to rest before reaching the supposed promised land. The instruments of science will be relegated to the caves of squirrels, and the wheel, symbol of industry and progress, will no longer be an object of fear.

Forms and Devices

García Lorca's strongly negative feelings about New York — its chaos, materialism, harshness, and brutality — necessitated a form or vehicle of expression that would lend itself to those feelings. García Lorca chose the vehicle of surrealism to express his strong reaction to the city and its inhabitants. Strongly within the surrealist tradition (surrealism is a movement in art and literature emphasizing the expression of the imagination as realized in dreams and presented without conscious control), "The King of Harlem," as well as the rest of the poems in the collection *Poet in New York*, relies almost exclusively on jarring rhythms, unexpected juxtapositions, and stark imagery and symbolism to convey its meaning.

The poem's imagery clusters around two focal points that are continually juxtaposed in García Lorca's poem: the "civilized" world of the white man and the natural world of the black man. For example, animals of Africa — such as crocodiles, monkeys, serpents, and zebras — are contrasted with animals of the city — such as squirrels and salamanders. García Lorca also contrasts the natural beauty of the African forest, with its "tattooed sun that descends the river" and "bristling flowers," to the "civilized" ugliness of the Harlem landscape, with its "putrid water," "rigid, descending skies in which the colonies of planets/ can wheel with the litter on the beaches," "chemical rose," and "black mire." The interior landscape of Harlem is also repulsive; apartments are cluttered with "feather dusters, graters, copper pans, and kitchen/ casseroles," "tarnished mirrors," and "elevator shafts."

The blood motif in the poem is connected not only with the black man's nature, his life and vitality, but also with his rage. In the course of the poem, the primitive vitality of the blacks is symbolized by gushing, pervasive blood imagery—"blood raging under the skin"; however, phrases such as "blood shuddering with rage" and "blood wrung from hemp and subway nectars," and the description of blood flowing "everywhere,/ and burn the blond women's chlorophyll" are images of the blood of anger that the black man carries within him, ready to explode at any time.

Themes and Meanings

Critics have pointed out that *Poet in New York and Other Poems* in general, and "The King of Harlem" in particular, is as much about the poet's own psychological state while he was visiting the city as it is about New York and the alienation of the black man from that city. García Lorca had come to New York hoping that the journey would distract him from a severe emotional crisis. Once he arrived, however, he slowly began not to recognize himself. Coming to New York immersed García Lorca in a culture that was as different from his native Andalusia (southern Spain) as any place could possibly be. In his personal alienation from the mechanized and dehumanized city, he identified with the black man in the poem; they were going through an identity crisis together.

Thus, the theme of alienation from one's roots is the dominant theme of García Lorca's poem. Harlem represents the extreme domination of culture over nature; like the poet, the city—as well as the black man—is divorced from an origin that, unlike humankind, it cannot even acknowledge. In the poem, civilization is repeatedly equated with barbarism and technological progress with physical violence and moral and spiritual regression. A general decadence, which the poet characteristically renders in imagery of violent fragmentation, disintegration, and decomposition, abounds. For García Lorca, these circumstances must be the accumulated effects of a cause; the dismembered bodies and disembodied emotions are the debris of some catastrophe or series of catastrophes. The black man is a slave to the white man; the white man is a slave to his own technological progress.

Of those of New York's citizens still endowed with vitality, the blacks, although geographically distant from their homeland, are pictured as being the least removed from their spiritual origin. These citizens, having incorporated potentially explosive tendencies, are dormant volcanoes waiting to erupt.

Genevieve Slomski

THE KINGFISHERS

Author: Charles Olson (1910-1970)
Type of poem: Meditation
First published: 1950; collected in *In Cold Hell, in Thicket*, 1953

The Poem

"The Kingfishers," a lyrical meditation on the ruins of an Aztec burial ground, is written in a bold style invented for this poem, which Charles Olson explained shortly after in his essay of 1950, "Projective Verse." The poem does away with such formalities as rhyme and regular meters, symmetrical stanzas, and the normal pattern of argument in which particulars move toward universals or vice versa. Instead, it proceeds through a succession of widely varying stanzaic units as information is brought into the discourse and a unifying perception is drawn from the array of accumulated facts and ideas.

The poem opens with a paradox taken from the early Greek philosopher Heraclitus, which states that only change itself is unchanging. Olson's rendering of the phrase emphasizes the *will* of change, which gives pretext to what follows. The poem cuts abruptly to a party in its last hour somewhere in Mexico, near the ruins of an Aztec city, perhaps Tenochtitlán, the old Aztec capital that is now Mexico City. A man is addressing a stunned audience of guests with remarks about the deterioration of Mexican culture, the downward path of change toward entropy. "The pool is slime," he concludes, and disappears into the ruins.

So begins part 1 of a three-part meditation on change and the poet's responsibility to heed the shiftings of reality in his calling as writer. Part 1, the longest of the sections, is divided into four smaller movements, each with its own set of relations to be worked out. Various principles are at work in the building up of the poem's content. In the first movement of part 1, the juxtaposition of elements is cinematic, a "jump-cut" technique of butting events together without transition markers.

The second movement combines elements of three different topics, each separate and sequential in the poem's exposition but increasingly part of some deeper unifying chord tying all three topics together. The *E* on the stone, the first topic, is an allusion to the description by Plutarch, the second century A.D. Roman writer, of a navel stone (*omphalos*) found at the temple of Delphi, site of the ancient Greek oracles. The second is snippets of Mao Tse-tung's speech before the Chinese Communist Party in 1948, on the eve of the revolution that drove out the regime of Chiang Kai-shek from mainland China, bringing to an abrupt end the long hold of Western imperialism there. The third is a technical description of the kingfisher bird, much of which is lifted directly from the eleventh edition of the *Encyclopædia Britannica*. All three mark points of change in time, with the kingfisher as the principle of unity in change. The ancient *E* is the last remnant of a great civilization; Mao's speech is the turning point of another civilization. The bird's mortal existence transcends the rise and fall of human civilization by means of some other agency of nature, which balances change with structural constancy of form.

The third movement is a commentary on human violence and aggression, in particular the conquest of Mexico by Hernán Cortés in A.D. 1517. Olson quotes from William H. Prescott's *History of The Conquest of Mexico* (1843), which itemizes some of the loot taken from the temples by Cortés' army, including two gold embroideries of birds, possibly quetzal birds, whose feathers were important in Aztec mythology and rituals. The Mexican quetzal is equivalent to the kingfisher in Amerindian cultures. "And all now is war," Olson remarks at the close of the movement, as he draws a line from the Spanish Conquest to the Korean conflict of his own time.

The fourth and final movement of part 1 raises the discussion of change to a principle: Nothing remains the same; everything is driven to the next stage of development or mutation. Change is the pervasive force running throughout nature, yet it cannot be abstracted or directed by human means.

Part 2 is a fugue that combines the information gathered in the opening part. It begins in the middle of a guided tour of an Aztec burial ground that has been partially excavated. The mounds contain the remains of Aztecs who had lived prior to Cortés' conquest; the figure in the grave recalls the young in the kingfisher's nest, the first connection. Mao's exhortation to rise and act is woven in. The discussion points up the frailty and haplessness of human notions of order against the lasting, vital orders of nature. The Mexican guide turns from the ruins to admire a yellow rose, the setting sun, the mystical figure of unity, spirit, and transcendent permanence within a realm of violent upheaval and chaos.

Part 3 is a coda in which the various themes of the poem are resolved in the form of a decision reached by the poet. He renounces the violence and errors of Western tradition, stemming from Greek and Roman civilization, and finds his true heritage among such rebel poets as Arthur Rimbaud, who left his own country to live in the deserts of the Middle East. Olson quotes a passage from Rimbaud's *Une Saison en enfer* (1873; *A Season in Hell*, 1932), which he translates immediately below, and closes the poem with a similar commitment to renounce Western culture and adopt the New World as his proper heritage.

Forms and Devices

One must "look" at an Olson poem as well as read it. Visually, it is an arrangement of words intended to convey the motion of thought itself. The term "projective" literally means to project the thinking process of composition onto paper and to reenact—a strategic term for Olson—the subtle motions of memory and association as they feed into the main discourse of imaginative activity. The poem is therefore "kinetic," even cinematic in its abrupt shift from scene to scene, in the "framing" that ensues as discourse contracts into a perception or lengthens out into narrative or description. Olson, like many other innovative American poets, based the new prosody of the poem on the techniques of filmmaking and emphasized motility and dramatic shift as the rhetoric of thought and articulation.

As many critics have noted in describing this poem, it is structured as an extended "ideogram," Ezra Pound's term for the elemental relations that constitute a poem's unity and force as language. The many separate parts of the poem are the clustered details that form a single structure of thought, the way a snowflake's radiations and delicate latticework constitute a single flake of snow. The challenge to the reader is to discern the connections and integrity of these many pieces as they cohere within a single flash of understanding.

Olson's poem runs the gamut of open forms, from the proselike strophes of the opening section, to the stepped lines showing the rhythm of Mao's words, to the steep descent of other passages in which the rhythm accelerates. The sprawling shapes of many of the paragraphs are indicators that the thought is labored or resistant, or that it emerges under conflict. It is not until the coda that one sees the resolution of opposites visually projected, the "balance" of the quatrains as they direct the reader to the declaration, "I hunt among stones."

Stylistically, the poem observes many of the conventions of verse discourse. Certain tropes predominate, especially the image of the kingfisher, which appears in every section of part 1 as its principal motif; another is the sun marking east and west, dawn and sunset, decay and renewal. The language is clean and spare, written in a stately tempo partly achieved through the use of pithy aphorisms and formal parallels, and partly by means of a series of stark assertions in tones ranging from scientific formality to the emotional declaration of his changed allegiance at the end.

Themes and Meanings

The poem is an analysis of the failures of Western expansion over the centuries, of the desire of one civilization to take possession of and exploit others. This vast subject provides the means by which the poet reaches his decision to change his cultural allegiance away from Europe to the New World. The poem's elaborate procedure of argument and analysis begins with the corruptions of modern Mexico, where a figure announces that the civilization that began with the achievements of the Mayas and Aztecs has been brought by Spanish conquerors to its present degradation.

Though Olson had not yet visited Mexico, he was becoming interested in modern archaeological diggings at some of the principal Aztec temple grounds, and had conceived this scene purely from his reading. Several months after writing the poem, he undertook an expedition to Mexico's Yucatán peninsula, where he resided for six months and wrote vigorous letters home about his own findings and speculations, later collected by Robert Creeley and published in 1953 under the title *Mayan Letters*. An important part of his ideas as a poet and cultural historian was derived from his studies of Mayan civilization. In "The Kingfishers," however, his interest lies principally in his view of modern Mexico as the victim of Spanish invasion and colonialization.

That focus on one victim of empire opens into a vision of the frailties of all human civilizations, their vulnerability to the decay of time or to the instinct of human violence to crush them. Hence, the *E* cut on the stone marks the last mysterious expression of a lost civilization marking one boundary of time, a point of origin along a continuum of growth and decay known as the Western tradition. The king-fisher, who flies into the sun to meet the westerning light and warm its breast against it, is thus a figure of enduring vitality that stands in vivid contrast to the tragedy of human history.

By the end of part 1, Olson has wrested a valuable lesson from his musings on history: Time is "not accumulation but change." Little endures of human nature but a few ruins; nature's vast backdrop is the stage on which human life plays out its tragedy. The Mongolian louse inherits the few possessions that were heaped in the Aztec burial mounds. Olson scorns the Western attitude that would destroy a civilization that lived close to nature. He senses in his own time a decay in social ideals and reads in the Korean conflict that had broken out in 1949 a continuation of Western violence against other cultures.

Arriving at the coda in part 3, the reader observes Olson's own ritual rebirth as a poet as he proclaims his new heritage and birthright as an heir to the New World, a descendant of Aztec roots. He sides with the victims of imperialism and claims them as his true ancestors. It is Olson's way of protesting against the nature of war and the aggressions of his own civilization. "The Kingfishers" is the first anti-imperialist poem written in an era that saw the end of many colonial states and the breakup of the major European empires.

Though "The Kingfishers" belongs to a long tradition of landscape and graveyard meditations, it turns this tradition around by meditating over the burial mounds of an ancient people who become, through the urgency of the poet's musings, his own ancestors and bloodline. With this poem, Olson may be said to have invented post-modernism, with its array of anti-imperialist arguments and its desire to reconcile contemporary Western art with ancient myth and ritual.

Paul Christensen

KITTENS

Author: Robert Peters (1924-   )
Type of poem: Lyric/elegy
First published: 1967, in *Songs for a Son*

The Poem

"Kittens" is a long poem written in free verse; its short lines are grouped into ten stanzas. It is an elegy, a poem written in grief or mourning. This poem is also a song, a lyric lament for Robert Peters' son Richard, who died suddenly in childhood. It laments unfulfilled wishes and lost promise. The poem is generated by the boy's wish to have kittens and his father's wish that his son had lived to experience more of the world.

The poem begins with the kittens that finally did come to fulfill the child's wish—after his death. They are filled with energy and life: "plump dark woolly cats/ with eyes like olives/ . . . tumbling/ on the floor . . ./ lapping up blue milk." Only "death-day/ morning" and perhaps the milk's tinge suggest an elegy. In addition, the stanza that follows, a finely paced account of the birth of the kittens, celebrates abundance and beginnings. The kittens, "fur wet like licorice," "fell/ into a land of honey." The description of the births, although precisely detailed, conveys the mystery of the event.

In stanzas 3 and 4, however, the poem moves with fortitude and resignation into the body of another mystery: death. The poet describes the breakfast conversation during which the boy expressed his wish for kittens. His last wish, however, was rejected that "wish-day/ death-day" by his father, who tried to explain about pets:

> "they die.
> Their little toes
> curl up like leaves,
> their waxy eyes go shut,
> their tails hang limp
> their whiskers droop."

Stanza 4 reveals a central admission. As if death itself were communicable (and parents are good at imagining that it is), the poet observes, "Dreading each death's/ advent, I sought to/ spare you." A fear of invasion emerges: "Each lost/ pet might break deep,/ deep within your heart" " —in almost the same way that an infestation might "crystallize" inside the boy "into long beads of rice/ to feed the worm." One senses the father's realization that he feared becoming a helpless witness to his son's death almost more than he feared the death itself. The stanza ends with a surprising tactile image—each pet's death might be "a buzz," like an eel's tail delivering "a fatal jolt!"

The following two stanzas document the deaths of Snake and Mouse, and their elaborate funerals. The father retells these tales to the boy in "proof" of the folly of keeping pets. Mouse, for example, left "sprinkling mortality/ like ivy-juice/ all over you that day." Again, the theme of contagion arises, as if mortality were a condition that one might carefully avoid, but death is one of the inescapable consequences of being born. Stanza 6 ends with a rumination on transformation; the bones of the mouse and the boy are imagined as ash slipping down between layers of rock in the "earthy crypt." These lines introduce a mood of calm acceptance.

The boy was not swayed by the scare tactics, his father's tales of "deep-felled nightmare," and although already carrying (invisible in his brain) "the hung smoke of the/ sleeping fatal fever," the delighted child snapped the wishbone to "free [his] wish." The poet looks back at this moment and confronts joy and loss simultaneously; as the bone breaks in the poem, one is aware of an instant of innocent yet fervent hope coupled with the father's sudden snap of agony over the boy's absence. Tenderness is accompanied by pain. The finality of the last line in stanza 8 echoes the suddenness and finality of the child's death.

The last two stanzas return to the present, a house filled with tumbling kittens, like tiny reincarnations of the boy's delight and movements. The kittens "do all the acts,/ make all the gestures that/ you knew live kittens make." These facts, the knowledge the boy took "into the night," are better than the "shouts of passion,/ war; the violence of cars," which he was spared. Sorrow is both relieved and rekindled in the end, as it has been throughout the poem. The poet mourns "the poetry that never/ broke itself against/ your ears," and although he struggles to accept Richard's loss, still wishes "that there had been more."

Forms and Devices

"My poems to my son were meant to give the illusion that a five-year-old child could understand them" says Peters. His language in "Kittens" is therefore direct, his rhythm plain, and his diction simple. Although the poem is not really written for a five-year-old (the metaphors and allusions are grown-up, and some of the vocabulary is too hard), the poem nevertheless is simple. This surface plainness allows a clear-eyed rumination on the boy's death, on life and death, which does not fall prey to gross sentimentality or overlush expressions of sorrow. The poet/speaker simply talks; on the surface, he shares what happened.

The poems in *Songs for a Son* grew out of an emotionally charged situation and thus are blessed with a sudden abundance of energy that peaks, seemingly paradoxically, and turns into musical celebration at precisely the moments of greatest sorrow and pain. A good example in "Kittens" is the indented final lines of the seventh stanza, which lead to the jumbly, joyful liveliness of the next stanza. The short lines help sustain this energetic movement; the poem moves quickly through thoughts and memories.

In "Kittens," the stanzas vary in length. Their form is loose enough to accommodate the varying needs and depths of the scenes. The poem's temporal movement from scene to scene (stanza to stanza) gives the poem a narrative shape. It has chronology and various settings, both of which are familiar components of storytelling. The narrative begins in the speaker's present, moves back in time to the death-day, moves further back in time to the funerals of Snake and Mouse, comes back to the death-day, and finally returns the reader to the present and the new kittens. Thus the poem is a cycle that examines, celebrates, and reveres, by means of the child's death, the basic cycle of birth, life, and death. The sections of the poem represent eras in the boy's short life.

What lends the poem further unity is that, like a talisman, *the wish*, which is directly referred to in four stanzas and is implicitly there in the rest, becomes almost an entity, a being with its own life that must be protected. An abstraction somehow concretized, it becomes an energy source in the poem, especially when it is fulfilled by the birth of the kittens.

Themes and Meanings

In this poem about things dying, the death of the boy's wish for kittens is mourned as heavily as the death of the boy. In fact, the poem seems almost to be, with its catalog of pets that die, an elegy for small pleasures. Pleasures often die or are lost to those who believe their daily routines are all-important. Possibilities for joy are also sometimes forsaken by those who fear taking risks—even small ones.

Thus one theme of the poem is to question the illusion of "safety" from life's horrors; there really was no way his father could have spared the boy from suffering, or even suffering only over each lost pet. The "blue, fatal jolt" can happen again and again in anyone's life. The poem suggests that only when one accepts life openly, with all of its risks, can one truly begin to live. Another suggestion is made about risks: that the boy, had he lived, would have dealt with the risks and dangers of his own life capably, and as a child, with a childlike openness that a wise adult might envy. Richard did not really need to be and could not have been protected from life. He "seized the dish," he was so eager.

As if to prove how futile it was for the father to refuse the boy his kittens, the kittens arrive anyway. They resurrect the boy's wish; in fact, they return the boy to the father in the vehicle of this poem. The kittens represent the acceptance of death, and therefore the acceptance of life.

JoAnn Balingit

KUBLA KHAN

Author: Samuel Taylor Coleridge (1772-1834)
Type of poem: Lyric
First published: 1816, in *Christabel*

The Poem

"Kubla Khan," one of the most famous and most analyzed English poems, is a fifty-four-line lyric in three verse paragraphs. In the opening paragraph, the title character decrees that a "stately pleasure-dome" be built in Xanadu. Although numerous commentators have striven to find sources for the place names used here by Samuel Taylor Coleridge, there is no critical consensus about the origins or meanings of these names. The real-life Kubla Khan, a thirteenth century Mongolian general and statesman who conquered and unified China, lived in an elaborate residence known as K'ai-p'ing, or Shang-tu, in southeastern Mongolia. Coleridge's Kubla has his palace constructed where Alph, "the sacred river," begins its journey to the sea. The construction of the palace on "twice five miles of fertile ground" is described. It is surrounded by walls and towers within which are ancient forests and ornate gardens "bright with sinuous rills."

Xanadu is described more romantically in the second stanza. It becomes "A savage place! as holy and enchanted/ As e'er beneath a waning moon was haunted/ By woman wailing for her demon-lover!" It is inhabited not by Kubla's family and followers, but by images from Coleridge's imagination. His Xanadu is a magical place where the unusual is to be expected, as when a "mighty fountain" bursts from the earth, sending "dancing rocks" into the air, followed by the sacred river itself. The poem has thus progressed from the creations of Kubla Khan to the even more magical actions of nature. The river meanders for five miles until it reaches "caverns measureless to man" and sinks "in tumult to a lifeless ocean."

This intricate description is interrupted briefly when Kubla hears "from far/ Ancestral voices prophesying war!" This may be an allusion to the opposition of the real Khan by his younger brother, Arigböge, which led eventually to a military victory for Kubla. Coleridge then shifts the focus back to the pleasure-dome, with its shadow floating on the waves of the river: "It was a miracle of rare device,/ A sunny pleasure-dome with caves of ice!"

The final paragraph presents a first-person narrator who recounts a vision he once had of an Abyssinian maid playing a dulcimer and singing of Mount Abora. The narrator says that if he could revive her music within himself, he would build a pleasure-dome, and all who would see it would be frightened of "his flashing eyes, his floating hair!" His observers would close their eyes "with holy dread,/ For he on honey-dew hath fed,/ And drunk the milk of Paradise."

Coleridge prefaces the poem with an explanation of how what he calls a "psychological curiosity" came to be published. According to Coleridge, he was living in ill health during the summer of 1797 in a "lonely farm-house between Porlock and

Linton, on the Exmoor confines of Somerset and Devonshire." Having taken an "anodyne," he fell asleep immediately upon reading in a seventeenth century travel book by Samuel Purchas: "Here the Khan Kubla commanded a palace to be built, and a stately garden thereunto. And thus ten miles of fertile ground were inclosed with a wall." He claims that while sleeping for three hours he composed two-hundred to three-hundred lines, "if that indeed can be called composition in which all the images rose up before him as *things*, with a parallel production of the correspondent expressions, without any sensation or consciousness of effort."

When Coleridge awoke, he remembered the entire poem and set about copying it down, only to be interrupted for an hour "by a person on business from Porlock." Returning to the poem, Coleridge could recall only "some eight or ten scattered lines and images." He claims he has since intended to finish "Kubla Khan" but has not yet been able to.

Forms and Devices

The most striking of the many poetic devices in "Kubla Khan" are its sounds and images. One of the most musical of poems, it is full of assonance and alliteration, as can be seen in the opening five lines:

> In Xanadu did Kubla Khan
> A stately pleasure-dome decree:
> Where Alph, the sacred river, ran
> Through caverns measureless to man
> Down to a sunless sea.

This repetition of *a*, *e*, and *u* sounds continues throughout the poem with the *a* sounds dominating, creating a vivid yet mournful song appropriate for one intended to inspire its listeners to cry "Beware! Beware!" in their awe of the poet. The halting assonance in the line "As if this earth in fast thick pants were breathing" creates the effect of breathing.

The alliteration is especially prevalent in the opening lines, as each line closes with it: "Kubla Khan," "pleasure-dome decree," "river, ran," "measureless to man," and "sunless sea." The effect is almost to hypnotize the reader or listener into being receptive to the marvelous visions about to appear. Other notable uses of alliteration include the juxtaposition of "waning" and "woman wailing" to create a wailing sound. "Five miles meandering with a mazy motion" sounds like the movement it describes. The repetition of the initial *h* and *d* sounds in the closing lines creates an image of the narrator as haunted and doomed:

> His flashing eyes, his floating hair!
> Weave a circle round him thrice,
> And close your eyes with holy dread,
> For he on honey-dew hath fed,
> And drunk the milk of Paradise.

The assonance and alliteration soften the impact of the terminal rhyme and establish a sensation of movement to reinforce the image of the flowing river with the shadow of the pleasure dome floating upon it.

The imagery of "Kubla Khan" is evocative without being so specific that it negates the magical, dreamlike effect for which Coleridge is striving. The "gardens bright with sinuous rills," "incense-bearing tree," "forests ancient as the hills," and "sunny spots of greenery" are deliberately vague, as if recalled from a dream. Such images stimulate a vision of Xanadu bound only by the reader's imagination.

Themes and Meanings

Much of the commentary on "Kubla Khan" has focused on the influence of Coleridge's addiction to opium on its dreamlike qualities, the "anodyne" he refers to in his preface, but no conclusive connection between the two can be proved. Considerable criticism has also dealt with whether the poem is truly, as Coleridge claimed, a fragment of a spontaneous creation. The poet's account of the unusual origin of his poem is probably only one of numerous instances in which one of the Romantic poets proclaimed the spontaneity or naturalness of their art. Most critics of "Kubla Khan" believe that its language and meter are too intricate for it to have been created by the fevered mind of a sleeping poet. Others say that its ending is too fitting for the poem to be a fragment.

Other contentions about "Kubla Khan" revolve around its meanings (or lack thereof). Some critics, including T. S. Eliot in *The Use of Poetry and the Use of Criticism* (1933), have claimed the poem has no veritable meaning. Such analysts say its method and meaning are inseparable: The poem's form is its only meaning. For other commentators, "Kubla Khan" is clearly an allegory about the creation of art. As the artist decided to create his work of art, so does Kubla Khan decide to have his pleasure-dome constructed. The poem's structure refutes Coleridge's claim about its origins, since the first thirty-six lines describe what Kubla has ordered built, and the last eighteen lines deal with the narrator's desire to approximate the creation of the pleasure-dome.

Xanadu is an example of man imposing his will upon nature to create his vision of paradise since the palace is surrounded by an elaborate park. That the forests are "ancient as the hills" makes the imposing of order upon them more of a challenge. Like a work of art, Xanadu results from an act of inspiration and is a "holy and enchanted" place. Within this man-decreed creation are natural creations such as the river that bursts from the earth. The origin of Alph is depicted almost in sexual terms, with the earth breathing "in fast thick pants" before ejaculating the river, a "mighty fountain," in an explosion of rocks. The sexual imagery helps reinforce the creation theme of "Kubla Khan."

Like Kubla's pleasure-dome, a work of art is a "miracle of rare device," and the last paragraph of the poem depicts the narrator's desire to emulate Kubla's act through music. As with Kubla, the narrator wants to impose order on a tumultuous world. Like Xanadu, art offers a refuge from the chaos. The narrator, as with a poet, is inspired by a muse, the Abyssinian maid, and wants to re-create her song. The resulting music would be the equivalent "in air" of the pleasure-dome. As an artist, the narrator would then stand apart from a society that fears those who create, those who have "drunk the milk of Paradise."

Michael Adams

LACE

Author: Eavan Boland (1944-   )
Type of poem: Lyric
First published: 1985; collected in *The Journey and Other Poems*, 1987

The Poem

A compact lyric in free verse, "Lace" consists of thirty-five lines irregularly divided into eight sections or verse paragraphs. The title evokes a strong visual image, the significance of which becomes clear only as the poem progresses; the tatted filaments of a piece of lace represent, for Eavan Boland, the interlacings of language, sound, and sense as she labors in her notebook to compose an ideal poem. "Lace," then, is a specialized kind of lyric, because it presents the reader with a version of the writer's poetics; it is a poem about how, in Boland's view, poems can be written.

The poem begins with a sentence fragment: "Bent over/ the open notebook—." Boland's first statement, lacking both a definite subject and verb, is elliptical and oblique. She tells the reader neither who is speaking nor whom the poem is describing, information that conventionally one might expect at the beginning of a piece of writing. Readers may feel dislocated by this immediate lack of grammatical sense and empathize with the poet's apparently halting efforts to express herself in words. Readers may also find themselves implicated in that same creative process; readers too, after all, are bent over the pages of an open book, like Boland's missing subject, trying to decipher her poem. The lack of a definite "I" or "she" permits poet and reader to be drawn more closely, though tenuously, together.

The second section of the poem offers a setting, both time and place. At dusk, light is fading and clear vision becomes more difficult. The poem is located, Boland says, "in my room" at the back of the house. She places herself in relative obscurity, in a dim corner, and introduces the lyric first person—at once the poet and the dramatized speaker of the poem—not as a confident "I," but obliquely, in a possessive pronoun.

In the third section, she connects the dusk around her to the lack of poetic insight she seems to be experiencing. Asserting herself at last as a subject—"I"—she continues to doubt her talents, claiming to be looking for a language with which to express herself. She is "still" in two senses of the word, both persistently striving onward and, paradoxically, unable to make herself go on.

The fourth section consists of a single word, bringing us at last to the poem's title: "lace." Boland finds the proper word or image to express her sense of what a poem is, but for her readers, that sense is far from crystal clear. She presents the reader with a conceit, a complicated metaphorical equation—in this case of lace and poetic language—that she must explain in the body of the poem.

The fifth and sixth sections provide that explanation. Boland invokes the figure of a baroque courtier for whom poetry resembles lace: an elaborate, elegant, and finely crafted play of words tossed off with *sprezzatura* (an appearance of ease) and savoir faire to impress his peers or lovers. Such courtiers, even if they were merely princes "in a petty court," possessed a seemingly natural talent for poetic form, a talent for which Boland herself longs.

The seventh section, however, returns to the initial setting, in the dark corner of a room, and Boland reminds herself that even the apparent ease of these courtiers involves the same secluded labor over a notebook that she has undertaken. Poetry, she realizes, has never come easily to anyone, nor are its complex interlacings of sound and sense simply a matter of careless grace.

The last section of the poem, again a single line, turns on a paradox. In attempting to gain insight into "the language that is// lace," Boland discovers what the poets who seemed to achieve that light, glittering language "lost their sight for." Her own well-wrought conceit emerges not from clarity of vision but from the relative obscurity of writing a poem. Poetry, she tells us, as it strives toward vision, puts forward an elaborate form of blindness.

Forms and Devices

Boland employs two types of language in "Lace." The poem begins and ends with a barren, simple form of speech. There are no elaborate metaphors here; the descriptions are direct and unadorned, and the vocabulary is limited and unpretentious, consisting mostly of blunt monosyllables.

This type of language stands in sharp contrast to the poetically complex, elaborate diction at the poem's center, in the fifth and sixth sections that follow the introduction of the image of lace. Boland here employs abstract polysyllables such as "baroque obligation" and poeticizes her vocabulary with highly charged metaphors, as in "the crystal rhetoric/ of bobbined knots/ and bosses." In this part of the poem, she twists words together like a complicated pattern of old-style lace. Her readers can hear in the poem's diction the difference between her presently uninspired state and the baroque cleverness for which she longs.

Boland employs a clipped line of no more than eight syllables, and includes only a few words per verse. The breaks between successive lines are not necessarily determined by grammar, punctuation, or meter, or even by the poet's sense of breath. Instead, the poetry seems broken, chopped, halting, as the poet feels her way precariously into words, pausing irregularly to search for a needed expression or image. The reader follows Boland's mind in motion as she scrutinizes her own creative processes and takes notes on the apparent breakdown of smooth, effortless form—what she calls "a vagrant drift of emphasis"—and the loss of poetic self-confidence.

In contrast to her fragmented lines, however, Boland exploits interlaced patterns of sound that draw the poem together, giving the reader a sense of wholeness. While there is no formal end rhyme in the poem, many words echo one another, giving the poem musical coherence. Series of words, such as "book . . . back . . . dark . . . dusk . . . look . . . shakes" or "wrist . . . thriftless . . . crystal . . . drift . . . kisses," contain assonances, alliterations, and half-rhymes—repetitions of vowel sounds, consonants, and whole syllables—which create threads of euphony that weave through the poem.

Boland presents her readers with two sides of the creative process. On the one hand, traditional forms seem to collapse and prove insufficient; the poet expresses frustration and anxiety about her inability to create. On the other hand, she succeeds in rebuilding the "interlaced" language she wants, by means of patterns of poetic music.

Themes and Meanings

Eavan Boland typically confronts in her poems the themes of hearth and history, her sense of herself as a woman in relation to home and family, and her sense of nationality and of the Irish tradition that lies behind much of her work. In "Lace," however, neither of these issues is engaged directly. The poem is set in "the house," but that setting is never made problematic and becomes, by the end of the poem, rather a comfort, a curiously vital link with lost baroque creativity. The courtier whom Boland admires is male, his sex necessitated by the patriarchal nature of the poetic tradition from which, at the poem's outset, Boland feels ostracized. Issues of gender are not at the core of the poem's concern, however, and the courtier's maleness is not called into question as it would have been in an earlier Boland volume such as *In Her Own Image* (1980) or *Night Feed* (1982).

Instead, "Lace" sets down a basis for creativity and poetic work that is, for Boland, independent of sex, nation, or historical period. The lyric deals with the struggle to see, to attain vision, and to liberate oneself, through poetry, from the confines of everyday life, which runs its course, metaphorically speaking, in dimness and perpetual dusk. Boland wants to make a poem something light, effortless, and beautiful, but wanting is not achieving, and she discovers that, despite appearances, poetry is made not from the seemingly crystalline, other-worldly language of bygone Renaissance men, but from the very dimness and blindness that characterize her life and that certainly characterized theirs. Poetry is not an escape into light and "thriftless phrases," but a means of confronting that blindness and coming to terms with one's own apparent inability to make something clever and perfect out of the world. Boland sees value in writing poetry not because it holds any visionary keys to understanding but because of the process of confrontation and self-scrutiny that it embodies.

Basic to Boland's poetry, even before she engages the problems of nationality and sexual identity, is this principle of self-scrutiny. The poetics that "Lace" offers present an alternative to the deceptive ease of the traditional lyric, as Boland builds a viable poetic music from her apparently blocked creativity and touches, with a very critical self-consciousness, the language that is lace.

Kevin McNeilly

THE LADY IN KICKING HORSE RESERVOIR

Author: Richard Hugo (1923-1982)
Type of poem: Lyric
First published: 1973, in *The Lady in Kicking Horse Reservoir*

The Poem

"The Lady in Kicking Horse Reservoir" refers to an actual site about thirty-five miles north of Missoula, where Richard Hugo taught at the University of Montana for the last eighteen years of his life. The poem, however, is not based on an actual drowning.

The fifty-six lines of the poem are divided into seven eight-line stanzas. The first-person speaker begins with a startlingly blunt line, mostly in monosyllables, in which he asserts that his hands, which once moved across the woman's body as the hands of a lover, have been replaced by the green algae and grasses of the lake. Instead of his ten fingers toying with her hair, ten bass "tease" it, as if they were macabre hair stylists. The poem is not a lament for his lost love, for the speaker says that he hopes to find her in the spring still tangled in the lily pads, stars reflected from her teeth.

In the second stanza, the speaker gloats in observing that while most lakes are dim a few feet down, this one is dark from the mountain range around it. He associates the woman's death with the songs of dying Indians, and he suggests that when her hands wave in the wind, they wave to the ocean, which he associates with their lost romance. In the following stanza he expands on the seashore, where they made love and where whales "fall in love with gulls." The "Dolly skeletons" of line 18 refer to Dolly Varden trout, whose watery death parallels the imagined death of the "lady" in the title. The music of the dying Indians now fades away as the "lover" bloats.

The fourth stanza begins with the terse understatement "All girls should be nicer." Instead of "windy gems," the "Indian rain" falls like arrows, and the speaker is haunted by dreams of regret and defeat; the arrows of rain sing, telling him there is no way to bring her back. In the next stanza, the speaker is reminded of a boyhood experience in which one boy was slapped and humiliated by another. The speaker in this nightmare episode recalls having tried to rescue him from the company pond. (In an interview, Hugo identified himself with both the slapped boy and the would-be rescuer who awakens to the "cold music" of failure and regret.)

In the fifth stanza, the speaker reflects on other failures: the factory that closed because "No one liked our product," the bison that multiply so fast they must be thinned out. The "hope" that he expressed so explicitly and grimly in the first stanza is now "vague," and he goes so far as to speculate that the woman's bones may be "nourished by the snow."

As the reservoir fills up with the spring run-off, the speaker imagines the woman spilling out "into weather," and he salutes her now as a "lover," not with the sarcasm of the third stanza, but in a literal sense. She has become a part of the lamented past. She is also a "mother," but in a perverse way: She will join in the irrigation of crops that "dead Indians forgot to plant." In releasing her and simultaneously associating her with unplanted crops and "dead Indians" (as opposed to the "dying Indians" of the second stanza), the speaker removes the "lady" from his obsessive anger.

The end of the poem finds the speaker "sailing west" with the arrows of rain, which now dissolve in the ocean, the site of their past romance. The "Dollys," which he envisioned in the third stanza as skeletons, are now seen as erotically "teasing oil from whales" with their tongues.

Forms and Devices

Although the free-verse line that Hugo employs in this poem varies from seven to twelve syllables, thirty-four of the fifty-six lines are within the range of blank verse (unrhymed iambic pentameter, the staple of William Shakespeare and John Milton), and it might be said that Hugo flirts with that form throughout. The first line, for example, is almost "pure" iambic pentameter, as are the last two lines of the third stanza and five lines of the sixth. Allowing for substitute and inverted feet, iambic pentameter lines occur frequently in the poem. In addition to the musical effects of this recurring but unpredictable metric regularity, Hugo often uses such sound devices as the assonantal (vowel) cluster in line 9, "lilly," "still," and "spillway," and the long *i* sounds of lines 3 and 4, "slime," "pile," and "ice." As is usually the case, such sound play creates music and adds emphasis to the statement.

What is most striking, however, is the image and metaphoric structure of the poem. A number of images and metaphors from the first three stanzas reappear, often with altered meaning or impact, in the last stanza. The recurrence involves the interplay between the landlocked reservoir and the ocean; the arrows of rain, which are connected with the defeated and dying Indians; and fish (bass, Dolly Varden, and whales—their actual status as mammals notwithstanding).

Certain key words also recur throughout the poem, and they are of special interest when they reappear near the conclusion: for example, "hope," "spillway," "lover," "foam," and "teasing." The "thundering foam" of the third stanza becomes the "dissolving foam" at the end of the poem. The ten bass that teased the woman's hair in the first stanza are transformed into the powerfully erotic metaphor of "naked Dollys" that tease oil from whales (perhaps one thinks of sperm whales here) with their tongues.

Themes and Meanings

Richard Hugo is often labeled a "regional poet," and there are strong regional elements in "The Lady in Kicking Horse Reservoir." The poem is specifically located in the Mission Range of the Rocky Mountains, and readers outside the Pacific Northwest might have difficulty with such references as those to the Dolly Varden trout, a predatory species known in the West as a bull trout. Donna Gerstenberger, in *Richard Hugo* (1983), observes that the Indians in Hugo's poems become "symbols for the dispossessed and the despairing." Hugo identifies himself with such symbols throughout his poems.

Hugo has described "The Lady in Kicking Horse Reservoir" as a "revenge poem," written from his pain and anger over a woman who jilted him and married another man. In the course of the poem, however, he exorcises the demon that has possessed him and filled him with self-destructive feelings of guilt and failure. Accordingly, the poem may be said to begin in psychological illness and end in a direction tending toward health. The dominant images of death yield to an almost comical metaphor of renewed sexual vigor.

Hugo spells out the autobiographical context of this poem in an essay from *The Triggering Town* (1979) entitled "In Defense of Creative Writing Classes." Yet it is more than a confessional cleansing ritual. Its richness has to do with the varied images and metaphors and with what might be called mythic and archetypal motifs of renewal and the return of fertility after the sterile death of winter. The ritualized symbolic death of the "lady" is similar in nature to that of the Fisher King encountered in T. S. Eliot's *The Waste Land* (1922). In that poem, Eliot draws on the ancient sacrifice of the Fisher King to assure the restoration of the land. Eliot closes his poem with apocalyptic references to a culture that disintegrates as the Fisher King, an "arid plain" at his back, shores up "fragments" against his "ruins." In the conclusion to this poem, however, Hugo associates himself with the forces of revival and renewal.

Ronald E. McFarland

LADY LAZARUS

Author: Sylvia Plath (1932-1963)
Type of poem: Lyric
First published: 1965, in *Ariel*

The Poem

"Lady Lazarus" is an extraordinarily bitter dramatic monologue in twenty-eight tercets. The title ironically identifies a sort of human oxymoron, a female Lazarus — not the biblical male. Moreover, she does not conform to society's traditional idea of ladylike behavior: She is angry, and she wants revenge. She is egocentric, using "I" twenty-two times, "my" nine. Her resurrection is owing only to herself. This is someone much different from the grateful man of John 11:2 who owes his life to Jesus.

Given Sylvia Plath's suicide, one might equate this Lazarus with Plath. Self-destruction pervades the poem as it did her life, but she has inventively appropriated Lazarus in constructing a mythical female counterpart that is not simply equatable with herself. This common tactic of distancing autobiography tempers one's proclivity to see the poem as confessional. As confession mutates to myth, subjectivity inclines to generalized feeling.

Lady Lazarus resurrects herself habitually. Like the cat, she allows herself nine lives, including equally their creation and cancellation. The first line may stress her power over her fate, but "manage" (line 3) suggests an uneasy control. It also connotes managerial enterprise, an implication clarified when the speaker's language takes on the flavor of the carnival.

The first eight stanzas largely vivify this ugly but compelling experience. The reader sees the worm-eaten epidermis and inhales the sour breath. More cadaver than person, Lady Lazarus intends terror, however problematic her bravado. Nevertheless, she will soon smile, when time restores flesh eaten by the grave. (The smile will not prove attractive.) For the moment, however, she is only a "walking miracle" of defective parts: a shell of glowing skin, a face blank as linen, a paralyzed foot. Almost spectral, she remains finely, grotesquely palpable.

Stanzas 9 to 19 present Lady Lazarus as sideshow freak, stripper, and barker. Her emergence from the winding-sheet (perhaps a straitjacket) is a "striptease." The "peanut-crunching crowd" thrills, pruriently. She alters the introductory "Ladies and gentlemen," but her phrasing retains the master of ceremonies' idiom. Reference to her "theatrical/ comeback in broad day" plays poetically with the jargon of show business and magic.

In presenting the history of her efforts to die, Lady Lazarus assures the reader of her honor. This integrity gives continuity, making her the same woman at thirty that she was at ten. It is nothing against her that her first attempt at annihilation was accidental; it was premonitory. Eventually, intention ruled — both descent and resurrection. In the eighteenth stanza, she says that each "comeback" is, however, to the "same place" and the "same brute/ Amused shout." The prosody allows "brute" to be a noun (hence, person) in the line, an adjective in the sentence. As it is the "same brute" each time, beginning with her tenth year, and as she finally intends the destruction of "men," this brute is always the father or his replica. This explains why Plath renders the customary "Ladies and Gentlemen" as "Gentleman, ladies."

Stanzas 19 through 26 clarify Lady Lazarus' victimization at the hands of "Herr Enemy" and "Herr Doktor," who are one and the same and merely the latest incarnation of the "brute" father. The German spelling of doctor and the choice of *Herr* create the stereotype of Germanic male authority. Lady Lazarus is this creature's "baby," more particularly his "opus." Thus, this menacing figure reminiscent of Josef Mengele, of the Nazi concentration camp at Auschwitz, fathers her "art" of dying. She sarcastically repudiates his inauthentic "concern" for her but allows him his role in her fiery death and resurrection. Because she was "pure gold," he expected profit from her. He pokes among her ashes for valuable residue, but she has reduced herself to "nothing" but a "shriek." Spiritually, however, she is a virtual reliquary, which turns the tables; "Herr Enemy" will pay, and dearly, for her victimized body and consciousness. There will be a "very large charge" for "eyeing [her] scars," for discovering that her heart "really goes," even for a "bit of blood" or a "word."

Having taken up the battle with the enemy on his terms, she concludes by warning the male deity and demon that when she rises from the ashes, she consumes men as fire does oxygen.

Forms and Devices

"Lady Lazarus" plays distinctively on the ear. It blends staccato, irregular versification with a dense mixture of highly patterned sounds. End and internal rhymes, both exact and slant, are rapidly mixed and steadily joined to consonance, assonance, alliteration, and sheer repetition. At the outset, Plath makes end rhymes of "again," "ten," "skin," "fine," "linen," and "napkin" before the eleventh line. She dares, in one line, "grave cave ate" and, in another, "million filaments." The "brute" that ends line 53 is followed at once by the only slightly dissimilar "amused." Plath's prosody ingeniously restrains the metronome while rendering sound almost childlike.

The nazification of the speaker's antagonist is a perhaps hyperbolic but crucial feature of the poem. Plath once said to George Macbeth, "I see you have a concentration camp in your mind too." For Lady Lazarus, the model of her victimization is the modern slaughter of the Jews. The "Nazi lampshade" refers to the commandant's practice at Buchwald of flaying inmates and stretching the skin, often tattooed, over a lampshade frame. The most notorious of the Nazi gas chambers and crematories were housed at Auschwitz, where blankets were made of human hair and soap from human fat. Those who emptied the ovens poked in the ashes for hidden gold wedding bands and for gold fillings missed by camp "dentists." It was at Auschwitz that the infamous and sadistically curious Doktor Mengele listened to the camp symphony, oversaw experiments on humans, and quizzically dropped in at the ovens. Hence the primal "brute" becomes "Herr Doktor" and "Herr Enemy." "Herr God" and "Herr Lucifer," two sides of the same coin, are but extensions of the Nazi male stereotype.

To this frame of reference, Plath adds an amusing filmic touch, after the fashion of the "vampire" and the "villagers" in her poem "Daddy." "So, so, Herr Doktor./ So, Herr Enemy" parodies the stereotypical speech of Nazi officers interrogating prisoners in American war films of the 1940's. That the words are Lady Lazarus' indicates that she is exorcising the victim within her and preparing to adopt her enemy's tactics against him. She had, of course, told her nemesis to "Peel off the napkin" of her "featureless face," the manifestation of her passivity, represented as a "Jew linen."

Themes and Meanings

People who return from the edge of death often speak of it as rebirth. "Lady Lazarus" effectively conveys that feeling. It is principally, however, about the aspiration to revenge that is felt by the female victim of male domination, conceived as ubiquitous. The revenge would be against all men, though the many are rendered as singular in the poem. The text forces the reader to take the father as prototype, which drives one to read it in terms of the Electra complex. Why, one asks, is the speaker malevolent toward the father rather than amorously yearning? What has he done to inspire the hatred which has displaced love?

The poem is mythic. It leaves the father's, the male's, basic offense at the general level of brutal domination. One might rest there, taking control and exploitation as the male's by nature, practiced universally and with special vigor toward spouses and daughters. The idea will come short of universal acceptance, but the text does not disallow it.

If one looks at the "Enemy" as modeled on Plath's own father, one finds something else, though certainly no Fascist. Otto Plath's blameless offense was his death in Sylvia's childhood, which seems to have left her feeling both guiltily responsible and angry, a common reaction. One normally expects the adult child to overcome this confusion by reasonably understanding it. This poem is not about that experience; it is about the wish, however futile, to turn the tables on the father and his kind. Its dramatic overstatement of male evil may be, for one reader, an offense against fairness. For another, it may not even pertain to that problem, but only represent the extremity of long-borne suffering.

Whether the poem depicts the onset of successful revenge is problematic. Lady Lazarus has surely arrived at the point of reversing roles with her antagonist. She understands and intends to exploit his means of violent mastery, and at the last, the prefatory myth of the halting Lazarus is altered to the myth of the ascendant phoenix, the bird which immolates itself every five hundred years but rises whole and rejuvenated from its ashes. Lady Lazarus' "red hair" suggests fire, which lives (easily) off oxygen. "I eat men like air," therefore, seems the foreshadowing of victory, in the restoration of the true self and the annihilation of its detractor(s).

For a person, however, the "eating" of air is not nourishing; also, Lady Lazarus confronts men in every quarter of the universe, and her battle plan is of their design. She is even nominally male herself. Whether the phoenix is male or female is even uncertain, though Plath preferred to think it female. Perhaps the poem ultimately envisions the tension created in the victim by the wish for revenge and the fear of its frustration.

David M. Heaton

THE LADY OF SHALOTT

Author: Alfred, Lord Tennyson (1809-1892)
Type of poem: Lyric
First published: 1832, in *Poems*; revised and collected in *Poems*, 1842

The Poem

"The Lady of Shalott," in both its original form of 1832 and in the revision of 1842, is divided into four separate narrative sections, each containing from four to six stanzas of nine lines each. The meter is predominately iambic tetrameter with an insistent and unusual rhyme structure involving double couplets and a triplet in each refrain. Alfred, Lord Tennyson took the poem's title and a few of its incidents from an anonymous medieval Italian novella variously identified as *Donna di Scalotta* or *Novella LXXXI* in the *Cento Novelle Antiche* (c. 1321). As is usual with Tennyson, this source is so altered in his retelling as to be largely unimportant for interpretation. What Tennyson retains from his source is simply a story of a lady's desperate love for the greatest of Arthurian knights, Lancelot, a love which ends in the lady's death.

The poem opens with a description of a riparian landscape: a river flowing between fields of grain down to Camelot and the sea; within this river, an island; within this island, a castle; and within the castle, the Lady of Shalott. There are enclosures within enclosures. About the island, ships sail and barges drift, but the Lady of Shalott remains unseen within the walls. Only her voice is sometimes heard by reapers at dawn; listening to her strange song, they refer to the mysterious lady as a "fairy."

This lady, the reader learns, weaves a tapestry of all the sights of the outside world that are reflected before her in a mirror hanging upon her wall. She will not look out at the world itself, only at its "shadows," for she has received a mysterious warning that if she looks to the city of Camelot, she will fall victim to a curse. The curse comes. Great Lancelot eventually rides by the window, and his splendid image in her mirror tempts the lady to look upon the man himself. As she does so, the tapestry rends, and the mirror shatters. Despairingly, in the midst of a blowing storm, the lady boards a small boat and drifts toward Camelot and death singing a final dirge. When the boat comes to Camelot bearing her silent corpse, all but Lancelot are terrified at this strange apparition. Lancelot, for whom she died loving, simply observes (almost flatly observes), "She has a lovely face/ God in his mercy lend her grace."

The narrative has the simplicity of a fairy tale, and, as in a fairy tale, causes and motivations are mysterious and obscure. The origin of the curse is never explained, and the lady has learned of it only by a strangely disembodied "whisper." Again, as in fairy tales, the transparency of the narrative surface hints at greater depths. The lady confesses after seeing a pair of lovers reflected in her mirror that she is "half sick of shadows," but her vision of the lovers is preceded by a vision of a funeral — significantly, for one later recognizes that her sickness among shadows ends finally with her death among realities. "The Lady of Shalott" remains one of Tennyson's most evocative and disturbing poems.

Forms and Devices

The most striking formal aspect of this poem is its remarkably vivid images. "The Lady of Shalott" was a favorite with Victorian painters and illustrators, who understandably delighted in picturing the crisis of the curse with its sprung tapestry and cracking mirror. Those images, and that of the lady's funeral barge at the poem's close, have been admired by many modern critics as early examples of poetic symbolism. While the magic mirror and tapestry belong to the machinery of legend and fairy tale, they seem more than props in Tennyson's hands. The lady's mirror, for example, reflects not only the outside world but also the condition of the lady herself as an outsider. Both the lady and the mirror capture images within frames, the mirror in its glass, the lady in her tapestry. This identification is pushed even further at the poem's close when the lady is described as having a "glassy countenance" as she gazes toward Camelot. Having preferred realities to shadows, having rejected the mirror's vision for her own, she becomes a mirror herself; her countenace now mirrors her coming death.

Tennyson's careful insistence on referring to the tapestry as a "web" suggests the idea of entanglement that is certainly part of the lady's condition. The insect connotations of "web" are also admissible, for this web is very much made from the lady's own substance: When it is disturbed, she dies. The careful texturing of these images reinforces, deepens, and extends their more conventional associations. The island's isolation and the temporal significance of the river current also gain by their participation in a symbolic pattern of such complexity. It is the combination of suggestive images with a relatively discontinuous, seemingly naïve narrative that lends this poem its disquieting power. The poem anticipates the modern understanding of dreams as symbol systems suspended in masking narratives. As in dreams, the narrative line is deceptively simple; the deeper significance is encoded in symbol. Since the poem is essentially about the power of dream and symbol, of image over life, its symbolic images embody the poem's theme rather than express it, which is very nearly the essence of modern poetic symbolism.

The collective effect of the symbol system in "The Lady of Shalott" is a powerful sense of narcissistic introversion. The Lady's attempt to break out of her insularity fails because she is incapable of escaping her enslavement to images. The image of Lancelot himself had been cast into her mirror from the river surface and is nothing more than another re-presentation of the reality she cannot reach. Trapped in the immobility of her island world of images, cut off from the world of transition and change—of life, love, and death—the lady rebels against her condition by casting herself adrift into the temporal tyranny of the river current. It pulls her into the world of living men and women, but she dies in transit, singing her own death song in a funeral barge emblazoned with her own name; her isolation is never broken.

The rhyme scheme of the poem is also a means for reinforcing the sense of inescapable isolation, for it is one of the most repetitive and insistent rhyme schemes to be found in serious English poetry. The sequence *aaaabcccb* is repeated throughout the poem, and all but one stanza end with the lady's name as the final rhyme. The obsessive repetition of the name drives home her own repetitive obsessions. Images and metrical organization work together to create claustrophobia, a terrified sense of compulsive ritual that is wearying and inescapable.

Themes and Meanings

"The Lady of Shalott" has most often been read as an allegory of the artist's condition in a society indifferent or even hostile to art. The Victorian age was not, by and large, especially sympathetic to art and artists. Many Victorians believed that poetry had had its day and could offer little of use in an age of serious scientific, industrial, and social effort. Put plainly, many Victorians believed that poetry "did" nothing, that it was merely idleness and frippery. Others, perhaps no more sympathetic to the real requirements of the artist, suggested that poetry could justify itself if it celebrated the serious social achievements of the modern age — if, in other words, it put itself to work providing moral edification for the reading masses. Certainly, many of Tennyson's contemporaries took him to task for writing poems remote in their imaginative wonders from the mundane struggles and triumphs of the passing hour. Tennyson had a strong tendency to idealize the isolated, self-absorbed artist rapt in his visions of unearthly beauty, and this "art for art's sake" doctrine came in for strong criticism from well-meaning Victorian critics. "The Lady of Shalott" is, in one dimension, Tennyson's allegorical rejoinder to those utilitarian critics.

In the allegorical scheme, Camelot represents the world of commerce, politics, social responsibility, and daily life. Lancelot himself represents the temptations of worldly fame and power to which the artistic temperament succumbs at its peril. The mirror and the web represent the arts, and the lady the artist. This schematizing is reductive but not inaccurate, for the poem is at some level almost certainly a dramatization of the artist's desperate condition in a world of commercial energies, democratic sentiment, and mass standardization. The artist, like the lady, is strong only in a world of images, and the price of this strength is isolation. Like the lady, the artist's connection to the busy world of real life can only be tangential; his or her songs are at most overheard in the bustle of politics and business. In an age making insistent demands on the strenuous efforts of individuals in cooperation with social ventures, the artist may inevitably feel misgivings about his self-absorption and isolation, but the artistic temperament also knows that no reconciliation with such a world is possible except at the cost of artistic integrity. Lancelot is desired at the cost of imaginative power.

If this is Tennyson's allegorical view of the artist's position, it is a view far removed from the strong poetic faith of his Romantic predecessors such as Percy Bysshe Shelley and William Wordsworth. The great Romantic poets had believed in the transforming power of poetry. They believed that it was strong enough to act upon the real world and that the poet was a person of might—not so Tennyson, at least in "The Lady of Shalott." If the lady is Tennyson's allegorized poet, then his poet is hiding out and is imperiled in a world of intractable fact. The lady is no match for the commercial power of Camelot; by comparison, her mirror is fragile and her web tenuous, and she turns from them only to be destroyed.

Whitney Hoth

THE LAKE ISLE OF INNISFREE

Author: William Butler Yeats (1865-1939)
Type of poem: Lyric
First published: 1890; collected in *The Countess Kathleen and Various Legends and Lyrics*, 1892

The Poem

"The Lake Isle of Innisfree," a twelve-line poem divided into three quatrains, is a study in contrasts. The most obvious contrast is between two places: one rural (identified in the title and described throughout much of the poem), the other (alluded to only in the second-to-last line) — by implication — urban.

Innisfree is a small island at the eastern end of Lough Gill in County Sligo, Ireland. William Butler Yeats spent part of nearly every year in Sligo while growing up; he often walked out from Sligo town to Lough Gill. His father having read to him from Henry David Thoreau's *Walden* (1854), he daydreamed (as he says in *The Trembling of the Veil*, 1922, incorporated into his *Autobiography*, 1965) of living "a life of lonely austerity . . . in imitation of Thoreau on Innisfree." In 1890, while living in London, he was "walking through Fleet Street very homesick [when] I heard a little tinkle of water and saw a fountain in a shop-window . . . and began to remember lake water. From the sudden remembrance came my poem *Innisfree*."

Yeats imagines escaping from the city to the solitude and peace of a pastoral retreat, there to live a simple life, close to nature. The first stanza states his intention and provides a prospectus for the home he will make for himself, specifying the rustic construction for his cabin and exactly how many rows of beans he will plant. The second stanza, more fancifully imagining what living there will be like, pauses over images that he associates with four different times of day: morning, midnight, noon, and evening. The third stanza reiterates his intention and for the first time suggests what motivates it: the (implied) urban setting and Yeats's nostalgia for Sligo.

The contrast between the matter-of-fact first and last stanzas and the fanciful middle stanza reinforces the contrast between the quotidian city, with its "grey" pavements, and the idealized country. The opening stanza employs no figurative language; the only figurative language in the closing stanza is the sound of waves "lapping" in "the deep heart's core." Otherwise, the language in these stanzas is straightforward and literal, emotionally neutral.

The second stanza, on the other hand, is brimming with metaphors and other figures: "peace comes dropping slow," as if it were dew; the morning wears "veils"; the cricket "sings"; the "evening [is] full of the linnet's wings." Language, imagination, and emotion all rise to a rapturous brief climax in this middle stanza before subsiding. The opening words of stanza 3, echoing the opening words of the poem, cue a return to the everyday world.

Forms and Devices

The poem's rhyme scheme is regular; all of its rhymes are exact. In each stanza, the first three lines are in hexameter, the last line in tetrameter. In these respects, the poem is perfectly regular. Its meter is iambic, though only the last line of the poem precisely conforms to the iambic pattern. In each of the other eleven lines, Yeats introduces an extra unstressed syllable just after the midpoint, and the extra syllable is in each case a one-syllable word: "now" in line 1; "there" in lines 2, 3, and 5; and so forth. Virtually all of these words could be deleted without altering the meaning of the poem. Their purpose, clearly, is to contribute not to the poem's meaning but to its sound and its tempo.

Yeats called "The Lake Isle of Innisfree" "my first lyric with anything in its rhythm of my own music. I had begun to loosen rhythm as an escape from rhetoric." The added syllables in lines 1 through 11 contribute to this loosening of rhythm (Line 3 adds still another syllable; line 6 adds two more syllables.); so, too, does Yeats's occasional relaxation of and variation from the basic iambic pattern. The loosening of rhythm prevented the poem's meter from being too mechanical. Absolutely regular cadence produces a monotonous, singsong effect (an aspect of what Yeats called "rhetoric"); and Yeats's "own music" was not timed by a metronome.

If "The Lake Isle of Innisfree" has something of Yeats's "own music" in it, it is not—he later realized—fully in his own voice. When he wrote the poem, he was young, and, as he recalled, "I only understood vaguely and occasionally that I must for my special purpose use nothing but the common syntax. A couple of years later I would not have written that first line with its conventional archaism— 'Arise and go'—nor the inversion of the last stanza."

"Arise and go" (in line 9 as well as line 1) echoes the parable of the homesick Prodigal Son: "I will arise and go to my father" (Luke 15:18). Alexander Norman Jeffares points out that line 9 also echoes Mark 5:5: "And always, night and day, he was in the mountains" (*A Commentary on the Collected Poems of W. B. Yeats*, 1968). Such scriptural sonorities, added to the Thoreauvian quality of the first stanza's humble images and the self-consciously "poetic" diction of the second stanza ("the veils of the morning" for fog and dew; "all a glimmer"), render the poem more literary, more "conventional" than a more mature Yeats would prefer.

Themes and Meanings

"The Lake Isle of Innisfree" expresses a set of desires familiar in the modern world: to escape, to achieve peace and solitude, to be at one with nature. Yeats says almost nothing in the poem about what he would like to escape from, but his reader can easily imagine the stressful conditions of modern, especially urban, life. Such desires have been common themes in Romantic literature since the beginning of the nineteenth century, and "Innisfree" is a good example of late nineteenth century Romanticism.

Many of Yeats's early (pre-1900) poems express the feeling that, in William Wordsworth's phrase, "the world is too much with us." Poem after early poem articulates a longing for peace, for escape. The refrain in "The Stolen Child" (1886) is a seductive call to "Come away" from the world (seen as "full of weeping") "To the waters and the wild." "To an Isle in the Water" (1889) differs from "Innisfree" by expressing a wish to go away not alone but accompanied by the "Shy one of my heart." Otherwise, the poem seems to be a study, a preliminary sketch for "The Lake Isle of Innisfree."

While "The Lake Isle of Innisfree" is an early poem, it is in some respects transitional, pointing toward Yeats's mature work. As its loosened rhythms contain something of his "own music," so its images and vocabulary reveal something of his own emerging language. Again, a contrast may be drawn between the middle stanza and those that enclose it.

The middle stanza is vague, not fully in focus. What, after all, do "midnight's all a glimmer" or "noon a purple glow" mean, exactly? One might guess that the glimmering is moonlight reflected on the lake, but it would be only a guess; and who can even hazard a guess about what glows purple at noontime? One cannot be sure whether "evening full of the linnet's wings" is meant to appeal to the mind's eye or ear. Yeats would eschew such imprecise images in his mature poetry. Similarly, "glimmer" is representative of Yeats's late Victorian diction, rife with such murmurous words which, after the turn of the century, all but disappeared from his working vocabulary.

Yeats never went to Innisfree, built a cabin, or laid out bean-rows. Instead of finding a refuge on an uninhabited island, he helped found and manage the Irish National Theatre; became the central, essential figure in the Irish Literary Revival; became a prolific playwright; became, indeed, a very "public man," an Irish senator and Nobel laureate. Although "The Lake Isle of Innisfree," with its escapist wish, offers no hint of these future developments, in form and technique it contains the seeds of his future poetry. He was to transform himself from a late Victorian dreamy Romantic into the dominant poet of the twentieth century, and the transitional "Innisfree" offers a preview of that transformation.

Richard Bizot

LAMENT FOR IGNACIO SÁNCHEZ MEJÍAS

Author: Federico García Lorca (1898-1936)
Type of poem: Elegy
First published: 1935, as *Llanto por Ignacio Sánchez Mejías*; collected in *Lament for the Death of a Bullfighter and Other Poems*, 1937

The Poem

Lament for Ignacio Sánchez Mejías is a long elegy divided into four parts corresponding to four dramatic movements. It was written to commemorate and celebrate the death of a man who many considered the bravest and most gallant matador of Spain. Ignacio Sánchez Mejías was also Federico García Lorca's great friend. In this poem, there is complete identification between poet and speaker.

The first part of the poem, "The Goring and the Death," starts at the very hour of the tragedy — "at five in the afternoon" — and proceeds to dwell on all the horrific details of the bull ring. A child brings a white sheet; lime is spread to soak up the blood; we can see and smell the chemicals of death, the chloride and the iodine. Surprisingly, what is missing is the fallen hero himself. It is as if the speaker cannot bring himself to look at his friend, lying bleeding in the sand, and instead must concentrate on what surrounds his body. The cadence is like that of a muted, tolling bell as after every stark image, the litany-like response "at five in the afternoon" is repeated.

The scene then shifts to Ignacio's deathbed, where the killer bull, "El Granadino," has become a bellowing nightmare that roars in triumph in the bullfighter's ears in his delirium. The clinical facts of a terrible death by gangrene poisoning are expressed poetically, but the agony cannot be hidden by beautiful words. Sensing that, again, after every image, the speaker drums into the listener the hour of the incident, until, finally, the poetic voice rises in protest at the significance of these "terrible fives."

The same fever pitch continues into the second section, "The Spilt Blood." The speaker shouts that he does not want to see Ignacio's blood in the sand and that no one can force him to gaze on it. (In this context, it is interesting to note that García Lorca did not witness the accident and later could not bring himself to visit his dying friend, even though their mutual acquaintances pleaded with him to go.) In the poem, the speaker wants night to come and, with it, the whiteness of the moon to hide the evidence of the truth from him. He tries to calm himself by invoking images of the living bullfighter who had always "walked with death on his shoulders," and he lauds his friend's courage, grace, wit, and intelligence.

Nevertheless, that is still not the real Ignacio, the man of flesh and blood who dies. The speaker is still trying to mask reality. In a further distancing technique — a further separation from the real, raw tragedy — Ignacio is now made the subject of medieval balladry. This entire section is written in the traditional Spanish ballad line, the romance. In addition, in another medieval echo, the poet imitates the famous cadences of another great Spanish elegy, Jorge Manrique's *Coplas por la muerte de su padre* (1492, Verses on the Death of his Father). García Lorca, however, does not have the philosophical or religious consolation of the medieval poet. Therefore, in the concluding lines of this section, the intensity of voice rises again as the speaker insists that nothing, no symbol nor image, "nor song nor flood of white lilies," can contain or justify that spilled blood.

In the third section, "The Body is Present," the verse line is lengthened as the speaker meditates on the finality and mystery of death. The stone on which the bullfighter lies is the symbol of the implacable laws of the universe, immutable for all living things: "Stone is a shoulder to carry time, with trees of tears and ribbons and planets." There is no life nor movement here, only the silence of this stone. The speaker, in protest, asks the strongest, those "men of hard voice," to stand in front of this stone, in front of this corpse and help him to discover another life for his friend and, in extension, for all humankind, but there is no hope. He then asks them to teach him a funereal song that may express adequately this horrible truth. Contrasted to the resignation of the final lines of this section, however, there still remains the lingering defiance of a friend who does not want Ignacio to accustom himself "to the death that he carries."

In the last section, "The Soul is Absent," the speaker talks quietly to the dead man. The "you" of his address is juxtaposed to the final "I" of the closing verses as the speaker insists that he is the only one who can, or wants to, remember the bullfighter. All other things and people of this world must forget, but the memory of Ignacio lives on because this poet can sing of his life and death.

Forms and Devices

The poetry of García Lorca is difficult to translate because of the complex associations of his verses, which are an amalgam of surrealistic images, personal trademark symbols, and traditional Spanish poetic and thematic echoes. His genius lies in the ability to fuse these disparate elements into one fluid, musical whole. *Lament for Ignacio Sánchez Mejías* is a master example of this poetical transmutation.

García Lorca was also a great playwright, and this poem can be described as a verse drama in four acts. Images and allusions are utilized as props or metaphoric icons which link the action and lead the listener/spectator to the artistic denouement. Two of these devices are color and the recurring image of the animal protagonist of the *corrida*, the bull.

Lament for Ignacio Sánchez Mejías starts *in medias res*. The reader is not actually present at the fatal goring; only its consequences are seen as if in a blurred black-and-white film. All color is stripped away as, one by one, dreamlike white objects appear and then fade away into others. The white of a sheet covering the body dissolves into that of lime, cotton wool becomes "arsenic bells," and the "sweat of snow," white eggs. These surrealistic images contrast sharply with the jarring simplicity of the refrain, just as white objects stand in contrast to the steady flowing of the red blood which the speaker cannot yet look upon or even bear to mention. Yet both he and the listener/spectator know it is there. In this first section, the animal that physically causes Ignacio's death announces the coming of this death. Agent becomes symbol.

In the second section, so resonant with traditional Spanish echoes, the roaring bull becomes plural and is transformed into the ancient stone bulls of Guisando, archetypal symbols of Spanish endurance and pride, and mute evidence of man's impermanence on earth. These figures, "almost death and almost stone," in their turn are metamorphosed into "the bulls of heaven." Celestial forces, they represent the fatality which seemed to surround Sánchez Mejías; they are the "black bulls of sorrow."

This black overcomes the white images of consolation which try to palliate the reality of death, but "no white frost of the light," that is, reason, can hide the blood which now "comes singing," forcing itself into the poet's sight. The speaker had asked the moon to hide with its white light the blood of his friend. The moon, as a symbol of death, is one of the definitive images of García Lorca's poetry. Here, its coldness cannot quench the fever of memory.

The dominant color of the third section is gray; the reds and whites mist away into "pale sulfurs" and "rain showers." Even noise and movement seem to harden into the cold gray stone on which Ignacio lies and which gives "no sound, nor crystal, nor fire." The speaker hopes without hope that his friend's spirit can break free of the physical death which fetters him. The bulls become part of the earthly impedimenta which weigh down on him, preventing his escape. (The living Sánchez Mejías could not resist this siren song; he had to return to the ring one more time.) "The Soul is Absent" has no colors, no bulls, no stone, nor indeed anything for Ignacio. These symbols are only for the living.

Themes and Meanings

The physical setting of *Lament for Ignacio Sánchez Mejías* is quintessentially Spanish: An Andalusian bullfighter, singled out by fate, dies defiantly in the ring. Its philosophical setting is a meditation on life and death. Two men, in the poem, must face this ordeal. Ignacio dies, but it is his friend who must deal with the implications of this tragedy. This personal poem symbolizes the universal dilemma of all human existence, what Miguel de Unamuno y Jugo called "the tragic sense of life." Human beings desire the eternal but are confronted with the seeming finality of death, which must come at a specific time and place. This sense of an implacable fatality is overwhelming in the first part as the reader is continuously reminded that Ignacio's death struggle must begin at a specific, inevitable moment (García Lorca was convinced that Sánchez Mejías had to die: "Ignacio . . . did everything he could to escape from his death, but everything he did only helped to tighten the strings of the net").

Much has been made of the ancient Spanish "culture of death," the idealization of those who deliberately place themselves in the greatest danger; much has been made also of García Lorca's identification with, and admiration of, this concept, in which (paradoxically) the continual defiance of death can be seen as an affirmation of life. It is appropriate to remember that García Lorca, criticizing those who wanted to abolish bullfighting, said: "I think it is the most cultured festival that exists anywhere in the world. It is the only place where one can go in safety to contemplate Death surrounded by the most dazzling beauty."

Sánchez Mejías, against the advice of all his friends, had come out of retirement because he missed the danger and excitement and was killed while performing a foolhardy maneuver in the ring. In the poem, García Lorca eulogizes Ignacio's "appetite for death and the taste of its mouth" and recalls the "sadness that was in your valiant gaiety." This sadness reflects the belief that man's existence is terminal; therefore, Ignacio's courage is all the more to be praised.

In *Coplas por la muerte de su padre*, Jorge Manrique compares the lives of men to rivers that flow into the sea, but this sea is not eternal oblivion. It signifies the passage from mortality to eternity. Fortified by his fate, Manrique's father accepts death with a Christian resignation. In García Lorca's poem, however, the poet keeps repeating, "Now it is all over," and in a direct rejection of the optimistic message of the earlier work, he cries out, "Go, Ignacio . . . Sleep, fly away, rest. Even the sea dies."

Nevertheless, in one important sentiment, the final message of both poems, so far apart in time and philosophy, seems to coincide. Manrique, although he stresses that all mortal things are transitory and worthless, still clings to the hope that his father will be remembered; Valiant deeds and a good life can endure, and his son's elegy will reinforce that memory. García Lorca, too, sings so that his brave friend will live on in his words, but there is one significant difference: García Lorca believed that poets were mediums, bridges between different worlds; consequently, only through a poet could the dead make themselves known authentically to the living. Together, poet and friend can overcome the oblivion of death.

This interlocking of destinies has provided a poignant, historical background to the reading and interpretation of this poem. García Lorca identified strongly with the death of his friend; "Ignacio's death is like mine, the trial run for me," he stated. It frightened him that the animal that killed the bullfighter was called "El Granadino" (the one from Granada), an epithet that was applied to García Lorca himself. *Lament for Ignacio Sánchez Mejías* has been interpreted as a premonition of its author's own death; García Lorca was murdered in 1936 by Nationalists in the Spanish Civil War. García Lorca's life and death have been inextricably woven into the metaphoric richness of this work.

Charlene E. Suscavage

LAMIA

Author: John Keats (1795-1821)
Type of poem: Narrative
First published: 1820, in *Lamia, Isabella, The Eve of St. Agnes, and Other Poems*

The Poem

Lamia is a narrative of 708 lines of rhymed couplets, divided into two parts of approximately equal length. The major source is a brief passage in Robert Burton's *The Anatomy of Melancholy* (1621) describing the marriage of Menippus Lycius, a twenty-five-year-old "philosopher" of "staid and discreet" decorum, to "a phantasm in the habit of a fair gentlewoman." She is exposed at her wedding by Apollonius as "a serpent, a lamia," upon which she, her house, and all who were in it instantaneously disappear. John Keats embellishes Burton's bare narration with the story of Hermes' love for a mysterious forest maiden, irresolvable thematic complexities, and passages of ornate description.

Lamia opens with words that echo the "Once upon a time" of the fairy tale, an appropriate beginning for a narrative that features nymphs, satyrs, and gods and has as its central figure a lamia, a supernatural creature represented as a serpent with the head and breasts of a woman and reputed to feast on the blood of children. Keats transformed this traditional demoniac figure into a character of considerable sympathy. Equally original is his depiction of the traditional classical wood deities being driven away by King Oberon and his fairy throng at some indefinite time after the action of this poem takes place.

The narrative begins with the ardent Hermes surreptitiously leaving his throne on Mount Olympus to find in the forest of Crete the beautiful nymph by whom he has been smitten. Even after a thorough search, he fails to find her, because a lamia has made her invisible to shield her from the lustful satyrs. Instead, he encounters "a palpitating snake . . . of dazzling hue." The snake (the lamia) agrees to reveal the maiden's presence if Hermes will restore her to her previous woman's form. Oaths are made. At once Hermes sees the "nymph near-smiling on the green." The beautiful creature begins to fade but is restored by Hermes, and the two fly into the green woods, never to grow "pale as mortal lovers do."

The lamia undergoes a violent metamorphosis into Lamia, a virgin of supernal beauty in love with young Lycius, a student in Corinth whom she has seen on one of the many psychic trips she made "when in the serpent prison-house." As quick as thought, she is in Corinth and meets Lycius, who is musing in "the calm twilight of Platonic shades." He falls in love with her at first sight and swoons "pale with pain" when she tells him that "finer spirits cannot breathe below/ In human climes, and live," ironically presaging her own demise and stating one of the poem's possible themes. Relenting, she "threw the goddess off, and won his heart/ More pleasantly by playing woman's part." On the way to her mysterious palace, unknown to any but "a few Persian mutes," they encounter the aged Apollonius, the sage teacher and "trusty guide" of Lycius. Lamia instinctively trembles, and Lycius for the first time in his life looks upon his "good instructor" as the "ghost of folly haunting [his] sweet dreams."

After living for an indefinite period of time shut off from the world with Lamia in her "purple-lined palace of sweet sin," Lycius is moved by pride to show her to his friends. Rejecting her pleas to continue as they are, he invites many guests to their marriage feast. Apollonius appears, uninvited, and with good intentions of saving his pupil from becoming a "serpent's prey," exposes Lamia. She turns deathly pale and vanishes. Lycius in turn dies, and the poem concludes as the guests wind "the heavy body" in "its marriage robe."

Forms and Devices

Lamia was written in 1819, Keats's wondrous year that began with "The Eve of St. Agnes" and concluded with *The Fall of Hyperion* (1856). In this period of creativity unparalleled in English poetry, Keats, ever the experimenter, mastered many literary forms and effects. In *Lamia* he returned to the pentameter couplet, which he had used two years earlier for the lengthy *Endymion* (1818). In the interim, he had studied John Dryden's couplets. Dryden's influence is seen in the heightened control of language over thought that is displayed in *Lamia*. Here there is little of that impression one has when reading *Endymion* that the progression of thought is often determined by the need for a rhyme, although Keats occasionally sacrifices English word order for the expedience of a rhyme, as in "Fast by the springs where she to bathe was wont" or "Soft went the music the soft air along." In this poem Keats minimizes the monotony of the couplet form by enjambment, internal stops, and frequent Alexandrines. The poem concludes with a triplet, which gives a strong sense of finality.

Lamia is rich in rhetorical devices: alliteration ("purple-lined palace of sweet sin"), allusion ("she lifted her Circean head"), metaphor ("a moment's thought is passion's passing bell"), simile ("His mind wrapp'd like his mantle"); personification ("Love, jealous grown of so complete a pair/ Hover'd and buzz'd his wings"), and periphrasis ("star of Lethe" for Hermes, "a bright Phoebean dart" for sun ray). The most important device is imagery. As in "To Autumn," Keats appeals to every sense (including a sense of motion) to involve the reader in the experience of the poem. Especially vivid are the descriptions of Hermes in quest of the nymph, the "gordian shape of dazzling hue," and Lamia's pleasure palace. These descriptions are as colorful and rich in detail as those of "The Eve of St. Agnes." "Green" and "pale" are motifs signifying vitality and death. In the last fifty lines, auditory images become particularly important as the sounds of pleasure in Lamia's palace are replaced by a "deadly silence" that is pierced by the shrieks of Apollonius.

Themes and Meanings

The possible meanings of *Lamia* have elicited extensive critical commentary.

While it is evident that Keats did not envisage the character of Lamia as the demoniac creature of tradition, it is far from clear whether she is a femme fatale or the fragile victim of Apollonius' rationality. The character of Apollonius is equally ambiguous: Is he the cold-hearted destroyer of beauty and joy or the good teacher of high ideals? Even Lycius is problematic. To what extent is the tragic ending attributable to his desire to provoke the envy of others? Further, does he hubristically reject human limitations to aspire to that pure pleasure known only by the immortals? These questions defy definitive answers.

The central conflict in *Lamia* may be taken to be either between responsibility and wanton hedonism on the one hand or between ethereal beauty and murderous rationality on the other. The problem is that, in either case, the text can support both views. Lamia's benevolence is illustrated by her protection of the beautiful nymph from the lustful creatures of the forest—but why was she imprisoned in a serpent's body in the first place? Apollonius' positive character is established by his desire to save Lycius from wasteful self indulgence—but why does he laugh maliciously when he discovers Lamia's identity?

It is probable that Keats himself was of a divided mind regarding his characters and their actions. Recurrent themes in his poetry are the power of art to capture the essence of human passions permanently, the power of the gods to enjoy for eternity the highest of human joys that last for but a moment on this earth, and the danger to humans of mingling with the gods. These themes are especially prominent in the poems of 1819, written only two years before his death.

The most problematic passage in *Lamia* is the one in part 2 that begins, "What wreath for Lamia? What for Lycius?" Keats appears to enter into the poem in a personal way, coming down on the side of Lamia against Apollonius, asking, "Do not all charms fly/ At the mere touch of cold philosophy" and asserting that "Philosophy will clip an angel's wings." These sentiments embody the anti-intellectual bias of Romanticism, a bias seen earlier in William Wordsworth's lines "Our meddling intellect/ Misshapes the beauteous forms of things: — / We murder to dissect." Keats's denunciation of rational inquiry, which he sees as destroying the mystery of beauty, is a personal intrusion upon a narrative which to that point had been as objectively delivered as one could reasonably expect. The passage does not answer the many questions which the poem raises, but it does suggest that Keats in his heart sided with Lamia.

Robert G. Blake

LANDSCAPE WITH TWO GRAVES
AND AN ASSYRIAN DOG

Author: Federico García Lorca (1898-1936)
Type of poem: Lyric
First published: 1940, as "Paisaje con dos tumbas y un perro asirio," in *Poeta en Nueva York*; collected in *Poet in New York*, 1955

The Poem

As one might imagine from the title, "Landscape with Two Graves and an Assyrian Dog" is an unusual poem. The title suggests a painting of some sort—not an ordinary one, but a Surrealist painting such as Federico García Lorca's fellow Spaniard Salvador Dalí might create. Such a painting almost always attempts to capture, on canvas, the illogical and imagistic nature of dreams.

García Lorca attempts something similar in his poem. The poem is relatively short, consisting of three stanzas easily contained on one page. It is written in free verse with lines of varying length. García Lorca also uses jagged, discordant language, which, when combined with the form and length of the poem, serves to mirror the ephemeral and illogical nature of a dream.

One thinks of dreams as making an appeal to the subconscious to discover or work out something. García Lorca makes the same appeal in his poem. The poem begins: "Friend/ get up and listen/ to the Assyrian dog howl." Each of the three stanzas begins the same way, by urging a friend to arise and listen. The poem is written in the first person, as are most of García Lorca's poems, and the speaker is most likely García Lorca himself. It is possible that García Lorca is trying to rouse a friend, but because of the commands, the reader feels that García Lorca is speaking directly to him or her, thus reaffirming this sense of urgency.

The poem shifts from this type of command to the poet's description of his surrealistic vision, about which he is warning the reader. In this vision, there are, among other things, "cancer's three nymphs," "mountains of red sealing wax," and a horse with "an eye in its neck." All of these images help build suspense and create an overwhelming feeling of terror.

García Lorca uses this technique effectively in stanza 2: "Wake up. Be still. Listen. Sit up in your bed." The poet does not plead or cajole; rather, he commands, as if he and the reader are in danger. And indeed, this seems to be the case because the howling of the dog is suddenly transformed into a "purple tongue" that disperses "terrifying ants and the liquor of irises." These images appear to represent two disparate elements—the frightening, swarming, regimented material world and the soft, pure, natural world. By transforming internal concerns into external symbols, García Lorca blurs the boundaries between the real and the symbolic.

This blurring of boundaries, the horrific images, and the fact that García Lorca urges his friend to arise, all suggest that the poem is a nightmare from which García Lorca is attempting to awaken his friend or the reader. The final stanza, however, is simply the first three lines of the poem repeated. The sleeper never awakens. Readers are left with the realization that the poem is not a nightmare, but the singing of the nightmarish quality of the real world, from which they will never "awaken."

Forms and Devices

The most striking aspect of "Landscape with Two Graves and an Assyrian Dog" is the imagery. The images García Lorca uses are not the picturelike images one finds in the poetry of William Carlos Williams (which one can literally picture, such as "a red wheel/ barrow/ glazed with rain/ water"), but images one can picture both consciously and subconsciously. García Lorca's images are images formed in the psyche. For example, when he says, "The grass of my heart is somewhere else," he is speaking of the vital, natural, basic elements that are dear to him but are now lost.

García Lorca does not use these images to describe something, but to convey a mood or to express emotion. In this poem, García Lorca is profoundly stirred, excited, and his mind is racing, making wild associations at the speed of light. The images are so strong that the poem revolves around them. The odd juxtaposition of the images, one of his most startling techniques, creates an odd poetic tension that infuses each line with power.

One's reaction to this poem is not intellectual, but emotional. Unlike many modern American poets, García Lorca does not attempt to encapsulate an idea in his poems, but instead attempts to translate the sensory nature of things into language. In "Landscape with Two Graves and an Assyrian Dog," this is especially evident, because we see García Lorca express the mysteries of being human through subconscious intuitions. He does this with such force and passion, the poem builds up so much momentum that it seems it could explode at any moment.

The result of García Lorca's insight is that he creates a new understanding, one more real than reality. The images do not make "logical connections"; instead, they cross boundaries and connect elements of the subconscious that appear frighteningly vivid and stark. For example, the first stanza closes with: "And the moon was in a sky so cold/ that she had to tear open her mound of Venus/ and drown the ancient graveyards in blood and ashes." Because of the odd juxtaposition of the already odd images, it is difficult to explain what this passage "means," but one can discuss the mood it conveys.

The aura surrounding this passage is one of death, which coincides with the title of the chapter in which this poem appears in *Poet in New York*, "Introduction to Death." In the poem, the moon mutilates herself, which in turn "drowns" (smothers) the graveyard in blood and ashes. This act of violence covers the dead (the graveyard) in traditional symbols of death (blood and ashes), as if to suggest that the dead are now more profoundly dead. This passage is a classic example of what García Lorca calls *duende* — which is the sense of the presence of death. He believes that for a poem to be truly powerful and magical, it must possess *duende*, which this poem does.

Themes and Meanings

Just as it is difficult to explain what a García Lorca image means, it is almost as difficult to attempt to offer the meaning of a García Lorca poem. "Landscape with Two Graves and an Assyrian Dog" is certainly no exception, but the tone of the language and of the images suggest that the poet is concerned with the recognition of horror and that this poem is a confession of that recognition.

García Lorca wrote this poem when he was staying on a farm in the Catskill Mountains in upstate New York. The owner of the farm, who was visibly suffering from cancer, owned a huge, half-blind dog that slept right outside García Lorca's room. The terror that these elements elicited in the poet became the genesis for the poem.

Though he has been labeled a Surrealist, in poems such as this one, García Lorca transcends Surrealism. The French Surrealist poets would remain in the dreamlike world mentioned earlier, but García Lorca breaks out of the nightmare to take the world head-on, shocking as it may be. What is horrific about the poem is not that it is the transcription of a nightmare, but that it is ultimately about reality. The horrors of deformity and of people suffering—the horrors of everyday life—are far more terrifying than the horrors of the imagination.

Reality frightens him so deeply because one can never escape it. One can wake up from a dream or simply stop imagining, but one cannot elude the suffering he or she must experience as a human being. This theme of unavoidable grief is reaffirmed in the second stanza of the poem. García Lorca warns his friend, and the reader: "Here it comes toward the rock. Don't spread out your roots!/ It approaches. Moans. Friend, don't sob in your dreams." Clearly something inescapable and terrible is coming and is bringing sadness with it.

García Lorca does not want the reader to remain sleeping, though; he urges him or her to wake up and listen to the dog howl: One cannot ignore the horrors of the world by living in a dream world or by covering one's eyes or ears. One must wake up and listen; one must embrace what one fears. For García Lorca, facing up to what he fears is his only method of conquering it, and it acts as his muse to create art. He writes with his eyes, his ears, his teeth, his hair, his heart, and his blood. Because his entire being is assaulted, his entire being composes poetry.

As stated earlier, this is a poem of confession. García Lorca confesses that to him the sky and the earth engender death, that he has lost something vital to his existence, that he loves, and that he is afraid. He confesses that he and a child he loves "lived inside a knife for a hundred years," suggesting that even his innocence has been ravaged. Essentially, the poet confesses to being human, and he accepts the tribulations of this responsibility through the force of his poetry which, to use his own words, even now remains "a conscious rocket of dark light, let off among the dull and torpid."

Dean Rader

LAPIS LAZULI

Author: William Butler Yeats (1865-1939)
Type of poem: Meditation
First published: 1938, in *New Poems*

The Poem

This fifty-six-line poem is dedicated to Harry Clifton, who gave to William Butler Yeats on his seventieth birthday an eighteenth century Chinese carving in lapis lazuli, an azure-blue semiprecious stone. It was a traditional scene representing a mountain with temple, trees, paths, and tiny human beings about to climb the mountain. Yeats uses the carving to meditate on the role of art in an essentially tragic world.

The poem begins by acknowledging certain complaints from "hysterical women" who say that they "are sick of the palette and fiddle-bow,/ Of poets that are always gay." The implication is that artists are frivolous and irresponsible, playing around in the face of imminent disaster instead of doing something to save the world. Unless something "drastic" is done, the hysterical voices go on,

> Aeroplane and Zeppelin will come out,
> Pitch like King Billy bomb-balls in
> Until the town lie beaten flat.

The second stanza does not deny the probability of violence, but it deplores the hysterical wailing and defends art as a way of coping with tragedy. Yeats uses the Shakespearean analogy that all the world is a stage and further states that the play enacted there is always tragedy. "There struts Hamlet, there is Lear,/ That's Ophelia, that Cordelia." All these Shakespearean characters die. Yet, when the curtain is about to fall, they do not "break up their lines to weep." They transcend their fate, for "They know that Hamlet and Lear are gay;/ Gaiety transfiguring all that dread." They are an expression of everyone's fate, for everyone dies.

The triumph of the tragic hero is to play that role with dignity and grace, finding beauty and inspiration in the performance. Even though the curtain drops on a "hundred thousand stages," tragedy "cannot grow by an inch or an ounce."

The third stanza presents a sweeping look at the course of history, with its endless succession of civilizations. The poet imagines them as a great caravan, coming on foot, by ship, on camels, horses, and mules. "Old civilisations put to the sword./ Then they and their wisdom went to rack." Moreover, their great art died as well. He gives one example: the superlative achievements of Callimachus, an ancient Greek sculptor, "Who handled marble as if it were bronze." Only a scrap of his art remains. "All things fall and are built again,/ And those that build them again are gay." In other words, the joy of life is in the process of creating; it exists in the journey itself, not in some goal or object at the end of the trail which is going to live forever.

The fourth stanza, shorter than the others, introduces the carving in lapis lazuli. Three Chinese men, one apparently a serving man carrying a musical instrument, are climbing toward a "little half-way house." Above them flies a long-legged bird, a crane, conventional Chinese symbol of longevity. The last stanza elaborates how the carving brings delight to the beholder. It evokes an imaginative journey that goes beyond the scene frozen in stone. The poet participates mentally in the climb and imagines the two old men sitting under flowering trees at the half-way house, listening to mournful music. They stare out on "all the tragic scene" below: "Their eyes mid many wrinkles, their eyes,/ Their ancient, glittering eyes, are gay."

Forms and Devices

The poet makes sensitive use of sound devices and connotations, the first stanza combining colloquial phrases ("sick of," "beaten flat") with explosive words and repeated consonants ("drastic . . . done," "King Billy bomb-balls") to suggest the hysterical, bombastic tone of the women. "King Billy" may have associations with English-Irish conflicts but also brings to mind "Kaiser Bill," a popular term for Kaiser Wilhelm II, German emperor during World War I. Although zeppelins, rigid-framed airships, were obsolete as war machines in 1936, when Yeats wrote this poem, he remembered the zeppelin bombing raids on London during World War I. In 1936, the Germans reoccupied the Rhineland; other events in Europe were leading up to World War II. The threat of war was real enough, therefore, but the tone of the first stanza suggests that a melodramatic, frenzied reaction to that threat is not helpful.

The poet ironically points to dramatic art as offering a better model for learning to bear human tragedy than public screaming and moaning or the condemnation of artists. He maintains the note of violence, however, by equating the real tragedy of modern war with the descending final curtain of the play. "Black out; Heaven blazing into the head:/ Tragedy wrought to its uttermost." The term "Black out" carries multiple, contradictory connotations. The final curtain blacks out the play, as a falling bomb blacks out human life. "Heaven blazing into the head," however, suggests enlightenment or transfiguration from that fatal blow that ends the play or the individual life. Thus, that which seems most terrible may be that which reveals heaven. The vision of heaven is itself an artifice, and it must be kept alive, often in defiance of the "real" world of political action and armed conflict.

The rest of the poem retreats into a calmer, more contemplative tone, assuming the viewpoint of eternity. The attention shifts from the everlasting recurrence of violence and death to the equally everlasting reality of life and creativity. Everything is in process. Even static arts celebrate and suggest motion: Callimachus "Made draperies that seemed to rise/ When sea-wind swept the corner." The poet's appreciation of the lapis lazuli carving does not rest in the reality of the stone itself but in the imaginative re-creation of a living scene it inspires. This is the magic of art — it leads the beholder beyond itself to partake again of the joy of creativity. The poet has not only defended art and artists but also demonstrated art in action.

Themes and Meanings

When Yeats uses the term "gay" in describing the old men's "glittering eyes," he is obviously not using the word in exactly the sense that the women do who speak of "poets that are always gay." The women intend some conventional meaning such as indulgence in wine, women, and song in utter disregard of the serious business of life. Yeats's meaning is closer to an intense consciousness, actually heightened by an understanding of the seriousness, indeed the tragic nature of life.

At about the same time that Yeats received the gift of the lapis lazuli carving, he wrote in a letter, "To me the supreme aim is an act of faith and reason to make one rejoice in the midst of tragedy." Moreover, in his rather esoteric prose work, *A Vision* (1925, revised 1937), in which he discussed his private psychological and historical mythology, he asserted, "We begin to live when we conceive of life as tragedy."

According to Yeats, each psyche is suspended mentally and emotionally between contraries, sometimes referring to some subjective inner validity, sometimes focused on some objective empirical evidence. Indeed, one cannot develop or expand consciousness except in a struggle to unify one's own contradictory interpretations of existence. Yeats says that "only the greatest obstacle that can be contemplated without despair, rouses the will to full intensity."

Obviously, the greatest obstacle one can imagine is death itself. The hysterical women are assuming that the threat of death is peculiarly significant in their particular, objective moment of history; therefore, one should suspend all other activities in the present emergency. Yeats is pointing out that the threat of death is the constant human condition, neither more nor less tragic than it ever was. What is needed is courage and a way to contemplate disaster with some measure of equanimity. Art, which may indeed seem to pull one into a different reality, may help one to "transfigure all that dread."

Another Yeats poem of this period, "Sailing to Byzantium," deals again with old men, but as more appropriately withdrawn into a subjective vision of reality:

> An aged man is but a paltry thing,
> A tattered coat upon a stick, unless
> Soul clap its hands and sing, and louder sing
> For every tatter in its mortal dress.

In warfare, persons of all ages become, like old men, more aware of the imminence of death. For them, there is an even greater urgency to transcend fate and to teach the soul to "clap its hands and sing."

The singer speaks for life, not death. As Yeats once ironically observed, "no actress has ever sobbed when she played Cleopatra." In "A General Introduction for My Work," Yeats wrote, "The heroes of Shakespeare convey to us through their looks, or through the metaphorical patterns of their speech, the sudden enlargement of their vision, their ecstasy at the approach of death." While social crisis should bring forth an active response to empirical danger, it should not silence the singers. Human beings must live in two worlds: the material, objective world where all men die, and the mental, imaginative world where the soul abides and joy is possible.

Katherine Snipes

LAST POEM

Author: Ted Berrigan (1934-1983)
Type of poem: Lyric
First published: 1988, in *A Certain Slant of Sunlight*

The Poem

In the work of Ted Berrigan, the mode of modernism sometimes called kitsch or camp, in which everything becomes jokey, a parody of serious intentions, received a new lease on life. In reading his work, one must keep in mind that the sentiment it contains is probably being mocked rather than uttered naïvely. Yet ultimately the sentiments are very likely being uttered with a degree of naïve genuineness that is protected by a campy tone; the poet can then deny having meant them too seriously. For all of his sophistication—Berrigan lived in Manhattan throughout his poetic career—he cultivated his naïveté and was able, behind his affectation of simple-mindedness, to stay simple to the end.

"Last Poem" is at once more and less than its title may suggest. The title is dramatic. Does the poem represent a deathbed dictation? Was it discovered in Berrigan's will? Is it a farewell to the pursuit of poetry? At the same time, it is flat in tone, uninspired, the merest chronological notation. From its position in *A Certain Slant of Sunlight* (1988)—about halfway through the book—one deduces that it is in no absolute sense a last poem, but rather the most recent poem Berrigan had written at that time. The title becomes another joke, an undercutting of readerly expectations and of the grand poetic tone of yesteryear that Berrigan so often targeted.

From one point of view, however, the title can gain more than these meanings. The poem concerns a strike and violent strike-breaking event in a working-class English community. It is dedicated to Tom Pickard, a poet from Northeast England, and by its vocabulary ("When you were just a wee insolent tyke") and other clues ("Management set upon us/ Jarrow boys"), one finds that "Last Poem" is a sort of dramatic monologue, with Berrigan speaking as if he were Pickard or one of Pickard's mates or forebears. (Jarrow is a shipbuilding center in Tyneside, near Pickard's home; there was a landmark strike and strike-breaking there.) The poem ends, "They/ outnumbered us 5 to 1; & each had club/ knife or gun. Kill them, kill them, my/ sons. Kill their sons."

Acted upon, this poem would become literally the last poem for those killed. On the other hand, one can see in a feud that spans generations the futility of all attempts at finality; every attempt to strike the final blow leads only to further acts of revenge. If read in this light, the poem becomes ironic in that its title is undercut by the events, or at least by the would-be events, referred to at its end. The poem then becomes a sympathetic yet ironically distanced act of comradeship, the American Berrigan understanding the social situation of his friend yet not wanting to allow him to continue in his attitude without trying subtly to show him something important that Berrigan has discerned about that attitude. Perhaps, however, Berrigan is simply saying that a time comes when poetry can do no more and the time for killing begins.

Forms and Devices

This eleven-line free-verse poem employs the dialect of Northeast England— Tyneside—on occasion to imply, rather than perform, a dramatic monologue. Although the subject, a strike-breaking, is serious, the tone is comic. "I am the man yr father & Mum was," it begins, making a man out of Mum. This confusion of genders yields to a confusion of dialect tones, for "wee insolent tyke" and other working-class terms are laid next to expressions such as "days of infamy" and "ensuing brouhaha," taken from journalistic diction. The "Kill them, kill them, my/ sons. Kill their sons" at the close has the violence of farce, not of tragedy, largely because of the lack of preparation for it. The farce shows the tragic aspect in another light—sublime vengeance becomes ridiculous mechanical reactiveness.

Berrigan's refusal to enter with formal seriousness any of the issues his poems raise operates as a critique of the conventions of serious poetry. By an ironic twist, this refusal itself becomes, therefore, a serious formal gesture. His homespun, slap-dash ways implicitly ask why others persist in climbing on a rhetorical high horse before addressing reality so earnestly, since reality happens anyway, like it or not. All the poems in *A Certain Slant of Sunlight*, in common with Berrigan's production overall, exude this casual, down-home air of spontaneity, and when one learns something of how they were written, this does not seem surprising.

Alice Notley, the poet's widow, in her introduction to this posthumous book, reveals that it was initially written on postcards, the postcards having been supplied by Ken and Ann Mikolowski of the Alternative Press. Berrigan's method of composition on these cards—of which five hundred were sent to him, each measuring 4½ by 7 inches—is also discussed by Notley, who says that her husband would give a handful of the cards to someone and ask that person to write a few words on them. Among those who collaborated in this way with Berrigan were Allen Ginsberg, Steve Carey, Greg Masters, Joanne Kyger, Steve Levine, Tom Pickard, Jeff Wright, Eileen Myles, Anne Waldman, and herself. It seems likely, therefore, that the poem dedicated to Pickard was also a collaboration with him.

Themes and Meanings

Berrigan collaborated with many poets in his lifetime, and a certain carelessness about ownership—of both words and possessions—was a part of the challenge that these poets raised to bourgeois society. Berrigan's poetry flourished in the 1960's and early 1970's, in the years when the counterculture had such momentum, and revolutionary possibilities were—to an extent—realizable. Such techniques of collaboration as the "exquisite corpse" method (each person writes a line, folds the paper over, and passes it to his neighbor) began with the Surrealists but were revived by Berrigan and his peers in the interests of encouraging community. A sort of utopianism, a kind of anarchy, and surely the old wish to shock the bourgeoisie were at once context and theme for Berrigan and his collaborators. These poets often composed while stoned on marijuana or hallucinogenic drugs; alcohol and amphetamines were also popular. To their detractors, this was mere self-indulgence, producing work of little consequence that would soon fade from attention. An illuminating hierarchy of precedence can be discovered for such a procedure, however, including Arthur Rimbaud's advice to poets to derange and disturb their senses, the better to see through society's false orders.

These writers, among whom Berrigan was prominent, might not have believed in possessiveness, but this did not mean that the material was a matter of indifference to them. Alice Notley remarks that postcards hold appeal as materials for poetry, being readily graspable, compact, and manageable. Indeed, the tendency of ownership to interfere with one's fascination with a given material, be it a landscape ("Get off my property!") or another person ("That woman is my wife, you cad!"), should be obvious enough to all, and one need seek no further for a connection between these two terms of an only apparent contradiction.

As for the way in which these themes connect with "Last Poem," the reader need only consider that what is being reported in the poem concerns a union, a brotherhood of shared concern, being beaten up and killed by thugs representing property owners. From this act of repression and murder flows endless harm, the poem reveals, corrupting even those who, as victims of violence, should best understand why violence ought not to be used.

David Bromige

LAST THINGS

Author: William Meredith (1919-   )
Type of poem: Meditation
First published: 1970, in *Earth Walk: New and Selected Poems*

The Poem

"Last Things" is a forty-seven-line meditation that is divided into four stanzas. Included in William Meredith's 1970 collection, *Earth Walk: New and Selected Poems*, "Last Things" is one of the thirteen new poems that make up the opening section of the collection; it is the last poem—the impact poem—of the opening section.

In the eleven-line first stanza, the poet observes a porcupine crossing a road. The porcupine's movements are described as reminding him of other "relics": "Possum, armadillo, horseshoe crab." They seem "arthritic with time." The porcupine and the other creatures are neither cute nor graceful, and "In all their slowness we see no dignity." The porcupine is "oblivious," though, to its standing on the evolutionary chart, and at the end of the stanza "he falls off/ Deliberately and without grace into the ferns." Meredith moves to a completely new location in the thirteen-line second stanza. He describes the situation of a different type of relic, old cars in a junkyard. The contents and arrangement of the junkyard are detailed. The "old cars" have been "kept for the parts"; there are "Fenders and chassis and the engine blocks." The rows in the junkyard conjure up the image of "an old orchard" that follows "the contours of the hill." The cars and their various parts are on display for the purpose of being picked clean to satisfy the needs of still-functioning cars. The last line of the stanza makes it clear what role the functioning cars play: "Cars the same age are parked on the road like cannibals."

In the fifteen-line third stanza, the poet transports the reader to Africa and focuses on "Statues of soldiers and governors and their queen" that were once erected by the Englishmen who had come to that continent. The statues now lie ignored in a field "where the Africans put them." Meredith speaks rather generously of the soldiers and governors, who "did their best" and who for the most part were not "plunderers." Nevertheless, those people and the statues of them that were left behind have been forgotten. The statues have "chipped extremities," rest "in a chipped regalia," and "lie at angles of unaccustomed ease." Only the African lichen confers any "grandeur" on the statues; lichen is a crustlike plant, consisting of fungus and green algae, that grows on rocks. The natural world may have given the statues a certain grandeur, but "men have withheld it."

The closing eight-line stanza introduces the ancient Greek world and the legend of Prometheus. The poet speaks of "fallen gods" that were chained to a cliff. This allusion refers to Prometheus, who, in Greek mythology, had committed a crime against the gods and therefore was chained to a mountain where a vulture would eat his liver by day; it was restored by night so that the process was never-ending.

Using the mythical story as the foundation of the last stanza, Meredith speaks of "Time" being "without forgiveness." "Time" also "intermittently" "sends the old, sentimental, hungry/ Vulture compassion to gnaw on the stone/ Vitals of each of us." No one is exempt from this process. Both old and young must be prepared "for the unthinkable/ Event he foresees for each of us—a reckoning, our own." The seemingly random subject matter of the previous stanzas is tied together by the reckoning foreseen for all things.

Forms and Devices

William Meredith began his poetic career by writing academic verse. Over the years, he slowly shifted toward a more open poetry that tends to be straightforward and personal. Like several of the other new poems of *Earth Walk*, "Last Things" flows with conversational ease. Meredith does not completely abandon formal constraints, though; he still capitalizes the first letter of each line, for example, but the line and stanza lengths vary. The balance of "Last Things" stems from the maturity of a poet who has learned to create poignant verse without always relying on formal poetic forms. Each stanza stands on its own as a description of a creature or object that, for whatever reason, has become a relic. In the first stanza it is the porcupine, in the second it is old cars, in the third it is statues, and in the last it becomes personal—it is "each of us." The cumulative effect creates a powerful conclusion. The title "Last Things" immediately introduces the reader to the idea of end results, and Meredith uses concrete images to build a moral case for his point of view.

In "Last Things," Meredith employs both metaphor and simile. "Tunnel of woods" and "freckled light," in the first stanza, enhance the description of the locale. When the creatures of the stanza become "like burnt-out galaxies," Meredith has chosen an appropriate simile to clarify the position these creatures have in the evolutionary scheme of things. In the second stanza, hills are described as being "as choppy as lake water," and rows of junkyard cars "are irregular only as an old orchard is." In the last line of the stanza, cars "are parked on the road like cannibals." The third stanza can be fully understood only with the reader having some knowledge of the English colonization of Africa. Meredith does not make vague references that would be understood only if footnotes were used—it is not his purpose to seem scholarly at the expense of the reader—but he does expect his reader to be schooled in the Western tradition. This becomes even more evident in the last stanza, where the mythological references enhance the personal perspective that concludes "Last Things."

Sound also adds to the power of "Last Things." Alliteration is used subtly; Meredith is never heavy-handed or showy. "Light," "Larger," and "life" are sprinkled throughout the first lines of the opening stanza. In each of the stanzas, sound casts its spell on the reader; well-chosen words make the conversational tone seem effortless. "Last Things" succeeds because of its seamless combination of all these techniques.

Themes and Meanings

"Last Things" is a poem of inevitability. Time seems always to control the race, but, as Meredith presents the story, there will be a "reckoning" in which "compassion" can be an ingredient in the final judgment. In each of the stanzas, the poet sees a relic and observes how it exists in the contemporary world. The porcupine of the first stanza seems ludicrous to the casual observer. "He moves with the difficulty of relics." The porcupine is "oblivious" to how it is observed. Meredith makes the point that how a creature is viewed by humans does not necessarily stand as the indicator of the true value of that creature. This only becomes clear, however, after one reads the entire poem. The porcupine moves at its own pace and answers to time accordingly. The junkyard of cars of the second stanza will be picked clean, so as to equip other cars that still ride the open road. The "old cars" are man-made relics, and they have become a feast for "cars parked on the road like cannibals." There is even an element of dark humor in the image of cars ready to strike "like cannibals." Yet Meredith has a larger—and more eternal—theme in mind, and the final two stanzas complete the moral picture.

The English soldiers and governors of the third stanza had struggled to make the best of things on the African continent. Meredith notes that the majority of them were "men of honor" and that the natural environment has conferred "an antique grandeur" on the statues left behind. Their own country forgot about them, and ironically, "more dreadful shapes of the ego" can be found "In the parks and squares of England."

In the final stanza, there is the image of the mythological "fallen gods" being "chained, immortal" to a cliff. The story of Prometheus is a gruesome one. He had taught people about fire and in doing so had angered the Greek gods. The gods therefore chained him to a mountain where a vulture would gnaw at his liver. In "Last Things," Meredith uses the mythological foundation to speak about time and how it shows no "forgiveness." Yet the vulture of "Last Things" is "compassion," and it will "gnaw on the stone/ Vitals of each of us." In a discomforting way, Meredith is presenting a comforting thought. There may be "an unthinkable/ Event," but it does not need to be feared by those who were neglected during their lifetime. The relics of "Last Things" all deserve better, and, as the poet presents it, all creatures and things will be judged by time. More "compassion" should be exercised by everything on Earth. Meredith is thoughtful without being ponderous, and in "Last Things" he has an effective moral voice without resorting to strident preaching.

Michael Jeffrys

LEARNING A DEAD LANGUAGE

Author: W. S. Merwin (1927-   )
Type of poem: Lyric
First published: 1956, in *Green with Beasts*

The Poem

W. S. Merwin's "Learning a Dead Language" begins with a stark and disconcerting statement that takes the breath from one's lungs: "There is nothing for you to say." The poem ends with the same statement. In between, the reader is told how to learn a dead language. One must listen and listen again, and remember even when what one remembers doesn't make sense. A language can only make sense, the poem implies, all at once. Imagine staring at Egyptian hieroglyphs before the Rosetta Stone was found, staring and staring again, memorizing the physical forms of the hieroglyphs but having no idea what they might mean. Then one clue makes sense of it all.

In second person throughout, "Learning a Dead Language" almost reads like instructions for a Buddhist spiritual exercise: "You must/ Learn first to listen . . . You must therefore/ Learn to be still when it is imparted,/ And, though you may not yet understand, to remember." In this discipline, one is told to practice one of the most strenuous forms of self-denial, that of silence, total and long, perhaps the lifetime of silence practiced by mystics both Eastern and Western. It is within the sound chamber of such a silence that one learns to listen. The poem suggests that what one hears when one listens is the dark, inarticulate presence of this dead language. This language constitutes a total order, a sense of self and world, that is unattainable until one learns the art of hearing a language that does not speak.

This will not be easy. The poem says that one must understand the whole language before one can understand any of its parts. Unfortunately, though, one "can learn only a part at a time," and to understand the least part, one has to "Perceive/ The whole grammar in all its accidence/ And all its system."

It appears that learning this dead language might, then, be impossible, and it is characteristic of Merwin's poetry that it asks the reader to abide within such paradoxes. In this, he is a mystic poet, evoking the dark that is light, the silence that speaks, the knowing that is unknowing, the enterprise that goes nowhere. The poem promises, only faintly, that silence and long listening may finally result in comprehension. At most, one might hope to hear the passion that once made the dead language live and thus bring oneself into partial accord with a form of wisdom that is inconceivable within the languages that now circulate the globe.

Forms and Devices

The most notable stylistic feature of Merwin's "Learning a Dead Language" is its remarkable flatness of tone, its lack of passion. The poem develops as a set of direct, cool, almost leaden statements. The deadness of tone seems deliberate, adopted to support one of the poem's chief thematic concerns, which is that the grammatical death of a language is also the demise of its formative, life-giving passion. The language of the poem tries—by means of its lack of tone and its lack of color, image, sensuous detail of any sort—to suggest the absence of this vitalizing passion.

Stylistically, the mode of direct statement is very different from Merwin's later distinctive style, which is oblique rather than direct, evocative rather than assertive, associative rather than sequential, and syntactically malleable rather than firm. Every aspect of style in "Learning a Dead Language" serves to make the language of the poem rigid, hieratic, and devitalized, almost as if "it," this language of the poem, *were* the dead language, awaiting the rebirth of one more passionate and more whole. The poem is, if anything, forbidding, like a closed iron door, challenging the reader not to enter.

Similarly, the structure of the poem is stolid and regular, unlike the "open forms" of Merwin's later work. Merwin, in fact, was one of those who tried to revive and reformulate what modernist poets called "free verse." For many contemporary poets, Merwin's was the most significant voice in defining the idea and practice of "open form" verse—poetry that was built upon temporal air rather than ideas of symmetry, regularity, measure, permanence, poetry that was composed of breath, emptiness, inconclusion. In distinguishing itself from modernist practice, which cultivated and parodied "cultural voice," Merwin's poetry sought an impossible voice, the voice prior to and uninformed by culture, the voice of pained and basic being in the world. This, primarily, is why he is often called a primitivist poet.

"Learning a Dead Language" is, unlike Merwin's signature work, filled with symmetry and regularity. The stanzas are all sestets, six lines long; the line lengths are regular and keep very close to iambic pentameter. Each stanza, after the first, begins with a clause that involves remembrance, usually its salvific and formative functions, so that there is a kind of refrain or chant in the poem of "Remember, remember, remember." Finally, the ending of the poem returns to the beginning: "There is nothing for you to say." This circular structure tends to close the poem. Such strong closure is very unlike Merwin's later work, which usually ends on a halftone, a faint or indeterminate utterance or image.

It may, however, be possible to read the ending of the poem more openly: If one has listened and learned, one is full and has no need to speak. The repetition may, then, be repetition with a difference.

Themes and Meanings

Though stylistically, "Learning a Dead Language" is a work in the formal style of Merwin's long and accomplished apprenticeship (in his first four books, he masters and exhausts formal style), it very much prefigures his major thematic concerns— his preoccupation with silence, with the inefficacies and failure of language and his desire to find a purer, more poetic, less implicated and virulent language than those that now flow from human tongues.

When Merwin evokes language in his later poems, it is often the "language" of silence rather than that of words. "What is the silence?" he asks in "Some Last Questions," and the answer is, "As though it had a right to more." In "The Cold Before the Moonrise" (another poem from *The Lice*, 1967), he says he would like to speak the language "Of frost stirring among its/ Stars like an animal asleep," a "language" that is wordless, to be sure, and almost inaudible.

Although "Learning a Dead Language" can be described quite literally as a poem about reviving a language that is no longer current, it can also be understood as a poem about discovering or rediscovering Edenic or Utopian language. Many of the poems in Merwin's later work are poems about finding or recovering a language that, so to speak, "really works." This language would be one that seems really to name the passions and the things of this world, and holds them without harming. It would be a language that is, in a way, disempowered, incapable of abusing the world and its creatures, and perhaps even dysfunctional, incapable of being reduced to communication or information, incapable of being commercialized and consumed.

There is in Merwin's work, both early and late, a deep, irremovable reluctance to speak. Speech is so often to the side of what one might say; speech is so often banal, ugly, manipulative, and, in poetry, exquisite but impoverished.

In "Learning a Dead Language" and in all of his poems that ruminate on language or the silence that language violates, W. S. Merwin is very much a voice of the twentieth century. While many contemporary voices speak of the joyous delights of language and how one might play with it, however, Merwin speaks of the grief that accompanies it.

Anne Shifrer

LEDA AND THE SWAN

Author: William Butler Yeats (1865-1939)
Type of poem: Sonnet
First published: 1924, in *The Cat and the Moon and Certain Poems*

The Poem

"Leda and the Swan" is a sonnet that, like the Italian or Petrarchan sonnet, divides into an octave that presents a narrative and a sestet that comments on the narrative. Although the rhyme scheme of the first eight lines follows the typical Shakespearean form (*abab, cdcd*), the next six lines follow the expected Petrarchan (*efg, efg*) rhyme scheme.

The octave essentially describes the god Zeus's forced and unannounced impregnation of Leda and her ineffectual human efforts at resisting this sudden implosion in her "loosening thighs." The sestet's first sentence has been called Yeats's most brilliant sentence and even the capstone of his magnificent *The Tower* (1928). This line reveals the consequent engendering of the Greek Age of Homer (but Aeschylus, Euripides, and even Vergil also profit), because springing from this union of the king of the gods and the mortal woman were both Helen of Troy, who caused the Trojan War, and Clytemnestra, who slew the returning, conquering Agamemnon at the war's end—primary themes of the Greek Age. The second sentence of the sestet poses a question not so relevant to the Greeks, who, thinking often of women as booty, rather accepted the inexorable, blind run of fate and the inevitability of tragic human destiny. The poem's final question, however, is highly relevant to Yeats's ultimate meaning:

> Being so caught up,
> So mastered by the brute blood of the air,
> Did she put on his knowledge with his power
> Before the indifferent beak could let her drop?

The fated and tragic character of the Greek mentality, in which superhuman deities (often all too human in their emotional rages of jealousy, anger, vengeance, and lust) would sport with nearly helpless human creatures, is immediately clear and powerfully felt at the opening of the poem: "A sudden blow." Zeus never courted Leda, never announced his coming (as, say, God told Mary through His archangel Gabriel), and never spoke a word throughout. The enormous tension is heightened by the seeming casualness of the nearly regular iambic pentameter of the first line. "Great wings" creates a midline spondee (a double-accented foot), in order to stress Zeus's overwhelming power. Leda, as a mere mortal (and a woman), has no active role in this drama: She suffers the divine play of human destiny to be acted out through the medium of her frail body. Like the Genesis story in which the woman causes the fall from grace, this is a male-dominated myth. Yeats, with his leading rhetorical questions, however, can at the same time retain the inextricable bond between mortal beauty and its tragic passing, even while he transcends the contexts of both the Greek and the Judeo-Christian myths.

Forms and Devices

The sonnet's extreme precision allows much to be said and implied, and Yeats further compacts this poem's terseness by using synecdoche: Only the "wings," "webs," and "bill" are attacking; only Leda's "fingers," "nape," and "thighs" are resisting. Only a "wall," "roof," and "tower" represent the Greek siege of Troy, though it was a war waged for ten years to recover Helen. The richness of the symbols, especially as they function organically within Yeats's overall poetic context, is astounding.

References to Helen of Troy, in particular, and to many enduring myths of the Greek, Celtic, Christian, Buddhist, or Byzantine eras abound in Yeats's poems. Because the central dedication of all Yeats's work as a poet-seer (the true bard of human culture) was always to the mystical, he was drawn constantly to the deep, still waters of humankind's most profound illuminations, which he tirelessly labored all his life to mold into a unity of vision. The framework upon which he would weave this unified tapestry of mythology was provided by *A Vision* (1925, 1937); however, the mystical "voices" who communicated the ideas of *A Vision* (through the medium of his wife Georgie's automatic writing) guided him carefully so that he would not take the finger (of the system) for the moon (of the mythological poetry): "We have come," they insisted, "to give you metaphors for poetry."

Yeats's *A Vision* is an elaborate system of the cycles of human ages, with archetypal as well as individual incarnations within the various gyres—both Helen, sprung from Leda, and Yeats's own beloved Maud Gonne, for example, appear in phase fourteen of the "Phases of the Moon." Yet grasping all the terrifying, vague features of Yeats's system may not be as important in this case as simply catching the large clues Yeats offers at the start of the final book of *A Vision*. There he explains that the present time, 1925, is nearing the peak of one "Historical Cone" of the gyre (the spiraling wheel of time that waxed from the year zero to the year 1050 and wanes to its nadir in the twentieth century). The text of this fifth book of *A Vision* starts off with the next critical clue, "One must bear in mind that the Christian Era, like the two thousand years, let us say, that went before it, is an entire wheel." As if to be certain that the complex gyres, wheels, phases, and cones of his visionary symbology do not intrude upon the poetry, Yeats calls the final book of *A Vision* "Dove or Swan" and reprints there, as a kind of epigraph to the final chapter, the entire text of "Leda and the Swan."

Yeats means for one to see "Leda and the Swan" in the broad context of *A Vision* if one is to understand its meaning: As the Swan-God's impregnation of Leda initiated the Greek age, so did the Dove-God's impregnation of Mary initiate the Christian age. Since mythic ages last about two thousand years, this age must be on the cusp of a new revelation—an idea Yeats explores in "The Second Coming."

Themes and Meanings

In Yeats's mythological poetry, the Christian revelation is not the only divinely inspired one; it is not unique. It does, however, share an honored place in concert with the world's other great religious myths — though its truth is not everlasting. Things thought to be true for too long (for Yeats, that time is about two thousand years) eventually can no longer be believed: Myth is symbols in motion, for Yeats as for William Blake, and the symbols must always be renewed. After their validity is exhausted, myths undergo change, flux, and rebirth. Indeed, the very heart of the prevailing myth contains the seeds of its own destruction. That is one reason why "Leda and the Swan," depicting the very inauguration of the predestined Greek era, concludes with the one question whose real answer is beyond the pale of the Greek imagination: Could Leda fathom Zeus's knowledge before being dropped? Perhaps more to the point, can the poem's reader comprehend the heart mysteries here? The real answer is beyond the merely logical categories of yes and no, since the real poem transcends the categories of the myths it utilizes to lead the reader to an inward vision. One might assume that no Greek would imagine Leda, being but a vessel for that august era, could "put on his knowledge with his power." The question simply would not pertain.

In sharp contrast to Leda, the Virgin Mary must have understood much, since she was given a choice: the Christian Annunciation is like a proposal, and Mary had free will in accepting the role of being the mother of God because Christianity cherishes informed free will as the Greeks cherished fated human destiny. Unlike the "brute blood of the air," the Dove of the Christian age is holy, aphysical, and otherworldly. To even think of the Virgin's "loosening thighs" would be sacrilegious, and any question of her sexual arousal would simply not pertain. There are built-in parameters, limitations, and presuppositions in every mythology, yet therein lies the nemesis of the Christian dispensation: Under Plato's influence, the body (the "mere flesh") for the Christian myth is all but irrelevant. In the end, the reign of the Dove, like the reign of the Swan, must pass away — for no myth can embody all truth, and certainly not for all time. If Leda, as mortal life, as vehicle for beauty that is inherently tragic, and as aesthetic affirmation, is momentarily thought of as the poet, the artificer of eternity, the bard of wisdom, then the implosion of the divine into the human can be understood in a yet more profound manner: as Annunciation not divorced from Epiphany.

Yeats intends ultimately to share with his reader the visionary truth of this conjunction of the divine and the human: It is not merely a symbol of what has already happened historically at Bethlehem or beneath some Olympian cloud, for both Dove and Swan pass away. The fortunate reader of Yeats, however, if not prejudiced against the brute flesh or biased in favor of the fleshless spirit, can, by meditating upon these symbols that pass away, attain the visionary moment of knowledge and power, the timeless now where (as Yeats described it in "Among School Children") the dancer need not be distinguished from the dance.

Paul R. La Chance

LEGEND

Author: Hart Crane (1899-1932)
Type of poem: Lyric
First published: 1926, in *White Buildings*

The Poem

"Legend" is a short poem of five stanzas of varying length. It is written in free verse and has elegiac qualities evidenced in the seriousness of the emotional statement being made about its topic: Hart Crane's lament for a homosexual experience or (more likely) relationship recalled from his youth. His lost love has now become "legend" to him, and the poet ponders the meanings of this passing.

Although the poem is written in the first person, the poet refers explicitly to himself one time only; he creates an aura of subtlety about his work by couching most of the important statements in passive voice. Crane does not much address or even seem aware of the reader; it is as though he were whispering a secret to himself.

The first stanza is the shortest one, containing only two lines. Crane positions himself in front of a "silent" mirror where, it "is believed," that "Realities plunge in silence by . . ." The redundancy of having a "silent" mirror in which reality plunges in "silence" is effective. His topic, in both its sexual and emotional nature, requires an absence of noise not only to preclude discovery but also to provoke an intensity in thought. Crane does not say who does the "believing," but the believer is identified in the next stanza, where he is revealed to be the poet himself.

The reader does not yet know that the implicit "now" of the second stanza refers to the poet in the "noon," or middle age, of his life. He asserts that he is not "ready for repentance." He is not sorry, by any means, for the experience which will be labeled "legend" in the last line of the poem. Nor is he ready "to match regrets" — a statement which may indicate that his lover had regretted the relationship, though not repented it. "Kisses" remain the most operant part of reality, the "only worth all granting."

The third stanza begins with another operative passive, "It is to be learned." The poet then defines the "It" as "This cleaving and this burning"; that is, he describes the intertwined sexual and emotional makeup of the love. "Cleaving" suggests an attempt on the part of the poet to hold on to his personal legend; just as readily, "burning" indicates the intensity of this relationship both in terms of its culmination in the past and unquenchable desire for its return in the present. The "one who/ Spends out himself again" is another indirect reference to the poet himself and a reference to masturbation.

The next stanza is the most enigmatic in the poem. The "Twice and twice" is explainable, however, in terms of the reference to the "unwhispering . . . mirror" at the end of the stanza. The poet counts himself as one and his reflection in the mirror of his soul as two; his love is compounded because the identity of his legend-lover is also embodied in his own, so there are two such reflections; that is, they are "Twice and twice."

The important part of the last stanza is the concluding two lines in which the poet explains the title of the poem by mentioning the "legend" — the personal love kept alive and made greater in love, emotion, and accomplishment in time. Crane attempts to expand the meaning of his expression by moving from the personal to the plural. He writes "for all those," and the personal legend of the title becomes, collectively, "their" legend.

Forms and Devices

The most important poetic devices in "Legend" are imagery and metaphor; each stanza contains elements that help the poet express the condition of his soul. The most important image is that of the mirror. Crane sees himself in the mirror, literally, but he also sees the reflection of his homosexual lover. Both are silent, and both are to be believed because the mirror does, in fact, reflect reality. The mirror is silent, "unwhispering," but it works to make "Realities" evident.

In the second stanza, the rather commonplace metaphor of the moth and the flame appears. A moth is attracted to the beauty of the flame which destroys it; such is the case of the poet and his legendary lover. The reflection in the mirror is both of himself and of his lover, but at least one of these will destroy the other. Later, in the fourth stanza, a "smoking souvenir" is mentioned, a reference to the burned remnants of the relationship. It is the result of the "burning" mentioned in the middle stanza.

Explicit and implicit sexual images abound in the poem. The mirror is indicative of masturbation and narcissism as well as homosexuality. The "cleaving and burning" of the third stanza literally and emotionally indicate the sex act, on one hand, and an intense longing for a departed lover on the other. The "Spends out himself again" is another reference to masturbation. The "smoking souvenir" of the fourth stanza at once refers to the burning moth of the second and to an expended phallus. The "Bleeding eidolon," or phantom, may be similarly explicated; it indicates a spent penis as well as the memory of his lost lover. Even so, the most explicit reference to the sex act occurs in the final stanza, where the poet records a "constant harmony" that has been achieved "drop by caustic drop." The reference is both to masturbation and to the following announcement of the "legend"-lover, the homosexual relationship of his youth. "Drop by caustic drop" can be explained as a reference to orgasm; the "constant harmony" means that the significance of such a relationship has never wavered or faltered. Finally, it is called a "Relentless caper," which ironically shows that it is not a caperish prank at all.

Themes and Meanings

The primary matter of "Legend" is the exposition of a mature man looking back to make a statement about a relationship of his youth in order to determine the lasting if not lingering effects. The poet expresses an intense desire for his return to this past relationship. At the same time, he explores its impact as a defining characteristic of his present identity.

The mature poet writing of a relationship from his youth knows that the way the relationship seemed then was not what he now considers it to be. Hence, there is the title and the use of the word "legend" in the last line of the poem. The love from his youth has, to a certain, insurmountable extent, made his love life, if not the essence of his being, what it is at the time the poem is being written—that is, in the "noon" of the poet's life. The relationship has left the poet fixed forever as one who can explain himself and the meaning of his existence only in terms of what had happened in his youth. He had not merely permitted but actually willed that this love would become a lover for all seasons and years and lives, one whose memory now could provide an unquenchable "constant harmony" not evident during the actual relationship of his youth.

As indicated in the fourth stanza, to believe in a mirror is to believe in oneself and the reality of oneself. The lover as object has become the lover as subject; one who is different, at least in memory, has become one who is the same. The result is a concord not only for the individual but also for "all those who step/ The legend of their youth into noon." The meaning of the poem is not universal, but it does have an audience and application far beyond that of the poet himself.

Finally, it must be maintained that the poem is not strictly about a homosexual relationship from the poet's youth, even though this factor gives clear sustenance to the poem's existence. The poem pertains to all individuals in the "noon" of their lives who would fondly look back at relationships from their youths in order to give them significance which they probably neither had nor deserved. Had they truly been what the poet romantically imagines them to be, then they would not be history. They can rightly be described as "Bleeding eidolons." They remove the lifeblood from one's present, denying temporal happiness.

Carl Singleton

A LEMON

Author: Pablo Neruda (Neftalí Ricardo Reyes Basoalto, 1904-1973)
Type of poem: Ode
First published: 1957, as "Oda al limon," in *Tercer libro de las odas*; collected
   in *Selected Poems of Pablo Neruda*, 1961

The Poem

"A Lemon" is an ode (an ode was originally a vehicle of praise, either civic or lyrical in nature, intended to be sung in public) written in highly flexible free verse and composed of four stanzas. Pablo Neruda wrote three volumes of what he called "odas elementales" ("elementary odes"), which were translated together into English as *The Elementary Odes of Pablo Neruda* in 1961. As in all those poems, the subject matter is a seemingly "unpoetic," simple, ordinary object.

The poem opens with a wild and sensuous image of "lemon flowers/ loosed/ on the moonlight." In the next several lines, the sense of smell dominates; the lemon blossoms become "love's/ lashed and insatiable/ essences,/ sodden with fragrance." As the poem moves from the sense of smell to sight, the blooming flowers are suddenly transformed into yellow lemons. Continuing the stanza's vertical movement (from moonlight to the tree to the earth), the lemons fall from their branches—which are likened to a planetarium—to the earth below.

Once the lemons drop to the earth, they are no longer described in romantic terms but rather in practical terms; they become the "Delicate merchandise!" referred to in the opening line of stanza 2. Thus the images of moonlight, love, and lemon blossoms alluded to in the previous stanza are superseded by images of bustling harbors and bazaars where lemon becomes "barbarous gold," a commodity to be bought and sold. The pace of the poem quickens.

Next the poet focuses his attention upon the individual buyer of the lemon. This person cuts the fruit and opens it, finding "the halves/ of a miracle" within. The simple fruit becomes elevated to the level of the extraordinary. Comparing the fluid that emerges from the cut lemon to blood flowing from a cut vein, the poet describes the fluid as "a clotting of acids." Alluding to the first stanza, in which the lemons are fixed like stars in the firmament, the second stanza describes how the juice of the lemon "brims/ into the starry/ divisions"—that is, the symmetrical divisions of the pulp of the cut lemon. Next the poet conjures up images of the creation of the world and the garden of Eden, referring to lemon juice as one of the essences of life, one of "creation's/ original juices." In the final lines of the stanza, the lemon's rind is compared to a house, the proportions of which are both "arcane and acerb," secret and bitter.

In the third stanza, the lemon is further endowed with a sense of reverence. The movement of the opening line continues the action of cutting the lemon, portrayed in stanza 2. Here the visual image is of another house, a "cathedral," that remains when the knife slices into the lemon's core. At this point in the poem, cutting the lemon becomes a religious experience. The sliced lemon contains "alcoves," "acidulous glass," and topaz-colored drops; these drops are described as "altars,/ aromatic facades."

The final stanza of the poem unites the religious and metaphysical imagery of the previous stanzas. For the first time in the poem, the poet addresses the reader directly, using the pronoun "you." The act of holding a cut lemon is likened to holding "half a world," "the gold of the universe." The lemon half returns its holder to the elemental forces of nature, to Mother Earth, with "a breast and nipple/ perfuming the earth." In the last two lines of the poem, there is a play on words that changes the biblical phrase "and the Word was made flesh" to "a flashing made fruitage."

Forms and Devices

Unlike the poems in Neruda's *Residencia en la tierra* cycle (1933-1947)—in which readers are always somewhat outside the system because of the complex language and content, mere spectators whose function is to admire the poet and his extraordinary experiences with the ordinary matter of, for example, wood, wine, and celery—the poems in the Elementary Odes series reverse the situation. These poems, including "A Lemon," are designed to draw the reader directly into the process of wonder and discovery.

The poem is designed as a didactic construct, helping the reader to see and to speculate on the extraordinary significance of the world in which he or she lives. For this reason, the poem (as is the case with most of the Elementary Odes) ends with a kind of philosophical maxim summarizing the lesson in order to help the reader comprehend the poem's practical import.

In "A Lemon," as in most of the poems in *The Elementary Odes of Pablo Neruda*, the basic formal pattern is as follows: The elemental subject is introduced, transformed, and then summarized at the end. At the outset of the poem, the subject announced by the title is metaphorized promptly so as to bestow it with a certain level of poetic dignity. It is introduced indirectly (with the hint of lemon-blossom fragrance), then directly in the object of the lemon itself. The subject is more completely transformed later in the poem; the juice of the ripe yellow lemon cut in half is associated with religious imagery and precious gemstones, elegant and noble points of comparison for a simple lemon. Instead of simply dropping to the ground when ripe, the lemon is depicted as traveling from the heavens (the planetarium) above to the earth below.

Finally, in the poem's conclusion, the religious/philosophical dimension predominates as the speaker philosophizes on the significance of the elemental. The speaker of the poem, addressing the partaker of the lemon directly, reminds him or her that partaking of the fruit connects that individual with the miracle of the universe and its creation in the garden of Eden. This individual is partaking of no simple, ordinary fruit but becomes part of the "diminutive fire of a planet."

Themes and Meanings

The major theme of Neruda's "A Lemon" is the unsuspecting and hidden poetry of ordinary objects surrounding humankind. Neruda saw in his new poetics (that is, the poetics following the *Residencia en la tierra* cycle) an aesthetic that resisted an excess of sophistication; its object was to draw the poet toward rather than away from everyday reality. This embracing of reality was a welcome return to the sources, to what was simply human: his family, his native village, the modest lives of his childhood friends.

In the poem "A Lemon," Neruda renders the elemental object of the lemon purely and directly. By gaining insight into the grandeur of the lowly and the sublimity of the trivial, the ode attempts to open the world to imaginative re-creation.

Although "A Lemon" is not an overtly political poem, as are the poems of the *Residencia* series, by his choice of subject matter, Neruda's poem conveys an ideological meaning. The return to, and exaltation of, nature in the poem is a political act, in that in praising what is positive and essential, there is a silent accusation against whoever would abuse and exploit the resources of the Americas. More important, in choosing the simple language and style for the Elementary Odes, Neruda was clearly motivated by a deeply held political belief: A leftist poet must reject "elitist" styles; he must write simply and clearly for the people. To Neruda, the poet should not be isolated in his or her ivory tower away from the human community but should be part of that community.

The new aesthetics exemplified in "A Lemon" aimed at strengthening the ties between the poet and the people. The elevation of common objects constituted a leveling of poetic subject and the breaking down of class distinctions, as if reducing all things to the same standard by investing the lowliest with a humble dignity of their own.

Genevieve Slomski

THE LEMON TREES

Author: Eugenio Montale (1896-1981)
Type of poem: Lyric
First published: 1925, as "I limoni," in *Ossi di seppia*; collected in *Selected Poems*, 1965

The Poem

"The Lemon Trees" is the second poem in Eugenio Montale's collection *Ossi di seppia* (*Bones of the Cuttlefish*, 1984) and the first poem of the series entitled "Movimenti" ("Movements"). It consists of forty-nine lines in free verse, divided into four stanzas of various lengths. In addition to introducing an important image in the poem—the lemon trees themselves—the title suggests a connection with the first composition of the book. First, it recalls the orchard mentioned in the opening poem and suggests to the reader that images of nature will continue to figure as prominently in the following compositions as they did in the first ("wave of life," "garden," "beating of wings," "solitary strip of land"). Furthermore, the Italian "I limoni" echoes the title of the first poem, "In limine" ("On the Threshold"), hinting that both poems together serve an introductory function in the collection.

As in "On the Threshold," the poet begins by addressing the reader with an imperative: "Listen." He thus impresses on the reader the urgency of his message and invites him to consider carefully not only what he has to say but also the way he says it, that is, the language of the poem. In the opening lines, he tells the reader that he will break with the laureate poets of the past and select for his poems objects, places, and language from his personal experience, rather than those dictated by tradition. He declares his individuality in the line "I, for my part, prefer." In the Italian, this declaration is strengthened by the use of the first-person singular pronoun in addition to the verb form. The poet then proceeds to take the reader down a path to "grassy ditches" where children hunt for eels and through cane fields to a lemon orchard. In the second stanza, he explains how "the war of the diverted passions" of his soul is miraculously calmed by the breeze in the "friendly boughs" and by the smell of the earth and the lemon trees. The orchard offers a haven to the poet and a point of contact with the elements of nature.

The poet begins the third stanza with another imperative, this time telling the reader to "see." He reveals at this time his desire to discover in the orchard the "ultimate secret,/ . . . the thread to disentangle which might set us at last/ in the midst of a truth," which will offer hope to him and other "dislodged Divinit[ies]." In the fourth stanza, however, his reverie is broken, and time brings him back to the present moment, in which his soul has grown bitter in the depressing winter darkness of the city. This spell is nevertheless broken one day when he chances to see, growing amid the ruin of the city, a lemon tree, whose golden fruit fills his heart with the song of sunlight.

Forms and Devices

Montale's strength as a poet lies in his ability to present the essence of an object or scene by paring it down to the core of its reality using a precise and exacting selection of diction, syntax, and composition. The objects in Montale's work are generally things common to most readers, but in the poems they take on a very personal meaning for the poet. Sometimes, the image or action of a poem can be traced to a specific event in Montale's life. Nevertheless, an understanding and appreciation of his poetry does not demand a thorough knowledge of his biography. Furthermore, Montale draws his images in such stark, graphic detail that he distances himself from the composition, allowing the individual reader to find his or her own meaning in the suggestiveness of the poem's symbols.

Several images appear frequently in Montale's poetry. For the most part, he takes his scenes from nature, in particular from the country and coast of Liguria, where he spent his youth. Montale often portrays nature as a harsh and brutal force, at times hostile, at times merely indifferent to humankind. In "The Lemon Trees," however, nature is a refuge for the poet from the harshness of modern society; it is a *locus amoenus* or a paradisiacal garden in which he hopes to find peace. Indeed, he describes the trees as "friendly boughs," and it is in the orchard that his impoverished soul finds its "share of riches/ and it is the scent of the lemon-trees." The city, instead, represents the barren, hostile world, which swallows up the individual and chokes off his life.

The lemon trees themselves play an important role in the poem. The poet knows the orchard well, and just as the scent of the fruit is "inseparable from earth" so are the memories, feelings, and thoughts associated with the lemons inseparable from his soul. When he sees the lemon tree in the courtyard at the end of the poem, he is able to transcend the decadent world in which he lives to find beauty and truth. In addition, Montale refers at the beginning of the poem to the classical poets' laurel, which to him represents a tradition void of life and without a voice for modern society. He breaks with tradition and chooses as his symbol the more common, more modest lemon tree, which for him is real, alive, immediate, and significant.

Another important image in "The Lemon Trees" is the boy (or boys, as in the Italian) mentioned in the first stanza. As in other of Montale's poems ("Dance of the Children" and "The End of Childhood," for example), the child symbolizes youthful vigor and curiosity, the simplicity of a past world unfettered by the concerns of modern society, and the power of the human spirit to survive. In "The Lemon Trees," the poet recalls his own childhood and finds in that memory the inspiration to continue down familiar paths to the orchard, where he hopes to find a way to rejuvenate his weary, adult soul.

Montale also uses the various elements of language to suggest the meaning of the poem. For example, because all the verbs in "The Lemon Trees" are in the present tense, the poem takes on a sense of immediacy. The poet's memories of hunting for eels, of going down into the orchard, and of seeing the lemon tree in the courtyard become present experiences through the act of poeticizing. The use of the present tense thus serves to erase the boundaries between past, present, and even future, much as the sight of the lemons in the courtyard lifts the poet out of the tedious world to which time has returned him into the timelessness of revelation.

Themes and Meanings

At the outset of his study *Eugenio Montale's Poetry: A Dream in Reason's Presence* (1982), Glauco Cambon says that *Ossi di seppia* ". . . is first and foremost a rhapsody of the four elements, Nature's essentiality confronted by a tried consciousness that keeps wavering between utter disenchantment and glimpsed ecstasy in the reiterated endeavor to regain contact with the lost bliss of childhood." Placed at the beginning of the collection, "The Lemon Trees" introduces the poet's search for something that makes sense of and brings meaning to his experience in the natural world and disperses the uncertainty in his soul. The narrator descends into the stillness of the orchard in hopes of finding there, by some miracle, an answer. He finds only "an unquiet sweetness," helpful but far from satisfying. It is only later, when the poet finds himself in the middle of the "clamorous cities," that he experiences the miracle of the lemon trees. Through a mistake of nature—a fruitful lemon tree growing in the middle of the wintery city—his soul is nourished and "the war of the diverted passions" is momentarily suspended. The answer is not complete, and one senses that the narrator will soon find himself again firmly planted in the world, but this burst of light and understanding, which has come only after a long period of darkness, enraptures his soul and encourages him to continue his search with hope. He cherishes the miracle all the more because of its unexpected arrival.

This poem is also the first step, the first movement, in the search for life to which the reader is invited in "On the Threshold." Like "Nature," as described in the third stanza of "The Lemon Trees," poetry often seems on the verge of giving up its secret, of revealing a thread whereby it can be understood, but in the end the reader is left somewhat disillusioned by the lack of a clear answer. Only in another time and place when one least expects it does a flash evoke the memory of the "song" and reveal its significance. In reference to the persona in Montale's poem "Arsenio," Ghan Shyam Singh, in *Eugenio Montale* (1973), notes that "Everything he sees around him—familiar sights and sounds as well as natural phenomena—becomes a means of self-discovery for him and represents a milestone in the exploration of reality. . . . In such a mood of metaphysical contemplation, he finds the distinction between the real and the illusory, the near and the far, the personal and the impersonal, momentarily annulled. . . . [His] profound and perspicuous awareness of himself as well as of the world outside him brings him in touch with the embryonic forces of life." In "The Lemon Trees," the lemons serve as a mediator between the poet's past and present, and his seeing them inspires him with understanding of his present life in terms of the past. Poetry is similarly the mediator between the poet and the reader, and it serves to unite them over the distance of time and space.

Cameron K. Deaver

LENORE

Author: Edgar Allan Poe (1809-1849)
Type of poem: Elegy
First published: 1831, as "A Paean"; collected in *The Raven and Other Poems*,
    1845

The Poem

"Lenore" is a poem of twenty-six lines in four stanzas, reflecting on the death at a young age of the fair Lenore. Most likely, the Lenore remembered in this poem is the same "rare and radiant maiden whom the angels name Lenore" who is mourned in another of Edgar Allan Poe's poems, "The Raven."

"Lenore" is a poem with at least two different speakers. The second and fourth stanzas are enclosed in quotation marks; the first and third, while not marked, are clearly spoken by a character or characters, not by an omniscient narrator. Beyond the quotation marks and a noticeable shift in tone and attitude, there is no indication who is speaking anywhere in the poem. Most critics have assumed that the poem presents a dialogue between Guy De Vere, Lenore's grieving lover, and the family or priest of the dead woman.

The first stanza is addressed to Guy De Vere. In formal and very poetic language, the stanza announces the death of Lenore. She is described as a "saintly soul" and "the queenliest dead that ever died so young," and yet there is no real mourning in this stanza. The stanza comments on the general sadness of a young woman dying, but there is no specific regret that Lenore herself has died. The tone is solemn and reverent but not truly sorrowful. The speakers ask De Vere why he has not cried.

The second stanza is spoken by De Vere. The tone here is much less restrained. The speaker rages against the speakers of the first stanza, calling them "wretches" and blaming them for their "evil eye" and their "slanderous tongue." They never loved Lenore, he tells them, but loved only her wealth. It would be shameful hypocrisy for them to read the burial rite or sing the funeral song. She died to escape from their unkindness.

The original speakers reply to De Vere's accusations in the third stanza. Again, there is little emotion in the speech. More platitudes about death and heaven are uttered, and De Vere is urged to calm himself. He is now only angry because Lenore has died, "Leaving thee wild for the dear child that should have been thy bride."

The fourth and final stanza is spoken by De Vere. He notes that Lenore's soul has risen to heaven from its turmoil on earth, and begs the others to leave off their rituals of mourning so that Lenore will not hear them. As for himself, he concludes, he is glad for Lenore that she is finally away from the "fiends" who tormented her in life. He will not mourn her at all but "waft the angel on her flight with a Paean of old days."

Forms and Devices

In revising "Lenore" for the final time in 1845, Poe made changes to emphasize differences in tone between the speakers of the poem. Death is a subject requiring great solemnity, but Poe worked within that framework to create drama as well.

Even the way the lines of the poem appear on the page contributes to the solemnity of tone. In an earlier version of "Lenore," each of the subsequent version's long lines was divided into two or three shorter lines. For example, the first stanza contained the lines "See, on yon drear/ And rigid bier,/ Low lies thy love Lenore!" The effect of these short lines is to lighten the tone. The "drear/bier" rhyme is emphasized because of the pauses that naturally occur at line breaks, and the iambic meter is heightened for the same reason. The resulting rhythm gallops—it is difficult to make the lines sound mournful. When Poe combined short lines into lines of iambic heptameter, he made them look and sound more dignified. The long lines and short stanzas look to the eye more weighty than do short irregular lines with complicated patterns of indentation.

More important, the revisions changed the sound of the lines, making them more suitable for exploring death and grief. Compare the three lines quoted above with their revision: "See, on yon drear and rigid bier low lies thy love Lenore!" The new line drops the internal punctuation and capitalization; the internal rhyme thus becomes less obtrusive—although it remains to add melody and beauty to the line. Read aloud or silently, the long line "sounds" more hushed, reverential.

Poe was a master at choosing words whose vowels and consonants would echo the feeling he was trying to convey. Consider the repetition of the *l* at the end of the same line: "low lies thy love, Lenore." The sound is quiet and formal as the empty rituals for Lenore are mouthed. The first stanza is full of these repeated consonants: "flown forever," "saintly soul," "dirge for her the doubly dead in that she died so young." The beauty of these words and sounds is undeniable—even though it is revealed in stanza 2 that the beautiful words are empty and false.

The second stanza, in which the grieving Guy De Vere rails against Lenore's hypocritical family, is harsher in sound as well as in meaning. Every line in stanza 1 is end stopped, contributing to the regular, formal rhythm and tone. The reader encounters frequent strong punctuation (primarily dashes) within the lines, and two of the five lines are enjambed. The stanza's third line, for example ("By you—by yours, the evil eye,—by yours, the slanderous tongue"), is punctuated five times internally and not at all at the end. The result is a much less regular rhythm. The sound is more like that of a man enraged, with abrupt stops and irregular phrasing.

Poe uses these devices throughout the poem to establish contrasts between the false formality of the dead woman's family and the sincere emotionality of Guy De Vere.

Themes and Meanings

Critics have been baffled by "Lenore" for more than one hundred years. There is no consensus as to what the poem is about, or who the speakers are, or even how many speakers there are. Most of the clues to the poem's meaning actually lie outside the poem, in Poe's other writings.

In "The Philosophy of Composition," Poe claimed that the most poetical topic was the death of a young woman. Further, he wrote, the best speaker to utter the mournful lines was the grieving lover. Poe went back to this idea again and again, creating poems such as "Ulalume," "The Raven," and "Annabel Lee."

The woman Lenore is typical of the dead women mourned in Poe's poetry. Her youth is emphasized; the phrase "died so young" occurs three times in the first two stanzas. Both the grieving lover and the other speaker refer to her innocence and her place in heaven. She is radiantly beautiful, in death as in life. Even the woman's name is identifiable as a Poe creation. Lenore takes her place with Annabel Lee, Ulalume, Ligeia, Morella, Eleonora, Helen, and others—the letter *l* seemed to Poe somehow fitting for the name of a dead, loved woman.

The identity of the lover as Guy De Vere seems clear enough from the first stanza of the poem. Since he is addressed directly in stanza 1, it seems only logical that it is he who speaks the next stanza and the fourth stanza, which are framed in quotation marks. De Vere might be expected to wish for the return of his love, but this mournful lover does not. Rather, he is glad that she has finally escaped the suffering inflicted upon her by false friends and family.

In fact, the "wretches" are never identified in the version of the poem Poe finally left. Yet two earlier versions of the poem provide clues to their identities. The earlier versions clearly blame "friends" and "false friends" for Lenore's suffering, and the 1843 version identifies Lenore as "yon heir," suggesting that family members are among the mourners.

The dramatic purpose of the poem, then, is to establish a contrast between the sincere feelings of Guy De Vere, Lenore's intended, and the false sentiments of her friends and family. The formal, ritualistic lines in stanzas 1 and 3 may be spoken by the group of mourners or perhaps, as has been suggested, by the officiating priest.

While critics have disagreed about its precise meaning, all agree that this poem—like many of Poe's poetical works—is more significant for its sound than for its thematic significance.

Cynthia A. Bily

THE LESSON

Author: Charles Simic (1938-   )
Type of poem: Narrative
First published: 1977, in *Charon's Cosmology*

The Poem

"The Lesson" is a short narrative poem in free verse, its seventy lines divided into six stanzas of varying lengths. The title suggests that the poem will focus upon an event or series of events from which the poet gained new knowledge. Such events are often characterized by irony, as they tend to overturn one's comfortable assumptions about the nature of things — sometimes violently, sometimes comically, sometimes, as in "The Lesson," both.

The poem is written in the first person, which gives the events that it describes the authority of actual experience and the poignance of personal recollection. One is encouraged to assume that the lesson mentioned in the poem's title was learned by the poet himself. He speaks directly to the reader in a tone both retrospective and confessional. As one reads, one believes that one is being taken into the poet's confidence and invited to share the knowledge he has gained.

The poem opens with a sudden, ironic revelation as the poet realizes that he has in some way been deluded his entire life, has been "the idiot pupil/ of a practical joker." The words that the poet chooses to describe his revelation foreshadow the complexity of the narrative he is about to unfold, as they accuse both his own foolishness and the cruelty of his experience for the ignorance which the poem will explain and dispel. Having realized himself to be the victim of a malicious joke, the poet intends to be a victim no longer.

In the next stanza, the poet recounts the foolishly passive ways in which he accepted as true and wise all that he was earlier taught. He revered his teachers unreflectingly. He repeated his lessons "like a parrot" — that is to say, with accuracy but without understanding. In happy ignorance, he accepted the proposition that his lot in life was constantly improving. The third stanza continues and brings to a climax the delusion which the poet mistook for education, detailing his conviction that life had some hugely felicitous "pattern" and purpose, that history itself was headed, as the "intricate plot/ of a picaresque novel" is headed, toward some inevitable happy ending.

Beginning with the word "unfortunately," stanza 4 signals the unraveling of the poet's delusion. As the evidence of his personal memory accumulated, it began to overshadow the memory of things learned merely by rote. The poet came to see, in all the details of life, ambiguous, troubling "beginnings" rather than happy endings. Ominous images, such as that of the urinating soldier and the "shadows of trees on the ceiling" were preludes to even more ominous situations, such as starvation. In stanza 5, the happy delusion is entirely replaced by the waking nightmare of the "prison train." Reality was no longer on the gladsome, ever-ascending path of a picaresque novel but rather on the iron tracks of a railway headed toward a frightening, unknown confinement.

The closing stanza defines this nightmarish awakening as the undeluded poet's new classroom. The practical joke is ended, and it is the poet who laughs. His situation is as terrifying and ambiguous as his laughter at "the memory of [his] uncle/ charging a barricade," but his situation is at last real, at last entirely his own.

Forms and Devices

As with all of Charles Simic's best poems, "The Lesson" expertly demonstrates what may be called the art of artlessness. Vivid but spare, direct but unrhetorical, the poem communicates its profoundly dramatic theme with seemingly little need for the traditional devices of poetry. "The Lesson" resonates with the qualities of actual, unrehearsed speech, and those qualities create an immediate trust on the part of the reader for what the poet recounts.

Yet there is an art to what "The Lesson" achieves, and this consists of a number of devices employed in their purest forms. Chief among these is the irony already discovered in the poem's title. From thence onward through every stanza, ironic reversals provide the literal energy for Simic's meaning. What was taken for knowledge turns out to be ignorance. What was revered as wisdom turns out to be folly. The implacable reality of human progress turns out to be a vain dream, as nightmare images (starkly recalled from Simic's own memories of his childhood in Nazi-occupied Yugoslavia) come to represent the sole and unprogressive reality of "The Lesson."

The poem concludes upon the richest and most disturbing of its ironies: The poet's own laughter at his "long and terrifying" delusion. In a situation where one might more reasonably expect to witness gestures of outrage or tears of shame, the reader is surprised by laughter, an irony which allows Simic to make the depth of his revelation as astonishing to the reader as it evidently was to him.

All the rest of the poem's devices function under the aegis of this irony. There are rich puns. The "pupil" in line 4 represents the poet not only as a student but also as an eye which takes in all that it sees without the judgment vital to real vision. The "plot" in line twenty-five suggests a conspiracy as well as the story-line of a novel. Such puns enable Simic's irony to function at the very basic level of language itself. Crucial metaphors—the teacher as "practical joker," the teacher's lesson plan as an entertaining but finally unrealistic "picaresque novel," and the poet's new, undeceived reality as a "classroom/ austerely furnished/ by my insomnia"—signal the various stages of the poet's awakening.

It is the imagery of "The Lesson," however, that embodies Simic's irony most effectively. These images, which the poem dismissively introduces as "trivial detail," turn out to be anything but trivial, as it is the "haircut of a soldier," "the shadows of trees," the "prison train," and the final image of the poet's uncle "charging a barricade/ with a homemade bomb" which accumulate in the poet's mind and there overwhelm the imageless, stale, and facile generalizations of his so-called education. The images are his real teachers, and as such they constitute the reality of "The Lesson."

Themes and Meanings

In keeping with the artful artlessness of "The Lesson," the themes of the poem are virtually identical with its techniques and the narrative it tells. What happens in the poem—the ironic transpositions of ignorance and knowledge—is the poem's meaning. "The Lesson" participates in the traditional expression of Western culture's most fundamental theme: the journey from innocence to experience.

The greater part of this theme hinges upon the identity of the "practical joker" of stanza 1. He can be God, history, society, or any source of ideology and idealism that sets itself apart from and above the stubbornly ambiguous realities of any life as it is lived in real time. However one pictures him, this practical joker is the source of the "wise pronouncements" and disembodied generalizations, the myths of progress and predetermined fate that the poet ingenuously parrots in stanzas 2 and 3. Like the tenets of Europe's Utopian Socialists and of America's doctrine of Manifest Destiny, these illusory precepts are as insidious as they are charming because they always subordinate historical means to supra-historical ends. They devalue reality in order to inflate the value of the dreams in which they so stridently and, in the case of the poet's teachers, so convincingly believe.

By countering such abstractions with the vital, animate images of the poem's latter half, Simic establishes the dignity of objects and of persons, no matter how unlovely, no matter how frightening, in a world which more often than not tends to degrade them in the name of supposedly higher purposes. Accordingly, "The Lesson" recounts a brief history that, in the context of the poet's life, details the excesses of history's idealism and the cruel practical joke which that idealism plays on people and things. It is the finally positive theme of this poem that asserts the victory of reality over idealism through the process of the poet's awakening. As he begins to linger "more and more/ over the beginnings" (represented by the poem's crucial images) and less and less over the ends preached to him in the classroom, the poet begins to understand the irreducible uniqueness of everything that exists. Every life is its own school, and its lessons cannot truthfully be translated into generalizations. That is why the poet exclaims, "Forgive me, all of you!" near the poem's end, for he had come dangerously close to imposing the tyranny of an ideal pattern upon the stubbornly independent objects in his life. "The Lesson" is a poem about the ways in which origins refuse to become ends, in which the infinite originals in any one life refuse to become stereotypes. Heard in this context, the poem's final laughter is indeed a laughter of joy, of liberation.

Donald Revell

LETTER FROM A DISTANT LAND

Author: Philip Booth (1925-   )
Type of poem: Epistle/letter in verse
First published: 1955; collected in *Letter from a Distant Land*, 1957

The Poem

"Letter from a Distant Land" is an epistolary poem of 163 lines in three stanzas. The title is derived from a quotation (which Philip Booth borrows as an epigraph) from Henry David Thoreau's *Walden* (1854). In this classic of American literature, Thoreau describes his adventure of living at Walden Pond, near Concord, Massachusetts, between 1845 and 1847.

In a brief passage, Thoreau, speaking to other writers, declares that part of a writer's work should be a simple account of his or her life, "some such as he would send to his kindred from a distant land." Booth makes images of Walden and nature central to his poem, and "Letter from a Distant Land" is Booth's response to Thoreau's challenge. Booth measures who and where he is in relation to who and what he aspires to be; Thoreau and *Walden* are his yardsticks.

To understand Booth's effort, it is necessary to know that in *Walden* Thoreau sought to discover the nature of true being, the essence of life. By withdrawing from society and living as a recluse, Thoreau lived in harmony with nature. As a result, he came to understand new spiritual truths; he discovered the oneness of creation and its manifold beauty. His message in *Walden* is that humanity needs to rediscover that core of value and meaning.

The first stanza of "Letter from a Distant Land" is dominated by the image of nature, the pleasant world in which the poet lives and in which he nurtures his spiritual strength. Booth quickly sounds his theme of "living halfway" in this world where it is difficult to feel comfortable and completely at home. At his back is the airfield with its gleaming jets that are a constant reminder of the world on the brink of war. Seeing them and hearing them mitigate his sense of being fully part of nature, where the woods are his "chapel" and where he half confesses and finds "absolution in the wind."

In the second stanza, the dominant image is of the jet planes that quickly metamorphose into "great sharks with silver fins that foul the ocean air" and prey on man. The jets represent the great destructive power of the modern state. As Booth meditates on them, he remembers his own participation in the "last war" (World War II) as a pilot and concludes that he "owes several debts" in relation to that participation. The remainder of the stanza deals with his efforts to live on and in harmony with the land, to protect nature, and to live by his own hard labor.

The long final stanza of eighty-four lines moves toward a resolution of the conflict facing the poet. The stanza opens with an image of radar and enemies, which the poet contrasts to the imagery of a walk through the woods, "half-way towards dawn." The lake is still "half Thoreau's," although the area has been made into a tourist attraction. The poet meditates on the transformation of Thoreau's world and ends the poem with an affirmation of hope despite these changes. He declares his love for the land, though he still feels like a stranger in it.

Forms and Devices

The form in which Booth expresses these ideas is the epistolary form of poetry, the letter, specifically a letter to a spiritual "kinsman." Booth adopts iambic pentameter as his primary meter and employs a complex pattern of off-rhyme in tercets (terza rima), rhyming *aba*, *bcb*, *cdc*, *ded* throughout the poem. This strict pattern accomplishes several objectives. The iambic pattern is that of speech and thus helps establish the sense that the poet is engaging in direct speech. The intricate pattern of rhyme provides for a tight structure of thought and image, but one that is disguised by the use of off-rhyme. The result is a carefully crafted poem, one suitable for delivery to a spiritual master.

Another formal device is the contrast of two sets of images: the mechanical and the natural, the jet planes and the birds and trees. These images are part of the structure of the poem's three long stanzas, yet they are subsumed under the more pervasive image of "halfway." Throughout the poem, this reference to halfway takes on new and richer meaning.

The entire poem is based on a sense of a half-realized life, a half-realized sense of purpose. This sense of half-realization is attributable in part to the allusion to *Walden*. Thoreau's vision of the complete life is very strict and demanding, and though Booth is attempting to live it, he falls short in his own estimation. *Walden* or no *Walden*, however, Booth sees himself at a halfway point with his life.

Where he is is not only a place but also a state of mind. Thus, when he describes the place he lives as "halfway between the airfield and your pond" he describes not only the physical location but also the fact that he has been able to free himself only in part from the concerns of the world, its history, its conflicts, and its stresses. That world is symbolized by the airfield and its jets that play so great a part in the development of the poem.

Themes and Meanings

The theme of the poem is the need of the poet to connect himself with a previous, perhaps more innocent, time and to establish a sense of himself in the present. Although he is ostensibly writing a letter to Thoreau, he is also using the poem as a vehicle to declare his own sense of connectedness and purpose, the "strange love in a distant land" with which the poem ends.

Part of the problem of identity for Booth is his perception of the encroachment of the machine that threatens the land, the chain saws that "rape a virgin stand to stumps" and that have "more power than has ever been seen before." They desecrate the natural landscape: "an orange oil tank flaws the spring; girders bloom with concrete blocks." In addition to the incursion of the machine, time has wrought additional havoc: wars, inflation, tourists, pollution. "Tight-paired jets" write "cryptic warnings on the thin blue air." The jets symbolize not only the present but also a future dominated by machines and by violence.

Booth's view of the mechanization of modern life is a step beyond that of Thoreau, who in *Walden* found a place for the railroad as symbol of the new age of the machine. Like Walt Whitman in *Democratic Vistas* (1871), Thoreau saw the machine as part and parcel of his transcendental vision. It was all part of the transformation of the world, a new vehicle for humanity to reach a state of higher development. Apparently neither Thoreau nor Whitman foresaw that modern science and technology would lead to the destruction of the environment. For Philip Booth, that destruction made great inroads on the quality of life and on the state of nature.

Booth takes this whole situation one step further: For him, the world is on the verge of war. This poem was written in the early years of the Cold War, in which the United States and the Soviet Union maintained hostile relations with each other and believed each nation sought the destruction of the other. The image of the jet overhead and the carcass of a "traffic-flat" skunk suggest a vulnerable world subject to imminent and total destruction. Booth recognizes, though, that war and death are not some new part of American life. He points out that Thoreau wrote *Walden* during a period of great violence and war. This was also the time when the issue of slavery was tearing the country apart.

Booth sees himself, a century after Thoreau, crossing "the middle-ground/ toward hope." Despite the fact that America has changed dramatically and that new and more potent dangers have emerged, Booth declares that he must make do with what he has and ask only that nature provide him with a home and the wisdom that was granted to Thoreau. Like Thoreau before him, he believes his salvation will come from hope and love derived from reverence for and appreciation of nature.

Richard Damashek

LETTER OF TESTIMONY

Author: Octavio Paz (1914-   )
Type of poem: Lyric/Meditation
First published: 1987; as "Carta de creencia: Cantata," in *Árbol adentro (1976-1987)*; collected in *Collected Poems of Octavio Paz, 1957-1987*, 1987

The Poem

"Letter of Testimony" is a long meditative poem in free verse. Divided into three parts, it is subtitled "Cantata" and concludes with a nine-line coda.

The poem begins at dusk, that uncertain moment between light and dark that can stand perfectly as a symbol for the flow of time. As day darkens, so does the page on which the poet is writing. Once again the reader is in touch with one of Octavio Paz's favorite scenarios for his long meditative poems: the writer writing at night.

Writing supposes a curious kind of conversation that is almost three-way: The poet talks to himself and to the woman he loves (in this case Paz's wife, the subject of most of his late poems). Writing, or the conversation that it stands for, should be natural, the way a tree talks to the air, or the way water flows or fire sparks. As always, however, Paz realizes only too well the multifarious nature of words. If words are bridges between objects in the world and human consciousness, they are also "traps, jails, wells." Nevertheless, as they define and describe, they do create meaning and character: "that word is you." Words are bridges to the past (as in the poem "San Ildefonso Nocturne"), and here they lead to a memory evoked by the author of his wife as a child, sleeping at the age of nine among the mimosa, near the city of Meknes in Morocco.

Part 2 reiterates the slippery nature of words but emphasizes that they speak to humans, reveal what they think and are. Love, a universal and particular theme for Paz, also requires a word that, like all others, is equivocal. Paz recalls, in poetic and sometimes unclear allusion, famous statements about love in Western literature and philosophy, some of which have their basis in the works of Plato and Dante and in Neoplatonism. In this tradition, love has been spiritualized, driven to ascend a ladder of perfection. Others, however, less fanciful, think of love as a fever, a kind of sickness. Paz insists on combining the physical with the spiritual, refusing to give precedence to either body or soul. He rejects the "Platonic One," the term for complete union, in favor of the notion that love is always a matter of two people, always searching, never quite finished.

Part 3 returns to specifics, the afternoon once more, the poet writing. The conversation (writing) is renewed, lovers are evoked in the figures of Miranda and Ferdinand from William Shakespeare's *The Tempest* (1611). In the coda, Paz says that although human beings have been condemned to abandon the Garden of Eden, perhaps a form of love is to learn how to walk through the world, to stand natural like a tree, and to continue talking (writing poetry).

Forms and Devices

Paz is at pains to underline what he conceives to be the musical structure of his poem. "Cantata" refers to a musical composition that can comprise a chorus, solos, and recitatives. It is music for voices and, in this case, for the conversation and meditation on the meaning of love and the fact that the spoken word is one of the ways that love defines itself. A "coda" is a passage that brings a composition to a close, and in this poem it contains Paz's statement that to learn to love is to learn to live in harmony with nature.

In terms of the contents, Paz also follows a musical pattern. He is fond of introducing a theme, developing it in the form of variations, and, at the conclusion of the poem, returning to the main theme. In "Letter of Testimony," the theme of time appears, followed by the writing of poetry, which cues a discussion of the slippery nature of words; love is introduced and confronted with time. Finally, the poem returns to the scene with which it began, now altered by the passage of time.

Paz's talent for metaphor is, as always, evident. One can see in the early lines a favorite device wherein he allows one metaphor to develop into another. The "page" on which he writes encourages the notion of a "leaf" and this, in turn, leads into the idea of a tree dropping its leaves. "Letter of Testimony" is part of a volume of poems called *Árbol adentro (1976-1987)* (1987; *A Tree Within*, 1988). The tree appears in the coda, and thus one can see that symbols and metaphors are stated, developed, and returned to, following the paradigm of a musical composition.

The afternoon itself at the opening of the poem stands for time, and the "dark river" that files away at the edge of things is Paz's expression of one of humankind's oldest symbols for the movement of time and life: the river.

In the midst of his flow of lyrical meditation, Paz is given to catching the reader's attention with a particularly striking metaphor. Above the nine-year-old girl sleeping in the arms of mimosa, a hawk circles. Paz notes the compulsiveness of this action by a wonderful line: "In love with geometry/ a hawk draws a circle." In part 3, the poet accents the importance of touch to lovers with the image: "To love is to have eyes in one's fingertips." In part 1, Paz indulges in an extended use of similes: "like running water . . ./ like a still puddle . . ./ like fire." The similes also function as anaphora, that is, the repetition of words at the beginning of a line.

Paz's love of pairing opposites, a characteristic feature of much of his poetry, appears also in this poem. To underscore the paradox of love, he gives it a series of contraries. Life is both a gift and a penalty, a rage and a holiness, a wound out of which blooms the rose of resurrection.

Themes and Meanings

"Letter of Testimony," as the title implies, confirms several of Paz's enduring themes: time, language, and love. Time hovers over nearly everything that he has written, an ever-present witness to human mortality. (It is interesting to note that Paz speaks very little about death, but much about time, the existence of which leads to the demise of individuals.) Time presides over "Letter of Testimony" in the first stanza. Throughout this poem, as in his other writings, Paz eschews the creation of moments outside time and even refuses the refuge offered to artists, that of claiming the immortality of art. Love (and of course art) can create a sense of timelessness, but the ultimate boundary is still time: "Love, timeless island,/ island surrounded by time." Love itself in its surges imitates living and dying.

The ability to use language is one of the defining characteristics of a human being and therefore makes humans dependent on what language can and cannot do. Philosophers and writers have made this one of the common themes of the twentieth century, and Paz in his essays and poetry has constantly discussed what it means to use words. Words are symbols, labels, but not the things themselves; nevertheless, they are all that human beings have, and they give to things a kind of reality. This is particularly true when it comes to distinguishing an individual: "That word is you,/ that word/ carries you from yourself to yourself." Language expresses us.

Writing poetry is one of the most special ways imaginable of employing language, and viewed in this light, it is easy to understand why Paz makes so much out of the writing of poetry in his work. Poetry thrives on the paradoxical reality of words.

In later life, along with the theme of language, love occupies a preferential place in the poet's themes. Paz's achievement as a poet has been to glorify love as an imperious life force without yielding to the temptation to romanticize it or indeed to over-idealize it. Love is part of history; like every other human activity it is time bound. One must distinguish it from lust. Desire (lust) is pointless (a mask of death) unless it permutes into love, which is barely an instant in biological history, but enough for invention (or transfiguration) to occur: "the girl turns into a fountain,/ her hair becomes a constellation."

One form of deifying love goes back to Plato and his enormous influence in Western civilization. It was to split the body from the soul and assign to the latter the highest stage of love. Paz recognizes that the corporal senses bring about love, and that the fusion of two bodies does not lead into the disappearance of both in the "Platonic One." Rather, "to love is two,/ always two," longing perhaps to be one but never complete.

The calm statement in the coda caps an impressive career: Love is perhaps a way of learning to see and to live in the world and to be in relationship with the world as are the elements of nature.

Howard Young

LETTER TO LORD BYRON

Author: W. H. Auden (1907-1973)
Type of poem: Epistle/letter in verse
First published: 1937, in *Letters from Iceland*

The Poem

"Letter to Lord Byron" was written during and after a trip to Iceland. W. H. Auden and fellow poet Louis MacNeice had approached Faber, the British publishing firm, and proposed a travel book; Faber accepted and gave the poets the money to finance the trip. Auden, not being a travel writer, had no real idea what to write on for the book, but he had brought a copy of Lord Byron's *Don Juan* (1819-1824) along to read. He decided to write a verse letter to Byron, informing the poet, who died in 1824, what was happening in the Europe of the 1930's. As such, "Letter to Lord Byron" has more digressions than it does Byron; indeed, one might claim that the poem is almost solely composed of digressions.

The poem comprises five unequal parts, all written in rime royal, all discursive and conversational in tone. The actual trip to Iceland that served as the occasion for the poem is mentioned, but in passing and at irregular intervals. References to the journey serve merely as a frame for what Auden really wants to say.

Part 1 begins with a direct address to Byron, apologizing for disturbing him. Auden—there is no point in insisting on a persona here, since the poet makes no pretense of developing any voice other than his own—mentions that he is in Iceland awaiting the arrival of the rest of his fellow travelers, and he discusses why he chose to address the letter to Byron. Auden had brought Byron's *Don Juan* and a novel by Jane Austen with him, but he finds both what he has to say and his medium for saying it more attuned to Byron. He talks about his choice of a form and then begins to give a defense of light verse, a form not highly prized in the literature of the twentieth century.

Part 2 initially describes a little of Auden's immediate reaction to Iceland, but soon he begins to talk of recent developments in Europe. He acquaints Byron with the changes of taste in England, the confusion of the class system because of industry—"We've grown, you see, a lot more democratic,/ And Fortune's ladder is for all to climb"—and then imagines how modern publicity would make a celebrity of Don Juan. After a quick glance at the art scene, Auden begins discussing "the spirit of the people," finding a conscious rejection of heroism for economic comfort: "'I may not be courageous, but I save.'" This spirit is inimical to that of Byron, so Auden next imagines Byron returned to modern realities, but this is not a heroic age: "In modern warfare, though it's just as gory,/ There isn't any individual glory."

Auden begins part 3 just before setting off for an excursion into the countryside of Iceland. Auden once again affirms his liking for light verse and announces that he shares Byron's belief that William Wordsworth is "a most bleak old bore." This observation leads naturally enough into a discussion of landscape, then proceeds to a lengthy consideration of the estrangement of the artist from society — an estrangement that Auden traces to the nineteenth century.

Part 4 begins on ship heading back to England. Auden quickly summarizes what he gained from the trip, his main accomplishment being learning to ride a pony. Then, triggered by his returning home, he begins to tell his own biography. Starting with a glance at his passport and his own Icelandic ancestry, Auden takes a general, and generally light-hearted, look at his own character, eventually pronouncing, " 'Your fate will be to linger on outcast/ A selfish pink old Liberal to the last.' " Then he begins to recount his upbringing, his early interest in machinery, school days during World War I, his adventures with headmasters (which allows him an attack on "Normality" and a defense of eccentric teachers), the incident that led him first to write poetry, his days at the University of Oxford, then his time spent in Berlin on family money, his return to England, and his teaching at a boarding school. He finally gets to his work in documentary filmmaking as the boat reaches the dock.

Part 5 is by far the briefest of the sections; Auden does, however, manage to touch on the coming war, labor difficulties, his essential Englishness, and the proper place to send his "Letter to Lord Byron." He finally pictures Byron lounging with other poets in heaven ("Are Poets saved? Well, let's suppose they are") and apologizes for the length of the "letter that's already far too long,/ Just like the Prelude or the Great North Road"; he then justifies the poem's size when he closes: "As to its length, I tell myself you'll need it,/ You've all eternity in which to read it."

Forms and Devices

"Letter to Lord Byron" is an obvious response to *Don Juan*, which Auden was reading at the time. Exactly why Auden chose a different form for "Letter to Lord Byron" is unclear. *Don Juan* is written in ottava rima, which consists of stanzas of eight lines of iambic pentameter with the first, third, and fifth lines rhyming with one another, as do the second, fourth, and sixth. The verse form is completed with lines 7 and 8 forming a rhyming couplet.

Auden claims, "I want a form that's large enough to swim in,/ And talk on any subject that I choose." Certainly, Byron found ottava rima appropriate for expansive, digressive verse. Auden acknowledges this: "Ottava Rima would, I know be proper,/ The proper instrument on which to pay/ My compliments." He states that if he did use it, however, he would "come up a cropper." Certainly such a claim should be taken with more than the proverbial grain of salt. First of all, rime royal, which Auden chose, is as difficult a form as ottava rima; second, even though at the time he was a poet still in his twenties, Auden had already shown himself to be a master of form. Clearly his claim of deficient skills should not be considered seriously.

Perhaps Auden believed that Byron had already done as much as one can with ottava rima in the comic mode. In choosing rime royal, Auden selected an expansive form that had not been utilized with any great success at length since Geoffrey Chaucer's *Troilus and Criseyde* (1382), which was not a humorous poem. Rime royal consists of seven-line stanzas of iambic pentameter, with the first and third lines rhyming and the second, fourth, and fifth lines rhyming. The verse then closes with a rhyming couplet composed of the sixth and seventh lines. In effect, the form is identical to ottava rima with the fifth line omitted. What this omission does is make the verse end with two pairs of rhyming couplets.

Regardless of the reason for his choice, rime royal left Auden with the repetition of rhyme and the drawing together of the closing couplet so helpful to humorous verse. Like Byron, Auden makes extensive use of feminine, or multisyllabic, rhyme, the bounce of which tends to have a comic effect: "At least my modern pieces shall be cheery/ Like English bishops on the Quantum Theory." He also echoes Byron in calling conscious attention to his supposed deficiencies in poetry: "Et cetera, et cetera. O curse,/ That is the flattest line in English verse."

Themes and Meanings

It would be impossible in this brief space to discuss adequately all the themes of "Letter to Lord Byron." The poem by design is without design; themes are introduced, dropped, and picked up again, sometimes merely touched on, at other times discussed in detail, and always with a lightness of tone. Topics include the psychology of twentieth century man and the isolation of the artist from society.

Auden tells Lord Byron that people have the "same shape and appearance" and "haven't changed the way that kissing's done" but that modern man is "another man in many ways." He says that the contemporary man is best portrayed by cartoonists such as Walt Disney. This man "kicks the tyrant only in his dreams,/ Trading on pathos, dreading all extremes;/ The little Mickey with the hidden grudge."

This is economic man, bred "on Hire-Purchase by Insurance," fearing admonishment by "tax collector and a waterboard." He makes no pretense to the heroic, as " 'Heroes are sent by ogres to the grave./ I may not be courageous, but I save.' " He dares to "give his ogreship the raspberry/ Only when his gigantic back is turned." He is caught in his fears, but he fears even more to escape into uncertainties, so his oppressor knows that his comfort makes him a slave: "The ogre need but shout 'Security,'/ To make this man, so lovable, so mild,/ As madly cruel as a frightened child." This is not a time for the disinterested hero, for those who risk their lives for the cause of others as Byron did for Greek independence.

Auden begins his consideration of the artist and society with the Augustan age. He speaks of two arts; one was dependent on "his lordship's patronage" and was more of an aristocratic pursuit. This form of "high" art Auden personifies in Alexander Pope. The other form of art was "pious, sober, moving slowly,/ Appealing mainly to the poor and lowly" and is personified in Isaac Watts. These arts were very different, but Auden is unusually emphatic as to the central point: "The important point to notice, though, is this:/ Each poet knew for whom he had to write." He makes the assertion that art must be attendant— that is, must serve a particular class with whom the artist shares similar concerns. What art must not be is independent.

Yet this is just what has happened. Auden writes that each man naturally wants his independence, but for the artist, such independence is disastrous. Until the Industrial Revolution, the artist had to depend on the patron and please the taste of the patron or the class: "He had to keep his technique to himself/ Or find no joint upon his larder shelf."

When the artist was able to declare his independence, however, he "sang and painted and drew dividends,/ But lost responsibilities and friends." At first there was great experimentation and euphoria; Auden writes of his imagined Poet's Party: "Brilliant the speeches improvised, the dances,/ And brilliant too the technical advances." Soon, however, the artist is ignored by the public that he scoffs at rather than serves and is left alone with only his technique. At the Poet's Party, some "have passed out entirely in the rears;/ Some have been sick in corners; the sobering few/ Are trying to think hard of something new." Technique is now everything; the audience is gone, and art becomes solipsistic.

Auden does mention that this applies more to the visual arts; even at "the Poet's Party," the majority "of the guests were painters." The case applies in a lesser way to literature, though the onus of meaning generally attached to words does make most writing more accessible than the other arts.

This is but one of many themes running through "Letter to Lord Byron," but it is particularly noteworthy in being one of the first instances where Auden is consciously rejecting the opaque style that brought him fame in his twenties and is attempting to reach out with plainer speech to a wider audience, in effect beginning to distrust the vatic nature of his early verse.

Robert Darling

LEVIATHAN

Author: W. S. Merwin (1927-   )
Type of poem: Narrative
First published: 1956, in *Green with Beasts*

The Poem

W. S. Merwin's "Leviathan" is written as "imitation" poetry. The poem replicates Old English poetry in both thematics and poetic technique. Merwin, following in the footsteps of Ezra Pound, has seen fit to describe the human condition in the twentieth century by using vehicles of poetry established during the Anglo-Saxon period some twelve to fifteen hundred years earlier. In particular, the lonesome, brooding qualities of figures in earlier English poetry are revisited as modern alienation, despair, and isolation. In the manner of Anglo-Saxon poetry, the poem is entirely in the third person, which permits the poet to comment about human nature while appropriately remaining detached himself. The title word "leviathan" means any large sea animal; it was originally applied to various animals such as crocodiles or sea turtles, but today it commonly signifies the whale, the meaning Merwin has in mind.

The first dozen lines or so of the poem provide a description of the leviathan, here seen initially as the "black sea-brute bulling through wave-wrack." The whale is then shown in action moving through the waves, creating vast havoc, and in his environment, where he "overmasters" the sea-marches to find "home and harvest."

The whale's size and actions make him "Frightening to foolhardiest/ Mariners." He plows through the ocean waves so as to create terror in the hearts of those who view him. All of nature receives the impact of his presence. When the whale is last seen, he is diving into the "cold deep . . . drowning."

The speaker of the poem then places the leviathan in the context of human history and identifies his association with man by listing a series of biblical references. Specifically, the reader is reminded that the whale was the first creature made by God and that Jonah was held by the whale for three days and nights. After describing him as the "curling serpent" of the ocean (yet another biblical reference, this time to the Garden of Eden), Merwin compares him to Satan himself in the phrase "lost angel." Finally, the main point of the poem is made: It is humanity that is the new leviathan; that is, humankind has now come to occupy the same position in the cosmos that was once held by the great whale. It is the human race that has come "to herit earth's emptiness."

In the concluding sentences of the poem, Merwin returns to the whale in action. The leviathan, now identified as both whale and humanity, is left in an isolated state, "cumbered with itself." The Creator, perhaps, has made no advancement in moving from whales to humans; both existences are isolated, functional, and mechanical. Both creatures dominate their environments, but neither experiences any peace or fulfillment.

Forms and Devices

"Leviathan" makes expert use of the themes and techniques of Old English poetry. Merwin exactingly captures the mood and atmosphere of the Anglo-Saxon mind-set in so far as brooding, isolation, and immobility (or at least pointless mobility) are concerned. The poem is an extended metaphor in which the life of man is compared, never contrasted, with the life of the whale. Humanity, too, is alone in a universe in which the environment is hostile yet sufficiently controlled; other creatures experience fear and dread in the presence of whales or humans; and there is an understood fear and dread of contact within the species.

As is the case with Old English poetry, the verse is highly alliterative; in this poem, in fact, every line contains alliteration, a feat not always accomplished by the ancients themselves. Every line has a marked caesura, a formal break, often rendered by punctuation, in the middle of the line. There is no end rhyming of the lines, and there is no fixed number of syllables. "Lines" are composed of four feet; four heavily stressed words or syllables are paired with unstressed ones. In addition, as is the case in Old English poetry, the language is forceful and direct, and kennings are used. In many Old English poems, Christian scribes later added Christian elements in an attempt to depaganize the themes of the poems. Merwin, too, has incorporated such elements into his work here. In every way, the poet has written a twentieth century poem by prescriptively following the requirements of form and theme used by the earliest English poets.

Themes and Meanings

The most important theme of "Leviathan" can be readily derived from the overall metaphor of the poem: Humanity has both replaced and displaced whales as the dominant being on earth, and its own existence is entirely similar to that of the original dominating animals. Both entities are large, pervasive, and given too much to thought; both are "hulks" in their own environments; both are frightening to other creatures, here called "mariners"; and, finally, both are trapped in the "dark of night," trying hopelessly to escape but unable to do so because the darkness is pervasive.

Humanity, then, is likened unto that which is leviathan. Like the whales, humanity lives trapped in the "emptiness" of life. Individuals wait in the stillness, trying to focus with one eye, unable to see because there is nothing to see. Existence is a struggle not so much for survival against nature, but for survival against the nothingness of life.

Merwin has taken the commonplace expressions about life voiced by the earliest English poets and has realized connections, associations, and direct applications between then and now. Alienation is the force against which all struggle and never win; the best to be hoped for is a benign acceptance of the emptiness that can only control and rule until the end of one's life. The poet does not provide a voice in the wilderness so much as a voice in the depths of the ocean of despair. Life has no meaning, purpose, or direction; each individual trapped in his own isolation and immobility, here represented only by the voice of the poet, lives like a "lost angel/ On the waste's unease."

Like the ancient poets, Merwin introduces Christian elements into this background with puzzling results that seem forced. The poet legitimizes the biblical creation, the story of Jonah and the whale, and Satan seen as lost angel. The end of the poem definitely recognizes the presence of a "Creator," although the reference is hard to understand. Traditional Christian belief would hold that mankind is the ultimate creation of God, his perfection and self-definition made in His own image. For Merwin, this is not so; the "sea curling . . . is the hand not yet content/ Of the Creator." Humanity, then, is not the final product of God's efforts, and mankind is far more akin to the beasts, represented by the whales, than to the Creator Himself. Appropriately, then, humankind "waits for the world to begin" because there is no evident or operant direction and plan to the present world, or to the present existence of human beings.

Essentially, the poem is "existential" in outlook, perspective, and meaning, although it is unique in poetry because of the poet's successful juxtaposition of an earlier form with contemporaneous thought and belief. Merwin's poem effectively serves to remind the reader that the recognition of an absence of meaning in life, as well as the understanding that each isolated individual must somehow discover and define life and its meaning for himself, did not start with nineteenth century pronouncements that God is dead. Such thinking has always been apparent in poetry written in English. All great thinkers and sensitive people have been aware that humanity can be rightfully compared to "that curling serpent that in the ocean is," knowing full well the earth is an empty place that must be filled with individual efforts made in isolation. Such was the life of leviathan when it dominated the planet, and such is the existence of each person.

Carl Singleton

LINES: COMPOSED A FEW MILES
ABOVE TINTERN ABBEY

Author: William Wordsworth (1770-1850)
Type of poem: Lyric
First published: 1798, in *Lyrical Ballads*

The Poem

This 160-line poem is autobiographical, written in the first person and in the poet's own persona. The poem is subtitled "On Revisiting the Banks of the Wye During a Tour." It is set at Tintern, a ruined abbey next to the River Wye in the West of England.

The poet opens with the observation that five years have passed since he was last there. He continues with a description of the peaceful landscape. Line 23 marks a transition in time and place. He recalls that in moments of weariness in noisy towns, the memory of this landscape has calmed and restored him in body and mind. These pleasant feelings promote kind and loving actions in life. They also bring with them a more sublime gift: transcendental experiences, beyond the everyday state of consciousness, which William Wordsworth was to refer to in his later poem *The Prelude* (1850) as "spots of time."

The poet describes such an experience as a serene and blessed mood capable of lightening life's burdens. The awareness leads into a state of such deep rest that the breath and heartbeat are suspended, though the mind is wide awake— "we become a living soul." In this joyful and harmonious state, the poet says, sense perception is directed inward. There are no objects of perception for the eye to see. Instead, the perception is opened to the inner spiritual life that informs creation.

At line 66, the poet shifts his attention to comparing his passionate, unthinking, animal-like enjoyment of the landscape five years ago with his more philosophical response now— underscored by "the still, sad music of humanity." Now, he is also aware of a spiritual presence imbuing nature's many forms and the mind of man, impelling both the perceiving consciousness and the objects of perception. This awareness inspires his mature love for nature, which fosters and nourishes his finest thoughts and feelings.

The final section of the poem centers on the poet's sister Dorothy, who accompanies him. In her "wild eyes," he recaptures the passion of his youth. He says a prayer for Dorothy, confident that Nature never betrayed the "heart that loved her." Nature's sublimating effect on the mind is proof against evil, unkindness, and world-weariness, and preserves one's faith that the world is full of blessings.

A prayer for Dorothy's old age begins at line 135. The poet asks that her mind might be a dwelling-place for beautiful forms and sounds, just as in the past he has been restored and uplifted by memories of this landscape. If her life should then be tainted with fear or pain, then the memory of his prayer will bring healing thoughts. If they are separated by then, she will not forget that they stood together on the banks of the Wye. Nor will she forget that on his second visit, this place was dearer to him, both because it had grown in significance in his mind and because Dorothy was with him.

Forms and Devices

The imagery of the poem in many cases brings out contrasts between opposites. For example, the "blessed mood" (line 38) is introduced, then defined in terms of its opposite value: In the lines that follow, the key words are "burthen," "mystery," "heavy," "weary weight," and "unintelligible." Then, in line 42, the burden built up over three lines is suddenly lifted in the resolution "Is lightened." The line rests in a momentary pause in which all tension is released.

The poet goes on to build an experience of an opposite kind—an account of the transcendental experience that nullifies the burden. The opposites within this description take the reader into the realms of the paradoxes of spiritual experience: The expected motion of the blood and breath is set against their state of suspension; the deep rest of the body is set against the alertness of the spirit. Also noteworthy is the "presence" (line 95) that "disturbs" him with "joy"—an apparent contradiction that makes intuitive sense.

A similar process of juxtaposition of opposite values is at work in the poet's tribute to nature. In rhetorical style and over several lines, the poet builds a sense of the power of nature to fortify the human spirit, in such words as "joy to joy," "inform," "impress," "quietness and beauty," and "feed with lofty thoughts." Then, in symmetrical structure, the negative influences are detailed. Evocative use of alliteration is made in "the sneers of selfish men," and "greetings" set against "no kindness" is a telling paradox. Yet the passage does not rest on the negative side: The reader is moved along to the resolution (lines 133-135), a moving affirmation of life's joys and fullness.

The poem is in the blank verse form of iambic pentameter, with five feet per line, each foot consisting of a weak and a strong stress. Though this metrical form closely approximates natural spoken English, it is capable of evoking immense grandeur, as one sees in the passage describing the "presence" of nature (lines 94-103). The music of this passage can be fully appreciated only when it is read aloud. The rhetorical device of repeating the introductory phrase "and the . . ." creates an ecstatic effect of an accumulation of blessings. The spondees (two consecutive strong stresses) combined with long vowel sounds add particular emphasis to certain images: The first two syllables of "round ocean," and "blue sky" are examples. The imagery also adds to the sense of the "presence" pervading nature as a vital being: A "dwelling" normally refers to something belonging to a person; the air is "living"; the spirit "rolls through all things."

Themes and Meanings

The central theme of the poem is typically Wordsworthian: the interactive relationship between the perceiving awareness, "the mind of man," and nature. In the poet's view, perception is as much active and creative as passive and receptive. Reality depends upon the quality of the onlooker's perception, and this changes with time. The poet's youthful perception of the area around Tintern Abbey was different from that of his mature view. Five years later, his mature perceptions are less passionate and more thoughtful. He no longer sees nature as divorced from the human condition (lines 91-94).

He has developed the ability to see a level of reality beyond sensory impressions — the spirit underlying the myriad forms of nature, which animates and unites perceiver and objects of perception. For example, the description of the Tintern landscape (lines 4-23) is noteworthy for the blurring of distinctions between objects: the orchards that melt into the woods, the farms green to the door, the smoke among the trees — all bespeak a synthesizing, unifying perception.

Central to Wordsworth's vision are "spots of time" (*The Prelude*) — profound spiritual experiences that he describes as having a renovating, uplifting, and nourishing virtue. In "Lines: Composed A Few Miles Above Tintern Abbey," worldly cares are twice referred to in terms of heaviness or burdens (lines 39-40, 55). Set against them is the ability of the "serene and blessed mood" to lighten their weight (line 42). More important, these experiences culture joy and harmony in the poet's awareness, allowing him to "see into the life of things." This theme is expanded in the extraordinary vision of the one spirit pervading nature and human consciousness in lines 94-103. The poet's moments of communion with nature endure, independent of inhospitable surroundings. Amid the noise of towns and cities, his spirit would turn to this landscape for regeneration — emphasizing the power of the human spirit to create its own reality.

Yet a tension runs through the poem that pulls against this affirmative theme. In Dorothy's "wild eyes," he recaptures his youthful passion, but one senses an underlying yearning for "what [the poet] was once" — and is no longer. Similarly, he prays that her memories will render her mind "a mansion for all lovely forms" in her later years, but he is preoccupied with the pain and grief she may suffer. He anticipates separation from her and his consequent inability to "catch from [her] wild eyes these gleams of past existence." Such thoughts reveal a deep anxiety about the passing of time and the decline and loss it may bring.

Many readers identify a lack of conviction behind Wordsworth's protest (lines 86-89) that he does not mourn the passing of the "dizzy raptures" of his youth and note a wistfulness in his references to that time being past (lines 84-86). In his assertion that maturity brings "Abundant recompence," he seems to be trying to convince himself that the gain is worth the loss. In this respect, this poem invites comparison with "Ode: Intimations of Immortality" (published in 1807). The "Ode" was inspired by Wordsworth's "sense of the indomitableness of the spirit within me" (annotation by Wordsworth, compiled in 1843 by Isabella Fenwick) yet at the same time is an elegy to the "visionary gleam" of his youthful perception of nature.

Claire Robinson

LINES: WHEN THE LAMP IS SHATTERED

Author: Percy Bysshe Shelley (1792-1822)
Type of poem: Lyric
First published: 1824, in *Posthumous Poems*

The Poem

"Lines: When the Lamp Is Shattered" is a poem of thirty-two lines expressing the loss of ecstatic poetic creativity in response to the loss of a beloved woman's affections.

The poem was written at the height of Percy Bysshe Shelley's poetic powers, in the last year of his short life, after he had anchored his restless exile from England in Pisa, Italy. There, in 1820, he at last found the semblance of contentment with his troubled wife and a group of close friends. Among Shelley's friends there were Edward Williams, a retired lieutenant of a cavalry regiment serving in India, and his charming common-law wife, Jane, with whom Shelley carried on a flirtation and to whom he addressed some of his best lyrics. Whether or not Jane Williams was the inspiration for "Lines: When the Lamp Is Shattered" remains a matter for conjecture. It was Jane's husband who was to drown with Shelley when a violent storm swamped their boat off the Leghorn coast on July 8, 1822.

The poem opens with a catalog of images expressing the shattered poetic creativity of the lovelorn male speaker made desolate by the loss of a beloved woman's affections. The desolation oppressing his creative imagination is like a broken lamp robbing the mortal poet of his vital genius ("The light in the dust lies dead"), like a dispersal of clouds breaking up a brilliant rainbow, or like a shattered lute unable to produce sounds to revive the memories of past love songs already forgotten by the lady of his hopeless affection (lines 1-8).

The second stanza elaborates on the images of the first stanza to explore the failure of the poet's joyous creativity in response to his failure in love. When lute and lamp cease, the inspiration for poetic sound and rhetorical brilliance cease, and the poet's broken heart and desolate spirit have no creative resources left to produce soaring, joyous verse (lines 9-12). The desolate poetic imagination, capable of only grief-stricken songs of death, is like a cramped ancient apartment in a wrecked monastery or like the doleful sea-wind and crashing waves that sound the death knell for a drowned sailor (lines 13-16).

The third stanza takes a new metaphoric and thematic tack and reviews the events of the romantic breakup by personifying Love as an eagle that bemoans the frailty of the heart's affections and yet perversely inhabits the nest or heart of the weaker of the two lovers (lines 17-24). The poet-speaker is the weaker of the two lovers. He is left to lament his heart-sickness and to wonder why Love made his heart its place of birth, development, and demise ("For your cradle, your home, and your bier"), whereas the still beloved lady, who no longer cares for him, escapes from being so enthralled.

The fourth stanza, continuing the personification of Love as a nesting eagle, warns that his heart will be an inhospitable domicile for Love. His lovelorn passions will act as a tempest blowing against nesting birds of prey (lines 25-26). His disenchanted intellect, like a brilliant wintry sun, will see through Love's tortures and delusions. The poet's embittered being will be but a rotting nest in the cruel winter season, exposing Love to the harsh elements of derisive disillusionment (lines 29-32).

Forms and Devices

"Lines: When the Lamp Is Shattered" is a delicate and melancholy lyric poem consisting of four stanzas, each with eight lines of alternating end rhymes. Shelley composed each stanza out of two sets of quatrains and made sure that weak, feminine end rhymes appeared in each stanza to capture the fluttering, evanescent quality of lost love through sound effects (for example, "shattered" and "scattered").

The poem's metrical system wavers between iambic tetrameter and iambic trimeter, both with many variations. The musical irregularity — the abrupt use of stressed sounds breaking, at intervals, the harmony of the iambic beat — works with the feminine rhymes to convey the discord of romantic bereavement through sound. Shelley also made heavy use of consonance and assonance (as in "The light in the dust lies dead") throughout the poem.

Shelley was a master of rhetorical fireworks, so much so that he has been criticized (often unfairly) for overdoing the artistry of poetry and for lapsing into incoherence and obscurity. Desmond King-Hele, in *Shelley: The Man and the Poet* (1960), adjudged "Lines: When the Lamp Is Shattered" to be too "trite and trivial" for its repeated appearance in anthologies of poetry; he was perhaps overly influenced in his severe verdict by F. R. Leavis' jaundiced opinion of the poem's diction and overall worth. Such criticism is excessive. Although "Lines: When the Lamp Is Shattered" may not rank with Shelley's greatest performances, it is an authentically desolate Romantic lyric on a typical Shelleyan theme of love and poetic creativity. The poem is not overly incoherent or obscure in its piling on of evocative images of his lovelorn state.

Cooperating with his complex sound effects is a series of metaphors and similes that are at the heart of the poem's achievement in communicating vividly the loss of love and ecstatic poetic creativity. The metaphors of the broken lamp, lute, and rainbow in the first stanza are implicit comparisons to the poet-speaker's lovelorn state of melancholy poetic inspiration in the second stanza, which concludes with two similes — explicit comparisons of his muted melancholy powers of imagination to narrow, wrecked cells and to doleful, death-dealing waves.

Finally, a new metaphor, comparing a personified Love to a nesting eagle, is central to the last two stanzas in describing the utter desolation of the romantically thwarted poet-speaker, who is still possessed by a strong emotional attachment. Stanza 4 employs two similes of storm and sun that are integrated with the pervasive eagle metaphor in order to communicate the poet-speaker's wintry embitterment with his failure in love.

Themes and Meanings

"Lines: When the Lamp Is Shattered" is about the loss of ecstatic poetic creativity in response to a failure in love. This is a theme close to the deepest concerns of Shelley as a radical thinker, artist, and proselytizer of love as the liberating force for an imprisoned humanity.

As Shelley wrote in his essay "On Love" (1815), "This is Love. This is the bond and the sanction which connects not only man with man but with everything which exists." A major vehicle for releasing an oppressed humanity from the chains of political tyranny and personal insecurity and hatred was the poet's imagination creating liberating visions of love in poetry that would inspire the human race. Shelley was not certain that poetry could accomplish this reformist goal, but he was certain that the artistic effort was worthwhile, if humanity was ever to progress and forsake a hopeless, self-created, and socially conditioned lethargy of spirit. As M. H. Abrams noted in the second edition of *Natural Supernaturalism: Tradition and Revolution in Romantic Literature* (1973), "the imagination for Shelley is the faculty by which man transcends his individual ego, transfers the center of reference to others, and thus transforms self-love into, simply, love."

If the great secret of moral good is love and the great instrument of moral good is the imagination—and if the great strength of the imagination is poetry—then "Lines: When the Lamp Is Shattered" is a despondent exploration by Shelley of the dissolution of his noble vision of love and poetic creativity. The poem is a beautiful statement of what happens when love fails, when the imagination cannot transcend self-absorption and sing a joyous love song for another, and when poetry must rest, not in an affirmation of universal love, but in a proclamation of disillusionment and a promise of bitterness.

Thomas M. Curley

THE LISTENERS

Author: Walter de la Mare (1873-1956)
Type of poem: Lyric
First published: 1912, in *The Listeners and Other Poems*

The Poem

"The Listeners" is a single-stanza poem of thirty-six lines, rhyming *abcb*. The title suggests the focus of the poem: It is not on the poem's human traveler, but on the phantom listeners who await him. The poem is written in the third person, to allow the reader to observe, objectively, the traveler first and then the listeners, and to remain behind with the listeners when the traveler hastily departs at the poem's close.

The poem begins *in medias res*, with the traveler knocking on a moonlit door in an unknown place. It is this sense of the unknown, with all its ambiguities, that controls the tone and mood of the poem. The place in the forest where the traveler finds himself is deserted and overgrown with brambles; the sense of isolation and strangeness causes the lonely human visitor first to knock on the door of the turreted house, then to smite it, and finally to smite it even louder, as his cries receive no response.

One soon discovers, however, that it is only he who is perplexed and lonely in this nighttime scene; nature ignores the phantoms, as is seen by his horse contentedly champing the grasses and by the bird in the house's turret being disturbed, not by anything eerie or frightening in the natural scene, but by his voice and loud knocking. The scene reinforces one of Walter de la Mare's common themes: Human beings are estranged from both the natural and the social worlds, and are puzzled and even frightened by the unfathomable mystery at the heart of life.

This sense of mystery is deepened by the power of hints and suggestions—in Wallace Stevens' terms, of innuendos and inflections. Why is the traveler here? Evidently to keep some promise, perhaps to those who are no longer alive, since he is "the one man left awake" (line 32). Something, though, has caused him to come to this lonely and isolated place in the middle of the night and compelled him to cry out repeatedly to a deserted house, without entering to see for himself who or what might be there.

De la Mare builds on the paradoxes and ironies inherent in the situation, opposing the "lonely" traveler to the "lone" house, and his standing "still" because he is perplexed and wondering to the "phantom listeners" who are "still" in the sense of being quiet (and perhaps dead). Yet even while the traveler feels in his heart their strangeness and stillness, his horse continues to crop the "dark turf," naturally oblivious to these human fears.

The poem ends with a shift in focus from the lonely traveler to the silent listeners; while he rushes to flee the scene, they remain behind in the returning silence. De la Mare's effort to coalesce verbal sounds and verbal symbols is nowhere more evident than in this poem, and especially in the soft sibilance of the *s* sounds in the final lines. Though the traveler has departed, readers are left wondering what has happened to those to whom he has made a promise as well as what this promise might be.

Forms and Devices

De la Mare uses several poetic strategies to make "The Listeners" effective. His language, for example, is quite simple and ordinary, an apt contrast to the strange and eerie quality of the setting. None of his words causes a reader to search out their meanings in a dictionary; it is as if he wants to convince readers that the world he is portraying is the actual world in which they live. With the exception, perhaps, of the turret on the house, none of the concrete details is exotic or arcane. The strangeness, in other words, is in the atmosphere created by the mind of the traveler, not in ordinary reality.

The repetition of words is also effective: knocking, still and stillness, and listening are prominent. There is a general absence of metaphor and simile as well; it is the language of the setting itself, dark, empty, still, listening, which creates a mood of sadness, loneliness, and emptiness.

It is perhaps the rhythm, however, which is the most striking stylistic component: de la Mare uses a basically anapestic rhythm (two unstressed syllables followed by a stressed syllable), more commonly used in rollicking ballads or sea chanteys, to communicate a sense of urgency and anxiety in the situation. Indeed, for many readers, it is difficult to be left behind in the forest at the poem's end. When the traveler leaves, one wishes to leave with him, rather than to stay behind with the phantom listeners.

Themes and Meanings

"The Listeners" is a poem about an unsuccessful quest for clarity and meaning in an inscrutable universe. Like Herman Melville and Stephen Crane, Walter de la Mare sees humans caught in a web of circumstance that drastically limits their personal freedom and prevents them from making full connections with either nature or other people. Yet, paradoxically, it is this yearning for a harmony and wholeness in the natural and social worlds which is always just out of reach that convinces people that personal integrity and fidelity to commitments, responsibilities, and attachments is what makes them most human, and what keeps them from the dark terrors of a universe which, while not openly hostile or malevolent, still ignores the human presence.

One question which occurs to many readers is why the poem is entitled "The Listeners" and not "The Traveler," since the initial focus is on the human traveler who comes to this distant and lonely scene. Although the focus is at first centered on "the one man left awake" or alive (line 32) who speaks with a "voice from the world of men" (line 16), that focus shifts in an important way to the "host of phantom listeners" (line 13) that dwell in this strange house. These listeners not only listen but also stand "thronging" (line 17) the dark stair that goes down to an empty hall, yet they answer his cries only with their "stillness" (line 22). Are they the ghosts of those persons the traveler is hoping to meet, and guardians of this lost house, those to whom the traveler made some promise that was so binding that he is coming to this forsaken spot in the middle of the night to keep his word? The reader cannot tell; de la Mare does not want readers to be sure, though they can perhaps guess. The poet wants readers to be left behind in this strange and eerie place, after the traveler has gone — left behind, alone, with the listeners.

The focus of the poem is much more on tone and mood than it is on theme. Like the traveler, readers experience the loneliness, bewilderment, and anxiety that is part of living in a world which they do not — and cannot — fully comprehend. In "The Listeners," Walter de la Mare has made excellent use of what Ernest Hemingway called "the fifth dimension" in literature: He has deliberately omitted details in the material, especially details which would explain the context of the situation. He does this not to confuse readers, but to cause them to wonder, and to engage with him in the mutual enterprise of seeking to comprehend at least partially what is finally incomprehensible: their nature as individual persons, their relations with one another, and their place in the physical world in which they live.

Clark Mayo

LISTENING TO THE MUSIC OF ARSENIO RODRIGUEZ IS MOVING CLOSER TO KNOWLEDGE

Author: Victor Hernandez Cruz (1949-   )
Type of poem: Narrative
First published: 1982, in *By Lingual Wholes*

The Poem

Victor Hernandez Cruz, who was born in Puerto Rico, grew up in New York City and remains in the forefront of the "Nuyorican" poetry scene that began developing in the late 1960's. "Listening to the Music of Arsenio Rodriguez Is Moving Closer to Knowledge" salutes Afro-Cuban music and the great musician in its title, as well as those who love this music. Rodriguez was a blind percussionist, player of the *tres* (a small nine-stringed guitar), composer, and bandleader. His impact on the mambo style in Cuba in the 1930's was immeasurable, and he was responsible for the mambo craze that took the Northeastern United States by storm in the early 1950's. In New York City, the Caribbean Hispanic community enjoys Afro-Cuban music under the general rubric of salsa. Nuyorican poets such as Hernandez Cruz, Sandra María Esteves, and Pedro Pietri are close to their musical culture; the study *The Latin Tinge* (1979) by John Storm Roberts offers valuable insights into the character and popularity of salsa.

Hernandez Cruz has written a free-verse poem of five stanzas that dispenses with nearly all punctuation. His speaker raves about the influence of Arsenio Rodriguez's music and ridicules those "researchers" who would attempt to study the results of its impact. The stuff of knowledge is in the music; to study its after-effects—the "puddles of water" that the listeners have become—is inane.

The speaker shares a humorous moment with a friend who also deeply loves listening and dancing to Arsenio Rodriguez; they seem to laugh at those who can only focus on "the puddles of water/ that we have turned into/ all over your room." Rodriguez's music causes the people to melt; even Doña Flores comes to the room from a neighboring apartment to enjoy the experience. All are so strongly affected by the rhythms and sounds that liquefying is the only possible response. The water they become is warm and "good." The music from the hi-fi could be said to wipe them out.

The imagery of stanza 4 has a surreal quality. The air opens, curtainlike, and "whistles/ in the thousands of afternoons/ that everybody is/ nervously plucking." The people undergo a metamorphosis as music propels them toward a safe haven for expressing the freedom that dancing provides. Ultimately, everything in them rises to meet the *son*, a dance rhythm that predated the rumba of the mid-1920's.

In stanza 5, "explorers" and researchers are one: They are incapable of understanding the magical power of the musical spirit and drive of Arsenio Rodriguez. They ask feebly at the close of the poem if it has rained and whether the windows are open, because they can find no one to explain the water on the floor.

Forms and Devices

Hernandez Cruz writes poems that mingle allusions and direct references to salsa and Latino culture, using speech patterns and idioms that are popular among Puerto Ricans in New York. He uses metaphor conventionally to illustrate that music allows one to attain knowledge and self-esteem. Arsenio Rodriguez's music is as magical, mystical, and vital as life-sustaining water. Its damage is constructive, not negative; here Hernandez Cruz reverses the usual meaning of the word "damage" in keeping with common practice in African-American and Northeastern Latino jargon, in which "bad" means very good.

When Rodriguez plays the tres, the listeners absorb the music by allowing his playing of their sensibilities to be the creative force of the music itself. That they are all "nervously plucking" means that they are approaching wisdom. The adverbial adjective "transformationally" is mock-intellectual slang.

The predominant figurative device used by Hernandez Cruz in this poem is little known to non-Hispanic people. It is "Spanglish," a deliberate form of slang that blends Spanish and English words or phrases, resulting in a colorful idiom. The poem contains three phrases that could be considered Spanglish: "to *liquidarse*," or liquefy; "flowers in the wind/ who know no *bossordomos*"; and "to *dance el son*," to dance the *son* rhythm. Hernandez Cruz himself may have coined *bossordomos* as a slanglike expression centered on the word *sordo*, meaning deaf.

Note that the first and third phrases use the English infinitive "to" in order to make the phrase. For the third phrase, one would say *danzon el son* or *bailar el son* in formal Spanish. The effect achieved by Spanglish is a tongue-in-cheek reconciliation of the two languages. It is a product of improvisation, and the improvisation that distinguishes music and language throughout the Americas is a creative force that ensures and sustains a culture's survival.

Hernandez Cruz uses a figure of speech known as metonymy when he says "Listen to the box." The box is the hi-fi set or radio transmitting the music, which is what Hernandez Cruz actually wants the reader to hear; it is the immediate source of the "damage" that Rodriguez's music creates for the benefit of the mind, body, and soul. Magical and surrealistic images characterize stanza 4, beginning with the air that whistles as it opens. The poet uses hyberbole when he speaks of "the thousands of afternoons" of listening, dancing, and living with the music. The wordplay of "transformationally swimming" reaffirms that the listeners are moved "to where it is safe to dance/ like flowers in the wind."

Themes and Meanings

The central feature of "Listening to the Music of Arsenio Rodriguez Is Moving Closer to Knowledge," from the title to the final line ("Has it rained?"), is its lightheartedness and sense of whimsy. Some things, it says, such as sensuous music, cannot by analyzed; they should simply be experienced. If one is not capable of experiencing the music directly, one is simply not going to understand it.

One moves closer to awareness, self-worth, and knowledge through Arsenio

Rodriguez's music because its power to liquefy makes one feel a union of water and knowledge. The intrinsic qualities of warmth and passion in the music have a special appeal to the Caribbean Latino sensibility.

The poem's vivid irony lies in the comparison of the researchers' scrutiny of the pools of water with the knowledge the speaker and his friends gain from directly experiencing the music. The poem satirizes the academicians' preoccupation with the puddles, since they are unaware of the water's essence and intangible qualities. Theirs is the kind of intellect that cannot rise to "*dance el son.*" The neighbors, represented by Doña Flores, love the music and willingly liquefy under its spell. *Flores* means flowers, and, as Mrs. Flores is affected, so are the flowers in stanza 4 that "dance/ . . . in the wind." The poem's organic spontaneity creates a bridge in stanza 3 between Flores and flowers—the people, who are lively and beautiful, and the metaphorical essence and spirit of the people. The water is warm because it is those who are alive in their exultation who are transformed.

The ending of the poem leaves the explorer-researchers seeking answers and understanding to absurd questions. They have missed the beauty and truth of the music of Arsenio Rodriguez: They will never be wise.

Ron Welburn

THE LITTLE CAR

Author: Guillaume Apollinaire (Guillaume Albert Wladimir Alexandre
   Apollinaire de Kostrowitzky, 1880-1918)
Type of poem: Lyric
First published: 1918, as "La Petite Auto," in *Calligrammes*; collected in
   Calligrams, 1970

The Poem

"The Little Car" is written in free verse, its forty lines divided into six stanzas, excluding the calligram inserted in the middle of the poem. It is autobiographical, relating the feelings and impressions of Guillaume Apollinaire as he thinks back on his journey with friends from Deauville across the French countryside to Paris, where they enlisted to fight in World War I.

By providing the date, hour, and location of their departure, Apollinaire establishes a specific setting and moment in time. The mention of the "little car" in the third line, and in the title, gives a sense of significance to a usually trivial detail. The following one-line stanza tells that the men in the car numbered three, a number that appears two more times in the poem.

In the next stanza, the poem shifts to a more profound level as the speaker suggests that their seemingly innocuous journey actually symbolizes the end of an entire "era." War is described in apocalyptic and prophetic metaphors as a wave of mysterious and otherworldly forces unleashed around the frail, helpless little car. Armies become "furious giants"; planes are "eagles" flying from their nests; submarines seem like "fish" ascending from the sea.

The poem shifts back to a more intimate focus in the fourth stanza. The "dogs" can be seen in two ways: literally, as dogs the speaker hears barking in the distance, or figuratively, as the dogs of war beckoning their destructive forces. The speaker expresses empathy with the battling armies in that he carries them within himself. The landscape on which the armies "meandered" suddenly transforms into the pleasant little villages and locales of the French countryside. The poem then expands its focus to encompass universal concepts. Contrasting sensations of beauty and horror are combined as the speaker again envisions war: those facing death hail "brightly colored life"; men fight at heights "higher than the eagles glide"; a fighting man "falls like a shooting star."

In the next stanza, the speaker expresses his feelings that the war will somehow transform the world. The mysterious dreamlike image of the "merchant" arranging a "showcase" and the giant shepherds leading "silent flocks" can be read metaphorically as rich and powerful men staging the war, leading people moved by the tyrants' rhetoric, feeding on their violent words. The poem then shifts back to a more intimate force, the dogs on the road.

Next, Apollinaire inserts a calligram, a device he used in many poems. A calligram is designed to appeal literally to the sense of vision by arranging the words in a picture that in some way deals with the poem. This calligram resembles two people riding in a little car down a winding road, as a chauffeur clutches a steering wheel. The text of the calligram describes more details of the quiet little journey.

The final stanza is a very direct telling of their arrival in Paris as the draft is being posted. Here, the speaker again expresses his sense of inevitable change the war will effect on both personal and worldly levels.

Forms and Devices

The most significant aspect of the poetic form of "The Little Car" is its freedom. Apollinaire wanted to divorce himself from the traditional poetic forms of the past, feeling they did not allow enough freedom for him to express himself in a spontaneous manner. The stanzas are not uniform in either line length or line number; he even offers a one-line stanza.

To further distance himself from the rigid forms of the past, Apollinaire removed all punctuation from the poem. One can see how lack of punctuation serves his purposes for the poem: Without punctuation, words and meaning become ambiguous; ideas and images flow and shift with more ease, just as images and impressions change and transform as they swirl through the speaker's mind during an emotional moment.

The most dramatic resistance against traditional poetic form is the inclusion of the calligram. Just as a poet uses imagery to help the reader form a vision in his or her mind, Apollinaire provides the vision by literally forming words into a picture. This concept stretches the poem's appeal to different senses. The effectiveness of the calligram is debatable, though, because the words seem subordinated to the image, their meaning obscured and impact weakened by the more powerful visual effect of the picture.

The frequent shifts in focus; the sense that the speaker is moving in and out of reality and dream, sometimes functioning in both at the same time; and the coupling of contrasts and incongruities all stem from Apollinaire's use of a technique dubbed "simultanism." This technique is similar to a painting style known as cubism. Cubism sought to expand conventional ways of seeing by showing every surface from all possible perspectives at the same time. For example, a cubist painting of a table would show the top, bottom, and all four sides of the table at once. Likewise, Apollinaire's poetry does not follow any conventional or logical approach of relating experience. The poem expresses contrasting perspectives and types of consciousness simultaneously. It subverts our conventional associations of death and war by combining contrasting sensations of beauty and horror in such images as a dying man falling like "a shooting star." Apollinaire believed that the simultaneous experience of both the splendid and the hideous, the refined and the vulgar, or the joyful and the sorrowful would expand one's perception in such a way as to reveal some truth of life, to help one better understand life.

Similarly, the poem exists in both a dream world and in reality simultaneously—two different types of consciousness. For example, following the elaborate and prophetic metaphor of the merchant and the shepherds, the "dogs on the road" bark at both the "silent flocks" of the dreamlike image that inhabits the speaker's imagination and at the actual tangible flocks on the French countryside, which the speaker is watching from the little car. Simultaneous experience also can be seen in the way the poem shifts focus back and forth from the trivial (happy forests, the little car, changing a tire) to the more profound (heading into a new era, horrifying prophecies of war).

Themes and Meanings

The dominant theme of "The Little Car" is war. At that time in history, the world was facing a war of such proportions and involvement as never experienced before. With hindsight, one sees that Apollinaire's predictions about the effects of World War I were correct. The world was embarking upon a new era. World War I not only significantly altered the geography of Europe, but technology made war less personal. Armies could hide in their trenches or fly high in their planes dropping bombs and shooting at nameless, faceless enemies who were hundreds, if not thousands, of feet away.

The contrast of this little car traveling along the French roads helpless against the overwhelming forces unleashed around it speaks to the powerlessness that many felt once war broke out. War, itself, seems to be a hideous, living force operating independently of the people who first provided the spark to let it live. Though people begin war, it eventually takes on a life of its own. People lose complete control of the entity. Apollinaire offers a vision of a demonic entity summoning his "furious giants" from the other world. All the world is victim to this apocalyptic chaos.

The nature of war reverberates throughout the poem. To many, war signals the approaching of judgment day, the end of the world. Almost every war in history has caused people to question the ability of humankind to sustain itself, to ask whether self-destruction is inevitable. Apollinaire's poem, however, envisions not destruction, but otherworldly transformation on a universal scale. The poem envisions great and mysterious powers encircling the earth, causing even the dead to tremble "fearfully in their dark dwellings." It speaks of "skillful new beings" arranging a "new universe" and "giant shepherds" leading "silent flocks."

"The Little Car" also deals with individual perception and involvement with war. The poem's tendency to shift between a narrow personal perspective and a broad focus encompassing all of humankind suggests the way an individual reacts to a momentous event. The speaker's life before the advent of war was centered around trivial details, such as the little car, but now he is thrust into concerns of universal consequence. Thus, at times the speaker mentions the gigantic supernatural forces of war encircling the world, but then mentions matters of more intimate concern, such as the travelers needing to change three tires during their journey.

There are also contrasts between specific immediate time and the timeless nature of war. The poem offers such specific references as "August 31, 1914/ A little before midnight I left Deauville" and "Farriers summoned/ Between midnight and one in the morning." "Furious giants" who rise "over Europe" or "dead" who "trembled fearfully in their dark dwellings" suggest eternal beings and timelessness itself. This contrasting perspective, however, is inherent in the title. That a poem entitled "The Little Car" actually is about the encroaching horror of war comments on the role trivial elements play in significant events. This irony inherent in the contrasting focus is embodied in the line ". . . the little car had driven us into a New era."

Heidi Kelchner

LIVE ACTS

Author: Charles Bernstein (1950-   )
Type of poem: Lyric
First published: 1980, in *Controlling Interests*

The Poem

"Live Acts" is a twenty-line poem in free verse. The title suggests a sign on a marquee outside a strip joint, one that would read in full, "Live Sex Acts." There is little in the poem, however, to bear out that legend; rather, the title resonates with the suggestions of something simulated—either the act itself or the passion of those engaged in it, as in a staged sex show. This resonance is often encountered in Charles Bernstein's poetry, in which the poet examines the question of sincerity and falseness in language and poetry.

Although the pronoun "I" is twice employed, it would not be accurate to characterize this poem as a first-person poem. The issue of the credibility of a poem (or of any statement) involves for Bernstein a questioning also of what it means to be a person. Bernstein tends to view the person as a social construct rather than as a natural fact and whatever has been put together by human agency can be dismantled by that same agency. Bernstein's poetry operates from multiple viewpoints in order to demonstrate his thesis and to embody it for a reader.

While personal experience is involved at one level in "Live Acts" (the experience of a number of persons), the reader is never allowed to forget that a poem's meanings are primarily generated by its language rather than by the experience to which that language points. Hence, no "scene" is offered—the sentences and phrases do not even lead from one to another in any usual sense of logical progression, but instead juxtapose in sudden and puzzling ways. Puzzling over these, the reader is to be made aware of the role he or she has in generating the meaning of the poem. Sometimes the poem emerges from its own fog to afford a glimpse of a figure who might be the author, uttering something profound: "The closer we look, the greater the distance from which/ we look back." Here, surely, is a clue to the procedures and to their aims. Faced with such a riddling work, the reader examines closely its abrupt changes, its startling juxtapositions, only to be thrust back, repulsed from any closeness to the text.

As with the "live acts" of a sex show, where the viewer, longing for closeness and intimacy, finds neither of these so easily achievable, so the promise of the poem—the promise that convention holds out for the poem, that it will be an understanding hand laid on the reader's shoulder, a kind ear, a sympathetic voice—is not kept, and the reader may well feel cheated. If one has the patience to reflect upon the experience of the poem, however, one may find that it makes considerable sense and is indeed a salutary parallel to and preparation for the real difficulties of a real life.

Forms and Devices

Bernstein's beliefs find adequate embodiment in the forms and devices of this poem. "What I want to call attention to is that there is no natural writing style," Bernstein explains in his essay "Stray Straws and Straw Men" (in his collected essays, *Content's Dream*, 1986). "Live Acts," with its various tones and dictions, bears this out, sounding more like something written by a committee than the self-expressive utterance of a single individual's "native wood-notes wild." The poem sounds learned, low-class, and smart-alecky by turns, a little like a George S. Kaufman script for the Marx Brothers rendered by an aphasiac professor of literature.

Yet Bernstein is "crazy like a fox," simulating all this and more in the interests of making the reader aware — even painfully aware — of the unexamined assumptions lurking in uniformities of diction, attitude, and interpretation. As the poem declares in its final sentence, "These projects alone contain/ the person, binding up in an unlimited way what/ otherwise goes unexpressed." One sense of "projects" is surely that they are the brief essays into varieties of tone and diction of which the poem is composed. These bind up — present in poetic form — what otherwise would go unexpressed, and they do it in an unlimited way — that is, in a manner that hints at its own illimitability, at the potential of this particular procedure to go on virtually forever. The range of dictions available for the poet to appropriate is wide indeed, and it is mimetic of the world itself — large, thronged and spherical, not at all to be contained in any discrete organization of words.

Themes and Meanings

Bernstein's poems have the awkwardness of the new, an unassimilability struggled for and wholly deliberate. Bernstein, who has written extensively on ideas of poetry, has admitted that such work as his and his associates' might prove a "discomfort" to customary expectations — expectations that would include transparency of language and intention, "personal communication," and the appearance of words "flowing freely" from poet to reader, a sort of "lisping in numbers" which sanctifies the notion of poet as Nature-inspired genius. To Bernstein, those and other devices are too easy, thus too glib, a means to emit poetic signals. It tends to reduce the poem to nothing more than the poet's personality. He wants the attention on the text, not on the character of the person who assembles the text. Even better, emphasis should be placed on the person who is immediately assembling the text: the reader. Bernstein wants to make texts that challenge readers to put the meanings together for themselves. He wants active engagement, not passive consumerism. Bernstein writes: "The cant of 'make it personal' & 'let it flow' are avoidances — by mystification — of some very compelling problems that swirl around truth-telling, confession, bad faith, false self, authenticity, [and] virtue."

These, then, are some of Bernstein's themes — in this poem as in his work generally — and the reader needs to see that they are implicit and tacit rather than spelled out and obvious. Bernstein does not believe in handing to the reader a poem precooked on a plastic platter; the meaning of a poem lies in the effort required to decode it. This much is clear: Bernstein's is a poetry of demystification, one that foregrounds language and not personality, and his poems are not to be "plugged into" "indiscriminately"; they must rather be wrestled with until their particular qualities become apparent to the reader-agonist.

To all of this, there is a political dimension, indicated by the poet in his interview with Tom Beckett. Bernstein speaks of his own poetry as concerned with the constituting power of language, as seeing language itself as the medium, which it foregrounds. He says that he is committed to changing society and that, since language controls how people think, he believes that people must be brought to examine their own words, phrases, and assumptions. This cannot be done through a perpetuation of past poetries, but through a poetry that calls the reader's attention to the ways in which it makes meanings. He notes that "objects are constituted by social values encoded in language." He also notes that reading and writing "can partake of non-instrumental values and thus be utopian formations." In other words, as "Live Acts" puts it,

> Impossible outside you want always the other. A continual
> recapitulation, & capture all that, against which our redaction
> of sundry, promise, another person, fills all the
> conversion of that into, which intersects a continual
> revulsion of, against, concepts, encounter,
> in which I hold you, a passion made of cups, amidst
> frowns.

David Bromige

LONDON

Author: William Blake (1757-1827)
Type of poem: Lyric
First published: 1794, in *Songs of Innocence and of Experience*

The Poem

"London" is a sixteen-line poem composed of four stanzas of alternatively rhyming short lines. "London" is included in the "Songs of Experience" section of William Blake's larger work, *Songs of Innocence and of Experience* (1794) and contributes to Blake's portrait of fallen human nature.

Blake focuses his attention on the condition of London, England, the capital not only of the country but also of "culture," yet, as the four stanzas make abundantly clear, Blake does not share the opinion that this city sets a positive example. Each stanza of "London" points out ways in which the British monarchy and English laws cause human suffering.

The poem is written in the first person and reports the narrator's observations as he walks through the streets of London. Stanza 1 opens near the River Thames, the heartline of the British Empire; it connects the capital city with the rest of the world. Here Blake observes that everything he sees is "charter'd"—owned by and bound to someone—including the river, which ironically should flow freely to the ocean. The narrator comments that everywhere he looks he sees unhappiness and people suffering.

The second stanza reports what the narrator hears as he walks these imprisoning avenues: human cries of anguish and fear. Not only does he find this suffering in individual misery, but Blake also says that the legal dictates he hears carry with them threats to human freedom. He concludes the second stanza by equating laws with "mind-forg'd manacles"—strictures that limit the human imagination, the human heart, and the human soul.

The third stanza maintains the focus on the sounds that Blake hears as he walks the London streets. He gives examples of persons who are enslaved by the British system of law, by economic boundaries, by the church, and by the monarchy. He says that each chimney sweep's cry is an affront to the Church of England, the state religion. The irony is that the Christianity Blake criticizes is founded on the principle of doing good to others, in particular the less fortunate; Blake says that the sweep's pitiful cry is a reminder to and a black smudge on the very institution that should be helping the child. Blake then lists a second victim of the British government and church: the "hapless Soldier" who fights to preserve the monarchy and whose death sigh bloodies the royal palace walls.

The final stanza of the poem is set in darkness—Blake is listening in the midnight streets to the cries of young prostitutes as they curse the men who victimize them, the wives who are equally victims, and the religion that forces people to think that they must marry and stay married no matter what. "London" ends on a pessimistic note in which Blake reviles the one sacrament that should offer hope to present and future generations: marriage. Instead of being predicated on love and mutual respect, Blake sees it as something that enslaves the body and soul in much the same way that stanzas 2 and 3 point out that English laws victimize the less fortunate.

Forms and Devices

"London" is a deceptively "simple" poem, in part because the language is plain, the lines are short, and the imagery is seemingly everyday. Yet the impact of this poem depends on the multiple layers of meaning that Blake expects readers to see in his choice of words and in the associations that readers will make. Furthermore, "London" is included as a part of a larger work: *Songs of Innocence and of Experience*, a collection of poems that examine and criticize the fallen world.

Because "London" is a "Song of Experience," it is set in contrast to the images that Blake presented in the first half of the work: "Songs of Innocence," poems that showed children frolicking, nature in bloom, people happy and loving, a world before Adam and Eve fell—an event that, according to Blake, brought law, government, monarchy, religion, and other "evils" into the world. "London" represents the antithesis to the world Blake showed readers in "Songs of Innocence"; "London" shows readers an urban landscape consisting of buildings. Nowhere in the poem does Blake include a reference to the natural world except to the River Thames, which he characterizes as "chartr'd"—owned and bound by British law. In this fallen world nothing is free, not even the minds and souls of the people. Throughout the poem, Blake makes use of layered meanings and references, as he does in the word "charter'd," which not only means "given liberty," but also refers to ownership and landholding.

Thus "London" depends for its impact on ironic contrasts. In the second stanza, Blake repeats this device by using the word "ban," which not only refers to an announcement of marriage—what should be an occasion for joy—but also implies bonds and enslavement rather than liberty. So when Blake, in this stanza, describes the pitiful cries of people enslaved by law and custom, he implicitly heightens the impact of his criticism by contrasting the antithetical meanings of the word "ban": political and legal prohibition and proclamation of a forthcoming marriage. Blake demands that readers make this type of connection; to miss these layers of meaning is to miss the harsh criticisms that Blake directs at the English monarchy, church, and legal system.

Finally, Blake uses appeals to the senses to heighten the poem's impact. By having the narrator walk through this sordid scene and report what is heard and seen, Blake forces the reader into an immediate confrontation with the human suffering the poet sees all around him. The speaker hears children crying in the person of the chimney sweep and in the diseased prostitute's blinded newborn; he hears despair in the dying sigh of the soldier; he sees death and suffering on every street.

Themes and Meanings

Blake's purpose in creating the *Songs of Innocence and of Experience* was to level criticism at late eighteenth century English society. In these poems, Blake contrasts the unfallen innocence of children with the sordid, repressed attitudes of the adult world—a world ruled by the church, the monarchy, and English common law. Blake viewed himself as a prophet whose task it was to shake people out of their complacent acceptance of their fallen circumstances. In "London," he turns his attack on the capital city, thus pointing out that the very heart of the English Empire is diseased and corrupt. By choosing syphilis as the symbol for all that is wrong with England, Blake is able to condemn institutions and emotions that are sacred to most people: love and marriage. He seems more antagonistic toward the civil and religious laws that sexually repress people than he does toward the husband who cheats on his wife by visiting a prostitute. Nor does he condemn the prostitute for her behavior.

He sees the prostitutes as physically, emotionally, and morally imprisoned by a system that makes them depend on their wealthy customers for their income. He also makes it clear that such victimization works both ways: The venereal disease that the men pass on to and contract from these young women also poisons innocent wives at home and the unborn children of both wives and prostitutes.

The poem concludes with the "youthful Harlot's curse": disease for the straying husband and his unsuspecting wife, syphilitic blindness for children of both women, and a condemnation of marriage as the institution that drives people to form loveless unions, that enslaves people instead of teaching them to love—emotionally and physically. There is angry irony in Blake's choice of words in the concluding line of the poem when he refers to the carriage carrying the young bride and groom from the church as the "Marriage hearse."

It is not only the church that draws Blake's anger in "London": The monarchy is also blamed for the people's woes. In part, the English government and the church are inseparable because the Church of England is the official state church. Of equal importance is the fact that, as the most powerful force in England, the government should protect rather than victimize its citizens. "London" shows that this is not the case. Soldiers who willingly lay down their lives to defend their ruler stand as testimony to their leaders' greed. This was especially pertinent in light of the recent bloody American Revolution, which Blake saw as a reaction against the greedy tyranny of the British monarchy. In poems such as "London," Blake hoped to shock his readers into demanding reform by pointing out the corruption and suffering that existed all around them.

Melissa E. Barth

LONDON

Author: Samuel Johnson (1709-1784)
Type of poem: Satire
First published: 1738

The Poem

London (the full title is *London: A Poem in Imitation of the Third Satire of Juvenal*) is a long poem of 263 lines written in heroic couplets. Samuel Johnson's first important writing and his second-greatest poem (after "The Vanity of Human Wishes"), this literary imitation of Juvenal's Satire III (part of Juvenal's *Satires*, from the second century A.D.) is neither a translation nor a paraphrase of the original. It is a genuinely new and vigorous composition about corrupt eighteenth-century London, "part of the beauty of the performance," Johnson himself wrote in 1738, ". . . consisting in adapting Juvenals Sentiments to modern facts and Persons." As such, the poem was a direct challenge to Alexander Pope, the supreme contemporary imitator of Horace, who supposedly welcomed the publication of "London" with the prophecy that its anonymous author "will soon be deterré." Johnson's satire against an urban wasteland did help to unearth him from literary obscurity and appropriately earned the praise of the great poet-critic T. S. Eliot two centuries later.

The poem opens with an unnamed narrator expressing mixed emotions about the pending departure of his friend, "Thales," from Greenwich, England, by boat to some rural retreat of primitive innocence in Wales. The narrator may regret losing Thales to "Cambria's solitary shore" but fully sympathizes with his friend's abhorrence of a physically and morally dangerous London.

From line 35 to the end of the poem, Thales utters a powerful diatribe against the city and, as Donald Greene notes in *The Politics of Samuel Johnson* (2d ed., 1990) makes use of all the commonplaces of contemporary opposition propaganda against the administration of the prime minister, Sir Robert Walpole. Bemoaning a city preoccupied with "vice and gain," in which learning goes unrewarded, Thales prays for his escape to an Edenic "happier place" far from pensioned politicians in the pay of Walpole's regime. Parliament itself is a major wellspring of national corruption, tainting the already "poison'd youth" of the land, spreading lies as truths, seeking a coward's peace with Spanish marauders of English trade who dared to cut off an ear of Captain Robert Jenkins, and enriching itself by controlling the populace through the government newspaper *The Daily Gazetteer* and the recent Stage Licensing Act, which was causing liberty-loving English drama to be displaced by depraved Italian opera.

By contrast, Thales is the truth-telling good man (*vir bonus*) found in classical satire, a true-blue Protestant Englishman who despises the corrupting invasion of foreigners—especially slavish Frenchmen, who win preferment by flattery, deceit, and an unprincipled readiness to do anything for the ruling class. In a money-hungry metropolis of topsy-turvy values, poverty is the only crime that provokes universal ridicule and neglect, whereas wealth causes an admiring nation to help rebuild rich Orgilio's mansion, gutted by fire. So widespread is urban violence from drunkards, street gangs, and murdering burglars that the amount of rope needed to hang this growing horde of criminals would use up all the reserves of hemp needed to rig the ships for King George II's annual visits to his royal mistress in Hanover, Germany. Consequently, Thales must bid farewell to London, and he promises that if his narrator-friend should ever retire to rural innocence in Kent, then Thales will leave Wales and join him there to help inspire the creation of satires against the vices of the age.

Forms and Devices

At the heart of Johnson's moral artistry is a moral realism that has roots in Juvenal's Satire III but that, influenced by a Christian-Renaissance vision of right and reasonable conduct, bears comparison with other eighteenth century works: Scribler satires, William Hogarth's prints, and Henry Fielding's novels. Claiming later to have had all sixteen of Juvenal's satires stored and poetically transformed in his mind, Johnson may well have composed "London" rapidly, mostly in his head, before he committed the verses to paper.

The poem was his first major bid for literary fame. It is much more of a poetical transformation of the Juvenalian satire than some previous commentators have recognized. The changes are an early indication of Johnson's distinctive moral vision and poetic voice. For example, in keeping with his Christian sense of moral decorum, he deleted Juvenalian references to sexual debauchery, homosexuality, slop basins, and wayward gods, and substituted sanitized generalizations and reverential references to a "kind heaven" protecting poor mortals.

Even more original was Johnson's creation of a political poem, replete with stock opposition propaganda and allusions to a glorious libertarian past, from a Latin satire relatively silent about Roman politics. Despite considerable restrictions on the eighteenth century press, Johnson enjoyed more freedom of political expression than Juvenal could assume under an imperial dictatorship. Even though Johnson acknowledged the irrelevance of his adaptation (lines 182-209) of Juvenalian verses on rebuilding burnt mansions to English manners, the rest of "London" was of immediate topical relevance to the current political scene and to his own bitter sense of being an outcast in the city.

Finally, Johnson's poem is far more compressed, more elegant, and more aphoristic than those of Juvenal, the angry but casual satirist of Rome. *London* is almost sixty lines shorter than Satire III, not only because of Johnson's omission of Juvenalian digressions and an entire section on crowded Roman streets, but also because of his remarkable rhetorical conciseness, which engenders summary moral generalizations. Thus, a single pithy and beautifully alliterated line, "And ev'ry moment leaves my little less," condenses almost two flaccid lines of Latin verse literally translated as "my means are less today than they were yesterday, and tomorrow will rub off something from what remains." Again, the well-known Johnsonian maxim, "SLOW RISES WORTH BY POVERTY DEPRESS'D," ennobles, with its antithetical verbs, this homely literal translation of the Latin equivalent: "It is no easy matter, anywhere, for a man to rise when poverty stands in the way of his merits."

Young Samuel Johnson in *London* proved himself a master of the closed pentameter couplet—better known as the heroic couplet—that John Dryden had refined and Pope perfected. In Johnson's hands, the closed couplet lines were at the magnificent service of his insistent search for moral order and rational control in a poem describing urban anarchy in vivid detail and striking generalizations that sometimes border on allegorical abstractions ("Behold rebellious virtue quite o'erthrown"). The intellectual density of some of his severely compressed lines can surpass the virtuoso poetic wit of even Pope. For example, Thales states a compulsion "To pluck a titled poet's borrow'd wing"—more prosaically, to expose an aristocratic poetaster's unoriginal literary productions under the metaphorically second-hand inspiration of a winged Pegasus, the mythological flying horse beloved of the Muses and all first-rate poets. Symmetry, balance, antithesis, and paradox provide a rhetorical harmony for the discordant subject matter: "Here malice, rapine, accident conspire,/ And now a rabble rages, now a fire."

Themes and Meanings

London is an idealistic outsider's view of England's depraved capital city, summed up in the poem's Juvenalian epigraph, "Quis ineptae/ Tam patiens urbis, tam ferreus ut teneat se" ("For who can be so tolerant of the city, who so iron-willed as to contain himself"). The theme of an idealistic or innocent youth's exposure to a corrupt city, in a journey to or from the country, surfaces repeatedly in Johnson's fiction—for example, in *Rasselas* (1759)—and in the works of fellow eighteenth century Englishmen: in William Hogarth's engravings of the 1730's of a rake's or harlot's progress to ruin, and in Henry Fielding's great novel *Tom Jones* (1749). The theme has classical roots in Greco-Roman myths of poetic escape to bucolic simplicity but also registers the genuinely bittersweet reactions of contemporary authors, so often born in the provinces, to the stunning realities of a fast-growing and fast-paced London.

Although Johnson later became famous for his love of London, this early poem strikes a note of repulsion. A thirty-year-old newcomer to the city born and reared in the provincial town of Lichfield, he surely felt neglect and endured poverty as a journalist-editor for Edward Cave's *The Gentleman's Magazine*. Fame and fortune must have seemed elusive to him as he struggled in the callous and crowded center of British culture, crime, commerce, and councils of state. Even though he interlards his satire with stock opposition propaganda against Walpole's regime, he also gives vent to heartfelt abhorrence of urban excesses and grinding poverty. Part of the poem's bitterness stemmed from the encouragement of his natural rebelliousness by his friendship with the charismatic and unstable minor poet Richard Savage, who is sometimes, perhaps erroneously, equated with Thales. Savage, too, was an erudite, hypersensitive, and poverty-stricken author who, like Thales, had to escape to Wales, and who, unlike Johnson, died in 1743 without achieving enduring fame and fortune in the big city.

Allied with the central theme of exposing the moral and physical horrors of the modern metropolis through ridicule for the reader's satiric instruction are two motifs of escape. The first is the classical myth of rural retirement from the city, adapted from Juvenal's Satire III to embrace British geography, including remote places such as Wales, Scotland, Ireland, Kent, and the banks of the rivers Severn and Trent. There is even a probable allusion to the new pauper colony of Georgia (lines 170-175), founded by James Oglethorpe in the early 1730's as a philanthropic and religious-oriented settlement in North America.

The poem's geographical escapism extends to an escapism in time. Juvenal's fleeting hints of an ancient golden age are nothing compared to Johnson's insistent and periodic appeals to visions of former English greatness as a foil to the stark national decline visible everywhere in the city. Radically innovating from Juvenal's original hints, Johnson created a new, more political poem of opposition propaganda that contrasts Robert Walpole's supposedly cowardly policies toward Spain and France during a looming "War of Jenkin's Ear" against the Spanish (1739) with the greatness of Queen Elizabeth I (lines 19-30), Edward III (lines 99-105), Henry V (lines 117-122), and Alfred the Great (lines 248-253). Indeed, Thales' very retirement to Wales is a re-creation of the flight of ancient Celtic Britons from foreign Saxon invaders (lines 7-8, 43-48). The pursuit and preservation of English liberty and Christian rectitude require an escape from the economic enslavement and ethical chaos generated in the capital city.

Thomas M. Curley

THE LOOM

Author: Robert Kelly (1935-   )
Type of poem: Poetic sequence
First published: 1975

The Poem

The Loom is a long poem of more than four hundred pages by one of America's most prolific and versatile poets. It takes up a thorny issue of contemporary poetry, the divided self, which is presented in many forms as the speaker ventures over the earth in search of a way to dissolve his own internal oppositions to become whole and imaginative in a new life. Robert Kelly's voluminous output as a writer is characterized by a lush and vivid imagination, a supple writing style that is clear, crisp, flexible in its command of a wide variety of experiences and topics, ranging from love stories to allegories, fables, romantic adventures, comic absurdity, myth, and occult lore. Hardly anyone compares with him for breadth of interest or facility with language or volubility. To date, his canon has expanded to over fifty volumes of fiction and poetry, and the pace of his output has even quickened in recent years with a series of short-story collections that have commanded high praise from critics.

The Loom is an early work that establishes some of the major themes of his subsequent poetry, in particular the complex relation between the sexes, which represents for Kelly not only the dynamics of love, but the terms of conflict between soul and self, ego and world. The Loom is an exploration of the identity of man and woman, self and soul, as these terms undergo a transformation through a loosely jointed quest narrative.

The poem, divided into thirty-six segments of narrative and commentary, is written in a fluid discourse of short lines, on a border between dramatic monologue and private revery. One is never quite sure where one mode of delivery ends and the other begins. The language is sinuous and moves effortlessly between direct address and dreamy introspection as one is drawn into the life of an intelligent, humorously candid man who shares his efforts to satisfy his sexual and emotional cravings.

The loom of the title is the imagination itself, which weaves into the design of its story the various myths by which a man slowly transforms himself from embattled opposites to serene lover of several women, each of whom represents an aspect of soul, his own and the world's. Though the quest has a long history in poetry, Kelly's version of it is modern and original. He begins the narrative by seating himself before a table, as medieval bards would do before reciting a long heroic epic. The reader learns immediately that there are "two rhythms" to harmonize, two realms of awareness to bring into phase, which Kelly identifies as "City & Language," "place & talk," or world and self. The table is parsed into its psychological root as *tabula*, the blank slate of mind on which experience makes its marks. It is also the table of seances, where spirits are summoned and made to talk across the border of death and sleep. Finally, the table is an altar where one partakes of communion with a holy spirit, and shares the ritual with others, his readers.

Kelly appropriates many of the conventions of epic narrative, including invocations to the muse and a ritual descent into the underworld of memory, from which heroes have traditionally set forth on their mythic voyages. Having deployed this classic machinery for his own narrative, one learns the essential purpose of the tale (the argument), that the sexes have been falsely polarized and separated from one another, and that wholeness resides in transposing sexual differences back into one human sensibility. Only then can *"we move/ naked at last/ beyond the garments/ male & female one/ & none."*

Each of the thirty-six sections of *The Loom* features a woman as the object of the quest. Her presence in the poem is a focal point of each tale or meditation; she figures as the lover, as goddess, muse, or as a dimension of the narrator's own self which he cannot bring into phase with the rest of his awareness. Woman here is both real and figurative, an actual woman, such as the wife he addresses as Helen, and the echo of mythic females whose historic or psychological significance reverberates behind the name of Helen. Sometimes, as in the case of Isabella, who appears twice in the sequence, in sections 3 and 16, she is like an Ariadne figure who helps Theseus, her lover, find his way out of the labyrinth at Minos. Lady Isabella is also a guide of sorts, a counselor to the ironic narrator as he plunges into the early stages of his journey toward rebirth.

The journey starts the moment the narrator is seated at his table and settled into his memory trance. Readers find him on the deck of an ocean liner, speaking to Lady Isabella, who is traveling with her father back to the island of Mallorca from Naples. Lady Isabella's father is founder of the Cabeza Foundation, an institute that studies the relation between the mind and the brain (*cabeza* is Spanish for head.) Readers see her through the ironic perspective of the narrator, who makes everything she says seem absurd, especially when she informs him that the motto of the institute is "To free the mind/ from the circuitry/ of the brain."

The Mediterranean, where the ship sails, is the locus of ancient mythology, and Homer's *Odyssey* (c. 800 B.C.) is the principal narrative from which Western journey and quest literature springs. The ocean liner fades into another, smaller, ship where the narrator meets Odysseus, who prefers his Roman name, Ulysses, and who introduces him to a new lover, Korinna. The narrator's brief relation with Korinna parallels the episode in the *Odyssey* where Odysseus falls in love with Calypso and lives with her on an island for ten years. Korinna is "much earlier than Odysseus," she tells the narrator, and she confides that she is one of the "blonde witches" of the Dordogne, the cave region of western France. "I had an odd feeling/ I wanted to worship her," he says, as he perceives in her the powers of a goddess. She, too, is a counselor and repeats the message of Lady Isabella that the "mind belongs to itself," and not merely to the logic of one's senses, the world of the brain.

Other episodes take a reader to California, to the mountains where he meets a young woman whose loyalty to an older man, a kind of Sisyphus who spends his life trying to climb a mountain, prevents her from becoming the narrator's lover. Her restraint is also a lesson in reserve, the soul's continence. The most striking of these early adventures occurs in section 11, where a hired hand on a ranch leads the cattle out into a field, slaughters a bullock, and throws a spell over the bewildered rancher and his family. The narrator behaves with godlike austerity as he makes his sacrifice. Already he is partly transformed into a mythological figure, a Dionysus.

Section 16 returns to the ship carrying Lady Isabella to Mallorca, where the narrator is her aggressive lover. At the point of seduction, however, they quarrel and he swims back to Los Angeles and returns home. In section 21, he is the "lame God," the figure of Pan or Eros, whose realm is a fertile garden, the pagan world of love and innocence. In other episodes, he meets Isis, the Egyptian goddess and sister/lover of Osiris whom she has restored to life. The narrator has traveled through his cultural memory to relive the experience of many heroes, and has undergone harrowing ordeals, such as his kidnapping and torture recorded in section 23, where he is buried and figuratively reborn. Finally, he returns home as Adam, first man, the link between the "creature world" of apes and the human world of anxiety and death. His skull looks back at him as the reminder of his mortality, but his mind has leaped free, as Lady Isabella said it should. The rains pour down into the desert as the sign of his renewal.

Forms and Devices

Although it is a complex work involving many references and allusions, the technical devices in *The Loom* are relatively simple. To allow for a quick flow of discourse in the poem, the lines are kept short and are enjambed in a loose, conversational rhythm of varying meters. Stanzas are irregular and can run for several pages. There is no set length of line but, on average, the lines do not exceed eight or nine syllables and are rarely fewer than two or three syllables. Sometimes a paragraph of prose will intervene. Kelly occasionally indents a line to mark a shift in tone or to separate units of thought or action in a stanza. These indentations vary and, perhaps, suggest the length of certain pauses in the flow of narrative. Otherwise, the poem is a graceful discourse, textured by occasional passages of verse from Greek, Spanish, and Provençal poetry and by the sheer exuberance of figures and place-names sprinkled throughout.

The discourse itself is a playful mixture of literal reminiscence, humorous commentary, hyperbole, and allegorical episodes. Literal and figurative events merge subtly in the language as the story unfolds; the characters are drawn realistically only to be elevated in the next phrase to their allegorical identities as gods, psychological functions, or as elements of human sensibility. Often the same figures are demoted back to their literal selves once more, as with Lady Isabella, Helen, and the protagonist himself.

The role of metaphor and symbol in the text is like the Double Axe of section 4, which has "Two blades, separate, wielded by one haft." They signal the double lives of events and objects in the narrator's memories, and thus bridge the separate worlds of fact and ideas, sense and imagination. Metaphors abound in the discourse as the vehicle of ambiguous reality, the double nature of things as phenomena in the sphere of mortality and death, and as ideas that live forever in the mind. Hence, gardens, flowers, women, adventures are all metaphorical in their capacity to mirror both sides of human existence.

Themes and Meanings

The Loom is a postmodern retelling of myth and fables; it does not pretend to serious intent or formality in its method of narration and argument, but recognizes its tradition through a complex allusiveness to epics by Homer, Vergil, and Ovid. The classical world of epic literature is a realm of mythical imagination which the narrator longs to repossess in his own words. The flight of mind from the world of mere sense and reason is achieved through the narrator's figurative descent into his cultural memory, where he merges tales of his own actual experience with those of epic narrative—hence, the figure of the loom as the metaphor of imagination, with its capacity to join the threads of different sources into the same woven fabric.

Kelly does not labor the familiar metaphor of the loom as imagination, but we see it constantly in the narrow strip of language that forms his poem. Its continuous presence, page by page, throughout the work is the woven tapestry created by the collaborative energies of mind and brain. One frequently returns to the speaker at his table in California to be reminded of the weaver at his work—that he draws the threads of narrative partly from his own store of facts about the world and partly from what he fabricates out of pure fantasy.

The modern character of this retelling of myth lies in its self-conscious attitude toward the narration; Kelly knows he is telling an epic journey and draws attention to the act of telling often throughout the poem. The emphasis is not on the adventures or the heroes involved but on the artist who conceives and propels his figures forward by means of other texts and his own ingenuity. Like other ambitious long poems by postmodern writers, Kelly's poem is as much about the effort to write as it is about what is written. Yet even as the writer draws attention to himself as the maker of his tale, the humor, vividness, compelling interest of the tales he tells lure one from disbelief into the spell of the work; this, too, is part of the humor and complexity of the poem. Magic has its ways, its will over the skeptical modern mind, despite the obvious artificiality of writing a poem and of reading it in a book.

The power of the tale lies chiefly in the myth it invokes. All stories have at their core some immutable and universal moment of truth about human nature contained in the myth or paradigm around which the story revolves. Each of Kelly's episodes in the poem is anchored by a myth in which all the literalness of the event dissolves into allegorical generality. The kidnapping that occurs in section 23 begins realistically and relates the details of his seizure and imprisonment. Gradually one sees the tale give way to a parable about the soul's powers to communicate with nature. The body in the muddy pit is isolated and helpless, until "a dream-guardian" stood over it and "taught me a song to sing," which gave it the power to call down the rain. In terms of the poem's own epistemological scheme, the brain is that part of us that only reckons with the phenomena of daily life and does not perceive the mythical moment transforming events. The mind (or soul) is that function of memory and spiritual perception that transforms information into great truths. Kelly would have readers believe that the women he presents are various embodiments of the mind and that his male persona is the commonsense brain longing to transcend its practical realm through love.

The Loom also presents certain ideas that Kelly first formulated in the early 1960's as a member of the group of "deep image" poets in New York, writers who had introduced the theories of the Swiss psychiatrist Carl Gustav Jung into American poetry. Language itself has its own memory, according to Kelly, and some of its terms are the descendants of a long line of antecedent terms composed of some of the same vowels and consonants. When used in poetry, such terms as "moon" and "ocean" reverberate with their long history as human sounds and signs, and confer mystery when placed in the modern sentence. Poetic language possesses incantatory powers to awaken the listener's or reader's unconscious; its terms derive from sacred liturgy and chant, spells and other magical rites, where repetition of vowels and certain repeating rhythms produced ecstasy or other religious states in the participants. The luxurious vowelness of the word "loom" itself promises, by its own dark sound, to draw one into an incantatory recitation of other rich images by which to escape from the mere quotidian world.

"Clean song," Kelly writes admiringly in section 24; "A light voice/ accurately lifted up,/ proclaiming the note/ dead on pitch." This is the ideal of poetry, the perfect execution of voice and idea together. The opposite is the merely adequate, the realm of information and dead act. "What will kill me/ is the adequate." The triumph of *The Loom* lies in its own magical intensity as fable, in its power to convey its readers to mythical worlds on the strength of its syllables and brief rhythmic phrases. The poem may, in fact, be a celebration of those powers by the poet, who, at the first writing of the poem, had turned thirty-six, the number of sections he gave to the poem. Readers leave him in the poem, back at his table where he began his work. Not only is the table the place of food, an altar, but it is also the desk where art is made. Outside, the quotidian world is glazed with newly fallen rain, where the desert has suddenly "crashed into flower."

Paul Christensen

THE LOST BABY POEM

Author: Lucille Clifton (1936-   )
Type of poem: Lyric
First published: 1972, in *Good News About the Earth*

The Poem

Lucille Clifton's "the lost baby poem" is an elegy — a poem written in mourning for one who has died — yet it is also a lyric of hope and a promise made to an absent presence: the lost baby.

The speaker is a woman who has been forced by her poverty to abort her baby. The "almost body" was swept out to sea with the sewage, she says — an observation both powerfully repulsive and grief-ridden. The questioning refrain, "what did I know about waters rushing back . . ." refers to her inexperience at the time. Could she have found some way to avoid her final choice? The line hints at her subsequent suffering: the terrible realization of what she has done, rushing back to her.

One recognizes that the waters are those "under the city," but they also represent female waters. The author alludes to the ageless link between the female spirit and reproductive cycle and to the cycles of the moon and tides. Thus "the waters" are also the waters of the womb, or life-giving waters. Apart from the the obvious, the "waters rushing back" may refer to her sorrow: "what did I know about drowning/ or being drowned." In stanza 1, however, the speaker wishes most simply to state what happened.

The second stanza explains further the circumstances that influenced the speaker's actions. The images are cold and bleak; the memory is difficult for her to confront. Yet in stanza 2, the woman refuses guilt, blame, and self-pity. Whereas the first stanza ends with a tone hovering near self-reproach and remorse, this section calmly explains the necessity of her decision: "you would have been born into winter/ in the year of the disconnected gas/ and no car."

The speaker goes on to imagine, if the baby had been born, the "thin walk" (the only walk) she and her baby might have made together on a day of bitter weather. The baby that would have been is imagined as "ice" and "naked as snow" — the coldness of death and the crystalline beauty and purity of snow combine in this image to suggest the persistence of a mother's love even after her acceptance of the loss.

The lines serve as a reminder that to lose the baby at birth would have been to endure another kind of death, still a terrible loss. The hard times "and some other things" weighed heavily enough to convince her that abortion was necessary, but her yearning for it to have been otherwise still exists.

The third stanza shifts in tone and perspective. The speaker looks forward to the unfolding of her life and the lives of her family. The lost baby's "definite brothers and sisters" will be fully nurtured; their mother vows never to be "less than a mountain" for them. For the "never named sake" of the baby, the speaker promises to be the mother now that she could not be in the past.

Her incantation—"let the rivers pour over my head/ let the sea take me for a spiller/ of seas" (should she fail her children)—underscores the gravity of her oath. Having been forced to go against the natural order of things once, and having suffered the consequences, she has no intention of invoking the waters' wrath again. Nor does she intend at any cost to allow the pressures of the world to induce her to take such an action again. The poem ends not in helpless sadness but with strength and with the conviction that she can now choose her sacrifices.

Forms and Devices

Because Lucille Clifton's work is rooted in the African-American experience, many of her poems have celebrated black music and paid homage to jazz and blues; "the lost baby poem," too, uses the sounds of the blues. Repetition of words and phrases suggests a percussive blues rhythm, as in the lines "I dropped your almost body down/ down to meet the waters" and the repeated phrases in "what did I know about waters rushing back/ what did I know about drowning."

The poem is also structured like a blues song, beginning with a statement in stanza 1, continuing in stanza 2 with an expansion of that statement—and a subtle adjustment in tone—and ending with a resolution or rebuttal. In the narrative line of the poem, the first part introduces the situation (with regret); the second provides details that sharpen that feeling of regret into proud indignation, even outrage perhaps; and the final part delivers the speaker from dejection—cures her blues—with an incantatory vow not to let life treat her (or her children) that way again. The wonderful paradox found in most blues lyrics is present here: Wrenching sadness and even despair are coupled with spirited and determined optimism.

Longer than many of Clifton's other poems, "the lost baby poem" is able to sustain unifying images through the three stanzas. The sewage/sea waters of the first stanza (which turn to desolate ice in the middle stanza) return in the third stanza as rivers—signifying revival or baptism. The monuments of the natural world are invoked throughout the poem—the sea, the north wind, winter snow, a mountain—to suggest the strength of the natural world and its order, of which human beings partake. Its specific place, however, is an urban landscape, reflecting as do many of Clifton's poems the experiences shared by people in many African-American communities in the United States.

The poem seems to begin in the middle of a conversation. This technique, and the use of the first person, allow the reader to share more easily the intimacy of the "conversation." In addition, the use of everyday language—black language—gives the poem a directness that engages one, comfortably or not. Thus, to witness and comprehend this very private self-confrontation is made possible by Clifton's choice of language. Its simplicity reflects the clear convictions of the speaker—her intention to cope, simply, without self-pity or bitterness.

Clifton has said of her style, "I have never believed that for anything to be valid or true or intellectual or 'deep' it had to first be complex. I deliberately use the language that I use." Her language is outwardly—and deceptively—simple. Seldom are her words longer than three syllables. The free, open verse is written in short lines, succinct and direct. Yet the compactness renders a great complexity of emotions. The very restrained ending of stanza 2 is an example: "if you were here I could tell you these/ and some other things." Its understatement is moving.

Themes and Meanings

Lucille Clifton's work is rooted in the black experience, in Christian idealism, and in her feminine sensibilities. "Femaleness" is the energy that informs many of her poems: she often writes about children, family, and keeping a household. She is interested in revealing personal joys and sadnesses in order to suggest the experiences people share—what makes human experience a continuous and collective experience.

Clifton is a self-proclaimed poet of black culture, and she clearly wishes to transmit values. As in her many children's stories, she wishes to convey the "good news" that despite dark days there can be and should be joy to look forward to, that ultimately the world is defined by possibility. This vision is strongly embraced in "the lost baby poem." The pledge of the third stanza clearly indicates that the speaker aims for better days. Also evident is the conviction that people *do* have choices.

The poem also resonates with communal and historic tidings: It re-announces and reminds readers of the plight that affects many women—many of them black and all of them poor. Not really a political poem (except in the sense that personal problems often lead to political action), it nevertheless takes on a topic that has become highly political. Clifton understands the complexity of the issue of abortion, and she offers no direct comment on the difficult maze of arguments surrounding it. She does offer her view, via the poem, that people must be allowed to nurture life—their own and their children's—for the good of the community and humanity.

The last cathartic stanza suggests that the mother's blues for the lost baby have somehow made a bright future possible for her other children. In that way the poem has served its purpose as a blues elegy—it has exorcised the speaker's sorrow and has validated, without devaluing the lost baby's life, her sacrifice. It is one of Clifton's most complex and lyrical poems.

The poem celebrates a reverence for life and the sacred will to continue life in the face of great hardships. One should note that no judgment of the speaker's choice to have aborted her baby is made. The poem cuts to the heart of this woman's dilemma and searches for understanding, forgiveness, dignity, and hope rather than passing judgments of right or wrong or voicing all-too-easily espoused solutions to the problems of poverty and the loss of self-esteem. As in blues music, the solitary personal journey is most important, and the individual voice that sings of its experience offers the most vivid, the most valuable, and the most comforting wisdom.

JoAnn Balingit

THE LOST PILOT

Author: James Tate (1943-   )
Type of poem: Elegy
First published: 1966; collected in *The Lost Pilot*, 1967

The Poem

"The Lost Pilot" is a poem in free verse, its forty-eight lines divided into sixteen stanzas, each of which is three lines in length. The title, along with the dedication to the poet's father (emphasizing the fact that the father died at the extremely young age of twenty-two), establishes a mood of loss both violent and tragic. The loss of a pilot suggests the loss of direction and control. The loss of a pilot/father foreshadows the great personal grief and bewilderment with which the poet will struggle throughout the length of the poem.

Appropriately, the poem is written in the first person, which allows great immediacy of emotion and brings the reader close to the intense and complex relationship of the poet to his lost father. The complexity of grief is at the very heart of the elegiac tradition in poetry, a tradition which seeks to reconcile the living to the reality of death. It is fitting, then, that this poem is addressed directly to the lost father, as only he can know the answers to those questions generated by his son's feelings and bewilderment.

The poem begins with a startling declaration: "Your face did not rot/ like the others." The sudden and shocking physical nature of this statement re-creates for the reader the emotional tenor of the pilot's death and the son's bereavement. It also characterizes the desperate tone of the elegy as the son seeks some consolation, however unlikely or grotesque. As the pilot died young and, presumably, in flames, his body did not suffer the deterioration either of age or of interment, fates which people in general and, as the poem goes on to explain, the lost pilot's surviving crewmen in particular, must eventually confront. Surely, this is a meager consolation, but then the unique circumstances of the poet's loss are bitterly deprived of ordinary comfort.

The poem continues as the poet gives voice to the injustice of his father's death, comparing the wrong he suffered to the sufferings of Job. Yet it is his own bereft situation to which the poet must somehow become reconciled, so in the body of the poem, he gives specific voice to his own doubts, hopes, and despair. He tries to talk his father down, out of the sky from which he never returned, hoping to receive from him the information and guidance every son desires from his father. In his desperation, he even bargains with the lost pilot, promising to keep their proposed reunion a secret from his father's widow and surviving crewmen. He receives no word in reply. In the closing stanzas, the poet is left alone with his grief, feeling that his eternally young, romantic father is somehow more alive in his mysteriousness than is he himself in his all-too-real bereavement. In the end, he accepts the silence of his misfortune only because he has no other choice.

Forms and Devices

The major encompassing form of "The Lost Pilot" is James Tate's unique version of the traditional elegy. It is this form which the poem fulfills through its general tones (anger and grief), its rhetorical methods (sorrowful exclamation and the interrogation of the lost pilot and of the facts of death itself), and final resignation. Ironically, it is the relationship of this poem to its elegiac forebears — works such as John Milton's "Lycidas" and Walt Whitman's "When Lilacs Last in the Dooryard Bloom'd" — that must substitute for the more intimate yet now impossible relationship between the poet and his father.

Presiding over the entire elegy is the metaphor of the lost pilot himself; it is into this metaphor that the poet's father has disappeared, never having had the time or life to be anything but a metaphor to his son. His lostness has many significant qualities which contribute to his mysteriousness: Being lost, he can only be presumed dead, thus leaving his son in a state of perpetual uncertainty; being lost, he represents a continual challenge to his son to find him, as Telemachus was challenged to find his father Odysseus in Homer's *Odyssey* (c. 800 B.C.); being a lost pilot, he represents an eternal contradiction as someone who is responsible for leading others and yet is lost himself. Toward the end of the poem, this metaphor finds its final shape in that of "a tiny, African god" forever orbiting the earth, eternally inscrutable, exotic, and out of reach.

The imagery of the poem serves to emphasize the distinctions between the mystery of the father's fate and the grim reality of the fates of those who survived him. His copilot's face has turned to "corn-/ mush," a bland and featureless foodstuff, while the lost pilot's is gemlike, having grown "dark,/ and hard like ebony." His blinded gunner's face is disfigured by "blistered eyes," while the lost pilot's face retains the smoothness of "an original page." Such contrasting images make the status of the living seem much poorer than the status of the lost.

While "The Lost Pilot" adheres to no formal pattern of rhyme or meter beyond its being divided into stanzas of equal length, it does make striking, if irregular, use of various musical devices. The proliferation of imperfect rhymes (such as "rot" with "co-pilot" and "life" with "sky") throughout the poem underscores the imperfect connections between the lost father and his son, connections the son is ultimately powerless to improve, much less to perfect. Finally, the fact that the end-stopped lines in the poem (such as "He was more wronged than Job.") are so overwhelmingly outnumbered by enjambed lines (that is, lines in which the thought runs over into the lines that immediately follow them) seems to maintain a continuous sense of imbalance, urgency, and precariousness, all of which are appropriate to the poet's emotional and psychological situation.

Themes and Meanings

"The Lost Pilot" is a poem about bereavement and the many improvisations that the heart performs as it seeks a way to hope and to live again after a shattering loss. The poet confronts a literal and figurative void as he mourns the disappearance of a father he never knew. Denied, by the unique and violent circumstances of his pilot-father's wartime death (1944 was the most terrible year of World War II), the consolations of a conventional funeral ritual, he is also denied the consolations of fond memory, as he has virtually no memories of his father at all. (The poet was less than one year old when his father was lost.) Without memories, the poet is forced to the abstract extreme of grief, an extreme at which his actions become the most vivid imaginable representations of the uncertainties and anxieties of human grief. One wonders in what ways every individual is an orphan. To what extent is every human being diminished by the universal and individual reality of death? The bargaining into which the poet enters with his orbiting father could be seen as emblematic of the ways in which all religions and philosophies seek to question and to cajole the unknown. Because his father cannot step down from the sky, the poet can only continue to state his case to the silence. In this, the poet suggests to the reader that everyone must find means to accept limitations to their individual lives and happiness which, though inevitable, are not necessarily endurable.

Losing a father means losing a point of origin, and Tate demonstrates how life can be suspended ("I feel dead") by a failure to devise a means to root one's life in personal and historical origins. Society can offer funeral rituals and time-worn platitudes to the bereft, but loss is finally a very personal, singular experience. An individual gifted with any sort of imagination is eventually compelled to use that imagination to express his or her own grief in all its singular intensity, and by so doing to root himself, if not in the irrevocably lost point of origin, at least in the total reality of his actual circumstances.

While the speaker of "The Lost Pilot" appears to conclude on a resignation to despair, the poem may not be entirely a hymn to hopelessness. The very fact that the poem is made at all and made so well, so intensely, represents a kind of victory. Grief has not destroyed the poet. Rather, it has made him eloquent and led him to a profound, if painful, self-knowledge and to the making of an urgent gesture of community with other living human beings.

Donald Revell

THE LOTOS-EATERS

Author: Alfred, Lord Tennyson (1809-1892)
Type of poem: Lyric
First published: 1832, in *Poems*; revised in *Poems*, 1842

The Poem

"The Lotos-Eaters" in its final form is 173 lines long. The first forty-five lines, the proem, are an imitation of the Spenserian stanza, a form used in Edmund Spenser's gigantic Christian allegorical epic, *The Faerie Queene* (1590, 1596). It is made up of eight even lines of iambic pentameter, plus a ninth line an extra iamb long. The rhyme pattern is *abab, bcbc, c.*

The proem describes a scene from the *Odyssey* (c. 800 B.C.) in which Odysseus and his men, after a terrible storm, arrive on the shores of the land of the lotos-eaters. His men are returning home to Ithaca after participating in the sack of Troy. It is known from Homer that in the end Odysseus actually will reach Ithaca and the others will die in the course of various adventures on the sea. Their difficult journey, however, almost ends on this island, because of the drugging effect of the lotos plant, a staple of the inhabitants.

In Homer's epic, Odysseus tells the story in a first-person narrative, saying, "My men went on and presently met the lotos-Eaters,/ . . . But any of them who ate the honey-sweet fruit of lotos/ was unwilling to take any message back, or to go/ away, but they wanted to stay there with the lotos-eating/ people . . . and forget the way home." Alfred, Lord Tennyson's version, on the other hand, is in the third person until line 46. The word "Courage" is spoken by Odysseus himself, as he directs his men to land their ship. Tennyson proceeds to describe in lyrical elaboration of the Homeric text the dreamy country of the lotos-eaters. His description is a frank imitation of several famous poems about magical lands. In these lands, sleep, reverie, inaction, and all that is the opposite of industry are the rule. Several places in *The Faerie Queene* come to mind, such as the cave of Morpheus, god of sleep, and the house of Despair, a personification who destroys men by sapping their will to live.

Another important influence is James Thomson's short epic *The Castle of Indolence* (1748), which is also based on Spenser. The Greek sailors, drugged by the lotos, lose their will to continue the struggle against the sea and decide to abandon their efforts to return home. Home, their families, and their domestic lives become bittersweet memories, sentimentally moving, but pale and powerless to motivate further heroic exertions. They sing a "Choric song" that evokes the gentle, aesthetic sense of indolence and restfulness, their drugged state of perpetual reverie and laziness.

The land of the lotos-eaters is not simply idyllic and pastoral. It is so restful that men become tired without working: "There is sweet music here that softer falls/ Than petals from blown roses on the grass." There is "Music that gentlier on the spirit lies,/ Than tired eyelids upon tired eyes." Under the effects of the lotos, the men of Ithaca find no reason to return to the sea. Their duty as sailors now seems too great a demand, and they complain of life's harshness, as if it were unjust that they should work so hard and continually struggle against the elements: "Why are we weighed upon with heaviness,/ And utterly consumed with sharp distress./ While all things else have rest from weariness?"

Stanza 3 of the choric song sounds like a pastoral appreciation of woodland beauties, but it is actually an aspect of the sailors' case against heroic adventure and industry: Why should they struggle on the sea, when the natural way of life is surrender to the cycles of nature? Great struggles are unnatural, for nature itself is free from effort: "The flower ripens in its place,/ Ripens and fades, and falls, and hath no toil, fast-footed in the fruitful soil."

Stanza 4 carries this argument further, pointing to the ultimate fruitlessness of great endeavors. Although when a flower falls, it leaves a seed to grow "in the fruitful soil," their human efforts are in vain. The sailors argue that the struggles of people only end in death, and so they turn away from the sea, a challenge to human courage and ingenuity and, thus, a symbol of ambition and goals: "Hateful is the dark blue sky,/ Vaulted o'er the dark blue sea." The effort to sail across the ocean to wage war is pointless. It is better to surrender, like the falling flower, to the cyclic laws of nature: "All things have rest, and ripen toward the grave/ In silence — ripen, fall, and cease:/ Give us long rest or death, dark death, or dreamful ease." So stanza 5 describes the restful alternative: It is better to dream and, in this dream, transcend the present to live in sweet memories of the past.

In stanza 6, they foresee the evil outcomes of the final return to families that are now in disorder — families that have changed beyond recognition after the men's ten-year absence at Troy. As is known from the *Odyssey* and Greek tragedies, they are right. Only doom awaits them.

The sailors swear to remain indolently in the magical land and live like gods in stanza 8. Verses 155 to the end evoke the luxurious and carefree life of the Greek gods as described by the Roman poet Lucretius (circa 96-55 B.C.) in his famous philosophical poem *De rerum natura* (c. 60 B.C.; *On the Nature of Things*). This passage presents Tennyson's version of the Lucretian epicurean cosmology and moral system, a system in which humankind is freed by philosophy from superstitious fear and in which an enlightened self-interest and acceptance of pleasure provide the thinker with spiritual peace.

The last lines summarize the poem, which turns out to have been one long argument against industry. The sailors imagine they are gods looking down on the life of humans. The Greek view of death does not give meaning to life; thus, one's actions, whether heroic or not, do not count in the long run. The sailors conclude by saying they will not return to the sea.

Forms and Devices

"The Lotos-Eaters" could be seen as a stitching together of imitations of several other epic poems Tennyson admired. The proem imitates those moments in Spenser's *The Faerie Queene* that describe reverie as an evil temptation to the Christian state, scenes that suggest a state of drowsiness and a sense of will-less dreaming. This effect is heightened by Tennyson's use of the Spenserian rhyme scheme to communicate languor and lassitude. The Spenserian stanza allows only three rhymes, *abab, bcbc, c.* Tennyson heightens this effect by simplifying the pattern further, rhyming, for example, "land" with "land" in the first quatrain. The other rhymes are also purposefully weak and unadventurous: "soon," "afternoon," "swoon," and "moon."

The streams, rolling hills, fields, and valleys of the lotos land give a sense of illusion because they are constantly connected with the verb "seem," connoting mere appearance. They are lit by a paradoxical dream light from the sun and moon, which appear in the sky at the same time. The similes also promote a sense of illusion by comparing the elements of this pastoral scene to vague and half-seen things. The descending stream is like smoke moving downward. It seems to pause in the air as it descends and is like "thinnest lawn." Lawn in this case is a kind of cloth used to represent waterfalls in the theater. There are numerous images of falling, slow descent, and settling.

"A land where all things always seemed the same!" is an allusion to a line from Lucretius in which nature argues with man that death and sleep are not so different from one another, and therefore death should not be feared even as life should not be clung to. The references to Thomson's imitation of Spenser have the same effect: "And up the hills, on either side, a wood/ Of blackening pines, ay waving to and fro,/ Sent forth a sleepy horror through the blood,/ And where this valley winded out, below,/ The murmuring main was heard, and scarcely heard, to flow."

The "Choric Song" is in theory a balladic genre. In contrast to the epic mode of the proem, its rhythms and rhyme scheme are shifting and melodic. This combination of epic and pseudoballadic verse is found elsewhere in Tennyson, particularly in "The Lady of Shallot" (another story that opposes an unreal, poetically beautiful world to a deadly daily reality).

The song, however, involves a sort of contradiction, for although its imagery and style suggest release, surrender, and passivity, its rhetorical structure argues initiative and careful thought. The sailors may be drugged, but they go to great trouble to make a strong argument for inaction. The rhetorical qualities of the "Choric Song" thus may foreshadow the sailors' leaving the island, abandoning their paradise of effortless living.

Themes and Meanings

Tennyson wrote several poems that, like "The Lotos-Eaters," were drawn from Greek epic materials. "Ulysses" — a monologue by the hero of the *Odyssey* in which he contemplates life after his return to Ithaca — is the most famous. There is also *Œnone* (1832, 1842), a lengthy poem about Paris' lamenting lover, abandoned by him for Helen; "The Sea Fairies," about mythic sea nymphs, the nereids; and "The Hesperides," from which material was taken for "The Lotos-Eaters."

These lyric poems drawn from epic narrative aimed to be "modernizations" of classical themes, updating traditional sentiments into the Victorian context. In "The Lotos-Eaters," the central theme is: Should a person live in a world of romantic vision and aesthetic reverie or turn from this dreamy life of art to the stable world of facts and hard work? For Spenser and Thomson, the moral is clearly drawn. The Cave of Morpheus and the Idle Lake are fascinating inventions, but they are places that a vigorous individual, filled with the Protestant ethic, should shun.

With Tennyson, one senses an ambivalence about the dream land, as if suspended between the Victorian love of the romantic and the insistent intrusion of scientific fact. In Spenser and Thomson, knights representing the virtue of hard work and stringent religious principles defeat the forces of indolence, but here the abandonment of the magical land is only implied. Although one knows that Odysseus' sailors finally left those shores to be destroyed in their further adventures, such heroism is not represented directly in the poem.

Robin Kornman

LOVE (III)

Author: George Herbert (1593-1633)
Type of poem: Lyric
First published: 1633, in *The Temple*

The Poem

"Love" (III), a relatively brief poem of three six-line stanzas, concludes the central section of George Herbert's *The Temple*, entitled "The Church." This collection of devotional lyrics is structured as a sequence that covers the inevitable fluctuations of religious experience as a person strives to lead a faithful life. "Love" (III) is the third poem by that name in "The Church." The first two, appearing early in the sequence, lament the fact that earthly love tends to attract more attention than the much more deserving holy love. By the end of "The Church," however, the persona created by Herbert is able to concentrate on sacred love, and "Love" (III) dramatizes a climactic meeting between a worshiper and God, imagined not as a remote figure of vengeance or stern judgment but as an inviting lover.

The speaker narrates an action that has evidently already taken place, but despite the past tense of the verbs, the experience described is powerful and immediate, in part because the poem is structured as a dialogue. Herbert is often thought of as a person of a secure and lasting faith, but many of his poems reveal that beneath such a faith is a large amount of tension and worry. In "Love" (III), the persona's nervous uneasiness is gradually overcome by the gentle words of a kind lover who has an answer for every question.

Herbert seems to be saying that divine love compensates for all human weaknesses. Instead of instantly accepting Love's invitation, the persona is hesitant, painfully aware that he is "Guilty of dust and sin," and is therefore unworthy to be in the presence of such a perfect host. As Herbert imagines it, however, divine love is not conditional: It does not deny the fact of human inadequacy, but renders it inconsequential. Humankind is indeed "unkind" and "ungrateful," but the resulting sense of shame serves no useful purpose. In fact, it reinforces one's turn from God: "Ah my dear," says the shameful man, "I cannot look on thee." Distance from God, not human weakness or guilt, is the real spiritual problem, and Love tries to remedy this by drawing closer and closer through the course of the poem.

One of the deepest ironies here is that the persona clings so resolutely to his sense of guilt and unworthiness. Despite every gentle assurance from Love, man seems to revel in confessing his own wickedness and yearns for punishment: "let my shame/ Go where it doth deserve," he says, even after Love takes him by the hand and smiles. Herbert shows much psychological insight in dramatizing how deeply embedded is the human resistance to love, a resistance that—at least in Christian terms—may only be overcome by the exemplary and loving sacrifice of Christ. Only when Love reminds the persona that he "bore the blame" for all human guilt by taking human form and suffering the Crucifixion is he properly humbled and prepared to accept the love he so desperately needs. The poem ends not on the painful spectacle of the Crucifixion, though, but on the joy of Communion, a celebration of God's love. After being exhausted by relentless, self-doubting questioning and gently overwhelmed by a divine figure who will not be outsmarted in debate or denied in love, the persona announces his capitulation and assent in a simple, monosyllabic assertion—"So I did sit and eat"—that is characteristic of Herbert's dramatic art of understatement. To say the least, this is no ordinary meal. In fact, it marks the intersection of the ordinary and the extraordinary, the human and the divine, desire and fulfillment.

Forms and Devices

Herbert is rightly regarded as a master of poetic form and language, and "Love" (III) is one of the best examples of how deceptively simple his lyrics are. Here Herbert reduces extremely complicated theological and psychological themes—the potentially devastating consequences of human sin and the avoidance of love—to a dramatic dialogue that is both a realistic debate and an allegory. One could call this a "love" poem, because in many ways it is deeply indebted to secular love lyrics, one of the most widely known and influential genres of Renaissance poetry. As in so many of his other poems, Herbert draws from this tradition basically to parody or reinterpret it.

The typical secular love lyric tells a tale of frustrated love, of a desiring man courting a mistress unable or, in most cases, unwilling to give in to his desires. Consummation of any sort is rarely achieved, and if it is, it prompts continuing worry rather than lasting satisfaction. Herbert's poem turns this pattern around: The personified Love is no flighty or indisposed mistress but an attentive, generous, and gentle divine being whose existence erases rather than intensifies human incapacity. Much like the illustrated religious emblem books of the time, Herbert pictures an allegory of the wooing of Amor (Love) and Anima (the human soul), and the key issue is not whether one can seduce or win someone's love but whether one can accept divine love that, unlike the love of a Petrarchan mistress, is freely given.

The language of "Love" (III) is, at least on the surface, remarkably transparent and direct. Herbert uses a relatively high proportion of monosyllables throughout the poem, increasing dramatically toward the end: About three-quarters of the words in each of the first two stanzas are monosyllables, and in the last stanza, only one of forty-seven words has more than one syllable. This heightens the colloquial sound of the poem and makes it read like an overheard conversation. Beneath this colloquial simplicity, however, is a subtle design. For example, Herbert structures the poem using alternating line lengths, and this formal technique helps convey the persona's evolving mood. One of the problems of the persona is that he tends to say too much: Instead of accepting, he argues with Love. His protests, however, gradually become quieter and briefer. In the first part of the poem, his voice dominates, at least insofar as he speaks at length while Love's brief statements fill only the short lines of the stanza. This is reversed in the final stanza, where Love speaks the long lines and the persona speaks the short ones, underscoring his move toward satisfaction and silence.

Unlike many other poems by Herbert and the so-called Metaphysical poets with whom he is usually linked, "Love" (III) does not rely heavily on elaborate or ingenious metaphors, but the poem gains resonance by his use of sacramental and biblical allusions which confirm that "Love" (III) is about no simple invitation to love or dinner. If the persona is a "guest," Love is implicitly the "host," not only a kindly benefactor but the substance of the Communion ceremony. The entire scene recalls Luke 12, where a guest is gently urged to sit and be served by Christ. Finally, especially in its place at the close of "The Church" and directly following a poem entitled "Heaven," "Love" (III) may also call to mind one's final entrance into heaven, described as a feast in Revelation 19:9.

Themes and Meanings

The problem of love is central to Herbert. Throughout the poems of "The Church" he repeatedly analyzes and dramatizes various aspects of this problem, particularly the recurrent failure of mankind to love God properly. Many poems catalog human evasiveness ("The Agonie"), attachment to earthly rather than heavenly ideals ("Frailty"), unwillingness to serve God ("Miserie"), and habitual (to use the titles of some other poems) "Unkindness," "Ungratefulness," "Vanity," "Giddiness," and "Affliction." To be sure, humankind has positive strengths and moods as well, and there are poems of "Assurance," "Grace," "Praise," and "Prayer," but the impression one may have after reading through "The Church" in its entirety is that the devotional life is a gradual ascent, often interrupted, to a precarious peak. Nothing seems to be accomplished "once and for all" in Herbert, including love— perhaps especially love.

This pattern puts much weight on the final poem of the sequence, which is in some respects both a triumphant ending and a conclusion in which nothing is concluded. The persona in "Love" (III) is chastened by a sense of his own sin. On the one hand, this is a lesson constantly reinforced by the poems of "The Church," and perhaps it is meant to be a good sign that the speaker at last apparently has no illusions about the limits of human power. Yet even at this late stage in the sequence, knowledge has not yet become wisdom. He has learned only half of the lesson: He is indeed "Guilty of dust and sin," but in the last analysis—and in the last moment of time—this does not matter. Human perfection or worthiness is not required by God, who simply smiles at the thought that anyone could actually deserve heaven on merit alone. The persona is so convinced that sin cancels love that he is blind to the basic Christian belief that love cancels sin. This should be a comforting doctrine, but Herbert suggests that it is nevertheless difficult to accept. Almost to the very end, the persona tries to assert his power and play a role in the ceremony. His offer, "My dear, then I will serve," is a touching confession of obedience but also a willful resistance to acknowledging that his primary role in the affair is to be loved, not to love, to be served by a figure of divine love that far overshadows any possible human love. One suspects that this is a lesson that needs to be learned again and again.

As uneasy and challenging as the poem is, it is still a triumphant conclusion to "The Church." The sequence of lyrics ends not on a fine point of theology but with what is simultaneously a subtle and commonplace observation about emotional and spiritual life: Love is difficult, chastening, and critical—"quick-eyed," in short— but all-embracing, redemptive, and the ground of humankind's being, if one can accept it.

Sidney Gottlieb

LOVE AMONG THE RUINS

Author: Robert Browning (1812-1889)
Type of poem: Lyric
First published: 1855, in *Men and Women*

The Poem

The design of this poem is similar to that of Robert Browning's powerful dramatic romance, *"Childe Roland to the Dark Tower Came"* (1855). In each poem a solitary youth, absorbed in his own reflections, is walking through a desolate landscape late in the day and eventually comes to a tower. In *"Childe Roland to the Dark Tower Came,"* however, a sense of ominous foreboding is relentlessly intensified until the very last line, whereas in "Love Among the Ruins" the scene is one of pastoral serenity with no sound but the tinkling of bells as drowsy sheep browse on lush green hills. As the title of the poem suggests, there are some traces of the ruins of a former civilization to be seen; nature is gradually reclaiming and healing the desecrated land.

According to the speaker, there had once been an awe-inspiring city on this site, dominated by an imposing palace, which was the residence of a king who could command an army of a million soldiers. No specific locale is named, but the repeated references to charioteers suggest that this was the site of an ancient civilization such as Troy, Babylon, or Persia. All of this was so long ago that the whole enormous complex with its palace and its hundred-gated marble wall is only a legend among the pastoral people who now inhabit the region.

The shepherd finally comes in sight of a little turret which is gradually being undermined and covered over by wild vegetation. This is all that is left of the great tower from which the monarch and his retainers used to view the chariot races and other war games. Here the shepherd has a rendevous with a girl with "eager eyes and yellow hair." His description of her youthful beauty and animation is in striking contrast to the futility of human aspirations suggested by the solitary turret and buried ruins surrounding it. As he begins to think about his beloved, the mental picture of the glorious city he had been reconstructing in his imagination seems to flicker and fade. Visualizing the woman he loves, who is awaiting him so eagerly, he reflects that her love and devotion are far more valuable to him than all the material possessions that might be obtained by men motivated by lust for gold and glory. The shepherd concludes with the three simple words that contain the moral of the entire poem: "Love is best."

Forms and Devices

The most striking thing about this work is the unusual juxtaposition of long and short lines. Browning wrote many of his most famous poems, such as the frequently anthologized "My Last Duchess," in blank verse; however, he was also a tireless experimenter with rhymes and meters. He seemed anxious to demonstrate his technical versatility and perhaps to compete in this respect with his famous contemporary Alfred, Lord Tennyson, who was better educated than the autodidactic Browning and was a master of all aspects of poetic composition.

The combination of one long line, which could be construed as trochaic pentameter with an extra syllable, or feminine ending, with a line of only three syllables, has several functions. The short line, which always rhymes with the preceding long line, is intended to suggest the sound of the sheep's bells as they "tinkle homeward thro' the twilight." The alternation of the long and short lines suggests the rolling hills that are an essential feature of the landscape. Since the long line is deliberately made to seem too long, the short line by contrast also suggests the remnant of a structure that has toppled because it became too lofty, like the Tower of Babel. The mismatched couplets suggest a contrast between the proud and overbearing ruler of the vanished empire and the rustic simplicity of the present inhabitants.

Some critics have complained that the ongoing contrast between such long and short lines is ungainly and that the continuous suggestion of tinkling sheep bells begins to seem annoying after a few stanzas. This is a matter of individual taste. Nevertheless, the radical innovation of contrasting such dissimilar lines in a couplet does help to evoke the scene and mood the author intended.

Browning was an ardent admirer of the great English Romantic poet Percy Bysshe Shelley. It can readily be seen that "Love Among the Ruins" is written in the same spirit as was Shelley's "Ozymandias." In that famous sonnet, Shelley depicts a ruined civilization, which the vainglorious ruler Ozymandias had thought he was establishing to last a thousand years. In both "Love Among the Ruins" and "Ozymandias," the moral is conveyed by using the verbal picture of a ruined civilization as a metaphor for the vanity of human aspirations.

Both Shelley and Browning frequently visited Greek, Roman, and other ruins, and the poets could not help but absorb the lesson those silent ruins convey. Centuries ago, ambitious, bustling populations had believed that their civilizations would last forever; eventually there was nothing but broken columns, crumbling walls, and silence. Shelley described a barren desert, while Browning's picture of a ruined civilization is softened with glimpses of fluffy sheep on rolling green hills and a beautiful young woman passionately in love with a young man. Just so, the poem of the pious and sentimental Browning poem reflects a more optimistic mood and suggests a more positive philosophy than that of the atheistic and suicidal Shelley.

Themes and Meanings

On the surface, "Love Among the Ruins" appears to have a very simple message. It is the same message that would be voiced a century later by antiwar activists during the late 1960's, whose slogan was "Make love, not war." When Browning wrote his poem, Great Britain under Queen Victoria was nearing its zenith as a military and mercantile power. In the words of the jingoistic English poet Rudyard Kipling in his poem "Recessional," his nation had established "dominion over palm and pine." The British Empire included huge portions of Asia, Africa, North America, and

Australia. The British boasted that "Britannia rules the waves" and "The sun never sets on British soil." In geographical area, it was by far the largest empire the world had ever seen.

There were Englishmen, however, who were questioning the wisdom of such extensive conquest and exploitation. Browning's poem can be read as a warning that Great Britain could go the way of Egypt, Persia, Greece, and Rome and end up losing all her territorial possessions. This was what actually began to happen a hundred years later in the aftermath of World War II.

"Love Among the Ruins" can also be read as a self-revealing rationalization on the part of the poet. Browning's love affair with Elizabeth Barrett, who became his wife in 1846, is perhaps the most famous love relationship that has ever existed between two such prominent literary personalities. The marriage seems to have had an inhibiting influence on Browning. Elizabeth was a more successful poet at the time of their marriage and continued to enjoy greater popularity than her husband for the rest of her life. During that period, Browning lived in her shadow.

Browning produced little poetry during the years of his marriage; he did not become lionized as a poet and as a public personality until after her death in 1861. "Love Among the Ruins" could be interpreted as a confession that Browning was willing to sacrifice fame and financial success for the love of his wife. One might conjecture that he may have felt that he would jeopardize their idyllic relationship if he were to compete with her too openly. Elizabeth Barrett Browning was a frail and sickly woman, but she evidently had a domineering personality. Her influence over her husband had both positive and negative aspects. Without her love and inspiration, Browning might never have become the great poet that he was; during their years of marriage, however, he seems to have been content to play a passive role. The ruined tower in "Love Among the Ruins" may even symbolize his own disappointed ambitions.

Bill Delaney

LOVE CALLS US TO THE THINGS OF THIS WORLD

Author: Richard Wilbur (1921-   )
Type of poem: Lyric
First published: 1953; collected in *Things of This World*, 1956

The Poem

"Love Calls Us to the Things of This World" is a lyric poem written in blank verse. The title is taken from Saint Augustine and gives theological support to the particular mood of acceptance significant to the poem.

The poem is set in the first awakening of consciousness after sleep in the morning. The time of initial dislocation between sleep and waking is often portrayed negatively in literature; at first waking, one can often feel alien to the world, even to one's own life. Indeed, even in this poem it is a "cry of pulleys" from clothes being hung out early in the morning that wakes the "astounded soul," hardly a pleasant way of being roused from sleep. Yet immediately the laundry is identified with angels in the awake but still-dreaming mind.

The poem next plays with the observer's imaginings of angels dressed in the bed-sheets, blouses, and smocks hanging on the line. As if on cue, the breeze begins and the laundry comes to life with "halcyon feeling" that fills the scene with a "deep joy of their impersonal breathing."

The waving laundry is next compared to white-water rapids in their rippled dancing until the breeze stops and the garments "swoon down into so rapt a quiet/ That nobody seems to be there." This sudden stillness brings the consciousness in the poem back to a realization that the "punctual rape" of the day is waiting, the day lived without the magic and delight of the angels that the half-awakened mind imagines. With this realization, the speaker in the poem wishes that he could remain in this pleasant waking fantasy.

Yet he knows he cannot. He does realize, however, that the daily round of common events has its own beauty, a beauty that contains the playful epiphany of the first moments of his morning. The soul of the man "descends once more in bitter love/ To accept the waking body"; the emotion may have bitterness in it, but it is also an emotion of love. As the soul must descend and accept the waking body, so the laundry must be taken down and worn, though it will be dirtied by doing so.

This "clean linen" will be worn by thieves, by lovers who are (like the laundry) "fresh and sweet to be undone," and by nuns. By choosing nuns to complete this earthly trinity, Richard Wilbur makes a particularly apposite choice. Just as the thieves and lovers contrast with each other, so do the nuns and angels. Nuns are creatures of this world as angels assuredly are not, but their existence speaks of the world of the spirit to which the man in the poem awakes. The nuns are termed "heaviest," but they walk in a "pure floating/ Of dark habits." They live in a world of wakened fact but also of the bodiless joy of the opening of the poem; so, by inference, do all humans.

Forms and Devices

On the page, "Love Calls Us to the Things of This World" appears at first to be semi-free verse, the lines metered but of indeterminate lengths. On close reading, however, one sees that the poem is actually written in blank verse. Typographically, the lines are scattered, and there are many dropped lines, much as one sees in William Shakespeare's plays when two characters share one line of iambic pentameter. Thus there is only one line—"Yet, as the sun acknowledges"—that is not a pentameter line, and this line is lacking only one foot. The effect is that a leisurely, seemingly loosely constructed poem does take a definite shape, much the same as the consciousness in the poem itself does accept a form. In both cases, the shape is one of discovery of meaning and correspondence.

The poem is about a joyous acceptance, and the poet indeed takes a delight in language. "Love Calls Us to the Things of This World" is full of playful language, perhaps most notably in its use of puns. The awakened soul fancifully seeing angels is described as "spirited from sleep." The laundry causes the morning air to be "awash with angels." When consciousness wins the upper hand and insists that these objects are not angels but laundry, the "soul shrinks." When the speaker rails against the "punctual rape of every blessèd day," there are two puns involved. The first is "blessèd," used as both an epithet and an affirmation of the sanctity of the commonplace. Second, the entire phrase is about the killing nature of habit. Yet the nuns "walk in a pure floating/ Of dark habits," which are reminders that one's daily actions are meaningful, that the things of this world are not only of this world.

The voice in the poem is another carefully considered construct of the poem. Only once is anything specific said about who it is who awakens in the poem; Wilbur writes in one line that "the man yawns and rises." In all other instances, nothing as particular is noted. Usually, the being in the poem is simply referred to as the "soul." There are two major reasons for this. The poem is about disembodied dreams that take a shape in common objects as the awakened consciousness ceases to dream. Therefore, as the consciousness in the poem gets out of bed, Wilbur refers to "the man" where he had twice previously used "soul." He has become once more of this world. Also, the poet wants the situation he describes to apply to all humankind, and too much particularization would be inconsistent with this goal.

Themes and Meanings

"Love Calls Us to the Things of This World" is a key poem in Wilbur's body of work and is typical of a vital concern of the poet. Wilbur has felt the appeal of philosophic speculation—indeed, there is much reference to philosophical texts throughout his work—but he has always insisted on the primacy of the objects of this world, "the world's hunks and colors," as he puts it in this poem. Meaning and beauty can be apprehended by the sense that is carefully attuned to observation. This poem is central to the poet himself—he chose to take part of its title for the volume in which it was collected, *Things of This World* (1956), which won a Pulitzer Prize.

Essentially, the poem is about the creative process, the relation of imagination to reality. The newly awakened soul at the beginning of the poem playfully makes the laundry into angels. This is emblematic of metaphor, seeing one thing in terms of another.

The soul takes such delight in the exercise, however, that the world itself seems a dull and uninspiring place where mundane actions seem a "punctual rape of every blessèd day." It is love, which is the central creative principle in Wilbur's work, that calls the soul back to "accept the waking body." The agent for this action may be a "bitter love," but it is love nevertheless.

The acceptance of this world by the soul does not imply a rejection of metaphor. Metaphor must be seen as the tool it is and not a displacement of reality. The speaker playfully sees the laundry as angels, then puts the notion aside and dresses. Yet once he has seen in this metaphoric fashion, the clothes will never feel the same on his back. Thus the mind can construct new metaphors from experience, so "the heaviest nuns walk in a pure floating/ Of dark habits." The soul called back to the world from sleep by love can bring with it a greater ability to see that each day is "blessèd."

In another poem, "Praise in Summer," Wilbur wonders why the poet so likes "wrenching things awry," why there is such delight in metaphor. He wonders if people have become so accustomed to everyday life that they do not really know it: "Does sense so stale that it must needs derange/ The world to know it?" "Love Calls Us to the Things of This World" may answer this question, one of Wilbur's central concerns.

Because one loves, one lives in and loves the world, but because of the imagination one is able to appreciate this world, to which one might otherwise become inured. Certainly the morning vision of seeing bedsheets as angels is a "wrenching things awry," but it is a metaphor that, once accepted as metaphor and not reality, allows one to view the world afresh. This is the central role for metaphor in Wilbur's work, and nowhere is it better developed than in "Love Calls Us to the Things of This World."

Robert Darling

LOVE IS NOT ALL: IT IS NOT MEAT NOR DRINK

Author: Edna St. Vincent Millay (1892-1950)
Type of poem: Sonnet
First published: 1931, in *Fatal Interview*

The Poem

"Love is not all: it is not meat nor drink" is a sonnet with a traditional structure of octave and sestet in its fourteen lines. Its focus is a personal message addressing the question of the depth, importance, and transitory nature of love. The reader may assume that the poet speaks directly to him or her concerning a message that is both emotionally and intellectually "suffered"—as traditionally expressed in a sonnet. Akin to much sonneteering, this poem bears no title except a number in both its original publication and in its collected version. Thus it is referred to by its first line, a practice dating back to Renaissance times.

The "love" discussed in this sonnet is not dramatically different from that in many Millay works, nor is the love unique in the long tradition of sonnet-making. It is partly the technique used that makes this poem singular and oft-repeated. The stark language and bold metaphors create an ambivalent tone and an uneasy resolution to the sonnet.

In the first six lines, the poet provides a negative definition of what love is not, ending with a transition that is somewhat startling: Without love, one "is making friends with death." The change causes the reader to stop suddenly to contemplate the clipped irony of the close of the octave. The lines seem almost final, as though the poet has abandoned the traditional format and divulged the sonnet's solution before the proper moment.

The sestet, or last six lines, reflects a new line of thought. The poet begins to wonder whether, in spite of the fact that lack of love can be related to death, she might trade love for life's necessities. If her situation became bad enough, she wonders if she would sell love for mental peace or trade love's memory for food. The sonnet ends on a surprisingly ambiguous note expressing deep doubts; the poet can say, "I do not think I would," but she cannot say with certainty that she would not.

Forms and Devices

"Love is not all: it is not meat nor drink" is tied closely to the revitalization of the sonnet observed in the work of nineteenth century English poet Elizabeth Barrett Browning. Browning and Millay share the limelight in returning the form to its traditional content—love. This focus is reflected in Browning's *Sonnets from the Portuguese* (1850). She not only revitalizes the intimate, personal direction of the love sonnet but also experiments with format, taking new liberties with old devices. "How do I love thee?" introduces a sonnet (Sonnet 43) by stating the problem quickly, in half a line, with the solution occupying most of the sonnet's remaining lines.

"Love is not all: it is not meat nor drink" opens in the anticipation that its format will conform to the traditional sonnet schematic, fourteen lines of iambic pentameter having a rhyme pattern suggesting compliance with the traditional Petrarchan scheme (that is, octave and sestet) or relying upon the English (Shakespearean) use of three quatrains and a couplet.

Millay, however, chooses pieces of both traditions. She employs an octave and sestet in content, wherein the problem (statement) occurs in the first eight lines and the solution (resolution) occurs in the last six lines. Her innovation is seen in the rhyme pattern, wherein Millay uses the Shakespearean pattern (*abab*, *cdcd*) instead of the rigorous *abba*, *abba* of the Petrarchan form. Flexibility in sound is gained by creating a fresh approach to the older Italian form.

In content, Millay strikes out rapidly (as sonneteers must) to make her point. Her negative metaphors ("not meat nor drink") create the illusion that she is suggesting that love is unimportant or not vital to life. She elongates the negative by forging more metaphors and encompassing essentials of life—food, shelter, and slumber.

In line 3, she begins a metaphor whose repetition strongly suggests the boredom of a life in which men "sink and rise and sink and rise again." Lines 5 and 6 continue the metaphor along the lines of illness and accident. Here too the author suggests that love is useless in any healing process.

It is line 7 that introduces the juxtaposition of an irony that negates all previous statements. Indeed, Millay clearly admonishes the reader that love may fail to feed, shelter, or heal; nevertheless, unless one attempts to love, one is flirting with death. The insertion of "even as I speak" emphasizes the urgency toward which she tries to persuade her reader. The octave closes with a seeming solution: love or die.

Opening the sestet, line 9 plods slowly and rhythmically to set up a dichotomy typical of much of Millay's work. The use of the expletive "It may well be" (a grammatical device delaying the real subject of the sentence) is an intentional delay tactic used by the poet to suggest the doubt that exists somewhere deep in her thought. The repetition of this phrase in line 14 reinforces the delay, the doubt, and the possibility that one may have to trade the best of love for another way of life, another kind of peace.

This technique, the use of a surprise ending that capitalizes on irony, exists in many of Millay's sonnets, especially the earlier offerings in *The Harp-Weaver and Other Poems* (1923). This trait is one reason her sonnets remain interesting and fresh through the years.

Themes and Meanings

That love poems, including sonnets, delve deeply into the poet's personal and intimate thoughts is an inherent aspect of the form. Indeed, lyric poetry in general has traditionally been an avenue for expressing a subjective thought or feeling. The Italian poet Petrarch, in the fourteenth century, developed the sonnet style now called the Italian sonnet; English poets, including Sir Thomas Wyatt and William Shakespeare, later adapted and altered the form. Within this long tradition, Edna

St. Vincent Millay relies upon some very traditional heritage while creating her own particular use of the form.

As a sonneteer, Millay dramatizes love in fresh and personal ways. Millay's candle "burns at both ends" (as she once wrote), and this light brings myriad reactions to love in her sonnets. Her first publication in 1917, *Renascence and Other Poems*, featured sonnets as well as the primary lyrics. This tendency continued, as Millay included sonnets in most of her major works.

"Love is not all: it is not meat nor drink" was a part of *Fatal Interview* (1931) and it may be an expression to one of her lovers. Edmund Wilson and Elizabeth Atkins maintain that, although this may be the case, the poem seems to be "the perfect expression of Millay's sentiments to her husband, Eugen Boissevain."

Some critics suggest that the octave represents sexual love, perhaps since the metaphors are so physical and the repetition of sinking and rising may allude to erection. The second portion of the octave may refer to Eugen's care of Millay during her various illnesses. The contrast of love with physical problems ("thickened lung," "fractured bone") is a departure from the metaphor of the first four lines, if one accepts Wilson's and Atkins' position, and could be construed as literal in meaning.

On the other hand, one might take the position that the second part of the octave is simply an extension of the earlier metaphors. This explication seems in keeping with the original problem that "Love is not all" and the idea that Millay wishes to extend her statement to a host of physical possibilities. This wide range builds intensity toward the irony to be delivered in the close of the octave.

To clarify the meaning of the sestet, one might conclude that Millay has reached a maturity in her life and writing. Many critics comment upon Millay's gradual growth toward more general themes and her departure from highly personal and intimate comments as she approaches universals; this may be endlessly argued. The literal meaning, if one assumes this posture, is a caustic, realistic view of life; one may be forced to give up "valued love" in search of either mental peace or a physical need, such as food. The mature Millay often writes in a similar surrendering fashion in her poetry. Life, she has discovered, is rife with the uncertainty of commitment. This position is supported by other sonnets in *Fatal Interview*; particularly noteworthy in this respect are the sonnets from this period that appear in the *Collected Sonnets* (1941). It is this understanding of the uncertainties of love and life that enriches the later poems of Millay.

Jeanette A. Ritzenthaler

LOVE POEM

Author: John Frederick Nims (1913-   )
Type of poem: Lyric
First published: 1947, in *The Iron Pastoral*

The Poem

"Love Poem" is a twenty-four-line poem in six stanzas of four lines each; the second and fourth lines of each stanza rhyme. Although the oddly generic title is an accurate description of the poem, its very generality also provides the reader with a subtle clue that this may not be a traditional example of love poetry.

Indeed, in the poem's first three words, the speaker directly addresses his beloved as "My clumsiest dear." The woman he loves, as the reader quickly learns, breaks nearly everything that encounters her "quick touch." Her hands wreak disasters — they "shipwreck vases" — and chip glasses. They are like proverbial bulls in a china shop, he says, and they catch in fine cloth like the burrs of weeds. The poem's first four stanzas follow an alternating pattern in which stanzas 1 and 3 depict the woman's clumsiness and stanzas 2 and 4 describe the qualities that make the speaker love her in spite of it.

In stanza 2, the tone suddenly becomes gentler as he states that her clumsiness disappears where "ill-at-ease" people with troubles are concerned. She can make a refugee, standing uncomfortably in the doorway, feel at home. She "deftly" steadies the drunkard for whom the very floor seems to be moving. Stanza 3 returns to her awkwardness in the physical world, humorously explaining that she has no depth perception — a dangerous situation when traffic is involved. She is "the taxi driver's terror." Having no idea how close anything is, she shrinks from distant approaching headlights but tries to dash across the street in front of streetcars that are practically upon her.

Yet in "traffic of wit," the poet says in stanza 4, she is an expert. When it comes to words and, more important, to "people and love," she can move with complete comfort and control. In the stanza's final line, he quietly states that this quality makes him love her, makes him devoted to her. Stanza 5 returns to the humorous tone, but now her clumsiness and his love for her come together in the same lines. Never mind the spilt coffee and lipstick stains on his clothes, he says; love creates a heaven that is unbreakable. Moreover, the bourbon that she spills will even provide the "glory" to buoy up their souls to that heaven.

In the final stanza, the breaking of glasses seems almost celebratory, like glasses purposely broken after a toast or during a marriage ceremony. The sound is music to the poet's ears because he realizes that the clumsiness is an inseparable part of the unique person whom he loves. The poem's final two lines provide the same sort of summation that the last two lines of a sonnet, that most traditional form of love poetry, often do: "For should your hands drop white and empty/ All the toys of the world would break." The poet drops the humorous tone that has recurred throughout the poem, admitting the seriousness of his love for the woman and confessing that without her, clumsiness and all, life would be silent and joyless.

Forms and Devices

One of the most notable features of "Love Poem" is its balance between humor and tenderness. John Frederick Nims uses the technique of hyperbole (extreme exaggeration) skillfully to help create that balance. Hyperbolic overstatement was once a common technique of traditional love poetry; the poet would declaim his lover's (or would-be lover's) overwhelming beauty and state that without her he would surely waste away and die. Nims, however, turns the use of hyperbole within the context of love poetry upsidedown: He exaggerates his beloved's faults.

The woman he is addressing does not merely accidentally break vases; her hands "shipwreck" them. Not a glass or two, but "all glasses" are chipped by her touch. Her reactions to traffic in the street are almost cartoonish; she "shrinks" in terror from distant headlights or "leaps" directly in front of streetcars. Nims expands her confusion to cosmic proportions, encompassing all time and space. Misjudging time (she is always late) and distance, she is "A wrench in clocks and the solar system." She has spilled enough bourbon to float their very souls. By the last stanza, she seems to be smashing glasses constantly, "early and late."

Yet Nims does balance those descriptions with the more traditional uses of overstatement. She may chip "all" glasses, but she is also adept at helping "all ill-at-ease fidgeting people." The poet himself is "all devotion." The final two lines provide the last hyperbolic statement and possess a seriousness that perfectly balances the poem's sense of whimsy; her death would break "All the toys of the world."

Nims is generally a traditionalist when it comes to poetic form, writing with careful attention to structure. "Love Poem" is written in four-line stanzas, the most traditional of forms in English lyric poetry. The second and fourth lines of each stanza rhyme; the rhymes are simple and unstartling. Within this framework, however, one finds effective use of imagery that is both precise and surprising. The word "apoplectic," for example, in "red apoplectic streetcars," personifies the inanimate streetcar while reiterating its red color and describing the panic of the driver hitting the brake at the instant the woman leaps in front of him. Similarly, in the image of her "lipstick grinning on our coat," the "grinning" both personifies the lipstick mark and implies the joy of their love.

Themes and Meanings

Although the poem puts a twist on the traditional love poem, there are precedents for a poem in which a poet takes pains to describe imperfect aspects of a lover. In Sonnet 130, William Shakespeare runs through a whole catalog of traditional praises while humorously stating that none of them applies to his love. Her eyes are "nothing like the sun," her hair is like "black wires," and her breath "reeks." Her cheeks are not rosy; she does not move like a goddess. Yet in the last two lines, he states that she is as wonderful as any to whom those comparisons are applied.

Similarly, eighteenth century English poet and dramatist William Whitehead wrote in "The 'Je Ne Sais Quoi' " that his lover (whom he gives the traditional name Celia) has neither a graceful face, shape, nor air. He, too, expresses his love for the woman he describes: He loves the "provoking charm/ Of Celia altogether." (The French phrase *Je ne sais quoi*, meaning "I know not what," refers to an unexplainable quality.)

At the center of "Love Poem" is the idea that no person is perfect and that love accepts and overcomes that fact. Whatever faults the person one loves may have are made up for by the qualities in him or her that one loves and respects. One has no doubt that the poet addresses a real person here rather than the unrealistic, idealized image found in some love poetry. He praises her talent for helping others and her quick mind even as he gently takes her to task for her "quick touch." Reversing the cliché that "love is blind," the poet states that sometimes love can see, accept, and thereby grow stronger. Also implied is the necessity of separating the important from the trivial: Wit and love for people are important; clumsiness is not.

Moreover, as Whitehead's poem does in referring to Celia "altogether," "Love Poem" recognizes that all aspects of a person are inextricably intertwined. It therefore does not begrudgingly accept the clumsiness, but finally, praises it joyfully. The last two stanzas express this paradoxically. First, it is the very bourbon that she spills that lifts them to "love's unbreakable heaven." Second, if she should die (therefore, one would think, making breakable objects safe), all toys everywhere would break at that moment. Ironically, those realizations bring the poet to the sort of devotion toward his beloved that would be perfectly at home in an Elizabethan sonnet. In stanzas 4 and 5, Nims uses the royal "we" to refer to himself, indicating that her love makes him feel like a king. He worships her at her knees, he says—thereby transforming her into a goddess. When he vows to "study wry music" for her sake, she even becomes his muse, inspiring him with the sound of breaking glasses.

Howard McCrea

THE LOVE SONG OF J. ALFRED PRUFROCK

Author: T. S. Eliot (1888-1965)
Type of poem: Dramatic monologue
First published: 1915; collected in *Prufrock and Other Observations*, 1917

The Poem

"The Love Song of J. Alfred Prufrock" struck readers as an astonishingly original poem when it appeared in Harriet Monroe's *Poetry* magazine in 1915. Although it belongs to an established genre — the dramatic monologue — the tone, the language, and the character of Prufrock are highly original.

The ironies of the poem begin with a title promising a "love song" from the lips of a person with a decidedly unromantic name. Still, a lover's name should not be held against him, and the first two lines of the poem do seem to promise a graceful lyric: "Let us go then, you and I,/ When the evening is spread out against the sky." In the third line, however, the reader is jolted by an unexpected and decidedly unromantic simile. The evening is spread out "Like a patient etherised upon a table."

After arousing, then abruptly defying, expectations, T. S. Eliot intimates that the "you" of the poem is not Prufrock's ladylove but a confidante — in effect, the reader — who will accompany him on a visit to some sort of evening party or soiree. The reader is led on a route through a shabby urban neighborhood on a foggy October evening to a place where "women come and go/ Talking of Michelangelo." Prufrock, who has "an overwhelming question" to ask, is fearful. He suspects that he will not be acceptable. If he starts up the stair to the party and then turns back, "they" will have a perfect view of his balding head. Clearly, Prufrock is a middle-aged bachelor — thin, fussy, and self-conscious. How can he "presume" to ask his question?

Although he shrinks from the inevitable scrutiny of the women in general, his question is for "one" who may refuse to respond favorably to it. The question is, it appears, a marriage proposal, or at least a declaration of love. He agonizes over the possibility of rejection and rehearses all the likely reasons for it. He is an insignificant man who has "measured out [his] life with coffee spoons." He is timid, ineffectual, and inarticulate, but he is driven by a desperate wish to escape the ranks of the men he has seen leaning out of windows along his route to the party.

Prufrock briefly fancies himself a heroic character: a beheaded John the Baptist, a Lazarus returned from the dead, a Hamlet who can assert himself and win the admiration of the woman and her friends. He quickly realizes, however, that he can never be "Prince Hamlet," only "the Fool." He makes a last effort to compensate for his failings. Perhaps he can comb his hair in such a way as to disguise his bald spot. Can he walk on the beach and attract the attention of mermaids in the surf? No, he concludes, and he wakens from his reverie with a sinking sense of drowning in reality. The question will never be asked, and Prufrock will remain a lonely and unhappy man.

Forms and Devices

Eliot's monologue differs markedly from those of nineteenth century poets such as Robert Browning and Alfred, Lord Tennyson. Unlike the protagonists of Browning's "My Last Duchess" and Tennyson's "Ulysses," Prufrock cannot control his situation, and he does not speak logically or coherently. Listening to him is more like overhearing one musing to oneself. The "you" of the poem disappears early; after line 12 ("Let us go and make our visit"), Prufrock is entirely self-absorbed.

The poem comprises 131 lines of various lengths with flexible rhythm and rhymes. Eliot uses couplets, cross rhymes, and unrhymed lines. The result is a blend of traditional poetic sound effects and free verse. The unpatterned nature mirrors the distracted state of Prufrock, who would like to produce a true love song but can manage only a confidential confession of his own ineptitude.

Prufrock's repetitions reveal his anxieties: "Do I dare?"; "how should I presume?"; "I have known them all." He also repeats the answer he expects from the woman if he ever does succeed in making his declaration to her: "That is not what I meant at all." Like other features of the poem, these iterations come at irregular intervals.

The poem's imagery is antiromantic: Like a "patient etherised upon a table." The city streets are tawdry and depressing; the women Prufrock will meet chatter meaninglessly of "Michelangelo"; he feels himself "pinned and wriggling on the wall." He contrasts "the cups, the marmalade, the tea" with the more momentous matters he would like to broach, but his grand visions always give way to bric-a-brac and bored tea drinkers. He sees himself as going down, descending a stair in defeat or drowning in the sea.

Eliot introduces in this poem a technique he would make famous in *The Waste Land* (1922): the ironic interjection of quotations from earlier poets. This poem commences with a six-line epigraph from Dante in which one of the denizens of his Inferno confides in his visitor because he cannot conceive of the latter ever escaping from hell, but whereas Dante will return to write his poem, Prufrock cannot escape his private hell. There are also references to or scraps from such varied sources as Hesiod's *Works and Days* (c. 700 B.C.), William Shakespeare's *Hamlet* (c. 1600-1601), Andrew Marvell's "To His Coy Mistress" (1681), and the Gospels.

When spoken by Prufrock, however, all sublimity drains from these passages. The comparison with Hamlet is particularly ironic. Hamlet, too, is an indecisive man who muses and delays, but he ultimately acts when sufficiently pressured. Prufrock has no prospect of such pressure: no ghostly father, no enormous wrong to rectify, not even an Ophelia—only a languid lady friend who will not take him seriously. He feels impelled to an antiheroic stance and compares himself to literary and biblical figures for the sake of denying any resemblance.

Themes and Meanings

Unlike the principal characters of most previous poets and storytellers, Prufrock is neither hero nor villain—he is simply a failure. Even heroes destined to fail normally begin with hopes and possibilities, but not far into "The Love Song of J. Alfred Prufrock," one senses the impossibility of this man fulfilling his aspirations. He is already middle-aged, set in his ways, and hopelessly irresolute; he is more like someone resigned to reading about heroes than someone who will ever take action.

Thus Eliot permits the reader no vicarious successful experience. Prufrock is a figure to be pitied, but he is also a disturbing presence because his weaknesses, his mediocrity, and his sense of isolation are all too common in the modern world. When an optimist such as Walt Whitman insisted that all people are potential heroes, he meant that they chiefly lacked recognition. The stuff of heroism abounds, Whitman would say, especially in a democratic society that permits the individual to develop a sense of personal worth. For the most part, these heroes remain anonymous; collectively, they constitute the strength of society.

Prufrock has something that Whitman's heroes lacked—a name—but he has precious little else. He has done nothing constructive with his freedom, and his keen awareness of his shortcomings destroys the self-esteem that theoretically ought to flourish in a free society. If Prufrock could compose a real love song, or any valid song, he would be achieving a victory of sorts, but he lacks the capacity to express his situation. "It is impossible to say just what I mean!" he exclaims at one point. The meaning emerges not from what he says but from what Eliot, through the images, the ironic quotations, and the obsessive repetitions, shows. The eloquence is Eliot's.

Prufrock lives in a world that is no better than he is. It is happier than he is, however, because of its capacity to avoid reflection—especially self-reflection—by busying itself superficially with culture (the chatter about Michelangelo), gossip, and social amenities. Lacking the talent for such unself-conscious distractions, he attempts to take refuge in literature and dreams, but they solace him only fitfully, and he must awaken to the oppressive reality of his life.

Prufrock's failure engages sympathy for him as a human being who must live with a residual sense of inadequacy. In his mediocrity, he is a more representative figure than Hamlet. Although he understands the mediocrity of his surroundings and of the society he frequents, he cannot rise above them. His plight raises the question of whether it is better to be a Prufrock than one of the presumably more well-adjusted people whom he so dreads confronting: Is disillusionment better than illusion?

To be a reader of Eliot's poem is not exactly to be a Prufrock or, for that matter, to become disillusioned. It is, however, to be greeted with what Herman Melville called a "shock of recognition" that forcefully counters the temptation to exist in a condition of complacent insensibility. It is difficult afterward to slip into the guise of one of those women "Talking of Michelangelo."

Robert P. Ellis

ERIE C. C. NORTH
REF PN1110.5 .M37 1992 **v. 3**
Masterplots II

3 4921 00122443 2